INFANTS AND TODDLERS

Development and Curriculum Planning

SECOND EDITION

Join us on the web at

EarlyChildEd.delmar.com

INFANTS AND TODDLERS

Development and Curriculum Planning

SECOND EDITION

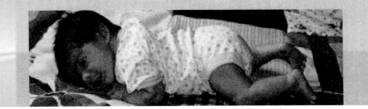

Penny Low Deiner
University of Delaware

DELMAR
CENGAGE Learning·   Australia   Canada   Mexico   Singapore   Spain   United Kingdom   United States

DELMAR
CENGAGE Learning

Infants and Toddlers: Development and Curriculum Planning

Penny Low Deiner

Vice President, Career Education SBU: Dawn Gerrain

Director of Learning Solutions: John Fedor

Acquisitions Editor: Christopher Shortt

Product Manager: Philip Mandl

Director of Content and Media Production: Wendy A. Troeger

Production Manager: Mark Bernard

Content Project Manager: Angela Iula

Art Director: Dave Arsenault

Director of Marketing: Wendy E. Mapstone

Senior Channel Manager: Kristin McNary

Marketing Coordinator: Scott Chrysler

ExamView® and ExamView Pro® are registered trademarks of FSCreations, Inc. Windows is a registered trademark of the Microsoft Corporation used herein under license. Macintosh and Power Macintosh are registered trademarks of Apple Computer, Inc. Used herein under license.

© 2009 Cengage Learning. All Rights Reserved. Cengage Learning WebTutor™ is a trademark of Cengage Learning.

Library of Congress Control Number: 2007922480

ISBN-13: 978-1-4283-1824-3

ISBN-10: 1-4283-1824-0

Delmar Cengage Learning
5 Maxwell Drive
Clifton Park, NY 12065-2919
USA

Cengage Learning products are represented in Canada by Nelson Education, Ltd.

For your lifelong learning solutions, visit **delmar.cengage.com**

Visit our corporate website at **www.cengage.com**

Notice to the Reader

Publisher does not warrant or guarantee any of the products described herein or perform any independent analysis in connection with any of the product information contained herein. Publisher does not assume, and expressly disclaims, any obligation to obtain and include information other than that provided to it by the manufacturer. The reader is expressly warned to consider and adopt all safety precautions that might be indicated by the activities described herein and to avoid all potential hazards. By following the instructions contained herein, the reader willingly assumes all risks in connection with such instructions. The publisher makes no representations or warranties of any kind, including but not limited to, the warranties of fitness for particular purpose or merchantability, nor are any such representations implied with respect to the material set forth herein, and the publisher takes no responsibility with respect to such material. The publisher shall not be liable for any special, consequential, or exemplary damages resulting, in whole or part, from the readers' use of, or reliance upon, this material.

Printed in the United States of America
1 2 3 4 5 6 7 11 10 09 08

To my husband John,

our children

Jamie Anne, Michael Seth, and Paige Lauren,

and their children,

Miles Benjamin, Maya Grace, Natalie Ann-Shing, and Isabella Franchesca,

who have kept me in touch with the world of infants and toddlers

contents

chapter 6   **Communication, Language, and Literacy / 231**

chapter 12 **Curriculum and Planning for Young Infants: Birth to Nine Months / 557**

chapter 13   **Curriculum and Planning for Mobile Infants: 8 to 18 Months / 604**

preface

This text provides a revised and up-to-date view of infant and toddler development and links this development to curriculum and planning. The text provides evidence-based knowledge and shows students how to use this knowledge to become better practitioners. The book integrates a variety of knowledge bases to present a holistic view of young infants, mobile infants, toddlers and their families. The book draws from the fields of child development, early childhood education, early childhood special education, psychology, sociology, medicine, nutrition, and physical education. It prepares students to use this knowledge to plan developmentally appropriate programs for infants and toddlers. It also increases their awareness of the joys and concerns that families have as they raise infants and toddlers, and supports their understanding of and communication with these diverse families.

All textbooks are greatly influenced by the author's beliefs and values. This book is no exception.

Evidence-Based Practice

The inclusion of both development and curriculum planning reflects my belief that these two areas are inextricably linked. Knowing where an infant or toddler is developmentally and knowing the next developmental step is the foundation for planning. This knowledge is based on the science of early childhood development. Moving from knowledge to application of knowledge is as necessary for college students as it is for infants and toddlers. This knowledge base allows early childhood educators to help parents and other professionals identify infants and toddlers whose development may be taking an atypical path.

New information about brain development and the importance of early motor development has changed how we think about the first three years of life. The pressures from standards and frameworks for infants and toddlers has made the role of early childhood educators important translators of what high quality means in caring for infants and toddlers. The move to evidence-based practice has also increased the level of skill and creativity that professionals who work with infants and toddlers are required to have.

VIEWING INFANTS AND TODDLERS IN CONTEXT

Infants and toddlers live and grow in families. Infants and toddlers come into the world different and the families they join are different. A large part of working with infants and toddlers involves working with infants and toddlers and their families. We, as professionals, need to become more aware of, acknowledge, and appreciate the impact of ethnic and cultural differences.

The changing context of families and communities impacts infants and toddlers. Early childhood educators must be able and willing to welcome all infants and toddlers. They must have the skills to include infants and toddler who are at risk for developing disabilities as well as those with identified disabilities. They must engage with infants and toddlers and families whose home language is not English and support them in learning their home language as well as English. They must welcome children who live in environments that place them at risk and create a safe, welcoming setting that allows children to grow and learn.

Most infants and toddlers will enter nonparental care during their first three years. High-quality early care and education can positively impact their development. Understanding what makes early care and education high quality and developing the skills and techniques to participate in this level of care are essential.

Infants and toddlers don't vote. They need advocates who understand the importance of the first thousand days. They need early childhood professionals to see infants and toddlers as our nation's most valuable resource. I would hope that students use the knowledge and experiences they have gained to think about infants and toddlers in a social and political context as well as a developmental one. Concerned adults need to ensure that the needs of infants and toddlers become a focal point as the nation moves forward. The needs of all citizens will be better taken care of if we ensure the best possible development for our infants and toddlers.

Major Revisions in the Second Edition

While building from the foundation of the first edition, information has been updated and revised. The book reflects the state of early care and education and the knowledge that supports it. It also supports developmentally appropriate practices. The first edition of the book had two parts: Developmental Processes and From Theory to Practice. These have been joined in the second edition and more clearly tied research and theory to practice. The reading level of the text has been monitored and lowered to make it usable for a broader range of students. All of the photographs and line drawings are new. Other revisions are detailed by chapter.

- **Chapter 1: Infants, Toddlers, and Caregiving** includes information on the science behind early childhood development, the importance of using evidence-based practice, standards for infants and toddlers, and the code of ethical conduct.
- **Chapter 2: Development Before Birth** has been updated, simplified, and organized to clearly focus on information students need to include all infants and toddlers in early care and education settings.
- **Chapter 3: Birthing and Newborns** is a combination of the first edition's Chapters 3 (Birth and the Birthing Process) and 4 (The Newborn). It provides more of a focus on newborn development and assessment as well as behavioral states.
- **Chapter 4: Physical, Motor, and Sensory Development** is a combination of old Chapters 5 (Patterns of Physical and Motor Development) and 6 (Sensory and Perceptual Development). Information about brain development has been expanded, a stronger theoretical base provided, and information about obesity and obesity prevention added.
- **Chapter 5: Cognitive and Intellectual Development** has updated and there is expanded coverage of Vygotsky's theory.
- **Chapter 6: Communication, Language, and Literacy** has been updated with additional information on children whose home language is not English and places a greater emphasis on early literacy.
- **Chapter 7: Social Development** has an updated and the section on attachment has been expanded. There is a greater emphasis on respectful relationships. It also includes more information about atypical social development, including autism.
- **Chapter 8: Emotional Development** has been updated with additional information on infant mental health and atypical emotional development.
- **Chapter 9: Early Care and Education** has updated information on who cares for infants and toddlers and where infants and toddlers are cared for. It provides more information on high-quality care, as well as the impact of care on infants and toddlers. It provides information about NAEYC's standards and guiding principles for early care and education. It also includes information about child care models used other countries.

❀ **Chapter 10: Partnering with Families of Infants and Toddlers** is a combination of Chapters 11 (Infants and Toddlers and Their Families) and 12 (Collaborating with Families of Infants and Toddlers), with additional information on the changing American family, including children in immigrant families and working with families in a cultural context. It includes information on families who adopt infants and toddlers.

❀ **Chapter 11: Inclusive Planning for Infants, Toddlers, and Twos** is a new chapter that focuses on the underlying concepts of infant/toddler curriculum. In addition to helping students develop a philosophy of teaching, it exposes them to a variety of curriculum models and approaches, including the Creative Curriculum, the Pilker/Gerber approach, Reggio Emilia, and the Emergent Curriculum.

❀ **Chapter 12: Curriculum and Planning for Young Infants: Birth to Nine Months** is a combination of old Chapters 14 (Planning for Young Infants: Birth to Eight Months) and 15 (Activities for Infants: Birth to Eight Months). This chapter has moved away from thinking about activities for young infants to focus more on experiences. There is more emphasis on individualized planning and knowing when and how to interact with young infants. There is more emphasis on scheduling, routines, and rituals.

❀ **Chapter 13: Curriculum and Planning for Mobile Infants: 8 to 18 Months** is a combination of old Chapters 16 (Planning for Crawlers and Walkers: 8 to 18 months) and 17 (Activities for Crawlers and Walkers: 8 to 18 months). The emphasis continues to be on planning individualized developmentally appropriate experiences and incorporating learning into routines and rituals, including an emphasis on self-regulation.

❀ **Chapter 14: Curriculum and Planning for Toddlers and Twos: 16 to 36 months** is a combination of Chapters 18 (Planning Programs for Toddlers and Twos: 18 to 36 Months) and 19 (Activities for Toddlers and Twos: 18 to 36 Months) It provides additional information on challenging behavior and routines, including toilet training.

Instructional Features in the Second Edition

❀ The **running glossary** defines terms used in the text. This feature ensures that students understand the terms used but also develops the professional vocabulary students need to be viewed as professionals in the field.

❀ **Why Study** helps to answer the "so what?" question. It focuses on why students need knowledge or skills in a particular area.

❀ **With Infants and Toddlers** helps students translate research and theory into practice.

- ❈ *Up Close and Personal* helps the text come alive with real stories from real people. All of the stories are real incidents that were either shared with the author or were written by the individuals for inclusion in the book.
- ❈ *Reflective Practice* provides students guidance in reflecting on a situation and confronting some of the dilemmas in the field.
- ❈ *Application Activities* provide both individual and problem-based learning opportunities for students to use the knowledge they have gained in real-life situations.
- ❈ *Chapter in Review* highlights what was in the chapter.
- ❈ *Resources* provides students with additional print and multimedia information to expand their learning in depth and breadth.

Ancillaries

e-Resource Instructor CD-ROM

The new e-Resource component provides instructors with all the tools they need in one convenient CD-ROM. Instructors will find that this resource provides them with a turnkey solution to help them teach. The CD-ROM introductory information provides information on how to design field placements and assignments that go with the text as well as information on how to support students in becoming more reflective practitioners. It provides a chapter preview and learning objectives. The key terms and concepts of each chapter are identified and defined, and a lecture outline is provided. There are a variety of suggested teaching strategies including those that employ problem-based-learning. Potential assignments have been detailed. Recommended readings to support the information in the text have been added. Audio-visual resources that support each chapter have been annotated as well as sources where these can be obtained if your college or university does not currently have these. Additional resources beyond those that were identified in the test are also annotated. PowerPoint slides for each chapter and, a computerized test bank that contains multiple choice and true/false, as well as essay questions with scoring rubrics complete the package.

Online Companion

The Online Companion for the second edition provides a chapter preview and learning objectives. The key terms and concepts of each chapter are identified and defined, and a chapter outline is provided. Recommended readings to support the information in the text have been included should students want additional information. Additional web resources are also provided. There are also sample test questions, multiple choice and true and false that students can use to test their knowledge. These questions do not overlap with the test questions in the e-source instructor CD-ROM.

Professional Enhancement Text

A new supplement to accompany this text is the Infants & Toddlers Professional Enhancement handbook for students. This resource, which is part of Delmar Learning's Early Childhood Education Professional Enhancement series, focuses on key topics of interest for future early childhood directors, teachers, and caregivers. Becoming a teacher is a process of continuing to grow, learn, reflect, and discover through experience. The Professional Enhancement text helps tomorrow's teachers along their way. Students will keep this informational supplement and use it for years to come in their early childhood practices.

ACKNOWLEDGMENTS

Although I am the sole author of this textbook, it could not have been completed without a strong support system. My family was a solid support for me. My husband John continues to support my writing as something that is important to me even when I complain about deadlines. Our youngest daughter, Paige, a journalist, provided insight into how to make some of the writing more interesting. Jamie and Michael continue to ask about the progress of the book and all three children generously allowed me to take photographs of them, their spouses and their children to help illustrate elusive concepts I wanted to convey. I particularly want to acknowledge Pat Childs whose progressive ideas continue to influence my thinking and awareness of the challenges that individuals with disabilities face and the skills that infants and toddlers will need to meet these challenges.

Graduate students Wei Qiu, Tina Kaissi, Dorit Radni-Griffin, and Tracy Evian contributed in many different ways, from contributing teaching strategies and test questions to the e-Resources Instructor CD-ROM to finding elusive references and helping with the bibliography. Wei Qui in particular was instrumental in writing the e-Resource Instructor Cd-ROM and the Online companion.

The experiences of many mothers, fathers, grandparents, teachers, friends, and colleagues contributed to the "Up Close and Personals," including Linda Clark, Cara Cuchinni-Harmon, Karen Rucker, Bahira Sherif-Trask, Wei Qiu, Gretchen Taylor, Paige Deiner, Michael Deiner, Suling Wang, and Jamie Deiner. They shared their experiences in a way that allowed me to make the book more authentic as well as interesting.

When I couldn't find needed photographs, graduate students and friends graciously allowed me to take photographs of them, their children, or grandchildren, including Laura Thompson Brady and Damien Brady, Lie Jiang and Wei Qiu, Paige Deiner and Rudy Oxlaj Cumes, Michael Deiner and Suling

Wang, Jamie Deiner and Rich Millman, Jessica and Tom Bain, and Ron and Donna Coffin.

The author and Delmar Learning wish to thank the following reviewers who commented on the first edition of the text as well as responding to the draft manuscript of the new second edition.

- Kristine L. Slentz, PhD, Western Washington University, WA
- Phyllis Gilbert, M.Ed., M.S., Stephen F. Austin State University, TX
- Helen Unangst, M.S., Imperial Valley College, CA
- Lynda Venhuizen, M.S., South Dakota State University, SD
- Elaine Wilkinson, M.Ed., Collin County Community College, TX
- Beverlyn Cain, M.Ed., Ed.D., Elizabeth City State University, NC
- Tracy Keyes, M.S., Kutztown University, PA
- Licia Watson, M.A., Penn Valley Community College, KS
- Berta Harris, M.S., San Diego City College, CA
- Elizabeth Schneider, M.A., Schoolcraft College, MI
- Marion Barnett, Ed.D., Buffalo State College, NY
- Karen Danbom, PhD, Minnesota State University, Moorehead, MN
- Debbie Stoll, M.Ed., PhD, Cameron University, OK
- Marci Hanson, PhD, San Francisco State University, CA
- Robin Hasslen, PhD, Bethel University, MN

They not only provided constructive criticism but also encouragement that the book was a worthy investment of their time and mine. They made an extremely positive contribution to the final version of this book. I appreciate and have enjoyed working with the people at Cengage. I particularly want to thank Philip Mandl who has been the developmental editor for this book. His insight into how to transform the book from a purely academic viewpoint to one that could come alive has been invaluable. He responded to my many phone calls and e-mails without fail and with good advice. I want to also acknowledge Erin O'Connor who had faith that a second edition was worthwhile, and to thank Angela Iula who has smoothed the production process for me.

about the author

Penny Deiner is Professor of Individual and Family Studies at the University of Delaware. Over the past 35 years, she has taught graduate and undergraduate courses in the areas of infants and toddlers, early childhood special education, early childhood education, and family studies. Deiner has supervised student teachers and students in field placements, and has run infant labs. She served as chair of the Department of Individual and Family Studies for five years.

Deiner received her PhD from Penn State. She has been the principle investigator in two federal grants, Delaware First and DelCare, which were designed to help family child care and child care centers include infants and toddlers with disabilities. She was instrumental in helping the University of Delaware develop a Center for Disabilities Studies. Deiner currently works with the University of Delaware and the Nemours Foundation's Division on Health and Prevention Services in developing an obesity prevention curriculum for early care and education settings for infants and toddlers. Deiner has been president of and served on the Delaware Developmental Disabilities Council, she has helped write the *Delaware Infant and Toddler Early Learning Foundations: A Curriculum Framework*. She is currently on the board of directors of the Parent Information Center of Delaware and the Children's Beachhouse. Deiner regularly presents at the professional meetings of the National Association for the Education of Young Children, Zero to Three, and the Division of Early Childhood of the Council for

Exceptional Children. She has also written numerous articles in professional journals. She is currently completing the fifth edition of *Resources for Educating Children with Diverse Abilities: Birth Through 8*, also published by Cengage. At a more personal level, watching her youngest daughter experience her first pregnancy (which occured during the writing and editing of the book), reinforced not only the empirical knowledge shared in the book, but also allowed her to relive the wonder a new birth brings to the entire family.

chapter 1

Infants, Toddlers, and Caregiving

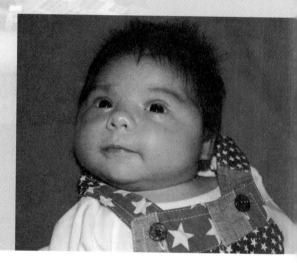

Chapter Outline

- Infants and Toddlers
- Historic Views of Infants and Toddlers
- Professional Organizations
- Evidence-Based Practice
- The Science of Early Childhood Development
- Quality of Child Care
- Foundations or Standards for Infants and Toddlers
- Advocacy and Social Policy
- Code of Ethical Conduct

One hundred years ago, parents had few resources to turn to in the tumultuous 40 weeks of pregnancy, or for the three years after birth. The Internet, with its vast amount of information on pregnancy and early childhood, did not exist. Medical doctors, if they were consulted, did not have tools like **ultrasound** that they do today. Expectant couples relied on parents and friends for advice—something many expectant mothers still do today.

Even since the 1980s, the field of infant and toddler development has been revolutionized by new technology and research. If your mother was pregnant during the 1980s, ultrasounds were rarely used and were prohibitively expensive. Now, they are an expected part of prenatal care. During birth, baby monitoring was invasive. Now, contractions and fetal heartbeats are measured with monitors smaller than a cell phone placed on the mother's stomach.

But even with the new technology, new diagnostic tests, and new procedures, a baby's development still seems like a "miracle" to most parents. On the first ultrasound, it may be difficult even to figure out that there is a baby; by the last one, parents can see eyelashes and fingernails. If they are lucky, they may even be able to watch the fetus suck her thumb. After birth, the changes become more dramatic, as the newborn who struggled to hold up his head becomes a toddler who can express himself—vehemently. Gradually, parents watch with amazement as this tiny infant grows up and becomes a college student like you. Parents frequently say, "It happened so fast! I remember when you … ."

WHY STUDY INFANTS, TODDLERS, AND CAREGIVING?

- The first three years are a pivotal period in the development of the brain, social relationships, and emotional development. What we know about development in these areas can make a difference in children's lives.

- The basis of caring for and working with infants and toddlers is based on evidence. To work effectively with infants and toddlers, you need to understand infant and toddler development and use science to support your interactions.

- Understanding families and the challenges they face will help you view infants and toddlers in the context in which they live and grow, and help you identify the skills you will need to support these children and their families.

- You can make a difference in the lives of infants and toddlers and their families.

Working with infants is a challenge. These challenges increase when a baby has developmental delays, the family faces economic hardships, or the parents discover they are not compatible. Raising infants is a complex business in a society that is child-centered but provides little support for parents and very young children.

This is where you come in. As a student and an eventual practitioner of infant and toddler care, you can help lead parents through the minefield of parenthood and possibly pregnancy. Like a soldier walking through a minefield, parents want to do the right thing for their baby—and, most of all, they do not want their actions to cause harm.

Adults come to parenthood with different backgrounds, beliefs, and experience. Parents want your expert advice on how they should teach their infant or toddler to live in an increasingly complex society. They may ask whether their infant needs *Baby Shakespeare* as well as *Baby Einstein*, if you recommend flash cards to help their toddler learn vocabulary words, and when they should expect their two-year-old to read. Another mother might ask if playing Metallica has the same benefit to brain development as Mozart. They may also question you about your curriculum for infants and toddlers. Parents have different concerns and beliefs, and the questions they approach you with will reflect those values and worries.

This textbook gives you the knowledge to answer most parents' questions, but, more important, it will give you the skills to teach, care for, and enjoy infants and toddlers. This book is designed to teach you about how infants and toddlers develop and learn, and to show you how to support them through these processes. The information presented is based on empirical evidence, developmental theories, program evaluations, and professional experience about what works and does not with very young children.

These first 1,000 days are unparalleled in growth. The brain changes, and early experiences influence the physical architecture of the brain itself. This architecture serves as the foundation for whom and what a child becomes (Lally, Lurie-Hurvitz, & Cohen, 2006). Relationships with parents, other adults and siblings, and infant and toddler educators are the architects who help build this foundation.

Development does not occur in a vacuum. Where a child spends her time—at home, early care and educational settings, and the community at large—plays a role in shaping her. Children must be understood in the context in which they grow and develop.

The foundation of balancing a checkbook, reading a textbook, or writing a love letter begins in infancy, long before preschool or kindergarten. A six-month-old infant cannot walk, but he can chew on the side of his favorite book, savoring not only the story but also the taste of the written word. Toddlers can grab a marker and scribble before they can write their names. They can find daddy's hat or mommy's briefcase. Infants and toddlers are learning about themselves and how they feel. They are acting on and reacting to the world around them. They are developing a sense of self, and expressing and regulating that self within their family and community.

Practice
is the techniques, methods, and processes used when working with infants and toddlers.

This text views very young children in the context of their environment. It considers the challenges some vulnerable families face as they rear infants and toddlers, and the challenges society itself faces in helping all infants and toddlers reach their potential. It also tells the story of the people behind the **practice**: mothers in labor, fathers caring for young children, researchers studying emotions and early language development, child care providers, grandparents, and the infants and toddlers themselves.

Each life brings joy, excitement, and hope into the world. Learning about infants and toddlers is not just about theories on nutrition or brain function and research about disabilities; it is also about the future of the world—yours and mine. You have the privilege and responsibility of learning about and caring for our most precious resource.

Throughout this book you will learn about infants and toddlers, and how to care for and educate them. I am passionate about the youngest, and often most vulnerable, members of our society and hope to share that passion with you. I hope to instill in you a respect and wonder for infants and toddlers and how they discover their world. I ask that you embrace diversity and become open to families who have different values and ideas than you. Ask yourself, "What can I learn from this situation and how can I best support this family and their children in a culturally appropriate way?"

To understand infant growth and development, you cannot just read about infants and listen to lectures. You need to observe infants, engage them, hold them, laugh with them, and play with them. As you learn about them and their families, you will learn a lot about yourself as well.

Infants are challenging to study and work with. They cannot tell you whether they are hot or cold. They cannot point to their diaper and say, "Change me." And they would not bring you a jar of baby food and say, "I'm hungry." Therefore, parents and caregivers must use their skills to interpret what a baby's behavior means. Babies are a mystery, almost like a human "whodunit," and you are the private eye figuring out the clues.

Most scholars who study infants and toddlers focus on just one aspect of development, such as language development. Caregivers, whether they are child care providers or parents, do not have that luxury. For the caregiver, infant behaviors may signal far more than whether a child is hungry, wet, or tired. A skilled caregiver identifies the bored baby and provides the right amount of stimulation to focus and attract her attention. She also understands the baby who is overstimulated and helps him regulate himself.

In addition to having been an infant yourself, many of you have had some experience with them. You have watched them in grocery stores, shopping malls, and restaurants. Perhaps you have even babysat one. Parents have babies without taking a course on infants and toddlers, and these infants have grown into adulthood. What is the difference, then, between caring for and loving infants and studying about them?

Many people believe that they instinctively know how to care for an infant, and that caring for children comes naturally. In part they are right; some child care is ingrained in our genes, but other knowledge comes with experience. (Eventually, you learn to distinguish between a baby's hungry cries and wet diaper cries.) However, caregivers now have access to a body of scientific knowledge that can help with making decisions about what to do and how to best care for infants and toddlers.

Loving, caring for, and respecting infants are the foundation of your work with our smallest community members. But you also need knowledge about how infants grow and develop, and how to translate that information into experiences that support development and are respectful of the child, family, and community.

INFANTS AND TODDLERS

Pediatricians
are medical doctors who specialize in the medical treatment of children from birth through age 12.

Pediatric nurses
are registered nurses who specialize in young children. They usually have additional training in developmental screening tools, family counseling, child care, and early intervention.

Child development
is the study of the growth and development (cognitive, language, social, emotional, and physical and motor) of children from birth to about age 12.

Early childhood educators
are professionals who provide care and develop and implement educational programs for children from birth through age 8.

Early childhood special educators
are early childhood educators with specialized knowledge of disabilities and early intervention.

Child development consultants
are master's-trained individuals who use assessment measures and often provide consultation in the home.

Developmental psychologists
are doctoral-trained individuals who administer psychological tests and other assessments.

In the past 30 years, the study of infancy has become a discipline of its own. A wide range of professionals study infants and toddlers. **Pediatricians** and **pediatric nurses** study medical aspects of infant's health. Professionals in **child development** focus on how infants interact with their world. **Early childhood educators** examine developmentally appropriate practices for very young children; **early childhood special educators** explore ways to identify infants and toddlers with developmental delays and design early intervention programs for them. **Child development consultants** typically work as itinerant specialists supporting families in the home and early care and education settings. **Developmental psychologists** study infant mental health and want to discover how infants perceive their world.

Although our knowledge of infants and toddlers has ballooned in recent years, infants and toddlers have existed as long as people have inhabited the earth. Knowing something about how infants and toddlers have been viewed and studied in the past provides us with a perspective on the future.

HISTORIC VIEWS OF INFANTS AND TODDLERS

Childhood has not always been seen as a distinct period of development, and, in some places in the world, it is still not. In medieval times, child labor laws did not exist. Young children had to grow and develop to enter the work force or find acceptance in society. Children became "adults" quickly because society at that time had no concept of adolescence. Because of these beliefs, scholars did not consider infants and toddlers worth studying. While scholars did not study very young children, they did examine families, and their research shows how different life was from today.

- ❋ Women had little knowledge of birth control (the Pill did not exist until the late 1950s), and consequently had many children. Mothers, especially poor ones, often viewed infants as a burden.

- ❋ Some parents did not name their infants until they were several months old, and tried not to become attached to them because the infants died frequently. (This is true today in some countries, like Ethiopia and Iraq, where the infant mortality rate is very high.)

- ❋ Wealthy families hired wet nurses to feed (using their breast milk) and care for the infant until weaning or beyond.

- ❋ Families abandoned or killed infants who were unwanted, malformed, or disabled.

Medieval Times to About 2000

Society's prevailing philosophies, like the concept of "original sin," influenced studies of infants and toddlers. In the Middle Ages, infants were viewed as sinners and the purpose of child rearing was to turn the sinful infants into God-fearing, competent adults. Parents often used hands, fists, and belts to accomplish this.

In the 1600s, the English philosopher John Locke (1632–1704) proposed that infants were born as a "blank tablet" (*tabula rasa*) to be written on and that everyday experiences influenced the baby's development (Koops, 2003). Locke believed the experiences of young children determined their success in life, and he encouraged parents to raise their children with the values they wanted them to have as adults.

French philosopher Jean Jacques Rousseau (1712–1778) gained acclaim at the end of the period of Enlightenment in England for his ideas about children. He felt that children were inherently good, and that teaching should be child directed and determined by the age of the child (Koops, 2003). He instructed parents to nurture children and allow their "innate goodness" to grow.

As economic conditions in Europe improved and knowledge about health and disease increased in the 19th century, interest in infancy also increased. Although there were some isolated studies of infants in the late 1700s, it was not until the late 1800s that there was sustained interest in studying infancy. Baby biographies, which recorded the daily activities of infants, documented a developing interest in infancy. Men usually made these "biographies" about their sons. Charles Darwin, the originator of the theory of evolution, and Wilhelm Preyer, a German physiologist, wrote some of the most famous baby biographies.

Baby biographers recorded observations about an infant over time (much as one might keep a personal diary). Through these observations, academics learned when a particular infant sat, grabbed for a bottle, or walked. Although these biographies proved useful, they did not help determine normal development for all infants.

Descriptive studies measure current behavior, but they do not predict future behavior.

By the 1920s and 1930s, **descriptive studies** of groups of children gave academics more universal information about children. These studies used groups of infants and toddlers, and focused on particular behaviors or sequences of behavior. Their goal was to describe development and document when particular behaviors happened and in what order they occurred. Researchers wanted to know at what age a baby crawled, walked, and talked. They investigated whether you could train a baby to do something like climb stairs or ride a tricycle before this would occur naturally.

Researchers continue to study the growth and development of children today. Some investigators focus on a particular aspect of development. Others are concerned more about the contexts in which children grow; for instance, the family and early care and education settings, and how these contexts have changed over time.

Infants and Toddlers in the Information Age

There is an explosion of information available to parents and caregivers. Rather than having too little information, we have a surplus of it—and we can get that information quickly. I put the word "infant" into a search engine, and in one second I had 6,609,874 results and suggestions for eight related topics to explore. Shenk (1997) refers to this as "data smog." He sees it as a menacing cloud of information that confounds rather than helps us understand. The problem is deciding what information to use to guide our practice with infants and toddlers.

Medical and academic professionals, books, blogs, and Web sites geared toward and sometimes written by parents are also gaining traction. Web sites offer pregnancy- and nutrition-tracking programs. There are sites that offer message boards where expecting mothers can chat about their pregnancy and get advice from other moms. Other sites give testimonies and advice from and for both parents and early childhood educators. Even major newspapers have gotten caught up in the interest in very young children. The *Washington Post* has an on-line column ("On Balance") that examines child rearing, working, and parenting.

This book provides information about choosing information and resources that are based on scientific evidence. One place to begin is with the professional organizations that support infants and toddlers.

PROFESSIONAL ORGANIZATIONS

Professional organizations share their information via public Web sites, as well as in newsletters, journals, position papers, and conferences. Founded in 1926, the National Association for the Education of Young Children (NAEYC) provides a forum for the discussion of major issues and ideas in the field. It is the world's largest organization working on behalf of young children, with nearly 100,000 members. It is dedicated to improving the well-being of children from birth through age 8, with a particular focus on the quality of educational and developmental services. It promotes professional growth and has also played a major role in the accreditation of early childhood programs and two- and four-year early childhood education college programs. Its journal is called *Young Children*. It also has an annual conference, which is often attended by 30,000 people interested in early childhood education. Its Web site is www.naeyc.org, and it is open to new members, particularly students in the field.

The Council for Exceptional Children (CEC) is the largest international professional organization focused on improving educational outcome for individuals with special needs, including infants and toddlers with disabilities and children who are gifted and talented.

The Division for Early Childhood (DEC) was founded in 1973, and is dedicated to promoting policies and the use of evidence-based practice to enhance the developmental outcomes of young children with developmental delays and disabilities or who are at risk for future developmental problems. Like NAEYC, it has an annual conference and encourages student membership. Its journal is *Young Exceptional Children*. It can be found on the web at www.dec-sped.org.

Both the NAEYC and the DEC have state chapters. Colleges and universities often have student chapters.

The national nonprofit organization Zero to Three (www.zerotothree.org) is a multidisciplinary organization that focuses entirely on the development of very young children. Its mission is to support the well-being and healthy development of infants and toddlers and their families. The organization publishes bulletins and provides a forum to discuss research, practice, professional development, and policy issues. Its policy agenda promotes good health, strong families, and positive early learning experiences.

Other nonprofit organizations, such as the Children's Defense Fund (www.childrensdefense.org), advocate for America's children, particularly those who face challenges like poverty, minority status, or disabilities. It is a voice for children because children cannot vote, lobby, or speak for themselves.

Other advocacy groups, such as the National Center for Children in Poverty, which is affiliated with Columbia University and the Mailman School of Public Health, focus on a particular issue such as ending child poverty.

GOVERNMENT INFORMATION ABOUT INFANTS AND TODDLERS

The U.S. government also tracks information about children and their families. The U.S. Census Bureau (www.census.gov) provides population statistics for both the nation and individual states. It also provides information about issues such as poverty and types of households. The National Center for Education Statistics provides a variety of information, but some of the most relevant to you is the data from the Early Childhood Program Participation Survey (ECPP) of the 2005 National Household Education Surveys Program (http://nces.ed.gov). This data informs us about such things as how many children are in child care, the type of child care parents use for infants and toddlers, and how important various aspects of child care are to parents. The Centers for Disease Control and Prevention (CDC) (www.cdc.gov) focuses on promoting health and improving quality of life by preventing and controlling injuries, diseases, and disabilities. The CDC focuses on such topics as **birth defects**, **Sudden Infant Death Syndrome (SIDS)**, and **autism spectrum disorders (ASDs)**. The National Center on Birth Defects and Developmental Disabilities (www.cdc.gov.ncbdd) is a source of additional relevant information.

It is clear that there is a lot of information about infants, toddlers, and caregiving, and that this information can be gleaned from government sources, advocacy groups, professional organizations, and scholars. This book brings these sources of information together for you. It supports you in teaching all infants and toddlers in a developmentally appropriate way. It increases your awareness of concerns parents have as they raise infants and toddlers, and supports your understanding of and communications with families and other professionals.

EVIDENCE-BASED PRACTICE

We need to think about why we do what we do. Scholars do research and practitioners educate and care for young children. How do we get the two together? How do we get the evidence to support our practice? We need scholars to do research that will inform our practice. It is a dilemma. Research usually focuses on what we do not know. Practice focuses on what we should do. Practice is now. Practice is what happens every day in every classroom. Infants cannot wait until researchers decide they have enough evidence to support a particular practice. For researchers to provide the evidence, they need money. Social policy determines where the money is given. There is tension between research, practice, and social policy (Buysse & Wesley, 2006).

Because of problems such as these, we classify information into three categories: established knowledge, reasonable hypotheses, and unwarranted and

---

Birth defects
are problems that happen while the baby is developing in the mother's uterus.

SIDS
is the sudden death of an infant less than one year of age that cannot be explained.

ASDs
are developmental disabilities identified by significant impairments in social interaction and communication and unusual behaviors and interests.

Peer review
is the process of giving research or writing to experts in the field for evaluation before it can be published.

irresponsible assertions (Shonkoff, 2000). Established knowledge is limited, has rigorous processes of **peer review**, and is very clear about what populations this particular research can be used for. Often this category has precise information that is difficult to translate into what happens in everyday practice. Reasonable hypotheses move beyond the limits of what we know, but are anchored in established knowledge (Buysse & Wesley, 2006). Anyone can make assertions that what they do or say makes a difference. They can do this in person, in books or articles, or on the Internet. They can sell products that make claims about the grand things that will happen if you just buy what they sell. Evidence-based practice builds the bridge between research and practice. It provides us with information we can have confidence in.

Buysse and Wesley (2006) offer the following definition of evidence-based practice: "Evidence-based practice is a decision-making process that integrates the best available research evidence with family and professional wisdom and values" (p. 12).

They see three major components to this definition:

1. Scientifically based research that focuses on the efficacy and effectiveness of specific early childhood practices and interventions.

2. Individual and collective wisdom of families and professionals gained through observation, experience, reflection, and consensus.

3. Characteristics of individual children and families, as well as local circumstances, values, and contexts that must be integrated into all practice decisions (p. 13).

Today we are concerned about the evidence that backs up practice rather than just practice itself. We want evidence to show that what we are doing works. We no longer do things merely to uphold tradition, or because our parents or our teachers did them in a particular way. Instead, we are interested in the practice that, based on evidence, will be more likely than other practices to elicit positive outcomes (see Table 1–1).

Peer-reviewed journals
are professional publications such as *Young Children*, the NAEYC journal, and *Young Exceptional Children*—the journal of the Division of Early Childhood of the CEC—to which researchers submit articles, which are then sent to experts in the field to determine whether or not to publish them.

Table 1–1 Questions to Ask about Evidence-Based Practice

- Are the practices based on research published in **peer-reviewed journals?**
- Have other researchers or setting found the same results?
- Are the practices endorsed by professional organizations such as the NAEYC, or the DEC of the CEC? These organizations have positions based on the consensus of the professionals who are part of their organizations.
- Have these practices been effective and do they produce the outcomes we want?
- How will the outcome or intervention be evaluated?

SOURCE: Strain and Dunlap (2006).

Evidence-based practice matters because, as professionals in the field, we want to do the best possible job. We need to be effective and accountable for our actions. This evidence was not available in the 1600s or even most of the 1900s.

Teachers use evidence of practices that work with infants and toddlers to guide their interactions.

THE SCIENCE OF EARLY CHILDHOOD DEVELOPMENT

In the past, information often passed from mother to daughter and father to son. Child care and rearing were based on tradition and what worked rather than on science. Today that has changed; research and science now form the backbone of early childhood education. An increasing interest in the science of early childhood development has led to the transition from "hand-me-down" knowledge to scientific knowledge (National Research Council and Institute of Medicine, 2000). While scientists have made great strides in their knowledge about child development, public policy and funding have been slow to react. Researchers discovered that 85 percent of core brain development occurs during the first three years of life, yet less than 10 percent of public spending on children focuses on this time frame (Lombardi et al., 2004). Our challenge is to use this knowledge to improve the lives of young children and their families. We begin with the science and then move on to practice. *From Neurons to Neighborhoods: The Science of Early Childhood Development*, (2000) by the National Research Council and Institute of

Medicine identified 10 core concepts that frame what we know about infant and toddler development.

1. **"Human development is shaped by a dynamic and continuous interaction between biology and experience"** (National Research Council and Institute of Medicine, 2000, p. 23). Humans are living organisms who act and react to their environment. Infants come into the world with different skills and talents. Some infants are quiet and serene, whereas others fight and kick their way into the world.

   The environments children enter are also different. Some families have many resources and openly accept any infant; other families have very specific ideas about the adult they want and plan to actively mold the infant to fit that image. Some families have fewer resources and face challenges related to housing and health care. The impact of the infant on the environment and the environment on the infant influences how the infant's brain grows and develops in his earliest years.

2. **"Culture influences every aspect of human development and is reflected in childrearing beliefs and practices designed to promote healthy adaptation"** (National Research Council and Institute of Medicine, 2000, p. 25). Culture influences values and beliefs. It influences what people eat and what music they like. It also influences who attends the birth of a baby, who delivers the baby, her name, and the care she receives after she is born. But this is just the beginning. Families in the United States have vastly different approaches to child rearing. Even though the differences are identifiable, researchers know less about their impact than many other aspects of early development.

3. **"The growth of self-regulation is a cornerstone of early childhood development that cuts across all domains of behavior"** (National Research Council and Institute of Medicine, 2000, p. 26). The ability to control one's behavior and physiological processes (both conscious and unconscious) is important in maintaining life and functioning in the world. Infants cry to signal discomfort or distress. As they develop, infants replace tears with other methods of communication. When children encounter discomfort they learn coping strategies to solve problems. If, however, children live in a situation where they cannot affect their environment, these coping strategies may not appear. That is, if toddlers talk and ask questions and there is no adult response to their talking, they may not see the utility of communication to get their needs met.

4. **"Children are active participants in their own development, reflecting the intrinsic human drive to explore and master one's**

Wired
refers to the way infants' brains work when they are born.

Early intervention
focuses on infants and toddlers with disabilities. It promotes development and learning, supports families, and helps to coordinate services with the goal of reducing or eliminating the need for special programs later.

Asynchronous
growth refers to the unevenness of development, with some children developing skills earlier than others (e.g., talking in two-word utterances at 12 months but not walking until 18 months).

Plasticity
is the lifelong ability of the brain to reorganize neural pathways in response to new experiences.

environment" (National Research Council and Institute of Medicine, 2000, p. 27). Infants are born **wired** to understand their world. They are intrigued and curious about the world in which they live. An infant's environment, his home or child care setting, can facilitate or impede growth and development. Regardless of whether a child prefers banging pots and pans or playing with the most expensive baby toys, he is born to construct meaning from his environment. **Early intervention** takes advantage of this intrinsic motivation for mastery. It is designed to help children overcome some challenges and to minimize others.

5. **"Human relationships, and the effects of relationships on relationships, are the building blocks of healthy development"** (National Research Council and Institute of Medicine, 2000, p. 27). The mutual attachment in the infant–caregiver relationship is the foundation for the development of subsequent relationships. Relationships are the building blocks of development. When caregivers accurately interpret and respond to an infant's signals, trust is born. If infants send out confusing signals, talented and trained caregivers sort out these signals, decide what they mean, and then respond appropriately. Interventions help caregivers learn and interpret these signals and adapt their responses to the idiosyncrasies of the infants for whom they are caring.

6. **"The broad range of individual differences among young children often makes it difficult to distinguish normal variations and maturational delays from transient disorders and persistent impairments"** (National Research Council and Institute of Medicine, 2000, p. 28). Growth is uneven or **asynchronous**. Infants who walk early have less need to talk early. Likewise, those who talk early might have a support system of "gofers" who will respond to their requests. Because of these variations it is difficult to decide what is asynchronous development and what might be a developmental delay. Each infant is different. Each has talents, and **plasticity** of the brain allows him to develop and meet the challenges of his environment. Understanding the pathways to learning and development is an essential part of working with infants and toddlers.

7. **"The development of children unfolds along individual pathways whose trajectories are characterized by continuities and discontinuities, as well as by a series of significant transitions"** (National Research Council and Institute of Medicine, 2000, p. 29). Some aspects of development are characterized by small, gradual changes, which then develop into larger, more dramatic changes. In most children, vocabulary acquisition (word learning) and memory are small, gradual changes that give way to written and spoken language. In other cases,

Disequilibrium
requires infants and toddlers to reorganize their thinking (and brain pathways) based on new learning.

the changes are more inclusive: Children's discovery of the relationship between objects and words (discontinuous) is unlike their discovery that something we sit on can be called a sofa, divan, or couch (continuous). Discontinuous discoveries require mental reorganization and are often fraught with psychological challenges, **disequilibrium** and vulnerability as children struggle to make sense out of their world. Challenging periods create the opportunity for intervention.

8. **"Human development is shaped by the ongoing interplay among sources of vulnerability and sources of resilience"** (National Research Council and Institute of Medicine, 2000, p. 30). A child's risk or resilience depends upon many different factors. Some are related to the child herself, whether she has a difficult or easy temperament, her environment (mother's education, quality of the child care setting), and other factors. The combination of the risks and positive features affects the child's development.

If a low-birth-weight infant is born to well-educated parents with well-paying, flexible jobs, and who are dedicated to promoting a positive quality of life for their infant, the prognosis is positive. If a single mom without a high-school education, steady job, or health insurance has the same child, the outcome is less likely to be positive. However, if this child receives early intervention services and is placed in a high-quality infant and toddler program, the outlook changes to a much more positive one.

9. **"The timing of early experiences can matter, but, more often than not, the developing child remains vulnerable to risks and open to protective influences throughout the early years of life and into adulthood"** (National Research Council and Institute of Medicine, 2000, p. 31). The concept of **prime time**, a time when the developing child is more able to change, is shaped by knowledge of human and other animal development. Initially, scientists thought particular ages were critical, inflexible periods for specific development and if a particular event did not occur during this period, it could never occur. (For example, if a child did not walk by 24 months he would never walk.)

Prime time
is the optimal time for learning a specific task or skill.

Now, researchers are less rigid about sensitive periods. They believe that because of the plasticity of the brain, advances can occur at any age. They may, however, occur more easily at some ages than others. There is greater potential for developmental adaptation in early childhood than in adulthood (National Research Council and Institute of Medicine, 2000).

10. **"The course of development can be altered in early childhood by effective interventions that change the balance between risk and**

protection, thereby shifting the odds in favor of more adaptive outcomes" (National Research Council and Institute of Medicine, 2000, p. 32). Children come into the world ready to learn and grow to their own rhythm. In a nurturing environment, this growth flourishes. When parents or caregivers do not support growth, children fail to thrive physically or psychologically, or develop in ways that do not support a positive trajectory into adult life. The objective of early intervention is to give a child the most positive trajectory possible: "It is the art of the possible, based on the science of early childhood development" (National Research Council and Institute of Medicine, 2000, p. 32).

Scholars have the science, but it must be used in ways that benefit infants and their families, and applied by professionals with the training to use the science and who are as respected and as well paid as educators of older children.

The science of early childhood development is interdisciplinary. Researchers depend on the knowledge of many different fields. This knowledge must be integrated and focused so that it applies to those who study growth and development and those who work with and care for infants and toddlers. Because infants and toddlers must be viewed in the context of their families, their early care and education settings, and the communities in which they live, scholars must be responsive to changing demographics to meet the needs of infants and toddlers.

QUALITY OF CHILD CARE

The science of early childhood focuses on the critical development of the first three years of life. The changing American family, with either both partners or single parents working outside the home, has necessitated that even very young children receive a great amount of care and education outside of their homes. According to the initial results of the 2005 National Household Education Surveys Program, many infants and toddlers are in at least one weekly nonparental care arrangement (see Table 1–2).

It is clear that many children enter care at less than a year and that these children are most likely to be in the care of relatives. With increasing age, the care shifts from relative care to center-based care. We know less about relative care than other types of child care arrangements.

We know that high-quality early care and education can have a positive effect on children's development. The impact is significant and long term, and influences how children develop, their ability to learn, and their capacity to regulate their emotions (Bowman, Donovan, & Burns, 2001; National Research Council and Institute of Medicine, 2000). Likewise, poor-quality care has the ability to harm very young children, and this impact is also long lasting.

Table 1–2 Weekly Care Arrangements

	Parental Care	Nonparental Care	Of Those in Nonparental Care		
			Relative	Nonrelative	Center
Less than 1 year	58%	42%	48%	33%	28%
1 to 2 years	47%	53%	39%	30%	43%
Below poverty threshold	49%	51%	44%	16%	57%

Note that the numbers of placements in nonparental care add up to more than 100%. This reflects the fact that some children have more than one nonparental care arrangement.
SOURCE: U.S. Department of Education, Initial Results from the 2005 NHES Early Child Care Program Participation Study (2006).

Here is where you enter the picture: You have the ability to change the future for yourself and the infants and toddlers you care for. To accomplish this goal you must be a consumer of research and information about infants and toddlers, a caregiver who can read and interpret toddlers' and infants' signals, and advocate for increasing the quality of care these infants and toddlers receive.

Researchers know that children in low-quality child care exhibit more aggressive behavior and show delays in language and reading, where as children in high-quality child care have fewer behavioral problems, greater mathematical skills, and better thinking and attention skills (Peisner-Feinberg et al., 1999). This is particularly true for **vulnerable children**. Investigators have evidence to show that high-quality child care makes a difference. The next step is to have people like you understand and implement the science behind early childhood education.

Vulnerable children are those whose circumstances (the child himself, the family, and/or the environment) place them at risk of poor developmental outcomes.

FOUNDATIONS OR STANDARDS FOR INFANTS AND TODDLERS

The educational reform movement created a renewed interest in children's academic development and the educational system's accountability for delivering it to them. Some people worry that this trend will move down to infants and toddlers and focus attention solely on the academic growth of young children rather than looking more holistically at the tasks young children need to master to succeed later in life. These developmental tasks include:

※ **Self-regulation**: Children move gradually from a state of dependence to one of independence. To become independent, infants and toddlers must be able to put themselves to sleep, eat appropriate amounts of food, be patient, manage their emotions and behavior, and focus on important tasks (National Research Council and Institute of Medicine, 2000).

☀ **Relationships**: Children must learn how to play with other children and develop friendships. Making and sustaining friendships are complex tasks that require many skills. The foundation for these tasks is set in the parent–child relationship (National Research Council and Institute of Medicine, 2000).

☀ **Communication and Language**: Children are born curious and motivated to learn about their environment, to solve problems, and to share this knowledge with others. Adults must support early language learning (National Research Council and Institute of Medicine, 2000).

Self-regulation, relationships, and communication comprise the cornerstone of early development. Some scholars feel that if the emphasis moves too far into the academic realm, some of the important early developmental tasks will be ignored or deemed irrelevant. Standards designed for young children should reflect these early developmental tasks.

Standards
is a broad term related to expectations about what children should learn.

Most states have developed **standards** for prekindergarten programs. The National Institute for Early Education Research (NIEER) (Barnett, Hustedt, Robin, & Schulman, 2004) has developed a quality standards checklist that looks at states' prekindergarten requirements for curriculum standards, qualifications for teachers, class size and staff–child ratios, as well as support services, screening requirements, and meal requirements. As of 2004, 11 states had no ratable programs and only one state, Arkansas, met all 10 of NIEER's quality benchmarks (Barnett et al., 2004).

Early learning standards
describe the expectations for learning and development of young children typically from birth to age 5.

Although states have standards for preschool children the concept of having **early learning standards** for infants and toddlers is off-putting on one level and a sign of our times on another. States are moving in the direction of developing standards, benchmarks, or foundations for children from birth to three years of age. Standards documents are neither an assessment tool nor a curriculum guide. Instead, most are designed around developmental domains such as cognition, communication, motor, social-emotional development, and creative expression. They are usually written to guide and be used by child care providers.

The NAEYC took a different tack toward standards. Although it acknowledges the inevitability of standards, it looked more at the principles that should underlie all position statements for young children rather than identifying particular **content standards**. It identified four essential features of all early learning standards in its position statement (see Table 1–3).

Content standards
are descriptions of what children should know and be able to do in particular areas such as language or mathematics.

When professionals began researching and creating standards, they discovered that children of color and those living in poverty lacked knowledge that their peers from middle-class Caucasian families have. Initially, research focused

Table 1–3 Essential Features of Developmentally Effective Early Learning Standards

1. Effective early learning standards emphasize significant developmentally appropriate content and outcomes (p. 4)

2. Effective early learning standards are developed and reviewed through informed, inclusive processes (p. 6)

3. Early learning standards gain their effectiveness through implementation and assessment practices that support all children's development in ethical, appropriate ways (p. 6)

4. Effective early learning standards require a foundation of support for early childhood programs, professionals, and families (p. 7)

SOURCE: NAEYC (2002).

on gaps among school-age children. Researchers believed that the lives of children before they enter public schools were outside the scope of public policy (Rouse, Brooks-Gunn, & McLanahan, 2005).

Children not only learn at different rates when they are in school, they come to school with different knowledge bases, and these differences mirror family income. Income is compounded by racial/ethnic identification, with more African American and Hispanic families in lower-income levels. Children from families in the lowest 20 percent of income levels enter kindergarten more than a year behind in reading, math, and general knowledge than children whose families are in the top 20 percent (U.S. Department of Education, 1998). Kindergarten teachers found African American and Hispanic children lagging in academic and self-regulatory aspects of school readiness (Rouse et al., 2005). High-quality child care can prevent and help close this gap.

Studies show that children living in poverty **and** with identified disabilities who received early intervention services during early childhood scored close to the same as children who did not have disabilities or did not live in poverty (Gamel-McCormick & Amsden, 2002). Studies such as this show that by enriching the environment of children living in poverty, they can achieve the same levels of knowledge as middle-class children. The quality of early care and education can be either a source of the learning gap or a potential solution.

ADVOCACY AND SOCIAL POLICY

Babies cannot vote, therefore many organizations have chosen to take on what they consider to be the most pressing issues affecting infants and toddlers and their families. Increasingly, individuals in advocacy groups, such as the Children's Defense Fund and foundations such as the Annie E. Casey Foundation and the Carnegie Corporation of New York, advocate for social policy changes that improve circumstances for infants and toddlers and their families.

Social policy is the government's plan of action that influences the welfare of its citizens. The United States has no comprehensive social policy that relates to families or infants and toddlers; however, it has many individual policies that both directly and indirectly affect infants and toddlers and their families. Some programs are related to child care and nutrition (Purchase of Care [POC]), the Child Care Development Block Grant (CCDBG)), others provide temporary aid to needy families (TANF), some programs serve infants and toddlers who live in or near the poverty level (Early Head Start), some focus on medical care (Medicaid), and others provide support for children with disabilities, Supplemental Social Security (SSI). There are many programs. One problem is that many of these are in different agencies and have different eligibility criteria.

In 2000, the CCDBG served an average of 1,040,600 families per month. This number decreased to 1,001,600 in 2004, while the number of families with children under 18 who are living in poverty increased from 4,866,000 in 2000 to 5,847,000 in 2004. Looking at all child care funding sources, in 2003 the federal government estimated that 2.5 million children received child care assistance. By 2004, this number declined by 200,000, and by 2010 it is projected to decline by 500,000 (Children's Defense Fund, 2006; U.S. Department of Health and Human Services, 2000). In the United States it appears that raising infants and toddlers is seen as a personal responsibility, not a joint one, as it is seen in some European countries (Gandini, 2001). At a time when we know about the importance of early development and its potential for closing the learning gap for very young children, the U.S. government is investing fewer and fewer dollars in child care.

High-quality early childhood programs are cost-effective in the long term. The Carolina Abecedarian Project (1972–1977) assessed children through age 21, and the Nurse Family Partnership: Elmira Prenatal/Early Infancy Project (1978–1982) assessed children through age 15. The Abecedarian Project had an internal rate of return of 7 percent with a benefit-to-cost ratio of $3.78 to $1.00. The Nurse Family Partnership had an internal rate of return of 23 percent with a benefit-to-cost ratio of $5.06 to $1.00. Some of the benefits relate to the children's higher reading and math achievement, lower retention, and less special education. There are also decreased rates of arrest for the child participants. There are also reduced welfare costs and less child maltreatment; the mothers earn more money and are less likely to be convicted of crimes (Heckman, Grunewald, & Reynolds, 2006).

Infants and toddlers learn and grow through the development of positive trusting relationships with parents and other caregivers. Programs such as Early Head Start make a difference. Early Head Start uses a variety of models: home-based, center-based, and a mixed approach with both home and center.

Children had the largest gains in the mixed-approach program. In these programs there was both intensive home visiting and quality center-based care (U.S. Department of Health and Human Services, 2006).

Policymakers not only determine what programs are going to be available, but also what the eligibility criteria will be for recipients. Some social policies support infants and toddlers in the context of their families; other policies do not. Increasingly, professionals concerned about infants and toddlers take their expertise into the political arena of their neighborhoods, communities, states, and nations, and become advocates for the needs of our youngest citizens. As you think about yourself and your career path, consider advocacy and public policy as potential arenas in which you can use your expertise.

CODE OF ETHICAL CONDUCT

Individuals who work with young children make decisions that have moral and ethical implications. NAEYC (2005) has developed a Code of Ethical Conduct and Statement of Commitment for those who work in early childhood education (see Table 1–4). It defines the core values of the field and provides guidance to individuals working with young children when they find themselves making

Table 1–4 NAEYC Statement of Commitment

To the best of my ability I will:

- never harm children
- ensure that programs for young children are based on current knowledge and research of child development and early childhood education.
- respect and support families in their task of nurturing children.
- respect colleagues in early childhood care and education and support them in maintaining the NAEYC Code of Ethical Conduct.
- serve as an advocate for children, their families, and their teachers in community and society.
- stay informed of and maintain high standards of professional conduct.
- engage in an ongoing process of self-reflection, realizing that personal characteristics, biases, and beliefs have an impact on children and families.
- be open to new ideas and be willing to learn from the suggestions of others.
- continue to learn, grow, and contribute as a professional.
- honor the ideals and principles of the NAEYC Code of Ethical Conduct.

SOURCE: NAEYC (2005, p. 13).

difficult decisions or deciding among conflicting obligations. NAEYC puts forth a conceptual framework that focuses on four different areas of responsibility:

1. Ethical responsibilities to children.
2. Ethical responsibilities to families.
3. Ethical responsibilities to colleagues.
4. Ethical responsibilities to community and society.

Although not an official part of the code, the Statement of Commitment acknowledges a willingness to embrace to the field of early childhood care and education and the profession.

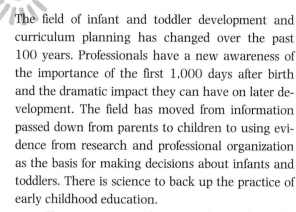

SUMMARY

The field of infant and toddler development and curriculum planning has changed over the past 100 years. Professionals have a new awareness of the importance of the first 1,000 days after birth and the dramatic impact they can have on later development. The field has moved from information passed down from parents to children to using evidence from research and professional organization as the basis for making decisions about infants and toddlers. There is science to back up the practice of early childhood education.

However, even with new evidence about the importance of the first three years of life, the quality of care for infants and toddlers is of concern to many in the field. One way of addressing this concern has been to develop standards for the field. This is both responsive to a dilemma and somewhat disconcerting. Many social policies affect infants and toddlers—some directly, others indirectly. Those that support infants and toddlers in the context of their family are the most positive. As with all fields in which decisions need to be made, there are times when these are difficult. Having the guidance of a code of conduct is useful.

CHAPTER IN REVIEW

* The period of infancy and toddlerhood has become a distinct focus for many professions, including child development, early childhood education, early intervention, developmental psychology, medicine, and others.

* Views of infants and toddlers and the importance of early development have changed significantly over time.

* Rather than working with infants and toddlers because of past practice, we are now looking at the evidence that shows what particular practices are the most likely to produce positive outcomes.

* The science of early childhood development provides us with a foundation on which to develop our practices with young children.

☀ High-quality child care can have a positive long-term impact on children's development, yet the quality of infant/toddler care is often poor to mediocre.

☀ A growing emphasis on academic achievement is now being applied to infants and toddlers. There is concern that this emphasis will destroy the holistic approach to early childhood and that important developmental tasks related to social and emotional development will be ignored.

☀ Young children who live in poverty come to school with fewer academic and self-regulatory skills than middle-class children.

☀ Professionals in the field need expertise in areas of advocacy and social policy to ensure that infants' and toddlers' needs are brought to the table.

☀ A code of ethical conduct provides guidance in making difficult decisions.

APPLICATION ACTIVITIES

1. Go to one government Web site (such as http://nces.ed.gov, www.census.gov, www.cdc.gov, www.cdc.gov.ncbdd) and one advocacy or professional type Web site (such as www.zerotothree.org, www.childrensdefense.org, www.nccp.org, www.nieer.org, www.naeyc.org). Compare and contrast the two sites and reflect on the differences. Decide which one you would use for a particular purpose.

2. Go the NAEYC Web site (www.naeyc.org) and look at its position statements. Read the Code of Ethical Conduct and Statement of Commitment. Decide whether or not you are willing to sign the commitment statement. If you are not willing to sign it as written modify it so that it reflects the commitment you are willing to make. Then follow through on your decision.

3. Go to your state's standards for infants and toddlers. If you do not know where they are begin with www.doe.k12.[state postal abbreviation].us/early_childhood. Evaluate these standards based on the NAEYC Essential Features of Developmentally Effective Early Learning Standards.

RESOURCES

Web Resources

☀ **Administration for Children and Families (ACF)** within the Department of Health and Human Services (HHS) is responsible for federal programs that promote the economic and social well-being of families, children, individuals, and communities. Their **About ACF** page provides a detailed introduction to ACF's mission, biographies, budget, fact sheets, functional statements, operating structure, key priorities, and regional offices. You can also read ACF guidance documents (downloadable) on federal legislation, and government policies on child care, child support, child welfare, developmental disabilities, families and communities, Head Start, information technology, welfare, and low-income assistance. http://www.acf.hhs.gov

❋ **Center for Law and Social Policy (CLASP)**, a nonprofit public policy and advocacy organization, has led successful efforts at the federal and state levels to improve the child support system and to establish child support as a major work support for low-wage families. CLASP posts detailed analyses of proposed federal and state legislations, laws, and regulations, in-depth reports, policy briefs, fact sheets, testimony, and much more, organized by topic area. Be sure to read *Starting Off Right: Promoting Child Development from Birth in State Early Care and Education Initiatives*. http://clasp.org/

❋ **Division for Early Childhood (DEC)** is one of seventeen divisions of the CEC—the largest international professional organization dedicated to improving educational outcomes for individuals with exceptionalities, students with disabilities, and/or the gifted. DEC is focused on children with special needs, birth through age 8, and their families. The **About Us** page provides information on DEC's mission, annual report (downloadable), strategic goals, members, and commitment to young children. http://www.dec-sped.org

❋ **National Association for the Education of Young Children (NAEYC)** provides information on issues related to early childhood education practice, policy, and/or professional development for which there are controversial or critical opinions. All position statements can be downloaded for free. http://www.naeyc.org

❋ **National Center for Children in Poverty** provides reports, fact sheets, and press materials focused on end child poverty. Its goal is to promote the economic security, health, and well-being of low-income families and their children. http://www.nccp.org

❋ **National Institute for Early Education Research (NIEER)** mission is to support early childhood education initiatives by providing objective, nonpartisan information based on research. This Web page includes information on goals, history, recent development, and contact information of NIEER. http://nieer.org/

❋ **Zero to Three** is the nation's leading resource on the first three year of life. It supports the healthy development of infants, toddlers and their families. Their Infant-Toddler Policy Agenda provides an overview of the policy agenda for infants and toddlers, with good health, strong families, and positive early learning experiences as the ultimate goal. http://www.zerotothree.org

Print Resources

❋ National Research Council and Institute of Medicine. (2000). *From neurons to neighborhoods the science of early childhood development*. Committee on integrating the science of early childhood development. J. P. Shonkoff & D. A. Phillips (Eds.), Board on Children, Youth, and Families, Commission on Behavioral and Social Sciences and

Education. Washington, DC: National Academy Press.

Robinson, A., & Stark, D. R. (2002). *Advocates in action: Making a difference for young children*. Washington, DC: NAEYC.

Seefeldt, C. (2005). *How to work with standards in the early childhood classroom*. New York: Teachers College Press.

Zero to Three. (2006). A policy agenda for babies. *Journal of Zero to Three, 26*(6), entire issue. National Center for Infants, Toddlers, and Families.

REFERENCES

Barnett, W. S., Hustedt, J. T., Robin, K. B., & Schulman, K. L. (2004). *The state of preschool: 2004 state preschool yearbook*. Rutgers, NJ: The National Institute for Early Education Research.

Bowman, B., Donovan, M., & Burns, M. (Eds.) (2001). *Eager to learn: Educating our preschoolers*. Washington, DC: National Academy Press.

Buysse, V., & Wesley, P. W. (Eds.) (2006). *Evidence-based practice in the early childhood field*. Washington, DC: Zero to Three.

Children's Defense Fund. (2006). *The state of America's Children 2005*. Washington, DC: Author.

Gamel-McCormick, M., & Amsden, D. (2002). *Investing in better outcomes: The Delaware Early Childhood Longitudinal Study*. Newark, DE: Center for Disabilities Studies.

Gandini, L. (2001). Reggio Emilia: Experiencing life in an infant-toddler center. In L. Gandini & C. P. Edwards (Eds.), *Bambini: The Italian approach to infant/toddler care* (pp. 55–66). New York: Teachers College Press.

Heckman, J., Grunewald, R., & Reynolds, A. (2006). The dollars and cents of investing early: Cost-benefit analysis of early care and education. *Zero to Three, 26*(6), 10–17.

Koops, W. (2003). Imaging children. In W. Koops & M. Zuckerman (Eds.), *Beyond the century of the child: Cultural history and developmental psychology* (pp. 1–20). Philadelphia, PA: University of Pennsylvania Press.

Lally, J. R., Lurie-Hurvitz, E., & Cohen, J. (2006). Good health, strong families, and positive early learning experiences: Promoting better public policies for America's infants and toddlers. *Zero to Three, 26*(6), 6–9.

Lombardi, J., Cohen, J., Stebbins, H., Lurie-Hurvitz, E., Chernoff, J. J., Denton, K., et al. (2004). *Building bridges from prekindergarten to infants and toddlers: A preliminary look at issues in four states*. Washington, DC: Zero to Three.

National Association for the Education of Young Children. (2002). Early learning standards: Creating the conditions for success. Retrieved April 8, 2007, from http://www.naeyc.org/about/positions/early_learning_standards.asp

National Association for the Education of Young Children. (2005). Code of ethical conduct and statement of commitment. Retrieved April 8, 2007, from http://www.naeyc.org/about/positions/RSETH05.asp

National Research Council and Institute of Medicine. (2000). *From neurons to neighborhoods the science of early childhood development.* Committee on integrating the science of early childhood development. In J. P. Shonkoff & D. A. Phillips (Eds.), Board on Children, Youth, and Families, Commission on Behavioral and Social Sciences and Education. Washington, DC: National Academy Press.

Peisner-Feinberg, E. S., Burchinal, M. R., Clifford, R. M., Culkin, M. L., Howes, C., Kagan, S. L., et al. (1999). *The children of the cost, quality, and outcomes study go to school: Executive summary.* Chapel Hill, NC: University of North Carolina, Frank Porter Graham Child Development Center.

Rouse, C., Brooks-Gunn, J., & McLanahan, S. (2005). Introducing the issue. School readiness: Closing the racial and ethnic gaps. *The Future of Children, 15*(1), 5–13.

Shenk, D. (1997). *Data smog: Surviving the information glut.* New York: HarperCollins Publishers.

Shonkoff, J. P. (2000). Science, policy, and practice: Three cultures in search of a shared mission. *Child Development, 71,* 181–187.

Strain, P. S., & Dunlap, G. (2006). *Recommended practices: Being an evidence-based practitioner.* Center for Evidence-based Practice: Young Children with Challenging Behavior. Retrieved December 7, 2006, from www.challengingbehavior.org

U.S. Department of Education. (2006). Initial Results from the 2005 NHES Early Child Care Program Participation Study. Retrieved April 8, 2007, from http://www.nces.ed.gov/pubs2006/earlychild/index.asp

U.S. Department of Education, National Center for Education Statistics. (1998). Early Childhood Longitudinal Study, Kindergarten Class of 1998–1999. Retrieved October 16, 2007, from http://nces.ed.gov/ecls/kindergarten.asp

U.S. Department of Health and Human Services, Administration for Children and Families. (2000). FFY 2000 CCDF Data tables and charts. Retrieved September 20, 2006, from http://www.acf.hhs.gov/programs/ccb/research/00acf800/chldser1.htm

U.S. Department of Health and Human Services, Administration for Children and Families. (2006). *Program models in Early Head Start: Early Head Start research and evaluation project* (Brochure). Retrieved September 20, 2006, from http://www.acf.hhs.gov/programs/opre/ehs/ehs_resrch/index.html

chapter 2

Development before Birth

Chapter Outline

- Pregnancy
- Prenatal Planning and Care
- Heredity and Genetics: Just the Basics
- Screening Techniques
- Maternal Diseases, Disorders, and Illnesses
- Exposure to Environmental Teratogens

Pregnancy can be both an exhilarating and a scary experience. Every woman comes to the experience with different concerns, expectations, and worries. Some really do not want to be pregnant, others cannot wait. Some have the support of a loving partner, others go through the experience alone. The only constant when studying pregnancy and development is that each woman and each pregnancy is unique.

WHY STUDY DEVELOPMENT BEFORE BIRTH?

※ Development starts at conception. When you are trying to understand an infant or toddler's behavior, you may need to know or ask about significant events that happened during the pregnancy.

※ As a professional in the field, others expect you to know and understand the implications of various prenatal situations and conditions and their effect on development.

※ Parents may ask you questions about what they should or should not do during pregnancy.

※ As a potential parent, you may want to know about some of the factors that affect birth outcomes.

PREGNANCY

The United States does little in the way of educating its young women and men about the life skills and healthy living habits needed before, during, and after pregnancy. When pregnancies are planned, the prospective mother and father can make positive changes in their lifestyle to prepare the environment. Such conscious decisions are crucial because prenatal development dramatically affects the infant.

A healthy lifestyle is a positive step, but it does not guarantee a successful pregnancy outcome. However, it should be a goal of all prospective mothers and fathers. Many prenatal risks can be prevented; others can be monitored or managed. Planning gives a woman time to ensure that her diet meets the nutritional demands of pregnancy. It provides time to stop using tobacco, alcohol, drugs, and caffeine, and to avoid harmful environmental exposure (Lowdermilk & Perry, 2003). These decisions are designed to increase the probability of having a normal, healthy, happy baby. Unfortunately, some prenatal risks are unknown. They cannot be prevented and may not be discovered until birth.

There are many factors that influence the development of the fetus before birth. These factors come from the genetic matter that forms the fetus, the environment in which the fetus grows and develops, and the developing fetus himself. These factors interact and influence each other and shape the developing organism.

As an educator, understanding prenatal growth and development helps you talk knowledgeably to parents and better anticipate how their child will grow and develop. This knowledge helps you to plan and better teach each infant. So, let us start at the beginning.

up close and personal

After two negative home pregnancy tests, my husband was sure I wasn't pregnant, but some instinct told me I was. I called an ob-gyn and went in for a pregnancy test. The nurse came back beaming—and I sat in the little cubicle for about 20 minutes. I was pregnant—a little person was growing inside of me.

It's hard to explain the myriad of emotions that flowed through me. I was ecstatic and terrified, excited and worried.

How were we going to pay for this baby? My career was just taking off. What would this mean to it? And the omnipresent thought in my mind: Would this baby make it? We had been pregnant 10 months earlier, but the baby had died 12 weeks into my pregnancy. My world had ended—I had wanted to be a mom so badly. I sat in the doctor's office with my hand on my tummy wondering if this baby would survive.

REFLECTIVE PRACTICE

How do you think this woman's experience will be different because she had a miscarriage 10 months earlier? If you were in her position what might you do or not do because of that experience?

Gestation
is the time between conception and birth.

The time from conception to birth is called **gestation** and usually lasts 40 weeks, or about nine calendar months. The most common way to think about the duration of a pregnancy is to divide the nine months into three trimesters. This is an outside-looking-in approach. In this section, we will focus on periods that are more significant to the developing organism: the germinal, embryonic, and fetal periods. This approach still breaks down the nine months into three periods, but the duration of each period is different: The germinal and embryonic periods correspond to the first trimester, and the fetal period corresponds to the remaining two trimesters.

Germinal Period

Each of us starts out as a single cell: the ovum, or egg. To develop from this single cell into the person you are today, several processes must take place: first, the egg must be fertilized by a sperm; cells then divide and increase in number; they differentiate to create different body parts (skin, bones, heart, etc.); finally, the cells initiate the systemic function of metabolism.

Ova
are the eggs produced by the ovaries.

Ovary
is an egg-producing female reproductive organ.

Fallopian tubes
are two very small tubes leading from the ovary to the uterus.

Uterus
or womb, opens into the vagina and is connected to both fallopian tubes.

Zygote
is a cell formed by the union of the egg and sperm.

Chromosomes
are very long continuous pieces (or molecules) of DNA that contain many genes and other regulatory material.

Cell receptor site
is a protein on the cell membrane or in the cell that binds to a specific molecule.

Nucleus
is a membrane that encloses the genetic material of the cell.

Cytoplasm
is a watery-like substance that fills cells.

Women are born with all of their reproductive cells. About two million eggs, or immature **ova**, are present in a female's ovaries at birth; however, only about 500 to 600 are used during the approximately 40 years in which a woman can bear children. The mature unfertilized ovum is the largest cell in the female's body. It is about the size of the period that ends this sentence. The ovum is large because of the nutrients it contains. These nutrients nourish the cells during their initial growth and development. Approximately once a month during a female's reproductive years, an egg ripens, is pushed from the **ovary**, drops into one of the **fallopian tubes**, and is available for fertilization. If the egg is not fertilized in 10 to 14 days, the woman's menstrual flow begins, washing away the egg and the lining of the uterine wall. This cycle repeats itself on a regular basis unless fertilization takes place.

While females are born with immature eggs, males begin producing sperm in puberty and continue into old age. Sperm are composed of a large head and a long tail. The head contains the cell nucleus, and the tail, or flagellum, is used for propulsion. During intercourse, about 300 million sperm are mixed with seminal fluid and deposited into the female vagina. Sperm travel the remaining length of the vagina and push through the cervix into the uterus. Midway into the menstrual cycle, mucus secretions of the vagina and the thinning of the cervix make it easier to penetrate, so fertilization is more likely.

Once in the **uterus**, the sperm must travel to the correct fallopian tube and then swim up the tube to meet the egg. The 200 sperm that make it to the fallopian tubes are viable for up to two to three days whereas the egg can only be fertilized for 12 to 24 hours after ovulation (Haffner, 2007). Sperm must travel approximately seven inches to reach the egg, a journey of about an hour. When one sperm penetrates the outer layer of the egg, the successful sperm prevents others from penetrating the egg. The unsuccessful sperm die within 24 hours (Hill & Haffner, 2002). Once inside the egg, the sperm's tail detaches, and the nucleus from the sperm and ovum migrate toward each other and then unite creating a **zygote**. Fertilization restores the number of chromosomes to 23 pairs and initiates cell division or cleavage. In humans, of the 23 pairs of **chromosomes**, there are 22 twin chromosomes, called autosomes, and one pair of sex chromosomes. The sex chromosomes are X for female and Y for male. The gender of the child is determined by the father. If the child is a girl, she will have two X chromosomes; if it is a boy, he will have an X and a Y chromosome.

We may begin as a single cell, but our bodies are made up of approximately 50 trillion cells. There are different types of cells, including nerve cells, skin cells, and white blood cells, to name a few. All cells have indentations called **cell receptor sites**, which allow them to receive information. Each cell, except for the red blood cell, has two components: a **nucleus**, or enclosed core, and an outer area, the **cytoplasm**. Red blood cells do not

DNA
is a nucleic acid that contains the genetic instructions or blueprint for development. Its main role is the long-term storage of information.

Genes
are a unit of inheritance on chromosomes that consist of a long strand of DNA and interact with other genes to influence physical development and behavior.

Mitosis
is the process by which a cell duplicates its genetic information (DNA) and generates two identical cells.

Meiosis
is the process of recombining the 23 chromosomes and then fusing them with another set to make the 46 chromosomes necessary for sexual reproduction.

Morula
is the earliest stage of embryonic development.

Blastocyte
is the second stage of embryonic development, it has both and inner and outer cell mass and it not yet attached.

Ovulation
is a process during the menstrual cycle (about the 14th day) when the ovum is released.

Progestrone
is a hormone that supports pregnancy.

have a nucleus. The cell nucleus houses the **deoxyribonucleic acid (DNA)**. The DNA, which is formed in threadlike double-helix strands called chromosomes, contains the genetic blueprint for development (Batshaw, 2007). Each chromosome is composed of smaller segments of DNA called **genes** that carry codes for inherited traits and are identified by their unique sequence of DNA.

All of the cells in the body divide. However, they divide at different rates, ranging from once every 10 hours in skin cells to once a year in liver cells (Batshaw, 2007). All cells except germ or sex cells divide through the process of **mitosis**. During mitosis, two daughter cells are formed from one parent cell. These are exact replicas of the original cell. Germ cells divide through **meiosis**. Meiosis is more complicated than mitosis and results in more abnormalities. Unlike mitosis, where two identical daughter cells are formed, during the first division in meiosis the chromosomes that come from the mother and father intertwine, allowing genetic material to be exchanged. This complexity increases the likelihood of genetic disorders, but it also enables children to be similar to, but not exactly like, their siblings. The fertilized cell makes a replica of itself through meiosis, changing from two to four to eight cells. This solid mass is called the **morula**. The egg mass continues to multiply as it moves down the fallopian tube. After five days it develops a hollow cavity and begins to change in size and shape. At this point, it is called a **blastocyte**. Although the cells were originally unspecialized, the embryonic stem cells differentiate to develop into three types of cells: the ectoderm, which evolves into skin, the spinal cord, and teeth; the mesoderm, which becomes blood vessels, muscles, and bones; and the endoderm, which develops into the digestive system, lungs, and urinary tract (Batshaw, 2007).

Following **ovulation**, other hormonal changes begin. **Progesterone** levels increase, and that in combination with other hormonal changes causes the lining of the uterus, the **endometrium**, to become thick, spongy, and ready for implantation. The follicle from which the egg was released increases in size and secretes progesterone to help maintain the pregnancy until the **placenta** is capable of producing enough progesterone on its own.

A week after conception, the blastocyst reaches the uterus. Of all fertilized eggs, only about half survive and reach the uterus; the body reabsorbs the others. Although it is possible for the blastocyst to implant, or attach, itself to the uterine wall in many places, it normally does so in the upper back portion of the uterus. The site of implantation is critical. If the blastocyst attaches itself to the bottom of the uterus, it may cause complications in the delivery or the placenta may detach too early. Sometimes implantation takes place outside the uterus, usually in the fallopian tube. This is called an **ectopic pregnancy** and results in a miscarriage (Batshaw, 2007).

Endometrium
is the inner membrane of the uterus whose glands and blood vessels increase in number and size during pregnancy.

Placenta
is formed out of the endometrium and supplies the embryo with oxygen and nutrients and takes away wastes.

Ectopic pregnancy
sometimes called a tubal pregnancy, occurs when the fertilized ovum implants in any tissue other than the uterus.

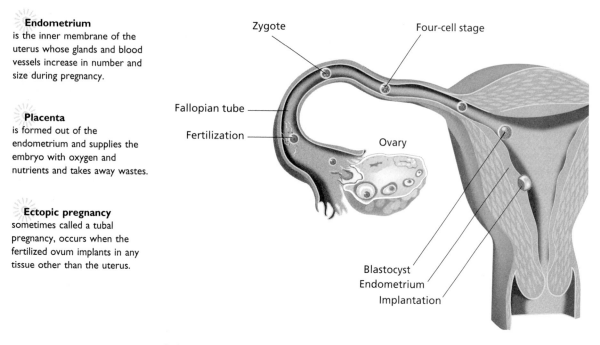

FIGURE 2–1 Ovulation, Fertilization, and Implantation
The ovary discharges an egg into the fallopian tube, where it is fertilized by a sperm. The resulting zygote begins to divide as it moves through the fallopian tube to the uterus, where it implants in the uterine wall.

Embryo
is the developing organism from implantation through eight weeks.

Until implantation is complete, the developing organism absorbs nutrients directly from the mother's cells (see Figure 2–1). Implantation is complete about 12 days after conception. The blastocyst becomes an **embryo**. The embryo produces a hormone, chorionic gonadotrophin, which prevents the mother from menstruating. During the time leading up to implantation, a woman may not even suspect that she is pregnant. Her suspicions usually begin once her menstrual flow is due but does not occur.

Umbilical cord
connects the embryo and later the fetus to the mother during pregnancy.

Embryonic Period

Amniotic sac
consists of a pair of tough, thin membranes that hold the embryo and later the fetus during pregnancy.

The eight weeks of the embryonic period are critical. For the embryo to survive, a complex infrastructure of supports must be developed to protect and nourish the growing organism. These changes, generated through cell differentiation, include thickening of the uterine lining and the development of the placenta, the **umbilical cord**, which attaches the embryo to the placenta, and the **amniotic sac**.

Amnion
is the inner membrane of the amniotic sac, which contains the amniotic fluid and the embryo or fetus.

The embryo is attached to the uterine wall by the placenta. The placenta is a highly specialized disk-shaped organ through which the fetus makes functional contact with the wall of the uterus. The embryo is connected to the placenta by the umbilical cord, which is hoselike and contains blood vessels. The **amnion**, a saclike membrane, is filled with a clear liquid called amniotic fluid. This membrane allows the embryo to move freely within the uterus, thereby protecting it from injury.

The mature placenta develops rapidly after implantation and covers approximately 20 percent of the uterus. There is a fetal and a maternal portion of the placenta and, although these intertwine, they do not intermingle. Once implantation is completed, there is a period of rapid growth because the embryo receives nourishment from the mother's blood through the placenta, a far more efficient process than absorbing nutrients from the mother's cells.

A placental barrier keeps the blood supplies separate. Even though small molecules can pass through this barrier, large molecules cannot. The exact exchange of substances is complex, but, in general, nutritive materials from maternal blood—oxygen, water, and salts—cross the placental barrier, while digestive waste products and carbon dioxide from the developing embryo can cross back. Large molecules, like red blood cells, most bacteria, maternal wastes, and many dangerous toxins and hormones, cannot pass.

Cephalocaudal
is the development and control of the upper part of the body before the lower part.

Proximodistal
is the development and control of the center of the body before the extremities.

Earliest development occurs in the head, brain, and sensory organs, followed by the trunk area (**cephalocaudal**). After two months of gestation, the head accounts for about half of the total body length; by birth, the head comprises only about one-quarter of the newborn's body length. In adults, the head is only about 10 percent of a person's height. Growth moves from the middle outward (**proximodistal**). Structures that are near the midline of the body, such as the spinal cord and heart, develop before the arms and legs, which develop before the fingers and toes.

Congenital malformations
are medical conditions that are present at birth.

The rate of growth is faster during the embryonic period than at any other time; all body tissues, organs, and systems develop during this period. While all of this is happening, a woman still may not yet realize she is pregnant. For this reason, many physicians recommend that women who are planning to become pregnant begin taking prenatal vitamins and that all women of child bearing age take folic acid to protect against a number of **congenital malformations**. It is also during this time that the embryo is most susceptible to the influences of disease, drugs, radiation, and other substances. Changes during this time are so precise and predictable that it is possible to determine when a certain problem occurred. For example, we know that if a child is born with a cleft palate, the defect occurred between the seventh and eighth week, when the palatal arches normally close (Haffner, 2007).

During the second month, the embryo becomes markedly less curved and the head increases in size; a face develops with a primitive nose, eyes, ears, and upper lip; and the neck lengthens. The tail-like projection almost fully disappears. Fully formed but extremely small arms and legs, hands and feet, and even fingers and toes appear. The heart and circulatory system is the first system to begin working, and by the end of the second month, the kidneys take over the function of concentrating and excreting urine. Although not yet functional, digestive and respiratory systems develop. The reproductive system also forms. A skeleton of cartilage develops, as do some of the finer features such as eyelids. The embryo is recognizable as a human being by the end of the second month of development, although it is somewhat strange–looking (Haffner, 2007).

Fetal Period

Fetus
is when all the major structures and organs have been formed; at about eight weeks until birth.

At the end of the second month the developing organism becomes a **fetus**. The early part of the fetal period is characterized by the development and growth of true bone. During the third month, the main organ systems (cardio-vascular, neurological, digestive, etc.) are established and differentiated. The fetus is about 3.5 inches long and weighs about an ounce. By the fourth month, with the fetus growing to about 6 ounces and measuring 10 inches, the mother can begin to detect movement (see Figure 2–2). Tissues and organs continue to develop, and the heart can be heard with a stethoscope or even by placing an ear on the mother's abdomen. During the fifth and sixth months there are more refinements in development (fingernails) and continued growth. By the end of the sixth month the fetus is about 12 to 14 inches long and weighs about 1 ½ to 2 pounds. With the support of neonatal intensive-care nurseries, infants born at 22 weeks or later are considered viable.

The major function of the third trimester is fetal weight gain. The fetus starts storing fat and life support functions are more fully developed. The brain continues to develop rapidly. The lungs begin to be capable of some limited gas exchange. The fetus grows to about 20 inches in length, usually weighs between 6 ½ and 8 pounds, and is ready to be born (Lowdermilk & Perry, 2003).

MULTIPLE PREGNANCIES

Dizygotic
or fraternal twins occur when two fertilized ovum are implanted in the uterine wall at the same time.

Usually the female releases only one ovum at a time. If two mature eggs are released and they are both fertilized (by separate sperm), fraternal or **dizygotic twins** will develop. The term dizygotic refers to the fact that there are two zygotes as well as two amnions, two chorions, and two placentas. Genetically,

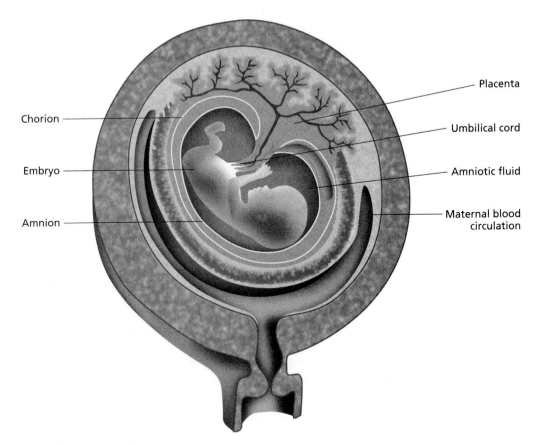

FIGURE 2–2 The Fetus at 4 Months
The fetal blood circulates through the placenta, picking up oxygen and discharging waste into the mother's blood. The amniotic fluid protects the fetus from shock and helps keep the temperature constant.

Monozygotic twins or identical twins develop from a single fertilized ovum that divides into two separate embryos.

fraternal twins are no more alike than other siblings. They are the result of different eggs and different sperm, yet they share the same uterine environment.

Identical or **monozygotic twins** develop from one fertilized ovum. These twins will be of the same sex and have the same genotype. The cell division resulting in monozygotic twins usually occurs between four and eight days after fertilization. When this division is early there will be two amnions, two chorions, and two placentas that may be fused (Lowdermilk & Perry, 2003).

Between 1980 and 2002, the rate of twinning increased from 1 per 53 to 1 in 32 and the rate of triplets rose from 1 per 2,703 to 1 per 543, representing an increase of 65 and 495 percent, respectively (Martin, Kochanek, Strobino, Guyer, & MacDorman, 2005). Multiple gestations accounted for 3.33 percent of all births in 2002 (Brown & Satin, 2007) and the rate is increasing. The incidence of fraternal twins varies with the age of the mother, whether or not there were previous births, racial background, and the use of assisted reproductive techniques. Mothers having babies later and the use of fertility drugs increase the number of multiple pregnancies or multifetal gestations. When couples use *in vitro* fertilization more than one embryo is typically implanted. Multiple gestations pose special risks, both long and short term.

PRENATAL PLANNING AND CARE

Once a woman knows that she is pregnant, the prenatal period provides her with the time to physically and psychologically prepare for the birth of the baby. It is a time of wonder and a time of learning—about oneself, the physical changes of pregnancy, and about commitment and significant relationships.

Women use this time to adapt to the maternal role and to prepare for their new role as a parent. They need to establish a relationship with the developing fetus. Women do this in a variety of ways. For some mothers, seeing the baby in an ultrasound makes it real. For others, the baby becomes real when they can feel it move. For others, it is giving the baby a name.

up close and personal

The day the ultrasound showed that we were having a girl instead of the boy I thought we were having, I decided "the blob" was no longer a suitable name. My husband is from Guatemala and I am from the United States, so we looked for a name we both liked and that would work in both Spanish and English.

We discussed names before we knew the baby was going to be a girl. I liked the name Lluvia del Lago (Rain of the Lake) because I thought it was pretty. My husband's response was to propose the name "Tree" if we were having a boy. I remember thinking to myself that some mean kid on a playground was going to ask to climb my baby.

Somehow, though, as we saw our little girl on the ultrasound, I knew that her name was not going to be Lluvia—and I smiled knowing that I would never have to call my child Tree. Her name was going to be Izabella—and so from about 17 weeks on that's what we've called her. Everyone who knows us refers to our unborn child as Izabella, and I love that this little person already has a name. Although I will admit that I frequently call her "Kicky" when she's pounding the walls of my tummy. It's nice that even my ob-gyn refers to our baby as Izabella, and the people at work ask about her by name. For us, giving her a name made her real.

REFLECTIVE PRACTICE

Medical professionals are concerned about helping mothers build a relationship with the developing fetus. This is particularly true for babies who are unplanned or unwanted. How would you help make a fetus a real person for a mother who was unsure about her feelings about being pregnant? How do you think this might impact her life style?

up **close** and **personal**

Oxlaj Family Birth Plan

Thank you for your help and support in bringing Izabella Franchesca Oxlaj into the world. We are so excited to become her parents and are grateful that you will be a part of her assimilation into our family.

We believe that by staying in the hospital we are not only increasing the health and safety of our child, but are also learning valuable skills that will aid us in better caring for Izabella. We look forward to learning as much as possible about breastfeeding, infant care, and calming techniques so that we can have the happiest, healthiest baby possible when she comes home with us.

We believe that bonding is an important part of welcoming our new baby into our family. To best accomplish bonding we request that

Both Edwardo and I are present at her birth, and that Edwardo can stay throughout the duration of the operation.

We can see and hold her in the operating room.

I can breastfeed in the recovery room or as soon as possible thereafter.

She rooms in with us.

She will not be given a bottle.

If breastfeeding is not working, that I can pump breast milk and that we can feed her through either a feeding cup or a syringe.

If it is deemed medically necessary to give her formula, that

We are informed of why this is necessary, and assured that all other options have been explored.

One of us can give her the formula.

The formula is soy based (I, my mother, and my husband were all allergic to milk as children).

We view any examination or assessment as an opportunity to learn and ask questions about our daughter. These questions, we believe, may help us become more informed parents, and, if any problems are detected, will allow us to make more appropriate and better decisions for our daughter. Because of this belief we ask that:

All assessments are done in our room if possible; if not, that one of us can be present during the assessment.

Procedures, no matter how routine, are thoroughly explained before they are performed.

If Izabella must be taken out of our room and we can not join her, we would like the following questions answered before she leaves our room:

Who is taking the baby, who will be caring for her during the assessment, who will bring her back, and who do we talk to if we have additional questions?

What does the assessment entail?

Why can't we watch the assessment, and why it is being performed?

Where will the assessment take place?

When can we expect her to be returned our room?

We would also like to be informed of the findings of any assessment not conducted in our presence.

I would also like

To have the anesthesiologist wait to begin administering any medications until *after* I've completed all paperwork processes (not doing so means I cannot give "informed consent" and any signed papers are legally null and void), to explain each medication as it is administered, and to take the time to address any concerns.

To have the urinary catheter inserted *after* the epidural (or spinal) has been administered.

To have my husband in the operating/delivery room with me at all times throughout the surgery/birth, whether or not I am conscious. (I understand that if an emergency situation develops, this may not be possible.)

To be able to wear my own clothes in the hospital.

We understand that in the case of an emergency that hospital personnel may not be able to follow our birth plan and that they will follow what they feel is medically best for the health of Izabella and me. Once the emergency passes we would like the birth plan followed as closely as possible, and any necessary deviation from it explained to us.

REFLECTIVE PRACTICE

This mother was planning for a Cesarean section. How did you respond to this birth plan? Did you think it was too much? Were there things you would have added to or taken away from the plan? How do you think it would be different if it had been a vaginal birth?

For low-risk women, the goal of birth planning is to provide choices. A woman can choose who she wants to have with her at the birth of her baby, where the baby is to be born, and whether she plans to have an epidural or use another type of pain relief during labor. Many women discuss these options with their physician or midwife, and some even write them down in the form

Babies are born into families. Families may have aunts and uncles, brothers and sisters and grandparents. Babies impact the families they are born into and families impact the growth and development of babies.

of a birth plan that they bring to the hospital with them. The plan usually functions as a guide for labor and delivery, but women are advised that the plan may not be followed if complications arise during the birthing process (Lowdermilk & Perry, 2003).

Partners, Relationships, and Pregnancy

Women may be the one carrying the baby, but there is a definite "we" in pregnancy. Men often joke that they have the harder job when their wife is pregnant. Although most pregnant woman (especially near the end) would disagree with this statement, most would agree that men's lives change a lot when their partner is pregnant.

Partners often find themselves in the role of being a support person—lifting heavy things, wrapping ice packs around swollen feet, and lending an ear to their partner's worries and concerns.

While they are adjusting to their changing partner, men are also coming to terms with the reality that they are going to become a father. Depending on the situation, some men may be excited and eager, others may be indifferent, and still others may be detached and hostile.

Partners also usually establish a relationship with the baby before he is born. They might do that by buying a fetal stethoscope to listen to the baby's heartbeat, placing their hands on their partner's tummy to feel the baby "kick," or by attending doctor's visits. Men also frequently attend childbirth classes with their partner, read books, talk to friends, and develop more intimate relationships with their own parents.

Siblings of the unborn child will have varying reactions to the pregnancy. Very young children may not be aware of the pregnancy and its implications. However, by age 2, children notice the change in the environment. They may become clingier and lose some of the developmental milestones they have just attained. Preschool children often want to be told what it was like when they were in their mother's "tummy."

School-age children have more pointed and specific questions about how the baby got in "mommy's tummy" and how she will get out. They often see themselves as the little mother or father to the baby. Adolescents, who are trying to establish their own sexual identity, may be embarrassed by the obvious evidence that their parents engage in sexual activity (Lowdermilk & Perry, 2003).

Prenatal visits to a medical professional usually begin after the first missed menstrual period, although women who are planning to become pregnant often consult a medical professional ahead of time. At the beginning of pregnancy, these routine visits occur monthly. As the pregnancy progresses, they become semimonthly and then weekly. For healthy pregnant women, prenatal care involves routine screenings for the relatively minor diseases or conditions that can affect both mother and baby. For women who are at high risk during pregnancy, the goal of prenatal care may include the prevention, detection, and management of problems and factors that adversely affect the health of the mother and/or fetus. Ideally, this care is multidisciplinary and involves physicians and/or midwives, nurses, nutritionists, social workers, and other professionals (Lowdermilk & Perry, 2003).

Genetics
is the science of genes, heredity, and their impact on organisms.

With the decreasing incidence of communicable diseases such as rubella, and our increasing knowledge of **genetics**, researchers and physicians have become more focused on genetic causes of disease and disability. To understand how children grow and develop, it is necessary for you, as a professional in the field, to have a basic understanding of heredity and genetics. This knowledge base will enable you to talk to other professionals and to ask the questions you need answers to so that you can work with infants, toddlers and their families.

HEREDITY AND GENETICS: JUST THE BASICS

Heredity influences the growth and development of human beings. It was once believed that hereditary factors were the only influences on development. Research has since indicated that this is not true (Travers, 2006). The genetic makeup of each individual plays a strong role in dictating specific developmental outcomes. The color of our eyes, our height, the size of our feet, the color of our skin, and even the diseases that we are susceptible to are influenced by the genes we inherited from our biological parents. However, the environment also plays a role in the expression of many genes. Most traits that humans are interested in are not located on a single gene, but are actually the interactions between genes and their environment. Personality and intelligence fall into this category. Genetics is a complex field and knowledge about inheritance patterns varies with particular traits.

Chromosomes and Genes

Human development is complicated. Because the process of development from conception to birth usually occurs without incident, we do not think about the complexities. However, the more we know about this process and the potential problems that can occur, the more amazing it is that most babies are born healthy, happy, and demanding attention from those who care for them.

Chromosomes

The human body is made up of cells. There are many different kinds of cells. We have skin cells, liver cells, brain cells, and so on. In the center of most of these cells (except blood cells) there is a nucleus, which contains chromosomes (see Figure 2–3). Humans have 46 chromosomes arranged in 23 pairs. To help identify the chromosomes, they are numbered. Chromosomes one through 22 are called **autosomes**. Although different in size, each is a matched pair. The 23rd pair of chromosomes are the sex chromosomes. The female chromosome is larger and in the shape of an "X," whereas the male chromosome is smaller and looks like a "Y" with a short tail. Females have two "X" chromosomes, whereas males have an "X" and a "Y" (National Human Genome Research Institute [HGP], 2007).

Autosomes
are nonsex chromosomes.

Chromosomal errors account for 2 to 3 percent of disorders in all live births. The actual number of problems that occur during pregnancy is much higher, but most fetuses with these chromosomal disorders die in utero (Batshaw, 2007). Most chromosomal abnormalities occur during meiosis. Damage can happen either to parts of a chromosome or to the whole chromosome. There are two basic types of chromosomal abnormalities: numerical and structural.

Numerical Abnormalities. In numerical abnormalities an infant is missing one chromosome from a pair, or has more than two chromosomes of a pair. In many instances this results in miscarriage. When it does not, the infants

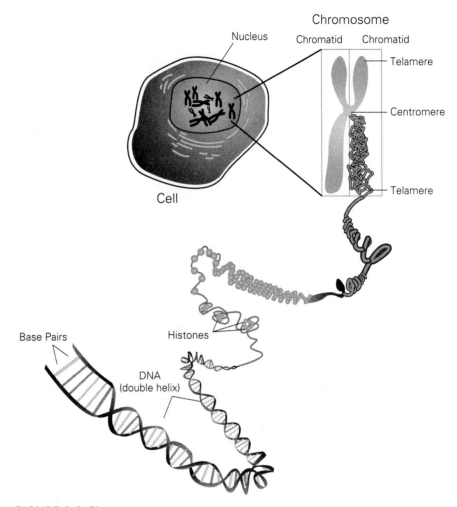

FIGURE 2–3 Chromosomes

Chromosomes are found in the cell nucleus. Humans have 23 pairs of chromosomes, which are made up of threadlike packages of genes and DNA.

have developmental problems. In trisomy 21, the most common form of Down syndrome, children have three 21st chromosomes (hence the "tri"; "somy" comes from chromosome), or a total of 47 chromosomes instead of the usual 46. The extra chromosome causes some of the distinctive features of children with Down syndrome, including a small head, flattened face, an upward slant of the eyes, and small ears, mouths, hands, and feet. Children with Down syndrome are born with developmental delays, and often have medical conditions requiring ongoing treatment, and typically need extra support throughout their lives (Roizen, 2007).

In some cases, a chromosome is missing. Turner Syndrome is an example of a disability where a chromosome is lost (resulting in 45 chromosomes). This syndrome results from the lack of one X chromosome, usually from the father. Girls have one X chromosome rather than the XX pair. This abnormality causes girls to be sterile; short in stature; have webbing at their neck; broad chests; compromised throat, trachea, and sinus; and often have heart and middle-ear problems (Batshaw, 2007).

Structural Abnormalities. In some cases a portion of the chromosome and hence the genetic information is missing (deletions); in other cases it may appear twice, which results in extra genetic material (duplication); in others, a portion has been broken off, turned upside down, and reattached (inversion). Sometimes information that should be on one chromosome is put on a different chromosome (insertion), and in other cases parts of two chromosomes are switched (translocation). For example, some of chromosome 20 ends up on chromosome four, and likewise some of chromosome four becomes part of chromosome 20 (HGP, 2007). In still other cases a portion of a chromosome is broken off and forms a circle or ring. Depending on the particular genetic material, this may or may not affect the infant's development (see Figure 2–4).

Most chromosomal abnormalities are accidental and are present in the egg or sperm at the time of fertilization. When this happens the abnormality is present in every cell of the body. If the problem happens later, after conception, some cells will be abnormal and others will not. This results in **mosaicism**. Because not all of the cells are affected, children who are affected will have a milder version of the abnormality.

Mosaicism is abnormal chromosome division that results in two or more types of cells containing different numbers of chromosomes.

Genes

Chromosomes are made up of genes (see Figure 2–5). Each chromosome has between 250 and 2,000 genes. Genes contain genetic material (DNA) that directs the body through the developmental process, one protein at a time. The human genome contains about 30,000 to 40,000 genes. In April 2003, the human genome was mapped. This mapping facilitates the study of hereditary diseases and the identification of single-gene disorders (HGP, 2007).

Genes have two core functions: They serve as a reliable template or blueprint for development and they have a transcriptional function. As a template, some genes regulate the development and functioning of the body, whereas others make specific products such as enzymes and hormones. Their transcriptional function is less well known. The transcriptional function allows the gene to affect the structure, function, and other biological characteristics in which it is expressed (Jensen, 2006). Every cell has the genes for your whole body.

Types of mutation

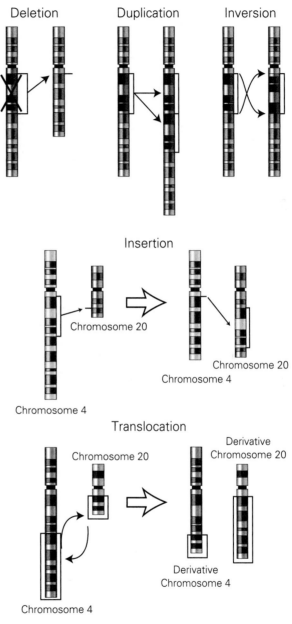

FIGURE 2–4 Types of Mutations
Chromosomes can have mutations during cell division. In some cases information is deleted, duplicated, or inverted. In other situations, parts of one chromosome are inserted on a different chromosome; other times, parts of two chromosomes are traded.

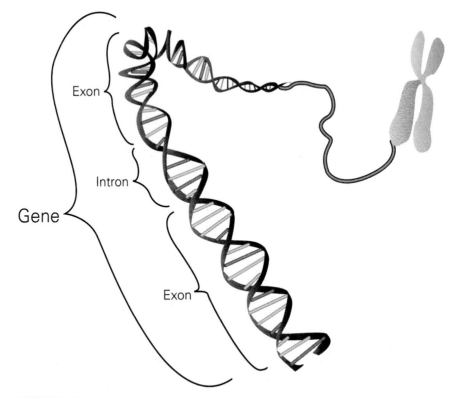

FIGURE 2–5 Genes
Genes are pieces of DNA. The exon is the region of the gene that has the code for producing the gene's protein. The intron is a noncoding sequence of DNA.

However, only a small portion of the gene is activated in a particular cell. For example, only the kidney-related function of a gene is expressed in the kidney cell; the other parts of the gene are repressed. Gene expression translates genetic information into action. Everyday factors such as emotional states, stress, exercise, and nutrition influence gene expression. The environment in which one lives and how one feels can affect gene expression. This is the basis for early intervention and the cause for our concern about toxic environments. Although genes provide the blueprint, just like the blue print for a house, there can be modifications in the structure and the house can be remodeled at a later date. The brain is highly experience dependent (Jensen, 2006).

A mutation, or error, in a gene can lead to a genetic disorder (Batshaw, 2007). Errors can occur at various steps in the process for many reasons. Some errors are irrelevant; there are enough checks and balances in the system to take care of them. Other errors, however, like those in the gene itself, disrupt subsequent steps. Approximately 1 percent of the population congenital malformations are caused by a single gene defect (Batshaw, 2007).

Mutation
is a different form or alteration of a gene.

A **mutation** is a change in a gene that occurs by chance. The larger the gene affected, the greater the probability of a mistake. Older parents have higher mutation rates. Some mutations occur spontaneously, others are related to radiation, chemicals, and viruses (HGP, 2007). The most common mutation is called a point mutation, where a single chemical is replaced with another chemical. In sickle cell anemia, a single substitution in the DNA base tells the cells to produce valine instead of glutamic acid at one spot on the hemoglobin protein. This leads to a painful disability where red blood cells are shaped like sickles instead of disks.

Now you have a basic understanding of how chromosomes and genes work and the role they play in development. The next step is to put this knowledge in the context of heredity and the infants who may inherit these genes and be present in your classroom.

Genetic Transmission

Some genetic traits follow a Mendelian pattern (see Figure 2–6), so-called because they were discovered by the Austrian botanist Gregor Johann Mendel. His findings were first published in the late 1800s. He did not study animals, but the laws he formulated while working with plants provided the basis for understanding inheritance patterns. Green and yellow plants fascinated Mendel, and he did not understand why, when he genetically mixed green and yellow plants, he did not get a chartreuse plant. Instead, he continued to create green and yellow plants, but he always had more green plants than yellow plants.

He concluded that some traits (green in this instance) are dominant, whereas others are recessive or hidden (yellow in this case). Scientists found that these same principles of dominant and recessive genes apply to human beings, and they help us understand how some birth traits and disorders are inherited (HGP, 2007).

Before getting into this let us talk about the language of genetics. When we talk about genetics we use a lot of prefixes. Breaking the words down makes it easier to understand what we are talking about. Let us start with the prefix *homo*. Homo means the *same*. Think about words you know that begin with homo. Homogeneous is an adjective that generally means composed of the *same* kind of parts. We homogenize milk to break up the cream so the fat globules are all the *same* size. And we are homosapiens because we are all the *same* species. Thus, when you encounter the prefix homo you can assume that it means the *same*.

Obviously there is a flip side to this: hetero. Hetero means different. Heterogeneous groups are different from each other. The term zygote is used for the developing individual who was created by the union of the egg and sperm. Think about eye color. Both the mother and father contribute genes related to eye color. If they both contribute the *same* eye color (both blue), the child will be

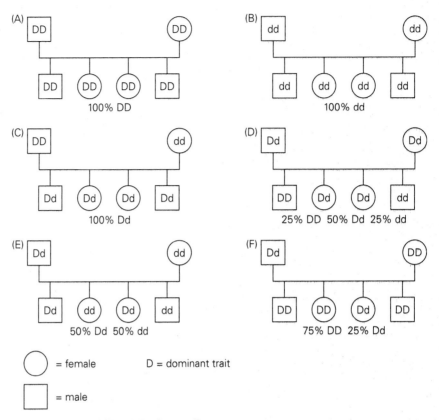

FIGURE 2–6 Mendelian Inheritance Patterns
Mendelian inheritance patterns are based on the predictable relationship between dominant and recessive genes on the autosomes. They illustrate the differences between the genotype and phenotype.

Homozygous
refers to two identical copies of a gene.

Heterozygous
is when two different alleles occupy the same place on a pair of genes.

Allele
is a DNA sequence, usually a gene that occupies a particular position on a chromosome.

homozygous for that trait. If they contribute different colors (brown and blue), the child will be **heterozygous** for that trait. Armed with this information, let us tackle heredity.

Two basic concepts will help you understand how inheritance patterns work: how genes are passed from parents to children, and the dominant and recessive characteristics of genes. We will start with the first. Genes, or **alleles**, always occupy a specific location on a chromosome. For example, the genes for eye color from each parent are in the same location on their respective chromosomes. Although the genes are in the same location, they may be for different eye colors.

Let us start with the assumption that you have blue eyes (we will get to brown eyes soon). Your blue eyes are somewhat of a mystery, because both of your parents have brown eyes. If you inherited the same coding, or alleles, from each parent (blue eyes) you are homozygous for that trait. If you inherited different codes (brown eyes from one parent and blue eyes from the other), you would be heterozygous for the trait and you would have brown eyes. So, obviously this did not happen. Something else is going on.

REFLECTIVE PRACTICE

If you have two brown-eyed parents and you have brown eyes (phenotype), what are the possible genotypes you could have?

Genotype
is the specific genetic genome or an individual's DNA.

We use capital letters (A) to indicate dominant forms of genes and small letters (a) to indicate recessive forms. There are two ways to be homozygous: You can inherit two dominant (AA) genes or two recessive (aa) genes. Knowing that you have blue eyes and your parents have brown eyes, and that brown eyes are dominant, we know that you received recessive genes from your parents. We also know that your parents are heterozygous for eye color. When there is one dominant and one recessive gene in a pair (Aa), the individual is heterozygous.

The basic genetic makeup of an individual transmitted from the specific genes of the parents at conception is called a person's **genotype**. This is the sum total of the genes transmitted to you from your parents, and the genes that you will pass on to future generations. However, you cannot tell a persons' genotype by looking at her. Think about your mother and father. Because of the dominant and recessive quality of genes, they were able to pass the gene for blue eyes on to you. So what you see is not necessarily what you get. The observable characteristics of an individual, both biological and behavioral, are a person's **phenotype**. The phenotype is partially the result of the interactions within the genotype of dominant and recessive genes. However, phenotypes can be determined by multiple genes and influenced by environmental factors. Knowing one or a few known alleles does not always enable prediction of the phenotype, particularly for more complex traits. The distinction between genotype and phenotype is important in understanding genetic transmission.

Phenotype
is an individual's physical appearance and constitution.

We have 23 pairs of chromosomes. Twenty-two of these are autosomes. The third pair are the sex chromosomes. Because genes can be either dominant or recessive and there are two different types of chromosomes, three different inheritance patterns are possible: autosomal dominant, autosomal recessive, or X-linked. The X-linked refers to those genes on the sex (X Y) chromosomes. Single genes control some of these characteristics (unifactorial inheritance). Approximately 1 percent of the population has a Mendelian, or single-gene, disorder (Batshaw, 2007). Single-gene disorders are caused by a change (mutation in one gene). There are more than 6,000 identified single-gene disorders. Although each disorder does not affect that many infants when grouped together, they account for about one in 300 births (Centers for Disease Control and Prevention, 2007e). Other disorders are caused by a variety of factors (multifactorial inheritance), including genes interacting with the environment.

Understanding inheritance patterns is a bit-like gambling—trying to figure the odds. We want to understand the probability of someone inheriting a particular genetic trait. If individuals understand the probability of a particular trait being passed on to their children, they can make informed decisions before deciding to have children. When you thought about applying for college, you may have been playing the probability game. You may have applied to one university that you really wanted to attend but did not think you could actually get into. You may have also applied to other colleges that you thought your odds were 50–50. And, to be safe, you may have applied to one school that you thought you had 100 percent probably of getting in. Some inheritance patterns have known probabilities. The focus in the next sections is on the inheritance of genes that cause disabilities in infants and toddlers.

Autosomal Recessive Disorders

There are approximately 1,700 different autosomal recessive disorders (McKusick et al., 2005). In general, dominant genes determine traits. However, if an infant receives a dominant gene (A) for a particular autosomal recessive disorder from one or both of her parents, she would not inherit the recessive disorder. For a child to inherit this type of disorder, she must receive an abnormal recessive gene (a) from both her father and her mother. The child would therefore be homozygous (aa) for the autosomal recessive trait. Autosomal recessive disorders typically relate to enzyme disorders. Enzymes break food down into fats, proteins, and carbohydrates. Children with phenylketonuria (PKU) lack the enzyme to convert phenylalanine to tyrosine. The phenylalanine is toxic to the brain and, if not treated, will cause intellectual disabilities. In autosomal recessive disorders the parents do not have the disorder, but they are heterozygous for it.

Autosomal Dominant Disorders

Autosomal dominant disorders relate to structural abnormalities in the individual. Unlike someone who is heterozygous (Aa) for an autosomal recessive disorder (and would therefore only be a carrier and not have the disorder), those who are heterozygous for an autosomal dominant disorder will be a carrier of *and* be affected by the disorder unless it is a mutation.

There are approximately 4,500 autosomal dominant disorders that have been identified and they effect about 1 in 500 births (McKusick et al., 2005).

Achondroplasia, a form of short-limbed dwarfism, is an autosomal dominant disorder. If only one parent has a dominant gene (Aa) for an autosomal dominant disorder (e.g., one parent with achondroplasia has a child with a person who does not have this disorder), the probability that the child will have the disorder is 50 percent. However, the probability is also 50 percent that the child will not be affected and will not be a carrier (aa). If both parents are heterozygous for the trait, the pattern would predict that the child has a 50 percent chance of having achondroplasia, a 25 percent chance of being unaffected, and a 25 percent chance of receiving two copies of the dominant gene. If the child receives two dominant genes (AA), the disorder will be more severe and may result in death. Autosomal-dominant disorders affect men and women equally, and most frequently involve structural (physical) abnormalities. About half of these disabilities result from mutations (Batshaw, 2007).

REFLECTIVE PRACTICE

You have just been told that an infant with achondroplasia is going to join your classroom. You know that this means an infant with a disproportionately short stature. You also know that it is an autosomal-dominant pattern of inheritance. What will you expect when you meet the parents? How will you understand what happened if the parents are not what you expect?

X-Linked Disorders

Approximately 900 X-linked disorders have been identified and described (McKusick et al., 2005). X-linked disorders typically result in physical disabilities and cognitive impairments. They include such disorders as hemophilia, Duchenne muscular dystrophy, fragile X syndrome, and red-green color blindness. These disorders are passed between generations by carrier mothers. That is, they are carried on the female sex chromosome (X), and they typically involve mutations of genetic information that are found on this chromosome. These disorders occur most often in males because the pairing of the XY chromosomes means that there is no second X chromosome in males to cover the problem. Approximately 25 percent of males with intellectual disability and 10 percent of females with learning disabilities have inherited these conditions from an X-linked transmission (Batshaw, 2007).

A carrier mother who reproduces with an unaffected male passes along the X-linked trait, the female offspring will either be a carrier (50 percent) or will not be affected (50 percent). A male child's situation is different. He has a 50 percent chance of getting the disorder and a 50 percent chance of not being affected. He cannot become a carrier—either he has it or he does not. In the situation where both parents are carriers, male children still have a 50 percent chance of inheriting the disease or being unaffected. But in this instance, the females have a 50 percent chance of being a carrier and a 50 percent chance of actually being affected by the disease (see Figure 2–7).

(A) Unaffected male and female

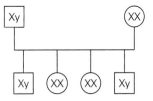

No males or females will be affected

(B) Unaffected male, female carrier

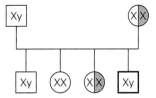

50% of the females will be carriers
50% of the males will have the disorder

(C) Affected male, unaffected female

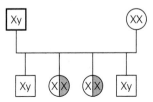

No males will be affected
100% of females will be carriers

(D) Affected male, carrier female

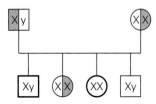

50% of males will be affected
50% of males will not be affected
50% of females will be affected
50% of females will be carriers

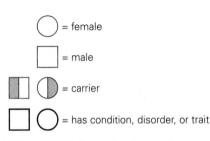

○ = female

□ = male

▮ ◐ = carrier

□ ○ = has condition, disorder, or trait

FIGURE 2–7 X-Linked Inheritance Patterns
Traits carried in the X sex chromosome follow a different pattern of inheritance, which is influenced by the gender of the offspring.

Multifactorial Inheritance

Genes from one or both parents may interact with each other and may be interfered with by environmental factors. The exact cause is not known and we understand less about these problems than single genes. These factors are more challenging to identify and beyond the scope of this book (Lowdermilk & Perry, 2003). Many common congenital malformations are a result of multifactorial inheritance, such as cleft palate and neural tube defects. Depending on the number of genes affected, these malformations can be mild or severe. In families in which this pattern of inherited disorders occurs, it usually favors one sex more than the other. Many traits not related to disabilities are also inherited in this way. Height is an obvious example of multifactorial inheritance. It is a result of not only genetics, but also such environmental factors as diet.

SCREENING TECHNIQUES

Many screening techniques are used routinely for detecting anomalies and other problems in the fetus. If the screening techniques indicate an abnormality, other, more complicated, precise, and expensive procedures are used to follow up. Only the most common procedures are detailed. The less invasive and more common screening measures are detailed first.

Maternal Serum Screening

AFP
is a molecule that can be obtained through the mother's blood; its concentration is measured to determine possible birth defects.

Maternal serum screening procedures use blood samples from the mother to determine the level of **alpha-fetoprotein (AFP)** in the fetus. AFP is a substance produced by the liver of the fetus that passes into the mother's blood stream by diffusion through the placenta and amnion. When the levels are found to be out of the expected range, the test is repeated and followed by other screening measures if the fetus is not beyond 20 weeks gestation.

Ultrasonography

Ultrasonography
is a technique for using sounds outside the range of human hearing to produce computer images.

Ultrasonography (ultrasound) uses the echoes from low-energy, high-frequency sound waves to produce a computer image of the fetus and his internal organs. Ultrasonography is used at different times during a pregnancy for different reasons. During the first trimester it is used to determine the viability of the fetus (to determine if the fetus is alive), to date the pregnancy, and to determine the number of fetuses and the position of the placenta. It is also used to measure nuchal translucency (the clear space at the back of the neck), because a fetus with abnormalities tends to have more fluid at the back of its neck during the first trimester, particularly those with Down syndrome. More subtle chromosomal abnormalities or genetic disorders, such as neural tube defects, abdominal wall problems, facial clefts, and skeletal abnormalities, are the focus of ultrasonography during the second trimester (Schonberg & Tifft, 2002). Most women in the United States have at least three ultrasounds during their pregnancy (Duck, 1999). Ultrasound is also used later in pregnancy when there is concern about the size of the fetal head relative to the mother's pelvis. Some debate remains about the possible maternal and fetal risks associated with the ultrasound screening procedure (Duck, 1999; Hershkovitz, Sheiner, & Mazor, 2002). When ultrasound examinations are performed and risks are found, followup counseling should be immediately available.

up close and personal

My daughter called today with the news: It's a girl. The news wasn't because she had delivered a baby girl, but the news was from an ultrasound taken at 16 weeks. She called from her cell phone on her way back to work. By 3:00 PM she had e-mailed me pictures of the ultrasound. I reflected on *her* birth. She was four days late, and after 20 hours of labor, her head appeared. As the doctor was suctioning her mouth, he and my husband were having a casual conversation about whether it was a boy or a girl. I was enraged. It's probably what gave me the energy to push the rest of her out!

REFLECTIVE PRACTICE

Childbirth and knowledge about birthing has changed dramatically since the 1980s. Few women used personal pregnancy tests to determine whether or not they were pregnant. Ultrasounds were very rare and parents did not know the child's sex until birth. What do you see as the positive and negative aspects of these changes?

Amniocentesis and Chorionic Villus Sampling

Amniocentesis
extracts fluid from the amnion to obtain fetal cells to look for genetic abnormalities that could lead to birth defects.

Amniocentesis was the first technique that allowed access to the intrauterine environment and is the most common invasive procedure for prenatal diagnosis. Amniocentesis, usually performed between 15 and 20 weeks of gestation, involves the removal of fluid from the amniotic sac. It is used as a followup to an ultrasound and is done using real-time ultrasound to avoid endangering the fetus and umbilical cord (Cunniff & the Committee on Genetics, 2004). Once obtained, fetal cells are grown in cultures and analyzed for chromosomal abnormalities, by-products of inborn errors of metabolism, and the presence of AFP. It takes approximately two weeks for the results.

CVS
takes chorionic villi from placental tissue to test for birth defects.

The outer layer of the amniotic sac is called the corion. **Chorionic villus sampling (CVS)** involves taking minute biopsies (pieces) of chorionic villi from placental tissue and testing it. CVS is performed during the period between the 9th and 14th week of gestation before there is enough amniotic fluid for an amniocentesis. This procedure is also done under real-time ultrasound with a needle inserted through the abdominal wall or the cervix. One advantage of CVS over amniocentesis is that it can be performed earlier in the pregnancy and the results take only two to seven days. It is used for diagnosing disorders involving single genes, chromosomal breakage, and some X-linked disorders. It can also detect most of the metabolic diseases that can be diagnosed with amniotic fluid.

Screening Series

Although these various screening techniques have been discussed individually, they are typically done in a series. For example, suppose 1,000 women had a maternal serum AFP test done. AFP levels might be elevated for 50 women, and the test would be repeated for those 50 women. After retesting, approximately 25 would have normal AFP levels. The 25 women who had elevated AFP would be given an ultrasound. The ultrasound might find some cases of multiple gestations, fetal death, or other problems that do not need followup testing. The remaining 15 women would than have some follow up, such as amniocentesis, CVS, or high-resolution ultrasound. Perhaps half of these tests would show that the fetus is at risk. These women's pregnancies would be consider high risk and would be monitored with more intensity than those needing routine prenatal care.

When the results of diagnostic tests show that the developing fetus has a major abnormality, parents must decide whether the fetus will be carried to term or if the pregnancy will be terminated. Parents who decide to carry an infant to term might use the diagnostic tests to select the members of the interdisciplinary medical team who will be needed during the birthing process. Regretfully, with all the information that we have, about 66 percent of the causes of congenital problems remain unknown (Hill & Haffner, 2002).

MATERNAL DISEASES, DISORDERS, AND ILLNESSES

There are many different maternal diseases, disorders, and conditions that affect the unborn infant. These can include infectious diseases, such as viruses and urinary tract infections. Infectious diseases work somewhat differently in pregnant women. Pregnancy alters the natural course of some infectious diseases. Group B streptococci, for instance, are rarely associated with infection in nonpregnant women, but can cause infectious diseases during pregnancy. In addition, some noninfectious chronic diseases of the mother, such as diabetes, may require different management techniques because of the physical demands of pregnancy. With good prenatal care, negative effects of these risk factors may be avoided or monitored, and the birth outcomes improved. Maternal infection and chronic illness account for 3 to 4 percent of congenital malformations (Hill & Haffner, 2002). Only the most common conditions are discussed.

S.T.O.R.C.H. and Other Infections

Prenatal infections account for 2 to 3 percent of disabilities in children (Hill & Haffner, 2002). Researchers group together a number of infectious agents that cause similar disabilities and refer to them as S.T.O.R.C.H. (or TORCH) syndrome. The acronym S.T.O.R.C.H. refers to syphilis (S), toxoplasmosis (T), varicella and other congenital infections (O), rubella (R), cytomegalovirus (C), and herpes simplex virus (H). When a mother contracts one of these agents, the infant may be born with visual or hearing impairments, damage to the central nervous system, or heart defects. Although the placenta acts as a barrier to some harmful substances, it does not prevent these infectious diseases from reaching the fetus.

Some congenital infections, such as influenza, mononucleosis, malaria, parvovirus, and enterovirus, result in increased maternal anemia, low birth weight, intrauterine growth retardation, premature deliveries, and infant mortality, but they do not seem to cause fetal malformations (Centers for Disease Control and Prevention, 2007c). Group B streptococcus (GBS) is one of the most common infections in the developed world.

Group B Streptococcus

Perinatal
refers to the period around the time of birth, five months before and one month after an infant's birth.

Sepsis
is a serious blood infection.

Meningitis
is an infection of the fluid and lining (membranes) of the brain and spinal cord.

Group B Streptococcus (GBS) was recognized in the 1930s and 1940s as a cause of postpartum infection, but it was not until the 1960s that the prevalence of the **perinatal** infections was recognized. Since the 1970s, GBS has been the most common cause of bacterial infections, 1.8 per 1000 live births (Brown & Satin, 2007). In the fetus, GBS is a leading cause of **sepsis** and **meningitis** during the first two months of life. About 20 percent of infected infants die, whereas others have neurological complications (Deering & Satin, 2002).

Approximately 30 percent of pregnant women have GBS in their genital tract, and 1 to 2 percent of their infants develop blood poisoning (sepsis). When this occurs there are two patterns. In about half of the cases the infant becomes ill in the first week of life. The newborn may get sepsis, pneumonia, and meningitis. In other cases the onset is later (a week to several months after birth), with meningitis more common (Centers for Disease Control and Prevention, 2007d).

Women should be screened for this infection routinely between 35 and 37 weeks of gestation. If GBS is discovered, the infected woman should be treated with antibiotics (penicillin). Because GBS can cause women to run a fever during labor or rupture their membranes 18 hours or more before delivery, women who experience these symptoms should also be screened for GBS and, if it is detected, given antibiotics. Antibiotics only help before the baby is born (Centers for Disease Control and Prevention, 2007d).

Chlamydia

Some sexually transmitted diseases pose serious threats to the fetus. One of the most common but least well known is chlamydia. Chlamydia is the most commonly reported bacterial sexually transmitted disease in the United States. The Centers for Disease Control and Prevention estimate that 2.8 million people are infected each year (Centers for Disease Control and Prevention, 2006). The infection is silent: Three-quarters of women who have the disease experience no symptoms. Chlamydia is potentially highly destructive and difficult to diagnosis. If a pregnant woman has chlamydia, the fetus will most likely be affected during the birthing process. Outcomes range from conjunctivitis (eye inflammation) to pneumonia, but it also increases the risk of HIV infection. Chlamydia also increases the risk of premature birth, stillbirths, and infertility (Lowdermilk & Perry, 2003). Chlamydia is responsive to antibiotics (Centers for Disease Control and Prevention, 2006).

HIV and AIDS

Today 90 percent of human immunodeficiency virus (HIV) transmission is vertical; that is, it is transmitted from mother to child. HIV can be transmitted in utero, during delivery, or through breast milk. It is estimated that in utero infection accounts for one-third to one-half of vertical transmissions, with most occurring during the birthing process. A number of therapeutic interventions have been tried. Voluntary screening, combined with the provision of antiretroviral prophylaxis and in some cases Caesarian section, has caused infection rates to decline from 25 percent to 1 or 2 percent (Lindegren, Steinberg, & Byers, 2000). Unfortunately, HIV-infected women with no symptoms can transmit the virus. Among children born to HIV-infected mothers, 25 percent will become infected without intervention. Many preterm infants are born to infected mothers, but whether HIV or other risk factors cause preterm births has not been determined. Infants with the infection can be diagnosed as early as day 2 and almost all by 2 months of age. Approximately half of infected infants show signs of the infection within the first year of life (Bell, 2007).

Maternal Weight and Weight Gain

The fetus is dependent on the mother for all of his nutrition. Her diet is the fetus' diet. Prepregnancy weight is a given and not amenable to change. There are few standards by which to evaluate weight as a risk factor. When a woman is either significantly overweight or underweight before becoming pregnant, or when the weight gain during pregnancy is too low or too high, there is concern (Lowdermilk & Perry, 2003).

Women who are overweight are more likely to have high blood pressure, hypertensive disorders, problems regulating blood sugar and insulin (**gestational diabetes**), and urinary tract infections. They are also likely to have infants who are large for their **gestational age**. Dietary manipulation is not advocated during pregnancy as it is viewed as having no benefit to the mother at this time and may be harmful to the fetus. The risk of having a child with a major problem that is present at birth (congenital) is double that of a woman in the normal weight category (Prentice & Goldberg, 1996).

Underweight women are likely to have infants who are small for gestational age, who may experience anemia or preterm delivery. Malnutrition affects the fetus differently depending on when it occurs. Intrauterine growth restriction (IUGR) is defined as a birth weight equal to or less than the 10th percentile for gestational age (Brown & Satin, 2007). Women who are anorexic or bulimic are advised to wait for the eating disorder to be in remission before becoming pregnant.

There are two major types of IUGR: proportional and disproportional. In proportional growth impairments (60 percent of the cases), the growth of the head and brain are affected. These growth impairments typically occur early in pregnancy and may be confounded by other impairments. Children affected by them often remain small, and have a small head and brain (**microcephaly**), cognitive impairments, and neurological impairments. In disproportional growth impairment (40 percent of the cases), the brain is not affected but the infants are at risk for low blood sugar (hypoglycemia), which can cause seizures and an excessive thickening (hyperviscosity), of the blood, which can lead to stroke. Although less stable at birth, these children have a good long-term prognosis (Farber, Yannni, & Batshaw, 1997).

Weight gain during pregnancy is a common concern for many women. A pregnant woman needs to consume about 300 additional calories a day

Gestational diabetes
is a form of diabetes that affects pregnant women who have never had diabetes, and is probably caused by hormones produced during pregnancy.

Gestational age
is the age of the embryo, fetus, or newborn, figured from the first day of the mother's last menstrual cycle.

Microcephaly
is a neurological disorder in which the head circumference is small and the brain is not well developed.

(Haffner, 2007). Recommended weight gain is dependent upon the appropriateness of the prepregnancy weight. For a single fetus, the recommendation is between 25 and 35 pounds. Overall, a weight gain of about 17 to 20 percent in body weight is the goal (Abrams, Altman, & Pickett, 2000). Thus, a woman with a prepregnancy weight of 100 pounds is considered fine even if she gained only 17 to 20 pounds, whereas a woman weighing 150 pounds might expect to gain 26 to 30 pounds. If the mother is underweight she should gain between 27 and 40 pounds; if she is overweight she should gain at least 15 pounds and up to 25 pounds (Lowdermilk & Perry, 2003).

The optimal rate of weight gain depends on the stage of the pregnancy. At the beginning of pregnancy, the weight gain is primarily in the mother (amniotic fluid; placenta; breast tissue; extra stores of fat, blood, and fluid). By the third trimester it is the fetus that is gaining the weight. During the first trimester a woman might gain about five pounds. In the second and third trimester, she might gain about a half a pound per week.

Chronic Maternal Illnesses

Some women become pregnant already possessing conditions that may affect the fetus; in other situations the pregnancy itself can precipitate risk conditions. Pregnancy causes complex metabolic changes in a woman that can alter previously controlled conditions, such as diabetes, lupus, cardiovascular disorders, anemia, and hypertensive disorders. These conditions increase the probability of preterm delivery and intrauterine growth retardation, accounting for 1 percent of congenital malformations (Hill & Haffner, 2002).

Diabetes Mellitus

Women with diabetes do not produce enough insulin. Before insulin was discovered, in 1921, little was known about diabetes or its effects on pregnancy. Since then, researchers have discovered that lack of insulin makes it more difficult to become pregnant. If a woman does conceive, the chances of complications during pregnancy are increased. Synthetic insulin has resulted in higher pregnancy rates in women with diabetes but managing insulin during pregnancy is challenging.

Pregnancy influences the amount of synthetic insulin a women needs. Early in pregnancy, diabetic women may have periods of hypoglycemia because of the fetus' heightened demands for glucose (sugar). Hormones produced by the placenta alter the mother's metabolism, and, in general, increase her need for insulin. Changes in the mother's metabolism produce periods of maternal hyperglycemia, resulting in the fetus getting too much sugar (**hyperglycemia**). Too much sugar (glucose) results in large babies (macrosomia) and places the

Hyperglycemia is having excessive amounts of sugar (glucose) in the blood.

Hypoglycemia
is having lower than normal amounts of sugar (glucose) in the blood.

infant at risk for **hypoglycemia** at birth when less insulin is required (Haffner, 2007). Diabetic women who receive optimal prenatal care often do well; those who do not receive this care are more likely to experience sudden and unexplained stillbirths; accounting for about half of perinatal deaths in diabetic pregnancies (Haffner, 2007). Even with optimal care, there is still an increased risk for major birth anomalies.

Women who are not diabetic may become so during pregnancy, particularly if they are overweight. This is called gestational diabetes and accounts for about 90 percent of all mothers with diabetes during pregnancy (Haffner, 2007). This usually occurs late in pregnancy. Diabetes can be diagnosed though urine and blood samples taken from pregnant women between 24 and 28 weeks of pregnancy (Deering & Satin, 2002). If well managed, birth outcomes are generally positive.

Hypertensive Disorders

Hypertension
is blood pressure that is chronically elevated (over about 140/90 or higher).

Some women have **hypertension**, or elevated blood pressure, before conception or before 20 weeks of gestation. These women may have high blood pressure because of personal heredity factors, excessive weight, or medical problems. Hypertension is the most common medical complication of pregnancy, affecting 1 to 5 percent of pregnant women. These women should be monitored carefully, because the fetus is at risk for intrauterine growth deficiency and premature rupturing of the placenta because of decreased maternal blood flow to the uterus, placenta, and kidney (Haffner, 2007).

When hypertension develops after the 20th week of gestation and is accompanied by the accumulation of fluid in the tissue (edema) and protein in the urine, it is called preeclampsia. The cause of preeclampsia is unknown, but for women with this condition the risks are the same as those for women who enter pregnancy with high blood pressure. Preeclampsia is a concern for the fetus because it may cause a low blood supply to the placenta, which is the fetal source of food and air. If preeclampsia is not treated, seizures (eclampsia) may develop. In some cases labor is induced if the mother's life is threatened by the probability of having seizures.

Anemia

Anemia is a disorder in which the blood has too little hemoglobin or too few red blood cells. The most frequent causes of anemia during pregnancy are iron deficiencies, folic acid deficiencies, and conditions such as sickle cells. Iron deficiency anemia is relatively common and affects about 20 percent of pregnancies (Lowdermilk & Perry, 2003). Iron is necessary to increase the number of the mother's red cells and to supply some to the fetus. To prevent anemia,

up close and personal

As soon as the doctor knew I was having twins, she told me to expect to have a cesarean section. The babies were not due until October, but I was ready to have them in August. I felt like a beached whale. Me, who likes to swim and hike; me, who ate organic food and who took such good care of myself. I gained 70 pounds. Can you believe it? The doctor was so pleased with me and I was so miserable.

The doctor became concerned about my blood pressure during the seventh month. By the beginning of the eighth month I had to see the doctor twice a week. Her nurse would take my blood pressure. She would come in and shake her head, and then send me to the hospital for blood work and a urine sample. It took hours, and I began to dread sitting in the hospital, waiting and waiting.

The third time we went through this, we were sitting and sitting and sitting, me with my fat tummy and swollen feet, trying to find a way to get comfortable. I told my husband we should just leave. Suddenly there was all this activity and I knew something was wrong. I looked around to see what all the commotion was about and realized they were heading our way. Apparently my tests results suggested that I could easily go into seizures (eclampsia). We did not go home to pick up my nicely packed bag; we went directly to the operating room. Less than an hour later I was the mother of twins.

REFLECTIVE PRACTICE

Women who are older and those with multiple gestations are more likely to have hypertensive disorder. How would you feel about going to the hospital for testing twice a week? How do you think this would be impacted by having a toddler, or several other children? Do you think you could continue to work? How might a job impact hypertensive disorder?

physicians prescribe iron supplements to anemic women, most prenatal vitamins include sufficient iron.

Fetal Hemolytic Disorder

Hemo is a prefix borrowed from the Greek word meaning blood. Individuals have one of four major blood types: A, AB, B, and O. Women have their blood typed and have an antibody screen during their first prenatal visit and after delivery. Hemolytic diseases are a result of incompatible blood factors in the mother and fetus. When the mother is type O and the fetus is A, B, or AB, there is the potential for ABO incompatibility. In addition to these blood types, there are other factors in the blood, called antigens, that must also be compatible between mother and fetus. The most common antigens are the Rhesus (Rh) family (D, C, E, c, e). Individuals who have this D antigen are Rh-positive, whereas those who lack the antigen are Rh-negative.

Rh incompatibility occurs only when a mother is Rh-negative and the fetus is Rh-positive. The only way the fetus can be Rh-positive is to inherit the D antigen from the father. An Rh-positive mother and an Rh-negative fetus is not a problem. About 10 to 15 percent of Caucasian couples have this incompatibility, about 5 percent of African couples, and it rarely occurs in Asian couples (Lowdermilk & Perry, 2003). Until there is an exchange of blood between the fetus and the mother, there are no problems. However, once this exchange has occurred and the mother has become sensitized, her body reacts to the infant's Rh-positive blood cells as if they are a foreign substance. She develops antibodies to attack the fetal blood cells, causing them to break apart. As a result, the fetus can experience brain damage or death.

Rh incompatibility with a first child is rare because the blood of the fetus must mix with the mother's for antibodies to be produced. This frequently happens during delivery, but rarely before unless the mother has had a mismatched blood transfusion. There is a slight risk earlier in an initial pregnancy of blood mixing through vaginal bleeding, amniocentesis, or abortion.

Initial attempts to control blood mixing earlier in pregnancy included administering fetal blood transfusions (in utero and directly after birth). These transfusions have been successful and are still used for infants with fetal hemolytic anemia. However, the development of RhoGAM solved the problem in a different way: It prevents the problem in the mother rather than controlling it in the fetus. RhoGAM is an anti-D **immunoglobulin** that prevents the development of the mother's antibodies (Ward & McCume, 2002). Nonsensitized mothers must receive RhoGAM no later than 72 hours after delivering an Rh-positive infant and are given it prophylactically at 28 weeks of gestation. This process must be repeated after every possible exposure to Rh-positive blood.

Immunoglobulin is an antibody that can identify and neutralize bacteria and viruses such as D.

EXPOSURE TO ENVIRONMENTAL TERATOGENS

Teratogens are nongenetic, extraneous substances implicated in causing malformations in the developing fetus. They adversely affect the development of the fetus, causing death, malformations, growth deficiency, or functional deficits. Common teratogens include alcohol, nicotine, and prescription and illicit drugs. The effects of many specific teratogens are known. Thalidomide, a drug used primarily in Europe in the 1960s, caused physical anomalies in children, such as missing or malformed limbs. The most pervasive effects occurred when the drug was used during the first two months of pregnancy.

Some teratogens have more effect at specific points during prenatal development, whereas others have debilitating effects throughout fetal development. This section focuses on the major teratogens that directly affect the fetus.

Among pregnant women, 5 to 10 percent abuse alcohol, 20 percent smoke cigarettes, 10 percent use marijuana, about 1 percent use cocaine, and 0.5 percent use opiates (Center on Addiction and Substance Abuse, 1996). According to the Center on Addiction and Substance Abuse (1996), three-quarters of individuals who abuse one substance are likely to abuse others as well. Polydrug use makes it difficult to determine the exact impact of a specific substance on the fetus. In addition, pregnant women who use drugs rarely have adequate prenatal care or good nutrition, and they may also have sexually transmitted diseases.

Alcohol

Alcohol use during pregnancy is the most common cause of preventable intellectual disabilities. Alcohol is abused more than any other drug in the United States. In the United States and in many parts of Europe, fetal alcohol spectrum disorders (FASDs) are the leading cause of intellectual disabilities. They are more frequent than Down syndrome, spina bifida, or fragile X syndrome. Fetal alcohol syndrome (FAS) is the most severe end of FASD. Infants and toddlers with fewer symptoms are still on the spectrum, but may have alcohol-related neurodevelopmental disorder (ARND).

Although prevalence varies among different populations, the Centers for Disease Control and Prevention estimate that FAS occurs in 0.2 to 1.5 cases per 1,000, and that FASDs are approximately three times that rate, putting them at 0.6 to 5.5 per 1,000 live births in the United States. Combined they constitute 0.8 to 7 cases per 1,000 live births (Centers for Disease Control and Prevention, 2007a).

Although alcohol was known as a teratogen that could cause irreversible damage to the fetus, FAS was not formally identified until the early 1970s. FAS is defined by four criteria: maternal drinking; prenatal and postnatal growth deficiency (low birth weight and poor muscle tone); facial anomalies (thin upper lip, flat mid-face, short nose, low nasal bridge, small head, droopy eyes); and brain damage (central nervous system dysfunction, irritability, hyperactivity, attention deficit, and intellectual disability) (Davidson & Myers, 2007). Timing of alcohol consumption affects the fetal outcome. If alcohol abuse occurs during the first trimester of pregnancy the risk is greatest, in addition to an increased probability of miscarriage, the physical signs of FAS are likely to be present

(Haffner, 2007). Alcohol abuse during the second trimester affects physical and intellectual growth, but not physical malformations. If abuse occurs in the third trimester, cognitive development alone is impaired. Maternal binge drinking (four or more drinks) has the most severe impact on cognitive growth (Davidson & Myers, 2007).

In a survey of American mothers, about 30 percent reported drinking alcohol at some point in their pregnancy (U.S. Department of Health and Human Services, 2003). When a pregnant woman drinks alcohol, her blood alcohol content and that of her fetus increases. They increase at the same rate, but the blood alcohol level of the fetus remains high longer because the mother's liver must remove the alcohol from her own blood before removing the alcohol from the fetus. The ethanol in alcohol crosses the placental barrier and goes into both the fetus and the amniotic fluid. Ethanol impairs the placental function of channeling essential nutrients to the fetus, and it also interferes with carbohydrate metabolism, resulting in growth retardation. By causing fetal malformations through chemical imbalances, alcohol affects the cells and the DNA of the fetus. Alcohol also affects fetal breathing and therefore levels of oxygen in the blood. If a woman ingests one drink per day throughout her pregnancy (270 days), she will have exposed her fetus to 135 ounces of absolute alcohol. This is the equivalent of feeding the baby 16 bottles (eight ounces each) of absolute alcohol (Burd, n.d.(a)).

Infants and toddlers who have been exposed to alcohol during pregnancy will have developmental delays particularly in the area of speech and language and impulse control. Toddlers may have problems following simple directions and understanding requests. They may also be clumsy and have motor delays. Executive function, which involves planning, sequencing, self-monitoring, and goal-directed behavior, is likely to be impaired. These children may need more support to acquire self-help skills. Toddlers may also display challenging behavior (Wunsch, Conlon, & Scheidt, 2002). These children are also more likely to be in the foster care system.

Tobacco Smoke

Smoking is the number one preventable cause of low birth weight infants. Birth weight is directly proportional to the number of cigarettes smoked per day or the length of time a woman is exposed to passive smoke (Klesges, Johnson, Ward, & Barnard, 2001; Wunsch et al., 2002). If a woman smokes one cigarette per day throughout their pregnancy (270 days), she will have exposed her fetus to 13 full packs of cigarettes. Smoking 10 cigarettes per day is equivalent of 135 full packs of cigarettes (Burd, n.d.(b)). Approximately 25 percent of pregnant women smoke (Fried et al., 2003). The Centers for Disease Control and

Medicaid
is a health insurance program for individuals and families with low incomes and few resources; it is funded by the state and federal government and is administered by state governments.

Prevention found that 3 to 13 percent of women not covered by **Medicaid** smoked during pregnancy, compared to 14 to 38 percent of women on Medicaid. The less education a woman had the more likely she was to smoke during pregnancy. White women are far more likely to smoke than black, Hispanic, or Native American women (Centers for Disease Control and Prevention, 2005).

Fetal tobacco syndrome is defined by three conditions: a mother who smokes five or more cigarettes per day, growth retardation of the fetus at term (less than five pounds, eight ounces if 37 weeks), and no maternal history of hypertension or other potential causes of fetal growth retardation (Schubert & Savage, 1994). Up to 8 percent of all neonates who die within a week after birth are due to problems related to their mother smoking during pregnancy (Centers for Disease Control and Prevention, 2005). Infants and toddlers whose parents smoke have more respiratory illness, bronchitis, and pneumonia than children of parents who do not smoke (Centers for Disease Control and Prevention, 2006). Children of fathers who smoked were twice as likely to develop cancer in adulthood as those whose fathers did not smoke (Huncharek, Kupelnick, & Klassen, 2001).

When a woman smokes, the carbon monoxide from her blood stream crosses the placenta and reduces the amount of oxygen available to the fetus. The nicotine causes the blood vessels to become smaller (constrict). In response to this, both maternal and fetal heart rates increase and fetal movement decreases. Cigarette smoking also interferes with the assimilation of essential vitamins and minerals. Nicotine has been found in breast milk, although the impact on the infant has not been well documented. Long-term monitoring has shown impaired intellectual and emotional development. In particular, infants born to smoking mothers are more likely to display hyperactivity and impaired school performance. Prevention involves explaining the risks of maternal smoking and advising women to stop or at least reduce the number of cigarettes they smoke. It is unclear what methods of raising awareness are most useful in assisting women to quit smoking.

It is difficult to effectively separate the influence of smoking on the fetus and postnatal exposure to passive smoke. Some research shows that ambient tobacco smoke contains twice the number of chemicals as inhaled smoke and may be more harmful to the developing brain than in utero exposure (Weitzman, Kananaugh, & Florin, 2006)

Drugs

Drugs are another commonly abused substance. Of those who use drugs, some pregnant women use illicit drugs, whereas others use only prescribed drugs. In the United States, the Food and Drug Administration (FDA) is considering methods of testing drugs to collect information about their effects on pregnant women and to provide new information about safety. The FDA uses potential fetal risk as its criterion for establishing guidelines for prescribing drugs to pregnant women. General concerns related to drug use during pregnancy are birth defects, spontaneous abortion, preterm labor, low birth weight, and fetal death. Drugs taken by the mother pass through her system to the infant via the placenta. Some over-the-counter drugs such as aspirin can cause problems. Aspirin interferes with blood clotting and leads to increased bleeding. High doses of aspirin can lead to more serious problems.

Illicit Drugs

Some pregnant women are recreational drug users (those who use narcotics sporadically) and others are addicted (they have a tolerance to the narcotic and show signs of withdrawal when they stop using it). When pregnant women were asked if they had used illicit drugs during the past month, 9.6 percent reported that they had. Eight percent of younger women (15 to 25 years) reported using drugs, whereas only 1.6 percent of those between 26 and 44 reported they had used illicit drugs (Substance Abuse and Mental Health Services Administration, 2005a). The actual incidence of use during pregnancy is much higher, ranging from 5 to 32 percent depending on whether the results are based on self-report or urine testing (Huestis & Choo, 2002; Mason & Lee, 1995; Substance Abuse and Mental Health Services Administration, 2005a). If a woman uses illicit drugs, the specific drugs and the magnitude of use must be determined. Women are routinely asked about their drug use, but about 25 to 50 percent deny using drugs even when they know they have just given a urine sample that will be tested for drug use (Mason & Lee, 1995). Given social desirability, the expectation is that the higher numbers are more accurate. The price for the infant is high. More than 75 percent of infants who have been exposed to drugs in utero will have major medical problems, compared to 27 percent of unexposed infants (Huestis & Choo, 2002).

Marijuana. Marijuana is the most commonly used illicit drug among middle-class women of childbearing age and, after alcohol and tobacco, is the most commonly used drug during pregnancy. Of young adults between 18 and 25 years old, 17.3 percent state that they have used marijuana in the past month (Substance Abuse and Mental Health Services Administration, 2005b). It is estimated that 10 percent of pregnant women use marijuana. More use it in the first trimester than in the third (Shiono, 1996), but these rates vary throughout the population. There is disagreement about the effects of marijuana on the development of the fetus. When confounding variables of race, education, income, marital status, and alcohol, and tobacco use were controlled, many findings about the detrimental effects of marijuana did not hold up (Kandall, Doberczak, Jantunen, & Stein, 1999; Lester, 2000). That is, prenatal marijuana exposure did not appear to have an important impact on postnatal development when it was used in isolation.

Cocaine. Cocaine is a frequently used illicit drugs and one of the most addictive. Of young adults between 18 and 25 years old, 2 percent state that they have used cocaine in the past month (Substance Abuse and Mental Health Services Administration, 2005b). Although its use is not as prevalent as alcohol and marijuana, fetal exposure occurs in 1 to 3 percent of pregnancies (Chiriboga, 1996). Although this drug is generally labeled "cocaine," it may take many forms, the concentration may vary, and it may be used in different ways: inhaled, smoked, freebased, or injected. These complexities make it difficult to reach conclusive statements about its effects.

The effects of cocaine are both direct and indirect. Cocaine affects the central nervous system as a stimulant and causes the blood vessels to constrict, which decreases the amount of blood and oxygen that can reach the fetus. The lack of blood and oxygen circulation then interferes with development, and the effect is magnified if the mother also smokes cigarettes or drinks alcohol. Structural defects associated with cocaine use are caused by the interruption of the blood flow to developing structures or previously developed structures (Covington, Nordstrom-Klee, Ager, Sokol, & Delaney-Black, 2002). Cocaine has been associated with premature birth and low birth weight, as well as neurobehavioral abnormalities (Wunsch et al., 2002). It can also cause contractions of the uterus and premature birth or spontaneous abortion. The constriction of the blood vessels can result in growth retardation, intracranial hemorrhage, malnutrition, reduced oxygen (intrauterine hypoxia), and a small head and brain (microcephaly) (Espy, Kaufman, & Glisky, 1999).

Children who have been exposed to cocaine prenatally are at biological and environmental risk. However, these risks may have been overstated. With differences in instruments used and inconsistencies in results, it is difficult to reach conclusions. Some of the differences that appear shortly after birth fade by seven months or so (Wunsch et al., 2002). Some abnormalities may not be apparent until school age (Singer et al., 2002).

Opiates. Opium and its derivatives, such as heroin, morphine, and codeine, can be ingested, injected, or absorbed through mucous membranes. Heroin addiction has decreased since the 1990s. Most heroin users administer it intravenously because of the immediate effect. Estimates are that one in 200 newborns are exposed to heroin or methadone each year (Glanz & Woods, 1993). Because menstrual abnormalities and low fertility are frequent by-products of heroin use, there are fewer infants born to pregnant women addicted to heroin.

The only drug available to treat pregnant heroin-addicted women is methadone. This can be taken orally, is long acting, and helps women maintain fairly consistent blood levels. The use of other opiates tends to produce rapid swings from intoxication to withdrawal, which adversely affects the fetus. Of babies born to heroin- or methadone-dependent mothers, 60 to 95 percent have withdrawal symptoms. Some experience neonatal abstinence syndrome (NAS) (Tran, 1999). Withdrawal from methadone can be more severe and prolonged than from heroin because of it longer half-life (Haffner, 2007). NAS is a nonspecific disorder that appears within 24 to 72 hours after birth (sometimes after the mother and baby have been discharged) and may last 7 to 10 days. The severity, timing of onset, and duration of NAS is related to total drug intake over the last trimester, as well as daily intake and levels at delivery (Wagner, Katikaneni, Cox, & Ryan, 1998). The most common signs of NAS in the infant reflect the disregulation of the central nervous system and include irritability, restlessness, sleep disturbances, sweating, vomiting, diarrhea, high-pitched cry, tremors, seizures, **hypertonicity**, and uncoordinated suck (Haffner, 2007; Wagner et al., 1998). If symptoms are severe, they may be treated with phenobarbital or paregoric.

Hypertonicity
is muscles that are tight, making the arms and legs difficult to move or bend.

Environmental Teratogens

Many factors within the environment of the pregnant mother can affect the developing fetus. People can be directly exposed to these contaminants (pesticides) or indirectly (eating fish with high levels of methylmercury and/or PCBs) (Davidson & Myers, 2007). Some of these environmental toxins include radiation, hyperthermia, and heavy metals. Data about the effects of environmental toxins on human development are limited and incomplete. There are individual differences in susceptibility to these toxins, as well as a threshold effect. Below a certain level, some toxins may not be harmful. It is important to have information about dose (total amount of exposure) and timing. Some toxins effect the fetal brain whereas others are more dangerous after birth and some are equally dangerous. Some exposure is chronic and other exposure is acute. All of this confounds our knowledge about the specific effects of environmental toxins (Davidson & Myers, 2007).

Radiation, Mercury, and Lead

Radiation is one of the most common toxins. Low doses of radiation have been found to be not harmful. The effect of radiation depends on the amount and timing of exposure. During the first weeks of pregnancy the embryo is either unaffected or its effects are lethal. During the next two months, if not lethal, exposure to radiation produces growth retardation. During the second trimester, excessive radiation can cause central nervous sensitivity, microcephaly, and eye abnormalities. Pregnant women should avoid x-rays when possible

Radiation
is energy in the form of waves or particles.

or wear lead capes to protect the fetus. All females should wear lead capes when exposed to x-rays to protect their supply of eggs from radiation.

Maternal exposure to **methylmercury** can occur from eating fish or from vaccines that contained thimerosal. Research in many different countries has documented adverse effects from both prenatal and postnatal exposure to methylmercury. It results in delays in meeting developmental milestones.

Methylmercury
is a heavy metal used in scientific equipment like thermometers and barometers; it is also present in fish and some vaccines. It is a neurotoxin that may lead to intellectual disability and deformities in infants and toddlers.

This pregnant woman is wearing an antiradiation maternity smock designed to protect pregnant women and their unborn babies from harmful radioactivity in daily life. It is assumed that we live in a high radiation environment—miscarriages and birth defects could be caused by electromagnetic radiation from cell phones and common household appliances such as computer monitors, televisions, refrigerators, and microwaves. The smock is very popular in China and almost every pregnant Chinese woman wears one at least during the first few months of pregnancy. Its effectiveness however needs further testing.

However, interpreting the results is complex as some research shows that nutrients in seafood may actually mitigate the potential adverse effects of methylmercury on brain development (Davidson & Myers, 2007).

Thimerosal, an organomercury compound 50 percent mercury by weight, was used as a preservative for vaccines; it has been removed from most vaccines, especially those children receive. Some parents believe that this substance is associated with higher incidents of autism spectrum disorders. Most studies have not found significant associations between thimerosal containing vaccines and autism (Davidson & Myers, 2007).

Lead
is a heavy neurotoxic metal that accumulates in soft bones and tissue and causes disabilities.

High ingestion of **lead** during pregnancy has been shown to cause brain damage in infants. Sources of lead exposure are slowly being eliminated in developed countries (lead additives in gasoline, lead paint, lead pipes, lead-glazed pottery, etc.). Lead levels as low as 100 micrograms per deciliter are associated lower IQ scores (Davidson & Myers, 2007). Prenatal exposure to lead also predisposes children to develop attention-deficit/hyperactivity disorder (ADHD) (Stein, Efron, Schiff, & Glanzman, 2002). Finally, the fetus' exposure to many different environmental pesticides, cleaners, paints, and other toxic substances increases his risk for developmental disabilities.

Hurricane Katrina brought a lot of the concerns about environmental toxins to the forefront. Concerns surfaced about carbon monoxide because of power outages, the chemicals in flood water, and even the use of insect repellent. There are not enough studies to know if N,N-diethyl-m-toluamide (DEET) is safe for pregnant women (Centers for Disease Control and Prevention, 2007b). It should not be used on infants.

Hyperthermia

Hyperthermia
is a condition in which the body absorbs more heat than it can get rid of, causing the body temperature to rise.

Hyperthermia, or exposure to high temperatures (over 102 degrees F), especially during the first trimester, is related to neural tube defects (Liptak, 2007). Because of the negative effects of hyperthermia, spas, saunas, and long hot baths are not recommended for pregnant women.

SUMMARY

Development before birth highlighted development from conception through the germinal, embryonic, and fetal periods. It looked at prenatal care and planning and their impact on the developing fetus. It covered the basics of heredity and genetics, including chromosomal and genetic problems, providing a background for understanding how disabilities occur and for understanding new information about the causes of disabilities. A variety of screening techniques were reviewed, as well as the maternal diseases, disorders, and illnesses that could affect the developing fetus.

CHAPTER IN REVIEW

☀ Every human being starts as a single cell. This cell contains the genetic information that will shape that individual and the genetic material that individual will pass on to future generations.

☀ Sometimes there are problems in the process of cell division, and chromosomes are added, lost, or moved to different locations. Some of these changes have significant consequences, others do not.

☀ An individual's traits, whether positive or negative, get passed to future generations in predictable ways. However, these traits also interact with environmental processes, which decreases the predictability.

☀ We use a variety of different screening methods to identify prenatal disorders and help families understand what these conditions mean.

☀ Some congenital problems cannot be prevented or diagnosed prenatally.

☀ In utero, the fetus has predictable patterns of development, and the majority of fetuses are born with the potential for a typical life trajectory.

☀ Maternal diseases, disorders, or illnesses can interfere with a fetus' developmental path.

☀ Teratogens such as alcohol, nicotine, and drugs interfere with interuterine development, as can teratogens in the environment.

APPLICATION ACTIVITIES

1. Interview a pregnant woman about her pregnancy, the advice she received from her physician, and the lifestyle changes she has made, if any.

2. Interview your mother or the mother of a friend who is about your age about her experiences of being pregnant. Ask about the advice her doctor gave her, her concerns at the time, and the lifestyle changes she made. Reflect on the differences between her experiences and what you have learned.

3. In a small group or with a group of friends, discuss feelings about pregnancy and find out what each knows about prenatal development. Share some of the concerns in the field today. Then develop a plan to educate young women about pregnancy and lifestyle that will improve birth outcomes.

RESOURCES

Web Resources

☀ **Kids Health** is a project of the Nemours Foundation. Its mission is to translate advances in health care to practical ways of improving health care for infants, children, and teens. It has a narrated pregnancy calendar slide show. Take time to look at the other aspects of the Web site. Note that information placed on this site is checked by a physician before being put on the Web. http://www.kidshealth.org

※ **National Center on Birth Defects and Developmental Disabilities** provides information about birth defects and their implications. http://www.cdc.gov

※ **National Institutes of Health and the National Human Genome Research Institute** provide information on heredity and genetics. They provide many different educational materials, including definitions, a talking glossary, and fact sheets, as well as information about the Human Genome Project. In addition to the genetics aspects, look as the issues related to privacy and ethics. http://www.genome.gov

※ **Parenting iVillage**, although a commercial site, provides a great slideshow that documents fetal development from six weeks to birth. This is free and the photos are furnished by GE Healthcare. http://parenting.ivillage.com

Print Resources

※ Batshaw, M. L. (2007). Genetics and developmental disabilities. In M. L. Batshaw, L. Pellegrino, N. J. Rosen (Eds.), *Children with disabilities* (6th ed., pp. 3–21). Baltimore, MD: Paul H. Brookes.

※ Davidson, P. W., & Myers, G. J. (2007). Environmental toxins. In M. L. Batshaw, L. Pellegrino, N. J. Rosen (Eds.), *Children with disabilities* (6th ed., pp. 61–70). Baltimore, MD: Paul H. Brookes.

※ Haffner, W. H. J. (2007). Development before birth. In M. L. Batshaw, L. Pellegrino, & N. J. Rosen (Eds.), *Children with disabilities* (6th ed., pp. 23–33). Baltimore, MD: Paul H. Brookes.

※ Zero to Three. (2006). Ones, Twos, and Threes, *26*(5). A major portion of his journal focuses on the experience of having an only child, twins, and triplets and their impact on parenting.

REFERENCES

Abrams, B., Altman, S. L., & Pickett, K. E. (2000). Pregnancy weight gain: Still controversial. *American Journal of Clinical Nutrition, 71,* 1233S–1241S.

Batshaw, M. L. (2007). Genetics and developmental disabilities. In M. L. Batshaw, L. Pellegrino, & N. J. Rosen (Eds.), *Children with disabilities* (6th ed., pp. 3–21). Baltimore, MD: Paul H. Brookes.

Bell, M. J. (2007). Infections and the fetus. In M. L. Batshaw, L. Pellegrino, & N. J. Rosen (Eds.), *Children with disabilities* (6th ed., pp. 71–82). Baltimore, MD: Paul H. Brookes.

Brown, J. E., & Satin, A. J. (2007). Having a baby: The birth process. In M. L. Batshaw, L. Pellegrino, & N. J. Roizen (Eds.), *Children with disabilities* (6th ed., pp. 35–45). Baltimore, MD: Paul H. Brookes Publishing.

Burd, L. (n.d.(a)). Drinking during pregnancy. Retrieved April 12, 2007, from www.cjsids.com

Burd, L. (n.d.(b)). Smoking during pregnancy. Retrieved April 12, 2007, from www.cjsids.com

Center on Addiction and Substance Abuse. (1996). *Substance abuse and the American woman.* New York: Columbia University.

Centers for Disease Control and Prevention. (2005). Preventing smoking during pregnancy. Retrieved April 12, 2007, from http://www.cdc.gov/nccdphp/publications/factsheets/Prevention/smoking.htm

Centers for Disease Control and Prevention. (2006). Chlamydia fact sheet. Retrieved April 12, 2007, from http://www.cdc.gov/std/chlamydia/STDFact-Chlamydia.htm

Centers for Disease Control and Prevention. (2007a). Fetal alcohol spectrum disorders. Retrieved April 12, 2007, from http://www.cdc.gov/ncbddd/fas/default.htm

Centers for Disease Control and Prevention. (2007b). Hurricanes—special populations, effects on pregnant women: Environmental exposures. Retrieved April 12, 2007, from http://www.cdc.gov/ncbddd/hurricanes/environmental.htm

Centers for Disease Control and Prevention. (2007c). Malaria during pregnancy. Retrieved April 12, 2007, from http://www.cdc.gov/malaria/pregnancy.htm

Centers for Disease Control and Prevention. (2007d). Newborns and group B strep. Retrieved April 12, 2007, from http://www.cdc.gov/groupBstrep/general/gen_public_faq.htm

Centers for Disease Control and Prevention. (2007e). Single gene disorders and disabilities. Retrieved April 12, 2007, from http://www.cdc.gov/ncbddd/single_gene/default.htm

Chiriboga, C. A. (1996). Cocaine and the fetus: Methodological issues and neurological correlates. In R. J. Koukol & G. D. Olsen (Eds.), *Prenatal cocaine exposure* (pp. 1–21). Boca Raton, FL: CRC Press.

Covington, C. Y., Nordstrom-Klee, B., Ager, J., Sokol, R., & Delaney-Black, V. (2002). Birth to age 7 growth of children prenatally exposed to drugs: A prospective cohort study. *Neurotoxicology and Teratology, 24*(4), 489–496.

Cunniff, C., & the Committee on Genetics. (2004). Prenatal screening and diagnosis for pediatricians. *Pediatrics, 114*(3), 889–894.

Davidson, P. W., & Myers, G. J. (2007). Environmental toxins. In M. L. Batshaw, L. Pellegrino, & N. J. Rosen (Eds.), *Children with disabilities* (6th ed., pp. 61–70). Baltimore, MD: Paul H. Brookes.

Deering, S. H., & Satin, A. J. (2002). Having a baby: The birth process. In M. L. Batshaw (Ed.), *Children with disabilities* (5th ed., pp. 55–68). Baltimore, MD: Paul H. Brookes.

Duck, F. A. (1999). Is it safe to use diagnostic ultrasound during the first trimester. *Ultrasound Obstetrics and Gynecology, 13*, 385–388.

Espy, K. A., Kaufman, P. M., & Glisky, M. L. (1999). Neuropsychological function in toddlers exposed to cocaine in utero: A preliminary study. *Developmental Neuropsychology, 15*, 447–460.

Farber, A. F., Yanni, C. C., & Batshaw, M. L. (1997). Nutrition: Good and bad. In M. L. Batshaw (Ed.), *Children with disabilities* (4th ed., pp. 183–210). Baltimore, MD: Paul H. Brookes.

Fried, V., Prager, K., MacKay, A., & Xia, H. (2003). *Chartbook on the trends in the health of Americans.* Hyattsville, MD: National Center for Health Statistics.

Glanz, J. C., & Woods, J. R., Jr. (1993). Cocaine, heroin, and phencyclidine: Obstetric perspectives. *Clinical Obstetrics and Gynecology, 36*, 279–301.

Haffner, W. H. J. (2007). Development before birth. In M. L. Batshaw, L. Pellegrino, & N. J. Rosen (Eds.), *Children with disabilities* (6th ed., pp. 23–33). Baltimore, MD: Paul H. Brookes.

Hershkovitz, R., Sheiner, E., & Mazor, M. (2002). Ultrasound in obstetrics: A review of safety.

European Journal of Obstetrics and Gynecology and Reproductive Biology, 101, 15–18.

Hill, J. B., & Haffner, W. H. J. (2002). Growth before birth. In M. L. Batshaw (Ed.), *Children with disabilities* (5th ed., pp. 243–262). Baltimore, MD: Paul H. Brookes.

Huestis, M. A., & Choo, R. E. (2002). Drug abuse's smallest victims: In utero drug exposure. *Forensic Science International, 128*(1–2), 20–30.

Huncharek, M., Kupelnick, B., & Klassen, H. (2001). Paternal smoking during pregnancy and the risk of childhood brain tumors: results of a meta-analysis. *In Vivo, 15*(6), 535–541.

Jensen, E. (2006). *Enriching the brain: How to maximize every learner's potential.* San Francisco, CA: Jossey-Bass.

Kandall, S. R., Doberczak, T. M., Jantunen, M., & Stein, J. (1999). The methadone-maintained pregnancy. *Clinics in Perinatology, 26*(1), 173–183.

Klesges, L. M., Johnson, K. C., Ward, K. D., & Barnard, M. (2001). Smoking cessation in pregnant women. *Obstetrics Gynecology Clinics of North America, 28*(2), 269–282.

Lester, B. M. (2000). Prenatal cocaine exposure and child outcome: A model for the study of the infant at risk. *Israel Journal of Psychiatry and Related Sciences, 37,* 223–235.

Lindegren, M. L., Steinberg, S., & Byers, R. H. (2000). Epidemiology of HIV/AIDS in children. *Pediatric Clinics of North America, 47*(1), 1–20.

Liptak, G. S. (2002). Neural tube defects. In M. L. Batshaw (Ed.), *Children with disabilities* (5th ed., pp. 467–492). Baltimore, MD: Paul H. Brookes.

Liptak, G. S. (2007). Neural tube defects. In M. L. Batshaw, L. Pellegrino, & N. J. Rosen (Eds.), *Children with disabilities* (6th ed., pp. 419–438). Baltimore, MD: Paul H. Brookes.

Lowdermilk, D. L., & Perry, S. E. (2003). *Maternity nursing* (6th ed.). St. Louis, MO: Mosby.

Martin, J. A., Kochanek, K. D., Strobino, D. M., Guyer, B., & MacDorman, M. F. (2005). Annual Summary of Vital Statistics–2003. *Pediatrics, 115,* 619–634.

Mason, E., & Lee, R. V. (1995). Drug abuse. In W. M. Barron & M. D. Lindheimer (Eds.), *Medical disorders during pregnancy* (2nd ed., pp. 465–486). St. Louis, MO: Mosby.

McKusick, V. A. (2005). Online Mendelian Inheritance in Man. National Center for Biotechnology Information, John Hopkins University. Retrieved October 19, 2007, from http://www.ncbi.nlm.nih.gov/sites/entrez?db=OMIM

National Human Genome Research Institute (HGP). (2007). All about the human genome project. Retrieved April 9, 2007, from http://www.genome.gov

Prentice, A., & Goldberg, G. (1996). Maternal obesity increases congenital malformations. *Nutritional Review, 54*(5), 146–150.

Roizen, N. J. (2007). Down Syndrome. In M. L. Batshaw, L. Pellegrino, & N. J. Rosen (Eds.), *Children with disabilities* (6th ed., pp. 263–273). Baltimore, MD: Paul H. Brookes.

Schonberg, R. L., & Tifft, C. J. (2002). Birth defects, prenatal diagnosis, and fetal therapy. In M. L. Batshaw (Ed.), *Children with disabilities* (5th ed., pp. 27–41). Baltimore, MD: Paul H. Brookes.

Schubert, P. J., & Savage, B. (1994). Smoking, alcohol and drug abuse. In D. K. James, P. J. Steer, C. P. Weiner, & B. Gonik (Eds.), *High risk pregnancy: Management options* (pp. 783–801). London: W. B. Saunders.

Shiono, P. H. (1996). Prevalence of drug-exposed infants. *The Future of Children, 6*(2), 159–163.

Singer, L. T., Arendt, R., Minnes, S., Farkas, K., Salvator, A., Kirchner, H. L., et al. (2002). Cognitive and motor outcomes of cocaine-exposed infants. *Journal of the American Medical Association, 287*, 1952–1960.

Stein, M. A., Efron, L. A., Schiff, W. B., & Glanzman, M. (2002). Attention deficits and hyperactivity. In M. L. Batshaw (Ed.), *Children with disabilities* (5th ed., pp. 389–416). Baltimore, MD: Paul H. Brookes.

Substance Abuse and Mental Health Services Administration. (2005a). The NHSDA Report: Substance use during pregnancy 2002 and 2003. Retrieved April 12, 2007, from http://oas.samhsa.gov/2k5/pregnancy/pregnancy.htm

Substance Abuse and Mental Health Services Administration. (2005b). Marijuana use and characteristics of users. Retrieved April 12, 2007, from http://oas.samhsa.gov/marijuana.htm

Tran, J. H. (1999). Treatment of neonatal abstinence syndrome. *Journal of Pediatric Health Care, 13*, 295–300.

Travers, J. (2006). Current views of life span development. In K. Thies & J. Travers (Eds.), *Handbook of human development for health care professionals* (pp. 3–18). Sudbury, MA: Jones and Bartlett Publishers.

U.S. Department of Health and Human Services. (2003). Fetal alcohol syndrome. Retrieved December 7, 2006, from http://www.cdc.gov/ncbddd/factsheets/FAS_alcoholuse.pdf

Wagner, C. L., Katikaneni, L. D., Cox, T. H., & Ryan, R. (1998). The impact of prenatal drug exposure on the neonate. *Obstetrics and Gynecology Clinics of North America, 25*, 169–194.

Ward, L. P., & McCume, S. K. (2002). The first weeks of life. In M. L. Batshaw (Ed.), *Children with disabilities* (5th ed., pp. 69–84). Baltimore, MD: Paul H. Brookes.

Weitzman, M., Kananaugh, M., & Florin, T. A. (2006). Parental smoking and children's behavioral and cognitive functioning. In P. W. Davidson, G. J. Myers, & B. Weiss (Eds.), *International review of mental retardation research: Vol. 30. Neurotoxicology and developmental disabilities* (pp. 237–261). San Diego, CA: Elsevier Academic Press.

Wunsch, M. J., Conlon, C. J., & Scheidt, P. C. (2002). Substance abuse: A preventable threat to development. In M. L. Batshaw (Ed.), *Children with disabilities* (5th ed., pp. 107–122). Baltimore, MD: Paul H. Brookes.

chapter 3
Birthing and Newborns

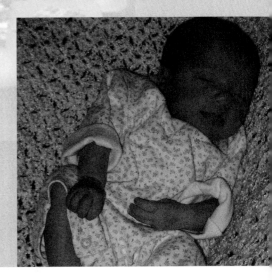

Chapter Outline
- Labor and Delivery
- Birthing Patterns
- Transition from the Womb
- Newborns
- Newborn Assessment
- Newborns at Risk
- Newborn Senses
- Newborn Development
- Transition to Parenthood

Birthing creates not only babies, but also mothers, fathers, grandparents, aunts, uncles, and cousins. Babies are born into families. These families can talk to others about the process of having babies as well as access numerous books, articles, Web sites, and videos that provide information on just about "anything you ever wanted to know" and perhaps even more about giving birth and adjusting to a new infant.

This chapter traces the infant's transition from womb to world. It highlights the science behind the complex process of infants moving from the watery, temperate intrauterine environment into a variable, often-cold-air extrauterine environment.

WHY STUDY BIRTHING AND THE NEWBORN?

⚜ Birth and the birthing process affect both the family and the newborn and how available they are to respond to their world. Knowledge about this process allows early childhood educators to have appropriate expectations of infants and helps them better work with families.

⚜ Infants are born with five working senses (hearing, seeing, feeling, tasting, and smelling). Understanding how these senses function for the infant allows educators to better care for and engage very young infants.

⚜ Infants come with reflexes that have survival value and form the base for future development. Early childhood educators monitor these reflexes as one indication of how the infant is developing.

⚜ The parent-child relationship that begins during this period influences the infant's future development and the role of the early childhood professional.

You do not need to be able to deliver a baby to be an effective caregiver, but you do need to know about the process of giving birth and how it affects the infant, mother, father, and other family members. The process of giving birth, although not uncommon, is a very personal one. In the past, women generally learned about birthing from their mothers or by assisting in the birthing process of other women. Today, trained professionals (obstetricians, nurses, midwives, doulas) inform families about the birthing process. Birthing is no longer the solitary affair it was in the 1960s and 1970s. The scene of the anxious father pacing the hall outside his wife's hospital room, waiting to be told whether he has a daughter or son, has been replaced by the father in the delivery room with the expectant mother; a birth coach or coaches, friends, and family members may also be with her during labor and delivery, in addition to her chosen medical support team. Today, many couples also know the gender of the infant before birth.

What is still a mystery is when the baby will arrive. The average pregnancy lasts 280 days, or 40 weeks. Figuring out when those 280 days begins is sometimes challenging, but about 85 percent of women deliver within 7 days (before or after) of their due date.

Many factors cause labor to begin. Most are chemical in nature, and the expectant mother is unaware of them. Some chemicals, like oxytocin, stimulate uterine contractions; others, such as epinephrine, cause uterine relaxation.

Basic knowledge of the role of different chemicals has allowed doctors to control the onset of labor to some degree. They are still uncertain about the role of *every* chemical or the interactions between chemicals.

Doctors know that some women experience a surge of energy near the time of birth (Lowdermilk & Perry, 2003). Some have called this a nesting instinct, because energy is often spent cleaning and preparing for the arrival of the new baby.

LABOR AND DELIVERY

Extrauterine environment is the world outside of the uterus, where the fetus has been growing and developing.

Preterm deliveries are those that occur before 37 weeks.

Postterm deliveries are those that occur after 42 weeks.

Labor is the process of regular uterine contractions that result in child birth.

Lightening is a gradual process of the uterus sinking downward and the fetus descending head first.

Engagement is when the largest part of the fetal head has passed through the mother's pelvic rim and into the true pelvis.

Contractions are the movements of the muscles in the wall of the uterus that push the fetus through the birth canal.

Dating a pregnancy is a crucial step in prenatal care. A pregnancy is full term if the baby is delivered between 38 and 42 weeks. The fetus is still small enough to fit through the birth canal and mature enough to cope with the **extrauterine environment**. Deliveries before 37 weeks are consider **preterm** and those after 42 weeks are **postterm**.

How does a woman know that **labor** is about to begin? An early sign of labor is **lightening** then **engagement** as the fetus moves into position for birth, with her head low in the mother's abdomen, close to the mother's cervix. As the cervix thins and dilates, tiny blood vessels break and give the mucus a bloody appearance, which may be seen on a mother's underwear as bloody spots. Also, the mother's "water" may break. This water is the clear amniotic fluid that that surrounds and protects the fetus while she is in the womb. The fluid rushes out following the rupture of the fetal membrane. The water can break conveniently at home or in the middle of the grocery store. It is like uncontrollable urination and can be embarrassing.

Contractions, or the movement of the muscular walls of the uterus that push the fetus through the birth canal and out of the woman's body, may also alert her to the impending labor. Initial contractions may be cramplike and come at irregular intervals. With time, these contractions become more intense, regular, and closer together.

The process of delivering an infant into the world is called labor. Most mothers would agree that this process is aptly named. Technically, labor involves discharging the fetus, placenta, and umbilical cord from the uterus.

According to Lowdermilk and Perry (2003), a typical labor occurs

- on or near the expected birth date;
- when there have been no complications identified during pregnancy;
- there is only one fetus;
- the head descends into the birth canal;
- the process is completed within 24 hours.

Labor is defined as regular uterine contractions leading to progressive cervical changes. These contractions are different from the Braxton-Hicks contractions (commonly referred to as false labor), which occur throughout pregnancy and are typically painless and do not lead to changes in the cervix. Three changes occur to the cervix during labor: it softens, shortens, and dilates. While theses changes are taking place, the fetus begins to descend through the birth canal (Brown & Satin, 2007). Labor is divided into three stages.

Stages of Labor

First stage
of labor begins with contractions and ends when the cervix is dilated and effaced.

The **first stage** of labor begins with the onset of contractions and continues until the cervix is completely dilated (about 10 centimeters) and fully effaced (thinned out) until paper-thin (Brown & Satin, 2007). The first stage is the longest stage of labor and can last from 1 to 20 hours. This stage can be further divided into three phases—latent, active, and transitional. During the latent phase contractions are mild to moderate, irregular, and not very painful. Women may be at home for some of this phase and it may last from six to eight hours. If they are in a hospital or birthing center, they may be encouraged to walk or stand and change positions frequently as these activities tend to shorten this phase of labor. Also during this phase, the cervix dilates zero to three centimeters and effaces, but the fetus descends very little. In the active phase, which lasts from three to six hours, the cervix continues to dilate up to about seven centimeters and the contractions become moderate to strong. At this stage of labor, women gauge their level of pain and their ability to control it. They may also experience fatigue. The transition stage lasts about 20 to 40 minutes, and the contractions are regular and strong to very strong, and the pain can be severe. Full dilation (10 centimeters) is completed during this stage. Generally, for first pregnancies this first stage of labor lasts from about 10 to 16 hours, for subsequent pregnancies it is approximately 6 to 10 hours (Lowdermilk & Perry, 2003).

Second stage
of labor begins when the cervix is dilated and effaced and ends with the birth of the infant.

The **second stage** of labor is the actual birthing of the infant. It begins when the cervix is completely dilated and effaced and ends when the baby is born. This stage can be as short as several minutes and as long as two hours. It too has three phases: latent, descent, and transitional. The latent phase is a resting phase when the woman waits for the urge to push. The descent phase is characterized by a strong urge to push. Lying down on a bed may suppress this urge. Squatting works with gravity and helps a woman to push more effectively. Squatting is considered to be the most effective position during this stage (Mayberry et al., 2000). The transitional phase begins when the fetal head is visible and ends with the birth of the baby (Lowdermilk & Perry, 2003).

Third stage of labor is the expulsion of the placenta.

The **third stage** of labor involves the separation and expulsion of the placenta or afterbirth. This normally happens with several strong contractions about five minutes after the birth of the baby (See Figure 3–1) (Lowdermilk & Perry, 2003).

Factors Influencing Labor

Many factors determine the ease of the birthing process and the birth outcome. The general physical and emotional condition of the mother plays an important role in the birthing process. If the mother has had good prenatal care, abstained from drugs and alcohol, followed a nutritious diet, and developed a good rapport with her obstetrician or midwife, the outlook is positive.

Childbirth education classes can help parents prepare mentally for the birthing process. These classes can also provide other important functions, such as

- encouraging the involvement of the woman's partner in the birthing process;
- heightening the parents' awareness of the impending transition to parenthood;
- exposing couples to a wider network of couples who share many of the same pregnancy concerns and experiences;
- offering parents information about the processes of labor and birth;
- teaching breathing and relaxation techniques and other practices that are useful during the birthing process.

The size of the fetus influences the birthing process. There is no accurate way to determine the exact size of the fetus in utero. An experienced physician can make a good guess, and ultrasound provides additional information. But the size of the fetus is only one factor that influences birth; in reality, the size of the fetal head in relation to the size and structure of the mother's pelvis is the important variable. If a woman has a larger pelvis, she can deliver a larger fetus.

Although the majority of deliveries occur as described, there are factors that influence labor that require additional measures for a vaginal delivery to be possible. In other cases, a cesarean delivery is necessary.

Delivery

Most deliveries are spontaneous vaginal deliveries. When the fetal head encounters the pelvic floor, the chin flexes, or tucks, to create a smaller diameter for descent. The fetus then rotates and the head crowns. The head, then the face and chin appear. While awaiting the next contraction, the obstetrician uses

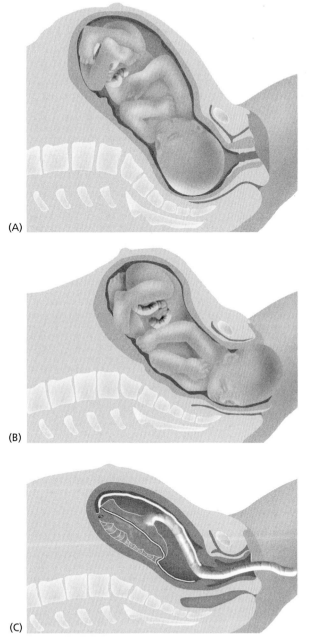

(A)

(B)

(C)

FIGURE 3–1 Labor and Delivery
By the end of the first stage of labor the fetus has descended, the cervix is effaced and dilation is complete (A). During the second stage of labor the head rotates, crowns, and extends with another rotation of the shoulders. The baby is born (B). The afterbirth follows (C).

suction to remove fluid from the baby's mouth and nose. Following the delivery of the head, there is an external rotation allowing the shoulders to pass though the birth canal, and, finally, the rest of the newborn appears. The length of this stage is determined by how long it takes for the mother to push to the point that the infant is deliverable. The umbilical cord is clamped and cut. The time of birth is the precise time when the entire baby is out of the mother's body (Lowdermilk & Perry, 2003). Usually the newborn is then given to the mother.

Fetal distress
is typically when the fetus is not getting oxygen or is experiencing some other complications.

If there is **fetal distress** or maternal exhaustion, it may be necessary to use other methods to speed up the process of a vaginal delivery. If the cervix is fully dilated, the position of the fetal head is known, and the fetus is far enough down the birth canal that he can be reached; either forceps or vacuum devices may be used to shorten the delivery. Both forceps and the vacuum are effective when the head is crowning; forceps are more effective if the fetal head is midway up the birth canal. In cases where the delivery is assisted by forceps, the second stage of labor is very long, or the baby is very large, the sphincter muscles or nerves can be damaged. The rectum is the last four or five inches of the digestive tract, which ends at the anus. The sphincter is the muscle that controls the fecal elimination. In some cases when a vaginal delivery is not possible, or when the delivery is not proceeding according to plan, a cesarean section is necessary.

Cesarean Section

Cesarean section
is delivering the fetus by making an incision in the wall of the abdomen and uterus.

A **cesarean section** is the delivery of the fetus through an incision in the abdominal wall and uterus. The purpose of the cesarean birth is to support the life and health of the mother and fetus. The most frequent indications for a cesarean section are fetal distress, malpresentation, dysfunctional labor, and multiple gestations (Lowdermilk & Perry, 2003). This process allows the baby to be delivered quickly, which is particularly important when the fetal supply of oxygen may be diminished.

up close and personal

Pregnancy for me was an unplanned detour. I was 25 years old and finally secure in my career and a relatively new relationship. Motherhood was never in my life plan. I had made my fiancé aware of this fact from the very first stages of the relationship. I was going to have a high-powered career and leave motherhood to my sister and brother, and would enjoy their children as my hectic schedule would allow. I went to the doctor because I was not feeling well and as a last resort she suggested that I have a pregnancy test. I laughed to myself, "No way, not me. This is not in my life plan."

I was overwhelmed. My fiancé was thrilled, as he wanted children. Not just one, "but a few." I spent the first month basically digesting that I was going to be a mother and would have to work this new little baby into my work schedule, as we are all programmed to do as career women. The second and third month were focused on just making it through the day and important meetings at work without being nauseous and having coworkers handing me crackers and offering helpful advice all day. I shut the actual "birth" stories out of my head during those months, as that date seemed so far away and I knew that I could not get through even menstrual cramps without wanting to just collapse. I envisioned labor pains like menstrual cramps— and how bad could that really be?

During the fourth month, it started to register that I had a baby inside of me who was growing and communicating through kicking and moving every day and most of the night. I somehow miraculously knew that my child was a little boy. Sometimes I would just sit in my office and talk to my baby about my day and my problems, and sometimes would just babble so he would know I was there and loved him.

I was constantly starving. During the eighth month I felt like I was going to explode. I gained 70 pounds and ate everything that was made for human consumption. It is amazing what tastes good when you are this pregnant. My favorite was a Burger King Whopper, but only at 11 pm! If I was not able to get a Whopper, a box of Bugles would do … literally, a whole box of Bugles. My back ached, my feet ached, and I was thrown into the reality of having to buy "baby things." This baby was coming out and soon.

I think I was still in partial denial despite the fact that I hadn't been able to see my toes for weeks. I just sort of assumed that I would be having a standard childbirth. I was two weeks shy of my delivery date when my water broke during my nightly relaxing bath. Terror finally set in that my little boy was coming out of me (*this is going to hurt!*) and into the world. This was the first thought of "labor" that I had let myself actually have during this pregnancy. As we rushed to the hospital I started to cry. I am still convinced I was crying because of the fear of being a first-time mom and not really knowing what was ahead for me or the baby. I had been in denial during my pregnancy and only glanced at the booklets and other helpful information given to new moms to guide us through the experience. During the ride to the hospital, I wished that I had actually read the booklets and prepared for the experience much like I prepared for important meetings at work.

In half an hour I was at the hospital, and doctors and nurses where swirling around me trying to figure out just how soon before my little boy would enter the world. At this point I had opted for no drugs, as I was going to do what was best for my baby. How hard can this really be? You just push. Women have been doing this for thousands of years. There was a lot of screaming in the room next to me, and I asked my nurse what was going on next door. The nurse informed me that the lady in the next room was two hours into her "natural" labor. That did it for me! I wanted to see the "drug menu!" I wanted all the drugs—now! What ever they had, I wanted it. Just about then, I had my first serious labor pain and I realized that if this was the first of many, I was in deep trouble. When a six-inch needle in your back is looking good, you know you are in a lot of pain!

This was big-time reality. Thirteen hours later, with all the drugs I could get, I was still pushing with everything that I had in my body to push with. Now, keep in mind that I'm normally 5′2″ tall and weighed 110 pounds. So, I'm a small-framed woman. By this time the doctors started to figure out that my baby was too large for a normal delivery. So, it was decided that I would need an immediate C-section. I was wheeled into a brightly lit operating room and had hospital-blue sheets draped up all around me, like a tent you make when you are a child.

Danillo was in the room, wearing a hospital gown and ready to experience his child being brought into the world. A little background about this guy: He loves bloody, gory horror flicks, so he was right

at home for the experience. I was blown away when the doctor asked me if I wanted to watch! There was no way that I could watch my stomach being cut wide open and my organs being tossed on a metal table, hoping they were all put back the exact way they went in! I, of course, declined the offer to watch. If I watched, I knew I would subconsciously feel the pain of being sliced open like a fish. I was drugged, so I remember everything in slow motion. After what seemed to be forever, I finally heard a baby cry. It took me a minute to realize that was *my* baby that was crying—all 10 pounds, 7 ounces of him!

I stayed in the hospital for four days. During those four days I can remember nurses checking my small-stapled incision and pushing on my stomach what seemed to be every hour. After the first day I was amazed that I was able to get up to hold my baby and try to walk around. I had no preconceived ideas about what I could or couldn't do after a normal childbirth, let alone a C-section. My family members and coworkers all seemed sympathetic that I had to go this route, as they felt it was much more painful and difficult to get back into a daily routine afterward. After years of knowing women who had normal child birth experiences, I tend to disagree. After a few weeks I had the staples removed. As far as I can remember, this was not as painful as I had expected. The sheer fact that I had been stapled seems amusing, which in actuality I had not found out until hours after the procedure. I was so squeamish that I couldn't even look at my incision for days!

I was up and doing for myself and the baby when I returned home. I was sore, but didn't have a lot of pain. I am not sure if I was just motivated to get back to my normal life or if I just healed really quickly. But at this point I was glad that I had the experience of the C-section rather than the painful experience of childbirth through normal methods.

There are six years between Mathew and Morgan. I had no notice with Morgan. At 3 PM I experienced a sharp labor pain, and by 4:30 PM she was born. Since I had already had a cesarean section, the emergency team at the hospital felt it was best if we just proceed the same way since Morgan was also a large baby. She was one month early and weighed nine pounds, six ounces, and measured 20 inches long! She probably would have made my son look tiny if she had gone full term. Again, I seemed to be back into my normal routine quicker and with less pain than my friends who had experienced normal childbirth. I personally feel that a cesarean section is a more controlled situation for everyone involved. My children were not scratched or bruised after the C-section. They looked like perfect little babies. I think my children experienced less trauma as babies the way they were brought into the world.

If someone today asked me what I would recommend, I would without hesitation say cesarean section. My physicians and all of the nurses were wonderful during my childbirth experiences. Some may feel that I missed out personally by not having my children the traditional way; I cannot believe the screaming and pain of the lady in the room next to me when Mathew was born. I keep flashing back to that experience. I identify with pain. I am able to focus on the birth of my children rather than the pain. I can remember being handed my babies and cuddling my babies during their first minutes of life; to me, those are meaningful experiences.

REFLECTIVE PRACTICE

Amber has very positive feelings about her cesarean section. However, professionals are concerned about the increasing number of children who are delivered by C-section. They feel that it puts mothers and infants at risk. How do you feel about this situation? Do you think women should be able to choose how to have their babies, or is this solely a medical decision?

COMPLICATIONS OF LABOR AND DELIVERY

Complications can affect the fetus and mother during the birthing process. Some complications arise because of the condition of the mother and her pregnancy, such as infection and high blood pressure (preeclampsia), others are related to the condition of the fetus; some conditions, such as fetal distress, relate to the delivery itself. Chapter 2 detailed the major maternal conditions, such as rubella, toxoplasmosis, group B streptococcus, HIV, maternal nutrition, and chronic maternal diseases that impact the birthing process. Although these are issues in and of themselves, one outcome of many of these conditions is that babies are born too soon and too small. Timing has a great deal to do with events that complicate labor and delivery.

Preterm Delivery

Preterm birth is the leading cause of infant death and serious complications (Agency for Healthcare Research and Quality [HQR], 2006). Of neonatal deaths not associated with congenital anomalies, 85 percent are attributed to preterm delivery (Brown & Satin, 2007).

Although some causes of premature labor are known, for the most part researchers do not know why labor starts too early in some situations, nor are we always successful in stopping labor once it has started. If labor begins between 24 and 34 weeks, tocolytic drugs are given to the mother to delay delivery. These drugs are used to stop uterine contractions or to help the uterus remain relaxed after a period of contractions. Although often successful in initially stopping contractions, it is not as clear whether or not they have any affect on continuing to maintain the stoppage (HQR, 2006). In addition to medication, pregnant women who experience preterm labor are usually put on bed rest and told to drink plenty of water.

If the birth can be delayed for only 24 to 48 hours, that is enough time to move the mother to a hospital equipped to support premature infants and their mothers, if necessary. The delay also provides the necessary time for the mother to be given an injection of antenatal glucorticoids, which accelerate the maturation of the fetal lungs (Lowdermilk & Perry, 2003).

Problems Related to the Membranes and Placenta

Abruptio placenta is the separation of the placenta from where it is implanted in the uterine wall before the delivery of the baby.

Preterm membrane rupture occurs in less than 2 percent of pregnancies but it accounts for 20 percent of all prenatal deaths that occur between 24 and 34 weeks (Perry & Strauss, 1998). Usually the placenta attaches in the upper third of the uterus, allowing it to stay intact during the birthing process and thus providing the fetus a source of oxygen. In **abruptio placenta**, the placenta is attached in the appropriate place but it detaches too early (Brown & Satin, 2007). Fetal distress develops quickly and a cesarean section may be necessary. Smoking significantly increases the risk for abruptio placenta. Trauma can also cause this problem.

In **placenta previa**, the placenta is implanted low in the uterus and is close to or covering the cervical opening of the birth canal. The incidence of placenta previa is approximately one out of 500 births. The incidence increases with each pregnancy and the risk is doubled with twins and multiples (University of Maryland Medical Center, 2005). This placement is detected early in pregnancy through ultrasound. Women may be prescribed bed rest to reduce the risk of hemorrhaging and premature labor. A cesarean section is almost always performed.

Placenta previa
is a condition where the placenta is implanted low in the uterine wall near or over the opening to the birth canal.

Delivery of Multiple Births

Women who carry multiple fetuses have increased levels of pregnancy hormones in their blood. They may experience an exaggeration of the usual early pregnancy symptoms of nausea and vomiting. These symptoms may arouse the first suspicion that it is a multiple pregnancy. Miscarriage is more frequent in multiple births than in singletons. There is also greater risk for anemia and

Twins
The number of multiple births is increasing.

hypertension because of increased fetal demands made on the maternal body. The probability of complications increases with multiple births. It is likely that the infants will be premature and small, and the risk of birth anomaly is greater. These conditions can influence delivery.

Some physicians recommend bed rest for women who are carrying multiples in order to delay delivery. Others do not see the value of the practice (Lowdermilk & Perry, 2003). Preterm delivery is a risk in multiple births complicated by intrauterine growth restriction. If birth can be delayed until 36 weeks, the risk for the neonate decreases. Although twins can be delivered vaginally, they are more frequently delivered by a cesarean section. This can be an emergency procedure or a planned one. Triplets and other higher multiple births are delivered through cesarean section.

BIRTHING PATTERNS

Birthing patterns are continuing to change. In the 21st century, for a noncomplicated delivery, women frequently go home in less than 48 hours after giving birth. In some hospitals, birthing is considered an outpatient process, and the mother and infant remain in the hospital for less than 24 hours. The brevity of this hospital stay could be problematic for the infant, because conditions such as **neonatal jaundice** peak the third or fourth day. It is a common condition and is usually part of the infant's process of making physical adjustments to being independent. If the new mother does not accurately judge the level of the yellow tinge of the infant's skin or the whites of his eyes, the condition may go untreated and result in **kernicterus**, which is caused by excess **bilirubin**. When the level of bilirubin is very high it moves out of the blood and is deposited in the brain tissue. This can cause neural problems, such as cerebral palsy, intellectual disability, or attention deficit (Lowdermilk & Perry, 2003). If treated it is entirely preventable. When infants stayed in the hospital longer, bilirubin levels were routinely monitored and the condition treated if necessary. It is imperative that infants who have been discharged early have followup medical care.

Some of the changes in birthing practices are the result of rising medical costs; others are the result of different beliefs and opinions about childbirth. It is difficult to determine the long-term effect of these changing patterns on infants and their families.

TRANSITION FROM THE WOMB

At birth, infants must make the transition from the dark, watery womb that was an almost a constant 99 degrees to a world of variable temperatures, light, and air. The infant must also move from a pulmonary (lung) and cardiovascular

Neonatal jaundice is an excess of bilirubin, which causes a yellow coloration of the skin and whites of the eyes of newborns.

Kernicterus is a form of brain damage caused by excessive bilirubin.

Bilirubin is a product of the breakdown of the hemoglobin in red blood cells.

Surfactant
is a chemical that keeps the air sacs in the lungs open during breathing.

(heart and blood vessels) system dependent on the mother and the placenta to one that is independent. The passage through the birth canal usually expels fluid from the lungs, and the infant's first cry usually inflates them. The chemical **surfactant** helps the lungs maintain their shape (Rais-Bahrami & Short, 2007). The pattern of blood circulation changes to allow the lungs to oxygenate the blood. These changes are tenuous during the first few hours and even days after birth. When the umbilical cord is clamped, additional circulatory changes allow the blood to pass through the liver for detoxification before entering the infant's heart. Infants also encounter the challenge of body temperature regulation. The wet infant enters the world with a large surface area and little body fat, so he needs to be warmed. The transitions are challenging for a full-term infant; premature birth can make the process even more difficult.

NEWBORNS

Neonate
is the designation for the first month of life.

Newborns are referred to as **neonates** for the first 28 days of their life. These 28 days are among the most dynamic and challenging for both babies and parents. Within minutes of birth, the newborn is assessed using the Apgar, which was developed by Virginia Apgar, M.D., in 1953. She wanted to create a simple, clear classification for newborns that could be taught easily to those working in the delivery room. Dr. Apgar chose five areas to focus on (see Table 3–1): heart rate as heard through a stethoscope; respiratory effort, observed by watching the movement of the chest wall; reflex irritability, obtained by gently slapping the soles of the feet; muscle tone, based on the degree of flexion and movement in the extremities; and color, determined by observing paleness and what parts of the body are blue and pink (Lowdermilk & Perry, 2003; Wood, 2005). Dr. Apgar concluded that the prognosis for infants who received a score of 8 to 10 was excellent, and the prognosis for those who received the lowest numbers—0, 1, or 2—was poor

Table 3–1 Apgar Scale

Sign	Score		
	0	1	2
Heart rate	Absent	Slow, less than 100	Over 100
Respiratory effort	Absent	Slow, weak cry	Good cry
Muscle tone	Flaccid	Some flexion of extremities	Well flexed
Reflex irritability	No response	Grimace	Cry
Color	Blue, pale	Body pink, extremities blue	Body/extremities pink

SOURCE: Lowdermilk and Perry (2003).

(Wood, 2005). These observations are made at one and five minutes after birth and can be performed by the nurse or other delivery room personnel.

Initial examination of the newborn is done while the newborn is being dried and wrapped in a warm blanket, outfitted with a hat, and lying on the mother's abdomen where she can hold and see him. This placement of the newborn affords the mother the profound experience of interacting for the first time with the new life that she delivered into the world. If the infant is alert, he will be curious and gaze with long intensity. When a parent stares into the eyes of her baby, it is usually love at first sight. The initial interaction between mother and baby might not be uncommon, as babies are born everyday, but the experience is unique and intense. A mother often has two conflicting responses—she wonders how anything so "enormous" could possibly fit inside her body, let alone get out, and how anything so "tiny" could be so perfect, especially those little hands, fingers, and fingernails. In addition to the emotional value of placing the infant on the mother's abdomen and covering him with a warm blanket, it also helps to regulate his temperature. Infants are put to the mother's breast soon after birth. Many hospitals choose to put the baby under a warmer to quickly warm and stabilize the baby. Also since many mothers choose to bottle feed, they must now request to breastfeed in the delivery room.

The first assessment relates to gestational age and birth weight. Newborns are assessed for physical and neurological well-being between 2 and 24 hours after birth. This gives the baby time to recover from the birthing process and occurs before some of the other significant changes that occur about 48 hours after birth are seen (Lowdermilk & Perry, 2003). Infants experience their first medical procedures soon after birth, when blood and urine samples are taken for screening. Different states have different requirements. Some states test infants for up to nine disorders, including phenylketurnia (PKU, a preventable form of intellectual disability), hypothyroidism, short stature, elimination, sickle cell anemia, HIV, cystic fibrosis, and others (Lowdermilk & Perry, 2003). Newborns are also screened for possible hearing loss.

What Does the Newborn Look Like?

Vernix
is the waxy or cheesy white substance found coating the skin of a newborn.

Newborns rarely look like their parents' dream baby, but parents usually do not care. The newborn is wet with amniotic fluid, his skin is wrinkled, and he may still be covered with the white cheesy substance called **vernix**. He may or may not have hair. His face may be asymmetrical from his trip through the birth canal, and his head may be cone-shaped from having been squeezed. His head circumference exceeds his chest circumference and it constitutes about 25 percent of his body length (in adults it is about 10 percent). He has a receding chin—the better to suckle. His arms and legs are bent or flexed and froglike and they are disproportionately short. His hands are in closed fists. His abdomen protrudes and there is no semblance of a waist. He is about 20 inches long and weighs about 7 ½ pounds. His skin may be a bit blue, his breathing rapid and even a little irregular, and his hands and feet cold.

Classification of Newborns by Weight and Age

One of the first questions that people ask about a newborn is, "How much did she weigh?" Unless, of course, the parents decided not to find out if the baby is a boy or girl before delivery. Birth weight is significant, especially in relation to gestational age. Birth weight and gestational age are the most widely used factors in determining neonatal risk. Neonatal risk often translates into infant risk. Information such as birth weight and gestational age will affect how you plan for infants and what your expectations are for their developmental patterns.

The average female newborn weights 3,400 grams (7 ½ pounds), whereas males average 3,500 grams (8 ¾ pounds). Because of water loss infants may lose 10 percent of their birth weight in the days after birth, but this should be regained within the first two weeks.

Newborns weighing less than 2,500 grams (or about 5 ½ pounds) are considered **low birth weight (LBW)**. Those weighing less than 1,500 grams (about 3 ⅓ to 5 ½ pounds) are **very low birth weight (VLBW)**. When an infant is born weighing less than 1,000 grams (2 ¼ to 3 ⅓ pounds) she is considered **extremely low birth weight (ELBW)**. Infants born at term weighing over 4,000 grams (8 ¼ pounds) are considered **large for gestational age** (see Table 3–2).

Infants born before 37 weeks gestational age are considered **preterm**. Being born too soon means that the infant has to make the adjustment from an intrauterine to an extrauterine environment with a less developed body and body systems. Common causes of preterm delivery are maternal infections and adolescence (Rais-Bahrami & Short, 2007). Infants born after 42 weeks are **postterm**.

LBW
refers to infants born weighing less than 5 ½ pounds.

VLBW
refers to infants born weighing less than 3 1/3 pounds.

ELBW
refers to infants born weighing less than 2 ¼ pounds.

Large for gestational age
refers to infants born weighing over the 90th percentile over their gestational age.

Preterm
infants refers to those who are born after 37 completed weeks of pregnancy.

Postterm
pregnancies are those that extend up to or beyond 42 weeks.

Table 3–2 Classification of Newborns by Birth Weight

Grams	Pounds (Approximate)	Classification
2,500–4,000	7 ½ to 8 ¾	Typical birth weight
1,500–2,500	5 ½ to 7 ½	Low birth weight (LBW)
1,000–1,500	3 ⅓ to 5 ½	Very low birth weight (VLBW)
Less than 1,000	2 ¼ to 3 ⅓	Extremely low birth weight (ELBW)
Over 4,000	8 ¼ and over	Large for gestational age

Few babies are born later than 42 weeks, because labor will be induced by then. In these instances, the estimated gestational age may be inaccurate.

Looking at gestational age and weight together provides additional information. Appropriate gestational weight (AGW) falls between the 10th and 90th percentile for the infant's gestational age. That is, an infant who was born at 36 weeks who weighed 2,268 grams (five pounds) (would be considered LBW but not **small for gestational age (SGA)**. If that same infant weighed 1,588 grams (3 ½ pounds) she would be SGA. Not all babies enter the world at full term ready to become active members of new families.

Small for gestational age refers to infants weighing less than the 10th percentile for their gestational age.

NEWBORN ASSESSMENT

The most widely used neonatal assessment tool is the Neonatal Behavioral Assessment Scale (NBAS) developed by T. Berry Brazelton in 1973, revised in 1984, and again in 1995 (Brazelton & Nugent, 1995). It can be used with infants from the first day of life up to two months. It was designed to provide an assessment of the neonate's neurological responses and behavioral repertoire. The scale evaluates the infant's potential for self-organization and his ability to control his state of arousal (alertness) as a response to the environment. The assessment tool requires a trained examiner and is most frequently used with vulnerable infants. The examination takes 20 to 30 minutes, and the examiner does the testing with the infant's parents, who help the examiner to assess the level of skill.

The measure is based on several key assumptions:

- Newborns have nine months of experience to draw on.
- Infants are capable of controlling their behavior to respond to their environment.
- Infants communicate through their behavior.
- Infants are social beings who shape and are shaped by their caregiving environment (Brazelton Institute, 2005).

Unlike most previous measures, the NBAS was conceived as an interactive assessment and the role of the examiner was to draw out the neonate's organizational skills and strengths. The emphasis is on establishing the newborn's capacities and limits, especially as they affect interactions with a caregiver. The infant's best scores are used, rather than his average performance. The test's requires that the examiner be knowledgeable of infants and also receive training in the test's administration.

The purpose of the assessment is to measure the infant's capabilities and to determine if she may need extra caregiving in some areas. The NBAS focuses on four major areas: the autonomic system, the motor system, state regulation, and social interaction (Brazelton Institute, 2005).

One of the first challenges newborns face is to regulate their temperature, breathing, and other parts of the autonomic system. High-risk infants may spend most of their energy just doing this and therefore have no energy left for other developmental tasks. They may be overtaxed by noise and visual stimulation.

Next, infants need to inhibit random movements and control their activity level. This includes the infants muscle tone, activity level, and reflexes. Swaddling can help babies control random movements.

State
describes levels of consciousness that range from quiet sleep to active crying.

State regulation is the next challenge. The ability of the infant to control her state determines how available she is to respond to her environment. The examiner looks at the state of the infant, looks at state changes, and the predominant state of the infant during the assessment process. Some infants can ignore stimulation or habituate to it. When babies cannot ignore it, caregivers need to evaluate the environment and regulate the amount of light and sound.

Finally, the ultimate developmental task: social interaction. The examiner looks at how infants respond to faces, voices, and even a ball. Because the parents are present at the assessment, they see what their baby can do. The examiner helps them see a profile of their infant that they can use to better care for her (Brazelton Institute, 2005).

NEWBORNS AT RISK

Some infants are born with conditions that place them and their future development at risk. The purpose of this section is not to identify all such conditions, but rather to increase your awareness of them and to help you think about how these conditions will impact how you will educate and care for these infants and toddlers.

Birth weight and gestational age are the most widely used factors in determining neonatal risk. The preterm infant comes into the world at a disadvantage. The immature organs may not be ready to perform the necessary tasks of independent living.

Preterm and LBW Newborns

Thirteen percents of infants are born before 37 weeks and 8 percent are born weighing less than 5 ½ pounds (National Center for Health Statistics, 2007). Preterm births and LBW babies occur in 11 percent of all pregnancies, yet they account for the majority of neonatal deaths and almost half of all neurodevelopmental disabilities that are present at birth (Hoyert, Freedman, Strobino, &

Guyer, 2001). The number of preterm births is rising. Common causes include maternal infections and adolescence, or both (Rais-Bahrami & Short, 2007).

Being born too soon means that not all systems are ready. Premature infants face risks that other infants do not face. Their immature immune system makes them more susceptible to infection. They have problems regulating their body temperature, coordinating sucking and swallowing, absorbing nutrients, they may not breathe regularly, and their heart may not beat rhythmically. They also look and sound different than term infants. They typically have fine hair, or *lanugo*, over their body (disappears by 38 weeks); their skin has a reddish tinge because the blood vessels are closer to the surface; their skin is more translucent; and they may lack breast buds, skin creases, and cartilage in their ear lobe. They may be floppy because their muscle tone is not well developed. These preemies may appear passive and disorganized (Rais-Bahrami & Short, 2007).

Respiratory Problems

Their respiratory system does not work as well or predictably as term babies. Their lungs may not expand because of the lack of the chemical surfactant. In mild cases, infants are given supplemental oxygen to help them until their system can produce enough surfactant. In more serious cases, infants are given surfactant replacement therapy, which begins to work almost immediately (Rais-Bahrami & Short, 2007).

Cardiovascular Problems

Patent ductus arteriosus is a hole that allows the fetal blood to bypass the lungs.

For some premature infants, certain necessary changes in the circulatory system may not take place. One of the most important is the closure of the **patent ductus arteriosus**, which the fetal circulatory system used to bypass the fetal lungs. In about 30 percent of premature infants, this closure does not take place. In term infants the first breath increases the oxygen level in the blood, which stimulates closure of this duct. Medication can be used to help this duct close (Rais-Bahrami & Short, 2007).

Neurological Problems

Apnea is a pause in breathing for 15 to 20 seconds.

Bradycardia is a drop in heart rate to below 80 to 100 beats per minute.

The preemie is also troubled by an immature central nervous system, which controls respiration and circulation. Getting oxygen into the lungs is a challenge. Two common problems are apnea and bradycardia. **Apnea** is a respiratory pause of 15 to 20 seconds associated with **bradycardia**; a fall in the heart rate to below 80 to 100 beats per minute, and is a problem for about 10 percent of preterm infants. The smaller the infant, the more likely the problem (Rais-Bahrami & Short, 2007).

Premature infants are more than twice as likely to die of sudden infant death syndrome (SIDS). Although apnea of prematurity is not a major predisposing factor for SIDS, infants who have persistent episodes of apnea and bradycardia are sent home from the hospital on an apnea monitor. Theses monitors sound an alarm if the infant stops breathing and may provide some reassurance to parents.

up close and personal

I had an emergency cesarean section, and Evan only weighed five pounds two ounces at birth. I was in my 34th week. He was in the Neonatal Intensive Care Unit (NICU) for a week. We begged to bring him home. They finally agreed after we had taken a course in Infant Cardiopulmonary Resuscitation (CPR). He came home with an apnea monitor. It has been a nightmare. I feel like I have my own little corner of the world. One of us sits here and watches him day and night. I watch during the day and we take three hour shifts at night. We know we can't keep doing this, but now it is the only way we have any peace. I know it would wake us up, as it is loud, but it is so scary. What if we didn't wake up? What if we didn't get to him in time? I heard a story about a woman who took a shower and didn't hear the monitor and her baby died.

It goes off all the time, but then he starts to breathe again or his heart beats or whatever is supposed to happen does. Only once did we have to press on his heart. They told us that he self-stimulates. I guess that means that after it stops too long it starts again. But it is always there. He is connected to a machine. I cannot decide if it gives me comfort or anxiety.

REFLECTIVE PRACTICE

How would you feel about having a baby with an apnea monitor in a child care center? Do you believe he should be there? Do you think you have the skills to care for a baby on an apnea monitor? If not, what do you need to learn?

In addition to heart and respiratory problems, premature baby's blood vessels are very fragile. Problems occur when the blood vessels that go to the ventricles (two sides of the brain) break. This causes bleeding or hemorrhaging in the brain. Most preemies have some degree of **intraventricular hemorrhage (IVH)** within a few hours after birth. The lower the birth weight and the younger the gestational age, the greater the probability of hemorrhaging. When hemorrhaging is limited, there are no adverse outcomes. More severe hemorrhages may lead to neurological impairment such as cerebral palsy and intellectual disability. Ultrasound is used to diagnose and classify IVH.

Ophthalmologic Problems

Premature infant's eyes should be checked because they may be at risk for problems, such as retinopathy of prematurity (ROP). ROP occurs when abnormal blood vessels grow and spread throughout the retina, the tissue that lines the back of the eye. These abnormal blood vessels are fragile and can leak, scarring the retina and pulling it out of position. This causes the retina to detach, which is the main cause of visual impairment and blindness in ROP. This is most likely to occur in newborns who weigh 2 ¾ pounds or less (National Eye Institute, 2006).

Gastrointestinal Problems

Many LBW babies cannot suck from a nipple. In premature infants the sucking reflex and the swallowing mechanism lack coordination. It is easy for the infant to wear himself out from sucking without getting the necessary calories and nutrients. A special high-caloric formula may be used.

Other Physiological Problems

Some problems directly relate to prematurity, others relate to the infant herself. Preterm neonates are more susceptible to problems such as hypothermia, hypo- and hyperglycemia, anemia, and jaundice. Losing body heat, or hypothermia, occurs because the preemie does not have as much subcutaneous fat, and because his higher ratio of body surface to body weight causes faster heat loss. This is why premature neonates are placed in warmed incubators. Premature infants have smaller reserves of glucose, which puts them at risk for hypoglycemia. This may cause lethargy, vomiting, and seizures. To solve the problem, these infants have early feedings, their glucose levels are monitored, and glucose may be administered intravenously. Because the preterm infant's liver is less developed, bilirubin can build up in his system, giving him a yellow, jaundiced appearance. Treatment typically involves phototherapy. The newborn's eyes are shielded and he is put under a light source. **Anemia** decreases the oxygen-carrying capacity of the red blood cells and may be treated by transfusion or medication.

Intensive Care Nurseries

Different hospitals have different levels of care that they can provide for newborns. Mothers who may deliver LBW babies are often moved to hospitals that have Level IV care, even if they are in labor. This is better than waiting for the infant to be born and then transferring him, which is a risk since about half of these babies must be delivered via cesarean section. Some premature infants and virtually all very-low-birth-weight neonates will need a intensive-care-nurseries (ICN) or neonatal intensive-care units (NICU) (Browne, 2003).

Neonatal intensive-care units are designed for high-volume, short-term acute care. They focus on medical concerns rather than social concerns. They are used in specially designated hospitals with highly trained staff and they have very advanced technological equipment. They are staffed not with pediatricians and pediatric nurses, but rather with **neonatologists**, medical specialists who concentrate only on the first month of life, and neonatal nurses, also specially trained to work with very small sick newborns.

Neonatologists are a subspecialty of pediatricians who care for ill and premature newborns.

The intensive-care nursery is a threatening place for most parents and not at all what their idea of parenting is all about (Browne, 2003). The equipment is daunting, as is the noise level, with monitors beeping and personnel moving quickly to handle emergencies. The infants in the ICN are often very small and are hooked up to equipment to help them perform a variety of life functions, from breathing to eating. Instead of being alone in a dimly lit room and being able to hold, cuddle, and love their baby, these parents must learn to look through a maze of equipment in order to see their baby, who needs the same love, cuddling, and holding.

Bringing a Preterm Infant Home

As threatening as the ICN is, parents may be more frightened of bringing their baby home. Most premature infants come home around their due date. This is not the same as bringing a full-term infant home. Preemies are not well organized internally. They may not give clear signals about when they are hungry, sleepy, or overstimulated. They may go from soundly sleeping to loudly screaming in a matter of seconds. It takes full-term infants several weeks to begin to establish predictable patterns of eating and sleeping. It takes preemies even longer.

Because the baby is not well organized, the adults need to be. The easiest way to do this is for parents to keep a chart of what the baby does 24 hours a day. This may seem unreasonable given the total situation, but the long-term payoffs are high. After two or three days a pattern may emerge. With a pattern, parents may be able to predict the baby's needs and determine how to meet them before the baby becomes disorganized.

The stress of coping with preemies is exacerbated by limited parental resources (money, transportation, education, etc.). Problems of developmental delays and neurological problems are greater for very-low-birth-weight infants whose mothers are 17 years old or under, have less than a high-school education, and are not married than for babies born to middle-class families (Moore, 2003). Premature and low-birth-weight babies have a far greater risk of being abused by parents or caregivers during infancy and early childhood (Sullivan & Knutson, 2000). This is true even when social class is held constant.

The possibility of developmental delays also looms. Overall, there appears to be a correlation between birth weight and developmental delay: The lower the birth weight, the greater the probability of a developmental delay. Delays appear more likely in the **perceptual-motor** areas that in verbal areas (Allen, 2002). The birth weight itself does not seem to be the major factor, but rather the complications such as hemorrhaging and other medical risk conditions.

Preterm infants usually sleep 18 hours a day or more. However, if they have been in an ICN there probably has been no attempt to mold their sleep preferences into a pattern of day and night. The ICN is very different from a home and the adjustment for both parents and infant is a major one. It may be necessary to experiment with the environment to help infants adjust. Some infants like the new peace and quiet, for others the adjustment is too great. Some infants may need to have the lights on and the radio playing softly when they go to sleep.

NEWBORN SENSES

Neonates, although dependent, are amazingly competent beings who are not at the mercy of their environment, but have a diverse repertoire of behaviors that enable them to adjust and adapt to their environment. Infants obtain information through their senses of hearing, seeing, feeling, smelling, and tasting. A sense is a system by which information outside the nervous system is translated into neural activity and thus gives the neonate information about the outside world.

Hearing

The newborn is auditory dominate at birth. The auditory system of the infant is among the most well developed bodily functions at birth. By the 15th week in utero the fetus has a well-formed ears and by 20 weeks he has an adult configuration, although it is not completely mature (Herer, Knightly, & Steinberg, 2002). Although infants cannot see in the womb, they can hear. Using real-time ultrasound has increased our understanding of the fetus in action and the skills that he brings with him at birth. Fetal responsiveness has been repeatedly documented. Although it was initially thought that the fetus did not hear until

Perceptual-motor development is the ability to mentally organize and interpret sensory information and then respond to it.

24 weeks, Hepper, White, and Shahidullah (1991) found that the fetus could respond to auditory stimulation at 16 weeks, perhaps even 12. This is before the hearing apparatus is functional. They hypothesize that perhaps very early in fetal life, specific receptor cells are responded to as stimulation by an undifferentiated neural system. In other words, the very young fetus responds to sensation but it is not sorted out into specific sensory modalities.

Even though the newborn can hear at birth, he hears differently than adults. This is in part because his outer ear (the visible part) is disproportionately small; secondly, his ear canal is plugged with a creamy white substance called vernix, which disappears in about a week; and, finally, the middle ear has fluid from the womb that takes the body a while to absorb. So, he is functionally hard-of-hearing; what he hears is thinner and duller than what adults hear, but he can hear.

The auditory cortex is immature. The newborn's brain does not have the ability to sort out the reverberations of sound waves, so what he hears is not the same as what we hear, much like what we see is not what the infant sees (Maurer & Maurer, 1988). He hears not only an initial sound like the slamming of a book on a table, but continuing vibrations as well. As adults, our brain ignores these further vibrations and "hears" a single sound. The newborn hears sound after sound after sound after sound.

Because what is heard is so different for newborns, some of the initial testing that was done using pure tones led to the conclusion that newborns could not hear at birth. However, given the right stimulus, such as a rattle, infants do respond and turn toward the sound of the rattle. Maurer and Maurer (1988) consider this not as locating a sound, but a reflexive orienting to the sound. That is, in response to a prolonged noise, the newborn will hesitate and then turn very slowly toward the source of the sound. He is not looking for the sound source, because he does this in the dark with his eyes closed.

Newborns locate sounds based on high frequencies. As women's voices are higher pitched than men's, the newborn may seem more responsive to his mother than his father. The newborn prefers his mother's voice to all other stimuli (Eklund-Flores & Turkewitz, 1996). Although he can hear both parents, he cannot accurately locate his father by his voice. Strangely, given all the newborn's disadvantages in the area of hearing, he has the ability to distinguish speech patterns. He can distinguish between vowel sounds (Moon, Panneton-Cooper, & Fifer, 1993), as well as discriminate between unfamiliar whispered voices, and remember speech sounds (Spense & Freeman, 1996) within two days of being born.

To speak, the newborn needs to hear speech, and the speech that best suits his needs is "parentese." In all cultures, when adults talk to babies their speech patterns change. They speak more slowly, more clearly, in a higher pitch, and have more variability in their pitch and intensity, using an almost singsong tempo. Their sentences are short and simple. This is what babies need. The pitch and rhythm gets their attention, the slow speed helps them sort out the sounds from the echoes, and the pauses help the infant hear the components of speech. Amazingly, adults do this automatically. Perhaps we are programmed to respond to infants in this way!

REFLECTIVE PRACTICE

Think about how you talk to infants. Does your voice pattern change? If not, given what you have learned, how will you change it?

Binocular vision uses two eyes at the same time.

Peripheral vision occurs outside the center of the gaze.

Retina is a thin layer of photoreceptor cells and neurons at the back of the eyeball.

Fovea is a small pit near the center of the retina that is responsible for central vision and visual acuity.

Visual cortex is the area of the occipital lobe that processes most visual information.

Occipital lobe is in the back of the brain and processes visual stimuli and contains most of the visual cortex.

Optic nerve transmits visual information from the retina to the occipital lobe of the brain.

Vision

The newborn's vision is different from adult vision, but it serves him well. Your knowledge of it will help you understand what to show very young infants and how to show it to them. The visual system is the most complex sensory system and it is also the least well developed at birth. The newborn can see at birth and he can visually track (Laplante, Orr, Neville, Vorkapich, & Sasso, 1996). However, as this is his first experience with light, he is hypersensitive to bright lights. Neonates do not have normal adult visual acuity (20/20). Normal visual acuity at birth is about 20/400, but the newborn has more functional vision than this would suggest (Glass, 2002). Although inhibiting for an adult, for infants this low visual acuity may have a protective quality and prevent overstimulation.

Newborns see best in dim lighting with high-contrasting colors. They are most attentive to black-and-white bull's-eyes, stripes, and checks. Pastels are really washed out, and infants do not notice them. Think about that as you look around the classroom or even as you buy a baby gift. Adults might like pink and light blue, but babies like red and black. Infants focus best on objects that are close to them. Newborns do not yet have **binocular vision** or the range of **peripheral vision** that adults have. Rather, it is almost as if he is looking through two separate tunnels that do not come together. The newborn can focus on the human face and has a field of vision of about 90 degrees. To get an approximation of what a newborn sees, take a piece of wax paper and hold it about eight inches from your eyes and look around. You will notice that everything looks blurred. That is what an infant sees.

This is caused in part because the **retina** is underdeveloped, particularly the **fovea**, which is responsible for visual acuity. The eye is connected to the **visual cortex** of the **occipital lobe** of the brain by the **optic nerve**. During the neonatal period the visual cortex is very immature. This immaturity influences the neonates gaze and his ability to follow objects. The infant watches whatever part of an object that catches his eye, but he does not visually explore the object. If the frame of a picture is higher contrast than the picture itself, the neonate will focus on the frame and not see the picture. Thus, the neonate will focus on your chin or hairline, but will probably not see your whole face until he is two to three months old. He sees slow-moving objects as photographs spaced at intervals rather than as a film or videotape that is continuous. Neonates also lack the coordination to follow rapidly moving objects. It is not just the eye that is developing; the visual cortex in the brain is developing more synapses. For young infants to see you, approach slowly and talk to them as you approach them. You do not want to startle them; rather, your goal is to connect with them.

Touch

The sense of touch is the first sense to develop in the early fetal period. With increasing size, the fetus comes into contact with the uterine wall, the fetus touches himself, especially his face, and the umbilical cord is constantly touching the fetus. At birth infants are not as sensitive to touch as adults; that is, they may not respond to a very light touch that an adult would feel. Through the combined integration of motor responses and reduction of immediate reflexive responses to tactile stimulation, the infants' involuntary response to touch decreases and is replaced by voluntary responses.

Tactile stimulation plays an important role in the emotional development of neonates. They crave tactile stimulation and like to be held. Touching is also an important element in the development of visual attentiveness and attachment behaviors.

Smell

The percentage of the human brain devoted to smell is much smaller than in most other mammals, leading one to believe it is a less crucial sense for humans. In addition, researchers have found the senses of hearing and vision more intriguing than smell. Consequently, relatively little is known about the infant's olfactory skills. Neonates appear to have a remarkably well developed sense of smell. They can discriminate between pleasant and unpleasant odors. They show a preference for fragrant odors and displeasure for noxious ones. Newborns can distinguish their mother's smell from the smell of other mothers by the end of the first week (Porter, 1991). They like the smell of their mother. By six days old, they can also distinguish between the smell of their mother's milk and another mother's milk. Some researchers (Blass, 1990; Engen, 1986) hypothesize that smell may be more important to the very young infant than previously thought. It may be that the infant's ability to learn and associate smells with familiar individuals and places is an important mediator of social behavior. This may initially be how neonates "know" familiar people, as their vision is not yet adequate to distinguish particular faces.

Taste

Taste was the subject of early investigations of newborns, but little research is currently being done in the area. The newborn has an adequate number of taste buds. Neonates can discriminate between sweet, acidic, salty, and bitter tastes. Infants much prefer sweet tastes, like salty fluids, and will spit out sour tastes. They can discriminate between intensities of these tastes also. Apparently the preference for sweet tastes is innate. Some research has shown that sugars, especially sucrose, may reduce the reaction to pain (Blass, 1990). A variety of measures have been used to determine preferences in taste. Some observe facial expressions, others sucking rates, and still others the heart rate. The latter two seem to be more reliable indicators (Lipsitt & Behl, 1990).

NEWBORN DEVELOPMENT

Newborns come equipped with a remarkable repertoire of skills. They can entertain us by moving their arms and kicking. They can get our attention by crying, and they like to hear their mother's voice. Newborns are competent at getting their needs met.

Motor Development

The newborn's motor development is characterized by two different types of movements: spontaneous and reflexes. Spontaneous movements occur without apparent stimulation, whereas reflexes are made in response to a specific stimulus (Haywood & Getchell, 2005). The spontaneous movements made by the newborn were initially thought to be unrelated to later movement, but **supine** (lying on the back) kicking is sometimes rhythmical and related to walking movements. Spontaneous arm movements show coordination. Although weak and lacking goal directedness, spontaneous movement could serve as the foundation for voluntary, functional movement (Jensen, Thelen, Ulrich, Schneider, & Zernicke, 1995).

Supine
is lying on the back with the face upward.

Reflexes
are an involuntary specific muscular response to a sensory stimulus.

The neonate is born with infantile reflexes. **Reflexes** are predictable responses to specific stimuli. They are controlled by the brain stem and the spinal cord. Some of these reflexes will disappear as the cortex of the brain matures and overrides them; others form the basis for coordinated, voluntary movement; and still others, such as the knee jerk, remain throughout life.

Reflexes are used in the diagnostic assessment of the newborn and infant. Trained examiners use the predictable pattern of infant reflexes for diagnosis of central nervous system dysfunction. As an early childhood educator you have an important role in this process. Your knowledge about reflexes and their importance should make you a keen observer. It is your role to alert parents if you see something that concerns you (see Table 3–3).

There are three different types of infantile reflexes: primitive reflexes, locomotor reflexes, and postural reactions (Haywood & Getchell, 2005). **Primitive reflexes** are the first observable reflexes. Some of the most primitive reflexes develop during the fetal period. Primitive reflexes essential for a newborn's survival include sucking, swallowing, blinking, urinating, hiccupping, and defecating. These reflexes are not learned; they are involuntary and necessary for survival. They are present in some form at or soon after birth. For example, a newborn sucks whenever a nipple, finger, or pacifier is placed in her mouth. It is unrelated to hunger or the nutritive value of what is being sucked. Gradually, the sucking reflex becomes more efficient; that is, the infant learns how much sucking is required for liquid to get into her mouth, and she coordinates sucking, swallowing, and breathing more efficiently and it becomes voluntary.

Locomotor reflexes are present at birth or shortly thereafter and relate to crawling, walking, and swimming. **Postural reactions** appear somewhere after two months and help the infant maintain his posture in response to changes in the position of his body.

Table 3–4 provides a summary of the reflexes, ages they are present, information on how to elicit them, and their significance. As you play with babies, check for the appropriate reflexes in the context of your play. Routinely stroke the infant's cheek to see if he turns, put your finger in his palm, and stroke the ball of his foot. There is no need to examine infants, but part of your role as a professional is to observe these behaviors. Knowing when reflexes appear and their expected trajectory helps you become a more alert observer of infant development.

Primitive reflexes
are inborn behavior patterns that develop during uterine life, are present a birth, and have survival value.

Locomotor reflexes
relate to body movement or locomotion.

Postural reactions
help the infant keep his head upright even when his body is at an angle and arm extension provides some protection when falling.

Table 3–3 Diagnostic Significance of Infant Reflexes

• A reflex persists beyond the age it should have been inhibited by cortical control.
• A reflex is absent.
• A reflex is too strong or too weak.
• A reflex is asymmetrical, that is unequal bilaterally with one side stronger than the other.

SOURCE: Gallahue and Ozmun (2002).

Table 3–4 Summary of Infant Reflexes

Reflex	To Elicit	Significance
Primitive Reflexes		
Rooting or searching	Stroke the cheek and the infant will turn toward that side.	Present from birth to 1 year. May be depressed in newborn because of drugs given in the birthing process. Absence or persistence after 1 year indicates neurological problems.
Sucking	Touch the face near the mouth with your finger and the infant will begin sucking.	Present birth to 3 months, changes into a voluntary behavior.
Palmar grasping	Touch the palm of the infant's hand with your finger and the hand will close, grasping your finger.	Present prenatal to 4 months, is of concern if it persists after the first year or is asymmetrical.
Babkin (Palmar-mandibular)	Put pressure on the palms of both hands. The infant's eyes will close, mouth open, and head flexes.	Present 1 to 3 months; diminishes gradually; Weak response, or return after it disappears, may indicate central nervous system dysfunction.
Plantar grasping	Stroke the ball of the foot just below the toes. Toes will curl around object or finger.	Present birth to 12 months; diminishes gradually. Strong in infants with cerebral palsy.
Babinski	Stroke the sole of the foot from heel to toes. The toes fan out, the large toes flexes.	Present birth to 4 months; absence indicates dysfunction of the lower spinal cord; concern if it persists after 6 months.
Asymmetrical Tonic Neck Reflex	Infant supine turn head to one side, same-side arm and leg will extend, the other side will flex (fencer "on guard" position).	Present prenatal to 4 months; concern if this happens on one side but not the other; persistence beyond 6 months may indicate motor immaturity or cerebral palsy.
Symmetrical Tonic Neck Reflex	First extend head and neck, then flex them; arms extend, legs flex; arms flex, legs extend.	Present prenatal to 6 to 7 months; helps infants get onto hands and knees; disappears as infant learns to crawl. Persistence of reflex prevents extension of legs when head is raised.
Moro	Infant supine, tap surface on each side of head; arms and legs extend with the fingers spread; then arms and legs flex.	Present prenatal to 3 months; absence, persistence after 6 months or asymmetrical response indicates dysfunction of the central nervous system.
Startle	Make a sudden loud noise or tap on abdomen; arms and legs flex.	Present from 7 to 12 months; merges with the adult startle reflex.
Locomotor Reflexes		
Crawling	Prone, apply pressure to the sole of one foot then the other; infant moves legs in crawling pattern.	Present from birth until 4 months; voluntary crawling appears around 7 months.

(continues)

Reflex	To Elicit	Significance
Stepping	Hold infant upright on a solid surface and tilt from side to side, infant will support weight and take alternating steps.	Present from birth to 5 months; strongest in first 6 weeks.
Swimming	Place infant above or in water prone; will exhibit swimming movement of arms and legs.	Present from 11 days to 5 months.
Postural reactions		
Labyrinthine righting	Hold infant upright and tilt forward, backward or to the side; head moves to stay upright.	Present from 2 to 6 months then is replaced by optical righting reflex into the first year.
Pull-up	Sitting upright held by one or both hands; tilt infant backward or forward; arms flex.	Present from 3 to 12 months.
Parachute and propping	Hold infant vertically and lower toward ground as if falling; extends arms and legs; tilt forward, sideways, and backwards; arms extend.	Present from 4 months for forward and downward positions, sideways 6 months, backwards 9 months.

SOURCE: Gallahue and Ozmun (2002); Haywood and Getchell (2005).

There are a variety of theories about reflexes, their value, and what happens to them. These theories can be divided into three general categories of explanations: functional, structural, and applied (Haywood & Getchell, 2005). A functional approach suggests that all reflexes are innate and that at some point they had survival, protective, or adaptive value in the evolution of the species. Some reflexes like rooting and sucking seem to have an obvious role in survival. Others like the asymmetrical tonic neck reflex seem far less obvious. A structural or neuromaturational approach (Eckert, 1987) contends that these behaviors are controlled by the lower brain (brain stem and spinal cord) and that as the cortex develops it inhibits the reflexes or modifies them and they come under voluntary control. The formation of the **myelin sheath** allows messages to be sent more quickly and to more isolated regions of the body, which in turn allows it to move with greater accuracy and precision (Gallahue & Ozmun, 2002). Applied theories focus on understanding the relationship between early reflexes and future voluntary movements.

Myelin sheath
is a layer of specialized cells that serve as an electrical insulator to speed the conduction of nerve impulses.

Cognitive Development

Before the 1960s there was little interest or research on the psychological capacities of the neonate. One of the challenges of studying cognition in the neonate is

Cognition
is the mental process of knowing including memory, attention, perception, problem solving, learning, and reasoning.

the rapid changes that are occurring in the brain itself, and the rate of physical and motor development. Increasingly researchers are interested in the infant's self-regulatory abilities and how these abilities impact long-term **cognition** and social adjustment (Williamson & Anzalone, 2001).

Some researchers interested in the neonate have focused their attention on whether or not newborns can "learn." Learning is defined as any relatively permanent change in an organism that results from past experience. Because learning is central to the way humans' function in the world it has been the subject of much investigation. The conclusion is clear: Neonates, even premature ones, can and do learn, and they can learn even before birth (Hepper & Shahidullah, 1992).

Habituation

Habituation
is a form of learning in which the infant quits responding after repeated exposure to a stimulus.

Habituation is the decrease in response that occurs to repeated stimulation. For example, if the newborn cried the first few times she heard a telephone ring, and after repeated rings did not cry, one would say that the infant had habituated. Habituation is one of the simplest yet most essential learning processes. Habituation is a central nervous system function that involves a primitive type of learning and memory. Habituation is essential for efficient function. It is this ability that allows humans to ignore familiar stimuli and pay attention to new ones. Habituation is correlated with later measures of language and cognitive development (Colombo & Saxon, 2002). Habituation allows the newborn to "tune out" some stimuli and not react to them. One stimulus neonates rarely tune out is the human voice when someone is talking to them.

Language Development

Language begins with the newborn's first cry. In addition to crying, newborns can make gasping sounds and vegetative sounds (murmurs and gurgles), which often accompany feeding. Newborns are responsive to the human voice, regardless of the language of the speaker. They prefer vocal music to instrumental. They also move to the rhythm of adult speech—if the speech is fast the infant's motion increases and, likewise, if the speech slows, the infant's motion also slows. The sounds that the newborn makes are relatively easy to identify and quantify. However, we are certain that newborns prefer to hear their mother's voice (DeCasper & Fifer, 1980). Remember that they have been hearing their mother's voice since 16 weeks of gestation or earlier. Interestingly, newborns are also sensitive to the rhythmic properties of their own language and can distinguish it from other languages (Moon et al., 1993). Babies do not know where they are going to live, so they must be prepared to recognize the sounds of all languages (Golinkoff & Hirsh-Pasek, 1999).

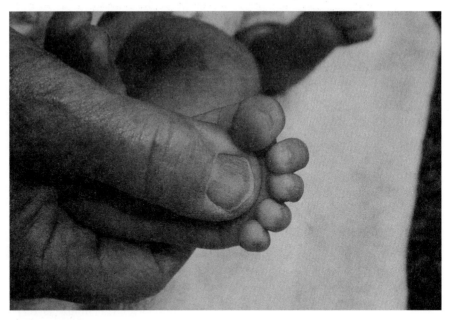

Plantar Reflex
To obtain the plantar reflex, stroke the ball of the foot just below the toes. The toes will curl around the finger or thumb.

WITH INFANTS AND TODDLERS

To find out first hand about infant's ability to imitate play the "O" game. Get close to a young infant and make your mouth into an "O" and say "oh." Hold it. Then do it again. If you catch the infant's attentions she will make her mouth shape like an "O" and imitate you. You can also play the stick-out-your-tongue game, which uses the same process.

Perceiving speech is a complex process. The neonate must be able to structure acoustical space and locate sound sources within it, speech must be distinguished from background noise, and sounds must be kept apart from each other when they originate from different sources but occur at the same time. Neonates apparently can locate a single sound source, but they do it slowly.

Social and Emotional Development

Some people believe that there is a critical period for mothers to bond with their infants and that this period is during the first hours or days after birth. Proponents of having fathers present at birth feel that fathers, too, bond during this period. Belief in bonding is one of the reasons people feel that mothers and their infants should not be separated in hospitals. The research does not consistently support this position, but rather a variation on it. Both timing and duration of contact seem to be more important than whether or not the father was actually present during the birthing process. Palkovitz (1982) found that the longer after delivery the father held the infant, the longer he held the infant in that first encounter. And the longer he held the infant at the initial encounter the more likely he was to be engaged in caregiving at five months. This would support the proposition that the duration of contact, rather than the contact being at the birth process itself, is the more important variable. Many parents expect that it will be "love at first sight," and for some it is. Other parents fall in love with their baby much more slowly and over a longer period of time.

The neonate does not really have an emotional attachment to anyone, as he cannot distinguish between himself and others. He prefers "familiar." To adults it may seem that he prefers his mother because she is typically the one who is most familiar with the infant and his routine. However, it is the familiarity the infant is responding to, not the mother. Much research has focused on the impact of parents on their newborn infant. Increasingly we are beginning to look at the impact of the infant on the parents. One of the areas that influence this impact is the "state" the infant is in and his temperament.

up close and personal

I suppose all babies are different, but when you have twins the differences are incredible. Julie is very active, awake more, and fusses if we are not fast enough. She even eats more. She is active even when she sleeps. She is already her daddy's girl. She calms to his voice. Sam is far calmer and is quieter. They were like that even in the womb. I would sometimes poke him to make sure he was okay. I knew Julie was fine because she was always kicking. At first I could not imagine life with them, now I cannot imagine life without them. And I cannot imagine that they were both inside me.

I fell in love instantly. It took my husband longer. He spent a long time lying down on his back with one of them on his stomach. He would just lie there. I think that is how it happened for him. He needed some time alone with them to think and feel.

REFLECTIVE PRACTICE

Infants come into the world different eliciting different response from parents. Adults who care for very young children must learn to identify these differences and develop ways of responding to them that is most likely to elicit the desired outcome. Think about how you will observe and identify infants' ways of being in the world and how this will affect how you approach and care for them. Reflect on this when you are ineffective in interacting with an infant. Is it you are not individualizing your approach?

NEWBORN BEHAVIORAL STATES

The newborn's self-organization is probably best reflected in his capacity for state regulation. Infant states vary from types of alertness to levels of sleep. When we as adults think broadly about what we do, we can distinguish at a gross level that we sleep and we are awake. Newborns sleep about 17 to 18 hours a day. They are awake and quiet for two to three hours, active for one to two, and cry or fuss the remainder of the time. It is the pattern of how these states occur that influences the family. The infant who sleeps for long periods at night, cries little, and is in a quiet alert state has a very different impact on a family than one who sleeps only for short periods, cries a lot, and is rarely quietly alert. The state an infant is in determines to a large extent how available he is for contact with the environment. Many researchers are interested in classifying infant states. However, not all agree on the number and definition of these states. Table 3–5 highlights some of the major aspects of state. Although many researchers use infants' states in research, they base their interpretation on the classic work of Prechtl (1965) and Brazelton (1979).

Most researchers describe several sleeping states, distinguished by the amount of movement. All seem to agree that there is a state between sleep and wakefulness. The awake states vary more and relate to the amount of activity, focus, and crying. This information is useful in identifying infants' state; it is the infant's capacity for regulating these states that intrigues researchers, as well as matching the state of the infant with appropriate adult behavior.

The neonate's ability to respond to the environment is influenced by the state she is in. Neonates differ in the amount of time they spend in each state. The degree to which a newborn can be in a quiet alert state and respond to adults is important for learning and establishing relationships. It is up to the adult to read the neonate's state, determine whether or not there is a pattern,

Table 3–5 Aspects of State

Deep sleep (non-REM)	Eyes are closed, breathing is regular; very unresponsive to external stimuli; full rest and little movement, amount increases with age.
Light sleep (REM)	Irregular sleep in which the eyelids may flutter; infant stirs, may grimace, chew, and respiration may periodically be irregular, there may be sobs, sighs, or smiles. Young infants are in light sleep every 15 to 20 minutes.
Drowsy	Appears when the neonate is waking up or going to sleep; the eyes open and close but are unfocused; the infant is not alert; little movement.
Quiet alert	Eyes open and bright, the face relaxed; little motor activity; focused, alert uncommon in newborns, increases with age, the infant is receptive to learning in this state.
Active alert	Eyes open, bright; bursts of motor activity; excited, energized, many free movements. Infants may become overstimulated and need adult to help them move to a lower state.
Fussy	The infant may be overwhelmed, hungry, hot, cold, tired, hurt, or even just cranky. Meeting the infant's needs, if possible, typically ends this state.
Crying	This is an infant's distress call. He needs an adult to help regulate his state.

SOURCE: Brazelton (1979); Butterfield, Martin, and Prairie (2004); Prechtl (1965).

and respond accordingly. One of the most difficult tasks adults face is helping newborns change states. When infants are crying, the goal is to lower their state of arousal. We do this by picking the baby up, murmuring soothing words, restraining her limbs (swaddling), or changing her position. We may sing a lullaby, turn down the lights, walk, sway, or whatever else we think will work. Over time we learn what comforts which baby.

The newborn's state influences parents, caregivers of newborns, and researchers who want to learn more about them. For example, if you wanted to find out how well newborns saw something, obviously you would not attempt such an experiment with a sleeping baby, but what could you conclude about a drowsy one or a crying one? The ideal is the quiet alert state, but it is difficult to schedule. The infant's state influences not only the family and researchers, but potentially even such things as medical care. It is difficult for physicians to examine sleeping or crying babies, although most have had experience doing it.

Crying, as an aspect of state control, is of particular concern to parents. An infant's cry is a signal to parents that she is in distress. This distress is disturbing to parents, particularly when they do all of the obvious things to provide comfort—such as picking up and holding the infant, rocking her, changing a wet diaper, and feeding her—and she still cries. Some newborns, especially premature ones, have unusual cries, particularly high-pitched and piercing.

All babies cry and most new parents are surprised at how long and how frequently they do so. During the first six weeks, most newborns cry about 2 hours each day, or about 15 minutes each hour that they are awake. Crying peaks at about six weeks, with infants crying between two and three hours daily (St. James-Roberts & Halil, 1991; Shelov, 1993). The overall amount of time spent crying gradually decreases, although the number of crying episodes stays constant. By the end of the first year, infants cry slightly less than an hour a day (St. James-Roberts & Halil, 1991). Infants tend to cry most between 6 PM and midnight.

Colic
is when babies cry for more than three hours, for three days for three weeks.

Some infants cry more than others. **Colic** is a condition in newborns indicated by a high-pitched cry accompanied by grimacing, clenched fists, knees that are either pulled up or rigid and extended, the passing of gas, and inconsolable crying. Colicky infants cry for more than three hours a day, three days a week, for three weeks during the first three months of life (Steinberg & Meyer, 1995). We do not really know what causes colic. Suggestions run from an immature gastrointestinal tract to food allergies to anxious mothers. About 20 percent of infants develop colic, usually between the second and fourth week (Shelov, 1993). The inability to stop an infant from crying is the most common reason given for abuse of infants. The most common abuse is to shake the infant.

Newborns have a large, heavy head and weak neck muscles. When they are shaken their brain bounces back and forth inside their skull, causing bruising, swelling, and bleeding in the brain that can lead to permanent brain damage, blindness, or death. Shaken baby injuries usually happen to infants and young toddlers. The long-term prognosis is not good (National Institute of Neurological Disorders and Stroke, 2007).

TRANSITION TO PARENTHOOD

The four to six weeks following the birth of an infant is unique. It has a name: the postpartum period. It is often a period of emotional upheaval and adjustment. Parents feel profound joy while struggling with lack of sleep. Many mothers feel the "postpartum blues," but fathers, too, may feel depression, mood shifts, irritability, and fatigue as they come down off the birth high and reality settles in. Americans have a very romanticized view of babies and parenthood. We picture a smiling, gurgling baby who is undemanding and on a schedule that is compatible with our own. The reality is that this tiny new "addition" can require drastic changes. This is a surprise to most parents, even those who thought they were prepared.

The transition to parenthood is difficult for several reasons. It is influenced not only by the birth of the baby, but also by the relationship the couple had before the birth and even before the pregnancy. For many couples the

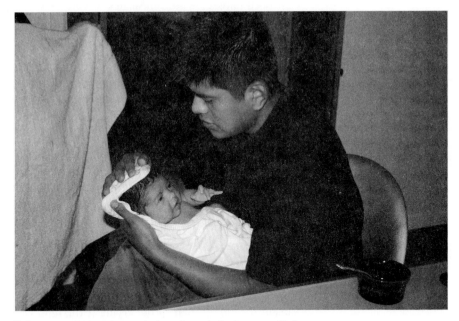

Fathers are taking an increasingly active role in the care of infants.

decision to have a baby is well planned, for others it just happens. Parenthood is irrevocable: There may be ex-spouses but there are no ex-children. Although the process of labor may seem long and difficult, it leads to a very abrupt life transition. One day there is no baby and the next day there is one. One day you can spontaneously run a half-hour errand, the next day you will need to negotiate having an adult at home to do the same thing. There is no time to ease into parenthood. Some view the transition to parenthood as a crisis. Parents may suffer from insecurity and intimidation when faced with the demands of their new baby and concerns about living up to unrealistic standards of being a "good parent." Some of the radical changes in lifestyle that parenthood brings include less sleep, sometimes chronic fatigue, less time together as a couple, and a changed social life. When asked, parents replied that they are "in love" with their baby, but also report that:

- 56 percent are stressed and worn out;
- 52 percent are afraid of doing something wrong;
- 44 percent are unsure about what to do "a lot of the time" (*Bringing Up Baby*, 1999).

The ability of the family to anticipate and respond to the ever-changing demands of an infant is a central feature in this transition (Newman, 2000). When the child's demands are ambiguous or the family cannot meet the infant's needs, families may become stressed. The challenge for the family is to synchronize the infant's needs with the rhythm and pattern of the family (Newman, 2000). The family must also constantly adapt to the infant's changing development. The first steps bring joy, but also require new vigilance, monitoring, and household adaptations. This high demand for flexibility and change may result in parental role strain and stress.

The extent to which the newborn is divergent from the family's hopes and expectations can be particularly stressful. Children both affect and are affected by the families in which they develop. The characteristics of the infant and the interaction of these characteristics with parenting styles are particularly important factors.

Having a baby requires many profound changes. Couples or individuals who are unprepared or unable to make these changes experience a great deal of stress in dealing with the baby and each other. Many couples feel that having a baby will pull them more closely together. This is unlikely to happen. Only 19 percent of 250 couples that participated in the Penn State Child and Family Development Project had more feelings of love toward their spouse, increased communication, or decreased feelings of ambivalence and conflict. Thirty percent remained unchanged, but did not gain a new sense of closeness. Fifty percent of the couples felt less love and communication, and more ambivalence and conflict (Belsky & Kelly, 1994). Successful couples were able to:

- surrender individual goals and needs and work together as a team;
- resolve differences about division of labor and work in a mutually satisfactory manner;
- handle stresses in a way that does not overstress a partner or a marriage;
- realize that however good a marriage becomes post-baby, it will not be good in the same way it was pre-baby;
- maintain the ability to communicate in a way that continues to nurture the marriage (Belsky & Kelly, 1994, p. 16).

Because the transition to parenthood is tumultuous and fraught with many difficulties, it is surprising that 90 percent of fertile couples do have children, and that this event is anticipated with such positive expectations. Some feel that the birth of a second or later child is less stressful than the birth of the first, but each birth brings its own unique stresses. With later-born children, parents must cope with siblings' reactions to the new baby, plus having extra work to do and trying to give adequate attention to the other children. One frequent but erroneous assumption is that the transition to parenthood is the same for the mother and the father, or that it is done as a couple. Some aspects of the transition are

Mothers and fathers fall in love with their babies differently.

gender-specific. Although men and women become parents at the same time, they do not become parents in the same way (Belsky & Kelly, 1994).

Mother's Transition to Parenthood

For mothers the transition to parenthood may begin with "love at first sight" as she gazes into the eyes of her newborn. Some women find this love so consuming that they cannot think about anything except the baby. Mothers frequently become worried that they are unattractive, housekeeping demands seem daunting, and the dirty diapers endless.

The mother's transition is affected by biological forces. The expulsion of the placenta dramatically reduces the hormones that were necessary for the maintenance of pregnancy (Lowdermilk & Perry, 2003). The mother's body begins almost immediately to rid itself of excessive fluid; however, it takes about six weeks for the abdominal wall to regain its previous elasticity. Some of the postpartum changes, including when a woman's menstrual cycle begins, depend upon whether or not the she is breastfeeding.

Changing hormonal levels also influence mood. Mood disorders are the most typical mental health problem that affects new mothers and they usually occur within a month of childbirth (American Psychiatric Association, 2000). Many women experience the **baby blues** after having a child. They cry easily

Baby blues are short-term mood swings that are caused by hormonal fluctuations after childbirth.

for no apparent reason; they feel depressed, sad, anxious, fatigued, and lonely. It is a period of emotional and physical vulnerability for new mothers, who may be overwhelmed by parental responsibility and just plain tired. The blues seem to peak around day 5 and decrease significantly by day 10 (Lowdermilk & Perry, 2003). There is concern if this lasts for more than two weeks. For 10 to 20 percent of new mothers, the condition is more severe and is called **postpartum depression (PPD)** (Mental Health America, 2007).

Postpartum depression is more serious and more pervasive than the blues. It has the same symptoms as clinical depression and may include specific fears, such as a preoccupation with the infant's health or concerns about harming the baby. It is characterized by irritability and may have violent outbursts or uncontrolled sobbing. The mother may reject the infant, and there may be concern about the mother harming the infant or herself. This is very frightening and obviously causes concern for those who are close to the mother of the newborn. Treatment involves both therapy and pharmacological intervention (Lowdermilk & Perry, 2003). Early identification can lead to early treatment, which is important to the new mother, the family, and the infant. Early childhood educators are concerned about maternal depression because these mothers are not available for their infants. These infants may be placed in child care to ensure that they receive the comfort and stimulation they need if others are not available.

Women are often anxious about the potential competition between their marital and maternal roles. Those who work have added pressure from that role, and over half (60 percent) of these women will return to work before their infant is a year old (U.S. Bureau of the Census, 2002). In the 1960s, the average father devoted 11 hours per week to being with his infant and caring for the home; in the 1990s this increased to 15 or 16 hours per week. A working mother exceeds this contribution to child care by 300 percent (Belsky & Kelly, 1994).

Father's Transition to Parenthood

The transition to parenthood for fathers seems to be more even-keeled. They experience fewer lows, but also fewer highs. Rather than falling in love instantaneously, it may take fathers days, weeks, or even months to fall in love with their child. It happens more gradually. The father may feel left out, or that he is competing with the baby for his wife's attention. His priority may focus on work and money. While he realizes that the work load has changed and perhaps even feels guilty about his lack of participation, and although he may be willing to modify his priorities, he still wants affection for himself, an active social life, and freedom to pursue his interests and see his friends (Belsky & Kelly, 1994).

From a father's perspective, he probably feels that he contributes far more to caring for his child than his father did for him. He feels that he should be appreciated for his help, rather than chastised for not contributing more or criticized for any inadequate skills. One of the relatively consistent research findings has been that although many fathers need to learn how to nurture and care for young infants, early participation in infant care by fathers was more likely to lead to later sharing of child care. Fathers and mothers contribute through different pathways in infant's development. Fathers spend less time in caring for infants but a greater percent of time in interactive play (Parke, 1996). Based on information from the National Institute for Child Health and Human Development Early Child Care Research Network fathers functioned as the primary caregiver about 23 percent of the time. Many fathers have a far more significant role in raising their children than in the past. Close to a third of total child care by dual-career couples was by fathers. Older men who see the role of "father" as important in comparison to other roles usually have an easier adjustment. Fathers who have high self-esteem are more involved in child care (National Institute of Child Health and Human Development, 2000).

The transition to parenthood is dramatic, but different for the mother and the father. The challenge is to move from a couple relationships into a family. One of the major decisions for parents is how they plan to feed their newborn.

Feeding the Newborn

Newborns need to be fed eight to 10 times in a 24-hour period (American Academy of Pediatrics, 2005). During the first two days of an infant's life he may not awaken this often. This is one time when infants should be awakened. They need to eat approximately every three hours during the day and four hours at night. Time between feedings is counted from the beginning of one feeding to the beginning of the next feeding. From the perspective of those doing the feeding, this often feels more like a two-hour schedule than a three-hour one because it takes infants a half-hour or more to eat. Sleepy babies do not suck well, and sucking is hard work and makes babies sleepy.

Choosing a Feeding Method

One decision families need to make before the baby comes is how the baby will be fed. Most physicians encourage mothers to breastfeed infants—or to at least try it, because one can decide later not to breastfeed, but it is difficult or even impossible to begin breastfeeding if the decision is made too late. The American Academy of Pediatrics in their policy statement of breastfeeding and the use of human milk recommend that infants be breastfed exclusively for the first six months (American Academy of Pediatrics, 2005).

Lactation
is the process of secreting milk from the mammary glands to feed infants.

The production of milk by the breast is call **lactation**. Until the 1940s, breastfeeding was common in almost all societies. With improvements in packaging, a greater variety of formulas, and arrangements between infant-milk manufacturers and health-care providers and hospitals, breastfeeding has decreased despite the recommendations of the American Academy of Pediatrics. Some women, however, do not want to or cannot breastfeed for a variety of reasons. Having the support of a partner in the decision is important.

up close and personal

I know that breastfeeding is great for my baby and great for me. It sounds so maternal and so easy. It wasn't for me. I knew I would have to have a cesarean section and went into the hospital at 12:01 AM. (If we went in earlier, they would have charged us for another day in the hospital.) The plan was for the C-section to begin about 9:00 in the morning. I had a problem with the anesthesia and stopped breathing. They delivered the baby in a minute and a half, but it took 37 staples to put me back together. In addition to the scar on my bikini line, I have one that goes up to my navel.

That day and the next are still vague to me. I know that I kept putting her to my breast, or rather, my husband put her to my breast so I could nurse. I was so out of it that I really didn't know how to do it. I hate hospitals—just when one of us finally got to sleep they would come in and want something. The hospital said they would put her in the nursery if my husband left the room, because I couldn't lift her. I wanted to go home. They said I could go home if I

could walk the length of the corridor. It took me an hour and 15 minutes, but I did it. We left the hospital and I still didn't know how to breastfeed, and at that point my little girl, who weight 7 pounds, 13 ounces, was down to 7 pounds, 2 ounces. The nurses wanted me to give her a bottle.

At home nursing wasn't any easier. I didn't like it, Franchesca didn't like it, and we were both tired and hungry. That was when I started to pump breast milk. She would drink it from a bottle, but not from me. I called the doctor, the lactation specialist with the insurance company, and anyone I knew. I learned a lot about breastfeeding, but I still wasn't having any success. Then the breast pump broke. I went to the store, but none of the pumps there were strong enough for what I needed. I finally rented one from a medical supply house. By the time we got home I thought I was going to explode. Even then I couldn't get her to nurse. It has taken six weeks. We are both better at breastfeeding, but I still give her breast milk in a bottle when she tires herself out. I like breastfeeding from the breast far better. The first six weeks were a struggle for both of us. Now I only have to get up once during the night to pump.

I had had a difficult pregnancy and was on bed rest for two months before she was born. I used up all my vacation and sick leave for two years. I had to go back to work when she was three weeks old. I was allowed to work from home for two weeks as I eased back into work. Then I had to go into the office. I asked where I could pump breast milk. I told them I needed an electrical outlet. They found a broom closet. Literally, a broom closet. I pump breast milk looking at mops, buckets, and brooms. They allowed me to put a sign on the door that says "Please knock" while I am using my closet.

I know why mothers quit breastfeeding. I was tempted many times. I know I will be again. For some mothers it is easy. For me it is challenging, but still worth it.

REFLECTIVE PRACTICE

As an early childhood educator, how do you see your role in supporting mothers who want to breastfeed their infants? Reflect on the changes that would be necessary at a societal level to increase the number of mothers who breastfeed their babies for a year.

Breastfeeding initiation rates have increased steadily in the United States since 1990. However, many women who breastfeed infants also use formula as a supplement, and exclusive breastfeeding has shown no increase. This is true at six months as well (American Academy of Pediatrics, 2005). In the United States, approximately 60 percent of infants are breastfed at birth, but by six months fewer than 25 percent of infants are still being breastfed. A goal of *Healthy People 2010* is that 75 percent of infants will be breastfed at birth, 50 percent at six months old, and 25 percent at one year old.

There are many reasons for the decline in breastfeeding. More women with younger children are working, although some find that with flexible scheduling, the use of a breast pump, or a combination of breast- and bottle-feeding they can continue breastfeeding. The length of hospital maternity stays has decreased to a day or two or less. Short stays mean that there are few opportunities for mothers to learn how to breastfeed their infants. Ironically, this decrease occurred at the same time that researchers are finding increasing long-term health benefits for breastfeeding. Table 3–6 highlights some of the benefits of breastfeeding.

Table 3–6 Health Benefits of Breastfeeding

- Breast milk, including colostrums, which comes before the mother's milk, provides infants immunologic protection from gastrointestinal infection, ear and upper respiratory infections, wheezing, diarrhea, vomiting, asthma, allergies, and eczema in infancy as well as protection from certain chronic diseases later in life such as diabetes, high cholesterol and obesity.

- Infants are not allergic to breast milk (although they can be allergic to the foods the mother ingests), and since milk production responds to the infant's consumption, it is rare to over or under feed a breastfed baby.

- Breast milk is the ideal food for infants. It contains sugar (lactose), easily digestible protein (whey and casein), and fat (digestible fatty acids) and numerous minerals, vitamins, and enzymes. Formulas can approximate the nutrients but not the enzymes and antibodies.

  1. Breastfeeding is a safety net against ill prepared, watered down, or too hot formula. It is also free (although the mother may eat more) and less expensive than formula. It is also convenient, no bottles to wash.

  2. Hormones produced during breastfeeding delay the return of fertility.

- Breastfeeding reduces infant mortality and may protect against obesity.

  1. Lactation also provides health benefits for the mothers it helps the uterus tighten up and return more quickly to it normal size, it uses up about 300 to 500 calories a day and helps the mother get back into shape physically. It reduces risk of breast, ovarian, uterine, and cervical cancer. It also appears to reduce urinary tract infections.

SOURCE: American Academy of Pediatrics (2005); Gavin, Sowshen, and Izenberg (2004); Lowdermilk and Perry (2003).

There are times when breastfeeding is not recommended. If a mother is ill, or takes certain medications or has a disease that would pass into the breast milk, breastfeeding may be dangerous to the infant.

Formula is a nutritious alternative to breast milk. It offers the mother more freedom and flexibility. The father and others can help feed the baby as well.

Regardless of feeding method, infants should be fed on demand, typically 8 to 12 times per day during the first month (Nemours, 2005). Adults are often concerned about whether or not the infant is getting enough to eat. During the first month the best way to tell if a breastfed infant's diet is adequate is through his elimination patterns. He should urinate about six to eight times a day and have several small bowel movements daily (usually after feeding). Because infants often lose 8 to 10 percent of their birth weight during the first week of life, weighing the infant is not a good indication of consumption (Lowdermilk & Perry, 2003).

Newborns need a little more than two fluid ounces of breast milk or formula each day for each pound of body weight. A 7 ½-pound baby needs 15 to 18 ounces a day, or about 2 to 3 ounces 8 to 10 or even 12 times a day. It is easier to see the bottle-fed baby getting this amount than a breastfed baby. Because it is easier to get milk from a bottle than a breast, it is easier to overfeed a formula-fed baby. Formula is digested more slowly than breast milk, so the infant may require fewer feedings (Gavin et al, 2004).

Some mothers find breastfeeding is easy; for others it is a challenge. When mothers pump breast milk, fathers can feed infants as well.

When you feed an infant a bottle, make eye contact with him, enjoy a feeling of togetherness, and make this a positive experience for both of you. The issue is not the source of the milk but the quality of the relationship between the infant and caregiver. Regardless of the method of feeding chosen, it is important to know when a baby is hungry. Most newborns cry or fuss when they are ready to eat. Some will withdraw into sleep as a way of dealing with the discomfort. However, adults who can read infant cues know that an infant is hungry before either of these occurs (see Table 3–7).

Table 3–7 Signs That Babies Are Hungry

When they
- make sucking movements or pucker their lips as if to suck.
- open their mouths.
- stick out their tongue.
- move their head from side to side.
- make hand-to-mouth or hand-to-hand movements.
- nuzzle against an adults breast and try to feed.

SOURCE: Nemours (2005).

Nutrition for Newborns

During this first month the newborn will grow about 1.5 inches and gain about 2 pounds. Like adults, infants need energy or calories to grow. For newborns this energy comes through breast milk or formula.

Human milk provides about 20 calories per ounce of breast milk. It consists of about 40 to 45 percent carbohydrates, 15 percent fat, and the remainder is protein. Formulas are designed to have a similar calorie count. In human milk the primary carbohydrate is lactose, which is easy for the infant to breakdown and absorb. In formula, corn syrup solids or glucose polymers are added to the cow's milk to increase the level of carbohydrates. Fat in human milk is easier to digest and absorb because of the arrangement of fatty acids and the enzyme lipase. In formula, the fat in cow's milk is removed and replaced by another fat such as corn oil. Fats also supply the essential fatty acids that are necessary for growth. Infants cannot digest the fat in cows' milk because it moves through their intestines too quickly. Without these calories the infant may not gain weight (Lowdermilk & Perry, 2003).

Infants need 2.2 grams of protein per kilogram of body weight. The protein in human milk is ideal for infants because it contains more lactalbumin in relation to casein. Lactalbumin is more easily digested. The amino acid composition is well suited to the newborns metabolic capacities. Most infant formulas are designed to closely approximate breast milk (Lowdermilk & Perry, 2003).

Young infants need about 80 to 100 milliliters of water per kilogram of body weight per day. However, they cannot afford to spend their energy drinking water when they need calories for growth. Breast milk is 87 percent water and solves this problem. Breast milk contains all the vitamins and minerals that an infant needs. Formulas are fortified with the appropriate vitamins and minerals. The infant himself will produce vitamin K, but that takes a while, so infants are routinely given an injection of vitamin K shortly after birth (Lowdermilk & Perry, 2003).

Cultural Considerations

Childbirth and the time after birth occur in a sociocultural context. Many health beliefs and practices are culturally based. Some Asian cultures believe that the mother and baby are in vulnerable state for several weeks after childbirth. Some women will eat only warm foods and drink hot drinks to restore the balance of hot and cold in their body (Lowdermilk & Perry, 2003). Other restrictions may be related to who the mother can and cannot see, how she should dress, and how she must take care of herself. There may also be traditional practices and celebrations.

up close and personal

I knew about the sleepless nights, crying, and diapers, but what surprised me the most were the cultural differences. My wife, Meihong, is Chinese. Her parents came over to the States before she was born. I knew that Meihong would want to incorporate her cultural traditions into raising Suehey, but I did not know her mother would be so involved.

My mother-in-law said she would be staying with us for the first month of Suehey's life.

I really didn't know how it would all work out. I didn't know my mother-in-law very well, but we had always gotten along fine when we were together. Meihong was adamant about having her mother stay with us, and I really could think of no reason why she shouldn't. I mean, our lives were already going to be turned upside down with a newborn around anyway. Plus, I knew that it would comfort Meihong to have her mother there.

In the Chinese culture, the one-month, or "first-moon," birthday is a big deal—for the mother and the baby. Typically, the maternal grandmother comes for the whole month to help take care of the mother and the newborn. The paternal grandmother would rarely undertake the first-moon caretaking job unless she already lives in the same house with her son and daughter-in-law, or "Lao Lao" is unable to come. Lao Lao is not her name it's like "grandma" or "nana" in English. In the Chinese language, there are quite a few ways of addressing the maternal grandmother depending on where you are from. People from northern China would call the maternal grandmother "Lao Lao," and most southern Chinese people would say "Wai Po."

The one thing that stood out the most during my mother-in-law's visit was the food she made. The Chinese believe that women become exceptionally weak after giving birth, so during the first month, foods that are regarded as very nutritious based on traditional Chinese standards are given to the mother.

I saw Meihong's mother make foods using fresh fish, ribs, whole chicken, and eggs. Let me assure you, I am no cook, but sometimes she used things that looked kind of unusual to me, such as pigs' feet and liver. Everyday, she made a special soup for Meihong. It contained dried jujube, dried longan, lotus seeds, white fungus, ginger, and brown sugar. Sometimes she might exclude one or two of those ingredients, but brown sugar was always added. She said these ingredients were very common in China and that they help the loss of blood and energy. I am an adventurous eater, so I tried the soup, but I eventually decided that pigs' feet and ginger soup weren't my thing.

I like Chinese food and we eat it a lot, but this was really unusual food. I am not sure if Meihong actually enjoyed the food that her mother prepared, but she always ate every morsel.

Despite my trepidations, the whole situation turned out to be extremely rewarding and helpful. When I got home from work, Meihong's mother would take Suehey if she was awake and Meihong and I would have time together. It really did give Meihong time to regain her strength and I felt taken care of.

The first month ended with a celebration dinner. In China, there would be a huge feast like those on weddings. Relatives and friends would be invited to celebrate the first-moon birthday of the newborn. The Chinese do not have baby showers, so people normally give money or presents to the mother and the baby at this dinner. The mother brings out the baby during or after the dinner and the baby has her first haircut in front of everybody. All the guests receive red eggs as gifts to take home. If the baby is a boy, the guests are given an odd number of red eggs. If it's a girl, they get an even number of eggs. I really enjoyed the celebration. Suehey got her first haircut and we distributed red eggs. I liked being exposed to these cultural traditions—they made the first few weeks of Suehey's life with us very special and helped to offset the stress of having a newborn. I became much closer with my mother-in-law and I could spend more time with Meihong.

In China the first lunar month after birth is considered a very crucial time for the baby. If the baby is able to survive it and becomes "one-moon-old," the family will be able to officially announce they have a new family member, which is why they have the celebration dinner.

REFLECTIVE PRACTICE

The first-moon birthday is a Chinese tradition. What do you think the implications would have been had Nathan not supported the traditions of the Chinese culture? Different cultures have different traditions surrounding the birth of a baby. Do you know other cultural traditions? Does your family have traditions and beliefs related to having a new baby?

SUMMARY

The end of pregnancy is marked by the birth and delivery of the newborn. Most women believe it is appropriately called labor. Traditionally babies have been delivered vaginally, but increasing numbers are being born by cesarean section. Although most deliveries go smoothly, there can be complications, particularly with preterm infants and multiple births. The transition from fetus to infant is a dramatic one. The newborn must regulate his own temperature and depend on his lungs to breath, his heart to circulate blood, and even his own feeding and elimination system. For infants who are born too small or too soon, these changes are challenging.

Newborns come into the world with all of their senses intact. They can hear, see, taste, touch, and smell, although their senses do not work as the same level as adults. They are very functional for the newborn. Newborns come with a variety of reflexes that have survival value to them. Infants can learn, they are interested in social interaction, and they have their own methods of communication that are effective. One of the challenges that newborns face is how to regulate their state.

Parents also face transitions as they move from a couple to a family. They need to find ways to welcome their newborn while keeping space for themselves and each other in the midst of new challenges and lack of sleep. One decision that parents must make is how to feed their newborn. During pregnancy, but particularly after birth, different cultures have traditions and rituals that affect the new family.

CHAPTER IN REVIEW

- The transition to parenthood is an abrupt one for both the parents and the newborn.

- Newborns are far more capable at birth than we once thought.

- Newborns' senses are functional but they are not as acute as an adult's.

- Newborns can learn and they have preferences.

- Newborns are tuned in to human language and have communication skills that help them to get their needs met.

- Newborns have different states and are unique in the amount of time they remain in each.

- Newborns get bored or habituate to stimuli that are repeated.

- Some newborns are born preterm and/or with LBW. They are different from full-term neonates in a variety of ways, have more complications, and may be placed in an intensive care nursery where medical specialists are trained to meet the specialized needs of these infants.

※ Physical and motor development are the most obvious aspects of early growth and development.

APPLICATION ACTIVITIES

1. Talk with your mother about your birth and what the experience was like for her and your father. Find out if she thinks things are better or worse now with regard to giving birth. Ask her what role she would expect to play if or when you or your significant other has an infant, and if there are family traditions around child birth. Ask her about her transition to parenthood and her experiences. Ask your father the same questions. If your mother is not the best person to ask, talk with someone about her age.

2. Discuss with both your female and male friends their expectations about childbirth and how they formed these views.

3. Think about your own expectations for birthing and the first month (whether or not you plan to have children). What do you know now that you did not before reading this chapter? What could you do to make the transition easier for you or a friend and a newborn?

RESOURCES

Web Resources

※ **The Brazelton Institute** is a good source for learning more about the Newborn Behavioral Observations System developed by Dr. T. Barry Brazelton. http://www.brazelton-institute.com

※ **Commercial sites**, which are designed for parents, are a way of seeing what they may be learning. Check out some of the following:

http://www.babycenter.com

http://www.parenting.ivillage.com

http://www.pregnancy.org

http://www.babyzone.com

http://www.pregnancy weekly.com

http://www.birthingfromwithin.com

※ The **Encyclopedia of Children's Health** provides information about various medical conditions, disorders, and pediatric diseases. It is structured into five main sections, which include immunizations, drugs, procedures, diseases and disorders, and development. http://www.healthofchildren.com/.

Print Resources

※ Dick-Read, G. (1959). *Childbirth without fear: The principles and practices of natural childbirth*. New York: Harper and Row.

❋ Karmel, M. (1965). *Thank you Dr. Lamaze.* New York: Dolphin Books.

❋ Lamaze, F. (1956). *Painless childbirth: The Lamaze method.* New York: Pocket Books.

❋ Leboyer, F. (1975). *Birth without violence.* New York: Knopf.

REFERENCES

Agency for Healthcare Research and Quality (HQR). (2006). Use of tocolytic therapy to stop uterine contractions can prolong pregnancy and prevent preterm birth. Retrieved April 13, 2007, from http://www.ahrq.gov/research/oct03/1003RA11.htm

Allen, M. C. (2002). Preterm outcomes research: A critical component of neonatal intensive care. *Mental Retardation and Developmental Disabilities Research Reviews, 8,* 221–232.

American Academy of Pediatrics. (2005). AAP policy statement of breastfeeding feeding and the use of human milk. *Pediatrics, 115(2),* 486–506.

American Psychiatric Association. (2000). *Diagnostic and statistical manual of mental disorders* (4th ed. Rev.). Washington, DC: Author.

Belsky, J., & Kelly, J. (1994). *The transition to parenthood.* New York: Delacorte Press.

Blass, E. M. (1990). Suckling: Determinants, changes, mechanism, and lasting impressions. *Developmental Psychology, 26,* 520–533.

Brazelton, T. B. (1979). Behavioral competence of the newborn infant. *Seminars in Perinatology, 3,* 35–44.

Brazelton, T. B., & Nugent, J. K. (1995). *The neonatal behavioral assessment scale.* Cambridge, MA: Mac Keith Press.

Brazelton Institute. (2005). Understanding the baby's language. Retrieved April 14, 2007, from http://www.brazelton-institute.com/intro.html

Bringing up baby. (1999). *Public Perspective, 10* (October/November), 19.

Brown, J. E., & Satin, A. J. (2007). Having a baby: The birth process. In M. L. Batshaw , L. Pellegrino, & N. J. Roizen (Eds.), *Children with disabilities* (6th ed., pp. 35–45). Baltimore, MD: Paul H. Brookes Publishing.

Browne, J. V. (2003). New perspectives on premature infants and their parents. *Zero to Three, 24(2),* 4–12.

Butterfield, P. M., Martin, C. A., & Prairie, A. P. (2003). *Emotional connections: How relationships guide early learning.* Washington, DC: Zero to Three.

Colombo, J., & Saxon, T. F. (2002). Infant attention and the development of cognition: Does the environment moderate continuity? In H. E. Fitzgerald, K. H. Karraker, & T. Luster (Eds.), *Infant development: Ecological perspectives* (pp. 33–60). New York: Routledge Falmer.

DeCasper, A. J., & Fifer, W. P. (1980). Of human bonding: Newborns prefer their mother's voices. *Science, 208,* 1174–1176.

Deering, S. H., & Satin, A. J. (2002). Having a baby: The birth process. In M. Batshaw (Ed.), *Children with disabilities* (5th ed., pp. 55–68). Baltimore, MD: Paul H. Brookes.

Eckert, H. (1987). *Motor development.* Indianapolis, IN: Benchmark Press.

Ecklund-Flores, L., & Turkewitz, G. (1996). Asymmetric head-turning to speech and nonspeech in human newborns. *Developmental Psychology, 29*, 205–217.

Engen, T. (1986). The acquisition of ordour hedonics. In S. V. Toller & G. H. Dodd (Eds.), *Perfumery: The psychology and biology of fragrance* (pp. 79–93). London: Chapman & Hall.

Gallahue, D. L., & Ozmun, J. C. (2002). *Understanding motor development: Infants, children, adolescents, adults* (5th ed.). New York: McGraw-Hill.

Gavin, M. L., Sowshen, S. A., & Izenberg, N. (2004). *Fit kids: A practical guide to raising active and healthy children—From birth to teens.* New York: DK Publishing.

Glass, P. (2002). Development of the visual system and implications for early intervention. *Infants and Young Children, 15*(1), 1–10.

Golinkoff, R. M., & Hirsh-Pasek, K. (1999). *How babies talk: The magic and mystery of language in the first three years of life.* New York: Dutton.

Haywood, K. M., & Getchell, N. (2005). *Life span motor development* (4th ed.). Champaign, IL: Human Kinetics.

Hepper, P. G., & Shahidullah, S. (1992). Habituation in normal and Down syndrome fetuses. *Quarterly Journal of Experimental Psychology*. Special Issue: *Comparative Studies of Prenatal Learning and Behavior, 44B*(3–4), 305–317.

Hepper, P. G., White, R., & Shahidullah, S. (1991). The development of fetal responsiveness to external auditory stimulation. *British Psychological Society Abstracts, 30.*

Herer, G. R., Knightly, C. A., & Steinberg, A. G. (2002). Hearing: Sounds and silences. In M. L. Batshaw (Ed.), *Children with disabilities* (5th ed., pp. 193–227). Baltimore, MD: Paul H. Brookes.

Hoyert, D. L., Freedman, M. A., Strobino, D. M., & Guyer, B. (2001). Annual summary of vital statistics: 2000. *Pediatrics, 108*, 1241–1255.

Jensen, J. L., Thelen, E.,Ulrich, B. B., Schneider, K., & Zernicke, R. F. (1995). Adaptive dynamics of the leg movement patterns of human infants: III. Age-related differences in limb control. *Journal of Motor Behavior, 27*, 366–374.

Karmel, M. (1965). *Thank you Dr. Lamaze.* New York: Dolphin Books.

Lamaze, F. (1956). *Painless childbirth: The Lamaze method.* New York: Pocket Books.

Laplante, D., Orr, R., Neville, K., Vorkapich, L., & Sasso, D. (1996). Discrimination of stimulus rotations by newborns. *Infant Behavior and Development, 19*, 271–279.

Lipsitt, L. P., & Behl, G. (1990). Taste-mediated differences in the sucking behavior of human newborns. In E. D. Capaldi & T. L. Powley (Eds.), *Taste, experience, and feeding* (pp. 75–93). Washington, DC: American Psychological Association.

Lowdermilk, D. L., & Perry, S. E. (2003). *Maternity nursing* (6th ed.). St. Louis, MI: Mosby.

Maurer, D., & Maurer, C. (1988). *The world of the newborn.* New York: Basic Books.

Mayberry, L. J., Wood, S., Strange, L., Lee, L., Heisler, D., & Neilsen-Smith, K. (2000). *Second stage labor management: Promotion of evidence-based practice and a collaborative approach to patient care.* Washington, DC: Association of Woman's Health, Obstetric and Neonatal Nurses.

Mental Health America. (2007). Postpartum disorders. Retrieved April 15, 2007, from http://www.nmha.org/go/information/get-info/depression/postpartum-disorders

Moon, C., Penneton-Cooper, R. P., & Fifer, W. (1993). Two-day-olds prefer their native language. *Infant Behavior and Development, 16*, 495–500.

Moore, M. L. (2003). Preterm labor and birth: What have we learned in the past two decades? *Journal of Obstetric, Gynecologic, and Neonatal Nursing, 32*(5), 638–649.

National Center for Health Statistics. (2007). Infant health. Retrieved April 14, 2007, from http://www.cdc.gov/nchs/fastats/infant_health.htm

National Eye Institute. (2006). Retinopathy of prematurity. Retrieved April 14, 2007, from http://www.nei.nih.gov/health/rop/index.asp

National Institute of Child Health and Human Development. (2000). Fathers with high self esteem more involved in child care, study finds. Retrieved April 15, 2007, from http://www.nichd.hih.gov/news/releases/fathers.cfm

National Institute of Neurological Disorders and Stroke. (2007). Retrieved April 15, 2007, from http://www.ninds.nih.gov/disorders/shakenbaby/shakenbaby.htm

Nemours. (2005). Feeding your newborn. Retrieved April 14, 2007, from http://www.kidshealth.org/PageManager.jsp?dn=nemours&lic=60&ps=107&cat_id=148

Newman, B. M. (2000). The challenges of parenting infants and young children. In P. C. McKenry & S. H. Price (Eds.), *Families and change: Coping with stressful events and transitions* (2nd ed., pp. 45–70). Thousand Oaks, CA: Sage.

Norwitz, E., Robinson, J., & Challis, J. (1999). The control of labor. *New England Journal of Medicine, 341,* 660–666.

Palkovitz, R. (1982). Fathers' birth attendance, early extended contact and father-infant interaction at five months postpartum. *Birth: Issues in Perinatal Care, 9,* 173–177.

Parke, R. D. (1996). *Fatherhood.* Cambridge, MA: Harvard University Press.

Perry, S., & Strauss, J. F., III. (1998). Premature rupture of the fetal membranes. *New England Journal of Medicine, 338,* 663–670.

Porter, R. H. (1991). Mutual mother-infant recognition in humans. In R. G. Hepper (Ed.), *Kin recognition* (pp. 413–432). Cambridge, UK: Cambridge University Press.

Prechtl, H. F. R. (1965). Problems of behavioral studies in the newborn infant. In D. S. Lehrman, R. A. Hinde, & E. Shaw (Eds.), *Advances in the study of behavior* (pp. 75–96). New York: Academic Press.

Rais-Bahrami, J, & Short, B. L. (2007). Premature and small-for-dates infants. In M. L. Batshaw, L. Pellegrino, & N. J. Rosen (Eds.), *Children with disabilities* (6th ed., pp. 107–122). Baltimore, MD: Paul H. Brookes.

Shelov, S. P. (Ed.) (1993). *Caring for your baby and young child: Birth to age 5.* New York: Bantam Books.

Spense, M. J., & Freeman, M. S. (1996). Newborn infants prefer the maternal low-pass filtered voice, but not the maternal whispered voice. *Infant Behavior and Development, 19,* 199–212.

St. James-Roberts, I., & Halil, T. (1991). Infant crying patterns in the first year. *Journal of Child Psychology and Psychiatry, 32,* 951–968.

Steinberg, L., & Meyer, R. (1995). *Childhood.* New York: McGraw-Hill.

Sullivan, P. M., & Knutson, J. F. (2000). Maltreatment and disabilities: A population-based epidemiological study. *Child Abuse & Neglect, 24*(10), 1257–1273.

University of Maryland Medical Center. (2005). Placenta previa. Retrieved April 13, 2007, from http://www.umm.edu/ency/article/000900.htm

U.S. Bureau of the Census. (2002). Statistical abstracts of the United States: 2002. Washington, DC: U.S. Government Printing Office.

Ward, L. P., & McCume, S. K. (2002). The first weeks of life. In M. L. Batshaw (Ed.), *Children with disabilities* (5th ed., pp. 69–84). Baltimore, MD: Paul H. Brookes.

Williamson, G. G., & Anzalone, M. E. (2001). *Sensory integration and self-regulation in infants and toddlers: Helping very young children interact with their environment.* Washington, DC: Zero to Three.

Wood, F. M. (2005). The Apgar score has survived the test of time. *Anesthesiology, 102*(4), 855–857.

chapter 4

Physical, Motor, and Sensory Development

Chapter Outline

- Physical Growth
- The Central Nervous System
- Motor Development
- Sensation and Perception
- Vision
- Hearing
- Kinesthesis

Every child is unique. Mustapha was born in Ghana to a Ghanaian mother and an American father. Shortly after his birth he moved to the United States. Muhmadid's family fled Iran during the war, after his father was murdered. His mother and two brothers gained asylum in the United States a few months after he was born. Gail grew up in the suburbs of Chicago, the daughter of two doctors. David's parents adopted him from Guatemala when he was seven months old.

Each of these children has a different cultural background. They speak different languages. They have different family structures and they have different socioeconomic backgrounds. But as different as they are these children, they actually have a lot in common. They have the same patterns of growth and development.

Physical growth refers to the quantitative changes that occur in children over time. Growth can be measured in inches or centimeters and pounds or kilograms. Development, however, is more complex and has many aspects. Development is "a continuous process of change in functional capacity" (Haywood & Getchell, 2005, p. 4). This process is cumulative. Although development is continuous, it is more obvious in very young children than it is in adulthood. Development is related to age but not dependent upon it, as individuals of the same age can have different rates of development. Development involves sequential change and results from internal changes within the child and the interactions of the child with his environment (Haywood & Getchell, 2005). Development focuses on the acquisition of skills.

WHY STUDY PHYSICAL, MOTOR, AND SENSORY DEVELOPMENT?

- Knowledge about patterns of physical development helps us identify typical and atypical developmental patterns. It can be the first step in identifying a disability or preventing obesity or in ensuring that underweight babies receive additional calories and nutrients.

- Motor milestones help us identify developmental patterns. They also guide our planning. If a child is too young to use visually guided reaching it may be frustrating to ourselves and the infant if we expect him to reach for and grasp an object. Knowing when crawling and walking emerge allows us to plan an environment that is safe and provides choices. Understanding the principles behind running and jumping we become better coaches.

- Knowledge about sensory development helps us choose appropriate objects for infants to look at and to change these objects when they are no longer appealing. It also tells us where to place objects so infants can focus on them.

- Knowing how the brain develops helps us to plan for infants and toddlers, to be aware of an environment that supports positive connections in the brain, and to insulate vulnerable children from negative outcomes.

Children come into the world "prewired" to grow and develop in a certain predictable pattern. Although this book focuses on cognitive, language, and social development in different chapters, these types of development are interrelated. As each chapter in the book progresses there is more discussion about the relationships between different aspects of development. Understanding the underlying principles of growth and development allows us to make predictions about whether future growth and development will fall within the normal patterns. It also allows educators to plan in a developmentally appropriate way for infants and toddlers. Most children follow this pattern; some follow at a slower or faster rate, and a few do not follow the pattern at all.

PHYSICAL GROWTH

The most rapid growth occurs in utero, when a baby develops out of a cluster of cells. Unfortunately people cannot readily observe this growth. The second-greatest period of growth occurs during the first year of life.

Height/Length

The average full-term infant is 19 to 21 inches long, with boys tending to be slightly longer than girls. Length at birth has little relation to adult height and is actually challenging to measure accurately. Up to age 2, children are measured while lying on their back (supine). When referring to this measurement we use the term body length (as opposed to height). Length increases by 50 percent during the first year, with the infant gaining about 10 inches (attaining a length of about 30 to 33 inches). By age 2 toddlers have reached approximately 50 percent of their adult height. Thereafter, growth continues to decelerate, with an average gain in height of 5 inches between 12 and 24 months, and about 3 inches between 24 and 36 months (to about 38 inches). See Figure 4–1 for the CDC's growth chart for boys birth to 3.

Weight

At birth infants weigh about 7½ pounds. Boys tend to be slightly heavier than girls. Infants typically double their birth weight in five months (to about 15 pounds) and triple it in a year (to about 22 pounds). During the first six months growth is primarily focused on filling out the baby rather than changing body proportions (Gallahue & Ozmun, 2002). The rate of change in the first year is startling if compared to similar changes for an adult. What would you be like if comparable changes happened to you? If today you were 5 feet 6 inches tall and weighed 120 pounds, in a year you would be 8 feet 3 inches; you would weigh 360 pounds.

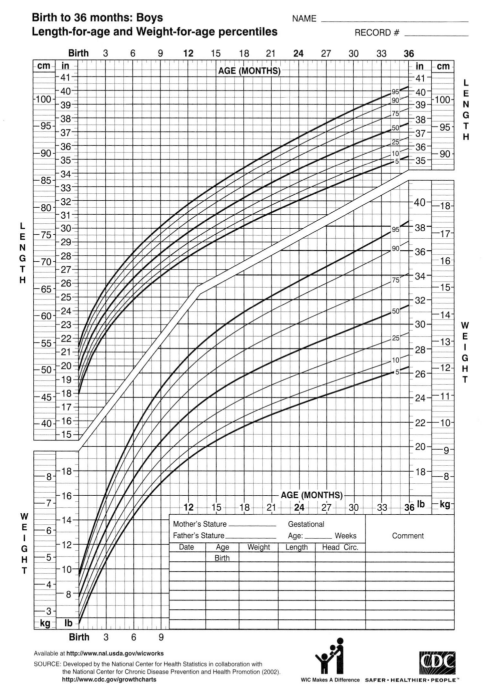

FIGURE 4–1

Height and Weight Charts for Infants from Birth to 36 months developed by the National Center for Health Statistics and the Centers for Disease Control and Prevention. Pediatricians plot individual growth charts for each child to look at growth pattern.

It is no wonder that infants need several sets of clothing during their first year and spend time adjusting to their body and learning how it acts and reacts. Growth gradually decelerates and toddlers gain about 10 pounds between 12 and 36 months. The timing of growth is largely genetic. The ultimate height and body type of an individual are determined by the genes she inherited from her parents and her environment. Some variation is not genetic, because genes interact with factors such as general health and nutrition patterns. Children who do not get enough calories or adequate nutrition may not reach their genetic growth potential. Children who are born to large parents are longer and heavier at birth than those born to smaller parents. Growth patterns are predictable, and deviations from them are significant. Pediatricians plot growth on a chart that compares an infant's actual growth with predicted patterns. Several growth charts have been developed by the Centers for Disease Control and Prevention (CDC). There are separate sets of charts for boys and girls. Although the patterns are the same, gender differences are clear, as is the decelerating rate of growth. For infants from birth to two years we plot length and weight. The expectation is that a child who is born weighing in at the 75th percentile will continue in that percentile, and there is cause for concern if his weight should drop to the 10th percentile. There is far less concern about an infant who is born at the 10th percentile and continues on that growth pattern, especially if her parents are relatively small individuals. In the first two years pediatricians want children to remain on their individual growth curves.

Premature infants are measured against percentiles designed specifically for this purpose, as their rate of growth is an important measure of risk factors. Long-term expectations are that their growth will plot normally, but during the first year at least they need different charts. When using norms for development with premature infants we often use an adjusted age, that is, the age of the child calculated from conception. (A five-month-old infant who was born two months prematurely would be compared to the expectations for a three-month-old infant.)

Pediatricians use a different set of charts to plot the growth of older children. For these children we use height and weight to determine and chart the **body mass index (BMI)**. BMI is determined by taking the weight in kilograms and dividing by the square of the height in meters. Children whose BMI is in the 5 percent or below category are considered underweight. Those between 5 and 85 percent are ideal, those who fall in the 85 to 95 percent category are at risk for becoming overweight, and those in the 95 percent category or above are classified as overweight. Weight is more susceptible than height to extrinsic factors such as diet, exercise, and illness.

BMI
is a measure of body fat based on height and weight.

We all love to see healthy, smiling babies and may think that chubby babies are healthier. There is a concern about the obesity epidemic in the United

States and globally. In 1976, of infants 7 to 23 months 7 percent were overweight. By 2000 this had increased to 12 percent. In 1990, 5 percent of children two to five years were overweight, but this had doubled to 10 percent by 2000. Looking at children longitudinally from two to eight years, Skinner, Bounds, Carruth, Morris, and Ziegler (2004) found by age 8 that 23 percent of the children were overweight. This was predicted by BMI at age 2. Obesity is a problem, and the problem begins in infancy.

Breastfeeding is one of the protective factors in preventing obesity. Breast milk is less energy dense than formula and may cause better self-control of food consumption. The longer an infant is breastfed, the less likelihood there is of obesity later on in life (von Kries, Koletzko, Sauerwald, & von Mutius, 2000).

The World Health Organization (WHO, 2007) is coordinating an effort to develop a child growth standard that will replace the one developed by the National Center for Health Statistics and published by the CDC. The WHO standards used breastfeeding as the norm and used a sample of healthy children from six countries (Brazil, Ghana, India, Norway, Oman, and the United States) (*Pediatric Basics*, 2007). These standards show the different growth patterns of breastfed versus formula-fed or **mixed-fed infants**. There was concern that many medical professionals were recommending that breastfeeding mothers give their babies formula so they gain more weight. Figure 4–2 provides a comparison ot the CDC and WHO growth charts. WHO's hope is that physicians in the United States will use this chart with breastfed infants to get a more accurate growth pattern.

Breastfeeding is a protective factor in preventing obesity in childhood and adolescence, but this protection does not continue on into adulthood. There are two thoughts for why this is the case. One has to do with the differences in composition of breast milk and formula. The other has to do with self-regulation. If we see that an infant has finished four ounces of a six-ounce bottle we are inclined to want the infant to finish the bottle. So the infant turns his head away and we follow after, putting the bottle back in his mouth. He spits it out; we try again. If we do this frequently enough he may learn to ignore the signals that his body is sending him that he is full. It is more difficult to see how much an infant is eating when he is being breast fed, so we are less inclined to want him to finish the last drop.

Early and rapid weight gain during the first six months in infancy increases the probability of obesity and earlier puberty (Dennison, Edmunds, Stratton, & Pruzek, 2006). This is particularly true for infants who are small for their gestational age. Our goal is to have these babies "catch up" (Ong et al., 2006). Physicians support this goal, as they are very reinforcing about how much weight the baby has gained. These children are the heaviest at age 5. It is the low-birth-weight babies who become larger in early childhood, not the baby who was nine pounds at birth.

Mixed-fed infants are those who receive both formula and breast milk.

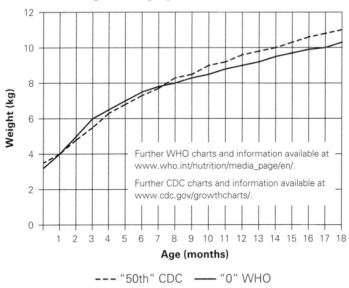

Weight-for-age girls, birth to 18 months

Further WHO charts and information available at www.who.int/nutrition/media_page/en/.

Further CDC charts and information available at www.cdc.gov/growthcharts/.

- - - "50th" CDC   ——— "0" WHO

FIGURE 4–2

Comparison of the Growth Charts Developed by WHO and the CDC (Adapted from the Editors. (2007). Growing Up to a New Standard: WHO Growth Charts Make Breastfeeding the Norm. *Pediatric Basics, 116,* 20.)

Our concern with preventing obesity has focused on what we feed infants and toddlers. The Feeding Infants and Toddlers study looked at 3000 children in the United States between 4 and 24 months of age. It found that soda was served to infants as young as 7 months. On a given day toddlers between 19 and

WITH INFANTS AND TODDLERS

We need to look carefully at our own behavior relative to feeding infants and toddlers. Are we responding to infants' cues that tell us when they are full? When they turn their head away do we follow? How often? Like adults, infants can change their mind, but we need to reframe how we think about feeding infants to ensure that we are respectful of their right to decide when they are full and that they develop the skill to convey that information.

When we think about snacks for toddlers we need to examine carefully the nutritional value of what we are feeding them. Juice and crackers is not a good choice. Juice has too much sugar, and most crackers are simple carbohydrates. Bread and crackers should have whole grains. Vegetables can be microwaved until they are soft enough that they are not a choking hazard. Toddlers need to taste a vegetable as many as 15 times before they begin to like it. So, do not get discouraged.

24 months usually had sweets, deserts, and salty snacks. However, 33 percent ate no healthy vegetables and 20 percent ate no fruit. The most commonly consumed vegetable was—you guessed it—French fries (Fox, Pac, Devaney, & Jankowski, 2004).

ASYNCHRONOUS GROWTH

Growth is uneven; different parts of the body grow and change at very different rates. This unevenness is referred to as **asynchronous growth**. The most obvious example of asynchronous growth is in body proportions. The head of the two-month-old fetus is half (50 percent) of his total body length; by birth it has decreased to a fourth (25 percent), and in adulthood it is about an eighth (10 to 12 percent). The head doubles in size between birth and adulthood. By age 4 the brain is more than 80 percent of its adult weight (Haywood & Getchell, 2005).

The limbs, at birth, are disproportionately short. To reach adult stature the arms quadruple in length and the legs quintuple in length. Trunk length triples. To achieve adult proportions the legs need to grow faster than the head or the trunk. Specific tissues and organs also grow at different rates. Internal differences are more difficult to see, but overall the proportion of the body that is water decreases and the amount that is made up by muscles increases.

Asynchronous growth is uneven, with different body parts growing at different times and at different rates.

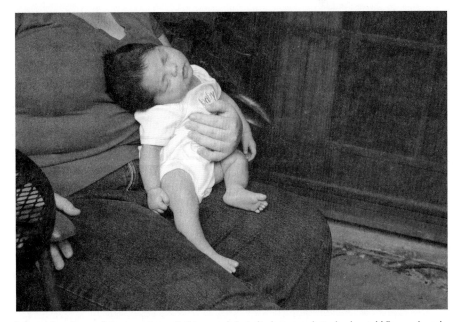

Infants' heads are disproportionately large and their limbs are relatively short. When relaxed they are floppy.

HEAD CIRCUMFERENCE

Physicians systematically measure and chart head circumference. As with height and weight, charts show the average head circumference for a newborn (13 to 14 inches) and how much head circumference should change over time. It grows about 0.5 inches per month for the first 6 months, to about 17 inches, then slows to 0.25 inches per month, so the head circumference is about 19 inches by the end of the first year (Mandleco, 2004). These measures have diagnostic significance. If the circumference is abnormally small physicians worry about intellectual disability. If it is more than two standard deviations below the average size, a diagnosis of microcephaly is made. Infants with microcephaly have brains that are too small or malformed, or elements of the brain itself are missing, causing developmental delays. When the head grows too quickly there is concern about hydrocephalus, or water on the brain.

Because the bones of the infant's head are not fused (or joined), the head can expand. The brain contains a watery liquid called **cerebrospinal fluid** that helps nourish and cushion the brain. If the flow of this fluid is obstructed, **intracranial pressure** builds up and size of the infant's head increases. Physicians are checking for hydrocephalus when they measure the infant's head circumference. This condition can be treated through medication or by surgically implanting a shunt (or drain) to decrease the pressure. If diagnosed early, children may not have their lives restricted, other than in terms of playing contact sports. For some infants, **hydrocephalus** may be related to other conditions that cause developmental delays.

Cerebrospinal fluid is a clear, salty bodily fluid that occupies the space between the skull and cerebral cortex and helps to cushion the cortex.

Intracranial pressure is the pressure exerted on the brain tissue, cerebrospinal fluid, and blood in the brain.

Hydrocephalus is a condition where too much cerebrospinal fluid causes pressure on the skull.

DENTAL GROWTH

Teeth typically begin to break though the infant's gums somewhere around four or five months. Usually the two bottom front teeth appear first, followed about a month or two later by the four front upper teeth. These top teeth are followed by two lower teeth. By about 30 months children have their full set of 20 primary teeth.

It is easy to see the young infant grow longer and increase in weight and even to see the first teeth come in. It is more difficult to understand the growth that we cannot see, such as that in the central nervous system (CNS).

THE CENTRAL NERVOUS SYSTEM

The central nervous system (CNS) consists of the brain, the spinal cord, and the nerves, which control voluntary and involuntary body functions. Different parts of the brain control different functions. The development of the CNS impacts

Ectoderm
is the outer tissue that forms the central nervous system and other organs.

Notochord
is a flexible rod-shaped body that becomes the backbone.

Midline
is an imaginary line that divides the body in half vertically.

Neural plate
is a flat region of neuroectoderm above the notochord.

Neural fold
is caused by the infolding of the neural plate.

Neurons
are cells of the central nervous system that are electrically excitable; they process and transmit messages.

Developmental delay
is a significant lag in an infant's or toddler's emotional, social, behavioral, or cognitive development in comparison to norms.

Glial cells
provide support and protection for neurons.

Myelin sheath
is an electrically insulating layer of glial cells that surrounds the axons of many neurons.

Synapse
is a small space separating neurons.

Neurotransmitters
are chemicals released from one neuron that cross the synapse to a receiving neuron.

the actions of the muscles, glands, and organs of the body, as well as motor and cognitive activities.

Early Development

Because of the importance of the brain and its role in early development, this section is detailed. In early fetal life the brain starts from the **ectoderm**, the outer layer of the embryo. The fetal brain undergoes a complex process of development. Through cell migration a solid rod called the **notochord** is formed down the **midline** of the embryo. This will become the backbone. By day 18 chemical signals cause the ectoderm to begin maturing and eventually become nerve cells (neuroectoderm). These cells also start replicating at a rate of 250,000 neurons per minute (Al-Chalabi, Turner, & Delamont, 2006). The neuroectoderm differentiates into inner and outer layers that are called the **neural plates**. These plates begin to fold over each other because of their fast rate of growth and become the **neural fold**. They differentiate into the neural tube and the brain. By the time the fetus is three months old, the basic structures of the brain are in place (Keating, Spence, & Lynch, 2002). Between three and five months' gestation, neurons from the neural tube rapidly divide and migrate toward the outer cell layers of the brain to form the cortex. **Neurons** are the specialized nerve cells that make up the CNS. If something interferes with this process, brain development will be impeded and the child will experience **developmental delays**.

The fetal brain consists of only one layer, whereas the adult brain is arranged in six layers. It is through the process of proliferation and migration that additional layers form. The sequence and timing of new layer formation are crucial. Brain cells must find their way up the cerebral walls. In addition to 100 billion brain cells, there are at least 10 times that many **glial cells**. Some glial cells are able to move around the brain consuming dead neurons; others form the **myelin sheath** around neurons, and still others direct information flow as they come into contact with various genes that define the neuron's identity, location, and mission (O'Shea, 2005). As brain cells migrate they can receive "misinformation" and die, or they can go to the wrong place, at the wrong time, and form the wrong **synapses**. **Neurotransmitters** carry messages across the synapse to another neuron. Exposure to teratogens such as drugs, alcohol, radiation, intrauterine infection, and poor nutrition can derail the process. Depending on the exact timing and nature of the problem, the child might develop a learning disability (Keating et al., 2002) or a neurological disorder such as epilepsy, autism, or schizophrenia. In general, the earlier that derailment occurs, the more severe the effects. The dynamic interplay of nature (genetic endowment) and the environment begins in the womb (Jensen, 2006).

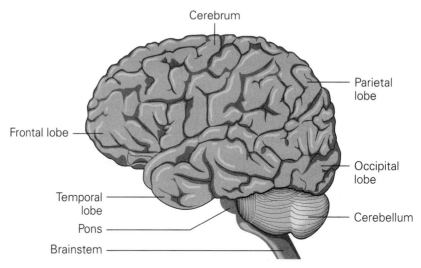

FIGURE 4–3

The brain has two hemispheres and four lobes

Corpus callosum
is a broad band of nerve fibers, axons, and cells in the cerebral cortex that connects the left and right hemispheres of the brain.

Cerebrum
is the largest part of the human brain and the source of thought and action.

Cerebral cortex
is the outer layer of the cerebrum.

Gray matter
comprises nerve cell bodies and their dendrites.

White matter
is made up of myelinated axons that connect gray matter areas and carry nerve impulses.

Myelin sheath
is an electrically insulating layer of glial cells that surround the axons of many neurons.

The Human Brain

The average adult human brain weight about 2.8 to 3.1 pounds and has about 100 billion neurons (McDowell, 2004). The brain's weight at birth is about 25 percent of its adult weight (about 12 ounces). It grows to 50 percent of its adult weight by 6 months and 75 percent by age 2 (Rosenblith, 1992). The brain is divided right down the middle into two hemispheres: left and right. Each hemisphere plays a major role in certain behaviors. The hemispheres communicate with each other through a bundle of 200 million nerve fibers called the **corpus callosum** (McDowell, 2004). If this does not develop properly or is damaged, this communication function is impaired. Other nerve fibers also connect the hemispheres. Figure 4–3 shows the cerebral cortex and the four lobes of the brain.

The Cerebral Cortex

The largest part of the brain is the **cerebrum**. It resides in both hemispheres of the brain. The outer layer of the cerebrum is called the **cerebral cortex**. If we look at the brain in cross-section, there are two distinct regions: the **gray matter** and the **white matter**. The gray matter consists of the nerve cell bodies, which are grayish in color. They cover the white matter and together make up the cerebral cortex. The white matter is the axons, which are covered in a protective fatty coating of glial cells called a myelin sheath. It is the myelin sheath that allows the rapid conduction of nerve impulses. The axons of newborns have little or no myelin. Development of the **myelin sheath** is necessary for the development of voluntary fine and gross motor movement. It is this process that moves the newborn from the primitive reflexes present at birth to the ability to walk, run, and pick up small objects.

The Four Lobes of the Cerebral Cortex

The cerebral cortex is further divided into four regions: the frontal, parietal, occipital, and temporal lobes. Each of the four cortical lobes is responsible for specific activities and functions. This is probably too simplistic a view of the brain, as it appears that far more areas are used in addition to the primary part of the brain most identified with a particular behavior (Al-Chalabi et al., 2006). However, discussing just the major components aids our understanding. Each of the lobes has many folds, which do not mature at the same time. Chemicals in the brain are released in waves that govern maturation, so different areas of the brain evolve in a predictable sequence (Jensen, 2006; Shore, 1997). This helps explain why there are prime times for certain types of learning and development.

The **frontal lobe** contains the motor areas of the brain. The left hemisphere controls the right side of the body. It is also involved in reasoning, planning, emotions, and problem solving. Humans have large frontal lobes relative to other species (McDowell, 2004). The frontal lobe is where high-level abstract thinking, planning, and organizing for the future take place. The completion of myelination is relatively late in the frontal lobe compared with other areas of the brain (Jensen, 2006). The frontal lobe is separated from the parietal lobe by the motor strip, or the **primary motor cortex**. The motor strip controls the intricate muscles necessary for speech, such as the tongue, and fine motor coordination as well as the muscles in the shoulders, knees, and trunk (Yaun & Keating, 2007). For motor activity to occur, a nerve impulse is sent from the primary motor cortex down the **pyramidal** or **corticospinal tract** that connects the cortex to the spinal cord, and ultimately to the appropriate muscle. Damage to either the motor cortex or the pyramidal tract can result in spasticity (cerebral palsy) or seizures.

The **parietal lobe** is the primary sensory area. There are distinct areas for vision, hearing, and smell. The parietal lobe also houses the sensory areas of perceived touch, pressure, temperature, and pain (McDowell, 2004). The parietal lobe is responsible for integrating other stimuli. Infants and toddlers with visual-perceptual problems and trouble with fine motor coordination, including children with learning disabilities and attention-deficit/hyperactivity disorder (ADHD), may have abnormalities in this area of the brain (Yaun & Keating, 2007).

The **temporal lobe** is involved in sensation and communication. The dominant hemisphere (for right-handed people, the left hemisphere) is

Frontal lobe
lies at the front of each cerebral hemisphere and plays a role in judgment, impulse control, language, memory, and problem solving.

Primary motor cortex
controls the planning and execution of movements.

Pyramidal tract
is a major nerve pathway that originates in the sensory and motor areas of the cerebral cortex and descends through the brainstem to the spinal cord.

Corticospinal tract
is a collection of long motor axons that run between the brain and the spinal column.

Parietal lobe
is involved in the perception and integration of sensory input.

Temporal lobe
is involved with auditory processing and verbal and visual memory.

Amygdala
controls emotions that are fundamental for self-preservation.

Hippocampus
plays a role in processing and packaging memory.

Limbic system
consists of the structures of the brain involved in emotions associated with memories and motivation.

Occipital lobe
is the visual processing center of the brain.

Brain stem
is the lower part of the brain, which connects to the spinal column.

responsible for the production and comprehension of speech. Areas are also devoted to auditory memory and visual experiences. The **amygdala** and **hippocampus** are small structures at the base of the temporal lobe. They are part of the **limbic system**, which reacts to stress and controls emotions. It is involved in sexual behavior, emotional reactivity, and motor regulation. The amygdala is the center for basic feelings, particularly fear and sexual response, and plays a crucial role in the control of major emotions such as love and rage. The amygdala also plays an important role in controlling the "fight or flight" response. The hippocampus plays an important role in memory and the ability to learn new information rapidly (Yaun & Keating, 2007).

The **occipital lobe** houses the primary visual receptive cortex. Damage to this area causes defects in the visual field (Yaun & Keating, 2007).

The Brain Stem

The **brain stem** controls more reflexive and involuntary activities such as blood pressure, heart rate, and regulation of body temperature, breathing, and other automatic processes. It is made up of the midbrain, pons, and medulla (Yaun & Keating, 2007). The midbrain is responsible for sleep and wakefulness, appetite/satiety, and arousal (watchfulness).

Some parts of the brain are not involved in either movement or sensation. These are called association areas. It is these areas that are believed to give individuals personality and a sense of humor (McDowell, 2004).

Connecting the Brain

Infants do not start with a small brain that just gets bigger and fills up with information. As discussed above, the brain is made up of nerve cells called neurons. Neurons are different and distinct from each other in physical and biochemical features. During early childhood the brain has amazing plasticity or malleability; that is, if one area of the brain is damaged, another part may be able to take over the function. For example, if a young child loses her language skills as a result of a stroke, she may recover these language skills because the brain cells move this function to another area of the brain. This is more possible in a younger brain than in an older one. In a young brain there are areas of the brain that are not yet committed to a particular function. There is an overproduction of synapses that are not in use and not designated for a particular use (Jensen, 2006).

Brain cells are like other body cells in that they contain a nucleus and cytoplasm. However, they are not the somewhat uniformly rounded shape we think of. They differ because they have an **axon**, a long snakelike fiber, that reaches out from the cell body and shorter, spiderlike **dendrites** that also

Axon
is a long slender nerve fiber that conducts electrical impulses away from the cell body.

Dendrites
are branched projections of a neuron that conduct electrical impulses to the cell body.

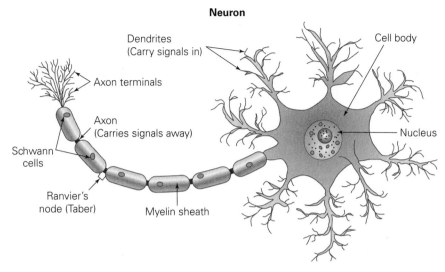

FIGURE 4–4

This simplified drawing of a neuron shows the cell body with the axon and the myelin sheath and the dendrite.

reach out from the cell body. The axon carries impulses away from the nerve cell body, and dendrites receive impulses from other neurons and carry them the short distance to the cell body. The tip of each axon, the growth cone, provides guidance for the growing axon and helps it reach its destination (Yaun & Keating, 2007) (see Figure 4–4). As axons grow, the dendrites respond by increasing the number of spines along their surface. This increased surface area allows for more elaborate and sophisticated communication between neurons (Yaun & Keating, 2007). Infants and toddlers with intellectual disabilities have fewer dendritic spines.

The axon of one cell body does not actually touch the dendritic spine of another cell body, there are spaces called synapses that separate the two. There are two types of synapses: chemical and electrical. Electrical synapses are closer together and there is communication between the cytoplasm of the neurons. This makes the electrical transmission rapid and the transmission is bidirectional (Yaun & Keating, 2007).

With chemical synapses the gap between the neurons is larger. Transmissions stop at the end of the axon, there are small vesicles in the neuron that hold **neurotransmitters**. Neurotransmitters are chemicals that relay, amplify or modulate electrical signals between cells. The neurotransmitter affects the postsynaptic cell by either exciting it or inhibiting it. The signal is unidirectional. This process continues until the signal reaches its destination (Yaun & Keating, 2007). If this seems like a long, complicated, and laborious process,

Neurotransmitters are chemicals that relay, amplify, or modulate electrical signals between cells.

with many steps, it helps explain why speed is important. Infants have immature dendrites and the process is very slow. It takes a long time for them to perceive sensation, send a message to the brain, process it, return with a message, and respond. This is why infants seem to react in slow motion.

As the child grows the number of neurons remains stable, but each one becomes bigger and heavier because of the increase in the number of dendrites. The key task in early development is the growth of these connections in the brain. Dendrites grow and make connections to other axons in the brain. One neuron can be connected to as many as 15,000 other neurons.

The connections formed are based on the child's experiences in the world and attachments to family and caregivers. In these early years, the child's brain forms twice as many synapses as it will need. By age 3, a child's brain has about 1000 trillion synapses. By late adolescence about half of all the synapses have been pruned, leaving about 500 trillion. If synapses are used repeatedly and are reinforced, they become part of the brain's permanent circuitry. If they are not used repeatedly or often enough, they are eliminated or pruned. Experience plays a crucial role in "wiring" the young child's brain (Shore, 1997). The brain works on something like a threshold level—when a part has been activated so many times (different numbers for different parts of the brain) it becomes exempt from elimination and is retained into adulthood. Much of the brain has a "use it or lose it" status.

Glucose
is a simple sugar that cells use as a source of energy.

The brain runs on **glucose** (sugar). Between birth and age 4 the cerebral cortex's use of glucose rises to more than twice the level of the adult brain's and stays that way for 10 years (Chugani, 1998). Children at this age also have higher levels of certain neurotransmitters. They are biologically primed to learn. Some areas are getting hard wired, and roughly 33 synapses are eliminated every second. The brain responds constantly and swiftly to conditions that promote (or inhibit) learning. Brain activity surges when a child addresses a difficult problem. It is virtually undetectable when a problem is easily solved (Shore, 1997).

Neurotransmitters play an important role in wiring the brain. Neurons use specific neurotransmitters. There are many different neurotransmitters; among the most important are serotonin, dopamine, and norepinephrine. A neuron's neurotransmitters are stored in pouches, presynaptic vesicles that border the synaptic membrane. When a depolarizing electrical current passes through the presynaptic membrane, these pouches open and release the neurotransmitters. The released neurotransmitters move across the synaptic cleft to the postsynaptic membrane of the dendrite carrying an excitatory or inhibitory neural impulse, much like an on/off switch. Each neurotransmitter also has an inactivator that can stop the transmission (McDowell, 2004). Problems related to neurotransmitters are implicated in a variety of disabilities such as autism,

ADHD, and some inborn errors of metabolism. Many of the drugs used to treat these disabilities as well as seizures, movement disorders, and depression act by altering specific neurotransmitters or their receptor sites (Yaun & Keating, 2007).

At birth, the infant's brain is still under construction. Experience is the architect that determines how blueprints are turned into reality. Brain development is an interplay between the genes the child was born with and the experiences he has. These early experiences shape not only the child's behavior but the child's brain itself. Synapses used repeatedly will remain; synapses used infrequently, or not at all, are pruned.

Unlike in other primates, which are born with the brain more completely formed, three-quarters of the human brain develops outside the womb. This is both an asset and a liability. How the brain develops is based on the interplay of nature and nurture. It seems obvious that trauma, disease, and abuse or neglect can change the brain. However, positive influences can impact the brain as well. An enriched, stimulating environment can change infants' brains not only in the area of cognitive development but also in the area of social development (Jensen, 2006).

The brain's ability to change and to recover lost functions is remarkable during the first 10 years of life. Early intervention takes advantage of the brain's plasticity. There are prime times for optimal development. These are periods during which the brain is particularly efficient at specific types of learning, or, in physiological terms, the periods when the brain's neurons create synapses most efficiently and more easily. This requires not only energy and neurotransmitters but space. The increased metabolic activity in the frontal cortex coincides with the ability of the infant to form attachments.

Although we use the plasticity of the brain to enhance the development of children, early experiences of trauma and abuse can interfere with development and impair the development of the brain. Negative early relationships can lead to a life-long limited ability, especially under stress, to regulate the intensity, frequency, and duration of primitive states such as rage, terror, and shame. The result can be antisocial behavior and personality disorders. Any factors that increase the activity or reactivity of the brainstem (chronic stress) or decrease the moderating capacity of the limbic or cortical areas (neglect) will increase the child's aggressiveness, impulsivity, and capacity to display violence. Violent behavior is most likely to occur when there is a lack of stimulation to the cortex and overstimulation of the limbic system.

Early intervention is based on the malleability of the brain and ways to change neural pathways to benefit children. To get the brain to pay attention we must program in a way that is congruent with brain development (See Table 4–1).

WITH INFANTS AND TODDLERS

The potential for early intervention is high. Individual experiences specifically designed for infants and toddlers can help them develop new capacities and change their brain. Using the principles outlined here, think about how you could design an experience for an infant or toddler that will change his brain. Start small: look at what the child is playing with. Decide what you could do to add a novel touch. You can make a significant difference in infants' and toddlers' brains. Identifying infants and toddlers who need additional support early and working during these prime times can and does make a difference.

Table 4–1 Strategies to Enrich Infant and Toddler Brain Development

- Infants and toddlers must be active participants in their learning. (The brain does not change as much from just observation.)
- Experiences must be novel, challenging and meaningful for infants and toddlers to learn. (The brain does not change by repeating what children already know, nor do meaningless experiences produce change.)
- Experiences must have both complexity and coherence. (The brain does not change from chaos or boring experiences.)
- Infants and toddlers need to strive for a goal that is attainable. (The brain does not form new synapse when uncomfortable and overwhelmed.)
- Infants and toddlers learn in the context of positive social relationships. (Unsafe environments cause the brain to be over vigilant and develop synapses that do not support learning.)
- Infants and toddlers need good nutrition to grow their bodies and their brains. (Both too little and too much food is not good for the brain.)
- Infants and toddler need time and repetition with minor variations. (The brain is rarely changed by just one experience unless it is traumatic.)

SOURCE: Jensen (2006).

The brain changes when infants and toddlers actively participate in a safe, interesting environment with adults they can trust. They learn, and their brain changes through active participation, so knowing how they develop motorically helps you plan better.

MOTOR DEVELOPMENT

There are few achievements that give parents, infant specialists, and infants themselves more joy than motor milestones. Motor development pervades all areas of development. Sensory stimulation provides the impetus for much motor development. Motor skills enhance social behavior and both benefit from and support cognitive development. It is important to know when different motor behaviors occur. This knowledge increases the infant's safety and helps to provide an interesting environment for growth and development.

The infant goes from having little control over his body at birth to sitting, standing, and walking in a little over a year. He goes from randomly flaying his arms to reaching accurately for something he wants, and from having his fist closed to being able to pick up a pea. This development happens in predictable patterns.

Motor development still follows the predictable sequence that was found by early researchers. Infants need to attain control of the head and trunk in sitting before they can walk.

Nature versus nurture
looks at the relative importance
of an individual's innate qualities
(nature) versus their personal
experience in the environment
(nurture) in shaping behavior.

The way motor development unfolds has long fascinated researchers and parents. The debate over **nature versus nurture** was intense regarding the development of motor skills. Some researchers felt that skills would emerge according to a biological timetable (nature), whereas other felt that infants and toddlers could be taught how to perform certain skills (nurture). We know that infants acquire skills slightly earlier than was established in the 1920s and 1930s, but the patterns of development researchers found then are still valid today. In addition to observing what infants and toddlers do, we are always curious about what causes behaviors. Why do children learn to walk at 12 months and not 6 or 20 months?

Maturational Perspective

The maturational perspective of motor development became popular in the 1930s. This perspective explains development as a process of maturation, particularly in the CNS. Researchers, such as Arnold Gesell and Myrtle McGraw, who followed this perspective believed that genetics and hereditary are mostly responsible for motor development and that the environment plays a very small role (Haywood & Getchell, 2005). Their results were primarily descriptive. The information served important practical purposes in the past and is still valued today. We use an updated version of the information about developmental patterns and ages at which typical behavior develops to decide what types of materials to use with infants of various ages and to determine whether infants are showing delayed or atypical patterns of development.

Cradle boards
are wooden baby carriers worn
on the back much like today's
back packs which are designed to
free the hands.

Maturationalists focused on infancy and early childhood. Wayne Dennis (1935, 1938, 1941), who restricted infants' ability to practice reaching, sitting, and standing, and who also investigated with his wife (Dennis & Dennis, 1940) the Hopi practice of placing infants on **cradle boards**, found that given the opportunity to practice skills they are maturationally able to perform, infants acquire these skills quickly. This gave rise to the question of whether intensive training could produce skills before they could be maturationally expected. Researchers such as Gesell and Thompson (1929) and McGraw (1935) looked at such skills as learning to climb stairs, cut with scissors, or ride a bicycle. Their co-twin control studies used monozygotic twins (who obviously had the same genetic make up) as a way of controlling for heredity. They then trained one twin but not the other in a skill such as stair climbing before it was maturationally expected. Overall, they concluded that motor development depends on the maturation of the brain and the development of muscles in the body. Yet these conditions are not sufficient. There has to be some opportunity to practice the behavior, but intensive practice before maturation is not effective. Patterns of development discussed later are largely based on the findings of these early researchers, whose results about the patterns of motor development have been confirmed and reconfirmed.

In the 1950s education became more focused on standardized tests and norms. The focus changed from patterns of development to scores and outcomes. Researchers were interested in how fast or how far the average young child could walk, run, or jump. They were also interested in the biomechanical description of movement patterns. They followed children **longitudinally** to see how such things as walking changed over time. They might describe beginning walkers, for example, as follows: a beginning walker has a short stride and holds her arms in a high guard position; to help with balance the feet are placed wide apart and the toes are pointed out; the arms do not swing (Haywood & Getchell, 2005).

The information-processing perspective began to be applied to motor development in the 1970s. This approach was used with young adults then children but rarely infants and toddlers. It focused on providing feedback to individuals about their performance to help them improve their motor shills. Researchers identified the processes that control movement and used this information to change development. Their approach was far broader than in the past as they included aspects of performance such as attention, memory, and feedback. This perceptual-motor approach linked learning disabilities to problems in attention and sensory and perceptual abilities (Clark & Whitall, 1989).

Ecological Perspective

The ecological perspective stresses the interaction of the individual, the environment, and the task (Haywood & Getchell, 2005). This perspective looks at individuals (toddlers), what they act on or with (a ball), and the task (kicking). Researchers are concerned about the size and weight of the ball relative to the toddler and his ability to kick the ball. This approach assumes that rather than being controlled by just the CNS (maturation), motor behavior self-organizes or emerges because of the interaction between the individual and the context in which the behavior is performed. As adults we walk because our body structure makes walking more appealing than creeping or crawling. We change the way we walk according to the terrain and our purpose for walking.

Let us get back to infants and toddlers and walking. Body systems develop at different rates. An infant begins to walk when the slowest developing of the necessary systems for that skill reaches a point where the skill can emerge. These are referred to as **rate limiters** or **controllers**. In walking, the muscles in the legs have to get strong enough to support the infant's weight on one leg. Muscular strength would be one rate limiter or controller for walking (Haywood & Getchell, 2005). What do you think others might be?

Longitudinal studies look at the same children at different points in time.

Rate limiter or **controller** is a system in the body that holds back or slows down the emergence of a motor skill.

Body scaling involves using a child's body proportions when making decisions about physical equipment and toys.

The relationship between a person and the functional use of objects or the environment must also be taken into account. For example, should you want to climb a set of stairs to get to the second floor, you raise your foot and, alternating feet, you go up. If, instead of the traditional spacing of steps, you find that the steps are three feet high, you might reevaluate how to go up the steps, especially if you are only five feet tall. This concept is referred to as **body scaling** (Haywood & Getchell, 2005). Going back to the original flight of stairs, an infant would not see a flight of stairs as climbable until her body proportions allowed her to raise her leg high enough to reach the next step. Using the concept of body scaling helps us choose the appropriate size chairs and tables for infants and toddlers as well as toys and materials.

The ecological approach encourages early childhood educators to look at motor development from a different perspective. Instead of being passive spectators waiting for motor development to occur and then supporting it, we can actively look at the environment and see how we can modify it to make some activities easier or more difficult for infants and toddlers.

The ecological approach helps us understand some of the cross-cultural studies of infant development that show differences in timing of motor events that are based on child-rearing customs and practices.

PRINCIPLES OF MOTOR DEVELOPMENT

Children follow similar patterns in motor development. What makes children different are the varying ages at which specific skills are acquired. The first year of life sees rapid growth in the acquisition of motor skills. During the next several years, the young child devotes time and energy to "fine-tuning" these motor skills to the point where intricate motor processes are possible. Motor development occurs as a result of the interaction of the developing infant with his environment and the particular tasks to be mastered.

Having good motor abilities is important for very young children. The infant learns from sensations acquired through movement. The acquisition of new sensations occurs through active involvement with the environment rather than through passive interactions. The infant is constantly receiving information about the environment from many sensory modes, including hearing, sight, and touch. Early motor development, then, is not only motoric but rather a more coordinated developmental effort integrating the senses and motor skills and the context in which these skills are performed (Haywood & Getchell, 2005).

Several principles underlie the development of motor skills in infants (See Table 4–2). The principles apply to all infants and toddlers. Knowledge of these aids in understanding normal developmental processes and is essential for developmentally appropriate programming.

Table 4–2 Principles of Motor Development

• Motor development is continuous. It begins in utero, with birth being only a marker in the process and continues into old age. Maturation of the motor system goes from gross motor to fine motor. Complex motor skills build on simpler motor skills.

• Almost all children follow the same pattern of motor development although the rate of development differs.

• Motor development generally proceeds from the head to the feet (cephalocaudal) and from the midline or spine outward to the extremities (proximodistal). Coordination of motor skills first develops close to the center of the body, with control of the neck and the shoulders then to the arms, and eventually, the fingers.

• Stability is the most basic category of movement.

• Control of body movements occurs first in the horizontal position and then moves to vertical orientation. Infants first learn head control while lying on their stomach. This skill is gradually integrated with sitting which requires control of the head and trunk, and then standing.

• Motor sequences are overlapping. Mastery of one skill is not necessary before others can begin, although skill ability does need to reach a functional level.

• Specific individual movements replace generalized mass activity. The development of motor abilities involves the disaggregation of gross movements into finer, coordinated, voluntary, specific motor responses.

• Motor development is the result of the child's ability to self-organize motor behaviors based on interactions between the child, the environment, and the task.

• **Neuromaturation** is one of many structural constraints that influence motor skills. Other factors such as body proportions, insufficient myelination, body weigh, muscular strength, and environmental conditions play a part in when skills emerge. Functional constraints such as fear of falling and even weather conditions also impact motor development.

SOURCE: Gallahue and Ozmun (2002); Haywood and Getchell (2005).

PATTERNS OF MOTOR DEVELOPMENT

Patterns of development can be typical, delayed, or atypical. Defining "typical" developmental pattern poses some difficulties. Children vary in the ages and rates at which they demonstrate abilities in certain skill areas. A specific skill that one infant may accomplish at a certain age, another infant may not accomplish until one, two, or even three months later. The later acquisition of skills does not necessarily mean that the second child is delayed. He may, in fact, be developing typically. The window of normal variation depends upon the particular skill. Walking has large variation in initial age acquisition, whereas lack of ability to uncurl one's fingers or eye-following patterns not being established within two months of expectation is cause for concern.

Walking is a good example of the variation of ages at which children acquire a skill. We know that, on the average, most children begin walking at around 13 months and that almost all children can walk by 15 months.

Neuromaturation
is the developmental level of the CNS

However, some children walk at 8 months of age, while others do not begin until they are 15 months old. This difference in age of acquisition indicates only that some children learn to walk early and some later. Those who do not walk at 18 months are of concern. Keeping this in mind, we can begin to create a picture of what constitutes the typical range of development.

Gross Motor Development

Antigravity positions
are all upright positions.

Large or gross motor development refers to the development and coordination of the large muscles of the body, including neck, trunk, arms, and legs. These muscles are necessary for all **antigravity positions**, such as sitting, standing, and walking. They are also necessary to stabilize the body as finer movements are performed. The general sequence of large motor development can be viewed as the infant moves from prone, to supine, to sitting, to standing, to walking.

Prone

Prone
is lying on the stomach with the face down.

At birth newborns are in a reflexive state. Before they can move around, infants must first develop voluntary control of their neck and trunk. In a **prone** position (lying on the stomach), newborns can lift their head to see what is happening around them. This is the beginning of their struggle against gravity. At this point the hands are still reflexively curled into fists and the forearms are tight against the body. As the infant's muscles strengthen and equilibrium responses improve, it is not just the head that is moved off the surface but the trunk as well. Gradually the forearms are used to bear weight (about two months). By three months, the infant can begin to lift both his head and shoulders, with legs extended. By the fourth month, he can support himself on flexed elbows, chest off the surface. Because of lack of control, infants sometimes flip onto their back. This is not true rolling, and once infants gain more control this rarely happens. Two further variations occur: the infant can lift his head, arms, and legs off the surface at the same time, and he can use one forearm for balancing while he uses the other to reach for an object.

SIDS
is the sudden unexplained death of an infant between one month and one year.

Some researchers are concerned that infants spend too much time on their back and not enough time on their stomach to develop the core muscles of the neck and back. Parents who know about the relationship between supine sleeping and **sudden infant death syndrome (SIDS)** are often reluctant to place their infants on their tummies. This results in many infants having very little tummy time. The question is whether this delays their motor development. The answer is "yes." Infants need more tummy time, particularly infants of higher social classes (Majnemer & Barr, 2005).

up close and personal

When Lucrecia was a baby I had a small catering business that I ran out of my home. Obviously, I spent a lot of time in the kitchen. At first I just put her in the bouncy seat and talked and sang to her. She was very content. A friend referred to her as the "containerized child." She commented that Lucrecia was in the bouncy seat, car seat, or sling of some kind all the time. I never put her down on the floor.

After I got over being offended, I thought about what my friend had said. I made a small play area for Lucrecia on the floor in the corner of the kitchen. I would lay her on her stomach surrounded by rattles and toys. At first she cried if I did not play with her all the time, and even when I did she would start to cry after a few minutes. I persisted. As I waited for timers to ding or when I had a break in the action I would sit on the floor with her and help her reach for little toys. I marveled how at first she could barely pickup her head and after a few months she could scoot her little body in a circle to find her toys

Life became more complicated when she learned to crawl, and I eventually had to hire someone to keep track of my moving munchkin.

REFLECTIVE PRACTICE

We are becoming increasingly concerned about the lack of time that infants spend on their tummies and how much time they spend "containerized" in bouncy seats, jumpers, swings, and car seats: about 60 hours a week! Think about the "back to sleep" policy statement released by the American Academy of Pediatrics in 1992 as a way to prevent SIDS and the impact that might have on infants' locomotion if parents and caregivers are concerned about putting babies on their tummies. Could this become a rate controller in early walking? Should we say, "Back to sleep, front to play!" As a professional in the field reflect on what you could do to encourage parents (and early childhood educators) to put infants on their tummies. What guidance would you give them if their infant did not like it? What would you to convince them of the importance of tummy time and how to make it fun?

Pivoting
is turning the upper body while the lower body remains in a specific place.

Infants begin to pivot at around five months when prone. **Pivoting** is moving the upper body in a circular pattern with the arms while the lower

Crawling
is moving using arms and legs with the stomach touching the ground.

Creeping
is moving on hands and knees with the stomach off the ground.

body stays at one spot. Infants begin to use their arms and sometimes their legs to make forward progress or crawl. Infants **crawl** with their chest and stomach on the floor. As control over the lower trunk and legs improves, the infant pushes up so that his weight is supported on his hands and knees. First he will hold this position, then begin to rock back and forth, and finally begin to make progress. This is **creeping**. The infant often goes backward before he goes forward. Initially, the legs work together (simultaneously). This is replaced by reciprocal arm and leg movements (Haywood & Getchell, 2005).

Many people use the terms "crawling" and "creeping" interchangeably. Technically, they are being inaccurate. Remember that snakes crawl as a way of reminding yourself that when infants' stomachs are on the ground they are crawling.

WITH INFANTS AND TODDLERS

Place infants on their tummies. Then get down on your tummy and talk to them. Make tummy time fun. Shake rattles, place them on interesting surfaces, and provide them with interesting things to look at. When they can better control their head and neck (about three months) hold intriguing toys above and to one side so that they need to support their weight on one arm to first look at the toy and then grasp it with the other arm. Offer toys on different sides so infants practice bearing weight on each arm. Gradually increase how high you hold the toys to improve their reaching skills. Infants sometimes need incentives for practicing skills. If there is nothing that requires them to push up on one arm and reach with the other, they may not do it. Use toys that vary in shape, size, and color but that can all be grasped. Praise the infants for reaching the toy but do not make them work so hard they become frustrated. Infants need tummy time every day. Keep increasing the amount of time you put infants on their tummies to develop these core muscles. And remember they want to have fun on their tummies; you are the one who knows it is important.

Supine

Supine
is lying on the back with the face up.

Visual following
is tracking a moving object with the eyes.

The infant is fully supported in the **supine** position (lying on her back), so the arms and legs move freely. Waving and kicking are the movement patterns most frequently seen in a supine position. The infant does a lot of **visual following** in this position, as objects and people move in and out of her range of vision. She may gaze at her hand before she gains the coordination to bring her hand to her mouth. Infants begin to roll from supine to prone at about three months. Infants

WITH INFANTS AND TODDLERS

When infants are on their backs encourage them to kick by saying, "Kick, kick, kick." Hold your hand out and say, "Can you kick my hand?" Try. Talk to infants and encourage them to kick, especially after you have changed their diaper. Take a minute to encourage them to kick and move their arms.

who spend much of their time on their back or in positions where their head is supported do not develop head control as quickly as infants who spend more time in a prone position.

Sitting

Newborns look like the letter "C" when placed in a sitting position. Their body is in flexion (bent at the joints). As body control improves, infants placed in a sitting position are able to raise their head. By three months the infant is able to sit with support. She can control her upper trunk, but it will take another month or two for her to gain control of the lower trunk (Gallahue & Ozmun, 2002). Between the third and fifth months, the infant struggles to keep her head at midline and needs adult support to stay in the sitting position. Between

Newborns have little head control and look like the letter "C" when placed in a sitting position.

the fifth and sixth months, the infant is developing back strength. Around the sixth month infants sit like a tripod, with their weight supported on their outstretched hands as well as their body. As trunk control increases hands are used primarily for balance, and then the hands become available for exploration. Although young infants can maintain a sitting position when placed there, it is not until later that they can push themselves into a sitting position. The infant eventually gains strength and balance, so by the ninth month he can begin securely to manipulate items, rotate and pivot, and complete coordinated tasks while in the sitting position.

Infants typically get into a sitting position from a prone or side-lying position, using their hands to push, rather than from a supine position. Their abdominal muscles are not strong enough for them to sit up from a supine position. Stable sitting and creeping allow infants to explore their environment in a different way: the infant creeps to a desired object, moves into a sitting position, picks up the object, and plays with it.

WITH INFANTS AND TODDLERS

When infants can reliably sit, at about six or seven months, sit in front of the infant and do the following "warm-up" exercises. Encourage the infant to copy what you do. Talk about what you are doing as you do it and encourage the infant to do it with you.

Look over your right shoulder, then your left; look at the ceiling, then the floor. Roll your shoulders, clap your hands, put your arms out at shoulder height and flap them. Touch your toes, pivot your shoulder left and then right, and so on. If the infant begins to slump, sit behind her and place your hands around her hips and lower back for a minute or two. This will give added support. Help move her body gently as you talk about what you are doing. Or place her between your legs facing you if she needs less support.

While you are doing this, look at the infant, call her name, describe what you are doing, and encourage her to imitate you. Infants will not be proficient at following you, but it is good exercise.

Gradually increase the amount of time and the number of opportunities infants have to sit independently. Trunk muscles need to be used to develop. Sometimes infants need encouragement to continue to develop these muscles. They need something to do while they sit. So be sure there are toys available. If an infant is encouraged to use her hands to play with toys or copy your motions, she is less likely to need them to help with balance.

Standing

Although newborns can support their weight on their feet, this reflexive weight bearing does not remain (unless it is consistently practiced). It is not until infants have attained a sitting position that they attempt standing. This upright control usually begins with the infant kneeling. He may get to a standing position by pushing back from a creeping position or changing to sitting position. From this kneeling position the infant uses furniture to pull to a standing position, using the strength of his arms. Over time this technique is replaced by one where the infant, from a kneeling position, shifts his weight to one knee, thereby freeing the opposite leg. He extends it and again shifts his weight. Initially a struggle, this movement becomes fluid with practice. The infant is able to bear his weight around the sixth month, with support. He begins bouncing, when held, by the seventh month. Around the eighth month the child can begin to pull himself up to a standing position, using a stable piece of furniture. Once the infant feels secure and has gained some sense of balance when upright and standing, he begins to take cautious steps. By the 11th month, the infant is **cruising** around furniture, holding on for support. Standing alone for an extended time usually takes place at about the same time as independent walking—about 11 to 13 months (Gallahue & Ozmun, 2002).

Cruising is walking sideways holding on to something stable such as furniture.

Walking

Independent walking starts with a few toddling steps and then an inevitable fall. Walking has a period where both feet are on the ground followed by a period of single-leg support. There is a **50 percent phasing** relationship between the legs (Haywood & Getchell, 2005). The toddler spreads his feet wide in an effort to establish a firm base and holds his arms up and out about shoulder height for balance and to protect against the fall that will surely come. At first each step appears to be independent of the next one; steps are short, with little leg and hip extension (Haywood & Getchell, 2005). As an infant moves toward mature walking several aspects of the process change: the speed increases, as does the length

Fifty percent phasing means that as one leg is half way through its motion the other leg begins.

WITH INFANTS AND TODDLERS

Once toddlers become steady walkers (about 15 months and beyond), have them participate in various types of walking. You may need to model the walk or to encourage the toddler by holding her hand.

- *Barefoot walk*: Toddlers can walk on grass, mud, sand, smooth rocks, concrete surfaces, and finally through a tray of water. Describe and ask about how each feels and the sensations involved. Inside use carpet squares, bathmats, woven doormats, foam pads, bubble wrap, and so on.

- *Walking a line*: Toddlers can walk a line forward and then backward, keeping each foot on, or near, the line. Have them walk pigeon-toed, turning feet out as far as possible, and crossing the front foot over the line each time.
- *Walking sideways*: Toddlers can walk to the right one step at a time, bringing their left foot over to touch their right foot. Reverse when moving to the left. If they walk in a circle it requires less space.
- *Animal walks*: For a duck toddlers can bend their knees and place hands behind their back; they walk forward one foot at a time, remaining in bent-knee position and, of course, quacking!

Support the toddler's attempts, and keep the distance short.

These are good rainy-day activities and fun ways of moving. Do not use these variations until children are confident walkers. Remember that novel ways of moving connect synapses in the brain. You are the architect.

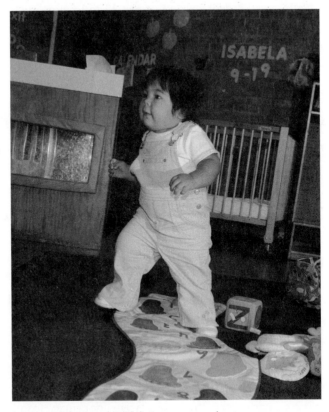

Early walkers have a wide base and hold their arms up and out.

of the step; the width of the step increases then decreases; the foot moves from pointing out to straight ahead; and the gait becomes smoother, more regular, and more synchronous (Gallahue & Ozmun, 2002). Toddlers begin to walk up and down stairs with help around the 18th month. By two years they can go up and down independently, two feet per step.

Running

Like walking, running has a 50 percent phasing relationship between the legs, but there is a time when neither foot is in contact with the ground. Infants' earliest attempts at running are really fast walking (no flight). Toddlers begin to run about six or seven months after they walk. Early running has some of the same characteristics as early walking (wide base, no arm swing). The range of motion is limited, and the stride length is short. Strength and balance are important controllers in early running (Haywood & Getchell, 2005).

REFLECTIVE PRACTICE

Think about the process of walking and how it is different from running or standing. What have you concluded? Walk around and think about the relationship of your feet to the ground and how you shift your body weight. What did you conclude? To run toddlers must propel themselves into the air with one foot and land on the other. This requires both strength and balance. Do you think you need to coach toddlers on how to walk, run, or jump? What could you do to support their development in this area?

Jumping

In jumping, a child propels her body from a surface with one or both feet and lands on both feet. Beginning jumping occurs when children jump down to a lower surface from a height of about 12 inches with one foot, landing on the other foot (e.g., jumping off the bottom step). This happens at about 24 months. This is followed by jumping off the floor with both feet, then from increased heights, and using both feet (Haywood & Getchell, 2005).

Fine Motor Development

The second pattern of development is small or fine motor development. Fine motor development involves the child's ability to use the small muscles of the arms, hands, and fingers. The development of fine motor skills is dependent on several interrelated skills. Vision plays an important role. Though vision is not a prerequisite for fine motor development, visual abilities function as a motivator for reaching and grasping. In addition, the ability to see objects allows children to direct their reaching more accurately. The major accomplishment for fine motor skills during infancy is the precise use of the hands for reaching, grasping, and manipulating objects.

Reaching

Reaching moves from gross movements of the arm to directed, precise touching of objects and the manipulation of those objects. The time from birth to four months is characterized as *prereaching*. At about four months infants can predictably bring their hands to their mouth. The sight of an object elicits arm movement, but this movement is typically not accurate enough to make contact with the object. It is often global and in the general direction of the object (Gallahue & Ozmun, 2002). Newborns do not use visual information to guide their reaching until around four months. Then they begin to shape their hand according to what they are reaching for. The infant can now bring her hands together in play. The infant reaches for objects placed directly in front of her. When held in a supported sitting position, the infant can reach for and touch objects on the table by the fifth month. Inability to reach for objects will greatly interfere with the child's ability to grasp and pick up objects. By nine months reaching is accurate and it may be done with one or both hands depending upon the object's shape and size (Haywood & Getchell, 2005).

Grasping

Prehension
is grasping an object.

Grasping, or **prehension**, proceeds from swiping and missing objects to accurately picking up tiny pellets and small items. The infant's early use of the hands is dominated by the grasp reflex; placing any small object (or your finger) in the infant's hand causes it to securely close around the object. This reflex is visible until around the fourth month. Around this time, the hand remains open and the infant begins to attempt to grasp objects voluntarily. However, it is not until the 10th month that the infant can voluntarily release the object in her hand. Children must be able to pick up and release objects successfully and voluntarily if they are to explore their world (Gallahue & Ozmun, 2002). Once the infant is able to release objects, it becomes a marvelous game if you are willing to pick up the object and play.

The development of the ability to grasp objects occurs in an observable sequence. However, the sequence is also related to the size of the child's hand relative to the object to be grasped. Early grasping is more like a squeeze or a "raking" motion in which the infant uses the whole hand in a fisted motion, raking up

Ulnar
prehension is using the little finger side of the palm to grasp.

Radial
prehension is using the thumb side of the hand for grasping.

Pronation
is grasping where the palm is facing down.

Supination
is grasping where the palm is facing up.

objects. This is followed by a grasping pattern described as **ulnar**-palmar prehension, whereby objects are held in the palm by all fingers flexing. If you placed a sock over your hand and grasped an object this would be the characteristic palm grasp.

The next stage in grasp development is characterized by the use of the ulnar (little finger) side of the palm and the three ulnar fingers—the middle, ring, and small fingers. Objects still appear to be raked in, but there begins to be some distinction between finger usage. The next stage sees a shift in the use of the hand from the ulnar side to the **radial** (thumb) side. The infant begins to use the thumb and first two fingers to grasp objects. This appears at about six months and is like grasping with a mitten on. This skill then progresses to the use of the index finger and thumb, identified as the inferior pincer grasp, by seven or eight months. Finally, the infant uses the tips of the fingers and thumb to pick up small objects. This is called the superior or neat pincer grasp. The superior pincer grasp can be expected to emerge at around 10 months. It is also at about 9 or 10 months that the infant is able to release objects in his hands voluntarily.

Development follows a **pronation** to **supination** pattern. Initially all activities involving the infant's hand involve use of that hand with the palm down (pronation). (You have a clue for this one. Prone is lying on the stomach.) Pronation refers to the orientation of the palm of the hand. As the child gains strength in the wrist, the hand rotates and the child is able to accept objects with his palm up (supination). (Supine is facing up; palm up.)

Given the progress in grasping skills, infants around seven to eight months old can hold onto and feed themselves finger food, bang objects on the

WITH INFANTS AND TODDLERS

Put about two inches of small seeds or water in a dish pan and add a variety of cups and spoons. Have one or two infants or toddlers sit on the floor in the middle of a plastic tablecloth. Place a dish pan in front of each infant or toddler and encourage him to fill up the cups and spoons and dump them. If necessary, place the infant's hands in the container and show him how to explore the medium before introducing the cups and spoons. This has the potential for simple exploration and is related to concepts of measurement and relative size. It provides the opportunity to use the rotational skills necessary in grasping objects and exploring them. *Note:* With infants and toddlers all materials used in "dump and fill" should be edible. They will be eaten. However, there is a concern in the field that there are communities where families may not have enough to eat, so it is inappropriate to play with food. Be creative in what you use, but the skills are developmentally necessary.

table, and transfer objects from hand to hand. However, they often seem far more interested in repeatedly dropping objects from their high chair than eating. It is not until about 10 or 11 months that infants become interested in placing objects into containers and taking them out. Preference for a particular hand appears at about one year, and two-year-olds have a decided preference. About 85 to 90 percent will be right handed. Further development refines and perfects the process of grasping and exploring objects.

Catching

The goal of catching is to gain control of and retain an object that has been thrown. Young children typically position their hands and arms rigidly to trap the object between their arms and their chest. They often close their eyes in anticipation of catching (Haywood & Getchell, 2005). This skill is not mastered during the first three years.

Infants' and toddlers' motor development is based on their ability to receive information from their environment and to make sense out of this information. Information is gained through the senses and sent to the brain for processing, then the body acts on the information obtained.

SENSATION AND PERCEPTION

Infants and toddlers use the five senses that we think of: seeing, hearing, feeling, taste, and smell. To be functional they have to organize their sensory world to take in, process, and act on sensory information.

Sensation, **perception**, and movement are highly integrated. Learning results from a collaboration of sensory input from the auditory, visual, and tactile-kinesthetic senses (Stockman, 2004). "Sensation is the neural activity triggered by a stimulus that activates a sensory receptor and results in sensory nerve impulses traveling the sensory nerve pathways to the brain. Perception is a multistage process that takes place in the brain and includes selecting, processing, organizing, and integrating information received from the senses" (Haywood & Getchell, 2005, p. 156). Early sensory experiences are important for the overall development of the child (Williamson & Anzalone, 2001).

Infants receive information about their world from motor and sensory feedback, but how do they go about making sense out of this information? Objects come in and out of their field of vision; they hear the sound of their mothers' voice, smell her perfume, and feel their own wetness before their diaper is changed. How do they develop patterns to make their world more predictable? How do they decide what to pay attention to, what is relevant, and what is not?

Vision provides the infant with information about what is interesting. Seeing objects and events motivates the infant to reach and move. Hearing

Sensation is the awareness of a stimulus that starts a biochemical reaction.

Perception is a mental process that responds to sensation.

up close and personal

Annette cries as her mother reaches down to lift her eight-week-old daughter out of the crib, saying, "Hey punkin, you're awake. Let's get your diaper changed and then we'll play." Annette smiles and coos as her mother places her on the changing table. However, as soon her diaper is removed her feet kick and her hands fist and she lets out a high-pitched wail. The use of the baby wipe only increases the intensity of the kicking and wailing. As soon as the diaper is replaced the wailing stops, her mother "raspberries" her tummy, and she is back to smiles and cooing.

REFLECTIVE PRACTICE

In the few minutes it took to change a diaper this infant went from crying to smiling to loud wailing to smiling in response to different sensory stimuli. If this diapering experience is typical, can you think of things you might do to make it a more pleasant sensory experience?

Proprioception
provides feedback on the internal status of the body and where various parts of the body are in relations to other parts.

Vestibular
or balance system provides input about movement and orientation in space.

provides the infant with information about his environment and the model to develop speech and language. Touch allows the infant to cuddle and mold his body to that of his caregiver and also to learn how different objects feel—a cuddly blanket, cold water, mushy food, hard plastic, and so on. Taste is part of mouthing, and the infant receives sensory information about objects by placing them in his mouth. The infant is sensitive to smells and develops associations with the sense of smell, particularly about his mother and other familiar caregivers. We know about these senses right from early childhood. We are less aware of the unconscious sensory information that comes from our own body: **proprioceptive** and **vestibular** sensations.

Older research concentrated on vision and hearing. Hence we know much more about these two senses than the others. Currently there is much interest in the role of movement or kinesthetic development in perception (Haywood & Getchell, 2005). Researchers are interested in the infant's ability to respond to sensory input, how they integrate this input, and how they use this input to perceive their world.

Sensory Stimuli

In addition to knowing how the sensory organs work we need to explore the sensations that are coming into the body to be perceived. It is useful to think of these as two entities: the sensory input or sensation, which is constant across infants, toddlers, and adults, and the perception that is the appraisal of the input, which is very individual (Williamson & Anzalone, 2001). Sensory input varies in intensity, duration, and location.

Intensity refers to the strength of a stimulus, and intensity varies among the senses. Duration refers to the length of time the stimulus is presented and also the duration of the effect that stimulus has on the CNS. Location focuses on the place on the body where the stimulus occurs or the location in space relative to the body. Before looking at the integration of the senses, let us look at the major components of sensory perception for each sense individually.

Vision

Though young infants do not have good visual acuity, they can see. To support infants' visual exploration, adults need to know how infants see, what infants are most likely to look at, how they visually explore objects, and how they process this information. From the infant's perspective, he needs something to look at, to keep it in his range of vision, and to focus on it.

The eye does not actually "see" any more than the ear "hears." The eye receives light, turns light into electrical impulses, and sends them through the optic nerve to the visual cortex of the occipital lobe of the brain. It is the brain that actually perceives visual images. If the relevant part of the brain is damaged, a child may not be able to see, even though the eye is completely normal. Damage in the brain or the optic nerve is not correctable. Defects in the eye itself, however, often are. The purpose of most visual aids is to compensate for defects in the eye so that a correct message can be sent to the brain.

Visual acuity
is the clearness of vision.

Visual acuity looks at how clearly one can see objects. At birth infants can see, but their functional vision is about 5 percent of adult visual acuity, or about 20/400, meaning that adults (with 20/20 vision) see at 400 feet what infants see at 20 feet (Haywood & Getchell, 2005). Vision improves and by the time an infant is independently mobile, at about six months, vision is adequate to keep the infant from bumping into things. Vision facilitates locomotion. Children have 20/30 vision by age 5 and adult levels by age 10 (Haywood & Getchell, 2005).

Visual Impairments

Decreased visual abilities affect a child's capacity to receive vital information. Visual impairments are relatively common among young children. Half to two-thirds of children who have developmental delays also have visual impairments of some type (Miller & Menacker, 2007). Parents and medical personnel can usually identify infants with total loss of sight. However, early childhood educators play a vital role in identifying less severe losses.

Researchers group visual problems into four major categories: problems with the physical mechanisms of the eye, problems with visual acuity, impairments to the muscular structure of the eye, and problems in visual perception (in the message pathway between the eye and brain). For most infants and toddlers, problems involving the physical mechanisms, acuity, and muscular structure can be corrected with medical techniques, glasses, and/or surgery. Problems involving the nerve pathways are difficult to remedy with medical intervention. Although there are a number of problems, only the most common are discussed here, as they affect more infants and toddlers and must be dealt with at an early age to prevent long-term negative consequences.

Retinopathy of Prematurity.

ROP
is an eye disease that affects preemies and is caused by the disorganized growth of retinal blood vessels, which can result in scaring or retinal detachment.

Retinopathy of prematurity (ROP) occurs primarily in premature infants. In premature infants blood vessel growth is incomplete. In the catching up process some blood vessels can grow to the center of the eye rather than along the back wall of the eye. These abnormal blood vessels eventually die in a way that produces scar tissue. If there are enough such blood vessels the scar tissue constricts so much that it can pull the retina from the back surface of the eye, detaching it, which results in loss of vision. Laser application can be used to reattach the retina. Although this procedure often results in improved vision, it is not necessarily perfect vision (Miller & Manacker, 2007).

Eye Muscles.

Eye muscles direct the eye toward an object and allow us to look in all directions without turning our head. Of the six muscles that control the eye, one is on each of the four sides of the eye, and the other two muscles help rotate the eye. When these muscles do not work as they should, misalignment of the eyes results.

Strabismus
is a condition where the eyes do not focus on the same object.

Strabismus occurs in about 3 to 4 percent of all infants, but it occurs in almost 15 percent of infants born prematurely (Miller & Menacker, 2007). The muscles controlling the eyes must work in coordination to result in clear vision. When the muscles are weak and lack coordination the child develops strabismus. At some point during development of binocularity, the eye appears to be subject to imbalance. Strabismus is usually identified between 18 and 36 months. The most common type of strabismus is **esotropia**, in which one or both eyes turn in toward the nose (cross-eyed). In **exotropia**, another form of strabismus, one or both eyes turn out (wall-eyed). Some infants and toddlers have these problems only intermittently, usually when they are tired. This is not a concern.

Esotropia
is a type of strabismus where one or both eyes turn inward.

Exotropia
is a type of strabismus where one or both eyes turn outward.

Amblyopia.

Amblyopia
or lazy eye is poor or blurry vision in a physically normal eye during infancy or early childhood.

Amblyopia occurs when the vision in one eye is blurred or lacks retinal images. Just as an unused muscle atrophies, unused neural pathways deteriorate. It can be caused by a number of conditions that interfere with vision: cataracts, refraction errors, and strabismus. In the latter two cases, the brain receives two different pictures, as each eye sees differently. To avoid double vision, the brain "turns off" the weaker eye, which leads to amblyopia. If the condition is treated early, the prognosis is good. To strengthen the weaker eye, the stronger eye is covered with a patch during the child's waking hours (infants can be patched only briefly), thus forcing the child to focus with the weaker eye. This is done as early as possible in a child's life. If patching is not possible, drops or lenses may be used to blur the vision of the good eye. Surgery can be used to correct the problem. Corrective lenses are almost always required as well. Amblyopia must be identified and treated before age 8 for acuity to improve significantly (Miller & Menacker, 2007).

Refractive Errors. For clear vision, the eyeball, lens, and the cornea must work together. Errors of refraction occur because of the shape of the eyeball or cornea or the strength of the lens.

Refractive errors are errors in the focusing of light by the eye that reduce visual acuity.

Hyperopia (farsightedness) means that the child can see distant objects better than relatively close objects. When the eyeball is too short or the refracting mechanisms (lens and cornea) are too weak, the focused image focuses behind the retina. The shorter the eyeball, the more out of focus the image will be and the more convex the lenses in the glasses will be to correct the problem (Miller & Menacker, 2007).

Hyperopia is when the eyeball is too short, resulting in an inability to focus on near objects.

In **myopia** (nearsightedness) the child can focus on near objects but not those that are far away. Myopia occurs when the eye ball is too long, or the refracting mechanisms of the eye too strong causing the image to be in focus before it reaches the retina. Myopia is corrected with the use of concave lenses. There is no mechanism to fine-tune vision for children with myopia. Therefore, these children may wear glasses from infancy if the myopia is severe (Miller & Menacker, 2007).

Myopia is when the eyeball is too long, resulting in an inability to focus on far objects.

Astigmatism is an error in refraction caused by the cornea's being more football-shaped than spherical. The image does not focus because the parallel light rays do not come together at one point. Cylindrical lenses that compensate for the irregular shape can usually correct astigmatism. This condition can also occur with other visual conditions. A child can be nearsighted or farsighted and also have astigmatism (Miller & Menacker, 2007). Corrective lenses may not be prescribed for infants and toddlers if the refractive problem does not interfere with daily functions.

Astigmatism is blurred vision because of an irregularly shaped cornea.

Cataracts. **Cataracts** are the clouding of the lens inside the eye. If the lens is clouded, light cannot reach the retina, which results in blurred vision. Some children are born with cataracts. A primary cause of congenital cataracts is maternal infection, such as rubella. Most cataracts can be removed surgically. If cataracts are small and stable, they may not need to be removed, but if

Cataracts are the clouding of the natural lens of the eye, making images look blurred or fuzzy.

WITH INFANTS AND TODDLERS

Infants and toddlers with visual impairments may show delayed development. They may have low muscle tone because children are usually stimulated to use their muscles by sight, so you must stimulate them with sound and touch. Infants with visual impairments need environments that provide varied auditory and tactile stimulation in addition to meeting their visual needs. Provide support so they can safely explore their environment. Have a variety of materials within reach (in a container such as a tub). Infants and toddlers with severe visual impairments may sit later and hitch instead of creep. Hitching is like scooting on their bottom, using the legs for propulsion. It is a safer method of locomotion as it protects the head from bumping into things. Toddlers typically walk with a wide stance for added support and may not walk until age 2 or later. Speech may also develop later, with less body and facial expression and little nonverbal communication.

Use toys that make a variety of sounds. Talk more and help infants interpret their world. Make a conscious effort to motivate children with visual impairments to reach for and grasp and explore objects. Help them use both hands to explore. Knobs on puzzles make them easier for children with very low vision. Children with visual impairment need to be active in their world beginning in infancy, and they need your help with this.

they become larger and denser, they will inhibit vision. Children with severe, unilateral cataracts have the best prospects of developing binocular vision if cataracts are removed before six weeks of age (Birch & Stager, 1996).

Visual Perception

Visual perception
is the ability to interpret visible light information for planning and action.

Vision and visual impairments relate to visual acuity. **Visual perception** is concerned with the ability to interpret visual information, to plan and act. Infants and toddlers depend upon visual perception to keep track of people and objects, to reach for and grasp objects, and to move about their world.

Scanning Patterns. What do you see when you look at someone's face? Obviously, a face is typically composed of eyes, nose, and mouth. You have the ability to scan and integrate the entire face. Newborns are not as skillful as you are. They tend to get stuck (fixate) at a relatively predictable spot such as the chin or hairline of a face, the corner of a triangle or square, or the external contours of an object. Although his scanning is not well developed, the neonate can regulate his looking behavior and avoid looking at visual stimuli as well as fixating on an object. Newborns tend to scan horizontally because this requires fewer eye muscles. They prefer looking at a vertical pattern of black and white stripes. These colors have the highest contrast and the stripes are interesting for horizontal scanning.

At around two months, the scanning pattern changes and the infant scans more of the total picture. The infant now scans all the corners and sides of a triangle or square and is drawn to explore the internal contours of the face, primarily the eyes and mouth. At two months his ability to make complex visual discriminations improves dramatically; also he begins to remember these patterns. Researchers believe it is at this point that infants begin to look for meaning in visual stimuli. These changes are related to the maturation of the cortex of the brain.

Beyond the age of two months infants are increasingly interested in looking at more complex patterns. They become bored with stripes and find a checkerboard, a bull's eye, or a picture of a person or object more interesting. Too much complexity, such as a very small checkerboard, or lack of contrast will not sustain scanning.

WITH INFANTS AND TODDLERS

For infants (two to six months) choose a book of simple black-and-white designs such as *White on black, Black on white, What is that, Who are they?* by Tana Hoban. Or make one by cutting poster board or paper into six pieces measuring 8.5 by 11 inches. On page 1, using a marker, make a bulls eye in the center and draw three thick concentric circles around the bulls eye; on page 2, using a ruler, divide the poster board square into 1-inch squares and color alternating ones black; on page 3, using a ruler, divide the paper into 1-inch stripes and color alternating ones black; on page 4, using a ruler, divide the paper into 1-inch diagonals and color alternating ones black; on page 5, draw a smiley face with the wide side of the marker; on page 6, draw a distorted face (mouth where eye should be) or caricature of a face. Or generate a similar design on the computer. Put these in plastic sleeve protectors and make a book out of them by putting them in a three-ring binder.

Now, sit in a comfortable place such as a rocking chair with the infant in your lap and enjoy yourself. Hold the book so the baby can see it (about eight inches from his face) and watch to see whether he focuses on the bull's eye. If not, tap it lightly to draw his attention and say, "Look, that's a bull's eye." Then turn the pages and point out the salient characteristics of each picture. Talk about each picture as long as the infant looks.

Get creative and make additional distorted or stylized faces on the poster board, or use black-and-white pictures of people's faces. Remember: high contrast, simple patterns.

Visual Tracking. Ocular control is the ability of the eyes to track objects smoothly. Controlled eye movements are necessary to find and track moving objects, to scan a room, to sustain eye contact with a person, and to shift focus from one object to another. It takes newborns longer than older infants to find and focus on a moving object, and even then the movement of the object must be slow. Within these limits newborns can track. However, the process is jerky. By two months the infant's tracking is smooth and continuous, with some anticipation of where a movement is going.

By about six months the infant can easily accommodate various speeds. Like scanning, eye control starts on the horizontal plane (looking from side to side). An infant can follow a horizontal arc by about six months and by four to six months he can follow movement using just his eyes, without turning his head. By five or six months the infant is visually attracted to more distant objects (Furuno, O'Reilly, Hosaka, Inatsuku, & Zeisloft-Falbey, 1987).

Facial Perception. There is much debate about infants' desire to look at faces or "facelike" patterns at a very young age. This goes back to the nature/nurture question. Some feel that newborns are prewired to focus on faces in preference to other objects. Others feel that this interest in faces is a function of general maturation and not innate. As the infant increases in age, there is far more agreement about his actual behavior. Research suggests that by about two months infants can discriminate between a typical facial pattern and one in which the features (eyes, nose, mouth, and eyebrows) have been rearranged. Interestingly, infants prefer to look at attractive faces rather than unattractive faces, regardless of the race and age of the individual faces (Hoss & Langlois, 2003). By three months they can distinguish a picture of their mother or father from one of a stranger.

Spatial perception
allows infants and toddlers to deal with the dimensions and distances of objects and the relationship of objects in the environment.

Depth perception
is the infant's or toddler's judgment of the distance from himself to an object or place in space.

Accommodation
is the process by which the eye increases optical power to focus an object on the retina.

Spatial Perception. **Spatial perception** allows the infant to look at the spatial properties of an object, its dimensions, and the relationship between objects in the environment. **Depth perception** relates specifically to the distance between oneself and an object or place in space (Haywood & Getchell, 2005). Current indications are that depth perception has a variety of aspects and is not a single entity that appears at a particular time. Some aspects of depth perception begin to appear as early as one month of age. It is unclear whether depth perception develops as a function of experience, is governed by a biological timetable, or derives from some combination of the two.

Accommodation is the ability of the eye to bring objects that are at different distances into focus on the retina. Young infants may use this as a depth cue. Some research on depth perception focuses on looming. A looming object is one that keeps coming closer and looks as if there will be a collision. The clue

With practice children use their vision for depth perception and to accurately guide their hands and fingers.

is the perceived increasing size of the object as it gets closer (accommodation). Infants under one month of age generally stare at looming objects but do not blink. After one month some infants begin to blink (Nanez & Yonas, 1994), and by four months virtually all infants blink and move their heads backward as objects approach. This argues that the three-month-old infant has depth perception based on kinetic information. Motion-carried information is a fundamental aspect of the visual system early in life.

Despite the fact that we have two eyes, through a process called fusion we see one image. Fusion occurs when two images are aligned on the retinas in corresponding positions. Four months is a transition point in the development

Binocular vision
is vision in which both eyes are used together to focus on objects.

Stereopsis
is the sensation of depth based on the slight difference between retinal images from the eyes because of their horizontal separation.

of **binocular vision**. **Stereopsis** involves the comparison of small differences between the images in the two eyes, which results in depth perception. Stereopsis emerges between three and five months (Kavšek, 2003). Because the eyes are horizontally separated on the face, we see a slightly different image in each eye. Differences between these two images give clues to depth. Some aspects of depth perception are based on environmental cues or pictorial cues. These can be observed in both two- and three-dimensional objects. In a picture, if one person is much smaller than another the assumption is that the smaller person is "in the distance." This is not related to movement as in "looming," or to binocular vision, since even if you looked at the picture with one eye closed you would reach the same conclusion. The ability to relate size and distance develops between five and seven months. It is not exactly clear how it develops, but it seems that visual experience plays a part. Spatial and visual perception provides infants and toddlers with information about their environment. Their ability to perceive and process this information increases with age.

Hearing

Auricle
is the outer ear.

Middle ear
contains three ossicles, which amplify the vibrations of the eardrum.

Inner ear
is the bony labyrinth that contains the cochlea and vestibular apparatus.

Vestibular system
provides information about movement and orientation in space.

Eustachian tube
links the middle ear to the pharynx (throat).

The ear is the organ of the body that we think of when we think of hearing. However, there is rarely a problem with the outer ear, or **auricle**. The auricle is the only visible part of the hearing system. It is connected to the **middle ear** and the **inner ear**. It is one of the least important parts of the auditory system, although it does function to keep foreign objects out of the middle ear.

In addition to hearing, the ear serves two other functions: balance and responding to differences in pressure. The **vestibular system** is located in the inner ear. The **eustachian tube**, a slender tube that runs from the middle ear to the back of the throat, equalizes pressure on both sides of the eardrum. When we change altitudes, it is the clearing of the eustachian tube by swallowing or chewing gum that keeps the eardrum from bursting. The ears essentially duplicate each other; the major benefit of having two ears is the ability to localize sound.

Auditory Impairments

We can reliably test auditory function shortly after birth, and many states require that that it is tested before the newborn leaves the hospital. Parents may be concerned about a hearing loss, but it is hard to pin down; just when parents think they should be concerned, the infant does something to make them think they are imagining things. Most parents do not want to appear overprotective and look foolish to their pediatricians. In addition, many parents continually adjust to and match their infant's emerging skills. As infants respond to more visual communication efforts, parents automatically use more gestures and expressions. This facilitates the child's language but makes the assessment process more difficult. Children with mild or intermittent hearing impairments are difficult to identify at an early age.

Parents who note the problem usually do so because the child does not reach developmental milestones in the area of speech and language. Unless there are other disabilities present, hearing loss itself does not interfere with the attainment of physical milestones such as walking and exploring the environment. One concern is that parents and educators may interpret the child's unwillingness to take turns verbally, looking away when someone is talking, and not learning the rules that govern language as a behavior problem.

Infants with hearing impairments make noises and babble like other infants up until about five months of age. After five months babbling imitates the language spoken at home. This does not happen among children with hearing impairments. They do not respond to auditory stimuli that are out of their range of hearing. An infant with a severe auditory impairment would not wake to a loud noise or try to seek out the source of sounds. The infant may, however, respond to vibrations such as approaching footsteps, making parents doubt their concerns. Adults may not recognize auditory impairments because the child does what is requested, but this child may be responding to cues from other children, not because he understands the request. As requests become more complex, the difference often becomes evident, but the noncompliance may be mistaken for oppositional behavior or a behavior disorder (Herer, Knightly, & Steinberg, 2007).

Auditory impairments severely affect the development of speech and language skills. Both speech and language depend upon hearing in the early years of development. Children organize language through listening, imitation, practice, and correction.

Conductive Hearing Loss. Many infants and toddlers who experience frequent ear infections have periodic hearing losses because of the fluid in their ear canals. This fluid interferes with the conduction of sound waves from the outer ear to the inner ear and is hence called a **conductive loss**. **Middle-ear disease**, or chronic otitis media, is the build-up of thick fluid in the middle ear that does not drain through the eustachian tubes. Middle-ear disease (infection and fluid) is the most prevalent illness in young children after the common cold. The National Institute on Deafness and Other Communication Disorders (NIDCD) (2002) estimates that 75 percent of young children will experience at least one episode of otitis media by their third birthday and that half of these children will have had three or more ear infections. This thick fluid, a prime target for bacterial growth, causes a hearing loss of about 60 **decibels (dB)**. Antibiotics cure the infection, but the fluid may linger for days or even weeks, prolonging the hearing loss. Fluid in the middle ear is related to dysfunction of the eustachian tube. Because of the problem's intermittent nature, it can be

Conductive loss
is a failure to transmit sound waves through the outer ear and eardrum to the middle ear.

Middle-ear disease
or chronic otitis media, is an inflammation of the eardrum and a build-up of fluid or pus behind the eardrum in the middle-ear.

Decibels (dB)
is a measure of the power or intensity of sound.

missed even among children whose hearing is frequently tested. An infant with fluid build-up hears sounds as if he is underwater. An infant with excessive wax hears sounds similar to a person wearing ear plugs. Sound is heard in each case, but acuity is poor.

If the problem is treated, there are usually few long-term implications from occasional ear infections. However, children who have repeated bouts of otitis media are at risk for permanent hearing loss, poor acquisition of language skills, and learning disabilities.

OME
is a build-up of fluid in the middle ear with no symptoms of infection.

More subtle, and even more difficult to diagnose, is **otitis media with effusion (OME)**. This condition often follows infectious otitis media, but it occurs without the infection. This means the infant or toddler has a conductive loss but no signs of fever or pain. Some feel this is caused solely by the malfunctioning of the eustachian tube; others that it is related to allergies. In addition, there may be a long-term relationship with learning disabilities. There is enough evidence to warrant investigating the possibility of allergies being a cause and looking for learning disabilities in this population (Hurst, 2007). As an early childhood educator you need to be aware of this connection and talk with parents about it as a possibility.

Sensorineural losses
occur where there is damage to the inner ear (cochlea) or the nerve pathways from the inner ear to the brain.

Cochlea
is the sensory organ of hearing and is shaped like a shell.

Auditory nerve
goes from the inner ear to the brainstem and then to the primary auditory cortex in the temporal lobe of the brain.

Sensorineural Hearing Loss. Other hearing losses involve damage to the inner ear, the auditory nerve, or both. These are called **sensorineural losses**. In cases of sensorineural impairments, sound vibrations are properly transmitted through the outer and middle ear, but something happens to the sound within the **cochlea** or **auditory nerve** pathway. At least half of sensorineural hearing losses in children are caused by genetic factors. Infections in infancy and early childhood can lead to sensorineural impairments. Bacterial meningitis carries the greatest risk, but common viral diseases such as chicken pox, measles, and mumps can also cause hearing loss. For children with nongenetic hearing losses approximately one third have additional disabilities (Herer et al., 2007).

Hearing losses in infants and toddlers prevent them from hearing sounds accurately. Conversations may be muffled, and good language modeling cannot occur as the children cannot hear much of what is spoken. Children with conductive losses frequently omit initial and final sounds of words. Children with mild to moderate losses are usually delayed in the development of speech and language and may need specialized help with articulation. In addition to delays in expressive language, infants and toddlers with severe and profound losses will also have problems with receptive language.

Residual hearing
is the hearing infants and toddlers have without amplification.

Early identification and amplification for sensorineural losses is essential. Brain pathways for hearing are immature at birth and will develop only with stimulation. The use of amplification can allow educators and children to exploit **residual hearing** and to develop communication skills.

WITH INFANTS AND TODDLERS

Help infants and toddlers develop an auditory way of life. Develop auditory awareness by drawing attention to everyday sounds and identifying them (a dog barking, a bell ringing). Draw a child's attention to a sound source then say, "Oh look, someone is at the door." Help them associate sound with meaning. Make noise by banging cans together, using musical instruments, or in any way you can and talk about it.

Parents decide whether they want to augment auditory input with visual forms of communication, such as **American Sign Language** or **cued speech**. As an educator it is important that you support the child's developing communication skills. Be sure to get the infant's attention before you begin speaking by establishing eye contact. Support eye/hand coordination and work on this skill area. It may be one of the infant's strengths, and it is important because children also use visual cues to interpret their world. Use picture books with clear illustrations. This does not mean that you should not talk as if children cannot hear; it means that your language should be simple, with supportive gestures. Help infants and toddlers by concentrating on the development of visual and tactile skills to keep them in touch with their world. Help them use these skills to interact with peers.

American Sign Language is a system of visual signs that has its own grammar and syntax and is different from the spoken word.

Cued speech is a system that combines the use of manual hand shapes with information from the mouth and face to make spoken language visual.

Auditory Perception

We know that infants hear and that the auditory nerve is well myelinated at birth. The myelination of higher parts of the brain such as the auditory cortex will continue for several years. Researchers are interested not just in how well infants can hear but in whether they can detect differences in intensity and frequency and whether they have auditory preferences.

Studying an infant's auditory perception, like studying his visual perception, is challenging. Infants respond differently to sounds depending on the complexity of the sound itself, how suddenly it begins, and the pitch. Once the newborn's ears are cleared of fluid, he can hear sounds of about 40 dB. Since conversation typically is this loud or louder the infant can hear the human voice.

Infants have preferences regarding the frequency of noises they respond to. They appear to like low-frequency sounds (200 to 500 Hz), which, interestingly, are the same frequencies as the human voice. Infants between one and four months can discriminate among speech sounds (p, m, and b) (Doty, 1974). Researchers have found that infants prefer a human voice to silence and that they prefer their mother's voice to all other voices. They find very high and very low sounds distressing.

Localization is the ability to detect the location of a sound and is based on the difference in the timing of the sound reaching each ear (Haywood & Getchell, 2005). Researchers now agree that newborns turn in the direction of some sounds, which is a primitive form of localization. What researchers finally realized was that infants could in fact locate a sound when they were given 12 seconds to respond and were kept in a position where they could turn their head, and when the tone itself was produced by a rattle. The duration of the tone (1 to 20 seconds) did not seem to matter (Mehler & Dupoux, 1994). This ability to orient to sound appears to dropout at around two months and to be replaced by voluntary localization at about four months. The reason that it was so difficult to confirm these results experimentally was that researchers did not give infants enough time to respond and erroneously concluded they could not.

By the time toddlers are about 18 months old they are able to locate a sound source precisely. The interest in localization is spurred by curiosity about whether newborns know that sounds are typically made by objects and whether an infant turning his head to the source of a sound indicates an expectation of seeing a sound-producing object. Although there is evidence that infants have this knowledge by three or four months, it is not clear whether younger infants do.

Kinesthesis

Kinesthesis is the sensation of movement, position of the body and body parts, and tension in the body. The **kinesthetic** or **proprioceptive system** is different from the visual and auditory systems as the receptors for this system, unlike the eye or ear, are all over the body. **Proprioceptors** are located throughout the body and can be divided into two types: **somatosensors** and the **vestibular apparatus**. Somatosensors are located in the muscles, muscle-tendon junctions, the joint capsule and ligaments, and the skin and underlying tissue. Their use creates memories that are necessary for automatic, learned movements such as going up stairs (Williamson & Anzalone, 2001). This memory gives rise to statements such as "Even if it has been 15 years you never forget how to ride a bike." Provided, of course, that you could ride a bike 15 years ago and did so regularly. The vestibular system is located in the inner ear and responds to the movement of the head in relation to gravity (Haywood & Getchell, 2005). This system also regulates our sense of balance and equilibrium.

The proprioceptive system provides internal awareness of where the body is in space and in relation to other body parts: what we typically think of as body awareness. The tactile system is the largest sensory organ and covers the body and the external surface of the internal organs (Williamson & Anzalone, 2001). This is the first sensory system to develop in utero and the most mature

Kinesthesis
is the sensation of position, movement, and tension in parts of the body perceived through the nerves in the muscles, tendons, and joints.

Kinesthetic or **proprioceptive system**
provides information about the position of the body in space, the body's movements, the position of body parts relative to each other, and the nature of objects the body contacts.

Proprioceptors
are found in tendons, muscles, ligaments and joints and provide information to the brain about adjusting posture and movement.

Somatosensors
are receptors located under the skin, in the muscles, at muscle-tendon junctions, and in joint capsules and ligaments.

Vestibular apparatus
houses the receptors located in the inner ear.

at birth. Infants are born with sensitive tactile abilities. There are a variety of sensory nerve endings just below the surface of the skin whose purpose is to convert mechanical energy to electrical signals that go to the brain. Some reflexes, including the rooting and stepping reflexes, are elicited by touch.

Semicircular canals provide information about rotation of the head.

The vestibular **system is** composed of three structures: the **semicircular canals**, the **saccule**, and the **utricle**. These structures in the inner ear are connected to the **vestibular nerve** (Haywood & Getchell, 2005). The function of the three semicircular canals is to register the speed, force, and direction of head rotation. They do this by registering the movement of hair cells that are embedded in a gelatinous mass. The saccule and utricle are sensitive to gravity and linear movement. Information provided by the vestibular system contributes to balance and equilibrium and the infant's state of arousal. It plays a role in regulating muscle tone and coordination. Eye movements help to maintain a stable visual field when the body is in motion. The vestibular system helps keep focus on what is important (attention) and helps to regulate emotional state (Williamson & Anzalone, 2001). Through integration of motor responses and the reduction of automatic responses to tactile stimulation, the infant's primitive reactions to touch decrease.

Saccule and utricle sense linear acceleration and head tilt (gravity).

Vestibular nerve is part of the eighth nerve, which also carries auditory information to the brain.

Laterality is the understanding that the body has two distinct sides. Infants and toddlers cannot identify the right and left sides of their body; however, laterality and lateral dominance impacts brain development. As early as three months infants begin to demonstrate hand preferences. This is true when reaching for an object and also as they manipulate objects at about seven months.

Laterality is the awareness that ones body has two sides that can move independently.

Coordinating body sides is necessary for the development of a dominant hand and also for the hands to work independently of each other on a given task—for example, for one hand to hold the jack-in-the-box and the other to turn the handle. The ability of the infant to cross the midline of the body with his hands is an indication that this coordination is developing. Infants also show the coordination of body sides when they transfer objects from hand to hand or bang two blocks together. Although hand preference appears early, hand dominance is not firmly established until about age 4.

Kinesthetic Impairments

Young children with atypical tactile responses are a diverse group. Overall, the protective aspect of touch predominates over the discriminative component. This limits children's ability to acquire tactile discrimination (Williamson & Anzalone, 2001). Some infants display extreme forms of tactile defensiveness. For these infants, it is unpleasant or even painful to be touched or to receive any form of tactile stimulation. Eating can be a difficult task, as the defensiveness produces the bite reflex and the gag reflex and can result in an infant's refusal to eat.

Infants with physical impairments such as cerebral palsy may react with primitive reflexes when touched. These reactions interfere with normal motor movements. Atypical tactile development can also be part of some emotional/behavioral disorders. Toddlers with autism tend to find tactile stimulation very unpleasant and will often avoid situations that may result in touching. Other infants exhibit little sensitivity to touch. They do not feel pain. These children frequently have severe emotional problems or profound disabilities.

Kinesthetic Perception

The tactile system serves two functions: protection and discrimination. The protective function plays an important role in the attachment of the infant to her caregivers. The discrimination function of the tactile system develops over time. "We learn discrimination through the integration of deep pressure, light touch, coordinated motion, and precise localization of touch" (Williamson & Anzalone, 2001, p. 7). The fingertips have the most receptors. Infants respond to tactile qualities and explore objects differently depending upon whether the objects are soft or hard, rigid or flexible. One of the earliest concepts of the body's spatial dimension that is mastered is up and down; this is followed by front and back and, finally, side (Haywood & Getchell, 2005).

The gentle and respectful touching, handling, and nurturing that is part of caring for a young infant is pleasurable and also provides a foundation for positive emotional interactions (Williamson & Anzalone, 2001). The tactile system is responsive to the infant's state of arousal. If an infant is tired and irritable she may respond to touch as a threat. The same touch may be interpreted as affection if the infant is alert and rested (Williamson & Anzalone, 2001). The protective aspect of the tactile system is what makes us withdraw our hand quickly from a hot surface.

Body awareness requires the interpretation of sensations that come from the muscles and joints of the body. This is how you know what position your body is in without visually scanning yourself. Proprioceptive feedback is important in learning to control the body. It helps a young child know how much pressure he is exerting on an object. A young child with poor body awareness (proprioception) may break toys because he does not know how much pressure he is using when putting things together or pulling them apart. When the toddler is using tools he may press a crayon too hard or too softly because of lack of proprioceptive feedback or the ability to interpret the feedback about how his arm, hands, and fingers are moving. Proprioception also provides feedback about our internal body systems. This is the system that signals the brain that we are "full" after eating (Williamson & Anzalone, 2001).

Young children can over- or under-react to touch. Children who are hyposensitive may not feel pain from bumps and bruises and also may not be able to manipulate materials well. Children who are hypersensitive may avoid tactile input and not want to be held or cuddled and not participate in tactile activities such as sand and water play. Vestibular information helps to regulate attention as well as posture and balance. Children who do not process enough information about their own movements may have trouble maintaining balance and need to spend conscious energy just to sit in a chair. Those who process too much movement information may become fearful or overstimulated.

WITH INFANTS AND TODDLERS

Use mats or blankets made of various textured materials (satin, cotton, fake fur, velvet, terry cloth). Textured mats are also commercially available. To make a blanket, sew together squares of various materials. Nine squares of 12 inches each make a good-size mat (36 inches square).

Place the young infant on her stomach on the mat. If it is warm enough, have her in diapers. Let her explore independently with her hands and body while you talk to her. Ask her how it feels? Is it soft or rough? Then take a corner of the mat and stroke her hand with it and keep talking with her about the texture of the material and how it feels. Use a different corner for another texture. If the infant is not mobile place her in different positions on the mat so it is easier to reach other textures. Have young toddlers slowly walk across the mat barefoot.

Some infants might not like some of the textures, so go gently, using smooth, soft textures. You can also use unsewn fabric squares. Help the infant explore the fabrics and gently rub one piece of fabric on her arm and talk about how it feels.

Gustatory Sense

We know less about the senses of taste (gustatory) and smell (olfactory) than other senses. Newborns have an adequate number of taste buds for us to assume that they have a fairly well-developed taste sensation at birth. A variety of measures have been used to determine preferences in taste. Some researchers observe facial expressions, other sucking rates, and still others heart rate. The latter two seem to be the most reliable indicators.

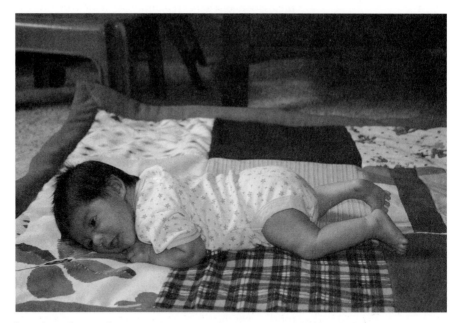

Providing infants with interesting textures gives them sensory feedback which is even better when there is something interesting to look at. It is a great way to enhance tummy time.

Gustatory Impairments

There is little information available regarding any disorders in the area of taste in infants. There are groups of infants who refuse to eat and others who decline any intake of fluids. Young infants spend a great deal of time mouthing objects they encounter in their environment, and the taste sensation may affect this activity.

GER
is a problem because the contents of the stomach come into the esophagus.

Gastroesophageal reflux (GER) is a problem for many infants. More than half of all infants experience reflux in the first three months of life, but most stop spitting up by 12 to 24 months (National Digestive Diseases Information Clearing House [NDDIC], 2006). Infants with GER may spit up, vomit, cough, be irritable, not want to eat, and have blood in their stools. It is difficult to diagnose, painful for the infant, and distressing for the parents. The problem is a plumbing issue. The ring of muscles at the bottom of the esophagus opens to release gas after eating. When this does not work properly, the contents of the stomach are not kept in the stomach. The stomach contents can move up into the throat. Some babies labeled as "colicky" may actually have GER. The most common problems of infants who are experiencing reflux are frequent vomiting, feeding problems, frequent awakenings, intense crying or bouts of screaming, and choking or gagging.

Interventions include such things as tilting the crib slightly so the head is higher than the foot and keeping clothing loose. If the infant is formula fed, change formula to ensure the infant is not allergic to the contents. A tablespoon of rice cereal may be added to expressed milk or formula. Holding the infant upright for 30 minutes after feeding is a possible solution. Medication may be used, but it is difficult to determine the appropriate medicine and dosage as most have been tested on adults. Most children without other developmental disabilities outgrow the symptoms.

Gustatory Perception

Infants can discriminate between sweet, acidic, salt, and bitter tastes and prefer sweet tastes. Newborns do not show a preference between water and a saline (salt) solution; around four to six months a preference begins to appear.

Olfactory Sense

Little is known about the infant's olfactory (smell) abilities, and most of the research has been done on neonates and has been reported in Chapter 3. Once it was determined that the sense of smell is well developed at birth and that infants are capable of discriminating between pleasant and unpleasant odors, most researchers lost interest in this area of research.

Olfactory Impairments

Since little is known about the infant's olfactory abilities, even less is known about any problems associated with this sensory ability. Learning is an important variable in reaction to different smells, and females may be more sensitive to odors than males.

Olfactory Perception

Infants show preference for fragrant odors and displeasure for noxious odors.

Researchers are curious about how infants perceive and integrate their world, but figuring out what infants do to make sense of their world is a challenge.

Sensory Integration

Our senses provide us with information about our environment. The role of the brain is to organize these sensations so they can be used to form perceptions, behaviors, and learning. Sensory integration involves putting it all together. Ayres (1979), a pioneer in sensory integration and an occupational therapist, used the analogy of eating. Food nourishes the body. However, just eating food is not enough, the food must be digested (for sensory information it is the brain that is important, not the stomach) and then distributed to the appropriate places in the body through the blood stream (nervous system).

Current research focuses more on some of the commonalities of sensation and perceptional rather than their differences. One aspect of development focuses on the infant's ability to self-regulate sensory integration and modulation. Williamson and Anzalone (2001) focus on four core abilities in behavioral regulation: arousal, attention, affect, and action. These processes interact and have a mutual regulatory function. Table 4–3 describes these core abilities.

Play engages infants and toddlers—not just their motor skills, but their brain. Crawling on a textured mat is fun for the first couple of times, but then infants need to crawl to obtain an object they desire or to get to a person who will hug them. Swinging is great, but if you want to activate the brain you have to put out your hand and see whether they can touch it with their foot. They need to line up cars to make a train, or take the train to the place on the track where "people" can board the train. The infant decides what is intriguing and fun; the adult, once the child has become comfortable with the skill, increases the complexity of the task. One of the best ways to increase complexity is to add different sensory stimuli.

It is the skill of an early childhood educator to be able to identify an infant's sensory-related behavior and their state and determine how to approach and play with each infant in the context of his own development. For some infants self-regulation is easy; for others it is challenging, and it is the skillful caregiver who can respond to each infant and tune in to their state.

Table 4–3 Core Abilities in Behavioral Regulation

- *Arousal* is the infant's ability to stay alert and to move or transition between different states of sleep and wakefulness. The ability to self-regulate in these states continues to be important throughout early childhood.

- *Attention* requires the infant to focus on a desired stimulus and to ignore other competing stimuli. For most infants the quiet alert state is the easiest one for them to attend, others may attend better in the active alert state. The aspect that is most important is the ability of the infant to sustain the state and to choose something to attend to for a short period of time. Infants and toddlers respond differently to sensory input. Some children may quiet to soft music others to being rocked or held; some to both, some to neither.

- *Affect* is the emotional aspect of behavior. Sensations elicit emotions. Some infants love to be tossed in the air and caught and respond with laughter, others scream in terror. Affect impacts social relations. If the child responds by screaming, the adult playing may decide to quit interacting with the infant rather than thinking about his arousal in the context of the level of interaction. Children who have unusual responses may make attachment difficult. Infants who stiffen when cuddled may not be cuddled and the opportunities for interaction may decrease. Children who have trouble regulating their sensory integration may feel anxious and withdraw from play situations or they may avoid sensory input.

- *Action* is infant's ability to engage in adaptive, goal-directed behavior (Anzalone, 1993). It requires the infant to organize perceptual and cognitive information and use that information in a goal-directed way. Action is more than just moving, it is purposeful. The best way to make actions purposeful and fun is play.

SOURCE: Williamson and Anzalone (2001).

SUMMARY

Early childhood educators need to view infant and toddler motor development in the context of the child, the family, and their environment. Their role is to motivate children to practice increasingly difficult developmental skills. Educators need to create a safe environment for infants and toddlers to explore. For young infants, this means bringing the environment to the infants. For mobile infants, it means arranging potential activities so children can make choices in a way that motivates them to use emerging skills. For toddlers, it means stimulating their curiosity while providing the scaffolding they need to comprehend and execute increasingly complex tasks.

Infants are born with all their senses operational. Over time they are able to fine tune these senses, regulate sensory input, and integrate the information that is received from different senses. Brain development is rapid and is use dependent. Sensory information that increases in complexity stimulates brain development.

CHAPTER IN REVIEW

※ Physical growth is most rapid during the prenatal period. However, physical growth and motor development over the first three years of life are phenomenal. There is no time in later life when the child will again grow at this rate.

※ Brain development is complex and involves cell differentiation and migration.

※ Neurons have an axon to send messages to other cells and dendrites to receive information.

※ Experience determines which synapses become part of the brain's permanent circuitry and which are pruned.

※ There are prime times for certain types of learning and development.

※ The plasticity of the brain allows it to process information in a variety of different ways. Early trauma can interfere with brain development and have life-long implications.

※ Infants are challenging to work with because of their behavioral states and their small repertoire of behaviors.

※ Growth is uneven, and some parts of the body grow at different rates than others. Although there are variations in *rates* of development, the *pattern* of development is relatively predictable.

※ Knowing and understanding patterns and principles of growth and development helps adults assess whether infants and toddlers are following typical patterns and allows them to plan environments that stimulate and match these emerging skills.

※ Researchers are interested in the infant's sensory abilities at birth and how these change. They are interested in understanding what the infant's world is like and how he makes sense out of it.

※ We know the most about visual and auditory perception.

APPLICATION ACTIVITIES

1. Sit in a place where you feel comfortable: a playground, a child care setting, a religious facility, or the eating area of a mall. Watch the infants and toddlers and see whether you can determine how old a particular child is on the basis of your observations of the child's size and motor development. Then, ask the parent or caregiver how old the child actually is. Continue watching to see how to refine your skills in this area.

2. Play with a young toddler (12 to 18 months) and try variations on creeping (different surfaces, over a pillow, etc.) and walking (furniture, holding one hand, two hands, pushing something, etc.). Play a fine motor game of exchanging blocks and putting them in a container, and then try having him mark paper with crayons. Note the energy involved and the quality of the movements. If possible, do the same activities with a child a year older and make a comparison of both the quality and quantity of their movements.

3. Go to a toy store and evaluate three toys for their usefulness in promoting fine or gross motor development in young children. Note the cost and the age range given on the box. Decide which, if any, of the materials you think are worth the price and give your rationale.

4. Explain to a parent what her infant's sensory capacities are and what type of stimulation the infant might like.

5. Explain to a parent why a one-month-old infant would find large newspaper headlines more interesting than the pastel prints that are typically used on crib sheets and baby blankets.

RESOURCES

Web Resources

※ The **Centers for Disease Control and Prevention** has developed growth charts for boys and girls as well as measures of body mass index. When you get into the site put in the words growth charts to look at how physical growth can be charted. http://www.cdc.gov.

※ **Gerber** hosts a web site for professionals which includes their journal *Pediatric Basics*. In volume 2007/116 the article on "Growing up to a new standard: WHO makes breastfeeding the norm" compares the growth charts from the CDC and WHO. http://www.gerber.com.

※ The **National Association for Sport and Physical Education** (NASPE) provides guidelines for physical activity for infants and toddlers. http://www.aahperd.org.

※ **Neuroscience for Kids** at the University of Washington is a great site for teachers and it is very useful in understanding the basics of the CNS. http://faculty.washington.edu.

※ The **Pathways Awareness Foundation** is a national non-profit organization dedicated to raising awareness about the benefit of early detection and therapy for infants and toddlers with motor delays. It provides information about children's physical development including a growth and development chart where you can track a child's physical, play and speech milestones from 3 to 15 months. www.pathwaysawareness.org.

※ The **Public Broadcasting System** provides information for parents on infants and toddlers. Focuses on how to make young children feel good about themselves and how to tell if they have special needs.

It is useful to see what sites focusing on parents are highlighting. http://www.pbs.org.

※ The **World Health Organization** has develop child growth standards and charts that are used to look at the growth of infants who are breast fed. These are used in many countries other than the United States. Put the words nutrition and child growth into the search engine to find their chart. http://www.who.int.

Print Resources

※ Gallahue, D. L., & Cleland-Donnelly, F. (2003). *Developmental physical education for all children* (4th ed.). Champaign, IL: Human Kinetics.

※ Gallahue, D. L., & Ozmun, J. C. (2002). *Understanding motor development: Infants, children, adolescents, adults* (5th ed.). New York: McGraw-Hill.

※ Haywood, K. M., & Getchell, N. (2005). *Life span motor development* (4th ed.). Champaign, IL: Human Kinetics.

REFERENCES

Al-Chalabi, A., Turner, M. R., & Delamont, R. S. (2006). *The brain: A beginner's guide*. Oxford, UK: One World.

Anzalone, M. E. (1993). Sensory contributions to action: A sensory integrative approach. *Zero to Three, 14*(2), 17–20.

Ayres, A. J. (1979). *Sensory integration and the child*. Los Angeles, CA: Western Psychological Services.

Bahrick, L. E., & Pickens, J. N. (1994). Amodal relations: The basis for intermodal perception and learning in infants. In D. J. Lewkowicz & R. Lickliter (Eds.), *The development of intersensory perception: Comparative perspectives* (pp. 205–234). Hillsdale, NJ: Lawrence Erlbaum.

Bertenthal, B., Campos, J., & Barrett, K. (1984). Self-produced locomotion: An organizer of emotional, cognitive, and social development in infancy. In R. Emde & R. Harmon (Eds.), *Continuities and discontinuities in development* (pp. 175–210). New York: Plenum Press.

Birch, E. E., & Stager, D. R. (1996). The critical period of surgical treatment of dense congenital unilateral cataract. *Investigative Ophthalmology and Visual Science, 37*, 1532–1538.

Chugani, H. (1998). A critical period of brain development: Studies of cerebral glucose utilization with PET. *Preventive Medicine, 27*, 184–188.

Clark, J. E., & Whitall, J. (1989). What is motor development? *Quest, 41*, 183–202.

Dennis, W. (1935). The effect of restricted practice upon the reaching, sitting, and standing of two infants. *Journal of Genetic Psychology, 47*, 17–32.

Dennis, W. (1938). Infant development under conditions of restricted practice and of minimum social stimulation. *Journal of Genetic Psychology, 53*, 149–158.

Dennis, W. (1941). Infant development under conditions of restricted practice and of minimum social stimulation. *Genetic Psychology Monographs, 23*, 143–191.

Dennis, W., & Dennis, M. G. (1940). The effect of cradling practices upon the onset of walking in Hopi children. *Journal of Genetic Psychology, 56*, 77–86.

Dennison, B. A., Edmunds, L. S., Stratton, H. H., & Pruzek, R. M. (2006). Rapid infant weight gain predicts childhood overweight. *Obesity, 14*(3), 491–499.

Doty, D. (1974). Infant speech perception. *Human Development, 17*, 74–80.

Fox, M. K., Pac, S., Devaney, B., & Jankowski, L. (2004). Feeding infants and toddlers study: What foods are infants and toddlers eating? *Journal of the American Dietetic Association, 104*(1), 22–30.

From the Editors. (2007). Growing up to a new standard: WHO growth charts make breastfeeding the norm. *Pediatric Basics*, 2007 (116). Retrieved April 21, 2007, from http://www.gerber.com/pediatricbasics/index.html

Furuno, S., O'Reilly, K., Hosaka, C., Inatsuku, T., & Zeisloft-Falbey, B. (1987). *The Hawaii early learning profile*. Palo Alto, CA: VORT Corporation.

Gallahue, D. L., & Ozmun, J. C. (2002). *Understanding motor development: Infants, children, adolescents, adults* (5th ed.). New York: McGraw-Hill.

Gesell, A., & Thompson, H. (1929). Learning and growth in identical infant twins: An experimental study by the method of co-twin control. *Genetic Psychology Monographs, 6*, S.5–S.124.

Haywood, K. M., & Getchell, N. (2005). *Life span motor development* (4th ed.). Champaign, IL: Human Kinetics.

Herer, G. R., Knightly, C. A., & Steinberg, A. G. (2007). Hearing: Sounds and silences. In M. L. Batshaw, L. Pellegrino, & N. J. Rosen (Eds.), *Children with disabilities* (6th ed., pp. 157–183). Baltimore, MD: Paul H. Brookes.

Hoss, R. A., & Langlois, J. H. (2003). Infants prefer attractive faces. In O. Pascalis & A. Slater (Eds.), *The development of face processing in infancy and early childhood*. New York: Nova Science Publishers, Inc.

Hurst, D. (2007). Middle ear disease and allergy: Why allergy? Retrieved April 25, 2007, from http://www.earallergy.com/

Jensen, E. (2006). *Enriching the brain: How to maximize every learner's potential*. San Francisco, CA: Jossey-Bass.

Kavek, M. J. (2003). Infants' perception of directional alignment of texture elements on a spherical surface. *Infant and Child Development, 12*, 279–292.

Keating, R., Spence, C. A., & Lynch, D. (2002). The brain and nervous system: Normal and abnormal development. In M. L. Batshaw (Ed.),

Children with disabilities (5th ed., pp. 243–262). Baltimore, MD: Paul H. Brookes.

Majnemer, A., & Barr, R. G. (2005). Influence of supine sleep positioning on early motor milestone acquisition. *Developmental Medicine and Child Neurology, 47*, 370–376.

Mandleco, B. L. (2004). *Growth and development handbook: Newborn through adolescent.* Clifton Park, NY: Thompson Delmar Learning.

McDowell, J. (2004). *The nervous system and sense organs.* Westport, CT: Greenwood Press.

McGraw, M. B. (1935). *Growth: A study of Johnny and Jimmy.* New York: Appleton-Century.

Mehler, J., & Dupoux, E. (1994). *What infants know: The cognitive science of early development* (P. Southgate, trans.). Cambridge, MA: Blackwell.

Miller, M. M., & Menacker, S. J. (2007). Vision: Our window on the world. In M. L. Batshaw, L. Pellegrino, & N. J. Rosen (Eds.), *Children with disabilities* (6th ed., pp. 137–155). Baltimore, MD: Paul H. Brookes.

Nanez, J., & Yonas, A. (1994). Effects of luminance and texture motion on infant defensive reactions to optical collision. *Infant Behavior and Development, 17*, 165–174.

National Digestive Diseases Information Clearing House (NDDIC). (2006). Gastroesophageal reflux in infants. Retrieved April 28, 2007, from http://digestive.niddk.nih.gov/ddiseases/pubs/gerdinfant/index.htm

National Institute on Deafness and Other Communication Disorders. (2002). Otitis Media (Ear Infection). Retrieved April 25, 2007, from http://www.nidcd.nih.gov/health/hearing/otitism.htm

Ong, K. K., Emmett, P. M., Noble, S., Ness, A., Dunger, D. B., & the ALSPAC Study Team. (2006). Dietary energy intake at the age of 4 months predicts postnatal weight gain and childhood body mass index. *Pediatrics, 117*(3), e503–e508.

O'Shea, M. (2005). *The brain: A very short introduction.* Oxford, UK: Oxford University Press.

Shore, R. (1997). *Rethinking the brain: New insights into early development.* New York: Family and Work Institute.

Skinner, J. D., Bounds, W., Carruth, B. R., Morris, M., & Ziegler, P. (2004). Predictors of children's body mass index: A longitudinal study of diet and growth in children aged 2–8 years. *International Journal of Obesity, 28*, 476–482.

Stockman, I. J. (2004). Introduction: The clinical problem. In I. J. Stockman (Ed.), *Movement and action in learning and development: Clinical implications for pervasive developmental disorders* (pp. 1–21). San Diego, CA: Elsevier Academic Press.

von Kries, R., Koletzko, B., Sauerwald, T., & von Mutius, E. (2000). Does breast-feeding protect against childhood obesity? *Advances in Experimental Medicine & Biology, 478*, 29–39.

Williamson, G. G., & Anzalone, M. E. (2001). *Sensory integration and self-regulation in infants and toddlers: Helping very young children interact with their environment.* Washington, DC: Zero to Three.

World Health Organization. (2007). Child growth and development. Retrieved April 21, 2007, from http://www.who.int/nutrition/topics/childgrowth/en/index.html

Yaun, A. L., & Keating, R. (2007). The brain and the nervous system. In M. L. Batshaw, L. Pellegrino, & N. J. Rosen (Eds.), *Children with disabilities* (6th ed., pp. 185–202). Baltimore, MD: Paul H. Brookes.

chapter 5

Cognitive and Intellectual Development

Chapter Outline

My husband and I were driving and I asked him what he thought our daughter's life is like inside my womb. I asked him, "Do you think she thinks about things? Do you think she has worries or expectations? Do you think she gets bored?" He was quiet for a couple of minutes. And then he smiled and said, "If there's a heaven, I think our baby's mind is in heaven listening to the angels. They're watching over her, keeping her company, and telling her about the new life that awaits her. I think her mind joins her body when she's born."

No matter what one believes a baby experiences in the womb, we know that most infants come into the world seeing, hearing, feeling, tasting, and smelling. What we are less sure about is how they construct meaning out of their world. Do they come "knowing," or must they interact with their environment to learn about it? Is this learning linear, incremental (where a bit at a time is added), or does knowledge sometimes spurt ahead and become qualitatively different from previous knowledge?

Cognitive processing changes during the first three years of life. The child progresses from the involuntary motor responses of early infancy to symbolic reasoning and abstract forethought. This is a giant cognitive leap for such a short period of time.

WHY STUDY COGNITIVE AND INTELLECTUAL DEVELOPMENT?

- Infant's experiences and learning determines how their brain will be wired and affects future learning.
- Understanding how infants and toddlers learn helps us to know the best ways to teach them.
- Understanding what infants and toddlers want to learn provides the basis for planning.
- Understanding theories about cognitive development impacts how and what we teach and when we teach it.

COGNITION

Cognition
is the ability to process information and apply knowledge.

The study of cognitive development has intrigued researchers for years. The act of knowing is called **cognition**. Cognition is the process of knowing in the broadest sense. It involves gathering information, categorizing this information, interpreting it, comparing it to previous information, and organizing it. Organization is critical for cognition; information and symbols must be organized so they can be retrieved in the future. Cognition involves a variety of other functions, including perception, memory, and learning. Cognition also involves nonmental processes such as personality, emotions, and social conscience. Cognitive researchers have focused on universals, rather than individual differences. The literature that does focus on individual differences falls in the area that is referred to as intelligence.

Intelligence
is the ability of an individual to change in response to the environment.

Memory
is the process of storing information for a short or long time.

Recognition
is identifying a known object or person.

Associative memory
connects information from several sources.

Recall
retrieves stored information.

Intelligence is the capacity of an individual to adapt to the environment. When one thinks of the characteristics of an "intelligent" infant or toddler, one typically thinks of a child who talks early, has a good vocabulary for his age, attempts to solve problems in interesting ways, is curious about the world around him, and adapts. Less intelligent children do not do these things as well. Intelligence is different from cognition in that it depends upon judgment and adaptation. Intelligence is therefore relative, depending upon the demands of varying cultures and the eras in which one lives. Researchers are interested in both the general aspects of intelligence as well as the specific ones. The latter part of this chapter focuses on intelligence.

Perception, as discussed in the previous chapter, is the aspect of cognition that involves organizing and interpreting sensory data. For perception to be effective you need memory. **Memory** is the mental process whereby information is stored for either a short or long time so that it can be retrieved. Without memory learning cannot occur. **Recognition** is the simplest form of memory and the aspect that is most used by very young infants. It involves recognizing a person or object that has been previously known. **Associative memory** involves connecting information about two events. Memory also involves **recall**—bringing back an experience without any cues. Recall is more complex than recognition because it requires the infant to think symbolically. Symbolic thinking apparently begins to occur about the time that an infant begins to use words, at about one year.

As you might guess, there are many different theories about how children learn about their world. These theories are becoming more complex. Theories, like knowledge, are not static. Theoretical modifications occur because of new information about growth and development and new insights by theorists. Theories are far more comprehensive, sophisticated, and relevant to the real world with real people than they have been in the past. Some theories overlap and find general points of agreement others do not. Some theories seem to have a central focus, such as cognitive development, yet also have implications for other areas, such as language or social development. Before looking at specific theories, there are some issues that all theories about early development must address.

Developmental Theories

Theories about development and issues related to these theories are changing. There was a time when theories were designed solely to help people think about issues in the field and were viewed as basic research. With increased interest in intervention and concern about the health and welfare of children, particularly as it is reflected in social policy, there is a renewed interest in applied research and theories that help focus research. Changing demographics have brought the question of the role of culture in development to the fore and have questioned the assumption of universals in cognitive and language development. Today's developmental theorists believe that some of the older theories (such as those by Piaget' and Freud') are too simplistic to explain the complexities of development that we now know about (Travers, 2006). Rather than present all of the developmental theories in this chapter, theories are presented in the chapter that most focuses on that particular area. For example, this chapter will include information about Piaget, but not Freud or Erikson. These theories will be addressed in the chapters on emotional development and social development.

Piaget was one of the first theorists to focus on cognitive development. He presented information that challenged how researchers had previously thought about cognitive development. Beginning in the 1970s, the field moved from validating (or not validating) Piaget's work to focus more on **metacognition**. He was concerned not just with what children know but with looking at the process of thinking they used in learning situations, such as how they approached tasks and how they figured out what they were learning. Beginning in the 1980s and continuing into the present, there is more of a focus on a theory of mind. We are interested in finding out how children not just think but also understand different activities related to the mind, such as memory, dreams, and imagination, as well as how children learn to understand that other people think and that they can understand what others think (Flavell, 1999).

Universal to Unique

The decision to focus on universals has affected not only the cognitive domain but language as well, and has taken the focus away from individuals and their families and the impact of culture and onto the "common" aspects of development. With the focus on what all children do, we have missed some important aspects of development that are unique to children or groups of children. The focus on the universal aspects of cognition that has been the focus of most cognitive theories about infants and toddlers has not taken into account how infants and toddlers acquire other knowledge, such as that about their **race**, **culture**, and **ethnic identity**.

The goal of **cross-cultural studies** is to provide information about the universals in child development; that is, the degree to which behavior patterns, values, beliefs, and products of a particular cultural group are similar and to what degree they are unique, culturally specific.

There is also knowledge that is discipline based. The discipline that you are currently studying is an aspect of child development. Many individuals have

Metacognition
looks at the process of thinking—thinking about thinking.

Race
refers to a category of people who share physical characteristics, such as skin color, that people feel are socially important.

Culture
refers to the behavior patterns, values, beliefs, and products of a particular group of people that are passed from generation to generation.

Ethnic identity
is a sense of group membership based on an individual interpretation of these variables.

Cross-cultural studies
compare children from one culture with children from other cultures.

no course work on and little academic knowledge about infants and toddlers, regardless of their cultural background. Others may have advanced degrees with infancy as a specialty. We know little about this specialized kind of knowledge and how it is acquired. Even within disciplines at an idiosyncratic level, it is not at all clear why some physicians become surgeons and others neurologists. Child prodigies are the most striking examples of idiosyncratic cognitive development. They move through the stages of development in the predicted pattern, but at an extraordinarily rapid rate (Feldman & Snyder, 1994). Cognitive theories in general are not concerned about, nor can they explain, unique cognitive achievements. Their focus has been on the universal, not the unique aspects of cognitive development.

Theories of Cognitive Development

This section focuses on the most influential cognitive theories. They include the theories of Piaget and Vygotsky, as well as theorists who have expanded on these theories—neo-Piagetian and neo-Vygotsky views. It also includes less-detailed reviews of other theories that have affected the field.

Piaget's Theory

Jean Piaget was a pioneer in studying cognitive development in young children. His work dominated the field for many years. Piaget's theory provides a great deal of information about cognitive development during infancy and toddlerhood; many later theorists compare their principles and findings to his. Piaget called himself a **genetic epistemologist**, because he studied the basis of knowing, or cognition. He concluded that cognitive development (the growth of the child's thinking skills and abilities) encompasses a complex variety of factors and variables that affect development. Although later scholars challenge parts of his theory, there is no doubt that he changed our view of infants.

Piaget believed that cognition is a dynamic, constructive process in which the infant affects the other people in her environment and they influence her. He viewed the infant as an active player in her own development. The child gains information about the world she lives in by actively interacting with it (Piaget, 1970). Researchers today see infants and toddlers as even more competent than Piaget theorized (Mandler, 2003; Moore & Meltzoff, 2004).

Piaget's theory about how children learn is considered a **constructivist approach**. He believed that children are actively searching and discovering information and hence they construct their view and knowledge of the world (Hulit & Howard, 2006). His underlying assumption was that problem solving is the basis for learning, thinking, and development. As infants and toddlers

Genetic epistemologist studies the development of knowledge and also applies developmental and historical knowledge to what is known.

Constructivist approach assumes the child is an active learner who, through interaction with the environment, solves problems and constructs and reflects on what is learned.

interact with their world and solve problems and figure out the consequences of their actions, they reflect on what has happened and construct their understanding of the process. Learning is an active process, not a passive one, and it requires a change in the infant or toddler. Piaget believed that infants and toddlers understand the knowledge they construct on a far deeper level than what they have been told. Some early childhood education programs use this approach as a basis of planning for young children.

Piaget made very careful observations of the behavior of his own three children as well as other Swiss children. From these observations he developed a theory about how infants learn. His writing recast the infant in the role of an active participant and problem-solver in his world. He focused on aspects of infant learning that others had not considered. He reached two conclusions that greatly influenced his work, and hence the entire field. The first is that children's mistakes are more interesting than their correct answers in understanding how children think. The second is that children must be understood from their point of view rather than that of an adult, and that it is possible to ascertain that point of view. Piaget focused on the universals in behavior and used stages as a way of describing how knowledge changes over time.

Piaget's goal was to use his observations to understand how infants define concepts that are precise, logical, and consistent. This goal not only influenced what he observed, but how he then organized his observations and made sense out of them. Present views of cognitive development are broader than this one aspect of cognition and are more context-bound; that is, researchers today are more reluctant to make broad generalizations from limited specific information. They believe that there are consistencies, but that they are loose and general and that specific behaviors must be viewed in context.

Piaget emphasized that cognitive development, like motor development, occurs in a recognizable and predictable progression, and that later development is based on the information the child learns during earlier stages of development and interactions (Piaget, 1963 [1952], 1970). He believed that the child's cognitive development begins at birth, and that cognitive growth is a function of consistent interactions with the environment. The majority of an infant's early behaviors are sensory and motor. Piaget's theory is detailed below with some later modifications and challenges noted. As you read Piaget's theory, keep in mind that his first passion was biology. Some of the terms he uses to describe processes are based on this background. His early study of mollusks led him to believe that not only genetics but also environment affects outcomes. Piaget was a gifted child who published his first paper at age 10 and had his doctorate 21. By that time he had published 25 professional papers (Wadsworth, 1971).

Components of Piaget's Theory

Piaget (1970) divided cognitive development into stages of intellectual growth that have learning processes. He described the key components of his learning paradigm. They are detailed below.

A **schema** is a concept or a mental category. The plural of schema is **schemata**. Children develop patterns of behavior, or schemata that function as organizing responses to environmental interactions. A schema develops as an organized behavior pattern is repeated frequently. Infants have a sucking schema. The young infant may first suck on a breast or bottle, then a pacifier or finger. As the infant adapts to these different objects the sucking schema is expanded and modified. The infant abstracts the commonalities in the sucking into a mental representation of sucking that is a schema. Infant schemata are based on sensory-motor actions. As the infant's opportunities to interact with different materials widens and he practices skills and modifies them, he progresses to higher levels of learning or cognitive activity.

A schema, then, is a mental representation, or intellectual structure, referring to a particular behavioral action sequence. Schemata are organizations of elements or ideas that are coherent, adaptive, and purposeful. Networks of schemata are developed that guide what the infant perceives and how he interacts with his environment. With increasing age, schemata become based on mental activity as the child develops knowledge from concept formation, reasoning, language, and symbols.

Think about a schema as a file folder on your computer. When your computer is new, the folder is empty. As you begin to use your computer, you file information in this file folder and the files fill up in an organized fashion, or schema.

Infants and toddlers come to know their world through experience and active participation. Their minds funnel information into the brain for processing (**assimilation**). All knowledge is connected with an action, and assimilation provides the basis of meaning. For example, an infant grasps all rattles the same way regardless of their size or shape. This grasping information is treated as "old" knowledge. That is, the child will use the same grasping motion for a cube that he did for a rattle. If the result is too divergent from his "old" knowledge, he will ignore it. He can make minor changes and adjustments but not major ones. Likewise, requiring the infant to stretch to reach the rattle provides slightly different information, setting the stage for accommodation.

Going back to our computer analogy, it quickly becomes apparent that this one folder is becoming unwieldy, so you might create subfolders to keep the information organized. You might start with a folder called infants and

Schema
is a mental concept or category that refers to a particular behavioral sequence.

Schemata
are mental concepts that grow and evolve through function.

Assimilation
is the process of taking in information for a schema or concept.

This toddler has developed a variety of schemata for grasping.

toddlers. This works for a little while, but then you decide that you want activities for infants and toddlers in a different place than your developmental information because this folder has gotten so big that you cannot find the activities you are looking for. So you create a subfolder. What happens when you want to file information that focuses on adolescents? Granted, adolescents are children, sort of, but they really are not infants and toddlers. You obviously need to create a new folder, this is accommodation.

Accommodation occurs when new information necessitates restructuring what was already learned. If the child cannot efficiently grasp the block using the previous pattern, then the child has to adjust. Accommodation is an inner reality. One might think of assimilation as a process of generalization, and accommodation more as a process of discrimination. If the information or

Accommodation
is the process of changing a schema or concept based on new information.

WITH INFANTS AND TODDLERS

If infants are to develop schemata and the goal is to have these serve as a solid foundation for the infant to build on, then we must think of ourselves as schemata builders. Let us think about a simple schema, like grasping. What are the principles involved in grasping? Begin with the obvious: size, shape, weight, and texture. In the classroom this means that we need to ensure that as infants are grasping different objects, we have varied the characteristics of these objects in a way that will allow the infant to develop a solid schema of grasping. He will have had the opportunity to grasp objects that are small, medium, and some so large that they require two hands; some of the shapes have corners, others are round, some even have holes in the middle; some are as light as feathers, others weigh so much they require concentration; some may be slippery and even slimy while other are rough and gnarly. All of these are objects the child has an interest in. This is how schemata are developed.

Adaptation
is the infant's new level of understanding based on enriched concepts or schemata.

requirements are too divergent, then no accommodation occurs. The process of assimilation and accommodation builds new schemata.

Assimilation and accommodation are separate yet complementary processes that result in new levels of adaptation. **Adaptation** involves change and is an ongoing process. An infant might develop two different styles of grasping based on his experience; that is, he might develop different grasps depending on the shape and size of what he is grasping.

Using the assimilation, accommodation, and adaptation sequence, Piaget concluded that the key to cognitive development is an environment in which there is a variety of similar, but not identical, experiences. This limited variety allows the child to assimilate past experiences. He then accommodates a new experience (if it is not too divergent from his past experience), and he develops a new level of adaptation that expands his repertoire of behavior. The next key to cognitive development is organizing knowledge in a meaningful way.

This analogy looks at a child who is learning related information over time with the ability to process the incoming information (assimilation) and to categorize it in the appropriate place. But what happens to the toddler if we bombard him with information about "green?" Not related information, like in the previous paragraph, but we just dump every green idea we have on him? It is likely that he will assimilate this information (provided we do it in a developmentally appropriate way). However, there will be so much new information that we throw the child's learning out of balance. The child's schemata will be so broad that he will be unable to categorize it. The opposite would happen if we

WITH INFANTS AND TODDLERS

Think about dramatic play in a toddler classroom. It is often a home setting. Good teachers know they need to start with experiences that are real for toddlers if they are to learn from the setting. A house in the dramatic play area is different from the toddler's house, but there are enough similarities that toddlers can construct new knowledge and "file" it. Field trips influence what toddlers find interesting and affect this assimilation-accommodation-adaptation sequence.

Let us say a toddler learns that green things outside are called plants. He also learns that there are different types of plants—some you can eat, some that hurt, and some that look pretty. Finally, he learns that different kinds of plants also have specific names (cactus, fern) that distinguish one plant from another. In each case, the child adapts previously learned information into a new, ever-expanding category of information.

Equilibrium
is a condition in which the competing influences of assimilation, accommodation, and adaptation are in balance.

Equilibration
is the process of building and maintaining balance.

focused solely on green plants. The toddler would accommodate the new information, but the schemata would be narrowly defined and the commonalities would not be apparent (Hulit & Howard, 2006). Teaching matters, it is not just common sense. It is based on evidence.

Learning is a result of interacting with the environment. Infants acquire new information by experimenting with materials and objects. Active learning is essential for the infant to practice and refine previously learned skills and to acquire new schemata. To do this toddlers need appropriate materials to experiment with. These materials must match their level of sensorimotor development. Piaget believes that children need a wide range of experiences in order to learn. What the infant learns about the world comes from physical experience and they acquire this knowledge through active participation.

Central to Piaget's theory is the understanding that assimilation, accommodation, and adaptation exist together in a balanced state called **equilibrium**. Equilibrium is dynamic; it requires almost constant recalibration and adjustment. The process of building and maintaining equilibrium is called **equilibration**. The interaction of assimilation and accommodation constantly changes the level of adaptation, which requires more complex organization and produces a new state of equilibrium. As the infant interacts with her environment, she must constantly reinterpret reality, therefore requiring new adaptations.

However, there are times when the infant or toddler begins to see things differently and things no longer fit into the old pattern and require significant reorganization. The first of these times is about 18 to 24 months, when the toddler moves from simpler sensorimotor-based schemata to the use of symbols.

Stage-Based Development

Piaget's theory is stage based. Each sequence or stage in development is a prerequisite to the next. Qualitative changes in the child's cognitive abilities occur as the child progresses through these developmental stages. Piaget divided the child's cognitive development into four stages. Each stage is identified and characterized by the occurrence of specific cognitive processes. The four stages are the sensorimotor stage, the preoperational stage, concrete operations, and formal operations. Stages are not independent, but more cumulative and integrated. Infants and toddlers are in the sensorimotor stage and the beginning of the preoperational stage.

Sensorimotor Stage (Birth to 2 Years). Piaget called the first stage of development the sensorimotor stage. Infants exploring their world with their senses and motor activity characterize this stage. This usually takes place from birth until about two years. Piaget did not emphasize age levels but rather emphasized the qualitative difference in cognitive abilities that occur in each stage or substage. He identified six individual substages in this stage. The end of the sensorimotor stage is marked by the emergence of symbolic functioning—that is, the ability of the infant to mentally represent events and objects and to solve problems through mental activity (Lamb, Bornstein, & Teti, 2002). The first two years of life create the need as well as the capacity for mental representation. At the end of this stage infants can link present experiences to past ones; they use their memory and perception of objects, people, movements to solve problems.

Newer research has proposed changes to Piaget's six stages of sensorimotor development and identified four states that are based on both behavioral changes observable in the infant as well as changes that occur in the brain itself. Noted are the significant changes in brain waves, sleep cycles, and perceptual abilities that coincide with behavioral changes noted at transition points at 3, 8, 12, and 18 months (Daws, 2000; Kellman & Banks, 1998; Nelson, 2003). The characteristics of the sensorimotor stages and the skills acquired in each stage follows.

Substage 1: Reflexes (Birth to 1 Month)

Reflexes such as sucking, crying, and grasping undergo assimilation and accommodation as the infant practices these skills. This is the origin of mental development. Later research does not view the infant as being so dominated by reflexes. The neonate's visual scanning, response to sound, taste preferences, and memory for smell suggest he is more capable and complex than Piaget thought (Aguiar & Baillargeon, 2002; Lou & Baillargeon, 2005). At birth and during the first three substages of the sensorimotor stage, the infant is

Egocentrism
is looking at the world as an extension of one's self.

egocentric. **Egocentrism** means the child sees and understands the world as an extension of himself. He does not understand that he is different from his mother or objects in this environment (Hulit & Howard, 2006).

Substage 2: Primary Circular Reactions (1 to 4 Months)

The infant's reflexes begin to come under voluntary control as cognitive abilities modify reflexes. Primary means first; circular reactions are repeated sequences of behavior, such as sticking the tongue out or thumb sucking. These are primary circular reactions because they do not require external objects. They involve the infant's body, and the infant's focus is on the action sequence, not on the object. The goal seems to be the repetition of the behavior sequence, not exploration of the object. Over the three months of this stage these primary circular reactions seem to become easier, requiring less concerted effort.

Unplanned interactions with the environment, combined with reflexive actions, lead the infant to continue the actions. Through this repeated practice a new skill is learned. An infant who accidentally hits a toy with his arm and sets it in motion may continue to make such arm movements. Through repetitive swiping actions, the arm movements become more accurate. Infants are curious; they imitate behaviors and vocalizations of others who imitate them. If the infant utters a sound and an adult imitates this sound, the infant will often repeat the sound. Some researchers believe that the infant cannot distinguish between herself and others at this stage of development, so that the infant really is not imitating at all but merely continuing a circular reaction. Others believe that this is true imitation (Meltzoff, 1999; Meltzoff & Prinz, 2002; Nadel & Butterworth, 1999).

The third aspect of this stage is typified by the gains in coordination and integration. Infants now know that objects can be explored in a variety of modalities. The infant turns her head to look at an object that makes interesting sounds. When the infant hears her mother, she also expects to see her. She now reaches for interesting objects to explore.

Substage 3: Secondary Circular Reactions (4 to 8 Months)

Secondary circular reactions begin as infants purposefully explore objects to see what happens, rather than merely for motor action. An infant shakes a toy and it rattles, the infant makes it rattle again and again. Secondary implies that the reaction is elicited from something in the environment other than the infant herself. When a new toy is offered the infant tries out all her available schemata: the toy is sucked, banged, grasped, dropped, shaken, and so on. If the child becomes intrigued with one of these schemata it is repeated. Infants begin to imitate simple actions, but only those actions they can see or hear; for example, hand waving or babbling (Miller, 2002).

Object permanence
is knowing that an object exists even when it is not in sight.

The first signs of object permanence occur during this stage. **Object permanence** is the knowledge that an object exists even when it cannot be

WITH INFANTS AND TODDLERS

Young infants can only imitate actions already in their motor schemata and that they can see themselves producing. Do you remember the "O" game? Make your mouth in the shape of an "O" and say "Oh" to an infant in substage two. Keep at it and see if she will imitate you. Or, try sticking out your tongue. Can she imitate you? What would Piaget say? Most researchers found that infants in substage 2 (one to four months) could imitate tongue protrusions (Meltzoff & Moore, 1997; Nadel & Butterworth, 1999).

seen. For example, if a toy is hidden with a portion showing from under the cover, the infant will search and may find the object. But if the toy is completely hidden, the infant loses interest in the object and will not search for it.

Substage 4: Coordination of Secondary Circular Reactions (8 to 12 Months)

Infants coordinating secondary schemata characterize this stage. The infant shows true "means-end" behavior. He moves a toy out of the way (means) to get to a favorite doll (end). The infant who jostles an adult's leg to continue the horsey ride, or pulls the adult's hands together to continue a pat-a-cake game, or holds up his arms to get picked up, understands this concept. Infant's imitation skills improve. She can now begin to imitate new sounds and facial gestures; late in this stage single words appear. The infant's ability to remember that toys and other items still exist when they are out of sight improves. The infant will search for objects he sees hidden. He begins to show distress when he searches for something and it is not there. Yet, if the object is not where he initially searched for it, he stops looking.

The learning that takes place around eight months is characterized by a change from accidental discovery to intentional behavior. The focus is on objects as opposed to self. Objects are significant as they mark the infants' knowledge of the differentiation of self and objects, and that objects can be acted on in intentional ways. Researchers struggle to understand the dimensions of object permanence and try to understand why infants this age show only partial object permanence. Piaget believed that infants stop searching because they think that the object no longer exists. Others offer different explanations: Perhaps the infants get "stuck" on one aspect, such as the location of where the object disappeared; perhaps it is a memory problem, or even that the infant has no other behaviors in his repertoire to call upon.

Overall, research confirms that initial indications of object permanence occur at about 4 months, and major improvements occur at approximately

8 and 12 months. It also seems clear that situational variables related to the objects themselves—what they are covered with, where they are placed, and the response required of the infant-influence infants' reactions (Aguiar & Baillargeon, 2002; Lou & Baillargeon, 2005).

Substage 5: Tertiary Circular Reactions (12 to 18 Months)

The circular (repetitious) quality of the past continues, but the tertiary stage involves first experimentation and then variation. Entirely new ways of doing things are learned through active experimentation. This is the "what if" stage. Mobile infants manipulate and explore materials to solve problems. They repeat actions and modify their behavior to see what happens. Problem-solving abilities are refined but still involve trial and error rather than forethought. Causal thinking is developing. Mobile infants search in new places for hidden objects but still need to watch the object being hidden to look for it. They build entirely new schemata during this stage. Mobility opens up new arenas for learning. As memory improves, children can learn from watching an event. With the advent of language, the mobile infants can and do ask questions.

A move from intentional behaviors to more systematic exploration and a more mature understanding of object permanence marks the transition to the next substage. Mobile infants use their entire repertoire of behavior to explore their environment.

Substage 6: Beginning of Thought (18 to 24 Months)

This is a transitional substage between the sensorimotor and preoperational stages. It is the stage of symbolic representation. Toddlers can now solve problems in their mind without going through the actual external problem-solving process. They can mentally represent objects and actions and invent new means to get objects without using trial and error. They can imitate models that are not present; wave "bye-bye" even if no one is waving back. A toddler can imitate gestures she cannot see herself make, such as scrunching up her face. She can search without needing to see the objects hidden. Pretend play begins!

This transition marks the shift in cognitive development from the sensorimotor orientation of infancy to the symbolic thinking that characterizes early childhood. Symbolic thinking allows the toddler to mentally represent, manipulate, and combine information, objects, and events. Growing memory skills allow the toddler to call upon past experiences to solve present problems. The challenges of object permanence are conquered as toddlers know that objects exist whether they are hidden or removed.

By 18 months, the toddler is capable of deferred imitation; that is, imitating an action seen in the past. Piaget believes that imitative ability is part of cognitive development. He sees imitation as a way of learning new behaviors. Once imitation has developed, he sees the process as primarily one of accommodation. When the infant imitates behaviors that are not part of his repertoire, accommodation takes place, then adaptation.

WITH INFANTS AND TODDLERS

Get an infant intrigued with a toy. Partly cover the toy with a cloth. Encourage the infant to find the toy. If he does not attempt to find it, point to the toy and again encourage him. If he still does not find it, take the cloth off, dramatically saying, "Here it is!" Play the game again. If he finds it when it is partially covered, cover it completely with a cloth and encourage the infant to find it.

As infants and toddlers become more competent, add an additional cloth. Again, start with a toy that intrigues the infant. Hide it quickly under one cloth, then move it to hide it under a second cloth (while the infant is watching), covering the toy completely. Initially, expect that the infant will hunt under the first cloth and then perhaps go to the second. Give verbal support for the search.

Experiences such as these support infants in developing the concept of object permanence. The concept has many aspects, so infants need increasingly challenging experiences to develop the concept fully.

It may now occur to you to ask, "So what? Who cares? Why should we be so concerned about imitation or object permanence?" Fundamentally, the issue is whether or not infants construct their own reality, as Piaget believes, or whether they are born with some innate knowledge. In addition, developmental information about imitation and modeling has direct relevance to working with infants. Knowing that infants imitate behaviors that are at, or just above, their cognitive level facilitates developmentally appropriate planning.

Preoperational Stage (2 to 7 Years). Piaget sees this as a major change in cognitive functioning. The toddler is no longer tied to a sensorimotor representation of the world. The child can now think using mental representations, or use symbols to represent the environment. The most obvious transition to this period is the rapid acquisition of language (Dapretto & Bjork, 2000; Miller, 2002). Words take on the form of signifiers of objects and events.

Thoughts are egocentric, with symbolic imagery highly individualized. The egocentrism in this stage differs from the sensorimotor stage. However, two-year-olds cannot yet take a perspective other than their own, and assumes that everyone likes what they like. Understanding of the concepts of past, present, and future begins to take shape. However, two-year-olds still have trouble seeing how steps of a project fit together to make a whole. They see each step of a process as separate. The child's play skills expand into more creative activities. Although two-year-olds have advanced far beyond the sensorimotor-based learning of the previous stage, their thought processes are still immature. Some of the significant changes that occur during this period are detailed below.

As children move from the sensorimotor period into the preoperational period their ability to use symbols increases as does their ability for pretend play.

Two-year-olds are just emerging into this five-year-long period. Consequently, many of the characteristics of the period will not be obvious.

Preoperational Themes. The preoperational stage also has themes that appear with developmental variation. These themes include egocentrism, centration, irreversibility, transductive reasoning, and concept formation. Each of these themes is detailed.

     Egocentrism. Unlike the egocentrism of the young infant who could not differentiate himself from his environment, at this stage two-year-olds are not able to view things from another's perspective. Their language reflects this egocentrism. Two-year-olds seem to believe that others know what they are thinking and they leave out important pieces of information. On the other hand, they cannot put themselves in another's place to figure out the strategies that someone else might use in a game or in problem solving.

⁂ **Centration**. This concept typifies the ability to concentrate on only one attribute of an object at a time. To solve problems successfully, children must be able to attend to many attributes of an object at the same time. The preoperational child's centration in thinking does not allow her to think of multiple attributes simultaneously. If presented with a liquid in a tall narrow glass that is then poured into a short fat glass, she will assume that the volume has changed even if she watched the pouring. Because young children focus on appearances, they may be frightened by people wearing costumes or those who dress up as holiday or cartoon characters, even if they watch them put on the costume. They do not realize that someone can simultaneously be two things and they overwhelmingly center on visual appearance.

⁂ **Irreversibility**. The preoperational child is not aware that logical operations are reversible. She is not aware that the ball of clay made into a pancake can be "reversed" into the original ball of clay. The knowledge that shape does not affect mass, volume, and so on is called **conservation**. Conservation requires that a child focus on the transformation from state to state in relation to mass, length, number, volume, and area. Of these, number appears first, but that is long after the child is three years old.

⁂ **Transductive Reasoning**. Logical reasoning requires the child to use both inductive (from specific to general) and deductive (from general to specific) reasoning. Transductive reasoning requires the child to recognize the stable commonalities of attributes despite perceptual changes.

⁂ **Concept Formation**. With the emergence of logical thought, children's problem-solving and decision-making abilities change dramatically. They can put events and objects in some useful order. They begin to understand the concepts of class (animals) and subclass (dogs) and the relationship between these.

Conservation
is the knowledge that a quantity remains the same (if nothing is added or taken away) despite the containers, shape, or size.

Conclusions about Piaget's Theory

Piaget was a pioneer whose work laid the foundation for later research. However, researchers today do not see Piaget's stages as being as "tidy" as he described, nor do they see the demarcations between stages as being so clear-cut.

There seem to be more shades of gray and variations on themes. Some researchers think children can exhibit different levels of maturity in different developmental areas, so they could be in different substages depending on the focus. The stages provide a useful way of organizing information. Their qualitative significance is not as well documented as the progression of development that they portray.

Today there are many studies with many variations to compare and contrast to Piaget's work. Overall, the conclusion is that some essential and basic cognitive skills appear earlier than Piaget predicted. However, when skills first appear they may not be useful in helping the infant understand her world. These findings are really not problematic, because one can simply adjust the ages. What is more important is the underlying assumption about *how* development occurs. Piaget's theory supports the proposition that children need to be actively engaged in their environment to learn. Some feel that infants come pre-wired to do certain things; that is, there is a genetic base for imitation and object permanence. Others feel that infants can also learn through watching and listening, not just by doing. Overall, Piaget's theory has generated a tremendous amount of interest and research in very young children. It provides a framework for understanding how children develop cognitively and can provide guidance in deciding what activities are appropriate for what age child.

Vygotsky and Neo-Vygotskian Theory

Jean Piaget and Lev Vygotsky believed that children actively participate in their own learning. However, their views of how this learning comes about are different. Piaget believed that children independently construct their cognitive world. In contrast, Vygotsky believed that a child's cognitive development was dependent on her environment and her culture; Piaget is the constructivist, and Vygotsky is the socioculturalist.

Both Piaget and Vygotsky were born in 1896. Vygotsky, a Russian developmental psychologist, died in 1934, at age 37, from tuberculosis (Hulit & Howard, 2006). Although exceptionally productive, his theory is not as extensive or well developed as Piaget's because he did not have the opportunity to reflect on it as he might have had. His successors have continued to develop his ideas, yet are not necessarily in agreement about how he would have continued (Cole & Cole, 2000; Karpov, 2005).

Vygotsky's emphasis is on the social world and social interactions and language as the foundation for cognition (Rowe & Wertsch, 2002). Vygotsky was tutored in his boyhood, but did not attend a formal school. His tutor challenged him to solve problems and to ask and answer questions. Vygotsky studied literature as his major field at the University of Moscow (Hulit & Howard, 2006).

It is not surprising that Piaget and Vygotsky approached cognitive development from very different perspectives. Vygotsky believed that cognitive development is driven by the interaction of the child's innate abilities and his experiences in his social/cultural environment. Vygotsky placed far more importance on language than did Piaget. Piaget was a biologist. Vygotsky's view of cognitive development is very compatible with the dominant view of language development, the social integrationist view (Hulit & Howard, 2006).

Social experiences are seen as shaping the child's way of thinking and interpreting the world. Adults mediate the development of mental processes in children as they interact with them socially (Karpov, 2005). Vygotsky sees this dialoguing with children as the way in which higher forms of mental activity are constructed and transmitted. **Tool** use is another aspect of Vygotsky's theory. Vygotsky's assumption is that systematic use of tools requires new levels of mental processes. His tools, however, are psychological tools such as language, concepts, signs, and symbols. Vygotsky distinguishes between lower mental processes of the very young child and higher mental processes that use these psychological tools (Karpov, 2005). For children to develop higher mental processes, adults must give these psychological tools to a child and teach him how to use them. In contrast, Piaget believes that children develop these tools themselves from independent, active engagement with their environment.

Language plays a critical role in development because that is how individuals communicate with each other and it is an indispensable tool for thought (Vygotsky, 1934 (trans. 1987)). Vygotsky distinguished three stages in cognitive development characterized by: preintellectual speech, preverbal thought, and the use of external symbolic means. He sees children under age 2 in a *primitive* stage of preintellectual speech, where they use vocal activity as a means of attaining social contact and emotional expression. They can perform systematic and goal-directed activities that do not require verbal operations. Neo-Vygotskian's (Karpov, 2005) have further broken down what they feel are these observations and views of early development into a more stage-based approach. Although time frames are attached to each stage, they are seen as approximate.

Tools in this context are mental abilities such as language, concepts, and symbols.

Vygotsky: Development of Infant–Caregiver Emotional Interactions

The First Stage: Birth to 1 Month. Infants come into the world with mostly negative reactions (crying and lack of emotional responsiveness). Caregivers must take the initiative by establishing emotional contact with infants and talking to them. With responsive care they begin to react more positively to their environment (Karpov, 2005).

The Second Stage: 1 to 2 ½ Months. Now the caregiver can evoke positive reactions. Initially this relates to gratification of physiological needs such as food, but toward the end of this period it becomes more social. Infants initiate smiling, an indication that the next stage has been reached (Karpov, 2005).

The Third Stage: 2 ½ to 6 Months. In addition to social smiling, an infant becomes excited when a caregiver approaches; if the caregiver responds, the baby expresses more joy and pleasure. Infants who have reached the third stage may briefly quit nursing or stop crying to respond to social interactions.

The earlier activity of the caregiver as the initiator of the baby's social interaction has been taken over by the infant if she has experienced this earlier responsiveness by the caregiver. Rather than the global response of excitement, the infant is fine-tuning her responses and may only vocalize or make noises as opposed to also the kicking and waving. Infants are also fine-tuning their reactions to people. As this stage ends, reactions to familiar people may be very positive, but strangers may no longer receive such a joyful response. This is an

up close and personal

Cody's grandmother lives about two hours away and sees her about once a month. She dotes on her six-month-old granddaughter and brings her more clothes that she can wear. When she came today, arms filled with gifts, she quickly put them down and made her usual grab for Cody. Instead of the eager smile she usually receives, Cody turned her face in my shoulder and wailed. Grandma was mystified. In the past Cody had been pleased to go to her. She demanded to know what was wrong.

We sat down with Cody on my lap and talked quietly for a while and I tried to explain to my mother-in-law that Cody now knows that Grimley and I are her parents and she is more attached to us and is reluctant to go to others. After muttering that Cody probably still liked my mother, we were able to gradually get Cody and grandma back together. However, whenever I got up, Cody's eyes would follow me. I decided it would not be a good idea to leave the room.

REFLECTIVE PRACTICE

This about Cody's reaction to her grandmother from the perspective of both Piaget and Vygotsky's theories. What might you conclude about Cody's development? How would you explain this to Cody's grandmother?

indication of attachment to primary caregivers and of moving to the next stage (Karpov, 2005).

The Fourth Stage: 6 to 12 Months. This stage marks a demarcation in development. Caregivers can use the foundation they have built to introduce playing with toys. This is also a time when caregivers can give infants a little more space. This transference of centering interest on the caregiver to object-centered activity is the hallmark of this period. Instead of being the infant's sole emotional support, the role of the caregiver changes to one of mediator of the infants' object-centered activity and develops as infant–caregiver joint object-centered activity. This also requires a change in communication patterns of infants and caregivers. The new role of the caregiver is particularly important at the end of this stage, when infants start imitating caregivers' action with toys, such as feeding a doll.

Learning and the assessment of this learning, according to Vygotsky's theory, involves two aspects of the infant's development: the infant's ability to independently use new psychological tools, such as language, to solve problems, and his success in using adults to develop higher levels of mental functions (Karpov, 2005). Adults can **scaffold** infants' learning by giving them feedback or encouragement, describing what is happening, or modifying the task.

These views contrast with Piaget's view that infants can only learn new ideas if they possess some understanding of the concept and that the approach to training requires interacting with materials (Siegler, 1991). Piaget's view sees instruction following development as opposed to leading it. Vygotsky believed that instruction and development were interrelated from the child's first day of life (Karpov, 2005). Instruction leads development. It does not target the child's actual developmental level, but rather his developmental potential. Infants are viewed as active participants in their social interactions, and it is in these interactions that adults act as facilitators. Instruction is an aspect of mediation (Karpov, 2005).

Vygotsky: The Development of Children's Object-Centered Joint Activity with Adults

The First Stage: 1 to 2 Years. During the first part of this stage, children continue to imitate the actions of adults with toys and objects. This is a continuation of the behavior from the previous stage. However, this behavior is limited to what they see adults do. As this stage progresses children transfer the actions they have imitated to different objects and toys. The importance is the generalization of the actions and the possibility that actions can be separated from the particular object to which they were tied. The easiest way to see this is when children substitute objects for other objects. Instead of just feeding the

> **Scaffolding**
> is a process by which an adult structures and supports a learning situation to lead an infant or toddler through the process.

baby doll, the toddler feeds the toy cat, and perhaps even the train (Karpov, 2005).

The Second Stage: 2 to 3 Years. The child now moves from using the same implements (a spoon) with other objects to being able to make substitutions in the implements (a stick). This ability typically grows out of a situation in which a two-year-old wants to do something (feed the baby doll) and he does not have the necessary implement (a spoon), so the adult asks, "What can we use instead?" At an earlier stage there would be nothing that could be used, but by this stage the child can make a substitution. It is adult mediation that introduces children to playing social roles. This happens at the end of stage one, what we would consider role-play (Karpov, 2005).

Practical intelligence begins around two years of age as the child's language reflects syntactical and logical forms. The child is beginning to use external symbolic means (such as language) to help with internal problem solving. Language can now be used to reflect and develop thought. Initially language is used to express emotions and maintain social contact, then to communicate, to make reference, to represent ideas, and then to regulate one's own actions (Bloom, 2002). Children who talk to themselves are viewed as regulating and planning mental activities. What Piaget would consider "egocentric speech," Vygotsky would call "overt self-regulation." With age, children replace these verbalizations with inner speech that serves the same function but is no longer observable.

Vygotsky and Neo-Vygotskian Themes

Like Piaget, Vygotsky has themes that run through his theory.

Self-Regulation. An important aspect of Vygotsky's theory focuses on the development of self-regulation. The National Research Council and Institute of Medicine (2000) defines self-regulation as the ability to gain control of bodily functions, manage powerful emotions, and maintain and focus attention. Self-regulation is apparent in all aspects of development, from sleeping to eating to talking. The process by which children learn self-regulation in all areas is a common one. Initially, adults structure the behavior and gradually the infant internalizes the structure and uses it to self-regulate. Little by little the infant learns that when she sees her mother or the bottle, this means that she is about to be fed; if she calms even before being fed, this is an indication of developing self-regulation. Young children learn self-regulation by being exposed to challenges that are manageable (Perry, 2005). Infants might be expected to wait for a minute while an adult is talking to them about what is causing the delay. They should not be expected to wait for five minutes with no support.

WITH INFANTS AND TODDLERS

With an infant or young toddler, using two fingers of your hand, start at the infant's fingers or toes and slowly walk your two fingers up the limb, saying the infant's name: "Garrett, Garrett, Garrett." As your fingers get closer to the trunk (belly-button area), say quickly, "Garrett, Garrett," and give the infant a gentle tickle and a big smile. As the game becomes more predictable, make the anticipatory time longer by going back down the limb and up again before quickly saying the child's name.

Learning to anticipate what is going to predictably happen is an important cognitive skill. Being able to sustain the self-regulation to wait is also important.

Vygotsky's focus is on the use of language signs and symbols to regulate behavior. Language has a social purpose that is designed to influence others. As adults use language to regulate infants' behavior, this leads to the internalization of language symbols. Gradually, infants and toddlers use language to regulate their own behavior. This starts out as "private speech" or self-talk. Young children use this speech to regulate their own behavior. They also use speech to regulate other's behavior. This is why sociodramatic play is such an important aspect of early childhood. It is critical in children's development of self-regulation. Play challenges children to find solutions to difficult problems, to control their own impulsive behavior, and to plan before they act (Vygotsky, 1978).

Language. Vygotsky views language as a multifunctional medium. Language serves a planning function and allows children to solve problems through speech and then carry out the solution. Through the interweaving of thought and language children move from a fragmentary use of language as a symbol system to mastery of using other symbol systems such as drawing, reading, and writing to enhance their understanding of the world they live in and how they think about it (Vygotsky, 1934 (trans. 1987)).

Self-talk
is a tool children use for self-direction and self-regulation; it is like thinking out loud, it is not meant as communication.

Private Speech. Piaget called **self-talk** egocentric speech, and he saw it as nonsocial and serving little purpose (Hulit & Howard, 2006). Vygotsky saw young children using self-talk to guide themselves through actions. A toddler might say to himself, "Red one," as he reaches for a red crayon. Self-talk is more like thinking out loud than external speech. With toddlers and two-year-olds Vygotsky believed that they were thinking through problems and tasks and deciding what to do. Vygotsky saw it as the first step to higher levels of thinking. "It helps the child learn how to pay attention, how to memorize and recall bits of information from memory, how to formulate and execute plans on solving problems, and in a very real sense, how to think, ponder, or muse" (Hulit & Howard, 2006, p. 93). Overall, the research tends to side with Vygotsky on the purpose of private speech. **Private speech** turns into **inner speech**.

Private speech
is used by a child to direct himself or to help him think through a problem.

Inner speech
replaces self-talk; as the child does not need to express himselves verbally, he does it internally.

Emotional referencing
is when a child looks to a trusted adult to determine how to feel in a given situation.

Instrumental referencing
is when a child looks to a trusted adult to determine what to do in a given situation.

Referencing. Infants use caregivers not only to introduce them to new objects, they use their body language to determine how they should feel about events. For example, if a stranger approaches, the infant might turn to a familiar caregiver to determine how to classify this new situation. He may look at his mother's facial expression, gestures, and actions to determine how to feel about new situations. If she smiles, he will react positively. If she tenses or looks worried, his reaction may be less positive. Researchers look at both emotional and instrumental referencing. **Emotional referencing** focuses on the "how do I feel" question. It develops at about nine months. **Instrumental referencing** focuses on "what do I do" (Feinman, Roberts, Hsieh, Sawyer, & Swanson, 1992, p. 28). Instrumental referencing develops at about one year of age. If a toddler encounters an unknown dog, he will look to a trusted adult to determine how to feel. If the adult is comfortable then the toddler will be comfortable as well (emotional); if the adult then speaks with the dog's owner and begins to pet the dog, the toddler may pet the dog as well (instrumental). Young toddlers can also be proactive by giving an adult an object that they cannot make work, such as a jack-in-the-box that will not pop up (instrumental referencing) (Rogoff, Mistry, Radiziszewska, & Germond, 1992).

ZPD
is the gap between what an infant or toddler can do independently and what he can do with adult guidance.

Scaffolding
is a dynamic system of providing support for learning.

Zone of Proximal Development. An important concept that Vygotsky has contributed to the field is his idea of a **zone of proximal development (ZPD)**. This refers to the range of tasks that a child cannot yet accomplish alone, but can accomplish with the help of adults or more competent peers. Or in Vygotsky's words, the zone of proximal development is "The distance between the actual developmental level as determined by independent problem solving and the level of potential development as determined through problem solving under adult guidance, or in collaboration with more capable peers" (Vygotsky, 1934 [trans. 1987], p. 86). To find the ZPD the adult must assess the child's abilities, plan activities that are slightly in advance of the child's ability, and then provide the necessary **scaffolding** for the child to perform the task. As the child's competence increases, the adult takes less responsibility for the task and allows the child more, while at the same time introducing increasingly difficult tasks that require scaffolding.

Scaffolding. According to Vygotsky's theory, cognitive development occurs because of social interaction with more competent partners. This adult guidance, called scaffolding, facilitates learning. In construction, scaffolding is a temporary framework that is built to support people and material in the construction or repair of buildings. As the building gets higher or different areas need to be worked on, the scaffolding is changed to allow workers access. Likewise, an infant or toddler can do some things independently, but there are other areas of development that are only possible for the child if he has the necessary supports or scaffolding. More mature partners who support infants and toddlers in their cognitive and language development by expanding and extending their knowledge base enhance their learning (Many, 2002). The support provided by adults is most effective if the child can use the same strategies to solve similar problems himself (Rogoff, 1998). If a toddler is working with a puzzle and the adult says, "Let's turn all the puzzle pieces right side up," this is something that a toddler can do—a strategy that can be generalized to other puzzles.

Because infants and toddlers grow, change, and learn at a faster rate than at any other point in their lives, it takes knowledge of developmental patterns and skill in scaffolding learning to create an optimal learning environment for young children. The focus of teaching should be in a child's ZPD. This is the dynamic region in which learning takes place. If you help a child with skills she has already developed, you are interfering with her mastery of the skills, or if you try to get a child to do a task the child cannot do even with adult support, the child will experience frustration and learn dependency.

Scaffolding is difficult, because as the adult provides scaffolding for a task, the child's functioning increases, then the adult must determine the next step in the learning process and provide support for the child in that area. Scaffolding is continually changing, which makes it challenging to teach people how to scaffold, especially for very young children. Table 5–1 provides a list of some of the methods you might use to scaffold learning for infants and toddlers (*text continued on page 211*).

(*text continued on page 211*)

Table 5–1 Types of Scaffolding

- Providing general feedback and encouragement helps infants and toddlers continue to work on challenging tasks.

- Asking open-ended questions such as, "What do you see?" or, "Oh, what happened?"

- Structuring the task cognitively by helping a child discover similarities, rules, and sequences. You can help activate a child's prior learning by asking questions such as, "Do you remember when ...," or, "How did you start ... ."

- Holding in memory by restating goals or summarizing what has been happening.

- Regulating tasks by matching them to the infant or toddler's ability and interest.

- Instructing children through modeling, direct questions, and participation.

SOURCE: Notari-Syverson, O'Conner, and Vadast (1998).

WITH INFANTS AND TODDLERS

Scaffolding is dependent on the child's level of development and the goals you have for the child. Some examples of what you might do in the classroom are provided below.

1. Irving is a two-year-old who grabs toys from other children. When a teacher is nearby and coaches him, he can say, "my turn." The ability to use words is within his ZPD. With practice he will be able to use the words even when an adult is not present. However, the level of scaffolding needs to change once Irving begins to use words to monitor his actions. If the adult keeps telling Irving to say, "my turn," when this should be internalizing to a higher level of understanding, then Irving will not have a chance to continue developing and stretching his skills in this area. This needs to be expanded to, "When Amy is done, you may play with it." or "Can you find another toy that you want to play with?"

2. Josefina, a one-year-old, is using a three-piece form board (circle, triangle, square). She has successfully placed the circle in the appropriate space. She is now trying to place the triangle in the opening for the square. You might do any of the following:

   - Take the circle out and give it to Josefina in exchange for the triangle. (Because Josefina knows how to put the circle in, no learning is taking place.)
   - Tell Josefina where to put it. (This is rarely effective with one-year-olds.)
   - Cover the opening for the square with your hand. (This means that Josefina will at least try the triangle in the appropriate place and this may be effective scaffolding depending on her level of skill.)
   - Move Josefina's hand so the triangle lines up more closely to the space. (This may also be effective depending upon her level of skill.)

There are no specific right answers when it comes to scaffolding, because it is dependent upon the adult's assessment of the child's skill.

3. Mary is a six-month-old in a chest-up position and is eying a toy that is out of her reach.

   - Give her the toy. (What does Mary learn from this? Probably not much.)
   - Push the toy closer to Mary but not quite within reach. (Depending on her ability, she will need to shift weight and grasp the toy. If this is challenging for her, it is scaffolding; if it is a skill she has mastered, then it is not.)
   - Verbally encourage Mary to try to get the toy. (If she makes an effort, evaluate the skill level and either keep encouraging Mary or place the toy where she can be successful and continue with the encouragement.)

Vygotsky believes that children learn most when they have adults or older children who can scaffold their learning.

Vygotsky believed that cognitive development occurred in a social and cultural environment. Although there are commonalities, there will be both individual and sociocultural variation based on what is valued and important in the particular culture in which a child is being raised.

Learning, and the assessment of this learning, according to Vygotsky's theory, involves two aspects of the child's development: the child's ability to independently use new psychological tools such as language and concepts to solve problems and the child's success in using new adult-assisted psychological tools to develop higher levels of mental functions (Karpov, 2005).

These views contrast with Piaget's view that children can only learn new ideas if they possesses some understanding of the concept, and that the approach to learning requires interacting with materials (Siegler, 1991). Vygotsky believed that instruction and development are interrelated from the child's first day of life (Karpov, 2005). Instruction is an aspect of mediation.

Behavioral Theory

Behavioral analysis is a systematic process of modifying observable behavior through manipulating the environment.

According to the **behavioral analysis** view of learning espoused by B. F. Skinner (1969), learning occurs because children systematically interact with a structured environment and are rewarded or positively reinforced for their successful accomplishment of tasks (Rosales-Ruiz & Baer, 1997). This perspective suggests that adults need to plan the "right" environment for young children and should respond to children's desired or appropriate behaviors with rewards. Responses that are rewarded will continue; those that are not will be extinguished.

The principles of behavior analysis are used extensively in the study of infant perception, an aspect of cognition. Behavior analysis highlights the fact that each problem has a unique history and hence needs a unique solution tailored to the specific problem behavior. The goal is to assist individuals working with young children to use empirically based learning procedures to modify or change targeted behaviors. Applied behavior analysis is used extensively in working with young children with disabilities and challenging behaviors. It requires educators to study behavior and then to change the environment as a method of modifying the behavior. Many of the techniques are useful in teaching infants and toddlers. Table 5–2 highlights some of the techniques.

REFLECTIVE PRACTICE

Compare the strategies used by applied behavior analysis with scaffolding. How are they the same and in what ways do they differ? Do you believe that both could provide you with tools and strategies for working with infants and toddlers?

Social Learning Theory

Social cognition emphasizes the impact that the environment (both physical and human) has on a child's cognitive development (Bandura, 1992). Like behaviorists, social learning theorists see the child strongly shaped by individual experience. Genetic factors and neural maturation are considered important. Social cognitive theorists view children as having vast potential, with behavioral outcomes influenced by the child's specific interactions with the environment. Social cognitive theory examines the interaction of the external environment with behavior, cognitive, biological, and other internal factors that can affect perceptions and actions. Each of these factors is seen as both acting on and reacting to each other component. Looking more closely at these interactions gives more insight into the cognitive development of infants and toddlers.

Social learning theory broadens behavioral analysis and looks more at the context of learning, and perhaps is even a bridge between cognitive theory and behavioral analysis. Bandura (1992) suggests that social learning occurs through observation, modeling, **vicarious reinforcement**, and self-regulated behavior. He believes that infants and toddlers can learn by observing others and by watching what happens to others based on their behavior.

Vicarious reinforcement is when someone the child is watching is rewarded for a behavior or task he is performing.

Table 5–2 Techniques from Applied Behavioral Analysis

1. *Task analysis* involves breaking a task down into its component parts, sequencing these, and then teaching them. This is particularly useful for tasks an infant or toddler must do frequently, such as putting on a coat, going to the bathroom, hand-washing, and so on.

2. *Backward chaining* uses task analysis but begins teaching the task from the last step. If step eight in putting on the coat is zipping it up, you would help with steps one through seven, then as the toddler begins to zip up the coat, say, "Great! You did it! You zipped up your coat." After a few days you might check if the toddler can start the zipper. This works well with infants and toddlers when there are many steps, because the reward is closer to the end of the task. For hand washing it might be throwing the paper towel into the wastebasket.

3. *Prompting* provides cues as to what has to be done. If a toddler is using a form board with a circle, square, and rectangle, you provide:

   - **Physical** prompting by using a hand-over-hand technique to help the toddler actually place the piece in the hole.

   - **Visual** cues, such as pointing to a particular piece and then saying, "Why don't you pick that one up?" or, "Try it here." Again, point to the place where it fits.

   - **Verbal** cues, such as saying, "Did you try the red one there?"

4. *Fading Prompts* is the process of eliminating (or fading) the prompts as the child develops the skill. Prompts are rarely faded all at once. You might move from a physical prompt to a visual one, then to a verbal one. The goal is for the child to learn the information or perform the task without prompts.

5. *Modeling* involves demonstrating how a particular task should be done. After an adult or older child models a behavior, the toddler needs the opportunity to practice the behavior and the adult should provide specific feedback and reinforcement.

6. *Generalization* involves using a skill in a variety of situations where it is appropriate. You will sometimes see this when a toddler does something such going to the potty, eating certain foods, or playing with particular toys either at home or at school, but not at both. Skills need to be generalized to be useful. If toddlers know colors using construction paper, then have them find colors in the environment with crayons, clothing, and so on.

7. *Shaping* involves gradually modifying undesirable behavior to the desired behavior. If your goal is to have the toddlers put away the toys they are playing with and they only put away one toy with your prompting, you might thank them for their help. Gradually you would not reinforce them until they had put several toys away and ultimately until all of the toys were put away.

8. *Reinforcement* is a response to an infant's or toddler's behavior that is designed to increase the behavior. To be a reinforcer the infant or toddler must desire it.

9. *Differential reinforcement* varies the level of reinforcement based on the child's behavior and the level of difficulty of the task. An easy task will be reinforced with less fanfare than a difficult one. Like prompting, reinforcement fades and the expected response is that natural, occasional social reinforcement will sustain the behavior.

If observation is an important source of learning for infants and toddlers, we need to check ourselves as role models and ensure that we model behaviors that we want infants and toddlers to learn. In addition, we want to ensure that our classrooms provide models that all children can identify with. In particular, if the infants and toddlers are from diverse ethnic and cultural backgrounds, materials that are part of their home environment need to be part of the classroom. The culture of the children is an important aspect of their social and cognitive learning.

Social learning theorists believe that young children learn more if they are interested in what they are learning and motivated to discover knowledge. For educators, this means that an important aspect of our role is to motivate children. We need to work within guidelines that are developmentally sound and compelling. We want infants and toddlers to wake up in the morning eager to come to school to try new and interesting things. We want toddlers to whirl around and have a difficult time deciding what to do first because it all looks so intriguing. And, under the excitement, that there are developmentally appropriate practices that take into account individualized goals for children.

WITH INFANTS AND TODDLERS

Social learning theory provides an interesting perspective for a problem such as putting toys away. Evan is putting toys away and Gannon is watching him but not putting any toys away. The teacher says to Evan, "Evan, you are a great help today. Thanks for putting the toys away. Are you ready to go outside?" The assumption is that Gannon can learn that Evan was praised (verbally reinforced) by the teacher for putting the toys away, and that this should increase Gannon's likelihood of participating in the future. If going outside sooner is also a reward, that should be an additional reinforcement.

Information-Processing Models

The information-processing approach to cognitive development sees cognition as a matter of organizing information to solve problems. It focuses on how information is selected, represented, stored, and retrieved. It views the human brain much as it might the central processing unit of a computer. Theorists of this approach sometimes use computers to test their hypotheses. They are intrigued with memory as both storage and control processes. They are interested in the particular strategies that children use in relation to the demands of the task (Klahr & MacWhinney, 1998; Siegler, 1998). In particular, they are intrigued with how young children encode and transform information in solving problems. Young children seem to have small, nonflexible repertoires of strategies for problem solving that they use somewhat randomly. With increasing age children use deliberate strategic approaches to problems and increased flexibility in applying strategies. Knowledge bases also increase with age (Case, 1998).

Many of the cognitive tasks used by information-processing models have a Piagetian base. Information-processing patterns have also incorporated concepts from social learning theory. Young children may have problems in different stages of this model. By breaking down the process into its stages, it is possible to pinpoint where in the system the child is having difficulty and to focus on those particular skills (Crick & Dodge, 1994; Joseph & Strain, 2003).

- **Encoding Information**: This involves sensory input: seeing, hearing, feeling, tasting, and even smelling a situation. It involves attention, sensation, and the perception of cues. Some children encode the wrong information. Instead of looking at another child's facial expression, they may encode the color of the child's clothing.

- **Mental Representation and Interpreting Information**: Given the sensory input, the next step is to process this information and create meaning from it. That is, to interpret the information and decide what it means. Typically, information is interpreted through experience, but infants and toddlers have little experience to draw upon. If one does encode facial expression and the child is frowning, it may not be a good time to try to join a group. Some toddlers may not interpret this nonverbal language accurately.

- **Generating Possible Responses**: Given the child's interpretation of the situation, she then generates potential responses. The problem is that young children have few available responses. The number of responses generated is dependent on the repertoire of skills the child has that are relevant to the situation. In general, the larger the repertoire of responses and the higher the level of her developmental appropriateness, the more effective the child will be in reaching her goal.

- **Deciding on a Response**: This is the evaluation and decision step. Given the repertoire of available responses, the child must decide which one has the greatest probability of success. Here the toddler must take into account the information gleaned from steps one and two, and then consider not only the available responses but also the consequences of these responses and the probability of their working.

- **Acting on a Response**: Having decided on a response, the child now needs to implement it. The response itself can be done skillfully, off-handedly, or even intrusively.

- **Self-evaluating**: The final step in the process is self-evaluation. This is the step that identifies a reflective child who can evaluate her own behavior and gain the knowledge to potentially modify future responses. Given the actions, what were the results? Were there consequences? What happened that was not anticipated? If the toddler just throws up her hands and leaves, she is unlikely to learn from her own behavior. Given very young children's ability to reflect, it is the role of the adult in the situation to describe what happened and what the consequences are, as well as other possible approaches: "Boyd doesn't like it when you take his shovel. He pushed you because he wants the shovel. If you want to play with Boyd, you need to find your own shovel or a truck so you can each have something to play with." It is the ability to evaluate and reflect on the process that will ultimately separate children with good social skills from those who do not have them. Children learn these skills from interacting with adults who know how to scaffold a child's learning and where in the system to start an intervention.

Theories of cognitive development seek to describe children's cognitive capabilities and limitations on a developmental continuum and explain how more advanced understanding grows out of less adequate comprehension. This chapter has thus far discussed how infants and toddlers develop cognitively, and has focused on the universals rather than on individual differences. Intelligence highlights the differences in cognitive development.

INTELLECTUAL DEVELOPMENT

Most researchers make a distinction between cognition and intelligence. Cognition has to do with knowing, whereas intelligence is the use of knowledge. Cognition is more abstract; intelligence is what we measure. Confusion about the meaning of intelligence and cognition is compounded because different people use the word intelligence in different ways. Psychologists view intelligence as the biological foundation for cognitive functioning that is responsible for individual difference in intellectual competence. The public view of intelligence relates to how individuals conduct their affairs and solve problems in their life and achieve success in academic, cultural, and career pursuits. The third meaning of intelligence is what the tests measure, and what we usually refer to as Intelligence Quotient (IQ) (Lamb et al., 2002).

Measuring Infant Intelligence

How do we measure infant intelligence, and for what purpose? Infants are assessed to determine whether or not intervention is necessary and to make predictions about how well infants will do intellectually later in life. Before looking directly at infant assessment measures, it is important to look at general issues related to infant assessment.

In the 1920s, there began to be interest in developing an intelligence test that could be used for younger children. Arnold Gesell at Yale, Mary Shirley in Minnesota, and Nancy Bayley in California all made important contributions to the development of such an infant assessment measure (Black & Matula, 1999; Teti & Gibbs, 1990). Gesell and Bayley both developed tests that are still used today.

Issues in Measuring Intellectual Development in Infants and Toddlers

There are two major dimensions that relate to the accuracy of infant intelligence measurement; the first has to do with issues relating to the test, the second is the challenge of the infant. The main reason for assessing an infant is to determine whether or not there might be long-term problems that could respond to intervention. In this case, the concern is the test's ability to detect problems that have long-term negative outcomes. Infant intelligence tests do a good job of identifying infants and toddlers with severe and profound developmental delays. They are not as effective, however, in identifying infants and toddlers with mild to moderate delays.

One critical testing issue concerns the relationship between scores obtained on infant intelligence tests and intelligence tests given at a later age. What we consider "intelligence" in infancy is not the same as "intelligence" in elementary school children or adults; that is, patterns of cognitive activities change at different ages (Meadows, 1993). Newer lines of thinking focus on infant alertness as shown in habituation tasks and attention as predictors of intelligence test scores in early childhood (Bornstein & Sigman, 1986), and tests that use visual recognition memory (McCall & Carriger, 1993). These types of tasks tap into basic cognitive abilities that underlie intelligence at any age. Because of the need for longitudinal data to confirm this hypothesis, it will be a while before we know the results of this approach.

The Infant. The infant himself poses concerns about accurate testing. The mother is almost always present, so she is part of the testing process and may affect outcomes. Her role may be active or passive, but she is part of the process. Scheduling is also an issue. An infant may only have an hour or two of alert time in a day, and that is obviously the ideal time for testing. At the very least, regular nap and feeding times should be avoided when testing. Flexibility is also a key ingredient. Because there is so little time, the examiner must be calm, gentle, and very efficient.

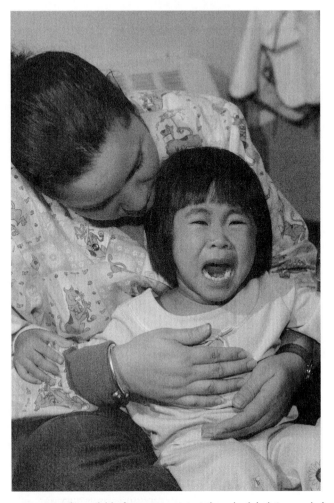

Children are not necessarily available for assessment at the scheduled time and place.

Psychometric Issues. Psychometric issues relate to the quality of measurement of intelligence or any other characteristics that are being measured. The question is how does one differentiate between "good" measures and "bad" ones? There are some basic characteristics of tests that determine the quality of the test regardless of what it is measuring.

Professional organizations, such as the National Association of School Psychologists and Zero to Three, advocate the use of dynamic play-based approaches to the assessment of infants and toddlers. Transdisciplinary play-based assessment is an integrated approach to assessment based on research showing that play encourages children's thinking skills, communication and language abilities, movement proficiency, and social-emotional development. It also lends itself to intervention (Linder, 1993a). Despite concerns about testing infants and toddlers using formal measures, they still seem to be the standard. Newer assessment tools hold the potential of being more developmentally appropriate and technically adequate (Ford & Dahinten, 2005).

Reliability focuses on the consistency of a measure. One way to determine if a measure is reliable is to give it a second time and compare the results. If the measure is reliable, the results should be the same or very close to the same. The infant who obtains a Developmental Quotient (DQ) of 100 on Tuesday should get the same score or one very close to it on Wednesday.

Validity has to do with whether a test is measuring what it claims to measure—that is, that the results are appropriate or correct for the inferences, decisions, or descriptions made. In reality, tests do not have validity; rather, it is the use of the test that determines whether or not it is valid. There are degrees of validity, and the question really becomes one of whether or not there is enough validity for a particular use. With infants we are most concerned with predictive validity. **Predictive validity** is the ability to predict the same or related characteristics in the future. We are concerned with how infants will perform in the future and if the problems were are seeing will affect their future.

What is an intelligent infant, and who cares? As practitioners, what we really want to know is if there are infants who could benefit from early intervention. To know who could benefit, we must be able to predict which infants will have delays in later childhood or adulthood. Overall, the predictive validity of infant intelligence tests has not been good. Predicting adult intelligence from infant intelligence requires longitudinal studies. Using reliable, well-standardized tests of infant intelligence, McCall (1983) found that these measures predicted only 1 to 2 percent of the variation in IQ in later childhood and adolescence. The study is old and the scales that were used then have been revised, but we still do not have good ways of predicting later intelligence (predictive validity) from infancy using these measures.

Reliability and validity are related. If you cannot consistently get the same results each time you measure something, the measuring instrument is not reliable. On the other hand, just because you can consistently measure something does not mean that the measurement is valid.

Objectivity is important in looking at measures and who is using them. To the extent that the requirements of a specific measure are not adhered to and that subjective evaluations are used, a test is less valid or reliable. A related issue is **bias**. There is concern about individual bias in a testing situation and cultural bias in the test itself. If clean, attractive, cooperative, and highly verbal young children consistently score higher than children who are dirty, poorly dressed, shy, or disruptive, bias might be operating. Cultural bias can occur if

Reliability
is the ability of a measure to obtain the same results time after time.

Validity
relates to whether or not a measure gets results that accurately reflect the concept being measured.

Predictive validity
is the extent to which the scale predicts scores on some measure or behavior that will exist in the future.

Bias
is a systematic error that favors one group over another.

all children taking a particular test have not had equal exposure to the material. We are particularly concerned about children whose home language is not English and whose cultural experiences are different from those children who were used in the development of the test.

Norm-Referenced and Criterion-Referenced Measures

Norm-referenced measures
compare scores to all of those who have taken the test.

In standardized **norm-referenced measures**, scores made by an individual child are compared to scores that other children have made. The "norm" for the **developmental quotient (DQ)** is 100. Infants scoring more than 100 are considered developing faster than the "norm," and those with DQs less than 100 are developing slower than the "norm." Testing and retesting many infants established the norm. For diagnostic purposes, norm-referenced tests are more useful. SATs are a standardized norm-referenced test.

DQ
is used instead of intelligence quotient for infants and toddlers.

Criterion-referenced tests rely on an absolute standard. For programming purposes, criterion-referenced measures are usually more useful. It is more helpful to know whether to expect an infant to sit independently for three minutes or stack three cubes than it is to know that he has a DQ of 110. The driving part of getting a driver's license is a **criterion-based test**.

Criterion-based tests
look at whether infants and toddlers can perform specific skills.

Assessing Intellectual Development in Infants and Toddlers

Intellectual development is rarely singled out for assessment, but rather instruments also measure other areas including language, motor, and social/emotional development, because these areas are so intertwined in infants and toddlers. The three types of measures used in these assessments are screening measures, standardized norm-referenced measures, and curriculum-based criterion-referenced measures.

Screening measures are used to decide which infants receive further testing and which ones do not. This is a crucial decision. Screening results that indicate children need additional testing when in reality they do not are considered false positives. Such results create overidentification, concern and stress in families and children, and a workload problem for professionals. False negatives occur when children who are at risk pass through the screening and are not identified for followup. This results in underidentification and hence lack of early intervention for infants and toddlers who could profit from it. False negative results cause parents and professionals to assume that infants and toddlers are developing normally when in reality they are not. It also denies them access to early intervention programs from which they might benefit (Salvia & Ysseldyke, 2007).

The *Ages and Stages Questionnaires* (ASQ) (Bricker & Squires, 1999) is a parent-completed child-monitoring system for children from 4 to 60 months old. It is a 30-item questionnaire completed at designated intervals and takes about 15 minutes. It looks at five developmental areas: communication, gross motor, fine motor, problem solving, and personal-social. Professionals convert the parent's responses into a code that determines whether children are at high or low risk in the various areas. *The Bayley Scales of Infant and Toddler Development, Third Edition (Bayley III) Screening Test* (Bayley, 2005) has cut scores by age for cognitive, language, and motor skills. It is designed for infants and toddlers ages 1 to 42 months. It must be administered by a trained professional and takes about 15 to 25 minutes. Both of these screening measures are standardized norm-referenced. If infants and toddlers are found to be at risk for poor developmental outcomes, then further testing is done.

The *Bayley Scales of Infant and Toddler Development, Third Edition (Bayley III)* (Bayley, 2005) also has a full scale inventory that can be used with children from 1 to 42 months. Its primary purpose is to identify infants and toddlers with developmental delays and to provide information for intervention planning. It has a cognitive scale, a language scale with receptive and expressive subtests, a motor scale with fine and gross motor subtests, a social-emotional scale and an adaptive behavior scale. It is designed to meet the requirements of the 2004 IDEA. It requires a trained examiner. *The Battelle Developmental Inventory (BDI-2)* (Newborg, 2004) can be used for children birth to 7.11 years. It is useful in the assessment of typically developing infants and toddlers as well as in identifying those with disabilities. It covers five domains: personal-social, **adaptive**, motor, communication, and cognitive. It matches the domains required by the IDEA. It requires a trained professional to administer it.

Adaptive
refers to self-help skills.

Criterion measures are useful in planning and in measuring small increments of development. They assess each child as an individual against specific developmental milestones. They are sometimes thought of as mastery tests. That is, for a given item the child either can or cannot do a particular task. Some measures will classify a skill as emerging if it is present but not mastered. This is a functional approach to assessment. It focuses on practical skills that infants and toddlers need to learn, and they are assessed in a context in which the infant or toddler is comfortable. Because the important people in a child's life are part of the assessment process, they come away with knowledge about how to interpret the child's behavior and to plan activities to meet his needs (Meisels, 2001).

The *Assessment, Evaluation, and Programming System (AEPS) for Infants and Children* is curriculum based and criterion referenced. The *AEPS Measurement for Birth to Three Years*, Volume 1 (Bricker, 1993), covers the areas of fine motor, gross motor, adaptive, cognitive, social communication, and social development.

The *AEPS Curriculum for Birth to Three Years* (Cripe, Slentz, & Bricker, 1993) provides curriculum goals and objectives in an activity-based intervention that are matched to the measurement.

The *Ounce Scale* (Meisels, Marsden, Dombro, Weston, & Jewkes, 2003) is a relatively recent curriculum-based criterion-referenced assessment designed to solve some of the problems specifically related to testing infants and toddlers. It can be used for children from birth to 3.5 years. It also has a far broader scope than just cognitive development. One of the goals of the scale is to make families and caregivers better observers of young children and to give them the skills to use their observations to enhance relationships and support development. It has three elements: the observational record, the family album, and the developmental profile. The observational assessment documents and measures infant and toddler growth, accomplishments, areas of difficulty, approaches to learning, and temperament. The observations focus on six areas of development: (A) Social and emotional development: (1) personal connections; (2) feelings about self; (3) relationships with other children, communication, and (B) language; (4) understanding and communicating, (C) cognitive development; (5) exploration and problem solving, (D) and physical development; and (6) movement (gross motor) and coordination (fine motor) (Meisels et al., 2003).

The *Transdisciplinary Play-Based Assessment* (TPBA) and the *Transdisciplinary Play-Based Intervention* (TPBI) (Linder, 1993a, 1993b), also a curriculum-based criterion-referenced assessment and intervention system, is designed for use by a team of different professionals (early childhood educators, early childhood special educators, physical therapists, occupational therapists, speech and language therapists) and the parents. Transdisciplinary teams require a high degree of coordination and trust. The goal of TPBA is to look at the child as a whole so that each professional can see her particular area from the view of others, particularly the family. It is also designed to be a more normal, natural situation in which to assess an infant or toddler. One professional typically takes the lead while the others sit around in a circle and watch, sometimes asking questions or making requests or suggestions. Done well, this is an excellent way for professionals and families to assess and plan for an infant or toddler.

DELAYED INTELLECTUAL DEVELOPMENT

Delayed intellectual development is cognitive growth that does not follow the expected rate. Infants and toddlers with intellectual disabilities will rarely reach the higher level of abstract thinking skills. It is often difficult to identify infants and toddlers with delayed cognitive development, especially when these delays are mild. Other variables, such as speech and language delays, or lack of environmental stimulation, may adversely affect test scores. Because of these identification problems, infants and toddlers who show delays in cognitive development are called developmentally delayed. This is a more tentative diagnosis than intellectual disabilities and it does not carry the same impact. Since it focuses on the child's developmental rate, it leaves open the possibility for alternative diagnoses; for example, learning disabilities or no diagnosis at all.

Infants and toddlers exhibiting extremely delayed development or when there is a known cause or etiology may be diagnosed as having an intellectual disability or mental retardation. The American Association on Mental Deficiency has developed the most widely accepted definition of mental retardation:

> *Mental retardation* refers to substantial limitations in present functioning. It is characterized by significantly subaverage intellectual functioning, existing concurrently with related limitations in two or more of the following applicable adaptive skill areas: communication, self-care, home living, social skills, community use, self-direction, health and safety, functional academics, leisure, and work. Mental retardation manifests before age 18 (American Association on Mental Deficiency, 1992, p. 5).

Because of concerns about labeling per se and criticism of the assessment process, the Association explains the assumptions behind its definition and how it is to be applied.

1. Valid assessment considers cultural and linguistic diversity as well as differences in communication and behavior factors.

2. The existence of limitations in adaptive skills occurs within the context of community environments typical of the individual's age peers and is indexed to the person's individualized needs for supports.

3. Specific adaptive limitations often coexist with strengths in other adaptive skills or other personal capabilities.

4. With appropriate supports over a sustained period, the life functioning of the person with mental retardation will generally improve (American Association on Mental Deficiency, 1992, p. 5).

Previously, the definition of mental retardation was based almost exclusively on IQ scores. Now, although an IQ of 70 to 75 or below is considered below average, there is consensus that additional measures must be used to verify these results and that the results should be reviewed by a **multidisciplinary team**.

Multidisciplinary team is made up of the different professionals needed to assess and plan for a particular infant or toddler.

Testing infants and toddlers requires tremendous skill and recognition of their schedules and life. When this does not happen, parents are upset and toddlers may not be assessed accurately.

Characteristics of Delayed Intellectual Development

Floppy
children have low muscle tone.

Spastic
children have high muscle tone.

In the first months of life, concern may arise because of inadequate sucking, **floppy** or **spastic** muscle tone, and/or lack of response to visual or auditory stimuli. Children may show little interest in the environment and not be as alert as other infants. As infants grow older and approach developmental milestones, it may be determined that the infant is not developing as quickly as most infants his age. It is often unclear whether this is just an individual growth pattern and that the infant will "catch up" in time, or whether the delay is of a more permanent nature. Medical consultation can identify some problems early, such as hydrocephalus, for which a shunt can prevent brain damage and educational intervention can promote early development.

Infants and toddlers with developmental delays have an overall slower rate of learning, poor memory skills, problems in abstract thinking, poor generalization skills, and lack of learning strategies (schemata). The most obvious signs are that these children are slower to talk than other children, may seem immature, and may also have been slower to walk (after 15 months). They may have a short attention span, and some are highly distractible. Language skills are also delayed, as is the acquisition of basic daily living skills (feeding, toilet training, and dressing). Children with more severe delays may lack social interaction skills, motivation, and a striving for independence. Infants and toddlers exhibiting extremely delayed development or for whom there is a known cause or etiology may be diagnosed before age 3. Because early intervention has proven to be successful, if you suspect delayed development, talk with the parents and encourage them to seek medical and educational intervention.

WITH INFANTS AND TODDLERS

Infants and toddlers whose cognitive development is delayed need an environment that provides individualized planning and stimulation, a low adult-to-child ratio, and adults who are sensitive to and know how to scaffold cognitive development. Infants and toddlers need to learn the adaptive skills that others are learning. Educators must also directly support infants and toddlers as well as teach and model necessary cognitive skills. Caregivers need to be dynamic and reinforce infants and toddlers as they successfully learn new skills.

☀ SUMMARY

Your beliefs about how infants and toddlers learn influence your curriculum and teaching methods. Caregivers whose philosophy agrees with Piaget's constructivist perspective need to be aware of children's innate abilities and stages of cognitive development and the quality of the environment available to the children. Teachers must provide a stimulating environment in which children learn by doing activities that interest them and match their level of adaptation.

Vygotsky's ideas contrast with Piaget's and provide a different model for the basis of early care and education. Children are in multi-age groupings, the teacher-to-child ratio is low, and teachers require extensive training in detailed diagnosis of skills, what skills fall in the zone of proximal development, and how to scaffold for and sensitively teach the required skills. Teachers have dialogues with children and older children scaffold the learning of younger children. Opportunities for play within a sociocultural context are supported and encouraged.

Although the philosophies themselves are different, most caregivers develop an eclectic philosophy that incorporates aspects of different theories. For example, if a caregiver uses Piaget as a guideline, she puts a favorite toy inside a hula hoop and encourages the child to pull the hoop. When the infant does not pull the hoop, the teacher models the behavior and exclaims when the child gets the toy (social learning theory). The teacher again encourages the child to try; when he is successful she rewards the behavior with a big hug (behavioral theory).

We measure intellectual development using norm-referenced and criterion-referenced measures. The major goal of assessing infants and toddlers is to determine which children can profit from early intervention. Children who are identified with intellectual disabilities may not reach higher levels of abstract thought.

☀ CHAPTER IN REVIEW

※ Infants come into the world seeing, hearing, feeling, tasting, and smelling, and are prewired to learn.

※ The child progresses from the involuntary motor responses of early infancy to the use of symbols and abstract thought in three years.

※ Piaget focused on infant cognition and emphasized that cognitive development occurs in a recognizable, predictable

progression, with later development dependent upon earlier stages of development.

※ Piaget believed that cognitive development begins at birth and is a function of sensorimotor interactions with the environment.

※ Vygotsky's theory focused on the role of language in cognitive development and social interaction.

※ Scaffolding and the zone of proximal development (ZPD) are contributions from Vygotsky's theory.

※ Recognition of the importance of early experience and the role of the environment has led to the development of measures to assess infant intelligence.

※ Some of the issues related to infant assessment include the infant herself, the definition of intelligence, and the reliability and validity of the measures.

※ Assessment is used primarily to identify infants and toddlers with delayed development.

※ Delayed cognitive development does not follow the expected rate of cognitive development.

※ It is difficult to accurately identify very young children who are mildly delayed because each infant and toddler's development is influenced by a multitude of factors, including the individuality of each child and the environment in which he lives.

APPLICATION ACTIVITIES

1. Play with an infant about eight months old and use Piaget's ideas about object permanence. Hide objects that interest the infant. Repeat this with both younger and older children. What conclusions do you reach about object permanence, age, and the usefulness of Piaget's theory?

2. Talk with the parent of a toddler. Ask the parent how intelligent they feel their child is and how they came to that conclusion.

3. Describe how you would develop a program for infants and toddlers if you believed in Vygotsky's theory. Discuss how this would be different from a program based on Piaget's theory. What would it mean for teacher preparation and how teachers spend their time?

RESOURCES

Web Resources

※ The **Centers for Disease Control and Prevention** (CDC) has information about infants, toddlers, and parenting. It also provides information about developmental screening and early intervention. http://www.cdc.gov/LifeStages/ infants_toddlers.html.

※ **Mathematica Policy Research, Inc**. collaborates in high quality, objective research to support decisions about the nation's most pressing social policy problems. Some of these include information about Early Head Start and other programs and policies that support infants and toddlers. They have one section devoted to early childhood. http://www.mathematica-mpr.com/.

※ **Medline Plus** is a service of the U.S. National Library of Medicine and the National Institutes of Health. It provides information about developmental milestones and links to numerous other sites that focus on infants and toddlers. http://www.nlm.nih.gov.

※ **Parenting: Babies and Toddlers** is one of a series of sites supported by the New York Times Company (About.com). It provides information on a variety of aspects of parenting including ways of supporting cognitive development. http://babyparenting.about.com.

Print Resources

※ Karpov, Y. V. (2005). *The neo-Vygotskian approach to child development*. New York: Cambridge University Press.

※ Ostrosky, M. M., & Horn, E. (2002). Assessment; gathering meaningful information. *Exceptional Children Monograph Series Number 4*, Longmont, Co: Sopris West.

※ Sandall, S., Hemmeter, M. L., Smith, B. J., & McLean, M. E. (Eds.) (2005). *DEC recommended practices: A comprehensive guide for practical application in early intervention/early childhood special education*. Missoula, MT: Division for Early Childhood.

REFERENCES

Aguiar, A., & Baillargeon, R. (2002). Developments in young infants' reasoning about occluded objects. *Cognitive Psychology, 45*, 263–336.

Bandura, A. (1992). Social cognitive theory. In R. Vasta (Ed.), *Six theories of child development* (pp. 1–60). London: Jessica Kingsley.

Bayley, N. (2005). *The Bayley Scales of infant and toddler development* (3rd ed., Bayley III). *Screening Test*. New York: Psychological Corporation.

Black, M., & Matula, K. (1999). *Essentials of Bayley Scales of infant development II: Assessment*. New York: John Wiley.

Bloom, P. (2002). *How children learn the meaning of words*. Cambridge, MA: MIT Press.

Bornstein, M. H., & Sigman, M. D. (1986). Continuity in mental development from infancy. *Child Development, 57*, 251–274.

Bricker, D. (1993). *Assessment, evaluation, and programming system AEPS measurement for birth to three years* (Vol. 1). Baltimore, MD: Paul H. Brookes Publishing Co.

Bricker, D., & Squires, J. (1999). *Ages and stages questionnaires*. Lewisville, NC: Kaplan Early Learning Company.

Case, R. (1998). The development of conceptual structures. In D. Kuhn & R. S. Siegler (Eds.), *Handbook of child psychology: Vol. 2. Cognition, perception, and language* (pp. 745–800). New York: Wiley.

Cole, M., & Cole, S. R. (2000). *The development of children* (4th ed.). New York: Worth.

Crick, N. R., & Dodge, K. A. (1994). A review and reformulation of social information-processing mechanism in children's social adjustment. *Psychological Bulletin, 115,* 74–101.

Cripe, J., Slentz, K., & Bricker, D. (1993). *Assessment, evaluation, and programming system AEPS curriculum for birth to three years* (Vol. 2). Baltimore, MD: Paul H. Brookes Publishing Co.

Dapretto, M., & Bjork, E. L. (2000). The development of word retrieval abilities in the second year and its relation to early vocabulary growth. *Child Development, 71,* 635–648.

Daws, D. (2000). *Through the night.* San Francisco, CA: Free Association Books.

Feldman, D. H., & Snyder, S. S. (1994). Universal to unique—Mapping the development terrain. In D. H. Feldman (Ed.), *Beyond universals in cognitive development* (2nd ed., pp. 15–38). Norwood, NJ: Ablex Publishing Corporation.

Feinman, S., Roberts, D., Hsieh, K., Sawyer, D., & Swanson, D. (1992). A critical review of social referencing in infancy. In S. Feinman (Ed.), *Social referencing and the social construction of reality in infancy* (pp. 15–54). New York: Plenum Press.

Flavell, J. H. (1999). Cognitive development: Children's knowledge about the mind. *Annual Review of Psychology, 50,* 21–45.

Ford, L., & Dahinten, V. S. (2005). Use of intelligence tests in the assessment of preschoolers. In D. P. Flanagan & P. L. Harrison (Eds.), *Contemporary intellectual assessment: Theories, tests, and issues* (2nd ed., pp. 487–503). New York: The Guilford Press.

Hulit, L. M., & Howard, M. R. (2006). *Born to talk: An introduction to speech and language development* (4th ed.). Boston, MA: Pearson Education, Inc.

Joseph, G. E., & Strain, P. S. (2003). Enhancing emotional vocabulary in young children. *Young Exceptional Children, 6*(4), 18–26.

Karpov, Y. V. (2005). *The neo-Vygotskian approach to child development.* New York: Cambridge University Press.

Kellman, P. J., & Banks, M. S. (1998). Infant visual perception. In W. Damon (Editor-in-Chief), D. Kuhn, & R. S. Siegler (Volume Editors), *Handbook of child psychology: Vol. 2. Cognition, perception, and language* (5th ed., pp. 103–146). New York: Wiley.

Klahr, D., & MacWhinney, B. (1998). Information processing. In D. Kuhn & R. S. Siegler (Eds.), *Handbook of child psychology: Vol. 2. Cognition, perception, and language* (5th ed., pp. 631–678). New York: Wiley.

Lamb, M. E., Bornstein, M. H., & Teti, D. M. (2002). *Development in infancy: An introduction* (4th ed.). Mahwah, NJ: Lawrence Erlbaum Associates.

Linder, T. (1993a). *Transdisciplinary play-based assessment (TPBA).* Baltimore, MD: Paul H. Brookes.

Linder, T. (1993b). *Transdisciplinary play-based intervention (TPBI).* Baltimore, MD: Paul H. Brookes.

Luo, Y., & Baillargeon, R. (2005). When the ordinary seems unexpected: Evidence for incremental physical knowledge in young infants. *Cognition, 95,* 293–328.

Mandler, J. M. (2003). Conceptual categorization. In D. Rakison & L. M. Oakes (Eds.), *Early category and concept development* (pp. 103–131). New York: Oxford University Press.

Many, J. E. (2002). An exhibition and analysis of verbal tapestries: Understanding how scaffolding is woven into the fabric of instructional conversations. *Reading Research Quarterly, 37,* 376–407.

McCall, R. B. (1983). A conceptual approach to early mental development. In M. Lewis (Ed.), *Origins of intelligence* (2nd ed., pp. 67–106). New York: Plenum.

McCall, R. B., & Carriger, M. S. (1993). A meta-analysis of infant habituation and recognition memory performance as predictors of later IQ. *Child Development, 64*(1), 57–79.

Meadows, S. (1993). *The child as thinker: The development and acquisition of cognition in children.* London: Routledge & Kegan Paul.

Meisels, S. J. (2001). Fusing assessment and intervention: Changing parents' and providers' views of young children. *Zero to Three, 21*(4), 4–10.

Meisels, S. J., Marsden, D. B., Dombro, A. L., Weston, D. R., & Jewkes, A. M. (2003). *The Ounce Scale.* New York: Pearson Early Learning.

Meltzoff, A. N. (1999). Origins of mind, cognition and communication. *Journal of Communication Disorders, 32,* 251–269.

Meltzoff, A. N., & Moore, M. L. (1997). Explaining facial imitation: A theoretical model. *Early Development and Parenting, 6,* 179–192.

Meltzoff, A. N., & Prinz, W. (Eds.) (2002). *The imitative mind: Development, evolution and brain bases.* Cambridge, UK: Cambridge University Press.

Miller, P. H. (2002). *Theories of developmental psychology* (4th ed.). New York: Worth.

Moore, M. K., & Meltzoff, A. N. (2004). Object permanence after a 24-hr delay and leaving the locale of disappearance: The role of memory, space, and identity. *Developmental Psychology, 40,* 606–620.

Nadel, J., & Butterworth, G. (1999). *Imitation in infancy.* Cambridge, UK: Cambridge University Press.

National Research Council and Institute of Medicine. (2000). *From neurons to neighborhoods: The science of early childhood development.* Committee on integrating the science of early childhood development. In J. P. Shonkoff & D. A. Phillips (Eds.), Board on Children, Youth, and Families, Commission on Behavioral and Social Sciences and Education. Washington, DC: National Academy Press.

Nelson, C. A. (2003). Neural development and lifelong plasticity. In R. M. Lerner, F. Jacobs, & D. Wertlieb (Eds.), *Handbook of applied developmental science, Vol. 1. Applying developmental science for youth and families: Historical and theoretical foundations* (pp. 31–60). Thousand Oaks, CA: Sage.

Newborg, J. (2004). *Battelle developmental inventory* (2nd ed.). Itasca, IL: Riverside Publishing.

Notari-Syverson, A., O'Connor, R., & Vadasy, P. (1998). *Ladders to literacy: A preschool activity book.* Baltimore, MD: Paul H. Brookes.

Perry, B. D. (2005). Self-regulation: The second core strength. *Early Childhood Today.* Retrieved December 7, 2006, from http://teacher. scholastic.com/professional/bruceperry/ self_regulation.htm

Piaget, J. (1963 [1952]). *The origins of intelligence in children.* New York: Norton (Original work published).

Piaget, J. (1970). Piaget's theory. In P. H. Mussen (Ed.), *Carmichael's manual of child psychology* (3rd ed., Vol. 1, pp. 703–732). New York: John Wiley.

Rogoff, B. (1998). Cognition as collaborative process. In W. Damon (Series Editor), D. Kuhn, & R. S. Siegler (Volume Editors), *Handbook of child psychology, Vol. 2. Cognition, perception, and language* (5th ed., pp. 679–744). New York: Wiley.

Rogoff, B., Mistry, C., Radziszewska, B., & Germond, J. (1992). Infants' instrumental social interaction with adults. In S. Feinman (Ed.), *Social referencing and the social construction of reality in infancy* (pp. 327–348). New York: Plenum Press.

Rosales-Ruiz, J., & Baer, D. M. (1997). Behavioral cusps: A developmental and pragmatic concept for Behavior Analysis. *Journal of Applied Behavior Analysis, 30*(3), 533–544.

Rowe, S. M., & Wertsch, J. V. (2002). Vygotsky's model of cognitive development. In U. Goswami (Ed.), *Blackwell handbook of childhood cognitive development* (pp. 538–554). Malden, MA: Blackwell Publishing.

Salvia, J., & Ysseldyke, J. (2007). *Assessment in special and inclusive education* (10th ed.). Boston, MA: Houghton Mifflin.

Siegler, R. S. (1991). *Children's thinking.* Englewood Cliffs, NJ: Prentice Hall.

Siegler, R. S. (1998). *Children's thinking* (3rd ed.). Upper Saddle River, NJ: Prentice Hall.

Skinner, B. F. (1969). *Contingencies of reinforcement: A theoretical analysis.* Englewood Cliffs, NJ: Prentice Hall.

Teti, D. M., & Gibbs, E. D. (1990). Infant assessment: Historical antecedents and contemporary issues. In E. D. Gibbs & D. M. Teti (Eds.), *Interdisciplinary assessment of infants: A guide for early intervention professionals* (pp. 3–14). Baltimore, MD: Paul H. Brookes.

Travers, J. (2006). Cognitive development. In K. Thies & J. Travers (Eds.), *Handbook of human development for health care professionals* (pp. 95–112). Sudbury, MA: Jones and Bartlett Publishers.

Vygotsky, L. S. (1934/1987). Thinking and speech. In R. Rieber & A. S. Carton (Eds.), *The collected works of L. S. Vygotsky: Vol. 1. Problems of general psychology* (pp. 37–285). New York: Plenum.

Vygotsky, L. S. (1978). The role of play in development. In M. Cole, V. John-Steiner, S. Scribner, & E. Souberman (Eds.), *Mind in society: The development of higher psychological processes* (pp. 92–104). Cambridge, MA: Harvard University Press.

Wadsworth, B. (1971). *Piaget's theory of cognitive development.* New York: McKay.

chapter 6

Communication, Language, and Literacy

Chapter Outline

- Communication and Language
- Theories of Language Acquisition
- Pragmatics
- Language Development
- Sources of Variation in Language Development
- Communication and Language Delays

The first cry, the first word, the first sentence! The infant's ability to move from crying, babbling, and cooing to an understanding of the complex rules of grammar in three short years is astounding. The light and dark that catches the visual attention of the infant moves into patterns that become incomprehensible squiggles that ultimately become letters and words in books. The turn–taking of infants and adults as they smile and gurgle at each other turns into conversations. Language allows toddlers to move from the past to the future and back again. So, how do children learn language? It starts in the womb!

WHY STUDY COMMUNICATION, LANGUAGE, AND LITERACY?

- ❋ Knowing how language is acquired enables you to support infants and toddlers in their language learning.

- ❋ Understanding language development helps you read infant's cues more accurately.

- ❋ To be successful readers, children need to acquire two new word meanings a day from the time of their first birthday. For them to do this, you must plan language learning experiences for each day.

- ❋ Strong language skills support cognitive development and vice versa. You need to provide infants and toddlers with both the experience and the language to talk about it as you plan.

- ❋ Many children come to school learning English as a second language. You need to know how best to teach these children and how to support their home language.

COMMUNICATION AND LANGUAGE

The womb is a noisy place. The constant lub-dub of the mother's heart and the blood rushing around the circulatory system sounds like driving on a crowded interstate with your windows down. The stomach groans and rumbles. And the fetus is underwater listening to the sounds that bombard him. And above all of this noise, the fetus can pick out loud, high-pitched sounds like a tired mother talking to her fetus. "Good morning, baby, don't you think it's a bit early to be up and about. I didn't sleep so well last night and I know you didn't." But amid all of this noise, how can researchers determine that the fetus "heard" his mother? When newborns see something interesting, their heart rate slows down and then returns to normal. Fetuses do the same thing in the womb, and they can hear their mothers talking to them (Fifer & Moon, 1989). Amazingly, the fetus can detect patterns of language before birth and remember them. The patterns differ based on the language that is heard.

This does not mean that more sound is better or that we should bombard the fetus with talk, music, poems, and anything else we can think of. Overstimulated fetuses tune out. However, as humans we are programmed to learn language, because over generations it has increased survival. The fetus is prepared to make sense of language from the moment he is born and even before (Golinkoff & Hirsh-Pasek, 1999).

Think about all the possible ways to communicate. There is obviously talking and writing, but we also communicate with our facial expressions, the clothes or perfume we wear, as well as other nonverbal gestures. This is just the beginning. Think about music and dance, and the list goes on. It is almost as if we cannot *not* communicate. We are constantly sending and receiving messages. **Communication** involves the sending and receiving of information, ideas, feelings, and messages (Hulit & Howard, 2006).

Language refers to a system of intentional communication that is understandable to others. It traditionally consists of sounds, signs, and symbols. These symbols are arbitrary and will change over time because language is evolving (Hulit & Howard, 2006). Language requires a system of rules whereby messages and ideas are transmitted. The capacity for language is innate, basic rules are shared by all languages, but specific rules must be learned for any given language. **Speech** is the oral expression of language (Hulit & Howard, 2006). A parrot can speak but he does not have language. A child with a profound hearing impairment has language but may not be able to speak.

Communication
involves sending and receiving verbal and nonverbal messages.

Language
is a system of sounds, signs, symbols, and grammar, which is used to communicate.

Speech
is the oral expression of language.

THEORIES OF LANGUAGE ACQUISITION

Just as scholars have different beliefs about motor and cognitive development, they also have different theories of how children develop language. Some of these theories are old friends by now and are highlighted briefly; others are discussed in more detail.

Billions of children learn to talk. They learn the language spoken by their parents. The question is how do they do it? Interest in identifying universals in language acquisition goes back to the familiar nature versus nurture issue. Do infants learn language by imitating adults, or do they learn because they have an innate biological propensity to develop language?

Researchers have approached the issue of language and its acquisition from a variety of theoretical and research perspectives. Some have studied the acquisition of a second language, others have looked at it from an evolutionary perspective, and still others have looked at children born without some of the senses considered necessary for language acquisition. Some theories focus on the function of language, others on the structure of language. Other theories focus on the relationship between cognitive and language development. There is general agreement that the genetic make up of the infant plays a role in language learning, and that the environment and culture into which he is born makes a difference. It is the relative importance of these and mechanisms for language acquisition where there is less agreement (Hulit & Howard, 2006).

Maturation Theory

Early studies of communications (1950s and before) used a normative or maturational approach. Researchers looked for patterns, or norms, by categorizing the sounds that infants made, counting the number of words children acquired, and looking at the length of sentences that children could utter in relation to their age. Later research, beginning in the 1960s, is more complex and concentrates more on the acquisition of language, the function of early communication, and the infant's ability to understand language.

Behavioral Theory

Scholars supporting the behavioral model focus on observable and measurable behaviors. They have little interest in the internal mental constructs of language. They believe that language is learned and that infants learn language through the processes of imitation and reinforcement. These two processes together explain why children who are reared in homes where English is spoken learn to speak English, while those in Spanish-speaking homes learn to speak Spanish. Infants utter sounds and sound combinations through imitation and chance. As adults reward, correct, ignore, or punish the toddler's emerging language, they influence the quality and quantity of language as well as the child's attitude toward communication (Osgood, 1968).

The role of reinforcement is a generalized one. As infants coo and babble, adults reinforce sounds that are close to words. A sound sequence such as "mamama" is reinforced and becomes the word "mama." Sounds that are not reinforced fade into extinction. As children utter sounds that are closer to words, adults "shape" these sounds into words by reinforcing sounds that successively approximate words until they are true words. As utterances increase in length, imitation takes a more important role in the process.

It is not as obvious from this theoretical approach why young children use words in ways that adults do not, if in fact imitation plays such an important role (James, 1990). For example, toddlers say, "Me go," "Mommy car," and "Sit chair," which they probably have not heard even in the simplified language that adults often use with young children. The adult's focus is on the external environment that shapes the child's language. Adults are the teachers and children are relatively passive recipients of this knowledge. To behaviorists, Skinner's principles apply: Learning language is like learning to tie your shoes. Although most scholars feel that learning explains some aspects of language acquisition, the theory as a whole explanation is too simplistic and leaves too many questions unanswered (Hulit & Howard, 2006).

Nativist Theory

Behaviorists place the major role of language in the nurture camp, whereas the nativist perspective takes the other end of the continuum—nature. As with cognition, a major goal of some researchers is to identify the "universals" that characterize language acquisition for all languages and all children. This theory supports the idea that language is universal and unique to humans (Hulit & Howard, 2006). Identification of invariant universals across languages would support the theory. Noam Chomsky (1965), a linguist, is most closely associated with this theory. He hypothesized that individuals have a predisposition to learn language. Not finding universals would bring this "innateness" into question. Support for this position uses the fact that infants babble sounds and noises used in languages they have never heard. Two-year-olds can utter complex yet understandable sentences they have never heard.

Another assumption of the nativist is that language is unique to humans. Although pygmy chimpanzees have learned sign language and the understanding of word order, they have not learned adult-like syntax (Rumbaugh & Beran, 2003). Nativists also believe that since language is acquired so quickly and so early in a child's life that learning alone cannot explain its occurrence (Hulit & Howard, 2006). One of the most compelling arguments is that language is functionally the same experience regardless of the language spoken or where people live. On the face of it, learning a second language may seem like a daunting task; however, the similarities among languages are astounding if you forget about the actual words. All languages have rules and these rules determine what words are necessary to make a sentence. They have subjects and predicates, tenses, and ways to make words plural. Different letters signify different sounds. I hope you have gotten the picture. Infants are born to talk.

Accepting these assumptions led to the concept of an innate, unitary **language acquisition device (LAD)** (Chomsky, 1965). The LAD is an innate language reservoir filled with information about the rules of language structure. Nativists contend that it should be understood as a real part of the brain specifically designed to process language. The LAD takes the syntactic information provided by the child's models and generates the grammar of that child's native language. Because no child is predetermined to speak any specific language, the LAD is driven by knowledge common to all languages (Hulit & Howard, 2006). As you might guess, some scholars do not believe in the LAD. The LAD focuses on the structure of the language and does not look at the interaction of structure and meaning.

Research to date has found variation in patterns both within and among infants and languages. Some of this variation seems to be related to the structural differences among natural languages. Within the same language group there are also different patterns of language acquisition. The basic nativist's contention that infants are born with an innate capacity has not been ruled out. What is under debate is the relative role of this innate capacity and environmental factors.

LAD
is an innate language reservoir filled with the possibility of learning the rules of any language.

Pragmatic Theory

Pragmatics
looks at how the context of communication influences what the speaker means and the actual words that are spoken—the difference between the speaker's meaning and sentence meaning.

In response to Chomsky's narrow view of the structure of language, other scholars focused on the functions that are served by communication—**pragmatics**. Although it began in the 1960s with the work of Austin (1962) and one of his students Searle (1969), pragmatics did not become well known until the 1980s and 1990s. Their research focused on the context of language and how language serves different functions for speakers depending on their goals and circumstances. "The study of the functions, purposes, or intents of communication is called pragmatics" (Hulit & Howard, 2006, p. 124).

Searle (1969) identified three different acts within interactions between the speaker and the listener: the locutionary act, the illocutionary act, and the perlocutionary act. Locution is based on the Latin word *loqui*, which means to speak. The **locutionary act** is the utterance itself. If you say to someone, "You had your hair cut," this is a sentence; it has a subject and predicate. But what does it mean? Is it a simple declarative statement, or are there other reasons for making this statement? The **illocutionary act** is concerned with the purpose or motive of the utterance. The speaker's motive might be, "I can't believe you had your hair cut," or "I've never seen such a bad haircut." Searle (1975) also refers to an *indirect speech act*. For example, if I said to you, "I'm thirsty," am I really just making a statement or have I implied in an indirect way that I would like you to get me something to drink? The **perlocutionary act** is concerned with the listener. It looks at the effect of the statement on the listener and whether or not the listener interprets the statement as being congruent

Locutionary act
is saying something, such as stating a fact, asking a question, and so on.

Illocutionary act
indicates how the speech or words should be interpreted, or the intentions of the speaker.

Perlocutionary act
is how the listener interprets the speech.

up close and personal

The following is a message on an answering machine made by a mother, Jamie, and her three-year-old son, Miles, because she is enlisting his help in leaving a message.

Miles: This is Rich, Jamie, Miles …

Jamie: and …?

Miles: Maya.

Jamie: (*Whispers.*) We are not here right now.

Miles: But we are here.

Jamie: (*Whispers.*) We can't answer the phone right now.

Miles: Why not?

Jamie: We'll call you back.

Miles: Yeah, we'll call back.

REFLECTIVE PRACTICE

Young children do not necessarily understand all of the functions of language. Think about conversations you have had with young children as it relates to the function of language. What ways do children use to increase their functional language? How will you support language development both formally and informally?

with the speaker's intent. If the listener knows that the speaker loved the listener's long hair, then she might interpret the statement differently than if the speaker was known to not care about hair length. This aspect of language can be extremely frustrating.

Cognitive Theories

The theories of both Piaget and Vygotsky look at the connection between language and cognition, albeit in very different ways. Piaget sees language developing out of active engagement with the environment. His theory does not focus on the role of language until children move into the preoperational stage, at about age 2. The transition to this stage is characterized by the rapid acquisition of language. Vygotsky, in contrast, sees language playing center stage in cognitive development with the emphasis on social interaction. He views language as one of the mental tools that children possess not only to communicate but also to use for internal problem solving and self-regulation. Vygotsky relies heavily on language acquisition as the impetus for the development of more complex cognitive and social interaction. He found that when children encountered obstacles and cognitive difficulties in tasks, their incidence of private speech almost doubled (Vygotsky, 1962). Although not identified as a social interactionist, Vygotsky's approach is very similar.

Social Interactionist Theory

Social interactionism focuses on the biological and environmental components of language development, particularly the social environment.

You have been watching the pendulum swing between nature and nurture, and structure and function in the previous theories. The final theory brings the pendulum back to the middle: **social interactionism**. Social interactionists believe that both biological and environmental factors play a role in language acquisition. However, they often disagree about the importance each plays. Interactionists focus on the function of language. Infants can communicate long before they can speak words. The upraised arms of the eight-month-old clearly communicates that she wants to be picked up. The adult can make one of four responses:

1. Ignore the infant's request.

2. Pick up the infant without comment.

3. Respond to the infant verbally, "Do you want me to pick you up?" and then pick up the infant.

4. Respond to the infant verbally, "I can't pick you up right now, I need to finish washing the dishes," and not pick up the infant.

The language outcome for the infant will be different depending upon the adult's response and how consistently these responses are given. If infants are ignored, they will make fewer attempts to communicate; if they live in an environment that is not rich with language they will have a smaller vocabulary. If their signals are responded to and reinforced with language, they will develop both language skills and attachment to their caregiver. The last response is more difficult and moves from language development into infant mental health and social development. The concern here is building a sense of trust between the child and the caregiver and the implications for attachment. Interactionists emphasize the importance of adults in responding to children's social and communicative initiations. They look at both the intent of the child and the language model of the adult (James, 1990).

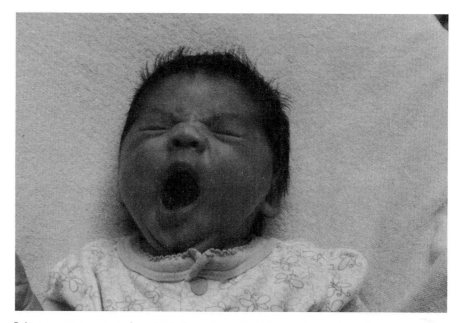

Babies can communicate from birth. Some infants have clear signals, others do not.

Parentese

Adults talk to infants differently than they do to other adults or even to older children. We call this **parentese**, or child-directed speech. No one teaches parents how to slip into parentese when they speak to infants; it seems to occur to most adults naturally and plays an important part in language acquisition (see Table 6–1).

Parentese helps focus the infant's attention on language. The same words are repeated frequently enough for the child to understand their function as well as to learn the words themselves. This is a tremendous help to the infant who is trying to figure out when speech stops and starts and the role different words play. For characteristics and examples of how adults can support emerging speakers, see Table 6–2.

These practices are useful for young children. Most adults use a variety of these techniques without consciously knowing that they are teaching language acquisition. Problems occur when adults continue speaking to toddlers in parentese when it is no longer necessary or useful and could be detrimental. For the young toddler all "fishlike" creatures might be referred to as "fishes." However, by 2 ½ children are ready to learn about minnows, whales, and dolphins.

Overall, social interactionists look at language acquisition in the context of the social environment. A variety of language components interact as infants and toddlers make meaning of their world and begin to affect it. We do not have consensus about how language is acquired, but the information we do have can help guide our communications with children in a productive way.

Table 6–1 Characteristics of Parentese, or Child-Directed Speech

- Use of short, simple sentences
- High-pitched and exaggerated intonation pattern
- Frequent questions and commands
- Frequent repetition of the adult's and child's utterances
- "Play-by-play" talk about what the infant is doing or playing with

EARLY COMMUNICATION

Infants do not hang around and wait to speak or learn about their environment. It is clear from the previous chapter that cognition and language develop in tune with each other. Piaget sees the move into the preoperational stage as the explosion of language. Vygotsky see the role of language more related to

Table 6–2 Characteristics and Examples of How Adults Support Toddlers' Speech

- **Sound**. Adults pitch their voice higher, speak both louder and slower, and enunciate more clearly when talking with infants. They also use a greater range of frequencies, high and low pitches, and more animation. When adults talk to toddlers they may use an unusual pattern of emphasis ("Yes, that is *Sam's* truck"). They may use unusual pronunciation of words ("*Sooo* big"), or they may echo a toddler's incorrect pronunciation. Thus, adults might echo a toddler's assertion that her sister played the "fa-lute." When mispronunciations are humorous, the attention they get is reinforcing.

- **Meaning**. When talking with toddlers, adults frequently use diminutives such as kitty, doggie, bunny, and so on, and substitute words such as choo choo for train. They may use nonstandard combinations, such as "choo choo train" and "moo cow," or use the words that the toddler has made up: "I have to get the vooom and clean this up." They frequently generalize in trying to make concepts easier for children to understand. Facial expressions may be exaggerated.

- **Rhythm**. The rhythm of parentese is different from that of normal speech. The rhythm is more regular than in adult speech. It is almost a singsong cadence.

- **Grammar**. Adults typically both shorten and simplify their utterances. They also frequently use nouns and pronouns in unusual ways. Instead of saying, "I'll do it," they may say, "Mommy do it." They may use plural pronouns instead of singular ones: "Let's eat up all our dinner." They may even purposefully misuse grammar, such as telling a combative toddler, "No hit!"

- **Conversations**. Adult conversations with young children generally relate to the immediate present and the child's immediate surroundings. Many conversations involve adults pointing out and naming items for toddlers. They ask toddlers many simple questions. They may provide both the question and the answer: "Are you hungry? Why yes, I can see that you are."

- **Expansion.** The process of extracting the meaning of a toddler's utterance and putting it into a more complex form is called expansion. A toddler's request for "more" might be responded to with, "Do you want more milk?" For a toddler using telegraphic speech, such as, "Me go," the expansion might be, "Where do you want to go?" or, "Are you ready to go now?" The objective is to provide a language model, not just answer, "Okay."

- **Extension.** Putting the toddler's statement in a broader context; that is, extending the meaning of the phrase is called extension. If the toddler says, "Me go out," the adult might respond, "If you want to go outside, you need to put your coat on." Using these techniques is particularly effective because the toddler has initiated the conversation and is prepared to listen to the response because it is meaningful to him. Adults can also extend children's language through intonation and emphasis ("What do you want to *do* outside?"). Expansion and extension are two techniques that encourage toddlers to use more complex language structures.

SOURCE: Hulit and Howard (2006).

cognitive development and clearly related to what we believe about language development.

Infants are born communicating! Initial communication is not intentional but does function as a signaling system. It is up to the adults in the environment to figure out what the signal means. Early crying seems to be related to the infant's generalized physiological state; in other words, comfort or discomfort. With increasing time vocalizations begin to be more intentional. Although there are many ways of studying the development of communication, a chronological approach seems to make the most sense, and looking at major milestones creates some logical divisions. Despite variations in the timing of language acquisition, like motor and cognitive development, there are major milestones that occur in a predictable sequence.

Infants are well designed to receive communication. Their sense of hearing is well developed at birth and they shows interest in human speech more than other sounds. At as young as three days an infant can recognize his mother's voice and distinguish it from others (DeCasper & Fifer, 1980). By one month he can discriminate among speech sounds. Visual and tactile perception seems to help focus the child and it is important in adult–child attachment. These are some of the general perceptual prerequisites for the development of speech and language. See Table 6–3 for the abilities infants need to speak.

The first two requirements were detailed as part of sensory and perceptual development. These skills are honed during the first year. To sequence speech sounds infants need to not only perceive them, but also remember them. Rudimentary memory skills are apparent as early as one month, and by four months infants can remember an object for five seconds (Owens, 2005). By about six months infants can respond to intonational patterns and even imitate them.

Distinguishing sequences of sound requires the infant to figure out when one sequence begins and the other ends, establishing boundaries. Although we do not know how infants go about making these boundaries, they appear to be able to do this by about seven months (Goodsitt, Morse, ver Hoeve, & Cowan, 1984). By about nine months the infant makes distinctions among speech sounds in her home language (Hulit & Howard, 2006). About this same time infants begin to match sequences of sounds they hear with those that are stored in their memory. "Dada" may be a familiar sound, but at this point "dada" may relate to all men, not solely to her father. When it becomes a word for an infant, and what the word really means to her is unknown. Intonation patterns play a role in interpreting language. The amount of meaning they convey is dependent upon the particular communication. Cognitive development, memory, and perceptual ability interact to support language acquisition.

Table 6–3 Skills Required for Infants to Develop Speech and Language

To speak infants need to be able to attend to speech
- discriminate among speech sounds
- discriminate among intonational patterns
- remember a sequence of speech sounds and the order they were presented
- discriminate between sequences of speech sounds
- compare a sequence of speech sounds to a model stored in memory

SOURCE: Owens (2005).

WITH INFANTS AND TODDLERS

Pick an infant up and hold her so she can see over your shoulder. Walk around the room and point out objects and events that are taking place and what other infants and toddlers are doing. With young infants, make the walk short and talk less. Use items that the infant is familiar with and start out with what she knows, like her own coat, then let her touch it. Use disparate items to continue, such as a book; allow her to touch this also. Only label one or two items and then stop if she loses interest. Label more items for older infants and talk about their function. Encourage the infant to touch the items and to imitate what you say. Vary what you say to include, "What are those?" Wait a few seconds and then say something like, "Those are Perry's boots!"

"That's the telephone. Sometimes it rings and I talk to people on it. (pause) There is Roxanna, she is playing with Dot. (pause) This is one of my favorite pictures. Aura painted it. See the beautiful red she used." (pause) Infants need to learn about and feel comfortable in their environment. The view from your shoulder is very different from their view from the floor. So it is important they see this, too, and learn the language that goes with these new perceptions. Although infants will not understand all the words you use, they will hear the different tones of your voice and begin to make associations, especially if you demonstrate what objects do. Do talk in parentese.

JOINT COMMUNICATION: AN ADULT–CHILD PARTNERSHIP

Communication does not develop in isolation; it is truly a joint venture. Babies want to communicate with their caregivers, because they have things to say. Caregivers want to initiate and reciprocate this communication. Language development is enhanced when skilled adults help infants focus on objects and attach names to those objects. For these children, vocabulary grows quickly. Vocabulary growth has the advantage that children can express themselves and make their needs known better. It also has long-term implications for literacy.

Literacy begins in infancy. Not with flash cards made with big letters but with the development of vocabulary. To be successful readers children need to need to have a stock of about 6,000 root words by grade two. This requires them to acquire about two new word meanings per day from one year of age (Biemiller & Slonim, 2001). **Root words** are common words and are defined as basic vocabulary as opposed to rare words that are specific and used infrequently. A root word is a real word and one you can make new words from by

Root words are real words, and new words can be made from them by using prefixes and suffixes.

Word families
are related words built by using a root word.

adding prefixes and suffixes. For example, the root word "use" can become useful, useless, using, user, usable, misuse, used, and so on. Together these words form a **word family**. Word families share the same root word, part of the spelling, and have a shared meaning. Using word families is a way of increasing vocabulary. One responsibility of the adults in a child's environment is to ensure that there are many opportunities for the development of vocabulary and that the adult and child jointly focus their attention on the same object or event at the same time (Owens, 2005).

There are a variety of ways in which adults support children's language learning. One strategy is that of *saying* the word. For example, if a toddler were playing with a train, the adult might point to the train and say, "Train." This may be followed by a request *asking* the child, "Can you say train?" A response to this question is hopefully followed by reinforcing statements such as, "That's close, good for you," or, "You certainly can."

At a later time there might be followup about the train where the adult *talks about* the properties of the train or the phonemic aspect of the word: "This train is moving on the track. I wonder where it is going?" Or, "Train starts with the sound /t/ like your name: /t/rain, /T/om." Other times, adults *define* the word: "All of this [*Gesturing*] is the train. This front part of the train that makes it move is called the engine. It pulls the other cars. The last car is the caboose." Sometimes adults *explain* a word by adding details and tying them into the children's experience: "When you come to school you cross over the railroad tracks. Have you ever had to stop and wait for a train to pass? Some trains are long and others are shorter. Some of the trains go very fast, but others seem to go back and forth and they take a long time. But all of the trains have to stay on the track. They can only go where there are train tracks" (Han, Roskos, Christie, Mandzuk, & Vuklich, 2005). Obviously what you would use from these techniques is dependent on the age of the child and the child's interest in the topic.

Does all this really make any difference in children's language acquisition? Yes. Will children who have language environments that are not as rich and responsive learn to talk? Yes. Are children who have language-rich environments more competent in language? Yes.

FIRST SOUNDS TO FIRST WORDS

The previous section focused on the receptive or input aspect of language and the interaction between children and adults. This section looks at output or expressive language. There is much preparation for speech before the first word is uttered. Early communicative acts are primarily reflexive in nature and are used to express basic bodily needs or states, such as hunger or pain. The interpretative aspect of the communication rests with the adult.

Reflexive Sounds

During the first few weeks, infants primarily cry and make "vegetative noises." Are babies' cries different depending on whether they are hungry, wet, or unhappy? The jury is out. Maybe some infants do have different cries, but it is also possible that adults read meaning into cries that is not really there. For example, if an infant cries at about the time he expects to be fed, and stops crying when he sees the bottle, we are likely to conclude it was a hungry cry. This conclusion might be more in response to context than to the crying itself. When researchers have studied crying they have not found differences in crying based on pain or hunger. They play tapes of infants crying and ask adults to predict why the infant is crying. However, as part of their controls, they have kept the length and intensity of the crying constant. It may be that the length of crying and a pattern of growing intensity are relevant signals for parents that were not part of the experimental conditions (Baron, 1992).

From birth until about two to three months, the infant's communication consists of reflexive reactions to internal and external stimuli. The caregiver

WITH INFANTS AND TODDLERS

Martin is tired, he is cranky, and everyone is busy. At six months he cannot get want he wants. But he is signaling, and no one is looking. He wants his blankie and he looks longingly at it, getting more upset. A caregiver notices his distress and comes over and tries to comfort him. He cries harder. You, the astute observer, notice the direction of his gaze. You get his blankie and say, "Is this what you wanted?" He takes it, smiles at you, puts his thumb in his mouth, and settles down. When infants communicate without words, it takes an alert, creative adult to notice the communication and then figure out the intent. If you focus on signals such as these you increase your ability to meet the needs of very young children and assure them that they are in a responsive world.

Morgan is 12 months old. She can get many things that she wants because she is a fast, efficient creeper. However, when she is being fed in her high chair, she is captive. When she is done eating, she clearly turns her head away when food is offered. She spits it out. These signals are clear. What she does want is her bottle. She can see it but she cannot reach it. She looks at you, makes eye contact, and then looks at the bottle. You are a little slow on the uptake this time, but she has not yet exhausted her repertoire. She vocalizes to get your attention and points to the bottle. Finally, you get it! Babies communicate with and without words.

responds to these signals or cues by increasing or decreasing stimulation, and talking to the infant in parentese. The infant in turn reacts to the tone of voice and facial expression, produces more consistent signals, and calibrates her states or moods (McLean, 1990).

Cooing and Laughing

At about two months cooing is added to the infant's repertoire. Contentment produces coos and vowel sounds. Discontentment produces crying; however, the crying has decreased in frequency and is more differentiated. The ku (coo) and gu (goo) sounds are physiologically very easy-to-produce sounds from the back of the throat. By two months, both the cries and other verbalizations start to take on more of the structure of human speech, and by about three months there are patterned vocalizations that are vowel-like (ah, ee, etc.) (Stark, 1979).

By four months laughter is added to the infant's inventory of sounds. Infants appear to interpret the intonation contours of adult speech accurately as well. Infants are now upset by angry voices and soothed by friendly ones. Around the fifth month infant utterances seem to take on the intonation and speech patterns of their native language. And infants now yell, squeal, and have more variety in their repertoire of vocalizations. Also around five months infants produce vocalizations that seem to bridge between cooing and true babbling, sometimes referred to as **marginal babbling** (Stark, 1979). These babbling sounds are produced when the infant is happy. They continue to be internal state responses and do not need stimulation to be present. About this time infants also get the idea of turn-taking in communications; that is, the adult speaks and then pauses, the infant vocalizes and waits, the adult speaks again. These become "conversations" between adults and infants. As the infant's vocalization sounds more like communication, sensitive adults respond to this cue and begin the turn-taking process.

Marginal babbling is the reflection of an inner state, not an attempt at communication.

Babbling

True babbling does not come in until six months or older (Stark, 1979). **Reduplicated babbling** is the systematic pairing of a consonant and vowel ("ma" or "dah") and then the repetition of that sound ("ma-ma-ma"). Different than spontaneous babbling, infants seems to find pleasure in recreating sounds they have heard themselves make. Infants tend to babble when they are investigating their surroundings or an object. Cooing is more social (Hulit & Howard, 2006). The initial consonant sounds used are those which are produced at the front of the mouth, such as /b/, /d/, /m/, /n/, /p/, and /t/. These sounds are easily produced by simple oral motor manipulation, and the child eventually

Reduplicated babbling is the systematic pairing of a consonant and vowel and the repetition of this sound.

Reading to infants and toddlers needs to be a planned part of every day. Reading is different from talking, and children need both.

develops the ability to voluntarily produce sound-blend combinations, like /ma/, /ba/, /da/, and so on.

The infant's sounds are becoming progressively become more refined. Between 8 and 12 months he begins to repeat sounds, syllables, or words heard in the environment. This repetition is called **echolalia**. He copies sounds and begins to experiment more with rhythm and inflection. But he does not yet attach meaning to sound. The ability to imitate environmental sounds becomes increasingly important. Infants with profound hearing impairments cry, laugh, coo, and babble spontaneously, but as the ability to imitate environmental sounds becomes progressively important, they do not hear or use these sounds.

Echolalia is the repetition of vocalizations made by other people.

WITH INFANTS AND TODDLERS

Beginning at birth, read to babies. Read, chant, or sing nursery rhymes as you turn the pages of a book with infants and toddlers. Use the books frequently so infants and toddler become familiar with the repeated sounds and learn the rhymes. Read books with simple nursery rhymes, such as *I'm a little teapot; This little piggy; Baa, baa, black sheep; Hickory, dickory dock.* Encourage toddlers to join you in saying the rhymes or parts of rhymes. Children often share an adult's enthusiasm and actions as they read. Share other books.

Jargon and Variegated Babbling

Variegated babbling uses more varied sounds (vowels and consonants) in a single utterance.

Jargon babbling begins to take on the intonation patterns of adult speech.

Vocables or **protowords** are sound patterns used consistently to refer to a particular thing or situation and are idiosyncratic to an individual child.

From about 9 to 18 months, babbling goes through another phase of more advanced babbling, called **variegated babbling**, where the infant varies the consonant vowel pattern in a single utterance. The pattern is typically either consonant-vowel-consonant or vowel-consonant-vowel. Infants' babbling is also taking on the intonational contours of adult speech, which is sometimes called **jargon babbling**. Although the words do not make sense, if you listen to the rhythm and stress it sounds like, you should be able to figure it out and even come up with an appropriate response. During this time, infants are moving from prelinguistic communication to language. They begin to produce **vocables** or **protowords**. These are "words" that are unique to a child, but are consistent patterns of sound that are used to refer to particular things or situations (Hulit & Howard, 2006). These are not words, but represent a transition between random vocalization and the purposeful use of a standard language.

PRAGMATICS

Pragmatics is the study of how context influences the meaning of communication.

As we move into language, our focus changes from the production of sounds to the intention or function of communication. We communicate for a purpose, often to get things done and accomplish particular goals. The study of the function or meaning of language in context is called **pragmatics**. Infants understand this aspect of communication before they can express language. Pragmatic theorists divided speech into three stages: perlocutions, illocutions, and locutions (Searle, 1969). Although infants do not participate in locution or speech until about a year, at birth they are in the perlocutionary stage. This stage lasts until about eight months. Infants show that they recognize the functional use of objects by using gestures, such as bringing a cup or spoon to their mouth. The illocutionary stage begins about 8 months and lasts until 12 months. It is a time when infants show intentionality and vocalizations by pointing or showing as well as using other gestures. By 12 months or so, infants are using all three aspects of language.

Perlocutionary Stage: Birth to 8 Months

At the beginning of this stage, communication is reflexive; by the end of this stage, infants use gestures as way of communicating (Hulit & Howard, 2006). This is the time in neo-Vygotsky theory when attention is moving away from the adult and to objects and interacting with them. In Piaget's theory it is in the transition between substages 3 and 4, which focuses on object permanence and the beginning of means-end behavior and goal-directed behavior.

Illocutionary Stage: 8 to 12 Months

Infants now use communication, gestures, and vocalizations to show intentionality. Infants point to objects they want or shake their head when they do not want something. The connection between communication and getting one's needs met or curiosity satisfied has been made.

Receptive language
is listening and understanding the meaning of communication.

Expressive language
is verbally communicating using words.

Comprehension of words (**receptive language**) begins before the production of words (**expressive language**). Comprehension and production are quite different processes. Comprehension requires that sound sequences be related to objects or events, whereas production requires retrieving from memory and articulating a sound sequence that relates to these object or events. Around 10 months infants begin to respond predictably to some words. The first of these are typically the infant's name and "no."

Why "no"? Why not "yes"? One reason is that children are likely to be told "no" far more frequently than "yes." One role of adults is to protect the new investigator from harm. This may require saying no many times, which one hopes is followed by suggestions of what can be safely done. Additionally, the /n/ is far easier than the /y/ for the infant to say.

Locutionary Stage: 12 Months and Up

Communication now takes on a social context. Words and gestures are combined. The infant now greets and initiates conversations. If adults react to children's communication as if it has communicative intent, infants learn more about the practical level of communications. When adults respond to and expand behaviors such as eye contact, gestures, babbling, and jargon as if they were purposeful communication, infants learn patterns of communication and produce them more frequently.

LANGUAGE DEVELOPMENT

Like cognitive development, stages in language development provide an essential organizing tool. The stages are continuous and the ages given are guidelines. The order in which language is acquired is more important than the age (Hulit & Howard, 2006). In addition to age there are other underlying organizational features used to understand language development. To understand the structure of language you need to understand the building blocks that are used to make up language itself.

Morphemes
are the smallest meaningful unit of language; they can be words, suffixes, or prefixes.

A **morpheme** is the smallest meaningful unit of language. At first thought you might say words are morphemes. In some cases this is true, but some words are made up of more than one morpheme. There are actually two kind of morphemes: free and bound. Free morphemes can stand alone and have meaning. Singular words like cat and dog are free morphemes. Bound morphemes must be attached to a free morpheme to be meaningful (Hulit & Howard, 2006). The letter *s* is a bound morpheme. If we bind it to cat, we change the meaning. Cat = one cat, cats = more than one cat. Prefixes and suffixes fall into the bound morpheme category. However, you need to be clear that the letters are actually being used as a prefix or suffix. The word *undo* means to release or untie something. Clearly *un* is a prefix that changes the meaning of the word *do*. However, the word *under* is a free morpheme, because the *un* is not used as a prefix.

MLU
is the average number of morphemes per utterance.

Another necessary concept is **mean length of utterance (MLU)**. Mathematically, the mean is the statistical average. The length of utterance is determined by the number of morphemes in the utterance. So, the morphemes are counted for each utterance and divided by the number of utterances. MLUs are rarely expressed as whole numbers. An MLU of 2.0 would mean an average of 2.0 morphemes per utterance. The stages that follow are based on those developed by Roger Brown (1973) with additions by Lloyd Hulit and Merle Howard (2006).

Stage 1: Words to Combinations of Words, 12 to 26 Months (1.0 to 2.0 MLU)

This stage begins when the child is producing meaningful words and ends when he can put words together. Another way of looking at it is he begins with an average of 1.0 morpheme per utterance and moves to 2.0 morphemes, a small difference, but a giant step in language development.

Early Stage 1: 12 to 22 Months (1 to 1.5 MLU)

Children's first words are not chosen at random. They are words that are meaningful to the child in her environment: objects, people, and actions. The words are usually one or two syllables or one syllable repeated: "bye-bye." They also have a particular structure. The most common are consonant-vowel (go) and vowel-consonant (ah) or a repetition of these (dada).

It is almost as difficult to decide when a "first" word occurs as it is to determine when the "first" step takes place. Many of the earliest "words" spoken by the infant are not traditional words. Initially there is no consistent word association, but eventually the idea of a relationship between word and object develops. In most instances, the child learns the meaning of the word before he begins to use it while communicating. See Table 6–4 for characteristics of real words.

As infants acquire words it is interesting to speculate how and why some words become part of the young child's vocabulary and others do not. Bloom (1993) gives three principles that govern which words are learned. The first principle is that of *relevance*—children learn words pertaining to objects or actions that have meaning to them. First words are often nouns and are the names of objects that children act upon, such as ball or shoe. Initially children seem to move from action to concept to words. Some young children place the most relevance on objects (nouns), whereas others learn words that help them initiate or maintain social interactions (greetings) (Nelson, 1973). What children are learning, however, is not just words, but the mental representation of what the words are about.

The second principle, *discrepancy*, has to do with the difference between the world as it is and the world as the infant wants it to be. The extent to which the child wants something creates the demand for language. The third principle, *elaboration*, reflects the increasing complexity of the child's world. With his increasing knowledge, he requires increasingly complex words and structures to express these ideas (Bloom, 1993).

As interesting as the words that toddlers use may be, the context in which they are used and the multifunction of the words are even more intriguing. Children's **overextension** is sometimes the most revealing aspect of their

Overextension is generalizing the use of words beyond their actual meaning.

Table 6–4 Characteristics of Real Words

- The same word is used to signal the same meaning. It can be arf-arf for the sound of a dog but not the sound of a cow.
- The word has to approximate the sound of the conventional word.
- The word is used with the intent to communicate, not in imitation.
- The word is used in a variety of settings to name objects the child has not heard someone else name.

SOURCE: Golinkoff and Hirsh-Pasek (1999).

cognitive classification system. One of my favorite posters is a two-year-old girl petting a dog and saying, "Nice kitty, nice kitty." To her, everything that is furry and has four legs is a "kitty." For most adults this is a humorous example. Parents find it less humorous when all men are called "Daddy" and all women "Mommy." Yet these are similar situations of overextension.

Underextension
is using a word to identify only one particular object in a category of objects.

The reverse of this overgeneralization process, **underextension**, is also fascinating. Toddlers sometimes refuse to generalize. The label "book" refers to one and only one book. Other books must have a different label. This is distressing to parents before they become aware of the one and only book or stuffed animal or whatever the appropriate designee is. One role of adults is to provide young children with enough examples that underextension is very rare.

Around 14 to 18 months children begins to experiment with new sound blends, using sounds heard in the environment, combining them, and producing new words. As children transition into two-word utterances the word order is not fixed. An infant may say "little doll" or "doll little" and the words themselves may not be related. Toddlers put two single words together, without intending a word combination, "cookie mommy." Gradually this is followed by two-word utterances that do relate, "Fall down." Utterances that leave out many words are often referred to as telegraphic speech. Early two-word phrases tend to be requests: "Mommy come?" "Daddy ball." "Want juice." The few words that toddlers can put together convey an amazing amount of information. Typically the adult has little difficulty understanding the meaning of these utterances.

Semantic features
are parts of meaning, such a plurals or nouns.

We are not really sure how children attach meaning to words. One hypothesis is that words have bits of meaning called **semantic features** (Clark, 1975). Many words have common semantic features but it is the particular set of semantic features that sets it apparent from others. The actual semantic features used are dependent on the toddler and her environment.

Functional core hypothesis
states that children categorize objects based on actions of things or their own action toward things.

Nelson (1974) proposed the **functional core hypothesis**. He feels that children categorize things based on their actions if they are animate objects, or actions they can perform on inanimate objects. Piaget would probably support this hypothesis because it directly relates to children actively constructing their knowledge by acting on objects in the environment. Bowerman (1978) found both of these approaches too narrow and proposed the **prototype hypothesis**.

Prototype hypothesis
states that children develop a prototype of a concept and test other information against the prototype, gradually fine-tuning the process.

Children use their experiences to build a model or standard for a particular concept and then "test" other words or actions against this mental representation. The toddler might start out with a prototype of "chair." It is likely to be a chair the child is familiar with. Initially a rocking chair or overstuffed chair might not fit the prototype. However, as the child expands and adjusts these prototypes to include and exclude information depending on its relevance, the concept becomes broader (Hulit & Howard, 2006).

Nominals
are words used to refer to objects (ball, book, cup, etc.).

General nominals
are used to refer to all objects in a category (balls could be big, small, rubber, plastic, beach balls, tennis balls, or baseballs).

Action words
describe someone doing something or demanding an action.

One of the things we do know about young toddlers as they develop language is that many of their words refer to objects. **Nominals** are words used to refer to objects. **General nominals** are used to refer to all objects in a category. That is, kitty for all cats and perhaps even dogs. Toddler's categories may be far broader than adults. Most of these nominals refer to objects that can be moved or manipulated or those of particular importance to a specific child (Hulit & Howard, 2006). Would Piaget have predicted this? **Action words** are another common category. These are words that describe or demand action, such as, up, go, and look.

It should be noted that there is much individual variation among children in their vocabulary development. This is true about the types of words children use and how they acquire vocabulary. However, once children hit the 50-word mark (about 18 months) they tend to experience rapid growth in vocabulary, especially nouns. But all children are different and may be acquiring vocabulary at their own unique pace. As children add words to their gestures they open up new communicative possibilities. Like other developmental areas, growth in language is asynchronous. Language development has intermittent spurts that vary with individual children. Toddlers around 15 to 18 months frequently experience such a developmental burst. Some have this burst as young as 10 months, others as late as 20 months (Cawlfield, 1992). During this language burst toddlers show a decreased interest in toys and playing independently and an increased interest in their primary caregiver. They are interested in books and labeling objects in pictures. They attempt to say words and concentrate on watching the adult's mouth. This period usually lasts about four months and the culmination seems to be the emergence of symbolic thinking, along with increased interest in toys and a longer attention span (Cawlfield, 1992).

As children's intentions become more complex, the relationship between the speaker and listener is more interesting. Children's speech is in the here and now. The listener may need an active and imaginative way to fill in the missing information. As toddlers move from one-word to two-word production, they are figuring out the rules.

Late Stage 1: 22 to 26 Months (1.5 to 2.0 MLU)

Rich interpretation
is the process of understanding toddler's utterances using context and other clues.

Toddlers begin to put two words together between 18 and 24 months. Although these combinations are not complex, they represent the beginning of syntax. Two-year-olds now have the ability to focus their communications and make them more meaningful. Moving from "no" to "no bye-bye" carries significantly more information. However, context is still necessary to interpret the meaning of the communication. Using context to interpret the meaning of these utterances is call **rich interpretation** (Brown, 1973) and has helped guide understanding of children's language development. Brown tied language and cognition together with the assumption that early language reflects what children know about the objects and actions in their lives and that their level of intellectual understanding is reflected in their language.

Toddlers are now participating in dialogue. They understand two-way communication and that one person speaks and the other listens. Their vocabulary is increasing. New words are learned quickly, though the correct pronunciation is not necessarily acquired during the initial stages. Two-year-olds begin to enter into simple conversations and initiate communication with peers or adults.

By 24 months communication may expand to two-, three-, and even four-word utterances. These may contain nouns and verbs, and even adjectives (Hulit & Howard, 2006). However, the toddler's speech may not be fully intelligible. Practice helps the development of the toddler's expressive skills. He needs adult support for this burst of language, and continued support as he uses his language with peers and in his play. Two-year-olds are purposeful. They use language to make requests and to get things done. They want to satisfy their needs and control those around them. They use language to learn. They want to learn about themselves and the world in which they live. The last language function to emerge is informative. To inform others you have to know more than they do. In early stages of language development everyone knows more. However at the end of this period two-year-olds feel confident in their knowledge and are eager to share what they know regardless of the adult's evaluation of the usefulness of this knowledge. One of their limitations as a conversationalist is their short attention span. By age 3 children can talk about a topic they are interested in for an extended period of time—perhaps beyond your interest.

Comprehension and expression are tied together; however, the relationship is not as straightforward as one might think. Initially it seems to be intuitive that infants and toddlers must hear and understand language before they can produce it. However, as children begin to produce language they use words they do not understand (remember the poster example). The relationship between production and comprehension changes as language develops. In the beginning comprehension is not based on language (Hulit & Howard, 2006). Comprehension is far more global than language. Comprehension is based on nonverbal experiences, actions, and the interaction of things and actions. It is based on the repetition of familiar routines with the addition of sound sequences that go along with these experiences. At some point the infant connects sounds and actions. A child's knowledge is based on her environment and her experiences in it. She creates mental representations of her world and gradually associates these representations with spoken words. The words help her retrieve the concepts or schemata (Huttenlocher, 1974).

Children comprehend names for people and things before they understand the words that describe actions and relationships (Hulit & Howard, 2006). The easiest scenario is the understanding of people and then objects that are present when talked about (12 months). By 16 months most children understand references to actions that are taking place. By about 20 months, toddlers understand some words referring to people and things they cannot see (Miller, Chapman, Branston, & Reichle, 1980). We may overestimate a child's level of comprehension because of his limited repertoire of behaviors. If we say, "Drink your milk," and the toddler does, we may assume that he knows what "drink your milk" means. The reality may be that he understood the word milk and the only thing he knows to do with milk is drink it, so he did.

According to Huttenlocher (1974), comprehension and production are different processes in the brain. When a child comprehends language, words are used to retrieve mental images or representations of the person, object, or action. In language production the child recognizes the person, object, or action and must retrieve the matching word. Thus production is a more difficult process once children understand more about people, objects, and actions than they have words to match them.

Language does not develop in isolation. Cognition and language develop in tandem. Hearing language alone is not enough. We do not know exactly how turn-taking, expansion, and extension aid in the acquisition of language, but we are clear that they do. It may be that is how children learn concepts such as plurals and possessives and other grammatical structures as well as the expansion of knowledge.

Stage 2: Elaborating Structure and Refining Meaning 27 to 30 Months (2.0 to 2.5 MLU)

Stage two is an elaboration of stage one. During this stage the child modifies the meaning of words. He does this by adding morphemes. With nouns we can modify the meaning by making them plural (boys) or possessive (boy's ball). With verbs we can use the past tense (played) or the present progressive (playing). The irregular past tense and nouns that do not follow the rules are more challenging. Initially two-year-olds overgeneralize. The plural of child is "childs," the past tense of go is "goed." By listening to good language models children learn the irregular forms.

Pronouns, words that take the place of nouns, are beginning to appear more frequently. Conceptually, pronouns are challenging to young children and even some adults. The child must know the gender of the referent (he, she) or lack of gender (it), the number of people referred to (I, we; he, she, they), and then of course there is you (singular) and you (plural). Pronouns also differ based

up close and personal

A family of four was standing looking into a mirror and the mother asked her 20-month-old daughter "Who is that?" pointing to the little girl's father. She appropriately replied "Daddy". The mother pointed to herself and asked "Who am I?" Maya responded "Mommy". Her mother next pointed to her older brother and she responded "Miles." When the mother finally asked, "and who is this?" pointing to the little girl, she promptly responded "My turn!"

REFLECTIVE PRACTICE

Children lean language that is useful to them. Think about the function the words "my turn" might have for a younger sibling.

on how they are used in the sentence. He is the subject, but the predicate is him, and the possessive is his. Two-year-olds come into stage two with several pronouns, typically *I, it, this, that*. They add *my, mine, me,* and *you* (Hulit & Howard, 2006). However, they might not always use them correctly.

As two-year-olds put words together to convey meaning, they must learn the basic components of sentences: phrases and clauses. There are two basic types of phrases: noun and verb. Noun phrases contain a noun and words that describe or modify it (Boy happy). Verb phrases contain a verb and words that modify it (Go home). Clauses have a subject and a predicate and a collection of related words (Boy go home) (Hulit & Howard, 2006).

Negations are becoming more prominent during stage two. In late stage one, the child uses the negation at the beginning of a phrase "no go." During stage two this position is modified by placing the negation in front of the verb and including a subject, "Me no go." It is not until the latter part of stage three that you might hear, "I not going."

Toddlers initially form questions by adding a rising intonation pattern to the last word in the utterance ("Go home?"). These are typically yes/no questions. In the latter part of stage two, children add the *what* and *where* and the inevitable *why* questions, although the child experiences some confusion among the *wh-* questions.

At 24 months the child averages 200 to 300 words in his expressive vocabulary. By about 30 months, the end of this stage, it grows to 400 words (Hulit & Howard, 2006). One explanation for the child's ability to acquire so much

Fast mapping is using context to gain information about the meaning of words.

information about so many words is the concept of **fast mapping** (Carey & Bartlett, 1978). When a child first encounters a new word, she uses the surrounding language and the context to gain some clues about the meaning of the word. She stores these bits of information. When the word is next encountered the child adds to her knowledge base about the word. This process works best when children hear the same word over a period of time. Drilling a child on a word is not effective because the context within the drill is the same each time and it is more difficult for the child to extract the bits of information necessary to form meaning. In the context of word knowledge, this means that children may have bits and pieces of information about a word, but not a complete understanding of it (Hulit & Howard, 2006). This is why so much programming for infants and toddlers uses variations on a theme.

Vocabulary increases dramatically, fluency is better, and improved grammar and syntactic skills appear throughout the second year. The toddler uses many new consonants. However, the most interesting aspect of language now is how children learn the structure of language. We know a lot about how children learn grammar from the mistakes they make using irregular verbs and plurals.

Toddlers begin to use the past tense around two years. They sort out some of the rules, such as adding "-ed." You are likely to hear the child say, "I comed home," "I blowed hard," and "I weared it today." This is a delightful stage as it is clear by these mistakes that young children have generalized the rules of the language. Initially they may use some irregular verbs correctly out of imitation. They have similar problems with irregular plurals that they have with irregular tenses: "Look at the mans." Word placement is a challenge, particularly with negations: "Why you aren't coming?" Some of the creativity is delightful as children grope to express themselves and become master wordsmiths.

SOURCES OF VARIATION IN LANGUAGE DEVELOPMENT

Not all children learn the same "language." A number of variables complicate learning language, such as the intelligence and personality of the child and the situation of the family in which he lives. Family factors include whether the child is a first, later, or only child, how responsive the family is to his verbalizations, and their beliefs about rearing children.

Families

As children are different, so are families. They have different expectations for their children and different ideas about the family's role in language development. Some families think children basically learn to talk on their own, so they are responsive to their child but do little initiating. Other families make more conscious efforts to stimulate language by pointing out and naming objects and reading to young children.

Adults provide most of the modeling and examples for young language learners. Parents who respond to a toddler's communicative attempts support and encourage these attempts. When adults do not respond to a toddler's sounds and gestures, they send a message that communication behaviors are not valued. It is important that the toddler's communicative efforts be responded to so they continue to communicate. Lack of reinforcement extinguishes behavior. Adult interaction is necessary for the development of the child's language abilities.

Parents are rarely the cause of delayed language, but they, as well as teachers, can often help children develop good language. Some types of adult speech, such as asking questions and showing approval of children's attempts at communication, are conducive to language development, whereas making disparaging remarks about children's language has negative effects on children's language development. Focusing on their deficits and not allowing children time to respond reduces children's self-esteem as well as their language output. Modeling grammatically correct speech, asking open-ended questions, recasting, and expanding their statements all encourage language development.

Position in the Family

Infant language development varies with the infant's position in the family, the educational level of the mother, the amount of reading and television watching, and other variables. As children begin to use identifiable words, they appear to take one of two approaches in learning additional words: a referential approach or an expressive approach (Baron, 1992). First children, especially those from middle-class homes, usually have a referential approach. These children often use words early (9 to 10 months) and the words generally refer to objects or people in their immediate surroundings. Other children begin talking a little later (12 to 14 months) and have more diverse utterances of an expressive style, such as a version of please or thank you. They tend to add to their vocabulary more slowly.

The child's style may reflect the parent's style. If the mother names objects for the infant, the infant will probably learn the names of objects. The presence of other children mediates the language that mothers use with infants. Older children are more likely to answer questions posed and "take over" experiences than younger children. With other children in the home, the mother may focus on having children play together in harmony, and, in an effort to request similar things of both older and younger children, may make more socialization requests. It is not clear how children who spend time in child care are influenced.

up close and personal

Our youngest daughter had a favorite blanket that she called, appropriately, "favorite." As she became attached to another blanket, we joked about an appropriate label for the "other" blanket, suggesting "Favorite II" and a variety of other labels—many of which were not appropriate, but we were having a great time with our ideas. She ended the appropriate-label discussion by simply calling the other blanket "other."

REFLECTIVE PRACTICE

Children focus on function. They sort out what is meaningful to them. This same child was once challenged by a family friend on her use of the word astronaut. Her response was "Astronauts can fly to outer space but they can't fly to New Jersey." You be the judge. Did she understand the word?

Gender

Pink for girls and blue for boys. Gender roles are socialized from birth or before. Language influences perception and perception influences language. Adults talk to boys and girls differently. There is some evidence that mothers talk to girls more than to boys, and that they are more likely to use words that relate to feelings and emotions with toddler girls than with their male counterparts. Mothers of girls asked more questions, repeated their child's utterances, and used longer sentences than did mothers of boys. Mothers of boys used more imperatives (Gleason, 1987). Girls tend to use language earlier and more frequently than boys (Zero to Three, n.d.).

We know less about the father's impact. However, it is clear that fathers can and do play an important role in early language and literacy. Fathers talk to their children, read them books, and help to ensure that infants and toddlers live and grow in a home environment that supports language and literacy (Gadsden & Bay, 2002). These differences show great cultural variation.

Personality

A child's personality influences how language is learned. Socially outgoing infants tend to vocalize more than quieter infants. Risk-taking toddlers are more willing to attempt new words regardless of their ability to say them, whereas more cautious toddlers may wait until they are more confident in saying a

Socially outgoing infants and toddlers vocalize more.

word. Some toddlers patiently listen as adults expand and use utterances that they have mispronounced. Others are quickly off to another topic or area.

Bilingual/Bicultural Infants and Toddlers

If all of the infants and toddlers speak English and the parents and child care providers also speak English, there is little doubt that English should be the spoken language. However, children whose home language is not English are the fastest-growing segment of the population. One out of every five children in the United States is an immigrant or the child of an immigrant parent (Capps, Fix, Reardon-Anderson, & Passel, 2004). Children's **first language** is the language

First language
is the language the infants and toddlers hear at home.

Monolingual
is speaking only one language.

used by their parents and the language that infants hear and overhear (Stechuk, Burns, & Yandian, 2006). Certainly the question that comes to everyone's mind, especially those of us who are **monolingual** and are not proficient in a second language, is, "Isn't exposure to two languages too much for an infant? Shouldn't he learn one language before attempting another?" The answer from the literature is no. The infant's brain is wired to learn language and it is not too great a challenge to learn two at one time—or even three.

Infants and toddlers are both directly and indirectly exposed to ways of thinking and acting. Parents use language to transmit cultural information. However, children are also parts of families and they observe the food preparation, meals, and family interaction; they are part of conversations and hear family stories, which also convey cultural and language information (Stechuk et al., 2006).

Adults often believe that learning one's home language is effortless and that trying to learn two languages will get in the way of learning a single language. They may believe that learning two languages will delay language acquisition or cause confusion in language use and linguistic representation. These beliefs may be different from children's internal processing of language. We really cannot identify how children represent their language or experiences and why some are retained and others are lost (Petito et al., 2001). The question is: Are these beliefs valid?

Infants who are exposed regularly to two languages are not different from infants who hear only one language. Infants who are exposed to two languages begin babbling and use the same number of vocalizations as monolingual infants (Oller, Eilers, Urbano, & Cobo-Lewis, 1997). Infants and toddlers who have good language models in two languages meet the same milestones as monolingual children relative to first words, two-word utterances, and the achievement of 50 words. Children's vocabulary was similar and they spoke in the language of their communication partner (Petito et al., 2001). There are different ways to count vocabulary. When counting the vocabulary of a bilingual child, you need to look at the vocabulary in each language and combine them. This may actually be an underestimation if the child knows the translational equivalents (*zapatos* in Spanish and *shoes* in English) of many words.

Code switching
is using two different languages in an utterance.

There is some concern that toddlers do not understand that they are learning two languages. This is especially true when they **code switch**, or mix the two languages. Young children do code switch. However, their switches are grammatically correct. Think about your language. What if you wanted to use the word "simultaneous," but you can not think of it, so you say "at the same time." That is how young children code switch. They use a word they know in one language to substitute for a word they do not know in the other. As their vocabulary increases this becomes less frequent.

Table 6–5 Ways of Teaching English as a Second Language to Infants and Toddlers

Total immersion: The entire day is in English; the goal is for infants and toddlers to learn English.
Culturally and language-enriched environments: The program is in English, but there is linguistic and cultural awareness.
Language classes: The program is English with a teacher who gives language lessons in the childrens home language.
Two-way immersion: Between 50% and 90% of the day is in English, with times or days specified for each language.
Partial immersion: About half of the day is in English and half in the specified home language.
Dual-language immersion: One teacher speaks in English, and the other speaks in the home language in a language-rich environment.

SOURCE: DeBay and Bombard (2007).

Home language
is the language that is spoken where infants and toddlers live.

There are several methods of teaching children whose **home language** is not English. See Table 6–5 for a summary of these options.

Regardless of the philosophy of the program, infants and toddlers need to value and feel positive about their home language and their culture. They need to be encouraged to communicate and never threatened. Any code switching should be accepted and not criticized. Children live in homes and need to be supported in learning their home language, particularly if that is how they communicate with their parents and extended family.

up close and personal

I came to United State at the age of 23. After more than a decade in this country, I still speak English with a Chinese accent. When I was pregnant with my son, I had planned to teach my son the Chinese language, which is spoken by a fourth of the population on earth. I asked my family in China to send me childrens books so that I could read to him even before he was born. I wanted to make sure that he would immerse himself in the Chinese language and culture. My plan was to speak and read to him only in Chinese. Good plan, right? Good luck to me.

It was not too difficult in the beginning. When he was little, I could read him anything and he would not protest. I have read all the Chinese children books and classics that my dear sister could afford to send me. I read to him while he was nursing, I read to him before bedtime, and I sang to him in Chinese. He was happy to hear my voice. Those were the happy, easy days. I was so sure that my son would be speaking Chinese as his first language for sure.

My husband, who is not Chinese, however, speaks to my son only in English. Even though English is not my husbands first language, he is more comfortable with it than his mother tongue, which is Urdu. I think that my husbands intention is to make sure that our son will be speaking English without a foreign accent like us. We have been teased and frowned upon more times than we care to remember.

My son is 2 ½ years old now. Every morning he greets me in English, he asks for his breakfast and milk in English, and he wants to watch the Barney DVD. I think his first word was DVD, and his second was TV. When I drop him off at the child care center, he will not respond to me unless I talk to him in English. All day long, he spends his time in an English-speaking environment. When I pick him up and start to converse with him in Chinese, he only responds to me in English. Then starts my desperate effort to engage my son in Chinese for a few hours before he goes to sleep. I know that he understand my Chinese because he can follow my commands and smiles at my praises of his good behavior. But somehow, it is so difficult to get him to speak the language. When I try to read to him bedtime stories in Chinese, he will cover his head with the blanket or cover my mouth with his hand. By the time he falls asleep, he may have heard about 10 minutes of Chinese spoken to him.

Every night I feel frustrated and wish that I had spoken a few more words in Chinese to my son. Now he can speak English in full sentences, but only phrases in Chinese. What happens to the assumption of acquisition of the mother tongue? He seems to pay more attention to me when I speak English. To be fair, I do speak English all day until I pick him up from child care. How can I expect him to speak Chinese when I do not speak it very often myself?

Despite the resistance on my sons side, I am still very committed to teaching him Chinese. The majority of the rest of the world can speak more than one language. Why cannot we? In the meanwhile, I am just going to press on and not give in. It feels almost like a battle between my son and me. The problem I am facing is that there is no environment that my son can practice Chinese. I just have to keep trying and not lose faith. When I have the time and money, I will take him back to China to spend a few months with my family. Perhaps he will pick up the language quicker this way.

I do hope that we can get more encouragement from society. Every time I speak to my son in Chinese, the child care providers ask me what I said. I do not want to appear rude or inconsiderate; therefore, I do not speak to my son in Chinese in public any more. It is also extremely difficult to find any books or videos in Chinese. These are the difficulties I am facing. The challenges are mine, and forward-minded shall I be.

REFLECTIVE PRACTICE

How do you feel about raising children bilingually? If you were in this child care setting, how would you respond to this mother's language dilemma? As you think of yourself as a professional in the field, what do you believe about bilingualism in early childhood? As you think about the possibilities of bilingual education, where do you place yourself?

Language Assessment

There are several approaches to language assessment. A traditional approach determines whether or not a child's language development is "normal" and, if it is not, identifies the areas in which it is deficient. Another approach uses language as a vehicle for finding out what children know and how they use this knowledge in everyday contexts (Lund & Duchan, 1993).

One must first determine the purpose of a language assessment. If the language assessment is to determine if a child has a language delay, then a normative approach or a developmental scale designed for this purpose is probably the wisest approach. There are several language measures available that have been standardized on typically developing children so that we know the mean length of response (MLR) for a child of a given age; which consonants should be mastered; whether or not children should use pronouns, prepositions, plurals, past tense, and so on. Examples of measures that fall in this category are *The Preschool Language Scale—Fourth Edition (PLS-4)* (Zimmerman, Steiner, & Evatt, 2005). Despite the name, the PLS-4 can assess children from birth to 6 years 11 months. For children birth to 2 years 11 months, there are items targeting interaction; attention, vocal, and gestural; as well as the expected receptive and expressive language. It takes 20 to 45 minutes to administer. The *Sequenced Inventory of Communication Development—Revised* (Hedrick, Prather, & Tobin, 1984) can be used for children 4 to 48 months and focuses on receptive and expressive language. Receptively, it looks at sound and speech discrimination and awareness. Expressively, it takes into consideration imitating, initiating, and responding, as well as the length and grammatical structure of verbal output and articulation. It takes 30 to 75 minutes to administer.

It would be rare to use only a measure of language development. It is likely that some of the measures discussed in Chapter 5 would also be used to get a fuller picture of what is going on with an infant or toddler. As language is emerging it is difficult to focus solely on it.

Once data has been obtained, it is up to a professional to determine how much of a delay there is and whether it is of concern. For example, is a child who is "below average" a concern? What about the child who is in the 25th percentile? The 10th percentile? Or the child who has a six-month delay? Test results have to be interpreted to be useful in making decisions, and they should be used with other measures to get a broader picture of the whole child and the context in which he grows and develops.

If a problematic language delay is determined, the next step is to find out what is causing the problem. Often a case history is taken from the parents to gain some insight into what the probable causes might be. The delay may be related to a psychological or physical problem (such as a hearing impairment, intellectual disability, or autism). There may also be information about a forceps delivery, teenage mother, low-birth-weight infant, and so on. Although this information may be helpful, knowing the cause of a language delay may not be useful in remediation unless the cause suggests an intervention.

It is therefore necessary to determine more specifically what the areas of deficit are. At a global level one might look at receptive versus expressive communications. The context in which the language is used is also important. One cannot necessarily assume that a child who shows an inability to make a plural on a test does not use plurals in spontaneous language or vice versa. It is also important to determine the discrepancies between what the child intends to communicate and what is actually communicated. Since children's language varies in different contexts, it may be necessary to gather more information about the child's language performance in a variety of contexts before reaching conclusions.

The next step is to determine the patterns or regularities in a child's language behavior. Again, this not only examines the language per se, but also the different contexts in which language is used. One may have to look at activities or events, the level of the child's familiarity with the events or individuals, the purpose of interactions, the child's role in the activity, and so on. This knowledge may influence the child's language production.

Using the gathered information, a professional can better assess a child's communication skills and, if necessary, design a program that will enhance the child's language development. Assessment of infants and toddlers is an ongoing process, and speech and language therapy is typically done in the social context where the language will be used.

COMMUNICATION AND LANGUAGE DELAYS

Unless it is related to a high-visibility disorder, such as severe cognitive disabilities or neuromotor abnormalities, it is difficult to diagnose a communication disorder at an early age. Communication disorders are high-incidence, low-visibility disorders and often not identified in infants and toddlers.

A toddler's ability to communicate is a critical factor in development and functioning. Communication is the key process through which individuals transmit and receive information, needs, wants, knowledge, and emotions. Disorders in the area of communication affect cognitive, social, and emotional development. There are two major types of concerns related to communications: communication delays and communication disorders. Children with communication delays have normal or close to normal speech and language form and function, but are delayed in their development. Children with communication disorders are impaired in their ability to generate or interpret language, and their speech is impaired. These disorders may appear singly or as part of other disorders. Communication differences are further divided into those that affect language, speech, or both.

RISKS FOR COMMUNICATION DISORDERS IN INFANTS AND TODDLERS

Many variables can affect an infant's ability to communicate. The child must have an intact sensory system for picking up relevant information in the environment. The child must have the capabilities for processing the information, understanding what was seen and heard, and remembering the important facts. Educators must provide an environment of adequate stimulation and reinforcement that impels a child to further communication.

In infants and toddlers, communication delays are typically part of another disorder, or may be a precursor to an emerging disorder. Hearing impairments are the leading cause of speech delays in very young children (Stuart, 2002). Infants born with chromosomal anomalies are at risk for communication disorders, as are those exposed to drugs and alcohol. One criterion for diagnosing autism is severe speech and language impairment beginning before three years of age. Infants who have self-regulatory problems beyond the sixth month are also at risk for communication disorders. Some children have diseases, traumas, and injuries that adversely affect communication abilities (Stuart, 2007).

It is estimated that about 3 to 7 percent of children will develop or be diagnosed as having a learning disability. This frequently involves a communication disorder. Those children who are later identified as having dyslexia may exhibit communication disorders as early as 30 months of age.

Language Disorders

Language delays are the failure to acquire language skills at the typical rate and within expected age ranges. Children with language delays acquire language along the same developmental patterns as typically developing children,

Semantics
refers to the meaning of words.

Syntax
is the rules that govern how sentences are formed in a language.

Congenital
is present a birth.

Acquired
is something that happens after birth.

Fundamental processing impairment
is the inability to process auditory stimuli rapidly.

but the acquisition of skills occurs over a longer period of time. A language delay can include a general delay in all dimensions of language or it can relate to skills in specific areas, such as **semantics** or **syntax**. Causes for delay in the acquisition of language can include physical or structural problems, such as a hearing impairment, and physiological or neurological problems, such as cerebral palsy, intellectual disability, or mental health problems. Some language delays have no specific cause and may be environmental.

Between 5 and 10 percent of all children have some type of speech or language disorder (Stuart, 2007). There are two major categories of language disorders: those that are present from birth (**congenital**) and those that arise after a child has been developing language at a typical rate (**acquired**). Congenital language disorders usually have some organic base. Hearing loss is a primary consideration. Increasingly researchers are searching for a better means of classifying language disorders, especially related to brain function, as a means of providing better intervention. One disorder, called a **fundamental processing impairment**, or auditory processing problem, falls into this category. Children with processing impairments are unable to integrate auditory stimulation despite having normal hearing. For these children, learning word meanings, sound combinations, and the specific order of words is flawed; hence, the child's internal models of language are inaccurate (Stuart, 2002). This results in the child making errors in communication and understanding. The most common cause of acquired language disorders is traumatic brain injury. The exact part of brain that is injured will determine the severity as well as the type of the disorder.

The two most common organic causes of language disorders are intellectual disability and hearing impairment. Brain damage is an organic cause of language disorders. Brain damage can interfere with a child's ability to receive, understand, remember, and recognize communicated information. These types of disorders are referred to as receptive language disorders. The child can hear adequately and has no expressive disorder, but the messages, once heard and transmitted to the brain, encounter interference and the message is not understood.

Physical disabilities can also affect both speech and language development. Motor impairments that prevent children from becoming involved with their environment—that is, they are unable to actively manipulate materials and receive sensory input—will result in a lack of experiences that help to build semantic language skills. Children with these impairments may be delayed in language acquisition and will require assistance in acquiring the knowledge or experiences to compensate. Physical disabilities can also affect the oral motor structures and musculature of the body. These infants and toddlers are capable of developing language, but may be unable to verbally express themselves in ways that others can understand. Alternative methods must be developed for these toddlers to express and communicate their thoughts and wishes.

Language delays or disorders can significantly affect social and emotional development. Communication difficulties interfere with social interaction. Interactions usually require give and take, and the inability to engage in social interactions can lead to isolation and poor interpersonal skills. Social isolation and weak interaction skills may result in a lack of social interactions, which provide models for later social interaction skills and help to build strong self-concepts.

Inappropriate environmental responses can discourage communication. Early communication development is intricately related to adequate and appropriate amounts of social interaction. During the cooing and babbling stages, adult responses to an infant's vocalizations stimulate further vocalizations. The failure of the environment to interact with the infant can result in a child who is uninterested in communicating. If attempts at communication continue to garner no response, the activity loses its appeal and fades away. Poor language models may also contribute to language delays. Because children learn language through imitation and experience, the lack of appropriate language for modeling will result in children who are deficient in language skills.

Emotional disturbances can also lead to language delays. Young children who exhibit moderate and severe emotional difficulties typically have problems with language expression. Emotional disorders may slow a child's development of expressive language skills to make thoughts known, or stunt the development of an inner language with which to think about received information. Some children with emotional disorders may develop their own language form, one that is unintelligible to the outside world. Young children with autism and severe psychotic disorders typically demonstrate severe language disorders, even though they may not experience speech difficulties.

The inability to communicate ideas and thoughts can frustrate young children. This is especially true for children with intact language systems but problems with speech output. If children know what they want to say but are unable to express their message, extreme frustration and stress may result. This may lead to behavioral problems or, for some children, a desire to withdraw from interactions altogether. In either case, these children need alternative means to communicate their messages.

Speech and Fluency Disorders

Speech disorders are interference in the production of specific sounds and/or sound blends that result in speech sounds that are inappropriate, irregular, or missing. Unless there is a physiological basis for a speech disorder, such as a cleft palate or cerebral palsy, it is very unlikely that infants and toddlers will

Language delays affect social, emotional, and cognitive development.

be classified as having a speech disorder. They do not yet have the ability to produce all of the speech sounds. More often, the lack of expected sounds is taken as an indication of other impairments (such as a hearing loss), rather than as an indication of a speech disorder per se.

In general, a child's speech is impaired when it deviates so far from the speech of other children that it calls attention to itself, interferes with communication, or causes the child to be self-conscious.

Articulation involves the ability to appropriately produce, orally, any one of a variety of vowels, consonants, and/or vowel-consonant blends. The inability to produce these sounds can be physiological—lack of tongue or mouth control, oral musculature difficulties, or a hearing loss. Articulation errors

Articulation
is the ability to produce vowels, consonants, and vowel-consonant blends.

occur when sounds are omitted, added, distorted, or substituted. Take, for example, *spaghetti*:

paghetti	(*s* is omitted)
spaghettiti	(extra *ti* is added)
speghetti	(*a* is distorted to *e*)
basaghetti	(*ba* is substituted for *p* and put at the beginning)

Articulation errors can happen at the beginning, middle, or end of a word. They may be the result of indistinct articulation. Slow, labored speech and rapid, slurring speech are both articulation problems. Some articulation problems are a natural part of a child's development. Infants and toddlers cannot make all of the sounds necessary to speak English. Caution must be taken to ensure that the problem is related to speech and not development.

One cause of articulation disorders is middle-ear disease resulting from chronic ear infections or ear blockages. This type of hearing loss prevents the transmission of higher-frequency sounds, especially the consonants. This results in children who hear only the middle parts of words: "-able," "-irl," "-abbi-," "-o wha-." This hearing difficulty causes children to omit sounds when speaking. Some children also substitute sounds to make up for what is missing; "dirl-girl." "*wellwo-y*ellow," "*wabbit-rabbit.*"

Fluency
is the joining of sounds and words in oral language without recitations or repetitions.

Fluency disorders are the abnormal flow of verbal expression and are characterized by impaired rate, rhythm, and emphasis that may include labored speaking (Stuart, 2007). The most common fluency disorder is stuttering. Stuttering occurs when the normal flow of speech is interrupted by abnormal repetitions, hesitations, and prolongations of sounds and syllables and avoidable struggle behaviors. Associated with stuttering are characteristic body motions such as grimaces, eye blinks, and gross body movements (The Stuttering Foundation, 2007). Occasional dysfluency is common in toddlers.

Four factors are most likely to contribute to the development of stuttering: genetics—over half of those who stutter have a family member who stutters; having other speech and language problems or developmental delays increases the likelihood of stuttering; neurophysiology—research shows that people who stutter process speech and language in different areas of the brain than those who do not; and family dynamics, especially where there are high expectations and fast-paced lifestyles (The Stuttering Foundation, 2007).

Most children experience some dysfluent between the ages of 2 and 5. In normal dysfluency, there is no struggle and the dysfluency is effortless. Normal dysfluency is also situationally specific: It increases when children talk with someone who speaks rapidly; when language use is more formal; or when they ask questions, use more complex sentences, or use less familiar words.

Table 6–6 Supporting Toddlers Who Are Stuttering

- Speak in an unhurried, slow, relaxed way.
- Do not criticize the toddler or tell him to "slow down."
- Comment on what the child has done rather than asking the child a lot of questions.
- Support the content of what is said by your expression and body language.
- Find a quiet time when you can play undisturbed with a toddler and let him direct you.
- Give the toddler your attention and do not interrupt, question, criticize, or speak quickly.
- Accept the child as he is.

SOURCE: Guitar and Conture (2007).

Stuttering is episodic and may occur because the child is upset, anxious, under pressure to communicate, or has a lot to say. Approximately 20 percent of children go through a stage of development when they stutter enough to concern their parents (The Stuttering Foundation, 2007).

The question is when should a child be referred to a speech and language pathologist based on stuttering? Toddlers who stutter may recover naturally without intervention, so there is some reason to wait and look for changes in the child's speech. If after six months there is no significant improvement, or if the child shows signs of becoming distressed by the stuttering, the child should be referred. During the early childhood years, treatment for stuttering is very effective and can result in children speaking as if they have never stuttered (Onslow, 2000). Table 6–6 provides helpful tips for how you can support a toddler who is stuttering.

SUMMARY

One of the major tasks during the first three years of life is learning to communicate. Infants move from first sounds to first words. To facilitate this process, early childhood education should provide an interesting and motivating language-rich environment. Although most infants do learn to speak and use language, there is disagreement about how this process happens. However, there are predictable stages that children go through in the language-learning process. The role of adults is important, and educators need to function as good language models and be responsive to young children's attempts at communication. As the skills of toddlers increase, educators modify their communication to enrich and extend their language. Some children have problems developing and using speech and language.

CHAPTER IN REVIEW

※ Infants must first be able to produce simple sounds, such as cooing and babbling, before they are able to coordinate the tongue and mouth to produce more complex sounds such as words and sentences.

※ Infants come prewired to communicate and learn languages.

※ Language acquisition is a major accomplishment achieved during the first three years of life.

※ Adequate communication and language play an important role in children's learning and subsequent cognitive and social development.

※ Motor development, cognitive ability, and the environment influence early communication and language development.

※ Failure to develop appropriate language skills can have profound effects on the development of important learning and social skills.

APPLICATION ACTIVITIES

1. Observe a toddler and write down the words that the toddler uses. Count the number of different words used, determine his mean length of utterance, and describe how the words were used. Compare this information to the normative information given in the text.

2. Play with a toddler and choose a word that you would like to teach her. Develop a plan for doing this and then implement it. Reflect on your success or lack of success.

3. Choose a book and read it to an infant or toddler. Think about the language characteristics of the book and modify your style based on the child's responses to the book.

4. Talk to an infant or toddler. Tape your conversation. Describe your speech patterns. Did you modify them? If so, in what way? Did you take turns? How did you know when to lead and when to follow?

RESOURCES

Web Resources

※ **The American Speech-Language and Hearing Association (ASHA)** has a Web site that provides information about and resources for speech, hearing, and communication. http://www.asha.org/.

※ **The British Broadcasting Company** provides information about infants and toddlers as well as music and poetry readings for young children. Their parenting section is particularly good. http://www.bbc.co.uk/.

※ **Families and Advocates Partnership for Education (FAPE)** is supported by the Office of Special Education Programs out of the PACER Center provides information on the types of assistive technology available for infants and toddlers to help them communicate and how to obtain these. http://www.fape.org.

※ **The National Child Care Information Center** has a lot of helpful information about literacy. http://nccic.org.

Definitions of literacy terms: http://nccic.org.

Literacy training initiatives: http://nccic.org.

Early language and literacy observation and assessment tools. http://nccic.org.

Print Resources

※ Bardige, B. S., & Segal, M. M. (2004). *The path to Literacy begins in infancy: Building literacy with love.* Washington, DC: Zero to Three Press.

※ Golinkoff, R. M., & Hirsh-Pasek, K. (1999). *How babies talk: The magic and mystery of language in the first three years of life.* New York: Dutton.

※ Hirsh-Pasek, K., & Golinkoff, R. M. (2003). *Einstein never used flash cards: How our children really learn—And why they need to play more and memorize less.* Emmaus, PA: Rodale.

※ Hulit, L. M., & Howard, M. R. (2006). *Born to talk: An introduction to speech and language development* (4th ed.). Boston, MA: Pearson Education, Inc.

※ Singer, D., Golinkoff, R. M., & Hirsh-Pasek, K. (Eds.) (2006). *Play learning: How play motivates and enhances children's cognitive and social-emotional growth.* New York: Oxford University Press.

REFERENCES

Austin, J. L. (1962). *How to do things with words.* Oxford, UK: Oxford University Press.

Baron, N. S. (1992). *Growing up with language: How children learn to talk.* Reading, MA: Addison-Wesley/Addison Wesley Longman.

Biemiller, A., & Slonim, N. (2001). Estimating root word vocabulary growth in normative and advantaged populations: Evidence for a common sequence of vocabulary acquisition. *Journal of Educational Psychology, 93,* 498–520.

Bloom, L. (1993). *The transition from infancy to language: Acquiring the power of expression.* New York: Cambridge University Press.

Bowerman, M. (1978). The acquisition of word meaning: An investigation into some current conflicts. In N. Waterson & C. Snow (Eds.), *The development of communication: International Child Language Symposium* (3rd ed., pp. 263–287). New York: Wiley.

Brown, R. (1973). *A first language: The early stages.* Cambridge, MA: Harvard University Press.

Capps, R., Fix, M., Ost, J., Reardon-Anderson, J., & Passel, J. S. (2004). *The health and well-being of young children of immigrants.* Washington, DC: Urban Institute.

Carey, S., & Bartlett, E. (1978). Acquiring a single new word. *Proceedings of the Stanford Child Language Conference, 15*, 17–29.

Cawlfield, M. (1992). Velcro Time: The Language Connection. *Young Children, 47*(4), 26–30.

Chomsky, C. (1965). *Aspects of a theory of syntax.* Cambridge, MA: MIT Press.

Clark, E. (1975). Knowledge, context and strategy in the acquisition of meaning. In D. Dato (Ed.), *Developmental psycholinguistics: Theory and application* (pp. 77–98). Washington, DC: Georgetown University Press.

DeBey, M., & Bombard, D. (2007). An approach to second-language learning and cultural understanding. *Young Children, 62*(2), 88–93.

DeCasper, A. J., & Fifer, W. P. (1980). Of human bonding: Newborns prefer their mother's voices. *Science, 208*, 1174–1176.

Fifer, W. P., & Moon, C. (1989). Psychobiology of newborn auditory preferences. *Seminars in Perinatology, 13*, 393–402.

Gadsden, V., & Ray, A. (2002). Engaging fathers: Issues and considerations for early childhood educators. *Young Children, 57*(6), 32–42.

Gleason, J. B. (1987). Sex differences in parent-child interaction. In S. U. Philips, S. Steele, & C. Tanz (Eds.), *Language, gender, and sex in comparative perspective* (pp. 189–199). New York: Cambridge University Press.

Gollinkoff, R. M., & Hirsh-Pasek, K. (1999). *How babies talk: The magic and mystery of language in the first three years of life.* New York: Dutton.

Goodsitt, J. V., Morse, P. A., ver Hoeve, J. N., & Cowan, N. (1984). Infant speech recognition in multisyllabic contexts. *Child Development, 55*(3), 903–910.

Guitar, B., & Conture, E. G. (2007). Seven ways to help the child who stutters. Retrieved May 4, 2007, from http://www.stutteringhelp.org/Default.aspx?tabid=38

Han, M., Roskos, K., Christie, J., Mandzuk, S., & Vuklich, C. (2005). Learning words: Large group time as a vocabulary development opportunity. *Journal of Research in Childhood Education, 4*(19), 333–345.

Hedrick, D. L., Prather, E. M., & Tobin, A. R. (1984). *Sequenced inventory of communication development–Revised.* Los Angeles, CA: Western Psychological Services.

Hulit, L. M., & Howard, M. R. (2006). *Born to talk: An introduction to speech and language development* (4th ed.). Boston, MA: Pearson Education, Inc.

Huttenlocher, J. (1974). The origins of language comprehension. In R. Soslo (Ed.), *Theories in cognitive psychology: The Loyola symposium* (pp. 331–368). New York: Wiley.

James, S. (1990). *Normal language acquisition.* Austin, TX: PRO-ED.

Lund, N., & Duchan, J. (1993). *Assessing children's language in naturalistic contexts* (3rd ed.). Englewood Cliffs, NJ: Prentice Hall.

McLean, L. K. S. (1990). Communication development in the first two years of life: A transactional process. *Zero to Three, XI*(1), 13–19.

Miller, J., Chapman, R., Branston, M., & Reichle, J. (1980). Language comprehension in sensorimotor stages V and VI. *Journal of Speech and Hearing Research, 23*, 284–311.

Nelson, K. (1973). Structure and strategy in learning to talk. *Monographs of the Society for Research in Child Development, 38*, Serial No. 149.

Nelson, K. (1974). Concept, word and sentence: Interrelations in acquisition and development. *Psychological Review, 31*, 267–285.

Oller, D., Eilers, R. D., Urbano, R., & Cobo-Lewis, A. B. (1997). Development of precursors to speech in infants exposed to two languages. *Journal of Child Language, 24*, 407–425.

Onslow, M. (2000). Stuttering: Treatment for preschoolers. *Current Therapeutics, 41,* 52–56.

Osgood, C. E. (1968). Toward a wedding of insufficiencies. In T. R. Dixon & D. L. Horton (Eds.), *Verbal behavior and general behavior theory* (pp. 27–56). Englewood Cliffs, NJ: Prentice Hall.

Owens, R. E. (2005). *Language development: An introduction* (6th ed.). Boston, MA: Allyn & Bacon.

Petito, L. A., Katerelos, M., Levy, B. G., Gauna, K., Tetrealto, K., & Ferraro, V. (2001). Bilingual signed and spoken language acquisition from birth: Implications for the mechanisms underlying early bilingual language acquisition. *Journal of Child Language, 28,* 453–496.

Rumbaugh, D., & Beran, M. (2003). Language acquisition by animals. In L. Nadel (Ed.), *Encyclopedia of cognitive science* (pp. 700–707). London: Macmillan.

Searle, J. R. (1969). *Speech acts: An essay in the philosophy of language.* Cambridge, UK: Cambridge University Press.

Searle, J. R. (1975). Indirect Speech Acts. In P. Cole & J. L. Morgan (Eds.), *Syntax and Semantics 3: Speech Acts* (pp. 59–82). New York: Academic Press.

Stark, R. (1979). Prespeech segmental feature development. In P. Fletcher & M. Garman (Eds.), *Language acquisition* (2nd ed., pp. 149–173). New York: Cambridge University Press.

Stechuk, R. A., Burns, A. S., & Yandian, S. E. (2006). Bilingual infant/toddler environments: Supporting language and learning in our youngest children—A guide for migrant and seasonal Head Start programs. AED Center for Early Care and Education. Retrieved May 3, 2007, from http://www.aed.org/toolsandPublications/upload/BITE_web1106.pdf

Stuart, S. (2002). Communication: Speech and language. In M. L. Batshaw (Ed.), *Children with disabilities* (5th ed., pp. 229–241). Baltimore, MD: Paul H. Brookes.

Stuart, S. (2007). Communication: Speech and language. In M. L. Batshaw, L. Pellegrino, & N. J. Rosen (Eds.), *Children with disabilities* (6th ed., pp. 313–323). Baltimore, MD: Paul H. Brookes.

The Stuttering Foundation. (2007). Facts on stuttering. Retrieved May 4, 2007, from http://www.stutteringhelp.org/Default.aspx?tabid=17

Vygotsky, L. S. (1962). *Thought and language.* Boston, MA: MIT Press.

Zero to Three. (n.d.). Brain Wonders: 18–24 months—Language. Retrieved May 3, 2007, from www.zerotothree.org

Zimmerman, I. L., Steiner, V. G., & Evatt, R. E. (2005). *Preschool language scale* (4th ed., PLS-4). New York: Harcourt Assessment, Inc.

chapter 7

Social Development

Social development focuses on relationships: their establishment, maintenance, and role in human life. The development of these relationships lays the foundation for later social interactions with both adults and peers. Social development focuses changes over time in the child's understanding of, attitudes toward, and actions with others. Social development begins at birth. Infants are born into a vast social network and one of their major life tasks is to understand and develop relationships with the people in their environment. Infants are born with the ability to tune into their social environment.

Social development can be divided into broad categories that focus on who the relationship is with and the purpose of the relationship. Categories include parent–child and adult–child relationships, sibling and other child–child relationships. Attachment is singled out because of its survival value and protective features.

WHY STUDY SOCIAL DEVELOPMENT?

❋ Infants are born into families, societies, and cultures. To work effectively with infants and toddlers you need to understand how these situations affect the children you work with and how that will modify what you do.

❋ Early social skills serve as the foundation for later social skills. Supporting infants and toddlers social interactions and helping them learn the basic social skills of sharing and taking turns is an important aspect of early childhood education.

❋ Infants and toddlers depend on adults to decide how to respond to situations. You are a role model for young children. They look to you for guidance. You need to be aware of this and reflect on your behavior in this role.

❋ Attachment provides the framework or blueprint for future relationships. Early childhood educators can help infants and toddlers develop secure attachments.

THEORIES OF SOCIAL DEVELOPMENT

Social development, as distinguished from emotional development, defines the growth of the infant or toddler's relations with others. Social and emotional development are intrinsically tied together, as are other areas of development such as language and cognition. Social development is also an integral part of cognitive development (Rochat & Striano, 1999). These additional connections are sometimes missed when social and emotional development are viewed together. Although there is overlap, these areas of development are so critical to the development of infants and toddlers that a chapter is devoted to each topic. When looking at early social development, we use the three Cs:

❋ *Context*, or the social environments in which children live

❋ *Comparisons*, between children and childhoods in various groups across diverse societies

❋ *Change*, both the transitions in children's lives and historical changes over time (Boocock & Scott, 2005, p. 7).

Much like motor development, early theorists saw maturation as the initial answer to all questions related to social development. When maturation was no longer considered the total answer to developmental change, the impact of adults on the developing infant became the focus. This set the stage for work, from the 1930s through the 1960s, in the area of infant social development. This work was influenced by the behavioral investigations of John B. Watson and the psychoanalytic theory of Sigmund Freud. They focused on the parents as the socializing agent but did not consider the role that peers and siblings might play in this process (Collins, 2002).

Later work has been influenced by the more cognitively based theories of Jean Piaget, Lev Vygotsky, and Lawrence Kohlberg. Kohlberg's (1969) work did not focus on infants and toddlers, but his views marked a shift in theories about social development and it was a major marker in viewing children in the context of their social environment and in looking at the child as an active player in his world (Collins, 2002). Cognitive theorists saw the young child as much more active in the socialization process. They saw cognitive conflict and its resolution as the method by which children moved from one stage of social development to the next. They also believed that peers played an important role in this development. Cognitive research has focused the field on three aspects of social development:

- the child's ability to regulate his own behavior and emotions
- the biological basis of control and regulation
- the use of the dyad as the unit of social analysis (Collins, 2002).

Early Theories of Social Development

Both behavioral and psychoanalytic theory view infancy as a critical time for the child to be socialized by adults to fit into society. Behaviorists viewed the infant as a passive being shaped by the external world. Psychoanalytic theory saw the infant as an active player in his development with biologically based instinctual drives that must be molded by society. Neither theory was concerned with individual differences or the impact of culture on socialization. Nor were they concerned about the impact of the infant on the adults. However, they did change how we thought about very young children then and what we think today. Because of their impact you need to have some knowledge of the early theories.

Behavioral Theory

From the behaviorist perspective, the child is socially a blank slate. The role of adults is to expose the child to the right values so that she grows into being a productive, self-sufficient member of society. Behaviorism focuses on power differences in the infant–adult relationship. The infant's dependency on the adult increases the probability that the infant will seek rewards and try to avoid punishment. Child rearing was seen as an almost businesslike arrangement. Parents were even cautioned not to become too involved with their young children. "Never hug and kiss them, never let them sit on your lap" (Watson, 1928, p. 81). Child rearing was viewed as a job: There is a correct standard of behavior that children were expected to adhere to. It was the parents' job to see that they do. Parents were clearly seen as responsible for their children's behavior and nurture clearly won the nature–nurture debate.

> Give me a dozen healthy infants, well-formed, and my own specific world to bring them up in and I'll guarantee to take any one at random and train him to become any type of specialist I might select— doctor, lawyer, artist, merchant, chief, and, yes, even beggar-man and thief, regardless of his talents, penchants, tendencies, abilities, vocations, and race of his ancestors (Watson, 1924, p. 82).

Current behaviorists do not have such an extreme position; however, it was the view of behaviorism put forth by Watson that influenced early research on socialization.

Psychoanalytic Theory

Sigmund Freud (1856–1939) was the initial architect of psychoanalytic theory. Freud was a medical doctor who specialized in neurology. He practiced in Vienna, Austria. His stage-based model placed great importance on early development. Rather than the passive infant of Watson's conception waiting to be molded, Freud (1940) saw the infant as active and filled with instinctual drives that placed him at odds with society. Withdrawal of parental love was the motivator in Freud's model. Freud believed that all individuals go through five stages in their **psychosexual development**. He hypothesized that at each stage of development there is one part of the body (erogenous zone) that gives more pleasure than other parts. According to Freud's theory, there is inherent conflict between these sources of pleasure and the demands of society. Personality development is based on how these conflicts are resolved.

Oral Stage (Birth to 18 Months). During this stage the infant's pleasure centers on his mouth, as evidenced by his sucking, mouthing, and biting. He uses these **oral** actions to reduce tension. If **weaned** too early or too late he might become fixated at this stage of development. Freudians would expect

Psychosexual development
is Freud's beliefs that sexual instincts and appetites play a major role in the formation of adult personality.

Oral
behaviors relate to the mouth, like mouthing and sucking objects.

Weaning
is when infants no longer use the breast or bottle for milk. They drink from a cup.

then that the infant might begin to suck his thumb or fingers as a way of relieving tension. Early researchers did find that infants who had been nursed less (whether breast or bottle) did suck their fingers more (Goldman-Eisler, 1951; Roberts, 1944). (Behaviorists would have expected children who had been weaned later to show more thumb sucking because it was a learned and positively reinforced behavior.) Freud felt that too much or too little sucking interfered with attachment.

Anal Stage (18 to 36 Months). The second stage focuses on the eliminative functions. In Freud's view, during this time span exercising the **anal** muscles reduces tension. Conflict at this stage revolves around toilet training, with training that is too early or too strict causing later personality problems. (Behaviorists would expect problems related to toilet training to cause bowel or bladder dysfunction; for example, constipation.) There was some evidence to show that harsh toilet training was related to negativism and aggression (Sears, Whiting, Nowlis, & Sears, 1953). The development of the characteristic anal character (punctual, precise, and parsimonious) was the expected outcome.

Anal
behaviors relate to the anus, such as going to the toilet.

Phallic Stage (3 to 6 Years). The child's pleasure during this stage focuses on the **genitals**. The young child typically finds self-manipulation enjoyable. This stage has great importance for Freud's theory, whereas feminists found it highly objectionable (Horney, 1937, 1945). The conflict at this stage for the boy is that he falls in love with his mother and has an intense desire to replace his father in her affections. This incestuous wish is called the Oedipus complex. (In Greek mythology, Oedipus unknowingly kills his father and marries his mother.) This results in castration anxiety because of fear of punishment by the father. As a response, this conflict is resolved by identification with the same-sex parent. The girl at this stage develops penis envy and holds her mother responsible for her lack of a penis. She becomes attached to her father with the resolution at about age 5 or 6 through identification with her mother. (This is called the Electra complex, based on a Greek myth about a girl who wanted her brother to kill their mother to avenge her father's death.) Lack of resolution results in fixation, which is characterized by aggressiveness and narcissism (the individual herself is the object of her erotic pleasure).

Genitals
are the male penis and female vagina.

Latency Stage (6 Years to Puberty). A stage of repressed sexually in which children's energy focuses on social and intellectual skills.

Genital Stage (Puberty and On). This is a time of sexual reawakening, but now the source is someone outside the family. Unresolved conflicts with parents reemerge.

Basic Structures. In addition to stages, Freud (1940) believed that personality has three basic structures, which also have a developmental base. The most primitive structure of the personality is the id. The **id** consists of instincts and contains an individual's psychic energy. The id is unconscious and pleasure seeking. Freud felt that infants are controlled by their id. As children grow they have to deal with the demands of reality. They begin to develop their **ego**. The ego is partially conscious and partially unconscious. The ego develops from experience and is the child's rational mind. The ego solves problems, evaluates risks, and makes rational decisions based on information. Neither the id nor the ego has a sense of morality. The **superego**, or conscience, is the last structure of the personality to develop.

The development of the superego is gradual and is accomplished by five or six years of age, although it may be modified later. The young child is subjected to frustration, some of which arises from parental demands. These frustrations generate hostility in the child. Yet because of anticipated punishment, especially loss of love and abandonment, the child represses the hostility. To maintain this repression as well as to gain parental affection the child adopts parental rules and prohibitions. He tries to emulate his parents' behavior to the point of punishing himself when he violates (or is tempted to violate) a prohibition. This self-punishment is experienced as guilt. Guilt feels like fear of abandonment, and the young child tries to avoid this feeling by acting in accordance with parental demands and by developing defense mechanisms to control impulses that get him into trouble (Hoffman, 1970).

We no longer believe that Freud's stages are representative of the actual stages of social development. However, Freud's work was the impetus for studying early development.

While Freud focused on problems related to fixation, Bowlby (1952) focused on the function of attachment for the development of the ego and superego. Bowlby felt that the infant is dependent on his mother to aid him in this capacity. She is his psychic organizer, and if the mother–child relationship is continuing and satisfactory, the child takes over this controlling and planning function. As long as the mother and child have a positive relationship, things go smoothly; when this positive relationship is lacking, the child is at risk for impaired ego development (Bowlby, 1952). Bowlby placed great importance on the first two years of life.

Like Bowlby, Erik Erikson appreciated the contribution of psychoanalytic theory, but he reframed Freud's stages into psychosocial stages that develop throughout the life span. His theory is discussed in detail in the next chapter.

Id
is the subconscious part of the brain that seeks pleasure.

Ego
mediates among the id, the super-ego and the external world.

Superego
acts as the *conscience* to maintain a sense of morality.

EARLY RESEARCH ON SOCIAL DEVELOPMENT

Early research in social development was based primarily on psychoanalytic and behaviorist theory. These theories influenced the topics that researchers chose to explore. Attachment and dependency received a tremendous amount of research, as did child-rearing techniques, sex typing, socialization, and aggression.

Margaret Ribble, René Spitz, and John Bowlby focused their attention on the development of infants in institutions. Children living in institutions had a high mortality rate. Of 10,272 children admitted to a Dublin foundling home between 1775 and 1800, only 45 survived (Kessen, 1965). By the 1930s, more infants in institutions were surviving, but displayed an alarmingly high level of psychological disturbances. The concerns about whether or not child care is good for infants and toddlers grew out of this research. We are still concerned about infants growing up in institutions. In the United States this concern led to the development of the foster care system rather than using institutions to care for young children. Spitz (1945) undertook a large-scale study to compare infants at two institutions who experienced good medical care but very different conditions in the visiting patterns of their mothers, availability of toys, and visual stimulation. The "Nursery" was an institution for infants of delinquent females who were in a penal institution. Infants in the Nursery were fed and cared for by their mothers or had full-time mother substitutes. They had toys and could see what was going on around them from their cribs. These infants had intelligence quotient (IQ) scores within the normal range and comparable to two control group of noninstitutionalized infants. Followup studies found development to be within the normal range. After 3 ½ years all the children were alive (Thompson & Grusec, 1970).

The "Foundling Home" was an institution for infants whose mother could not support them. Infants in the Foundling Home had few toys, and, because sheets were hung over the crib rails to control germs, they could see little of what was going on around them. They were interacted with only at feeding time by busy nurses.

> They lay supine in their cots for so many months that hollows were worn into their mattresses and, by the time they were physically able to turn themselves in their cots (about seven months of age), these hollows prevented them from doing so. Thus, at the age of 10 or 12 months, they were observed lying only on their backs and playing with the only toys they had—their hands and feet (Thompson & Grusec, 1970).

Deprived of their mothers, toys, and visual stimulation, their IQs dropped dramatically by the end of their first year, and they displayed unusual reactions to strangers, ranging from extreme friendliness to blood-curdling screams. Despite impeccable hygiene, the infants were very susceptible to disease; many succumbed to a measles epidemic.

Conditions for infants at the Foundling Home improved. However, in a two-year followup study, Spitz (1946) found only a small portion of the original infants alive. Those located displayed retarded physical development, toilet training, speech, and self-help skills. The conditions experienced during the first year of life seemed to have produced irreversible effects. Spitz (1945) attributed the infants' condition to lack of human contact—a mother or mother substitute. Others felt the results could be attributed to lack of environmental stimulation, inherent differences in the two groups, respiratory problems based on inactivity, poor genetic background, poor prenatal care, and other causes (Pinneau, 1950).

Ribble (1944) studied 600 infants who were deprived of adequate "mothering" and described the undesirable and often fatal symptoms she found as **marasmus** or a wasting away of the body. Ribble, too, attributed the effectives of institutionalization to maternal deprivation. Her data and theoretical treatment were also criticized.

Bowlby (1940, 1944) believed that if an infant lacked the opportunity to form attachments to a mother figure during the first three years of life, if he was deprived of a mother figure for a limited period of time, or if there were changes from one mother figure to another, the result world be an affectionless, psychopathic character (Thompson & Grusec, 1970). He concluded that maternal deprivation before the age of six months was less detrimental than that occurring later.

The research of Bowlby, Spitz, and Ribble led scholars to focus on adult-child interactions. This research was published near the end of World War II. It had a profound impact on caring for children outside the home.

In countries such as Romania infants are still being raised in and adopted from institutions, and we worry about the impact of their institutionalization on their long-term development. Research in the United Kingdom looked at more than 100 Romanian children who were adopted into the United Kingdom and compared their development with 50 children who had not been deprived. The children who were adopted from Romania experienced severe early deprivation and were less likely to be securely attached and showed atypical patterns of attachment. The older the children were at adoption (closer to 42 months), the more likely they were to have atypical patterns (O'Connor, Marvin, Rutter, Olrick, & Britner, 2003). Marked adverse effects for many of the children who were over six months when adopted continued at least until age 11. There was no difference for those who were between 6 and 42 months at adoption (Beckett et al., 2006). These children had IQ scores that were 15 points lower than those

Marasmus
is severe malnutrition caused by too few calories and resulting in very low energy.

Parents and caregivers frequently use pacifiers to soothe infants, especially when they need to accomplish other tasks.

under 6 months at 6 and 11 years. For children over 18 months, even if they had minimal language skills (they could imitate speech sounds) when they arrived, their prognosis was stronger for language and cognitive outcomes, but not social, emotional, or behavioral outcomes (Croft et al., 2007). Although most of the children did not have clinically identified levels of conduct, emotional, or behavioral problems, many of the children did experience inattention and over- or hyperactivity. Their attention deficit and hyperactivity had different characteristics than those of nondeprived children (Kreppner, O'Connor, Rutter, & Romanian Adoptees Study Team, 2001). The duration of the deprivation was the important variable in all of these problems. The longer the children experienced deprivation, the more likely they were to have some type of problem; six months seemed to be when the cumulative effect began. Whether it is the 1930s or today, institutions are not places where young children grow and develop well. Interestingly, Bowlby (1940, 1944) concluded that material deprivation before the age of six months was less detrimental than if it occured later, but that by 36 months there would be long-term consequences. The Romanian studies support his contention.

During the depression of the 1930s, the government became involved in child care. Child care was one aspect of the Works Progress Administration (WPA) program. The purpose was threefold: It provided work for unemployed teachers, care for children whose mothers were working because their husbands were out of work, and it used up surplus food that the government was buying from farmers. The federal government's interest in child care continued through the end of World War II. With the men coming home from the war to assume new jobs and to create families, wives and mothers exited the workforce. Although some child care centers remained open, the majority of them closed in the late 1940s (Barclay, 1985). Research on the implications of institutionalization of very young children was extended to child care, and there was grave concern about the impact of child care on infants and toddlers. This legacy continues today.

With the baby boom in the late 1940s, research continued to focus on parent-child interactions. The classic work of Sears, Maccoby, and Levin (1957), *Patterns of Child Rearing*, focused on issues related to how and when parents wean, toilet train, and discipline their children. They also looked at how parents dealt with sexual expression and aggression. Much of the concentration was on whether parents used power assertion, which included physical punishment, deprivation of objects or privileges, or the threat of these (behaviorism), or whether they used nonpower-assertive techniques such as love withdrawal (psychoanalytic theory).

Baumrind (1967), in another classic study with 134 preschool children and their parents, observed children and parent-child interactions, and interviewed parents. She described three general categories of parental control: authoritarian, authoritative, and permissive (see Table 7–1).

Data from Baumrind's observations indicated that parenting style was related to patterns of children's behavior (Baumrind, 1967). Parents who were authoritarian were more likely to have children who were classified as conflicted and irritable (fearful, moody, passively hostile, etc.). Parents who were authoritative generally had children who were energetic and friendly (self-reliant, cheerful, cooperative, etc.). Parents who were permissive were likely to have children who were impulsive and aggressive (rebellious, low self-control, domineering, etc.). Baumrind's terminology and general categories are still used today.

Table 7–1 Parenting Styles

- *Authoritarian parenting*: Restrictive parenting style that includes many rules and expectations of strict obedience, and uses punishment or love withdrawal to gain compliance.

- *Authoritative parenting*: More flexible style in which children are allowed a degree of freedom within set limits and relies on power or reasoning to gain compliance.

- *Permissive parenting*: A laissez-faire style of parenting that includes few limits, a great deal of child freedom, and few attempts to control behavior or gain compliance.

SOURCE: Baumrind (1967).

CONCERNS WITH EARLY THEORIES AND RESEARCH

Research centered on the idea of parental control predominated and continued into the 1960s. However, by the late 1960s and early 1970s, it became clear that not all infancy scholars embraced this view of socialization. Opposition to the theories centered on three themes: infant competence, individual differences in infancy, and mutuality of influence (Feinman & Lewis, 1991).

Behaviorists viewed the infant as incompetent and undirected, whereas psychoanalytic theorists saw the infant as incompetent and misdirected. With new research on infants' sensory competencies and their ability to learn, even while in the womb, earlier views of incompetence were no longer considered valid. Researchers began to focus on the competent infant. Individual differences and variations in infants finally caught the attention of researchers, as opposed to the continuing search for **universals**. Some of the early work of Thomas, Chess, and Birch (1968) that focused on differences in temperament of infants helped in the move away from universals.

Universal behaviors are the same for all infants in a given situation.

Finally, researchers were beginning to look at the role of fathers and to include information on a range of family constellations. This led to a growing recognition that the mother–child relationship exists in the context of family relationships. These relationships affect the way mothers care for their infants and hence impact the infants' development. There has been expanded interest and research into the father's role in infant development. Research also emphasized the impact of siblings and grandparents. The role of other adults, such as child care providers, was also seen as important. The move was toward viewing infants in the context in which they live and grow and looking at the effect of all caregivers on the infant and the impact the infant on those caregivers.

The realization that infants are competent, active, and unique both complicated and fragmented research in social development. Researchers recognized the problems with previous conceptualizations, but lacked a replacement. Researchers who focused on the infant began to move closer to a developmental psychology framework, while those interested in social aspects of early childhood moved closer to social psychology (Feinman & Lewis, 1991). Early childhood research began looking at the effects of television, superheroes, and war play on children's socialization. Infancy researchers are still struggling to rework the behaviorist—psychoanalytic model of socialization or build an alternative model. Rather than developing a general theory of social development, researchers now tend to focus on specific aspects of social development, such as relationships or attachment, and concentrate their work in one area.

LATER THEORIES AND RESEARCH

Researchers in the 1960s and 1970s and the impact of the translation of Piaget's and Vygotsky's work into English helped to refocus the area of early social development.

Social Learning Theory

Differential reinforcement involves positively reinforcing behaviors that are appropriate for the child and ignoring or punishing those that are not.

Social learning theory has its base in behaviorism and psychoanalytic theory. However, in social learning theory the role of the parents is a major one. The idea that children's gender development is based on the identification of a young child with his same-sex parent is a foundation of social learning theory. Children learn to be boys and girls because of **differential reinforcement** of behavior and because of modeling the same-sex parent (or significant person) (Bandura, 1992). We think that boys learn to be boys and girls learn to be girls by observing many different role models and noticing which behaviors are performed by each sex. Parents treat boys and girls differently, dress them differently, and encourage infants and toddlers to play with sex-typed toys. The question is whether parents are causing this behavior or responding to their child (Golombok & Hines, 2002).

Cognitive Theories

Cognitive theorists see young children playing a more active role in their own social development. They develop gender schemata in the way they develop other mental representations of their world. By age 2 or 3, children label themselves and others by gender. From then on children organize relevant information based on gender. Younger children tend to develop strong gender stereotypes that become less stereotypic with age. Cognitive theorists focus on the child's acquisition of gender knowledge. Social cognitive theory is more concerned about the translation of this gender knowledge into gender-related behavior (Golombok & Hines, 2002).

Genetic Influences

Gender development and gender differences begin in the womb. Hormones affect the development of the internal and external genitalia. These same hormones impact the development of the brain and, yes, boys and girls do have regions of the brain that are different based on gender. These hormones influence toy choices, playmate preferences, and gender identity (Golombok & Hines, 2002). The question remains: Are adults supporting sex-typed behavior or responding to it?

RELATIONSHIPS

Forming relationships with others is the core of social development. There are many ways to look at these relationships. One can focus on the individuals involved, such as adults, peers, and infants and toddlers. One can also look at relationships based on the degree of intimacy or connectedness between individuals, such as infants and fathers. One might look at the intimacy of relationships as ranging from love relationships to friendship, acquaintances, and strangers. Obviously all these categories of relationships can be subdivided. There is little doubt that gender and age influence relationships, beginning at birth. When we add that relationships must be viewed as complex, **transactional**, and embedded in a social context, we seem to have muddied the waters even more.

Transactional relationships acknowledge the two-way interaction of relationships.

Development of Relationships

To understand different types of relationships, it is necessary to look at how relationships develop. Most believe that there is some innate genetic basis for the formation of social relationships and that they grow out of early adult-child social interactions (Pike, 2002). Focusing on social interaction, the question becomes how these initial adult-child interactions transform into a relationship. Both Freud and Piaget assumed that infants begin life with no sense of self. The concept of **self-permanence** is established around 9 to 12 months. With the establishment of self-differentiation and self-permanence, the infant conceives of himself as an independent person regardless of the setting, the people he is with, or the interactions that are taking place. This process results in the establishment of the "self-other" schema. This schema is necessary for the development of other aspects of "self" and provides the basis for more complex social cognitive processes.

Self-permanence is the infant's belief that he is an independent person and exists regardless of where he is.

up close and personal

I see myself as an enlightened father. I wanted to be honest and up front with the twins and I planned to tell it like it is, even at age 3. One evening, as I was bathing Michael and Michele, Michael asked me about the difference between boys and girls. I saw my opportunity. I calmly replied, "Well, why don't you look." The initial comments related to the fact that Michele had long hair and Michael's was shorter, hers was blond, his darker. Michele's bellybutton was an "inny" whereas Michael's was an "outy." This went on and they seemed to observe a variety of characteristics, but not the relevant ones. I finally pointed to Michael's penis and said, "Michael has a penis and Michele has a vagina." I went on to explain that men have a penis and women have a vagina. I confirmed that I am a man and I have a penis and, yes, their mother is a woman and she has a vagina. The children then asked about the next-door neighbor, Mrs. Harris, and the children confirmed that she is a women and she has a vagina. At this

point I was still very proud of myself. I was a father who could speak about sex with his children. I heard them talking in their bedroom after I had put them to bed. It became a game. One would name a person, "Mr. Roberts," and the other would respond, "He's a man," and the initiator would proudly say, "He has a penis!" This went on until they fell asleep.

Well, I won't add what my wife thought of their game. But the next day, Mrs. Harris came over to bring the children some cookies she had just baked. They looked at each other and Michele said, "Mrs. Harris." Michael responded, "She's a woman." Michele sang back, "She has a vagina." Needless to say, Mrs. Harris put the cookies down and exited. The game continued for about a week, and I kept apologizing to the neighbors. My wife wanted me to punish them for what they were saying, but I didn't think that was a good idea. I assumed that when the game lost its shock value they would quit. It was a very long week.

REFLECTIVE PRACTICE

What does this conversation tell you about the children's concepts about gender development? How would you have handled this situation? How do you think this situation would have been different in 1970?

Gender identity is knowing whether you are a boy or girl.

One part of the development of "self" is **gender identity**. By age 2 most children can tell you whether they are boys or girls and use the terms boys and girls to talk about their peers. However, they are still visually grounded and can be confused by appearance. A girl with a boy's name

Gender constancy
is the belief that ones gender is permanent.

Gender stereotypes
are social expectations for male and female behavior.

Decentration
is the ability to focus on more than one aspect of a situation.

who looks boylike would be considered a "boy." Although they are aware of their gender, they have not yet attained **gender constancy**, the belief that they will remain the same gender for life (Huston, 1983). However, by age 3 they are beginning to know the sex or **gender stereotypes** and behave following those patterns: Boys like rough-and-tumble play and use trucks and blocks; girls like housekeeping and play more quietly with dolls. Two-year-old boys may play in the doll corner, but by three and beyond this is less likely. Overall, boys tend to be more stereotypic in their play than girls. Some believe this stereotypic concept of gender roles may be necessary and serve as the foundation for later nonstereotyped behavior (Lobel & Menashin, 1993).

The development of the categorical self or a self-schema allows toddlers to relate to others, particularly their peers, in different ways. Toddlers learn that they are beings with wants and needs and likes and dislikes. As they attribute these feelings to themselves, they begin the process of learning that there are also other "selves" who have wants and needs and feelings. Other children are not inanimate objects. In cognitive theory, this process is called **decentration**. The toddler must overcome his egocentric idea that he is the only person in the world and begin to attribute the same feelings, wants, and needs that he has to others. This knowledge is necessary for the development of two prosocial skills: empathy and sharing, the foundation for building relationships (Lewis, 1987). Having either empathy or sharing requires that toddlers develop not only self-awareness but also awareness of others.

Informed early childhood educators help children in this process by pointing out the wants and needs of others and requiring children to share and take turns. They also help children see the consequences of their social actions, both positive and negative.

ATTACHMENT

Attachment
is an infant's emotional bond with an adult and is used as a framework for developing other relationships.

Attachment is the development of the human bond between infant and parents or other caregivers. Attachment has been studied in more detail than any other aspect of social development in childhood. Some see the development of attachment as the most important early social event to occur in the child's life. Attachment is not present at birth, but develops over time and progresses through stages. Much of the research in this area has focused on mothers and infants.

The underlying assumption of attachment is that young children use attachment as an internal working model for relationships. Its purpose is to make the relational world more predictable, meaningful, and shareable (Bretherton, 2005).

Theories of Attachment

Psychoanalytic theory is the basis for much of the early work in attachment. Freud believed that the mother–child relationship was unique and that the mother is the child's first and strongest love object. In addition, this relationship is the prototype for later love relations. He believed that the basis of this relationship is sucking. Because of the importance of sucking, weaning is a threat to the mother–infant relationship: if weaning is either too severe or too lenient, the infant's later interpersonal relationships are at risk.

Erickson extended, revised, and reframed Freud's ideas. He felt that interactions other than sucking influence the development of relationships and he generalized it to a "trust–mistrust" continuum. He felt that good mother–infant relationships promote basic trust, whereas poor mother–infant relationships led to mistrust. His trust and mistrust concepts related not only to individuals but extended to generalized trust in institutions.

Both Freud and Erickson placed great importance on the mother–child relationship, not just because of the relationship itself, but also as a prototype for relationships throughout life. Those who had insecure attachments were forever doomed (without specific intervention) to inadequate relationships, especially in their own marriage and parenting. Although the concept is central for them, neither Freud nor Erickson actually used the specific term *attachment* for this mother–child relationship.

Ethological Theory

Ethology
is the scientific study of animal behavior.

Ethological theory, which looks at behavior in evolutionary terms, views attachment as a biological survival mechanism for animals and humans. Species with long periods of immaturity need some way of keeping their young safe until they are old enough to care for themselves. Infants' attachment to mothers is seen as providing this necessary protection. As infants became more mobile the attachment figure becomes a secure base from which infants can explore their environment (Bowlby, 1989). Similarly, being wary of strangers and protesting separation increases chances of survival.

Current thinking about attachment is influenced by the work of ethological theorists, primarily the work of Bowlby and Ainsworth. John Bowlby was a psychiatrist based at the Tavistock Clinic in London. He worked for the World Health Organization after World War II and visited children who were orphaned. He was struck by their fear and apathy, and concluded that children need a warm, continuous relationship with a mother figure. Without this, they would be emotionally damaged. Mary Ainsworth, a psychologist, systematically investigated the theory of attachment through the development of the strange situation (Penn, 2005). Ethological theorists suggest that to ensure the survival of the species, infants are equipped with behaviors that increase their probability of survival: the ability to cry, cling, call, smile, lift their arms to be picked up, creep, and follow after a departing adult. These behaviors are the basis for the attachment of adults to infants.

This information may not sound startling today, but when Bowlby first presented his conceptualization of the attachment process (*The nature of the child's tie to his mother*, 1958) the assumption was that the basis of attachment was feeding. Bowlby's paradigm was very different. His definition is: "Attachment behavior is any form of behavior that results in a person attaining or maintaining proximity to some other clearly identified individual who is conceived as better able to cope with the world" (Bowlby, 1989, p. 238). The biological function attributed to attachment is protection, and this behavior can be seen throughout life, particularly in emergencies.

Bowlby (1989) envisioned two interrelated processes: attachment and exploration. When a child of any age feels securely attached, he can freely explore his environment. For young children these explorations are limited by time and space. The concept of a secure base is the fundamental foundation underlying this exploration. When a close, caring, intimate relationship is formed, infants can balance feelings of security with their need to explore. Deep security in being cared for allows free exploration and focused play. When this security is lacking, the infant's quality of play suffers (Honig, 1993). As children get older, they increase their time and distance of separation. With increasing age, children can productively be away from their attachment figure for increasingly longer times.

For the attachment process to operate efficiently, the infant must have information about himself and the attachment figure. He needs to know how likely the other is to respond as environments and conditions change. By the end of the first year, the infant has a considerable amount of knowledge about his world and organizes this knowledge to form a "working model" that includes models of self and adults in interaction with each other (Bowlby, 1989). The infant uses these models to plan his behavior. When caregivers abuse or neglect infants, or when the relationship is disrupted by events such as death or foster care placement, the model does not function as intended (Dozier, Dozier, & Manni, 2002). The more accurate and adequate the infant's model, the better adapted the behavior.

Stages of Attachment

Like cognitive development, attachment is stage based. The first three stages occur during infancy and toddlerhood (Ainsworth, Salter, & Wittig, 1967). These three stages are widely accepted and appear to be invariant. Bowlby (1969) suggested a fourth stage that appears during the third year.

Indiscriminate attachment
is the establishment of an emotional bond with caring adults regardless of their level of familiarity.

Stage 1: Indiscriminate Attachment. The first stage of attachment is called **indiscriminate attachment**, or undiscriminating social responsiveness, and is present from birth to approximately four to six months. The infant enjoys being handled, approached by people, and engaging in social interactions. There is no special responsiveness to the primary caregiver; young infants enjoy being held by anyone. The infant produces orienting behaviors (tracking, listening, postural adjustment, and signaling behaviors that include smiling, crying, and vocalizations).

Infants who are placed in early care and education settings between six weeks and four to six months seem to make a marvelous adjustment. They do not protest being left alone and often adapt well if they can maintain their internal schedule.

Discriminate attachment
is an emotional bond established with familiar caring adults and some distress with unfamiliar adults.

Stage 2: Discriminate Attachment. Once the infant develops the ability to identify familiar adults (four to eight or nine months), the process of **discriminate attachment** or discriminating social responsiveness can begin. During this second stage, children show a marked change in social behavior. They respond differently to one (or a few) familiar individuals than they do to

Young infants are indiscriminately attached. As long as they are held comfortably, they are willing to be held by anyone.

strangers. The infant may visually follow an attachment figure, fuss when she leaves, and smile more at that person than others. Although the initial attachment figure is usually the mother, there is no biological reason for this. Attachment develops through contact and familiarity.

Infants who are placed in care during this stage appear to have a more difficult time adjusting. Cognitively, this means that the infant is on target in developing discriminate attachment. Practically, it means that the infant often cries when being dropped off at an early care and education setting. Infants who were previously "well adjusted" may also begin to cry at being left. It is important to be able to tell families that their child is developing well and that this is to be expected and why. Encourage them to leave a family picture so that you can show them their family and remind them that someone in their family will return soon.

Stage 3: Active Initiation. Although the first two stages are well documented (Ainsworth, 1969), they have not intrigued researchers the way the third stage has. The third stage builds on earlier attachment behaviors, but is characterized by the infant's initiative in seeking proximity and contact with the attachment figure and is referred to as **active initiation**. The timing of this phase is dependent on specific motor and cognitive developments. First, to seek proximity, the infant must have some locomotion skills. At a cognitive level, he requires the concept of object/people permanence. Both of these skills begin to develop around eight or nine months. Because this stage is so intriguing and has been researched so extensively, it is discussed in further detail.

Active initiation
is a stage where infants use a trusted adult as a secure base from which to explore the environment.

Stage 4: Goal Directed. The final stage is identified as **goal-directed**, or *goal-corrected partnership*, and usually appears in the third year. It is characterized by the child's understanding of factors that influence adult's behavior. This knowledge allows the child to interact with adults in a more sophisticated way (Ainsworth, 1973; Lyons-Ruth & Zeanah, 1993). Children play as more equal partners in games, where the adult might be the "baby" and the child might go off to work, telling the "baby" she will be back to get her soon.

Goal-directed
attachment reflects the child's understanding of adult behavior.

Active Initiation Stage. Because of the importance placed on secure attachment, researchers have been interested in not only describing attachment and its evolution but also measuring it. In an attempt to quantify attachment at the active initiation stage, Ainsworth (1963) developed the **strange situation**. It involves the mother and child entering an unfamiliar setting, the mother leaving for a short time, the entrance of a stranger, and the mother returning (see Table 7–2).

Strange situation
is a method of measuring attachment during the active initiation stage.

Table 7–2 The Strange Situation

1. A mother and child (between 12 and 24 months) enter an unfamiliar room that contains two chairs and a few appropriate toys for the child to play with. The mother stays with the toddler for 3 minutes and then leaves.

2. A stranger enters and stays for 3 minutes.

3. The mother returns and the mother and infant are reunited.

SOURCE: Honig (1993).

This procedure allows observation of the child's behavior before, during, and after separation. Observations focus on behaviors related to proximity seeking and maintaining contact as well as more negative behaviors of protest. Theoretically, a securely attached child would protest strongly at separation and score high on proximity seeking at reunion. However, once having connected with the secure base, the child would then be ready to leave the security of his mother and go back to exploring the toys.

Some have questioned whether a child's protest when his mother leaves or when a stranger approaches him is an adequate measure of attachment. Part of the concern is that these negative behaviors indicate positive attachment. Others even question whether protests are a measure of attachment at all. Many feel that stranger anxiety may not be a valid measure of attachment because young children have very individual experiences with strangers. Young children in child care see many different caregivers, as well as the parents of the other children. Ainsworth (1973) herself raised some of these questions. It may be that fear of strangers is more related to fear of the unknown than to attachment per se.

Leaving aside the challenge of evaluating the role of the stranger, there were some additional problems. One was that from a theoretical perspective attachment should be a stable trait. That is, the behaviors of a "securely attached" child at 12 months should remain at two years. Likewise, the attachment should hold in a variety of settings. This did not happen. Ainsworth (1973) argued that the problem was not the concept of attachment but rather the measurement of it. Further, that attachment was more wisely thought of as a pattern of behavior rather than a particular behavior.

Over time several different methods have been devised to measure attachment and to extend the age at which it is measured. Coding systems have been developed that focus more on the reunion episodes and how the child organizes her behavior toward her mother. The age range has been expanded to six years. Other researchers have tried story-completion tasks, Q-sorts, and doll-play situations. Although the methods of measuring attachment have been a concern, most researchers agree that attachment is an important concept not only in infancy but also throughout life.

Types of Attachment

Ainsworth (1973) described three patterns of attachment: secure, ambivalent, and avoidant. A fourth pattern, disorganized/controlling attachment, has also been established (Lyons-Ruth, 1996). All infants are attached to their caregivers. The differences are in the security of the attachment and the particular pattern an insecure attachment may take (see Table 7–3).

Patterns of attachment in children appear to be far more stable over time than specific behaviors. However, they were less stable for infants from economically vulnerable families or in families where mothers entered into employment during the attachment process. It appears that the mother–child relationship has to be renegotiated at this time. Research continues in the area of attachment in an effort to understand and classify attachment behavior. The picture emerging is one of developmental complexity (Sroufe, Egeland, Carlson, & Collins, 2005). Infant attachment alone does not predict later relationships, but in the context of other information, it provides important information. Combining early attachment information with peer experiences enhances our knowledge of the impact. Secure attachment histories provide a base for toddlers to accept parents' limit setting. When there is insecure attachment or anxious attachment, parents have greater difficulty setting limits and boundaries and providing the support during the struggles that toddlers have with autonomy (Sroufe et al., 2005).

Attachment Disorders

Failure to develop appropriate attachment patterns may cause toddlers to withdraw or shun social interaction. They may exhibit cranky and whiny behaviors. Social responsiveness may be limited. These children fail to develop appropriate interaction patterns with adults and peers. They do not respond as expected to social stimuli. The combination of these behaviors typically results in further isolation, as both adults and peers tend to ignore or dislike these children and refrain from interacting with them.

Attachment problems can also be related to the behavior patterns of the caregiver, who plays a crucial role in the development of attachment. Parents who are depressed or under great strain may find it difficult to respond to their infant's cues, or they may respond in inappropriate ways. Separation between the child and caregiver during early infancy can also affect the attachment process. Children needing frequent hospitalizations when young are at risk for attachment difficulties.

Parents who are psychologically unavailable or hostile result in infants who are not securely attached. Although rare, children who experience markedly disturbed and inappropriate social relatedness before age 5 can be

Table 7–3 Types of Attachment

- **Secure attachment**. Toddlers showing secure attachment protest at being left alone or with a stranger in an unfamiliar place. They may show the obvious distress of crying or fussing, the disruption of play behavior, or unwillingness to be comforted by a strange adult. When the mother returns, the child calms quickly, seeks proximity, and returns to play and exploration. Parents of securely attached infants appear to be sensitive and responsive to the infant's signals. They seem to feel secure in their own attachment patterns. Children who are securely attached seek out their mother for comfort when they are scared, hurt, or even hungry. These children use their mothers to help them settle down (Dozier et al., 2002).

- **Avoidant Attachment**. Toddlers who display avoidant behavior neither protest when their mother leaves nor do they immediately acknowledge their mothers' return. Rather, they become busy exploring the surroundings and make overtures toward the unfamiliar adult. At first glance, these look like mature behaviors. However, most feel that this is a strategy for dealing with the stress of separation rather than lack of stress per se. It is viewed as an organized defensive strategy. Parents of these infants tend to minimize or dismiss the importance of attachment and to avoid confronting negative behavior. When children come to their parents because they are scared, they may be told, "There is nothing to be scared of," or, "You have to grow up; this is silly," or, "Don't bother me." If parents consistently do not comfort and reassure their young children, they learn that they do not respond to their concerns. They may look and then turn away based on their memory of previous experiences. The childrens' behavior may be adaptive for the situation they are in (Dozier et al., 2002).

- **Resistant Attachment**. Toddlers displaying this type of attachment are distressed at separation from their mother and contact her when she returns, but the contact is one of anger. They do not seem to be comforted by the mother's return and they do not seem to be able to resume play. This behavior has been interpreted as the toddlers' response to inconsistent caregiving. Parents of ambivalent toddlers show similar ambivalent feelings about their own parents. They saw their parents as overly involved, and felt unable to please their parents. They appeared preoccupied with attachment relationships (Dozier et al., 2002). Avoidant and resistant attachment patterns are seen as organized consistent strategies of response to stress that are adaptive for young children in some situations.

- **Disorganized/Controlling Attachment**. Toddlers with disorganized/controlling attachment lack a consistent pattern in response to stress. This behavior is typically in response to caregivers whose behavior is frightening to them. Parents' behavior can be frightening for many reasons. Toddlers' responses can be based on experiences of abuse or neglect, or they can be responses to threats of abandonment. Toddlers' responses may be idiosyncratic, but typically include alternations of approach and avoidance of their mother. They lack an organized way of seeking comfort and security when stressed. Parents of these infants appear stressed and seem to be dealing with unresolved loss or trauma. Parents who are depressed, abusive, alcoholic, or having serious psychosocial problems may respond in ways that frighten young children and make them unable to respond in a consistent way. Some researchers feel that these children are at the greatest risk for later psychopathology (Dozier et al., 2002). Children with both avoidant and resistant attachment have figured out a system that works for them, not ideal but workable. Children with disorganized/controlling attachment are vulnerable for both internalizing symptoms, such as anxiety and depression, as well as externalizing symptoms such as acting out (Lyons-Ruth, 1996).

Reactive Attachment Disorder of Infancy or Early Childhood is a markedly disturbed and developmentally inappropriate social relatedness in a variety of settings.

diagnosed with **Reactive Attachment Disorder of Infancy or Early Childhood** (American Psychiatric Association [APA], 2000). This is usually caused by pathological care, which is care that does not meet the infant's basic emotional and physical needs. The effects of such treatment on infants are pervasive and devastating. A related but somewhat different disorder focuses on separation.

Separation Anxiety Disorder

As the name suggests, anxiety results from separation from familiar people, usually parents, or from leaving home. The reaction is excessive and usually occurs regardless of the general intellectual level of the child. Separation anxiety and generalized anxiety are strongly associated (Warren, 2004). Separation anxiety may be a precursor to adult anxiety.

All young children react to separation. Some children cry, others want their parent to stay, some withdraw and some act out, some hesitate to enter a new setting and, when left, keep returning to the door, some look stressed, and some bring attachment objects. It is the recurrent excessive distress on separation and persistent and excessive worry about losing or having harm befall the attachment figure that characterize this disorder. It may involve sleep disturbances, both not wanting to go to sleep as well as having nightmares about separation. It may involve physical symptoms such as vomiting, headaches, or nausea upon separation or knowledge of separation (APA, 2000). The condition must last at least four weeks to be considered a disorder.

up **close** and **personal**

When you teach two-year-olds you expect separation problems. We have a goodbye window where children can watch their parents leave and look in anticipation of their return. We have had some difficult separations, but not in the same category as Rebecca. She started school in September, and her mother stayed in the classroom with her on the first day, which is pretty typical. The next day her mother planned to leave, but Rebecca protested so violently that her mother stayed. I tried to coach the mother to have her say goodbye, leave for five minutes, and then return so Rebecca would get used to the separation. She cried the whole time her mother was gone. The next day, Rebecca came with her father. This was more difficult, and we again tried the five-minute routine. The family was desperate for her to be in school because they were expecting another child in several months. Rebecca's father did mention that she and her mother were very close. Rebecca didn't like her mother to close the door when she went to the bathroom. And although Rebecca had her own room, she cried to the point that she either slept with her parents or one of them slept with her in the double bed in her room. Her father said they were always tired. As long as he stayed and talked with us, Rebecca was fine. When he left, she cried. We tried variations on leaving, bringing attachment objects, and everything else we could think of. It was difficult to tell at the beginning if this was a power struggle or if it was a genuine separation anxiety dis- order. By the end of the third week we were all exhausted. We had a parent- teacher conference and mutually decided that Rebecca would be withdrawn from the program. I suggested that some family counseling might be helpful. They were non- committal. I feel a bit guilty, but I felt like the other children were paying such a high price and I really thought that I had done all I knew how to do. This situation required more skill than I had.

REFLECTIVE PRACTICE

Separation is an issue with infants and toddlers. As you think about the skills you have to apply to this situation, what might you do that the teacher did not do? How would you have handled this situation? How long would you let it continue?

Attachment and Early Care and Education

The impact of routine nonmaternal care in the first year of life on the security of the infant's attachment to her mother has sparked interest and debate. Bowlby's theory (1973) was interpreted and perhaps misinterpreted to mean that mothers should stay home with their children, and if they did not they risked insecure attachment (Penn, 2005).

Some researchers feel that the early use of nonmaternal care for very young infants may disrupt the attachment relationship. They see infants in child care as having internal models of attachment that are characterized by insecurity and avoidance. Although the data is not completely consistent, there appears to be an overall pattern that young infants who are in nonmaternal care for more than 20 hours per week are more likely to be insecurely attached. The data is less clear on the type of this attachment, but it shows an increased incidence of avoidant attachment (Barton & Williams, 1993). How- ever, are we asking the right questions? We need to know which infant/toddler outcomes are associated with which patterns of maternal and nonmaternal care, under what conditions, and the variables related to these outcomes.

The National Institutes of Child Health and Human Development (NICHD) answered these questions in its study on early child care and youth development. It did not find that hours (less than 10 and more than 30 hours per week) spent in child care invalidated the strange situation. It did find that children's attachment security was related to their parents' sensitivity and responsiveness, particularly at home, and also to the parents' positive psychological adjustment. Overall, the study found no significant differences in attachment related to being in child care. However, when low-quality, unresponsive child care was combined with low maternal sensitivity and lack of responsiveness the effects were cumulative, and these children had the highest rates of insecurity. Findings also showed that less sensitive and responsive parenting and more time spent in child care placed children at risk for insecure attachment. High-quality child care served as a compensatory function for children with insensitive home care (NICHD Early Childcare Research Network, 2005). The ongoing parent-child interaction appears to be an overriding variable, whether or not young children are in child care. The important variable does not appear to be child care but the quality of child care.

Secure attachment is the blueprint for other attachment relationships, including peer relationships. Secure attachment provides young children with a motivational base to expect positive peer relationships, connectedness, and rewarding relationships. Young children expect others to respond to them. As they become more competent and see themselves as change agents they expect to explore their world and discover how it works. Emotionally, children learn to modulate their arousal and regulate their emotions. They also expect a stable relational base from which to develop relationships and explore their environment. They expect reciprocity from peers, empathic care, and to respond empathically to others (Sroufe et al., 2005).

WITH INFANTS AND TODDLERS

Infants learn to feel secure through close sensitive contact. They build trust when you respond quickly and respectfully to their distress. This is not spoiling infants but building trust. Play with infants by humming, singing, or chanting songs or rhymes. Traditional rhymes like "This little piggy went to market," "I'm going to get your nose," "Hickory Dickory Dock," and "Rock-A-Bye Baby" work well. Even if you don't sing well, infants like to hear you sing. As they get older, add songs with motions, such as "Pat-A-Cake" or "Johnny Hammers with One Hammer." At the beginning, hold the infant on your lap and gently move his body.

We do not know as much about the effects of child care on infants as we would like to. We do know that quality matters and individualizing the care of infants is an important aspect of quality.

Child's Perspective of Attachment

From the child's perspective, the goal of attachment is to keep the attachment figure close. He attempts to use the skills he has that are likely to bring or maintain contact. Children typically experience many separations, from being left at home with one parent while another goes to work, to being left with a babysitter, or to staying with an adult relative or friend. Separation also occurs when children enter early care and education settings. Although we use separation reactions in the laboratory to better understand the attachment process in naturally occurring situations, the goal is to use what we know about attachment to support children.

Young children want a sense of predictability and control over their world. Explaining to young children what is going to happen before the parent leaves gives them this information, but may produce a predictable separation reaction. Children whose parents try to "sneak out" to avoid this reaction are likely to experience increased separation anxiety. Even young children who initially seem to separate easily may have problems at varying points; for example, with the birth of a sibling or if parents go away for a weekend.

up close and personal

I was teaching a group of two-year-olds several years ago. It was March and I thought that I had dealt with all the separation issues I was going to have. On a Monday morning, Ashley's mother brought her to school and explained that they had left Ashley with her grandmother over the weekend while they celebrated their fourth wedding anniversary. She said that she was clingy and hadn't wanted to come to school that morning. This was unusual behavior for Ashley because she was typically one of the bouncy, outgoing children.

I was busy with the other children and happened to look over and see Ashley sitting in her cubbie with her coat on.

I went over and helped her take her coat off, and explained that we were going to play for a while, then go outside, have a snack, and then have some time to play inside, and then her mother would come. A little while later I saw her again in her cubbie with her coat on. I helped her take it off and went through my litany again. We then all put on coats to go outside. We came in for a snack, washed hands, and after the snack she was again sitting in her cubbie with her coat on. I went over to her primed with my speech and she looked me in the eye and said, "I'm cold." I let her keep her coat on and sat with her for as long as I could.

REFLECTIVE PRACTICE

What would you have done in this situation? What might the teacher have done earlier to support her? What would you say to her mother when she came to pick her up?

Toddlers can use symbolic play with adult guidance to play out the separation paradigm. This involves games of having objects disappear or hide and then reappear. These games, with sensitive verbal support, help children cope with fear of abandonment. The major issues involved are whether or not the parent will return and who will care for the child in the interim. Children need repeated reassurance on both of those issues.

Symbolic play also offers children the opportunity to play out their feelings about being left. Some young children think they are placed in early care and education settings because they were "bad." Parents may inadvertently support this idea by telling children they are going to child care because they got "so big." Young children may play out this theme (sending things away because they get too big) as a way of coping with separation anxiety. Explaining to children that they are in care so their parents can work is rarely useful and does not address children's concerns or misconceptions.

WITH INFANTS AND TODDLERS

Encourage toddlers to play with and care for the dolls. Be sure to have male and female dolls as well as multiethnic dolls. Help children notice the differences in the ways the dolls look. Join the toddlers' play and actively encourage exploration of the doll. Help children to gently feel the doll's hair, eyes, and clothing, and to move its body parts. Name the body parts and clothing for children. Encourage toddlers to carry, cuddle, feed, sing to, and rock the dolls. When toddlers are ready, introduce new ways of playing with the doll in an appropriate way. Encourage toddlers to play together and talk about what each is doing with their doll and why. Encourage them to think about what the doll might want or need. Support them in leaving the doll and coming back to play. Have them think about what the doll will do while they are away. See if older toddlers can imitate more difficult skills, such as pretend feeding with a spoon or combing the doll's "hair." Help children use their imagination with the doll: Have a tea party, take the doll for a walk in a wagon, and wash the doll in a small tub, then dry the doll off, and so on. Play out separations and reunions.

Children may need to be taught caregiving skills. Toddlers are struggling to develop their own identity, independence, and self-concept. It is useful for them to explore different roles with the dolls and to practice prosocial behavior as well as playing out separation scenarios.

One reason that there is such concern about the development of attachment is that secure parent–infant attachment has been linked to positive outcomes in later years. A secure attachment does not prevent behavior problems in preschool children any more than insecurity causes them. The concern is when insecurely attached infants live and grow in families with few social or emotional resources and are placed in child care settings that are not responsive to their needs.

ADULT-CHILD INTERACTIONS

Social development is an interactive process that involves the infant and adult attending to and responding to each other.

Joint Attention

Joint attention
is when an infant and adult focus on the same object.

Joint attention refers to the ability of individuals to coordinate attention with a social partner focusing on a third object or event (Mundy & Acra, 2006). Although this may sound very technical, it is probably a common part of your behavior. If I wanted you to look at a photograph in this book, I might do something as profound as point to the photograph. If you in turn looked where I pointed, we would have just engaged in joint attention. This capacity emerges between 3 and 6 months, and becomes more complex through 18 months. It begins with such behaviors as eye contact and pointing. These same behaviors may be used to obtain help or to communicate wants and needs.

Joint attention is an important contributor to social competence. Social competence contributes to many adaptive behaviors: resiliency, school readiness, and academic success. With infants, we typically study the behaviors that we believe affect social competence such as attachment, temperament, emotional regulation, and executive function (Mundy & Acra, 2006).

The development of joint attention skills is a major milestone in infant development. It is a self-organizing facility that supports social and cognitive development. The preverbal infant can use these joint attention skills to provide a cognitive platform for language development. If the infant points to an object, or even looks at an object, and an observant adult responds, "That's a ball." The infant has been an active player in his own learning. As a 15-month-old smiles and gazes back and forth between a product he has created and an adult, it is clear that he believes emotions can be shared. Children with autism show a disturbance in the development of joint attention suggesting a biological base for the development of this and related skills (Mundy & Acra, 2006).

Social Referencing

Social referencing
occurs when a child refers to a trusted adult to decide how to interpret a situation.

Social referencing is a process whereby one person utilizes another's interpretation of a situation as a knowledge base (Gilliam & Mayes, 2004). It is a form of active communication that occurs when an infant or toddler encounters a situation of uncertainty and looks to a trusted adult for an emotional signal to resolve the situation. For a very young child this facilitates or reduces stress in everyday life. For example, an infant may be startled or frightened by a jack-in-the-box, but a sensitive adult will make an exaggerated facial expression showing surprise and say, "Did you see that clown?" This then provides the infant with information on how to respond to this new experience.

During the first six months the infant presents emotional information. The caregiver uses this information to meet the infant's needs. By the latter part of the first year, the infant uses emotional expressions from adults to resolve uncertainty. Facial expressions of familiar social partners provide information to infants. By one year of age infants use the facial expression of adults as a form of social referencing. When encountering an unfamiliar situation, infants will turn toward an adult to determine whether or not to approach. If the adult looks wary, the infant is less likely to approach. Infants vary in their use of social referencing; securely attached infants are more likely to use this behavior. Infants look more often at the adults who are the most emotionally expressive (Camras & Sachs, 1991). This is also why the famous "teacher stare" is effective in preventing some behavior.

WITH INFANTS AND TODDLERS

Place the infant in front of a large mirror that is mounted where she can easily see herself, or hold the infant on your lap with an unbreakable mirror in front of her so she can see herself. Talk about what she sees in the mirror: "Look, there's Jia! I see you!" Tap her image in the mirror (joint referencing). Say, "Look, this is you. Don't you look gorgeous?" With an older infant or toddler, point to and name facial parts when she looks in the mirror. Ask her to point out these parts on her own face. Play imitation games in the mirror, such as opening and closing your mouth, patting your head, tugging your ear, and making silly faces!

Infants enjoy looking at themselves in the mirror. Because many mirrors they encounter are too high for them to see, accessible mirrors are a good way to show them what they look like. Mirror rattles, especially larger ones, are also useful because infants can manipulate them themselves.

INFANTS' CUES

Of course, infants cannot control their world; they cannot get their own food or change their own diapers. Infants send cues to their caregivers to modify their environment. However, they do not have a vast repertoire of behavior with which to work. They depend upon such cues as sleepiness, fussiness, alertness, hunger, changes in body activity level, distress, and others. Some infants send cues that are clear and easy to read. Other infants send ambiguous or confusing cues that make it more difficult for their caregivers to respond appropriately. The infant whose eyelids get heavy, yawns, cuddles up, and then falls asleep is easier to read than the infant who opens his eyes and appears to be awake, yet when he is picked up fusses and returns to sleep. Premature infants and those with disabilities often are less alert and responsive in their early months and their cues are more difficult to interpret.

Responding to Infants' Cues

Caregivers must be able to read infants' cues to respond to infants' need. Some adults are more sensitive to infants' cues than are others. However, this is a learned skill. Therefore, even those who do not seem to be innately sensitive can improve their ability to read infants' cues by being given specific information about these behavioral cues. Knowing an infant's schedule can give you some initial hints about the meaning of cues. If an infant has not eaten in three hours, and she is opening and closing her mouth and sticking her tongue in and out, the best guess is that she is hungry.

Some cues infants use signal distress, such as crying. The caregiver must recognize the distress signal and decide on an appropriate action to alleviate the distress; that is, determine whether an infant needs to be changed, fed, held and comforted, or taken to a less stimulating environment.

The more quickly, accurately, and sensitively that caregivers respond to and alleviate distress, the more quickly the infant will be comforted. Caregivers who are under stress may not be sensitive to infants. Infants respond to "depressed" caregivers and may mirror that depression (Honig, 1986). Some caregivers believe that responding to infants quickly will spoil them and make them more demanding. This is not correct; in fact, the opposite is true. When infants are responded to quickly, the infant even begins to anticipate help and may stop crying at the sight of the caregiver, knowing that his needs will be met.

Alleviating distress is important for the infants' well being; however, it is only a small part of the challenge of working with very young children. The ability to play with infants and to respond to and initiate social interaction and support cognitive growth requires far more caregiver adaptation than mere disaster relief.

WITH INFANTS AND TODDLERS

So much of the time with infants is devoted to routine care that it is important to embed learning experiences into such things as diaper changing. It is easy to work in a massage as you change a diaper. Sometimes you may just want to massage the hands and arms or legs. Place the infant on the changing table or floor. Undress an infant down to his diaper. (Be sure it is warm enough.) Place some lotion in one hand to warm it, and then put the lotion on the infant's body. As you massage the infant's body with the lotion, talk to the infant about his body. "Adolpho, now I'm going up and down your arm. Let's check out that hand. You've got five fingers. I'm going to count them. One, two, three, four, oh, actually this one is a thumb." Continue to talk to the infant as you massage his body.

Massaging the infant's body increases body awareness. It is also good for relaxation and for establishing closeness between infants and their caregivers. It is important that you are comfortable with this, and that the parents are as well. Check with the parents before doing infant massage. Some parents may consider this a too personal and sensual activity for caregivers to perform. Others may be overjoyed that you are joining with their infant.

Joint Socialization

When adults respond accurately to the infant's cues an interaction take place. The infant then "reads" the adult's response so that he can modify his behavior. That is, the infant cries to signal the caregiver, the caregiver responds by picking the infant up, cuddling him, and then changing his diaper, and the infant in return responds by a cessation of crying and perhaps making eye contact. If the infant does not respond to the caregiver then adaptation is not possible. No infant responds every time, and likewise, no caregiver always accurately interprets infant signals. However, to the extent that interactions are consistently inappropriate, because of either the infant or the caregiver, the relationship becomes a concern.

The progressive development of the interaction patterns between the infant and adult is the result of several factors. These include the child's temperament, the child's communication cues or signals, the adult's interaction style, and the adult's personality, skill, and emotional investment in the child's upbringing. The development of social behaviors within a child is a result of a combination and interaction of these factors. A fussy infant with a calm and caring parent can develop into a relatively stable preschooler. A fussy infant with an intrusive, abrupt, and unaffectionate parent may develop into an older child with emotional difficulties and social behavior problems.

Vygotsky's (1962) zone of proximal development provides additional insights for understanding social referencing. In Vygotsky's theory, the infant or toddler uses the adult as a guide to learn about her world. The adult role is to help the young children find connections between what they already know and what is necessary to deal with a new situation. With very young children this scaffolding might include modeling, verbal labels to help classify objects and events, nonverbal emotional cues to help assess the situation, and so on. Young children are very astute observers and use social referencing as an effective means of learning information.

Initially, young children require a great deal of redundancy in scaffolding to understand a concept. If an adult were playing ball with a young toddler, the adult might show the toddler the ball, slowly roll the ball, encourage the toddler to roll the ball, while at the same time saying, "Do you want to play with the ball?" "Can you roll the ball" "This ball is red. The ball is round and red and rolls." The continued use of the word ball when one would normally substitute a pronoun, and the verbal and nonverbal support are the redundancy in the scaffolding. As the child becomes knowledgeable about the properties of balls, the redundancy in the scaffolding is reduced. Success depends on the skill of the adult in matching the child's changing world. Although typically most of the adults in child care are female, the importance of male interactions with children must be emphasized. We need more males in early care and education.

Fathers

Professional and popular literature both portray a "new breed" of fathers who have high involvement and increased commitment, and spend greater amounts of time and energy in child-centered activities. The new style of fatherhood has been labeled "involved fatherhood," "highly participant" fatherhood, "androgynous" fatherhood, or simply "new fatherhood" (Palkovitz, 1992). At the same time, the public is also being inundated with stories about the uninvolved "deadbeat" father who ignores his parenting obligation, resulting in a "good dad–bad dad" dichotomy.

Fathers have both a direct and indirect effect on their children. Directly, children who have involved, caring fathers have better educational outcomes. When fathers actively play with and nurture their children, these children develop better linguistic and cognitive skills (Pruett, 2000). Children who have involved fathers—that is, fathers who respond quickly to their cries and play with them—are more securely attached, allowing them to more freely explore their environment. Indirectly, fathers who have good relationships with the mother of their children tend to be more involved and have children who are healthier emotionally and psychologically (Rosenberg & Wilcox, 2006). Mothers observe and imitate father's positive interactions with infants, and vice versa. Mothers often feel more supported when their husband is actively involved in parenting and, in turn, interact more positively with the child themselves.

Studies of fathers and infants show that fathers play and interact with infants differently than mothers. Fathers tend to spend more time playing with their infants than mothers do. Through father's play, infants learn how to regulate their feelings and behavior without losing control of their emotions (Pruett, 2000). Fathers often promote independence and an orientation to the outside world, while mothers stress nurturing. Fathers are more likely to bounce and tickle younger infants and engage in more rough and tumble play as infants turn into toddlers. Mothers spend more time in routine caregiving behaviors (like diapering and feeding) while fathers tend to play more often in physical ways.

Fathers typically become more involved as their children become older, when less time is spent in routine care and there is more time to play and explore. The different interactions of mothers and fathers are important and work together to enhance a children's development. Although father attachment has been studied far less than the infants' attachment to their mother, it is clear that children are attached to their fathers and that fathers can be involved, sensitive caregivers (Rosenberg & Wilcox, 2006).

Lamb, Pleck, and Levine (1987) found four factors crucial to understanding variations in the degree of father involvement: motivation, skill, support of the mother and culture, and institutional support. Motivation—that is, the extent to which the father wants to be involved with his children—affects involvement. However, motivation, is not enough. Men also need skills and sensitivity, along with the self-confidence to use them to interact with their young children. Level of paternal involvement is also related to support, particularly from the mother. There is some question about how much mothers actually want fathers to be involved. This may be related to the father's perceived lack of skill; it may be an area where mothers feel they have authority and do not want to give up; or it may be related to attitudes and values. Middle-class cultural values are clearly changing in this area. The fourth factor is related to institutional practice; fathers typically work outside the home. One might expect that fathers whose wives worked would be more involved; however, paternal involvement levels show very little relationship to the mother's employment status or work schedule (Marsiglio, 1991).

Some biological fathers live with their children; others have different arrangements with their children and the mother of their child. Relationships can become challenging when there are multiple fathers involved in a household. Concerns arise over who is responsible for the safety of the children and who is the psychological "dad." In some cases, boyfriends fill the role of father to a child, and in other cases stepfathers play this role (Rosenberg & Wilcox, 2006).

Fathers play with infants differently than mothers.

Parenting

Human parents everywhere share a common set of goals for their children (see Table 7–4). These goals are hierarchical in nature; that is, if an infant's or toddler's physical survival is threatened, then survival takes precedence over all other goals.

Table 7–4 Parents' Goals for Their Children

- Physical survival and health.
- Increasing the capacity for economic self-sufficiency in maturity.
- Enhancing the ability of their children to succeed based on their culturally defined beliefs, norms, and ideologies of the culture in which they live.

SOURCE: LeVine (2003).

up close and personal

When Laura was about 2 ½, she had a cold, so we took her to the doctor. Because it was near the holiday, we wanted to make sure our celebrations were not interrupted with too much coughing. The doctor became alarmed when she felt Laura's spleen. After some tests—and attempts at being "normal" for our six-year old, we discovered that Laura had neuroblastoma. That was how our roller coaster with cancer began. I do not know where it will end. They operated to remove the cancer and then began chemo. We know she is likely to have hearing loss from the chemo cocktails, which are like eating lead paint with a few other heavy metals thrown in for good measure. Life is a priority.

I didn't realize how much her cancer would change our entire household.

Certainly we expected the hospitalizations, the lethargy, her hair falling out and how stressed we would be. The other strain was keeping the rest of the family healthy. She had no immune system so if we became sick she might get sick. We have hand sanitizers in most rooms, I spray the house with an antibacterial spray every day. I spray the telephone, doorknobs, and light switches several times a day. I wash the counters with an antibacterial spray. It is hardest on our six-year old, Linda. She was use to being able to have friends over whenever she wanted. Now I have to screen them. Some mothers have just given up on us. For Laura to be safe we have to be healthy. We are truly dancing with the devil.

REFLECTIVE PRACTICE

After 12 months Laura's cancer is in remission. Because of the trauma she has been through and her small stature her parents have decided to place her in a two-year-old class-room. How would you feel about being her classroom teacher? What would be your wor-ries? How would you adapt your programming? What precautions would you take?

Although it is easier for us to see the culture of others, each of us has a culture and all of us are the product of one or more cultures (Lynch & Hanson, 2004). Culture is an integral part of all of our lives. It influences the food we eat, the clothes we wear, the language we speak, and what we think and believe. Although culture is powerful, it is just one of many influences on life. Gender, educational attainment, socioeconomic status, and personality, as well as many other attributes impact individuals and groups and their attitudes and beliefs. Culture is dynamic, it is not static (Lynch & Hanson, 2004). Think about the values and beliefs of your parents and grandparents. All cultures change. People embrace culture in different ways. We cannot assume that because we have met one person from Mexico that we now understand the Mexican culture. Within all cultures there is great variation. Cultural varia-tions, migration, and poverty influence family structures and functions.

Different cultures have different goals in having children, and raise them differently based on their culture. In the United States we tend to focus on sepa-rateness, self-sufficiency, and self-confidence (LeVine, 2003). With these values there is a tendency to have fewer children and to invest more in these children. In more agricultural settings, the value of children is their potential to work. To be useful in this setting, children stay at home longer and work under the super-vision of family or community members. How children are raised and the values and beliefs they will have are determined by the culture in which they are raised (LeVine, 2003).

Child-to-Child Interactions

Little child-to-child interaction occurs early in infancy. Infants do not have the necessary social or motor skills to interact with each other. Infant are inter-ested in their peers and look, smile, and touch them. They like to be near some social partners more then others and repeat play sequences. It is not until in-fants can safely venture away from adults that the potential for more involved social interactions begins. Older toddlers may have one or more friendships. They may play together or in reciprocal roles such as run and chase; and in establishing some private time where they exclude others from play (Buysse, Goldman, West, & Hollingsworth, 2008).

Siblings

Siblings play an important role in socialization. Young children are attached to their siblings, particularly younger siblings to older ones (Mercer, 2006). Sibling relationships are the longest-lasting family relationship. Siblings play a variety of roles depending on gender, age, spacing of siblings, and family and cultural expectations. Siblings share the same parents and the same environment, and the infant's early experiences of sharing and turn-taking often occur with siblings. Infants and toddlers learn many skills through watching and imitating older siblings. Siblings often serve as playmates.

Much research on siblings focused on such family structure variables as gender and birth order to explain either similarities or differences in sibling socialization. They contributed little to our understanding of sibling relationships. Recent research has begun to view siblings as experiencing a microenvironment within the family. In trying to elucidate differences in the socialization of siblings, researchers have identified four different classes of sibling experience: (1) differential parenting, (2) differential experiences with other siblings, (3) differential experience in peer groups, and (4) differential exposure to life events (Bussell & Reiss, 1993).

Research seems to support the observation that parents react differently to each child in the family and that children feel they are treated differently from their siblings. Very young children closely monitor the mother's interactions with siblings and react to those interactions. Young children who experienced greater maternal control or less maternal affection than their siblings were more likely to be anxious or depressed (Dunn & McGuire, 1994).

Parenting changes over time. In their longitudinal study, Dunn and McGuire (1994) noted that although parenting with a single child was not consistent over time, the parenting of a child when he was two was similar to the parenting of his sibling when he was two. It may be that parenting is more consistent based on age of the child than previously thought, and that although we see parents behaving differently with each of their children, it may be that we need to think of parenting as varying appropriately with the age of the child rather than overall consistency. This may also be why children perceive their parents as treating them differently from their siblings.

As children get older or go to early care and education centers, they encounter children their own age who are unrelated to them. These interactions are often different from interactions with siblings, because the children are closer to the same age.

Play and Peers

Play contributes to cognitive, physical, social, and emotional development and to the well being of infants and toddlers. There is concern as our world becomes more hurried and pressure increases for academic achievement at a younger age that the importance of play is being devalued. Play is an essential part of childhood, and all infants and toddlers need unscheduled time to interact with their world (Ginsburg & the Committee on Communications and the Committee on Psychosocial Aspects of Child and Family Health: American Academy of Pediatrics Policy, 2007). For an infant, play does not require fancy toys. You are the infant's favorite playmate (Lerner & Greenip, 2004). As children move into toddlerhood, you step back a bit.

Play is not one size fits all. Some infants love to be thrown in the air and caught, or to have a mobile that moves and makes noise; others prefer a home that is stable and quiet. In homes where schedules are tight, we need to ensure that infants and toddlers have time to play and explore their environment without the pressure of accomplishing a particular task. Likewise, in homes where there is little stimulation, attending a more organized program might be beneficial if it provides time to play and explore.

Classification of Play

A majority of early social interactions with peers centers on play and play activities. The quality and type or level of interaction that occurs between children in play activities develops sequentially, increasing with age and maturation. Researchers have been intrigued with this process. Mildred Parten constructed a developmental categorization of play in 1932 that is still used today.

Parten classified play based on the child's level of social participation and the level of organization of the play itself. She saw a social developmental progression in play, but noted that even older children could be in different levels of social participation at different times.

For about the first two years, children participate in **unoccupied**, **onlooker**, or **solitary play**. Young infants need adult involvement in play as they lack the motor skills to play independently. The length and quality of independent play increases as their motor and cognitive skills develop. Early play is centered on sensory exploration of materials and the environment.

Around 18 months, many children begin to view other children with interest, but interaction is typically minimal. At this stage, children see other children as objects rather than people. Toddlers may pull, pinch, hit, or bite others. For some children this behavior may last through 30 months or later. At around 24 months, toddlers often become involved in **parallel play** activities, in addition to maintaining their interest in more solitary play. At this time,

Unoccupied play occurs when the child is not focused on his surroundings or the other children.

Onlooker play is when the child is watching other children play but not actively participating.

Solitary play occurs when the child is playing independently.

Parallel play occurs when the child is playing near other children using similar materials, but playing in his own way.

children are not yet ready for cooperative play. They are still involved in independent play, but these activities now occur in close proximity to other children. Children closely watch each other's play activities and may imitate them (see Table 7–5).

Howes and Matheson (1992) note some variations between Parten's level of parallel and associative play. In **parallel-aware play**, children not only use similar materials, but they also become more social and make eye contact with each other. As contact increases, children may smile at and talk to each other and perhaps exchange toys, turning it into **simple-social play**. Children want to use the same object and attempt the same play activity. Two children can

Parallel-aware play occurs when children use similar materials, but watch other children near them.

Simple-social play occurs when children interact as they play, although the play itself is independent.

REFLECTIVE PRACTICE

Think about how your knowledge of the levels at which two-year-olds play will affect how you set up the environment for them. If you have many different toys, it will be difficult for two-year-olds to participate in parallel play. If, on the other hand, you put out several similar toys at the same time, you are supporting their parallel play, and with your support they may move into simple social play. Decide on the types of materials you would use to support this move.

Table 7–5 Parten's Classification of Play

Level	Definition
Unoccupied behavior	The child is not playing in the usual sense, but watches activities of momentary interest or plays with his body.
Onlooker behavior	The child watches others play. He may talk to, question, or offer suggestions to the children who are playing.
Solitary play	The child plays alone with toys that are different from those used by other children; there is no verbal communication with other children.
Parallel play	The child plays independently, but among other children and with similar toys and materials.
Associative play	The child plays with other children; all are engaged in similar activities, but there is no organization or roles assigned.
Cooperative play	The child plays in a group that is organized for a purpose, to obtain a goal, or to dramatize adult life; formal games are included in this classification; there is a definite division of labor and a sense of belonging to the group.

SOURCE: Parten (1932).

both be in the block area, using the same-size blocks and building roads, yet the entire play activity occurs independently for each child. With increasing age, two-year-olds play with other children in small groups but they do not reach the **associative** or **cooperative** levels of play.

Smilansky and Shefatya (1990) conceptualized play differently from Parten. They, too, focused on the child's development, but they were more interested in cognitive aspects of play. They used Piaget's ideas about cognitive development as the basis for their stages. Their conceptualization of the development of play meshes well with Parten's levels of social interaction. In Smilansky and Shefatya's framework, a child can engage in **functional**, **constructive**, or **dramatic play** alone, near others or with others.

As children's play develops, their social interactions move to peer relationships rather than adult–child relationships. The toddler is developing more precise control over both his large and small muscles and his motor skills are increasing. Cognitively, he is becoming able to **decenter**; that is, focus on more than one aspect of an object, which allows for the manipulation of toys and objects in a social context. Increasingly, children are learning to participate in reciprocal relationships with peers. The development of symbolic play goes through a predictable sequence.

The ability to "pretend," or pretense, emerges at about one year. Pre-pretense is more in the mind of the adult than the child. As the one-year old lies down, the adult says, "Oh, you're sleeping, I better be quiet," and then tiptoes away. In Vygotsky's zone of proximal development, this represents a nudge into symbolic play. Initially, actions are directed toward the child himself (self-pretend) as he "pretends" to comb his hair or drink from a cup. Over a period of several months, this ability at pretense extends beyond the self (other pretend). Now, a toddler might pretend to comb a doll's hair or even have the doll hold the comb and pretend to comb her own hair. See Table 7–6 for the different types of play.

Decentering is the ability to understand different aspects of a toy. The child now knows that he can roll, drop, or throw a ball.

Table 7–6 Types of Play

Level	Definition
Functional play	Repetitive movements that appear playful and usually involve objects (shaking a rattle, dump and fill, etc.)
Constructive play	Using objects or materials to make or create something (putting together a puzzle, block play, painting, etc.)
Dramatic play	Pretend play that may or may not have props and frequently involves assuming a role (eating/drinking pretense, family role-play, using dolls, etc.)
Games with rules	Activities that require compliance with particular requirements and may involve competition (simple board games, ball games, hide and seek, etc.)

SOURCE: Smilansky and Shefatya (1990).

An important aspect in the development of symbolic play is the ability of the child to participate in substitutional behavior; that is, a child can pretend that one object is another, such as a block for a car (object substitution). The ability for single substitutions (block for car) appears at about 24 months. The ability for double substitutions (a block for a car and a string for a gas hose) emerges later (Gowen, 1995).

Around age 2, children incorporate imaginary objects and beings into their play; however, they need the support of real objects. They can imagine the tea, but they need the teapot and cup to pour it into. Toddlers become capable of a different form of object substitution (**active agent**). They "animate" the object. Instead of just feeding the doll, they become the doll and say "yucky" in response to being fed. Puppets, dolls, and stuffed animals support the emergence of this level of symbolic play (Gowen, 1995).

Active agent
is when the child pretends to be a toy, such as a puppet, and begins to take the part of the toy (rather than himself) in play.

WITH INFANTS AND TODDLERS

For toddlers, use easy-to-use animal or people puppets, such as sock puppets. Play with one child with a puppet; you take the lead and have the child respond to your initiations. Encourage the child to put the puppet on her hand and use the puppet to talk to you or another child. Help children find ways to play together by suggesting simple roles they can take or ways of interacting with their puppets that will prolong the play. They will need your scaffolding for play to continue. Encourage two children to play together with different but related puppets; for example, two animal puppets, such as a turtle and a fish. Sometimes toddlers who are reluctant to talk or play socially with others are more willing to play using puppets. Be sure to find ways of including reluctant talkers in puppet play. If you have a multi-age group, encourage older children to use puppets with younger children. Talking with puppets encourages peer interaction as well as the development of language skills.

As children's symbolic play develops, it becomes more integrated. The transition to integration is where the child repeats an action with different recipients (Gowen, 1995). She feeds different dolls or the doll and herself. This develops into related behaviors when she pretends to put the food in a dish and then eats, or pours the tea and then drinks it. These sequences begin to appear at about 15 months, but increase in frequency and complexity (Gowen, 1995). Asking questions about the child's drama is one way of increasing the complexity. As children gain sophistication, planning plays a more important role. Planning is an important aspect in play. Children decide what they are going to do and how they will go about doing it before they actually do it.

Sociodramatic play is theme-related and includes at least one other child.

Smilansky and Shefatya (1990) make a distinction between dramatic play and **sociodramatic play**. In dramatic play the child takes on a role and imitates a person with the aid of real or imagined objects. For toddlers, these roles are typically self-related; often they pretend to be their mother or father. Sociodramatic play involves a theme of some type and at least one other child to participate (Smilansky & Shefatya, 1990). As children progress from age 2 to 3, they go from self-based to shared make-believe play, and they begin to participate in shared play themes. Their play becomes increasingly more complex over the preschool years.

The focus of this section has been on the social and cognitive aspects of play. Children's work is play. Play is the major focus of the infant and toddler curriculum. Yes, because it is fun, but also because it is the way infants and toddlers learn. As the concern about the development of academic skills is being pushed down to infants and toddlers professionals are worried that there will be less time to learn through play. Through play, infants and toddlers can try out new skills, explore their imagination and creativity, and learn about relationships. They can learn key scientific concepts, such as sinking and floating; mathematical concepts, including how to balance blocks to build a tower and how to count the blocks; and literacy skills, such as trying out new vocabulary or storytelling as children "act out" different roles (Lerner & Greenip, 2004). Play cannot be replaced by adults telling infants and toddlers what to do nor can watching these experiences being performed by others on television fulfill the learning that occurs through play.

MEDIA USE

A 1999 national survey showed that virtually all American families have at least one television set and a VCR in their homes, 81 percent of American families own two or more television sets, and three-quarters of American families subscribe to cable or satellite channels. Although ownership of other media items is not as saturated as televisions or VCRs, the majority of American children live in homes furnished with computers (63 percent) and video game consoles (52 percent). The typical American child between the ages of 2 and 3 is likely to live in a household where there are three television sets, two VCRs, one video game player, and one computer (Roberts & Foehr, 2004).

The American Academy of Pediatrics (2001) recommends that children under two should not watch any television, and that all children over two should be limited to one to two hours of quality programming per day. Despite this recommendation, 70 percent of American children under two do watch television on a typical day and spend an average of two hours and five minutes in front of the television. One-fifth of children from birth to two years have a television in their bedroom (Vandewater et al., 2007). Children's media use begins at a very early age. Infants as young as six months are exposed to television for an average of one to two hours per day (Vandewater et al., 2007). Given the omnipresence of electronic media in children's lives today, it is not surprising that they become heavy users of media at an early, impressionable age. Certain and Kahn (2002) found that children who watched more than two hours of television per day at age 2 were more likely to watch over two hours per day at age 6.

There is particular concern about television viewing in low-income families and families in which one parent is depressed. Children ages 4 to 35 months whose parent had no signs of depression watched 1.6 hours of television a day. This rose to an average of 2.1 hours when one parent suffered from mental distress (Thompson & Christakis, 2007). Irregular naptime and bedtime schedules are also associated with increased television viewing (Thompson & Christakis, 2005). Less-educated parents reported that their children watched more television than recommended (Certain & Kahn, 2002).

In a national survey on children's media use conducted in 1997 (Wright et al., 2001), infants and toddlers were observed to watch whatever the adult caregivers or older siblings were watching and spent a lot of time in **secondary viewing**. Many families do not consider this as viewing television because it is not for the child. As children grow older, their secondary viewing declined. Others are concerned that children are exposed to material on the television that is very inappropriate for them. In a national survey, two-thirds of parents reported that they are "very" concerned about the amount of inappropriate content in the media (Rideout, 2007). However, almost half (43 percent) of parents of young children (ages 2 to 6) find media mostly a positive influence with only 17 percent having negative opinions. And 56 percent of parents of young children feel that baby videos have a positive effect on development (Rideout, 2007). For children from ages 2 through 7, video game playing increased with age, particularly for boys.

Programs designed for children are less likely than others to show any long-term negative consequences of violence (5 percent do), and they often portray violence in a humorous context (67 percent) (National Association for the Education of Young Children, 1996). Instead of helping children develop a sense of autonomy and connectedness to each other, television portrays autonomy as being related to fighting and the use of weapons. Conversely, helplessness and altruism are related to connectedness. Other concerns revolve around empowerment and efficacy, gender identity, appreciation of diversity, and morality and social responsibility (Levin & Carlsson-Paige, 1994).

If one looks at the distribution of violent portrayals over the time of day and the day of the week, the situation looks even worse for young children. Most young children watch television on Saturday mornings, in late

Secondary viewing is when infants and toddlers are in a room with the television on with the programming selected for someone else in the room.

afternoons, or in early evenings, when the highest proportion of violence is shown (Comstock & Paik, 1991).

The prevalence of violent media content has aroused great concerns among parents as well as early childhood professionals. The National Association for the Education of Young Children (1994) officially condemns all violent media directed at children. According to its position statement, "exposure to media violence leads children to see violence as a normal response to stress and as an acceptable means for resolving conflict" (p. 2), and those "who are frequent viewers of media violence learn that aggression is a successful and acceptable way to achieve goals and solve problems" (p. 2).

Media for children over two can have a positive impact on social relations. This kind of media content is referred to as "prosocial" and promotes a wide range of positive outcomes, including friendly interactions, imagination, buying books, library use, safety activism, and conversation activism (Hearold, 1986). Rideout, Vandewater, and Wartella (2003) investigated media use among 1,065 infants, toddlers, and preschoolers and found many parents valued media because of its potential positive effect on educational skills. Of all the types of **electronic media** included in the survey, parents were most enthusiastic about the educational potential of computers. Despite criticisms parents made of television, parents believe that television helps even very young children learn and that various kinds of educational media are very important to infants and toddlers' intellectual development, including educational television, educational videos, and educational computer games.

Electronic media includes television, video players, and computers.

PROMOTING PROSOCIAL BEHAVIOR

Social development was seen as the core of the early childhood curriculum until the 1960s, when the emphasis shifted to cognitive development. The goal of early childhood programs was to promote prosocial behavior and positive child-to-child interactions. Prosocial behaviors include helping, giving, sharing, and showing sympathy, kindness, affection, and concern for others (Wittmer & Honig, 1994). Prosocial behaviors are no longer core goals for many programs.

Concerns about prosocial behavior have come for a variety of reasons. Some researchers have found that full-time child care beginning in infancy may be associated with increased aggression and noncompliance (Honig, 1993). There are concerns about war play and superheroes and how this play is moving down to include younger children, and there are overall concerns about the amount of violence young children are experiencing (Osofsky, 1994).

Prosocial behavior does not just happen it must be learned. Modeling prosocial behavior sets the tone for young children. Empowering toddlers by giving them choices enhances their prosocial behavior. Likewise, making them conscious of other children and their feelings promotes prosocial behavior as well.

Toddlers struggle with the ideas of sharing, turn taking, and ownership. You can help promote prosocial behavior by specifically identifying these behaviors: "I like the way you and Carla are taking turns using the markers." Comments should be specific and not used to the point that the purpose of prosocial behavior becomes external reward rather than an internal standard. Emphasize cooperation rather than competition to promote prosocial behavior (Honig & Wittmer, 1996). Help children take the perspective of another child, especially in situations where one child hurts another. "She is crying because you hit her. What can you do to help her feel better?" This both points out the consequences of the behavior as well as helping children understand what might make a distressed child feel better. Children need to accurately identify the emotional state of another child before they can act in a prosocial way toward her (Wittmer & Honig, 1994). Most toddlers respond prosocially to peers in distress. However, toddlers who have been abused may be impassive or react with anger. Vulnerable children need support in specifically developing prosocial behavior. Choosing children's literature with prosocial themes may be a place to start (Honig & Wittmer, 1996).

ATYPICAL SOCIAL DEVELOPMENT

Some infants fail to develop secure attachment patterns with adults. They do not respond as expected to social stimuli. They may be irritable, not easily comforted, dislike affection, and may be withdrawn. These infants may have difficulties in their signaling systems that interrupt the early attachment process. They may cry continuously, have a piercing scream, arch their bodies to physical touch, and show no response to soothing interactions from adults. They may have poor eye contact and lack interest in social interaction. They are frequently described as "difficult" infants. The presence of these behaviors can cause parents or caregivers to think that the infant does not like them. They may also find it unpleasant to be around the infant due to these behaviors. The result may be the failure of the adult and the child to develop secure attachment.

The identification and detection of atypical social development is difficult with young children. Diagnosis includes a subjective judgment of what is inappropriate. Assessment must consider cultural and child-rearing differences. The first signs of atypical social development are identified as infants and toddlers try to master basic developmental skills or social responses. There is concern when an infant cannot be comforted, when a toddler does not talk, when a child continues to show extreme anxiety around strangers, or when a young child does not demonstrate any responsiveness to adults. These responses are warning flags for social development.

Social Problems in Infants and Toddlers

Some common social problems are addressed below. What differentiates social problems from disordered social development is when the behaviors are exhibited more frequently, persistently, and at ages that are no longer appropriate or beyond the stages at which such behaviors are expected.

Victimization and Its Developmental Implications

As children grow and develop they both acquire and lose characteristics that put them at risk for atypical social development. Infants and toddlers are dependent on the adults in their world to fulfill their basic needs; they are vulnerable in ways that older children are not. They can easily become victims of inappropriate adult–child relationships.

In an effort to move beyond the literature that focused solely on child abuse and neglect and to find a developmental framework for viewing social situations in which children are at risk, Finkelhor (1995) proposed the concept of "victimization." He saw the need to develop a means for understanding social traumas within a developmental framework.

The most clearly dependency-related form of victimization is neglect (Finkelhor, 1995) and parents are the adults responsible for such neglect. Even when others are aware of neglect, it is the parents' responsibility to care for their children. Child neglect is the most common type of child maltreatment. It frequently goes unreported. Defining neglect is challenging because it is based on the age and the developmental level of the child. In 2004, approximately 8 out of every 1,000 children in the general population were reported as being neglected (Children's Bureau, 2006). Rates of child abuse and neglect are double for infants and toddlers. In 2003, 16 per 1,000 infants and toddlers were victims of abuse or neglect (United States Department of Health and Human Services, 2005).

This view of victimization (Finkelhor, 1995) uses the disruption of developmental tasks of childhood as a basis for understanding vulnerability. Development of attachment to a primary caregiver is a major social task of infancy. Victimization interferes with this task when abuse is perpetrated by the caregiver. The result is insecure attachment and the expectation is that the effects of this insecure attachment will be carried into later phases of development and other relationships. There may also be physiological alterations in endocrine functioning and neurological processes that permanently affect a range of cognitive and behavioral development (Putnam & Trickett, 1993). The effects of abuse do not end in early childhood. Infants and toddlers who have been maltreated show more symptoms of anxiety and depression in adulthood (Kaplow & Widom, 2007).

Dissociation
is a mental state where certain thoughts, sensations, or memories are compartmentalized because they are too overwhelming for the conscious mind.

As children become a little older and are capable of mental representation, they develop the ability to **dissociate**. They fantasize, developing imaginary playmates, and deny things they clearly have done. Children victimized as two-year-olds or preschool children use dissociation as a defense mechanism and can develop chronic patterns of dissociation, such as memory loss, a tendency for trance-like behavior, and auditory or visual hallucinations (Macfie, Cicchetti, & Toth, 2001; Putnam, 1991).

Assessing the results of victimization for young children is different than adults. When adults are victimized, they typically display post-traumatic stress symptoms that are relatively short term and primarily affect the behavior associated with the experience. Young children, too, show such behaviors as fearfulness, nightmares, avoidance of violence on television, fear of adults who resemble the offender, and fear of returning to the place where the victimization occurred (Finkelhor, 1995). Almost all traumatic situations result in some increased sense of fearfulness. In addition to traditional post-traumatic stress symptoms with very young children, victimization interferes with typical developmental processes. Although specific developmental problems vary, the effects of victimization can result in impaired attachment; problems relating to others; poor peer relationships, often in the form of aggression toward peers with lack of remorse; and problems coping with stress and anxiety (Briere, 1992; Cicchetti & Lynch, 1993).

Autism Spectrum Disorders

The term *autism spectrum disorders* (ASD) refers to a continuum of neurodevelopmental disorders related to impairments of social interaction, communication and narrow repetitive patterns of behavior (Matson & Minshawi, 2006). The APA (2000) uses the term pervasive developmental disorder (PDD) which includes autism, Asperger's syndrome, Rett's disorder, and childhood disintegrative disorder. Pervasive developmental disorder–not otherwise specified (PDD-NOS) is used as a classification when symptoms are present but do not meet the specific criteria of in a particular category. These disorders are grouped because they share an essential feature of all PDDs: impaired social reciprocity. Children with these disorders also have problems with communication and repetitive behaviors. The social limitations usually result in limited play skills. PDDs may coexist with other disorders and there is often some degree of intellectual disability (APA, 2000; Hyman & Towbin, 2007).

For purposes of education the IDEA 2004 defines autism as follows:

Autism means a developmental disability significantly affecting verbal and nonverbal communication and social interaction, generally evident before age three that adversely affects a child's educational performance. Other characteristics often associated with autism are engagement in repetitive activities and stereotyped movements, resistance to environmental change or change in daily routines, and unusual responses to sensory experiences.

Autism does not apply if a child's educational performance is adversely affected primarily because the child has an emotional disturbance.

A child who manifests the characteristics of autism after age three could be identified as having autism if other criteria are satisfied.

The APA (2000) has developed diagnostic criteria for autistic disorder. To be diagnosed with autistic disorder, its onset must be before age three, with abnormal functioning in one of the following areas: social interaction, language as a communication skill, or symbolic play. To meet the criteria, the child must display six or more items from the list in Table 7–7, with at least two coming from A and one each from B and C.

Table 7–7 Criteria for Diagnosis of Autistic Disorder

A. *Qualitative impairment in social interaction*
- impairment in using multiple nonverbal behaviors such as eye-to-eye gaze, facial expression, gestures, and body postures to regulate social interaction
- inability to develop appropriate peer relationships
- lack of spontaneous sharing of enjoyment, interests, or achievements with others
- lack of social or emotional reciprocity

B. *Qualitative impairments in communication*
- delay in, or lack of, spoken communication
- inability to use speech to initiate or sustain conversation
- stereotyped and repetitive use of language or idiosyncratic language
- lack of spontaneous make-believe play or social imitative play

C. *Restricted, repetitive, and stereotyped patterns of behavior, interests, and activities*
- preoccupation with stereotyped patterns of interest (intensity or focus)
- adherence to specific nonfunctional routines or rituals
- stereotyped and repetitive motor mannerisms (hand flapping)
- preoccupation with parts of objects

SOURCE: American Psychiatric Association (2000).

The term PDD–NOS is a source of confusion for parents and professionals. It is a vague designation that does not have specific criteria. Some use it as a diagnosis for children who have a basic impairment in relating and communicating, but do not meet the criteria for autistic disorder. Others use it when it is not clear whether the criteria (before age 3) have been met or when the child is too "mild."

Some professionals do not like the term *PDD–NOS* and would prefer to use the term *autistic spectrum disorder*. There is certainly a gray area where high functioning children with autism are labeled and PDD–NOS begins. Greenspan and Wieder (2006) particularly object to this label. They prefer to use the term *neurodevelopmental disorders of relating and communicating*. They feel that this term more accurately defines the regulatory-sensory processing problems with the significant developmental delays and dysfunctions that derail the child's ability to relate and communicate.

Greenspan and Wieder's research (2006) shows a different pattern of development than that noted by the APA (2000). Their research shows children having seemingly normal development for about the first 12 to 15 months. At this time, the toddler begins to show oversensitivity or becomes less reactive to sounds and touch. Language development stops and existing language seems forgotten. Greenspan and Wieder (2006) see these behaviors as falling along a continuum rather than fitting into clear diagnostic categories. They see each child as having a unique profile relative to sensory reactivity, sensory processing, muscle tone, and motor planning or sequencing.

Greenspan and Wieder (2006) feel the disorder is triggered by the environment and that two events derail the child's development between 16 and 24 months. The first is the child's emerging capacity of higher-level presymbolic, symbolic, and cognitive function. These new capacities are built on a weak foundation. They overwhelm the child and cause him to regress in the areas of self-regulation, behavioral organization, interpersonal patterns, motor control, and language abilities. At the core of this regression is a weak capacity for intentional two-way affective communication. Although this alone may impact development a second event which stresses the child such as the loss of a caregiver, parent's return to work, birth of a sibling may be overwhelming. The more difficult the child becomes the more frustrated the parents' feel. They feel that it is a biologically based problem in forming an early sensory-affect-motor connection that leads to the challenges and symptoms observed in ASD.

There has been a lot of controversy about whether the ethylmercury-based preservative thimerosal used as a preservative in pediatric vaccines before 2001 could be associated with the rise in cases of ASD. At this point there is not scientific documentation for a causal relation between these variables although clearly some parents believe this is true (Hyman & Towbin, 2007).

Identification of children with ASD is determined by their behavior in three areas: social reciprocity, communication, and repetitive behaviors (APA, 2000). Delays or abnormal functioning in social interactions, not using language as a tool for social communication, and not participating in symbolic or imaginative play serve as markers (APA, 2000).

- *Social Reciprocity.* Social interactions form the core of getting along with others. Social interactions are complex. They involve being able to read and respond accurately to the cues of others. These social skills emerge as children learn about themselves as individuals and eventually, about the thoughts and feelings of others. Children with autism are inept at learning these skills. They may not respond, have limited responses, or be clumsy in their attempts, but they do not have good social interaction skills.

- *Communication Skills.* Children with autism have some degree of communication impairment. Expressive language may show more **echolalia** (repetition of what is spoken) than spontaneous speech. Personal pronouns are often confused. Speech may be higher pitched, and may have unusual rhythm and intonation (Hyman & Towbin, 2007). Receptively, children may have problems with more complex communication. Traditionally, they are visual learners.

- *Stereotyped Behavior.* Children with autism do not know how to play, especially when toddlers move into pretend play. They often get into rituals, routines, and schedules, but spontaneity is beyond their capacities. They become upset if their routines are disturbed. They may display stereotyped movements and self-stimulating behaviors such as arm flapping, pacing, running in circles, rocking, hand waving, and so on. They may have sleep disturbances, mood changes, and unusual responses to sensory input.

Echolalia is repeating what another person says rather than responding to the communication. In response to, "I like you," a child would echo, "I like you."

REFLECTIVE PRACTICE

Think about how you would modify your classroom to include a two-year old with autism. Knowing that these children are visual learners, I might have pictures I could point to. I might use exaggerated facial expression and ensure that my expression and tone were congruent. I might evaluate my play space to ensure that it is not visually confusing. I would be respectful if children have problems with touch and learn the level of touch that works best. I would partner with parents for a shared understanding on approach and what works. What else could you do?

Failure to Thrive

Failure to thrive
is a medical condition that is characterized by poor weight gain and physical growth failure over an extended period of time during infancy.

Failure to thrive is the modern-day equivalent of marasmus, or wasting away of an infant. The main cause of failure to thrive is that infants do not get enough food and, as a result are failing to meet the standards for age in both growth and development. It is, in effect, more of a symptom than a diagnosis (Beker, Farber, & Yanni, 2002). In infancy, it also means deficits in nutrition to the brain and diminished physical energy for exploring and learning. Malnutrition reduces the number of brain cells.

SUMMARY

The study of social development has been influenced by psychoanalytic and behavioral views of development as well as social and cognitive theories. Relationships are the cornerstone of social development. The development of attachment between an infant and trusted caregivers serves as a blueprint for the development of future relationships.

Adults respond to infants' cues to determine what infants want and need. Likewise, infants use adults to get their needs met and to determine how to respond to particular situations. Infants are born into families and all members of the family including the siblings play a part in social development. In addition to the family, many children are in the care of others during these early years. Peer relations begin during the infant and toddler years as children become interested in each other and interact by playing near and with other toddlers. Media also has an impact on social development. Some are concerned about the impact of media violence on young children, but many also acknowledge the potential of media to support prosocial skills and to learn. Some infants and toddlers have problems in social development and some are identified with social disorders such as autism.

CHAPTER IN REVIEW

* Social development begins at birth. It focuses on relationships: their establishment, maintenance, and role in human life.

* Social development lays the foundation for later social interactions with both adults and peers.

* Behaviorism and psychoanalytic theory provided the theoretical basis for early work in social development.

* Early research focused on such areas as child-rearing techniques, sex typing, and socialization. As the knowledge base about infancy increased, scholars began to question the efficacy of these theories.

* Current research focuses on relationships and the development of these relationships.

* Attachment is an essential element in social development.

* Infants are born with behaviors that support attachment, but they need sensitive

- adult support for secure attachment to develop.

- Not all infants develop secure attachment behaviors to their primary caregivers. Some infants display avoidant attachment, others ambivalent attachment, and still others disorganized/disoriented attachment.

- Infants are not only attached to their parents or primary caregivers, but also to their siblings.

- Research is increasingly focusing on the role of fathers, siblings, and culture in early socialization and the joint socialization of infants and caregivers.

- Atypical social development is difficult to diagnose because of the natural variability of infant behavior.

- As infants become toddlers their social interactions reach beyond their family to peers. This interaction is based on play behavior.

- As toddlers learn to use symbolic play they increasingly interact with peers.

- Play becomes a basis for social development and increases in complexity with age, and the interactions demand new levels of self-awareness from young children.

APPLICATION ACTIVITIES

1. The AMA recommends no media for children under age 2. Ask your friends when they think it is okay for infants to begin watching television. Also ask them if they think it is okay to have an infant in the room when adults are watching television. Discuss how their responses relate to what you know to be best practice.

2. From reading this chapter you know that a six-month-old infant cannot be spoiled and develops a secure attachment from being responded to consistently and quickly. Ask your friends if they believe a six-month old can be spoiled. Note their responses. Also ask them if they think it is important to always respond to an infant's cries or if it is better to let the infant "cry it out." Reflect on how their answers relate to what you know.

3. Given what you know about the importance of attachment, discuss how this will impact your interactions with infants and toddlers and their families. How will it affect your behavior should you decide to have children?

RESOURCES

Web Resources

- The **Administration for Children and Families** at the U.S. Department of Health and Human Services is highlighting the positive role that fathers play in *The importance of fathers in the healthy development of children.* http://childwelfare. gov.

- The **Center on the Social and Emotional Foundations for Early Learning** at Vanderbilt University focuses on promoting social and emotional development and also looks at challenging behavior. They provide training as well as a series of *What works briefs* on specifics topics. These can be downloaded or purchased for a small fee. http://www.vanderbilt.edu.csefel.

- The **Child Welfare Information Gateway**, a service of the Children's Bureau, provides access to information and resources to help protect children and strengthen families. It has links to many sites that have a similar mission. http://www.childwelfare.gov.

- The **National Center for Children in Poverty** publishes articles that are helpful in working with high-risk families. A particularly useful one is *Helping the most vulnerable infants, toddlers, and their families*. nccp.org.

- **Zero to Three** provides a section on key topics, including social and emotional development, and it also provides tips for building relationships. The article "Social Emotional Development" is of particular interest. zerotothree.org.

Print Resources

- Balaban, N. (2006). *Everyday goodbyes: Starting school and early care—A guide to the separation process*. New York: Teachers College Press.

- Brown, W. H., Odom, S. L., & McConnell, S. R. (2008). *Social competence of young children: Risk, disability, and intervention*. Baltimore, MD: Paul H. Brookes.

- Honig, A. (2002). *Secure relationships: Nurturing infant/toddler attachment in early care settings*. Washington, DC: National Association for the Education of Young Children.

REFERENCES

Ainsworth, M. D. (1963). The development of infant-mother interaction among the Ganda. In B. M. Foss (Ed.), *Determinants of infant behavior* (Vol. 2, pp. 67–102). London: Methuen.

Ainsworth, M. D. (1969). Object relations, dependency, and attachment: A theoretical review of the infant-mother relationship. *Child Development, 40*, 969–1025.

Ainsworth, M. D. (1973). The development of infant-mother attachment. In B. M. Caldwell & H. N. Ricciuti (Eds.), *Review of child development research* (Vol. 3, pp. 1–94). Chicago, IL: University of Chicago Press.

Ainsworth, M. D., Salter, D., & Wittig, B. A. (1967). Attachment and exploratory behavior of one-year-olds in a strange situation. In B. M. Foss (Ed.), *Determinants of infant behavior* (Vol. IV, pp. 111–135). New York: Wiley.

American Academy of Pediatrics. (2001). Children, adolescents, and television. *Pediatrics, 107*(2), 423–426.

American Psychiatric Association. (2000). *Diagnostic and statistical manual of mental disorders: DSM-IV-TR* (4th ed.). Washington, DC: Author.

Bandura, A. (1992). Social cognitive theory. In R. Vasta (Ed.), *Six theories of child development* (pp. 1–60). London: Jessica Kingsley Publisher Ltd.

Barclay, L. K. (1985). *Infant development*. Fort Worth, TX: Holt, Rinehart and Winston.

Barton, M., & Williams, M. (1993). Infant day care. In C. H. Zeanah Jr. (Ed.), *Handbook of infant mental health* (pp. 445–461). New York: Guilford Press.

Baumrind, D. (1967). Effects of authoritative parent control on child behavior. *Child Development, 37*, 887–907.

Beckett, C., Maughan, B., Rutter, M., Castle, J., Colvert, E., Groothues, C., et al. (2006). Do the effects of early severe deprivation on cognition persist into early adolescents? Findings from the English Romania adoptees study. *Child Development, 77*(3), 696–711.

Beker, L. T., Farber, A. F., & Yanni, C. C. (2002). Nutrition and children with disabilities. In M. L. Batshaw (Ed.), *Children with disabilities* (5th ed., pp. 141–164). Baltimore, MD: Paul H. Brookes.

Boocock, S. S., & Scott, K. A. (2005). *Kids in context: The sociological study of children and childhood*. Lanham, MD: Rowman & Littlefield Publishers, Inc.

Bowlby, J. (1940). The influence of early environment. *International Journal of Psycho-Analysis, 21*, 154–178.

Bowlby, J. (1944). Forty-four juvenile thieves. *International Journal of Psycho-Analysis, 25*, 1–57.

Bowlby, J. (1952). *Maternal care and mental health* (2nd ed.). Geneva: World Health Organization: Monograph Series, N.2.

Bowlby, J. (1958). The nature of the child's tie to his mother. *International Journal of Psycho-Analysis, 39*, 350–373.

Bowlby, J. (1969). *Attachment and loss: Vol. 1. Attachment* (2nd ed.). New York: Basic Books.

Bowlby, J. (1973). *Attachment and loss, Vol. 2: Separation, Anxiety, and Anger*. London: Hogarth Press.

Bowlby, J. (1989). The role of attachment in personality development and psychopathology. In S. I. Greenspan & G. H. Pollock (Eds.), *The course of life: Vol. 1 Infancy* (pp. 229–270). Washington, DC: U.S. Government Printing Office.

Bretherton, I. (2005). In pursuit of the internal working model construct and its relevance to attachment relationships. In K. E. Grossmann, K. Grossmann, & E. Waters (Eds.), *Attachment from infancy to adulthood: The major longitudinal studies* (pp. 13–47). New York: The Guilford Press.

Briere, J. (1992). *Child abuse trauma: Theory and treatment of lasting effects*. Newbury Park, CA: Sage.

Bussell, D. A., & Reiss, D. (1993). Genetic influences on family process: The emergence of a new framework for family research. In F. Walsh (Ed.), *Normal family processes* (2nd ed., pp. 161–181). New York: The Guilford Press.

Buysse, V., Goldman, B. D., West, R., & Hollingsworth, H. (2008). Friendships in early childhood: Implications for early education and intervention. In W. H. Brown, S. L. Odom, & S. R. McConnell. *Social competence of young children: Risk, disability, and intervention* (pp. 77–97). Baltimore, MD: Paul H. Brookes.

Camras, L., & Sachs, V. (1991). Social referencing and caretaker expressive behavior in a day care setting. *Infant Behavior and Development, 14*, 27–36.

Certain, L. K., & Kahn, R. S. (2002). Prevalence, correlates, and trajectory of television viewing among infants and toddlers. *Pediatrics, 109*(4), 634–642.

Children's Bureau. (2006). *Child neglect: A guide for prevention, assessment and intervention: User Manual Series.* Retrieved November 17, 2007, from http://www.childwelfare.gov/pubs/ usermanuals/neglect/chaptertwo.cfm

Cicchetti, D., & Lynch, M. (1993). Toward an ecological/transaction model of community violence and child mal treatment: Consequences of child development. In D. Reiss, J. E. Richters, & M. Radke-Yarrow (Eds.), *Children and violence* (pp. 96–118). New York: The Guilford Press.

Collins, W. A. (2002). Historical perspectives. In P. K. Smith & C. H. Hart (Eds.), *Blackwell handbook of childhood social development* (pp. 3–23). Oxford, UK: Blackwood Publishers Ltd.

Comstock, G., & Paik, H. (1991). *Television and the American child.* Orlando, FL: Academic.

Croft, C., Beckett, C., Rutter, M., Castle, J., Colvert, E., Groothues, C., et al. (2007). Early adolescent outcomes of institutionally-deprived and non-deprived adoptees. II: Language as a protective factor and a vulnerable outcome. *Journal of Child Psychology and Psychiatry, 48*(1), 31–44.

Dozier, M., Dozier, D., & Manni, M. (2002). Attachment and biobehavioral catch-up: The ABC's of helping foster infants cope with early adversity. *Zero to Three, 22*(5), 7–13.

Dunn, J., & McGuire, S. (1994). Young children's nonshared experiences: A summary of studies in Cambridge and Colorado. In E. M. Heatherington, D. Reiss, & R. Plomin (Eds.), *Separate social worlds of siblings: The impact of nonshared environment on development* (pp. 111–128). Hillsdale, NJ: Lawrence Erlbaum Associates.

Feinman, S., & Lewis, M. (1991). Influence lost, influence gained. In M. Lewis & S. Feinman (Eds.), *Social influences and socialization in infancy* (pp. 1–22). New York: Plenum Press.

Finkelhor, D. (1995). The victimization of children: A developmental perspective. *American Journal of Orthopsychiatry, 65*(2), 177–193.

Freud, S. (1940). *An outline of psychoanalysis.* New York: Norton.

Gilliam, W. S., & Mayes, L. C. (2004). Integrating clinical and psychometric approaches: Developmental assessment and infant mental health evaluation. In R. DelCarmen-Wiggins & A. Carter (Eds.), *Handbook of infant, toddler, and preschool mental health assessment* (pp. 185–203). Oxford, UK: Oxford University Press.

Ginsburg, K. R., & the Committee on Communications and the Committee on Psychosocial Aspects of Child and Family Health: American Academy of Pediatrics Policy. (2007). The importance of play in promoting healthy child development and maintaining strong parent-child bonds. *Pediatrics, 119*(1), 182–191.

Goldman-Eisler, F. (1951). The problem of "orality" and its origin in early childhood. *Journal of Mental Science, 97,* 765–782.

Golombok, S., & Hines, M. (2002). Sex differences in social behavior. In P. K. Smith & C. H. Hart (Eds.), *Blackwell handbook of childhood social development* (pp. 117–136). Oxford, UK: Blackwood Publishers Ltd.

Gowen, J. W. (1995). The early development of symbolic play. *Young Children, 50*(3), 75–84.

Greenspan, S. I., & Wieder, S. (2006). *Infant and early childhood mental health: A comprehensive developmental approach to assessment and intervention.* Washington, DC: American Psychiatric Publishing, Inc.

Hearold, S. (1986). A synthesis of 1043 effects of television on social behavior. In G. Comstock

(Ed.), *Public communication and behavior* (Vol. 1, pp. 65–133). New York: Academic Press.

Hoffman, M. L. (1970). Moral development. In P. H. Mussen (Ed.), *Carmichael's manual of child psychology* (Vol. II, pp. 261–360). New York: John Wiley & Sons, Inc.

Honig, A. S. (1986). Stress and coping in children. In J. B. McCracken (Ed.), *Reducing stress in young children's lives* (pp. 142–167). Washington, DC: National Association for the Education of Young Children.

Honig, A. S. (1993). Mental health for babies: What do theory and research teach us? *Young Children, 48*(3), 69–76.

Honig, A. S., & Wittmer, D. S. (1996). Helping children become more prosocial: Ideas for classrooms, families, schools, and communities. *Young Children, 51*(2), 62–70.

Horney, K. (1937). *The neurotic personality of our time.* New York: Norton.

Horney, K. (1945). *Our inner conflicts.* New York: Norton.

Howes, C., & Matheson, C. C. (1992). Sequences in the development of competent play with peers: Social and pretend play. *Developmental Psychology, 28*, 961–974.

Huston, A. (1983). Sex typing. In E. M. Heatherington (Ed.), *Handbook of child psychology: Vol. 4. Socialization, personality, and social development* (pp. 387–467). New York: Wiley.

Hyman, S. L., & Towbin, K. E. (2007). Autism spectrum disorders. In M. L. Batshaw, L. Pellegrino, & N. J. Rosen (Eds.), *Children with disabilities* (6th ed., pp. 325–343). Baltimore, MD: Paul H. Brookes.

Individuals with Disabilities Education Improvement Act of 2004, Pub. L. No. 108–446, 118 Stat 2647, 20 U. S. C. 1400. 2004.

Kaplow, J. B., & Widom, C. S. (2007). Age of onset of child maltreatment predicts long-term mental health outcomes. *Journal of Abnormal Psychology, 116*(1), 176–187.

Kessen, W. (1965). *The child.* New York: Wiley.

Kohlberg, L. (1969). Stage and sequence: The cognitive-developmental approach to socialization. In D. A. Goslin (Ed.), *Handbook of socialization theory and research* (pp. 347–380). Chicago, IL: Rand McNally.

Kreppner, J. M., O'Connor, T. G., Rutter, M., & English and Romanian Adoptees Study Team. (2001). Can inattention/overactivity be an institutional deprivation syndrome? *Journal of Abnormal Child Psychology, 29*(6), 513–528.

Lamb, M. E., Pleck, J. H., & Levine, J. A. (1987). Effects of increased paternal involvement on fathers and mothers. In C. Lewis & M. O'Brien (Eds.), *Researching fatherhood* (pp. 109–125). London: Sage.

Lerner, C., & Greenip, C. (2004). *Power of play: Learning through play from 0–3.* Washington, DC: Zero to Three.

Levin, D. E., & Carlsson-Paige, N. (1994). Developmentally appropriate television: Putting children first. *Young Children, 49*(5), 38–44.

LeVine, R. A. (2003). A cross-cultural perspective on parenting. In R. A. LeVine (Ed.), *Childhood socialization: Comparative studies of parenting, learning and educational change.* CERC Studies in Comparative Education, Comparative Education Research Centre, Hong Kong: University of Hong Kong.

Lewis, M. (1987). Social development in infancy and early childhood. In J. D. Osofsky (Ed.), *Handbook of infant development* (2nd ed., pp. 419–493). New York: John Wiley & Sons, Inc.

Lobel, T., & Menashin, J. (1993). Relations of conceptions of gender-role transgressions and gender constancy to gender-typed toy preferences. *Developmental Psychology, 29,* 150–155.

Lynch, E. W., & Hanson, M. J. (2004). *Developing cross-cultural competence: A guide for working with children and their families* (3rd ed.). Baltimore, MD: Paul H. Brookes Publishing Co.

Lyons-Ruth, K. (1996). Attachment relationships among children with aggressive behavior problems: The role of disorganized attachment patterns. *Journal of Consulting and Clinical Psychology, 64,* 64–73.

Lyons-Ruth, K., & Zeanah, C. H., Jr. (1993). The family context of infant mental health: I: Affective development in the primary caregiving relationship. In C. H. Zeanah Jr. (Ed.), *Handbook of infant mental health* (pp. 15–37). New York: Guilford Press.

Macfie, J., Cicchetti, D., & Toth, S. L. (2001). Dissociation in maltreated versus nonmaltreated preschool-aged children. *Child Abuse and Neglect, 25*(9), 1253–1267.

Marsiglio, W. (1991). Paternal engagement activities with minor children. *Journal of Marriage and the Family, 53,* 973–986.

Matson, J. L., & Minshawi, N. F. (2006). *Early intervention for autism spectrum disorders: A critical analysis.* Oxford, UK: Elsevier Ltd.

Mercer, J. (2006). *Understanding attachment: Parenting, child care, and emotional development.* Westport, CN: Praeger.

Mundy, P. C., & Acra, C. F. (2006). Joint attention, social engagement, and the development of social competence. In P. J. Marshall & N. A. Fox (Eds.), *The development of social engagement: Neurobiological perspectives* (pp. 81–117). Oxford, UK: Oxford University Press.

National Association for the Education of Young Children. (1994). Media violence in children's lives: A position statement of

NAEYC. Accessed May 5, 2007, from www.naeyc.org/about/positions/pdf/PSHEVI98.pdf

National Association for the Education of Young Children. (1996). The national television violence study: Key findings and recommendations. *Young Children, 51*(3), 54–55.

NICHD Early Child Care Research Network. (Eds.) (2005). *Child care and child development: Results from the NICHD study of early child care and youth development.* New York: The Guilford Press.

O'Connor, T. G., Marvin, R. S., Rutter, M., Olrick, J. T., Britner, P. A., & English and Romanian Adoptees Study Team. (2003). Child-parent attachment following early institutional deprivation. *Developmental Psychopathology, 15*(1), 19–38.

Osofsky, J. D. (1994). Introduction. In J. D. Osofsky & E. Fenichel (Eds.), *Hurt, healing, hope: Caring for infants and toddlers in violent environments. Zero to Three, 14*(3), 3–6.

Palkovitz, R. (1992). Changes in father–infant bonding beliefs across couple's first transition to parenthood. *Maternal Child Nursing Journal, 4,* 141–154.

Parten, M. B. (1932). Social participation among preschool children. *Journal of Abnormal Psychology, 27,* 243–269.

Penn, H. (2005). *Understanding early childhood: Issues and controversies.* Berkshire: Open University Press.

Pike, A. (2002). Behavioral genetics, shared and nonshared environment. In P. K. Smith & C. H. Hart (Eds.), *Blackwell handbook of childhood social development* (pp. 27–43). Oxford, UK: Blackwood Publishers Ltd.

Pinneau, S. R. (1950). A critique on the articles by Margaret Ribble. *Child Development, 21,* 203–228.

Pruett, K. (2000). *Father-need*. New York: Broadway Books.

Putnam, F. W. (1991). Dissociative disorders in children and adolescents: A developmental perspective. *Pediatric Clinics of North America, 14*, 519–531.

Putnam, F. W., & Trickett, P. K. (1993). Child sexual abuse: A model of chronic trauma. In D. Reiss, J. E. Richters, & M. Radke-Yarrow (Eds.), *Children and violence* (pp. 96–118). New York: The Guilford Press.

Ribble, M. A. (1944). Infantile experience in relations to personality development. In J. M. Hunt (Ed.), *Personality and the behavior disorders* (pp. 621–651). New York: Ronald Press.

Rideout, V. (2007). *Parents, children and media: A Kaiser family foundation survey*. Menlo Park, CA: Henry J. Kaiser Family Foundation. Retrieved November 6, 2007, from http://www.kaiserfamilyfoundation.org/entmedia/upload/7638.pdf

Rideout, V. J., Vandewater, E. A., & Wartella, E. A. (2003). Zero to six: Electronic media in the lives of infants, toddlers and preschoolers. Menlo Park, CA: The Henry J. Kaiser Family Foundation. Retrieved July 18, 2004, from http://www.kff.org/entmedia/loader.cfm?url=/commonspot/security/getfile.cfm&PageID=22754

Roberts, D. F., & Foehr, U. G. (2004). *Kids and media in America*. Cambridge, UK: Cambridge University Press.

Roberts, E. (1944). Thumb and finger sucking in relations to feeding in early infancy. *American Journal of Diseases of Children, 68*, 7–8.

Rochat, P., & Striano, T. (1999). Social-cognitive development in the first year. In P. Rochat (Ed.), *Early social cognition: Understanding others in the first months of life* (pp. 3–34). Mahwah, NJ: Lawrence Erlbaum Associates, Publishers.

Rosenberg, J., & Wilcox, W. B. (2006). *The importance of fathers in the healthy development of children*. Washington, DC: U.S. Department of Health and Human Services, Administration for Children and Families, Administration on Children, Youth and Families, Children's Bureau, Office of Child Abuse and Neglect.

Sears, R. R., Maccoby, E. E., & Levin, H. (1957). *Patterns of child rearing*. Evanston, IL: Row, Peterson.

Sears, R. R., Whiting, J., Nowlis, V., & Sears, P. (1953). Some child rearing antecedents of aggression and dependency in young children. *Genetic Psychological Monographs, 47*, 135–234.

Smilansky, S., & Shefatya, L. (1990). *Facilitating play: A medium for promoting cognitive, socio-emotional, and academic development in young children*. Gaithersburg, MD: Psychosocial & Educational Publications.

Spitz, R. A. (1945). Hospitalizm: An inquiry into the genesis of psychiatric conditions in early childhood. *The Psychoanalytic Study of the Child, 1*, 53–74.

Spitz, R. A. (1946). Hospitalizm: A follow-up report on investigation described in volume I. *The Psychoanalytic Study of the Child, 2*, 113–117.

Sroufe, L. A., Egeland, B., Carlson, E., & Collins, W. A. (2005). Placing early attachment experiences in developmental context: The Minnesota longitudinal study. In K. E. Grossmann, K. Grossmann, & E. Waters (Eds.), *Attachment from infancy to adulthood: The major longitudinal studies* (pp. 48–70). New York: The Guilford Press.

Thomas, A., Chess, S., & Birch, C. (1968). *Temperament and behavior disorders in children*. New York: New York University Press.

Thompson, D. A., & Christakis, D. A. (2005). The association between television viewing and irregular sleep schedules among children less than 3 years of age. *Pediatrics, 116*(4), 851–856.

Thompson, D. A., & Christakis, D. A. (2007). The association of maternal mental distress with television viewing in children under 3 years old. *Ambulatory Pediatrics, 7*(1), 32–37.

Thompson, W. R., & Grusec, J. E. (1970). Studies of early experience. In P. H. Mussen (Ed.), *Carmichael's manual of child psychology* (3rd ed., pp. 565–654). New York: John Wiley & Sons, Inc.

United States Department of Health and Human Services. (2005). Adoptions with Public Agency Involvement by State. Washington, DC: U.S. Department of Health and Human Services, Administration for Children and Families, Children's Bureau.

Vandewater, E. A., Rideout, V. J., Wartella, E. H., Huang, X., Lee, J. M., & Shim, M. S. (2007). Digital childhood: Electronic media and technology use among infants, toddlers, and preschoolers. *Pediatrics, 119*(5), 1006–1015.

Vygotsky, L. S. (1962). *Thought and language.* Boston, MA: MIT Press.

Warren, S. L. (2004). Anxiety disorders. In R. DelCarmen-Wiggins & A. Carter (Eds.), *Handbook of infant, toddler, and preschool mental health assessment* (pp. 355–375). Oxford, UK: Oxford University Press.

Watson, J. B. (1924). *Behaviorism.* New York: Norton.

Watson, J. B. (1928). *Psychological care of the infant and child.* New York: Norton.

Wittmer, D. S., & Honig, A. S. (1994). Encouraging positive social development in young children. *Young Children, 49*(5), 4–12.

Wright, J. C., Huston, A. C., Vandewater, E. A., Bickham, D. S., Scantlin, R. M., Kotler, J. A., et al. (2001). American children's use of electronic media in 1997: A national survey. *Journal of Applied Developmental Psychology, 22,* 31–47.

chapter 8

Emotional Development

Chapter Outline

- Emotions
- Theories Relating to Emotional Development
- Emotional Development
- Temperament
- Sensory Integration and Behavioral Regulation
- Atypical Emotional Development

Emotional development is one of the least studied and least understood areas of early child development, especially compared to areas like language and cognitive development, but even in comparison to social development. Many texts link social and emotional development together in their coverage and refer to social-emotional development. There is little doubt that social and emotional development are related, and that emotional development needs to be viewed in a social context. However, combining social and emotional development obscures the specific ties that emotional development has to other developmental domains.

WHY STUDY EMOTIONAL DEVELOPMENT?

※ Emotions are the motivators of human behavior. To understand not just what and how infants and toddler do specific things, you also need to know why. Your role is to make learning interesting and to motivate children to learn.

※ Self-regulation is a cornerstone of early development. Adults must help infants and toddlers regulate their behavior by arranging a physical and social environment that provides manageable developmental challenges. You need to develop the skills to scaffold this regulation.

※ Infants are born with different temperaments. Understanding a child's temperament helps you know how to interact with individual children and to make predictions about how they will react in new situations.

※ Interpreting facial expressions is one key to emotional competence. Helping infants and toddlers pay attention to the significant emotional cues that others give requires you to have skill and knowledge in this area.

Babies are born with certain qualities, which may be called drives, motives, inborn tendencies, or even "prewiring," and these have adaptive survival skills. At a general level these include skills for self-regulation, activity, becoming interested in the world, participating in human interactions, and seeking positive affect (Trevarthen, 2005). Another way of stating this is that nature equips infants with loud cries, dazzling smiles, endearing coos, and other behaviors that elicit caring and cuddling from significant adults. Infants want to connect with others, to explore their world, and to be separate, competent individuals (Butterfield, Martin, & Prairie, 2004).

Infant and toddler emotions develop in the context of relationships. It is through imitating, initiating, and responding to adults that young children learn about their emotions. Infants have a built-in tendency to become attached to their caregivers. They are capable of establishing relationships with several caregivers. Sibling bonds, too, are characterized by strong emotions. With increasing age, children develop friendship patterns and have ties to a peer group.

REFLECTIVE PRACTICE

Think about yourself as you are reading this book. What if the telephone rang and a friend said he saw your family's car in an accident as he was driving by. He did not know if anyone was hurt, but he wanted you to know. What would this do to your concentration? Emotions matter.

EMOTIONS

It is easier to describe and feel emotions than to define them. How many are there? Which emotions are the basic ones? When do children first feel emotions? Lack of agreement about these issues has led researchers to conceptualize emotions differently. Some have focused on the expressive characteristics of emotions, particularly facial expressions. Their research has looked at infants' facial expressions to determine when emotions are expressed and helped older children better interpret facial expressions of others. Some have looked at the cognitive aspects of emotions and focused on empathy. Others focused on the physiological aspects of emotions and looked at heart rates and the parts of the brain that are activated in different situations. Still others looked at the subjective experiences of feeling emotions.

Emotions reflect underlying physiological states that play a key role in the ability to adapt to the environment. From an evolutionary perspective, the more evolved the species, the more important emotions are (Nadel & Muir, 2005). Humans have complex and elaborate emotional structures. Emotions shape our world. They are how we signal others about our wants and needs. We also use the emotions of others in deciding how to react. If a stranger rapidly approaches a nine-month-old infant, the infant may react with fear. He looks toward his mother, and if she opens her arms and greets the approaching stranger with a warm hug and friendly greeting, the infant may reevaluate his initial response. If she responds to the stranger with a look of concern or fright and moves away, he is likely to cry. Reading the emotions of others helps infants adapt to situations and shapes what they attend to.

The lack of scholarly information about emotional development reflects the complexity of studying such a complicated, elusive area, rather than a belief that it is less important than other developmental areas. Recently, however, there has been a burst of interest in studying emotions and new technology to support this interest (Panksepp & Smith-Pasqualini, 2005).

The definition of emotion is still elusive, and it is sometimes difficult to differentiate emotions from the display of emotions, or **affect**.

Affect
is the outward display of emotional states.

"An emotion is experienced as a feeling that motivates, organizes, and guides perception, thought, and action" (Izard, 1991, p. 14).

"...Emotions—characterized by neurochemical, expressive, and experiential components—are the fundamental motivator of human behavior and that each of the basic emotions has unique adaptive functions, including a significant role in the organization of the developmental processes" (Izard & Malatesta, 1987, p. 494).

We view emotions as complex, subjective experiences that have many components, including physical, expressive, cognitive, and organizing, as well as highly personalized, subjective meanings (Greenspan & Greenspan, 1985, p. 7).

Affect is typically considered to reflect the feelings associated with emotional processes, which are related in presently unknown ways to the other major components—expressive, autonomic, and cognitive (Panksepp & Smith-Pasqualini, 2005, p. 24).

What seems clear in these definitions is that emotions play a role in the organization of, and motivation for, development. The study of emotions goes beyond facial expressions and accelerated heart rates. Emotions are the inborn link to learning (Butterfield et al., 2004). Emotions generate motor activity and cause experience—they are motivators! Emotions determine what we are interested in, and cognition determines what we learn about our interests. Emotions lead infant to explore objects; cognition comes after the fact (Trevarthen, 2005). Emotions draw others into social interactions with the infant.

THEORIES RELATING TO EMOTIONAL DEVELOPMENT

Some theories focus directly on emotional development; others have a broader scope. Much early thinking about emotions was not developmentally oriented, but related more to the evaluation and significance of the expressions of emotion, causes of emotions, or sequences of physiological events related to emotions (Izard & Malatesta, 1987).

Psychoanalytic Theory of Psychosocial Development

Eric Erikson's work provides a foundation for understanding emotional development as it relates to psychoanalytic theory. He expands and reframes Freud's theory. Erikson proposed a stage dependent theory in which each stage depends upon the previous stage and contains the seed for succeeding stages. The stages are developmental and he views them as a series of psychosocial crises, with the successful resolution of these crises having positive social/emotional outcomes. Table 8–1 describes these stages.

Erikson frames the conflict inherent in the psychoanalytic model as related to **psychosocial crises** rather than stemming from the erogenous zones that Freud proposed. Erikson felt that the crises were more responsive to the social context in which individuals grow and develop. Individuals struggle with

Psychosocial crises are the conflicts generated by moving through Erikson's developmental stages.

Table 8–1 Psychosocial Crises

Age	Psychosocial Crisis	Successful Resolution
Infancy	Trust vs. Mistrust	HOPE
Early Childhood	Autonomy vs. Shame, Doubt	WILL
Play Age	Initiative vs. Guilt	PURPOSE
School Age	Industry vs. Inferiority	COMPETENCE
Adolescence	Identity vs. Identity Confusion	FIDELITY
Young Adulthood	Intimacy vs. Isolation	LOVE
Adulthood	Generativity vs. Stagnation	CARE
Old Age	Integrity vs. Despair, Disgust	WISDOM

SOURCE: Erikson (1989, p. 49).

the conflicting pulls of each crisis, with the resolution of each crisis resulting in basic strength of character, or "ego" quality (Erikson, 1989). If the struggle is not successful, then the individual psychologically withdraws and future psychosocial development is at risk. Thus, if infants do not develop trust in infancy it will be difficult for them to establish autonomy in early childhood. Infants learn trust when their needs are met.

Most young children learn trust from responsive parents. When this does not happen or when children spend much of their time in child care centers, it is the role of caregiver to build trusting relationships. Caregivers provide continuity that builds trust. They do this by being responsive to the child's signals. Although it might seem that anticipating what the child wants and needs is ideal, this is not how trust is established. It is important that infants and toddlers learn to express their needs and to have these needs responded to. When children signal and their needs are ignored, they may give up or withdraw (Butterfield et al., 2004).

Erikson sees the infant's ego, or concept of self, develop through the internal struggle to establish basic trust. To develop, this trustfulness must be nourished by responsive and sensitive care. The development of trust is related to the development of hope. "Hope is, so to speak, pure future; and where mistrust prevails early, anticipation, as we know, wanes both cognitively and emotionally" (Erikson, 1989, p. 61). When trust is not developed the infant withdraws and loses hope. Erikson's explanation for infant deaths in foundling homes would be that the infants did not develop trust, and hence hope, that they psychologically withdrew from their environment and, even with good medical care, died from lack of hope.

Toddlers' growing independence and their need to do things themselves focuses the next psychosocial crisis. This stage is characterized by the toddler's struggle between autonomy and shame and doubt. The toddler bounces back and forth, trying to balance free choice and self-restraint. The toddler develops his will

WITH INFANTS AND TODDLERS

Talk to the children about what they do during the day. Then tell them that you are going to make up a song about what they do. Encourage them to decide on motions to go with the words. If this is taking a long time, suggest appropriate movements to go with the verse. Try to get several related concepts. Ask them what happens first in the morning. (Have a sequence that will work in your mind before you start, and only do as many verses as there is interest.) Sing to the tune of "Here We Go Round the Mulberry Bush." With younger toddlers, take photographs of the various tasks you plan to sing about and show them as you sing. You can sequence the photos as well as the singing.

This is the way we wash our hands, wash our hands, wash our hands. This is the way we wash our hands so early in the morning.

Morning

Get out of bed	Wash our hands
Brush our teeth	Comb our hair
Put on our clothes	Eat our breakfast
Come to school	

Substitute an activity, such as cleaning the house

Sweep the floor	Vacuum the rug
Make our beds	Wipe the table

Another variation is to ask children what they like to play with and incorporate their names into the song.

This is the way Juan plays with the ball, plays with the ball, plays with the ball. This is the way Juan plays with the ball, and plays with all of his friends.

Helping children sequence their day increases their self-awareness. Stress what toddlers can do. Support their suggestions. After children have participated in experiences like this, they become more active in offering suggestions and thinking about themselves as actors in their environment.

as he struggles between doing what he wants to do when he wants to do it (impulsiveness), and regulating his behavior and emotions in a socially acceptable way (compulsion). The toddler is moving from "oral sensory dependence to some anal-muscular self-will and to a certain trust in self-control" (Erikson, 1989, p. 60).

The third psychosocial crises is played out during the preschool years as children work through relationships with parent figures in an atmosphere of play. Children come to grips with the opposing pulls of initiative and guilt. Positive resolution of this conflict results in purpose. Young children who do not work though this conflict between initiative and guilt are extremely inhibited. Lack of a positive outcome at this stage is seen as the foundation for many of the psychoneurotic disturbances, such as hysteria, which are rooted in this stage (Erikson, 1989).

Although psychoanalytic/psychosocial theory does not have the support it once did, it has had a tremendous influence on the field of early childhood. The emphasis on developing self-help skills during early childhood and giving toddlers the satisfaction of completing tasks and viewing themselves as competent is based on this theoretical approach. There is also grave concern about caregivers who shame toddlers into compliance and the effect that this type of discipline has on their development.

There have been two general theoretical views about emotions in infancy. The cognitively oriented perspective is that basic emotions do not exist in the first months of life, and come about only after the infant has the ability to attribute cognitive meaning to an event and when he can distinguish himself from others. Early emotions are seen as undifferentiated. The second approach, differential emotions theory, sees emotions as present at birth and serving adaptive functions that organize cognition, action, and communication. These theorists believe that basic emotions emerge on a predictable timetable and that interventions should focus on helping children learn to read facial expressions (Soussignan & Schaal, 2005).

Emotional Stages and Milestones

Greenspan and Greenspan (1985) identified six stages, or major milestones, in emotional development. Their conceptualization is a stage-based theory, with overlapping stages or milestones. While the infant is mastering one stage, he is simultaneously exploring another stage of emotional development. The Greenspans (1985) do not focus on distinctions between stages of emotional development for classification purpose; they see a continuous flow, with the end of one stage blending into the next.

The first emotional milestone has three components: The infant must (1) feel tranquil in the midst of sensory stimulation, (2) organize his sensations, and (3) reach out actively into the world. Reaching out leads to the second milestone. The infant becomes interested in the sights and sounds of his new world. The third stage brings the infant further into the human world, as events are not only intriguing, but also enticing, pleasurable, and exciting. At this stage infants between about 3 and 10 months want to interact with their world. They want to play simple turn-taking games with adults. They want to be part of actions and reactions. Their emotions are evident, as pleasure produces a smile, and anger and protest are seen in their refusal to give up (Greenspan & Greenspan, 1985).

By 10 to 12 months, the fourth stage begins to emerge. Infants connect small units of feeling and social behavior and learn that these bits develop into more complicated patterns of behavior. Near the middle of this stage mobile infants become capable of more complex behaviors. Now they go beyond simply being able to express pleasure or displeasure. If a mobile infant wants a particular toy that is out of reach, rather than just crying to express his displeasure at not having what he wants, he organizes and focus his feelings on what he wants (the toy). He develops a plan of action based on his intentions (takes his mother's hand and leads her to the desired toy and points to it), and has a sense of satisfaction at getting his needs met through his own planning and actions (playing with the toy). He understands the symbolic meaning of objects. He also realizes that objects have functions, as do people. If you place a telephone in his hand he will talk into it. He more clearly comprehends the distinctions between animate and inanimate objects and that these serve different functions. All of this occurs before the age of 2 (Greenspan & Greenspan, 1985).

The fifth stage incorporates the advances the toddler has made in cognitive development. The toddler moves from understanding how an object functions to being able to imagine the object in his mind. He creates in his mind's eye a picture of the ball or the dog. He can play imaginatively and even dream. However, he has difficultly distinguishing dreams from reality (Greenspan & Greenspan, 1985).

During the sixth stage of emotional development, older toddlers are able to separate make-believe from reality; they can play with ideas, plan, and even anticipate what will happen. They are expanding their world of ideas to include emotions. They have moved beyond the more generalized emotions of pleasure to curiosity, the ability to set their own limits, to express empathy and love (Greenspan & Greenspan, 1985).

The association of verbal symbols to feeling states, emotion-cognition relations, represents another developmental milestone. Toddlers begin to label emotions during their second year. By 18 months most toddlers have considerable skill in this area. By age 3 children can demonstrate rather sophisticated knowledge of emotions and their causes and sequences.

The Greenspans (1985) believe that children, like adults, may reach different levels of functioning in different emotional areas because of emotional constrictions or limitations. A young child may show warm, trusting feelings, but be unable to lead or assert himself. He may show overall adequate functioning, but have setbacks in a particular area. Some children do not reach adequate levels of functioning. They do not know how to relate to others, and therefore play alone. They are only able to express frustration through aggression and temper tantrums, and are not able to talk or even scream about their problems. Failure to attain emotional milestones is associated with difficulties at subsequent emotional stages (Greenspan & Greenspan, 1985). Helping children attain emotional growth and development from the earliest stages is the best way of ensuring positive emotional development.

Differential Emotions Theory

Caroll Izard and his colleagues developed the conceptual base for differential emotions theory. The central premise of the theory is that emotions, which are characterized by neurochemical, expressive, and experiential components, are the fundamental motivators of human behavior. Basic emotions have unique adaptive functions. *Interest* allows the infant to learn about his world. *Disgust* keeps him from eating things that might make him sick. *Distress* brings someone to care for him. Like ethological theory, the basis for the attachment research, the theory of differential emotions emphasizes the survival value of emotions.

Differentialists
are those who support the differential emotions theory.

Differentialists believe emotions are critical building blocks and prime movers in organizing and motivating developmental processes and all significant human behavior (Izard & Malatesta, 1987). They identified seven principles that serve as the foundation of this theory (see Table 8–2).

Table 8–2 Differential Emotions Theory

Principle 1	Facial expressions connected to basic emotions have regular forms, emerge at predictable times, and have adaptive functions. Interest, disgust, and distress are present at birth.
Principle 2	The emotions system can function independently; however, the interaction and interdependence between the emotions system and the cognitive system increase and become more complex with development.
Principle 3	Infants change from having instinct-like expression to more restricted and controlled expressions because of maturation and interaction with the environment.
Principle 4	Infants are born with an innate expression-feeling concordance; that is, what an infant feels internally and how he expresses that feeling are congruent (e.g., if he is happy he smiles).
Principle 5	The socialization of emotional expressions contributes to the regulation of emotional feelings.
Principle 6	Emotions are the same over the life span, but the causes and sequences of these feelings change with development.
Principle 7	The concordance of facial expressions and expression of feelings helps children learn about the feelings of others.

SOURCE: Izard and Malatesta (1987).

From birth to three, infants learn to regulate their emotional states and to develop more complex behavioral strategies to cope with emotionally challenging situations. These strategies develop through maturation, emotional signaling, and shared relationships. Emotions, both positive and negative, change the brain's chemistry. Emotional regulation is the cornerstone of initiating, motivating, and organizing adaptive behavior (Nadel & Muir, 2005). Scholars agree that effective communication plays a crucial role in early social and emotional development as well as cognitive development (Oster, 2005). As adults we need to become skilled observers and learn how to use touch and voice to help stabilize and organize young children's emotions.

EMOTIONAL DEVELOPMENT

To understand development, scholars have tended to separate it into separate domains and skill areas, as I have done in this text. Although this separation makes understanding the developmental process easier to conceptualize, it sometimes neglects the interrelatedness of developmental areas and the functional interrelationships among the different domains. This multidomain approach increases the complexity of understanding children's development, which is further complicated by the need to look at infants as part of family systems that embrace certain cultural values. Although it is useful for our understanding to study cognitive, language, motor, social, and emotional development separately, when we look at the whole child we cannot separate these domains because they interact and influence each other.

One long-term consequence of this approach is that assessment, treatment, and intervention focus on particular developmental areas as if they could be treated in isolation. For example, an infant with cerebral palsy would probably be referred to a physical and/or occupational therapist to help him achieve motor milestones. It is unlikely that he would be referred to a mental health professional to support the motivational and internal mental organizations needed to perform motor tasks.

Patterns of Emotional Development

With increasing age infants develop an increasing array of emotional resources. It is difficult to know when young children begin to understand emotions. Some studies report that infants as young as six weeks can distinguish between facial expressions (e.g., happy versus angry), but there is little indication as to what this actually means to infants. Identifying developmental patterns involves two related issues. The first involves identifying the links between children's early understanding of emotions and language. The second relates to how children's understanding of emotions is linked to interactions with others (Kuebli, 1994). The developmental timetable for the emergence of emotional states is fairly well agreed upon (see Table 8–3).

We are less knowledgeable about the emergence of emotional experience. Emotional experience probably develops gradually with the child's self-differentiation and becomes integrated into his self-concept. Adults often take an active role in the socialization of young children's emotions. Adult behavior can reinforce the child's expression of emotions. Telling Maggie, "I like your smile," rewards that behavior. On the other hand, saying, "It can't hurt that much," sends the message that either displaying emotions is not okay or denying the relationship between the emotion and the experience, either of which, if

Table 8–3 Timetable for the Emergence of Emotional States

1. *Birth to 4 months*: Infants display the emotions of interest, distress, and disgust at birth; enjoyment emerges at about 1 month. By 4 to 6 weeks there are "just for fun" emotional exchanges between affectionate parents and infants. Infants expect to have sensitive reciprocal responsive conversations with their caregivers by 2 months of age and are confused by responses that do not meet their expectations.

2. *4 to 7–8 months*: Infants are curious and experience pleasure in discovery. They laugh. They also become bored. Infants' motor skills improve and adults become more animated as they seek attention from infants. Communication becomes more playful and emotional exchanges include rhythmic body play, singing songs, and chanting. Teasing and joking routines grow as infants and adults interact. Infants are interested in exploring their surroundings and playing simple one-on-one games with adults.

3. *7–8 to 9–10 months*: The emotions of surprise, sadness, fear, and anger emerge at about 7 months. This marks a transition from person-to-person to object play. The infant now may be fascinated with a ball and how it rolls, and will begin to roll the ball with an adult, but may miss some of the fine points, like rolling it back. Infants may "show off" for company, or for their own enjoyment while watching themselves in a mirror.

4. *9–10 to 12 months*: Cognitively, infants know that objects and people exist outside of their view. This knowledge creates the possibility for separation anxiety and fear of strangers. It also opens up the possibility for more interactive play with adults and objects. Behavior is more purposeful. Infants imitate gestures and actions. With new memory skills infants want pleasurable experiences repeated. The readiness to communicate is apparent.

5. *12–24 months*: Emotional development moves from awkward dependency to wanting independence but not having all the necessary skills to follow through. The emotions of shame, shyness, guilt, and contempt emerge between 12 and 18 months, followed by embarrassment and pride at 18 to 24 months. The first emotion words are appearing (happy, sad) and toddlers use emotion words spontaneously in conversations with others. Toddlers can reliably associate facial expressions with simple emotional labels. Happiness appears to be the easiest emotion for them to label.

6. *24–36 months*: Toddlers' emotional vocabulary increases rapidly. They can label simple emotions in themselves and others. They talk about emotions they have experienced in the past, what they are feeling now, and how they might feel in the future. They identify emotions associated with certain situations and talk about the causes and consequences of emotions. By 36 months, children can imagine how they might feel in various hypothetical situations. They use emotion language in pretend play.

SOURCE: Hyson (2004); Izard and Malatesta (1987); Kuebli (1994); Trevarthen (2005).

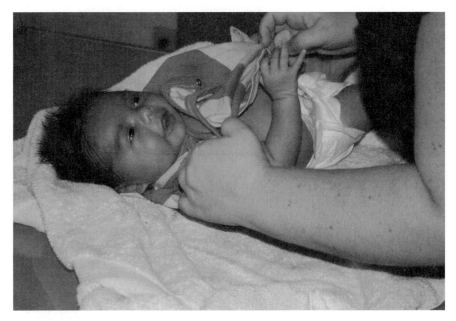

By 1 month infants begin to show interest. They are intrigued with their world and the routines that are part of it.

repeated, tells the infant to not respond to his feelings (Butterfield et al., 2004). Adults can also directly teach children about social conventions for expressing emotions. The common but ill-advised "boys don't cry" is a prime example of direct teaching. Emotional expression is also taught indirectly through "contagion" (when one child laughs, others "catch" it), through social referencing, and through observation and modeling (Kuebli, 1994). Sometimes emotional beliefs are influenced by expectancy or foreshadowing, such as when adults tell children they are going to "love" a new experience, whether it is a new book or a new teacher.

Forms of emotional expression are embedded in cultures and subcultures. Different cultures support or condone the expression of certain emotions and when, how, and with whom these emotions can be expressed. Families, too, differ in their acceptance of emotions and the language they will allow to express emotions. Within families there are gender differences in how parents talk to young children about emotions. Both fathers and mothers talk about a greater number and variety of emotions with daughters than with sons (Kuebli & Fivush, 1992).

Talking about emotions with young children provides them with the foundation to learn about feelings. Table 8–4 identifies seven major trends that characterize children's emotional growth.

Table 8–4 Trends in Children's Emotional Growth

- Wider, more complex emotional relationships
- More varied, complex, and flexible ways of expressing emotions
- Better coordination and control of emotions and emotion-related skills
- More ability to reflect on their own feelings and those of others
- Representation of emotions through language, play, and fantasy
- Linking individual emotions to culturally valued skills and standards
- An integrated, positive, autonomous, but emotionally connected, sense of self

SOURCE: Hyson (1994, pp. 59–60).

TEMPERAMENT

Although the basic processes by which children learn about and develop emotions are similar there are vast individual differences in the display of emotions and emotional states in young children. Temperament is one aspect of emotional development that has received much attention. Each child has a unique personality. Part of an individual's personality is their temperament. Infants are different, exhibiting their own personalities early in life. Some infants smile all the time no matter what happens, and some infants are difficult to soothe once they are disturbed or frustrated. Some toddlers are shy around strangers, and some feel comfortable and secure wherever they are.

Temperament affects how an infant relates to his world. Temperament includes the infant's general mood, activity level, regularity, approach/withdrawal, adaptability, physical sensitivity, intensity of reactions, mood, persistence, and resistance/distractibility. Just as adults respond to situations in fairly predictable ways, so too do infants and toddlers. It is the predictable pattern of response and preferences that makes up an infant's temperament.

Dimensions of Temperament

All children exhibit the following characteristics to some extent; it is the extremes in these areas that characterize children who show emotional and behavioral vulnerability. Thomas, Chess, and Birch (1968) interviewed parents and observed children to identify nine dimensions and three styles of temperament they felt had stability over time. Identifying these particular characteristics in children may help you individualize programming for children. It is the pattern of these dimensions that make up temperament.

Activity Level. This refers to the amount of time an infant or a toddler is active or not active. Children who are always on the go and cannot sit still are at one end; children who are inactive and just sit are at the other extreme.

Regularity. Infants and toddlers have an internal biological clock that can be either regular or unpredictable. For those children who are *very* regular (they get up at the same time, eat at the same time), it is important to look at the match between adult expectations, programmatic demands, and the child's typical pattern. To the extent that these are mismatched, these infants or toddlers can be more difficult than unpredictable children. Unpredictable children do not have a strong internal rhythm.

Approach/Withdrawal. Children have a typical response to new experiences. The extremes are to approach without caution or to avoid at all costs through crying or clinging to adults. Most children approach new experiences with some degree of caution. For infants and toddlers who have had many or recent new encounters that were painful, the avoidance response may be predominant.

Adaptability. Some infants and toddlers find it easy to adapt to change; others find it very difficult. Young children who are change-resistant may find new routines, a different caregiver or teacher, a new sibling, or even a new child entering the classroom extremely stressful. Especially at celebrations, holidays, and transitions, slow-to-adapt children need extra time and support.

Physical Sensitivity. Some children are aware of slight changes in the environment; others respond only to major physical changes. Infants and toddlers who are highly sensitive can become overstimulated by too much noise, touch, light, and so on. They need support in regulating their environment.

Intensity of Reaction. Many situations evoke reactions in infants and toddlers; it is the intensity and length of the response in relation to the event that needs to be evaluated. One child may cry violently for 20 minutes when another child takes a toy, whereas another child may fuss only briefly.

Mood. Children have a range of moods that are a balance of positive and less positive moods. Some infants and toddlers are in a predictable mood most of the time; others vary considerably. Infants and toddlers who are predictably negative may make adults feel guilty or angry. Rather than receiving the extra attention, love, and support they need, these children may be avoided.

Persistence. Persistence is the amount of time an infant or toddler attends to or persists with a task. It is related to how difficult the task is and how interested the child is in the task.

Resistance/Distractibility. Resistance measures the ability of the child to return to an activity after an interruption. Resistance focuses on longer breaks for such things as toileting. Distractibility relates to momentary interruptions and how the child reacts to extraneous stimuli. Distracting sights and sounds cause some children to lose concentration others can continue.

WITH INFANTS AND TODDLERS

Using Table 8–5, observe and record the behavior of a particular toddler for parts of several days or as long as you feel you need to establish a pattern. If possible, ask the child's teacher or parents for their input about the child's temperament. Compare your observational results with their perceptions and reflect on the similarities and differences. Identify the child's temperament style. Decide how this might impact your programming for this child.

Table 8–5 Assessment of Temperament

Activity Level	Active	1	3	5	Quiet
Regularity	Regular	1	3	5	Irregular
Approach/Withdrawal	Approach	1	3	5	Withdrawal
Adaptability	Adaptable	1	3	5	Slow to adapt
Physical Sensitivity	Not sensitive	1	3	5	Sensitive
Intensity of Reaction	Low intensity	1	3	5	High intensity
Mood	Predictable	1	3	5	Not predictable
Mood	Positive	1	3	5	Negative
Persistence	Long attention	1	3	5	Short attention
Resistance	Returns to task	1	3	5	Does not return
Distractibility	Not distractible	1	3	5	Highly distractible

Temperament Style: flexible (40%); feisty (10%); fearful (15%); typical (35%).

Temperament Styles

Thomas and his colleagues (1968) have organized these dimensions of temperament into three basic temperament categories or styles:

1. *Easy children* are those who rate moderate in intensity, adaptability, approachableness, and rhythmicity, and have predominantly positive moods. They are usually calm and predictable and tend to eat and sleep on a schedule, although they can adapt the schedule to some extent. They smile frequently, typically approach new experiences positively, and show little negative emotion. They tend to be easygoing and highly sociable. They adapt quickly to change, and have low to medium intensity of reactions. Their biological rhythms are regular and they are (or were) easy

to toilet train and sleep through the night. Chess and Thomas (1977) classified about 40 percent of their sample as easy children. Some see these as *flexible* children.

2. *Difficult children* are at the other end of the temperament scale. Difficult children often display negative emotions: They cry a lot and are fearful or withdrawn in the face of new experiences. They are unpredictable, have mood shifts, and are easily distracted. Although they set their own eating and sleeping schedule, they do not have a predictable schedule (Chess & Thomas, 1990). They shift states quickly and may go from sleeping to screaming in seconds. These children are slow to adapt and change, are

A child's temperament affects the way she approaches her world. A child who is tentative or slow-to-warm-up needs adult support to explore her environment.

nonrhythmical, have intense reactions, and often have negative moods. Their biological rhythms are irregular and they are difficult to train to sleep through the night; toilet training also is a challenge. They are also movers: They crawl, walk, or run, rarely staying in the same place for long. They are less sociable than other children. Chess and Thomas (1977) found that about 10 percent of their sample was difficult children. These children are more positively characterized as *feisty*.

3. *Slow-to-warm-up children* share some of the characteristics of difficult and easy children. They initially appeared to have the characteristics of difficult children, but do not show the intensity or persistence. Initially, their response to new events is negative, but given time, they do in fact "warm up," although it takes them longer to adapt than easy children. They have negative moods, but the intensity is low or mild. They can have either regular or irregular biological rhythms. Fifteen percent of Chess and Thomas's (1977) sample fell into this category. Some refer to these children as *fearful* or shy.

Approximately 35 percent of children did not fall in any of the three categories and were classified as typical.

A child's temperament is sometimes a challenge to adults. Some parents find it comforting to know that infants are born with different temperaments and that they are not the cause of their infant's or toddler's temperament. Temperament affects the child's development because it affects how she approaches her environment, as well as how the environment responds to her (Brazelton, 1992). Difficult children and easy children evoke different responses from adults. However, they do not get the same response from all adults. The key is the interaction pattern between the child and the adult, or the "goodness of fit" (Thomas & Chess, 1980).

Goodness of Fit

The concept of goodness of fit looks at the match between the expectations and interactions of the adult and the child's behavior in relationship to these expectations. A parent or educator who is up and on the go, wants to do things and not sit around, and is not disturbed by crying and temper tantrums might be delighted with a difficult child and find an easy child boring. A parent or educator who has a cautious approach to new ideas and patience may find a slow-to-warm-up child enchanting, whereas with either a difficult or easy child, she may feel overwhelmed or unnecessary. It is not possible to evaluate child outcome on temperament alone. Chess (1983) stresses that the interaction between the adult's expectations and the child's responses is a key factor in assessing the quality of the adult-child relationship. Concern focuses around children who are slow-to-warm-up and those with difficult temperaments who need extra adult understanding, but who may actually receive fewer positive responses from adults who do not understand and know how to work with these children. Consider the following two scenarios:

1. Maggie is a two-year-old who is fearful, shy, and cautious. She has never been in a group child care setting before. One morning, her mother wakes her up earlier than usual, feeds her breakfast with admonitions to hurry, and, without telling her where she is going, takes her to an early care and education setting. She and her mother arrive at a strange building, which her mother, who is in a hurry, pulls her into. When Maggie is not moving fast enough, her mother picks her up and carries her into a room with eight other two-year-olds and two unfamiliar adults. The other children are playing with toys and the adults are talking to each other. Maggie's mother takes her over to the adults and says, "Here she is." Maggie tries to cling to her mother, but she loosens her grasp and hurries away. One of the adults takes Maggie over to some blocks and tells her to play with three other children.

2. Morgan is another two-year-old who is fearful, shy, and cautious. She has never been in group care either. One morning, her mother gets her up earlier than usual. While she is eating breakfast, her mother reminds her that this is the day she is going to stay with Miss Irene and the other children while Mommy goes to work. Morgan knows Miss Irene because her mother has taken her there for short visits to see her and the other children twice before. This time, her mother explains that she will stay until lunch time, which is when her mother will come back to get her. While Morgan and her mother go to the center, her mother talks about what Morgan will be doing during the morning. When they walk into the room, they see eight other two-year-olds and two adults, all of whom look familiar to Morgan. Miss Irene comes over to Morgan and her mother and tells them how happy she is to see them. She then mentions several activities that Morgan might join if she would like to. Morgan's mother sits in one of the chairs for about 10 minutes before telling Morgan that she will be back to get her at lunch time. She then leaves (Adapted from Franyo, 1998).

The first scenario is an example of *poorness of fit*. The child was being pressured into adjusting in a way that was incompatible with her temperament. The situation made demands on the child that are not possible for her to adapt to and meet successfully. The second scenario is an example of *goodness of fit*. The adults in the child's world adapted to help the child have a successful experience. Children who experience a pattern of poorness of fit in their environment may develop ways of coping that are problematic.

REFLECTIVE PRACTICE

Go back to Table 8–5 and rate yourself on the scale. What is your temperament style? Which children do you like to teach most? Which children are you most comfortable working with? Which children are most difficult for you? Which children have the greatest goodness of fit for your style? Once you know this, do some hard thinking about children who may not fit as well. The adult and the environment need to be as flexible as possible to include children of all temperament types.

Educators need to be observant of and responsive to children's temperament. The goal is not to change their temperament (which is genetic and not likely to change), but to work with children in ways that are supportive of their development. This means finding time to give the easy child attention, supporting the fearful child as she learns to joining groups, and setting limits and finding ways to help the feisty child calm down. It also means acknowledging that young children have issues that impact their emotional and mental health, and being aware of these and knowledgeable about the resources to support these children.

The ability to regulate emotional expression develops gradually and unevenly (Hyson, 2004). Through interest and self-regulatory capacities working together, the infant gradually gains control over his emotions. His "interest" prompts him to visually explore his environment. If his environment becomes too stimulating, he can use his skills in self-regulation to avert his gaze or to visually find a caregiver's face. He can also listen to a soothing voice or respond to gentle stroking and rocking to help regulate his state.

Young infants learn what they can do to comfort themselves, and before the end of the first year many have individualized these strategies. By about a year old, infants can exercise conscious, voluntary control over their emotions and even deliberately intensify or reduce their emotional expression (Hyson, 2004). Children also learn to respond to cultural norms for the expression of emotion.

Emotional Relationships

The focus of this chapter so far has been on the emotional development of infants and toddlers. This development does not happen in isolation. Adults play an important role in this. From birth, an infant is tuned in to the emotions of those who care for him. The caregiver's face, tone of voice, and the way they touch and hold him send messages about his world. Your face, body language, and tone of voice send messages to infants and toddlers whether or not you intend them to (Butterfield et al., 2004).

Emotional connections are powerful; therefore, your connection with infants and toddlers is a powerful one. Emotions can be positive or negative. Different emotions are processed in different parts of the brain. Positive emotions stimulate different neural pathways than do negative emotions (LeDoux, 1996).

Shared positive emotions give infants and toddlers pleasure, closeness, and feelings of acceptance. These feelings allow them to explore their world and set the stage for learning and forming positive relationships (Butterfield et al., 2004). Caregivers share positive relationships by smiles, positive comments, happily observing, and being with children and joyously enjoying them. Shared positive emotions help organize and focus infants and toddlers. When these shared positive emotions are calm and quiet they can change the emotions of a fearful or injured child. They form the foundation for resiliency, for helping children find solutions within themselves (Butterfield et al., 2004).

Negative emotions are also powerful. They tie into our survival instincts and elicit the adrenaline rush that triggers the "fight, flight, or fright" response. Instead of leading to feelings of connectedness, they lead to distrust. In pervasively negative environments infants and toddlers are on alert, unsure and hypervigilant, and ready to protect themselves (Karr-Morse & Wiley, 1997). Shared negative emotions make children feel distrust and uncertainty, and feel rejected and ashamed (Butterfield et al., 2004).

All children (and adults) have bad days. Sometimes it is difficult to tell if a child is having a bad day or week, has a difficult temperament, is having a short-term behavior problem or one that is long term. It is hard to decide if the child is going through a "stage" or responding to environmental stress. As with all behavior, it is important to look for patterns and to examine the roots of the behavior. It is also important to look at ourselves. Challenging behavior is that which challenges the teacher. What is challenging for me may not be challenging for you. However, some behaviors, because of their intensity, duration, or potential for harm, cause concern.

SENSORY INTEGRATION AND BEHAVIORAL REGULATION

Sensory integration is the ability of the infant or toddler to take in information through the senses (vision, hearing, touch, movement, taste, and smell) and to combine these perceptions with information stored in the brain to organize it in a way that is useful and can produce meaning. Sensory integration looks at the information that comes from the senses and into the child's brain and how the child acts based on this information. The ability to integrate this information and act on it is central to how infants and toddlers react and act on their world. Sensory integration puts it all together. Infants and toddlers get meaning directly from their senses and move their body in response to these sensations. That is one reason why this time period is referred to as the sensory-motor period. Infants and toddlers want to move because the sensations of movement nourish their brains (Ayres, 1979). Sensory integration is considered part of infant mental health because of its tie to behavioral regulation.

Heredity provides the baseline for **sensory integration** in infants and toddlers, but children develop sensory integration by interacting with objects that

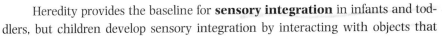

Sensory integration takes in information through the senses and organizes it to be meaningful.

To increase sensory-motor integration, an infant's behavior has to be goal directed. He needs to decide what he wants and figure out how to do it.

require adaptation. Responding to these challenges change both the child's body and his brain. Adaptive responses are purposeful, goal-directed responses to sensory experiences. An infant waving his arms is not adaptive. An infant trying to reach a rattle is adaptive. The complexity is increased when an infant must stretch his body because the rattle is just out of reach. This reach takes organization and regulation and builds connections in the brain (Ayres, 1979).

Learning to regulate themselves and their behavior is an important part of learning during the infant and toddler years. At this time their brain is making synaptic connections, and the connections that regulate behavior are far more important in the long term than a two-year-old's ability to say the ABCs. Their brain isn't designed for memory (Butterfield et al., 2004). It is designed to organize.

The core of behavioral regulation in infancy is the four A's: arousal, attention, affect, and action (Williamson & Anzalone, 2001). Understanding these concepts helps us reframe discipline and offers alternative explanations when infants and toddlers behave in ways that are not conducive to learning. It also provides insights into ways we can change the environment to make infants and toddlers more available to learn.

Arousal is the ability of the infant to maintain an alert state and to make the transition between states of sleep and wakefulness (Williamson & Anzalone, 2001). Infant states were described in detail in Chapter 3. Briefly, they are deep sleep, light sleep, drowsy, quiet alert (when the infant is most receptive to learning), active alert (when the infant is energized and excited), fussy, and crying (Butterfield et al., 2004). Observe infants as they are transitioning through states of alertness. Learn what works best for individual infants and try to plan an environment that supports their transitions. If a toddler needs quiet to make the transition to sleep, try to ensure that he is one of the last toddlers to go to sleep. For children who take a long time to wake up, plan so that they have this time available and are not rushed.

Attention is the ability of the infant to focus on a desired task or event and to ignore other stimuli. Most infants attend best in the quiet alert state, although for some children the active alert state works as well (Williamson & Anzalone, 2001). When an infant or toddler is in an alert state, note what time of day it is and what else is going on. This knowledge can help you keep each infant in this state longer and take advantage of it when it occurs.

Affect is the behavioral aspect of emotions. Infants have different responses to sensations. Some infants love to be touched; others recoil at a touch. Some laugh when adults roughhouse with them; others cry. Some infants have extreme responses; others show a narrow range of responding. It is the infant's and toddler's ability to manage or organize body sensation that is important. Affect is the behavioral response to these sensations (Williamson & Anzalone, 2001).

Arousal
is the infant's ability stay alert and transition between behavioral states.

Attention
is the infant's ability to selectively focus on a task or event.

Affect
is the emotional component of infant's behavior.

Learn how individual infants and toddlers respond to their environment so that you can provide them with a level of sensory input they can manage.

Action is the infant's ability to engage in adaptive goal-directed behavior (Anzalone, 1993). To act purposefully, an infant not only needs to organize the motor aspect of movement, but also maintain the goal and attempt to achieve it (Williamson & Anzalone, 2001). Play is one of the most important ways that infants and toddlers learn goal-directed actions. Provide uninterrupted time for infants and toddlers to explore the developmentally appropriate environment that you have designed for them.

The four A's are the basis for behavioral regulation; however, it is the child's ability to manage sensations that is important. **Sensory modulation** is the ability to manage and organize reactions to sensations in an adaptive way. There are three major aspects to sensory modulation: sensory threshold, the rate of recovery from sensation, and the ability of the child to maintain a receptive level of arousal (Williamson & Anzalone, 2001).

Sensory thresholds vary between infants and toddlers and within a particular infant or toddler depending on the particular type of sensory input. For most children these thresholds fall between a lower limit that allows the perception of subtle change and novelty and a higher limit that can tolerate the complexity of home or an early care and education setting. When stimulation is below the child's threshold, he will not react to it. When stimuli are above a child's threshold, the child may throw a tantrum, "melt down" or withdraw. When you are working within a child's threshold, the child is alert and focused. The sensory threshold is not a discrete point, it is dynamic. Optimally there is a wide zone between the high and low sensory levels that children can work in. However, this zone is likely to be smaller when an infant or toddlers is tired or on the verge of being sick.

Children receive a lot of sensory input. A parent may be actively dancing with a toddler as they listen to rock and roll songs being belted out, and then they are joined by a preschooler who dances and bumps into them because she wants to be part of the action. Sensations accumulate and they vary in type and intensity. When the music stops, it is useful to know how long it takes the toddler to return to an optimal state of arousal. That is the **rate of recovery from sensation**, or the duration of the effect (Williamson & Anzalone, 2001).

Understanding the concept of sensory thresholds provides information about how much sensory input an infant or toddler needs to attain an optimal level of arousal. It is also important to know how long a child can **sustain a receptive level of arousal**, or the amount of time the child can stay in the **zone of responsivity**. When children get outside their personal zone of optimal arousal, they become behaviorally disorganized and overstimulated (Williamson & Anzalone, 2001). The longer children can remain at an optimal

Action
is the infant's ability to engage in adaptive goal-directed behavior.

Sensory modulation
is the child's ability to manage and organize reactions to sensation in a useful way.

Sensory threshold
is the zone in which the child is attentive to stimuli, with stimuli below the threshold going unnoticed and those above causing overstimulation.

Rate of recovery from sensation
is the amount of time it takes an infant or toddler to move back into a state of alertness, particularly after sensory overload.

Sustaining a receptive level of arousal
is the ability of the infant or toddler can stay at an arousal level where they are organized and available to learning.

Zone of responsivity
is the area within which a child can maintain an optimal level of arousal.

level of arousal, the more available they are to learn about their environment and the interesting people who are part of it.

When infants or toddlers have a very narrow zone of optimal arousal, or when they stay in the extreme ranges of threshold, there is concern. These children can easily be under- or overstimulated (Ayers, 1979). Children with very low thresholds are easily overstimulated and are sometimes referred to as **sensory defensive**. These children may be overwhelmed by the sensory input from daily life and from a typical early care and education setting. They are reluctant to participate in sensory experiences that are a regular part of the infant/toddler curriculum. At the other end of the spectrum are infants with high sensory thresholds. There may not be enough sensory input to reach their threshold. They may seem passive and elicit less stimulation when they actually require more (Williamson & Anzalone, 2001).

Sensory modulation is an important aspect of sensory integration. It looks at how children receive information and organize it. Because infants and toddlers have less information stored in their brain with which to integrate sensory information, many situations that are familiar to older children are novel to infants and toddlers. **Praxis** is the ability to conceptualize, organize, and perform new purposeful actions. Praxis has three components: ideation, motor planning, and execution (Williamson & Anzalone, 2001). Ideation is the cognitive aspect of praxis. The infant or toddler must establish the goal for the action. What does he want to do? Motor planning requires the organization of sensory input. The infant or toddler must figure out the motor sequence necessary to attain the goal and then perform or execute the motor skills. The hallmark of praxis is flexibility and creativity. Children with **dyspraxia** can have problems with the ideation, motor planning, or execution of these actions. Because so much of what is learned during the infant and toddler years has a base in sensory and motor activity, these children are at a great disadvantage. The effects are pervasive.

ATYPICAL EMOTIONAL DEVELOPMENT

Classification of infants with atypical emotional development is a challenge, and requires a systematic and multidisciplinary point of view. The purpose of classification is to accurately communicate knowledge among professionals and to help infants and toddlers.

Zero to Three, National Center for Clinical Infant Programs (1994) developed a system for classifying mental health disorders designed specifically for very young children: *The Diagnostic Classification of Mental Health and Developmental Disorders of Infancy and Early Childhood (DC: 0–3)*. The goal of assessment is to accurately diagnose infants and toddlers so that timely intervention is possible. The short-term goal is to alleviate infants and toddlers distress; the

Sensory defensive infants and toddlers are those who have low arousal thresholds and are easily overstimulated.

Praxis is the ability of the brain to conceive of, organize, and carry out a sequence of unfamiliar actions.

Dyspraxia is a poor ability to conceive, organize, or carry out novel actions.

Table 8–6 Axes of the DC: 0–3

Axis I:	Primary Diagnosis
Axis II:	Relationship Disorder Classification
Axis III:	Medical and Developmental Disorders and Conditions
Axis IV:	Psychosocial Stressors
Axis V:	Functional Emotional Developmental Level

SOURCE: Zero to Three, National Center for Clinical Infant Programs (1994).

long-term goal is the prevention of maladaptive patterns of functioning (Lieberman, Barnard, & Wieder, 2004). Assessing infants and toddlers is difficult the context of their emotional relationships with the people they live with and who care for them must be considered. Although children come into the world with different temperaments and biological characteristics, emotional relationships with sensitive caregivers can help children moderate these vulnerabilities. Infants are also born into families with styles of child rearing and teaching that are deeply embedded in their cultural values (Lieberman et al., 2004). These variables need to be taken into consideration in the assessment process.

A short overview of the DC: 0-3 is given to provide insight into the types of behaviors that are of concern for infants and toddlers. It looks at behavior from a variety of different dimensions, which they call axes (see Table 8–6).

Once the primary diagnosis has been made, the different axes are used to understand the context in which the behavior is taking place, with the assumption that the child may have no needs in some areas, and that other areas need to be addressed as part of the intervention.

Axis I Primary diagnosis looks at seven main categories: traumatic stress disorders, disorders of affect, adjustment disorders, regulatory disorders, sleep behavior disorders, eating behavior disorders, and disorders of relating and communicating (Lieberman et al., 2004).

Traumatic Stress Disorder

Traumatic stress disorder is defined as a continuum of symptoms, and is classified according to whether the disorder relates to a single event (acute, single event), whether it is a connected series of traumatic events, or if those events are repeated (chronic, repeated) (Lieberman, Wieder, & Fenichel, 1997). A child who broke his arm in an automobile accident and had to be taken to the emergency room would be expected to have short-term disturbances, such as nightmares and a temporary fear of riding in cars. A child who is repeatedly abused or neglected is at risk for more pervasive interference with development (Finkelhor, 1995).

Disorders of Affect

Disorders of affect focus on the infant's experiences and on symptoms related to the child's general functioning rather than to specific situations or relationships (Lieberman et al., 1997). Disorders in this category include anxiety disorder, mood disorders (including prolonged bereavement or depression), mixed disorder of emotional expressiveness, gender identity disorder, and reactive attachment deprivation or maltreatment disorder of infancy. Educators can help parents who have children with these disorders to read infant cues more accurately, to improve the organization and predictability in the young child's environment, and to increase the availability of a primary caregiver.

Adjustment Disorders

Adjustment disorders focus on the length of time it takes infants to adjust to change. In this case, there is a clear environmental event that can be tied to the infant's behavior (Lieberman et al., 1997). For example, an infant or toddler who cannot adjust to child care after four months would be of concern in this area. Specialists in infant mental health may have to be consulted to work with infants and their caregivers to provide support and guidance to work with these problems.

Regulatory Disorders

Regulatory disorders focus on an infant's need to adjust his behavior to fit into the world around him. Infants who have trouble doing this are often referred to as "fussy." Sometimes these behaviors go beyond fussy; these infants need help regulating themselves. Regulatory disorders are characterized by disturbances in regulating physiological, sensory, attentional, motor, or affective processes and in organizing a calm alert positive state (Lieberman et al., 1997). There are three basic types of regulatory disorders. With hypersensitivity, children display fearful and cautious behavior, or negative and defiant behavior. Under-reactive children are withdrawn, difficult to engage, self-absorbed, and motorically disorganized. Children with impulsive behavior may crave sensory input and employ poor behavior control.

Sleep Behavior Disorder

Sleep behavior disorder is diagnosed when sleep is the child's only problem and it is not a symptom of another disorder more typical of older children. The diagnosis applies to children who have trouble initiating or maintaining sleep. They may also have problems in self-calming and making transitions between one state of arousal to another (Lieberman et al., 1997).

Eating Behavior Disorder

Eating behavior disorder is diagnosed when children have difficulty in establishing regular feeding patterns that result in adequate food intake. As with sleep disorders, the diagnostician must distinguish between the disorder per se, and the disorder as a symptom of another regulatory dysfunction.

Disorders of Relating and Communicating

Disorders of relating and communicating are similar to the DSM-IV-TR (American Psychiatric Association, 2000) conceptualization of pervasive developmental disorder (autism) or multisystem developmental disorder (Lieberman et al., 1997). Children show, in varying degrees, an impairment in the ability to form and maintain an emotional and social relationship with a primary caregiver. In addition, they have problems developing and/or maintaining communication with others, so they may have auditory processing problems as well as problems processing other sensations and in motor planning.

SUMMARY

Emotional development is a complex area that overlaps other areas and also serves as a motivator for cognitive, motor, and social development. Although there are theories of emotional development, there are fewer general guiding principles than there are for other areas of development. There is general agreement of what emotions are and how they affect development. Temperament is an important aspect of emotional development. It is not just temperament alone, but the goodness of fit between the infant or toddler's temperament and environment in which he lives and grows. Infants and toddlers need goal-directed behaviors to develop sensory integration and praxis. Infant mental health is how we currently view atypical emotional development. The goal of infant mental health is to identify infants and toddlers who are at risk and to help their short-term distress while preventing long-term problems.

CHAPTER IN REVIEW

- Emotional development is one of the least-studied areas of child development, reflecting the complexity of studying emotions rather than a belief that it is less important than other developmental areas.

- Erikson proposed a stage-based developmental theory, within which psychosocial crises and the resolution of these crises are seen as affecting social/emotional outcomes in children.

- Ethological theorists and differential emotions theorists believe that there are basic emotions that have unique adaptive functions in continuing the species.

- Differentialists feel that emotions serve as a foundation for organizing and motivating developmental processes, including cognitive, language, and motor functions, as well as all significant human behavior.

- The Greenspans view emotional development in terms of a stage-based theory, with overlapping stages or milestones.

- Theories are not necessarily incompatible, but they focus on different aspects of emotional development.

- Emotions are easier to describe than to define.

- Temperament affects how children relate to their world. Based on their characteristic patterns of behavior, children can be classified into four basic temperament types: easy, difficult, slow to warm up, or typical.

- Sensory integration and behavioral regulation are important parts of early development.

- Atypical emotional development is the concern of the field of infant mental health.

- DC: 0-3 identifies major diagnostic categories of atypical development. Infant mental health specialists find these categories helpful when treating infants and toddlers with atypical emotional development.

APPLICATION ACTIVITIES

1. Have a conversation with a young toddler that focuses on emotions. Draw a simple happy and sad face and ask if the toddler can identify the emotions. Then see if she has developed a causal relationship between events and emotions. Ask how she would feel at her birthday party and so on, and then ask how she might feel if she fell and hurt herself.

2. Using the information given in the text, talk with a parent who has more than one child. Try to determine the temperament types of her children and how the parents act and react to the children differently because of these types.

3. Observe a toddler from another culture. Can you pick out any obvious differences in emotional expression and preferences from those of your own culture?

RESOURCES

Web Resources

- **FACETS (Family-guided Approaches to Collaborative Early-intervention Training and Services)** is a collaborative outreach program for infants and toddlers with disabilities focusing on early intervention. This joint project, funded by the U.S. Department of Education, between the University of Kansas and Florida State University, provides training for family-guided, activity-based intervention strategies. It provides modules that can be used and other resources. http://www.parsons.lsi.ku.edu.

- ☀ **Parent Training and Information Centers** in each state provide training and information to parents of infants, toddlers, school-aged children, and young adults with disabilities and the professionals who work with their families. This assistance helps parents participate more effectively with professionals in meeting the early intervention needs of infants and toddlers with disabilities.The Technical Assistance Alliance for Parent Centers and the National Technical Assistance Center is located at the PACER center in Minneapolis, MN and provides support for all parents centers as well as information on the location of state parent centers. http://www.taalliance.org.

- ☀ **Research and Training Center on Family Support and Children's Mental Health** at Portland State University, Portland, Oregon is designed to promote the transformation of mental health care by increasing knowledge of supports, services, and policies that build on family strengths, are community based, and family driven, promote cultural competence, and are based on evidence of effectiveness. http://www.rtc.pdx.edu/.

- ☀ **TaCTICS (Therapists as Collaborative Team members for Infant/Toddler Community Services)** is an outreach training project funded by a U.S. Department of Education Grant. It provides tools to embed intervention in the child/family's daily routines, activities, and events as a context for assessment and intervention. http://tactics.fsu.edu/.

Print Resources

- ☀ Butterfield, P. M., Martin, C. A., & Prairie, A. P. (2004). *Emotional connections: How relationships guide early learning.* Washington, DC: Zero to Three.

- ☀ Guerin, D. W., Gottfried, A. W., Oliver, P. H., & Thomas, C. W. (2003). *Temperament: Infancy through adolescence.* New York: Kluwer Academic Publishers.

- ☀ Hyson, M. (2004). *The emotional development of young children: Building emotion-centered curriculum* (2nd ed.). New York: Teachers College Press.

- ☀ Lieberman, A. F. (1993). *The emotional life of the toddler.* New York: The Free Press.

- ☀ Williamson, G. G., & Anzalone, M. E. (2001). *Sensory integration and self-regulation in infants and toddlers: Helping very young children interact with their environment.* Washington, DC: Zero to Three Press.

REFERENCES

American Psychiatric Association. (2000). *Diagnostic and statistical manual of mental disorders: DSM-IV-TR* (4th ed.). Washington, DC: Author.

Anzalone, M. E. (1993). Sensory contributions to action: A sensory integrative approach. *Zero to Three*, *14*(2), 17–20.

Ayers, A. J. (1979). *Sensory integration and the child*. Los Angeles, CA: Western Psychological Services.

Brazelton, T. B. (1992). *Touchpoints: Your child's emotional and behavioral development*. Reading, MA: Addison-Wesley.

Butterfield, P. M., Martin, C. A., & Prairie, A. P. (2004). *Emotional connections: How relationships guide early learning*. Washington, DC: Zero to Three.

Chess, S. (1983). Basic adaptations required for successful parenting. In V. Sasserath (Ed.), *Minimizing high-risk parenting* (pp. 5–11). Skillman, NJ: Johnson & Johnson.

Chess, S., & Thomas, A. (1977). Temperamental individuality from childhood to adolescence. *Journal of Child Psychiatry*, *16*, 218–226.

Chess, S., & Thomas, A. (1990). The New York Longitudinal Study (NYLS): The young adult periods. *Canadian Journal of Psychiatry*, *16*, 218–226.

Erikson, E. H. (1989). Elements of psychoanalytic theory of psychosocial development. In S. I. Greenspan & G. H. Pollock (Eds.), *The course of life: Vol. 1. Infancy* (pp. 15–84). Washington, DC: U.S. Government Printing Office.

Finkelhor, D. (1995). The victimization of children: A developmental perspective. *American Journal of Orthopsychiatry*, *65*(2), 177–193.

Franyo, G. (1998). *Early childhood educators and temperament: What they think and how they learn more*. Newark, DE: Dissertation from University of Delaware.

Greenspan, S., & Greenspan, N. T. (1985). *First feelings*. New York: Penguin Books.

Hyson, M. C. (1994). *The emotional development of young children: Building an emotion-centered curriculum*. New York: Teachers College Press.

Hyson, M. (2004). *The emotional development of young children: Building an emotion-centered curriculum* (2nd ed.). New York: Teachers College Press.

Izard, C. E. (1991). *The psychology of emotions*. New York and London: Plenum Press.

Izard, C. E., & Malatesta, C. Z. (1987). *Perspectives on emotional development I: Differential emotions theory of early emotional development*. Oxford, UK: John Wiley & Sons.

Karr-Morse, R., & Wiley, M. S. (1997). *Ghosts from the nursery: Tracing the roots of violence*. New York: The Atlantic Monthly Press.

Kuebli, J. (1994). Young children's understanding of everyday emotions. *Young Children*, *49*(3), 36–47.

Kuebli, J., & Fivush, R. (1992). Gender differences in parent-child conversations about past emotions. *Sex Roles*, *27*(11), 683–698.

LeDoux, J. (1996). *The emotional brain*. New York: Touchstone Books, Simon & Schuster.

Lieberman, A., Wieder, S., & Fenichel, E. (1997). *The DC: 0-3 casebook: A guide to the use of zero to three's "diagnostic classification of mental health and developmental disorders of infancy and early childhood" in assessment and treatment planning*. Washington, DC: Zero to Three.

Lieberman, A. F., Bernard, K. B., & Wieder, S. (2004). Diagnosing infants, toddlers, and preschoolers: The zero to three diagnostic classification of early mental health disorders. In R. DelCarmen-Wigging & A. Carter (Eds.), *Handbook of infant, toddler, and preschool mental health assessment* (pp. 141–160). Oxford, UK: Oxford University Press.

Nadel, J., & Muir, D. (2005). *Emotional development*. Oxford, UK: Oxford University Press.

Oster, H. (2005). The repertoire of infant facial expressions: An ontogenetic perspective. In J. Nadel & D. Muir (Eds.), *Emotional development* (pp. 261–292). Oxford, UK: Oxford University Press.

Panksepp, J., & Smith-Pasqualini, M. (2005). The search for the fundamental brain/mind sources of affective experience. In J. Nadel & D. Muir (Eds.), *Emotional development* (pp. 5–30). Oxford, UK: Oxford University Press.

Soussignan, R., & Schaal, B. (2005). Emotional processes in human newborns: A functionalist perspective. In J. Nadel & D. Muir (Eds.), *Emotional development* (pp. 127–159). Oxford, UK: Oxford University Press.

Thomas, A., & Chess, S. (1980). *The dynamics of psychological development*. New York: Brunner/Mazel.

Thomas, A., Chess, S., & Birch, C. (1968). *Temperament and behavior disorders in children*. New York: New York University Press.

Trevarthen, C. (2005). Action and emotion in development of cultural intelligence: Why infants have feelings like ours. In J. Nadel & D. Muir (Eds.), *Emotional development* (pp. 61–91). Oxford, UK: Oxford University Press.

Williamson, G. G., & Anzalone, M. E. (2001). *Sensory integration and self-regulation in infants and toddlers: Helping very young children interact with their environment*. Washington, DC: Zero to Three Press.

Zero to Three, National Center for Clinical Infant Programs. (1994). *Diagnostic classification of mental health and developmental disorders of infancy and early childhood*. Arlington, VA: Author.

chapter 9

Early Care and Education for Infants and Toddlers

Chapter Outline

- History of Early Care and Education in the United States
- Issues in Early Care and Education
- Types of Early Care and Education Settings
- Quality in Early Care and Education
- Including Infants and Toddlers with Developmental Delays
- Work/Family and Early Care and Education
- Professional Preparation

High-quality care is essential for infants and toddlers. In the past this care was most frequently provided at home. With changing American demographics, more than half of families with children ages 3 and under share the care and education of their children with others.

WHY STUDY EARLY CARE AND EDUCATION?

- ❋ The first three years are important in and of themselves and make an impact on future development. How infants and toddlers are cared for affects their current and future lives.

- ❋ More than half of infants and toddlers will be cared for outside of their homes.

- ❋ Overall, the quality of early care and education for infants and toddlers is poor to mediocre.

- ❋ We know how to translate information from theory and research into care and education practices.

- ❋ Care and education for infants and toddlers should be evidence based. You need to know the evidence and use it to guide your practice.

Joining with parents in the care of their infant or toddler is an awesome responsibility. Parents are in the process of adjusting to their new role as parent of an infant. They are struggling to read his cues, and at the same time they are fatigued from lack of sleep. Although they know they must have someone care for their child, they may be conflicted over who that should be. Physicians recommend that women need at least six to eight weeks away from work to recover after pregnancy and childbirth. Child development experts recommend four to six months as the length of time critical for fostering healthy infant attachment and development. Most mothers would like to remain home for about six months (Ring, 2001). Why then, given the feelings of mothers and recommendations of professionals, are children as young as six weeks of age in early care and education settings? Economic necessity requires women to go back to work far earlier than they did in the past. The lower the person is on the economic scale, the more crucial child care becomes (Ring, 2001).

The issue of nonparental child care is complicated and controversial. At the root of this problem are the beliefs we have about the role of parent. Before the baby is born, the mother thinks about what her baby will be like and a physical and emotional bond is formed. The mother is there 24/7. She was there when he was conceived and she is of course present at his birth. She wants to be there for her child. Perhaps this is a central factor that makes the decision to place an infant in child care so difficult—the notion of the "other woman" who may take her place in her baby's world (Clarke-Stewart & Allhusen, 2005). Although we know that children can and do form relationships with their father and other caregivers, it is still difficult for many mothers to leave their infant in the care of others.

Putting a baby in child care conflicts with the 1950s view of the traditional family, with the mother as homemaker and child rearer and the father as breadwinner. She has friends who "sacrifice" so they can be home with their baby. She might read a newspaper article about an infant in child care who died because he was placed on a mattress that was too soft and could not turn his head (Clarke-Stewart & Allhusen, 2005). At some level, child care is seen as un-American. In 1971, the House and Senate of the United States passed a bill called the Comprehensive Child Care Act. It would have provided five months of paid maternity leave for working women and subsidized child care for infants and toddlers. It was vetoed by President Richard Nixon. He viewed it as an attempt to "Sovietize" our youth (Lally, 2001).

Governments of other nations, including Italy, Sweden, Norway, Denmark, and France, for example, made very different decisions about their role in child care. They provide paid maternity leave and subsidize child care. Initially infant care was seen as a right of working families. Gradually, programs in these countries moved out of health and social welfare departments and into education. The psychologists who were concerned about the child's separation from his mother began to look for new and better ways to build connections between families and child care providers. By the 1980s a new system was emerging in Europe, particularly Italy (Mantovani, 2001). The United States was not even in the competition.

HISTORY OF EARLY CARE AND EDUCATION IN THE UNITED STATES

The field of early childhood education evolved from multiple sources, including maternal and child health services, child development, compensatory education and the nursery school movement (Meisels & Shonkoff, 2000). Preschool or nursery school was designed as an enrichment and socialization program for children of upper-middle-class and upper-class mothers who did not work outside the home. It was typically a half-day program. By the 1930s, there were approximately 200 nursery schools in the United States, about half of which were associated with colleges and universities (Peterson, 1987).

Child care's history dates from the mid-1800s. It was initially a philanthropic endeavor by upper-class women to care for children of the working poor and recent immigrants. Children stayed in child care all day (Handel, Cahill, & Elkin, 2007).

The federal government became involved in child care during the depression of the 1930s. Child care was one aspect of the Works Progress Administration (WPA) program. Its purpose was threefold: It provided work for unemployed teachers, care for children whose mothers were working because their husbands were out of work, and it used up surplus food the government was buying from farmers. The federal government's interest in child care continued through the end of World War II. Then, although some child care centers remained, the majority of them closed in the late 1940s. As more women began reentering the workforce in the 1960s, child care again became, and continues to be, an important issue. In the United States there is a clear tie between parents' need to work and the need for child care.

Child Care in Italy

In Italy, the early care of infants and toddlers is no longer viewed as a necessary service to allow mothers to work, but a way of sharing the tasks of infant and toddler care and education. Italian parents, even those who do not work, see infant-toddler centers as the best solution for care for children under three—if they can get their children into them (Mantovani, 2001). Infant and toddler caregivers are consultants to parents and provide support on educational matters. Caregivers have a delicate and complex role. They have moved their focus away from the primary caregiver for the child to having responsibility for both the child and the parents. When the well-being of the child is the common goal, the roles of parents and caregivers become clearer. They work together to become competent professional partners (Mantovani, 2001). This is possible partly because caregivers stay with the same group of children for up to three years. They develop a genuine partnership with the family. There is little turnover because caregivers who work in public infant-toddler centers have paid vacation time, usually the month of August, and full benefits. Their salaries are similar to preschool teachers. See Table 9–1 for the distinctions between the Italian system and current practices in the United States.

Table 9–1 Comparison of the United States and Italian System of Early Care and Education

1. Paid parental leave. Infants in Italy rarely enter care before 6 months of age. In the United States, with no paid parental leave, children enter care as early as 4 to 6 weeks.

2. Conceptualization of child care. In Italy, caring for infants and toddlers is seen as beneficial to the child, intellectually stimulating, and enriching the lives of the child, family, and caregiver. In the United States we typically see it as a service to help families so they can work or a support for other factors such as poverty or parental illness.

3. Child care is seen as a profession in Italy, and child care providers are educated professionals. Their role is to determine the best possible way to support each infant and toddler in their care and their families. In the United States many feel that child care providers are glorified babysitters who need little training and receive little pay.

4. In Italy child care is subsidized and parents pay on a sliding scale based on their ability to pay. Child care in the United States is not subsidized. It is a business arrangement.

SOURCE: Lally (2001).

REFLECTIVE PRACTICE

Think about the differences between how Italy and the United States view early care and education for infants and toddlers. Do you plan to work with infants and toddlers when you graduate? Would you make a different decision if the philosophy of the United States and the pay was similar to Italy?

In the United States, educating children is seen as a shared responsibility when children reach age 5 or 6 and enter public schools. There are requirements for public school teachers and a clear move to having highly qualified teachers based on the requirements of the No Child Left Behind Act of 2001 and the Individuals with Disabilities Education Improvement Act of 2004.

ISSUES IN EARLY CARE AND EDUCATION

The early history of child care has had a direct impact on the issues in the field. Some important issues remain unresolved, relative to both the impact of early care and education settings on infants and toddlers and issues related to the settings themselves. It is difficult to differentiate these issues cleanly because the quality of a setting influences the impact on the infant or toddler. The distinction between child care and early education is one such issue. The historical connection of child care to the welfare system caused much stigmatization. Child care was viewed as part of a service system that provided custodial care for children of families who needed help. Child care allowed mothers to work and hence kept them off welfare while preserving the family unit.

Over time, the nursery school movement began to overlap with the child care movement. An important distinction between the two is that the nursery school movement was based in education, not social welfare. This grounding significantly influenced child care in two ways: Educators were interested in affecting the curriculum for children so that it moved beyond custodial care, and, at the same time, such education was recognized as a service to the general public, not as a welfare issue.

Some professionals in the field see child care and early education as different but overlapping services for young children. Others, such as Spodek and Saracho, see no distinction. "Indeed, children's development is considered at risk if they are denied an educational program while they are attending a child care center" (1992, p. 189). Lack of agreement about the relationship between child care and early education has led to confusion and disagreements about quality, particularly in relation to personnel preparation, staff training, teacher–child ratios, and pay. I clearly believe in early care **and** education.

Some confusion also relates to the "target population." Who are services provided for? From an early education perspective, it is clear that nursery school or preschool is designed for young *children*, typically between the ages of 3 and 5. Child care, on the other hand, is seen as a service designed to meet the needs of *parents* of young children. Sometimes the needs of parents and children are pitted against each other when funds are limited: High-quality care is better for children but more costly for parents. To keep costs down for parents, quality for children is often sacrificed.

Having infants and toddlers in care presents additional challenges. Do infants and toddlers need teachers or "mother substitutes"? Infants and toddlers are just forming their identity and learning about themselves. Adults play a role in this definition of self. Infants develop a sense of self, not based on educational activities, but on caring, sensitive relationships. To support infants in this process, caregivers need a sound grounding in the developmental aspects of infancy as well as knowledge and experience with infants and toddlers in group situations. Does this now make them highly trained caregivers or teachers? As a society we value "mothering," and more recently "fathering," and in a more generic sense, good "parenting." We offer classes to teach parenting skills and acknowledge the stresses involved in parenting. We label caregivers "unskilled."

Other issues relating to child care have changed. In the 1960s we asked whether or not children should be in child care. In the 1980s we asked what constituted quality child care and what the effects of early care and education were on infants and toddlers and their families. In the 2000s we are asking how to provide high-quality child care for infants and toddlers and we are focusing on work/family issues.

TYPES OF EARLY CARE AND EDUCATION SETTINGS

Child care comes in many varieties and sizes, but at least five distinct types of child care can be identified: (1) parental care; (2) child care by family, friends, or neighbors (either in their home or the child's home); (3) family child care; (4) child care centers; and (5) other types of care, including babysitters, housekeepers, and nannies. The care of infants is more variable than for older children. Families determine the type of care they feel best fits their needs. This may ultimately be determined by what is available. Some professionals feel that family child care is preferable for infants and toddlers and, as children reach preschool age, that center-based care provides more variety.

Table 9–2 provides data from the U.S. Department of Education, National Center for Educational Statistics (NCES) (2001) on the distribution of care for children under three. It appears clear that many infants and toddlers are

Table 9–2 Distribution of Care for Infants and Toddlers in the United States

	Less than 1 year	1 to 2 years
Parent	60%	44%
Nonparent	40%	66%
Child care center	8%	21%
Nonrelative arrangement	14%	19%
Relatives	21%	23%

SOURCE: U.S. Department of Education, National Center for Education Statistics (NCES) (2001).

cared for by individuals other than their parents and that at least some of this care takes place in institutional settings. As infants and toddlers become pre-schoolers, the probability of this care being in a child care center increases to 56 percent (U.S. Department of Education, 2001).

Another way of looking at this is to look at the caregivers. On any given day approximately 2.3 million caregivers are in the paid child care work force. Of these individuals 35 percent are paid relatives, 28 percent are family child care providers, 24 percent work in center-based settings, and 13 percent are paid nonrelatives. There are also approximately 2.4 million individual providing unpaid child care during a given week. Of these, 93 percent are unpaid relatives (Burton et al., 2002).

Families who use family, friend, and neighbor care choose so for a variety of reasons. Nonstandard working hours is a major reason. Parents who do not work 9-to-5 jobs or parents who have fluctuating schedules that work either predictable or unpredictable nights, days, and weekends do not find standard child care an option. Convenience, transportation and cost also play a role (Annie E. Casey, 2006). Overall, black families are most likely to use family, friend, and neighbor care (37 percent), although white families also rely on it (27 percent). In addition to these more measurable factors for some families it come down to trust, personal comfort, culture, language, and preference. Hispanic families are more likely to rely on exclusive parent care. If they do use out-of-home care they are more likely to use family, friend and neighborhood care than center-based care (Annie E. Casey, 2006).

Because there are different methods of collecting data on the number of children in child care, the National Institute of Child Health and Human Development (NICHD) followed 1,364 children born in 1991 through elementary school. Although old, this data provides additional information about how child care changes from birth to three years. The average age at which a child entered non-maternal care was just over three months. By 12 months, 69 percent of infants had received regular nonmaternal care and 80 percent had been in regular nonmaternal care for some portion of that time (NICHD Early Child Care Research Network, 1997). When infants first entered care, fathers or partners (25 percent) and grandparents or other relatives (25 percent) were most likely to be the nonmaternal caregivers, with only 13 percent cared for in their homes by nonrelatives and 13 percent in child care centers. By the end of the first year, the number of children in child care homes was 27 percent and in child care centers 17 percent. This means that during the first year, the majority of children in nonparental care experienced two child care arrangements, and over a third had three or more arrangements. At 12 months, about half of the infants were in nonmaternal care for 30 or more hours a week (NICHD Early Child Care Research Network, 1997). This causes some concern about the development of secure attachment.

By 36 months, 92 percent of children had experienced some form of nonmaternal care and 80 percent were in nonmaternal care, with half of these children in care for 30 or more hours a week. That is about the same number of hours that infants are in care. However, there is a major shift in where children are cared for. At this point 44 percent of the children are in center-based care, 25 percent in family child care homes, 12 percent are cared for by their father or mother's partner, and 9 percent by grandparents (NICHD Early Child Care Research Network, 2000).

up close and personal

When I was pregnant I made the decision to put Serena in child care. I went to various child care centers and knew which one I wanted her to attend. But after she was born, I couldn't do it. I never thought I would have such a hard time, but every time I thought of leaving my little girl with perfect strangers, tears welled up in my eyes and I felt a strange constriction in my chest.

I didn't have a choice about going to work, because I am the one with health insurance—and the newspaper I work for doesn't offer paid maternity leave. At six weeks I had a decision to make: Place Serena in child care or work out a schedule where her dad and I could care for her.

We get little sleep—I work from 7 AM to 3 PM, plus an extra two hours on Mondays. My husband drops the baby off at work at 3:00 on his way to work, and then I take her home and we play. Serena still doesn't have a regular schedule, and there are days when I function on less than three hours of sleep, and moments where I have cried out of sheer tiredness. But the constriction in my heart hasn't returned. Serena gets talked to and cared for by the people who love her most in the world—her parents. And I have no fears about what will happen when I'm not around, because I'm leaving my baby girl with her father.

REFLECTIVE PRACTICE

What are your feelings about having young babies in child care? Can you empathize with the hard choices some mothers and fathers have to make? What choice would you make if you had to make it now?

Parental Care

Approximately half of children under three in the United States are cared for by their parents in their own homes. We actually know less about this care and its quality than we do about other types of care. At one level, we assume that biological parenthood automatically assures sensitive and thoughtful care; at another level, we know this is not true. The assumption seems to be that separation and attachment are a nonissue when parents themselves care for their children. Sometimes parents care for their children at home and work as well by juggling their work schedules so someone is always home, or sometimes the child is taken to work or a parent does some work at home.

Relative Care

Approximately 20 percent of infants and toddlers are cared for by relatives, either in their homes or in the child's home. These arrangements are not subject to regulations of any kind. As with parents, we assume that the care given by relatives is automatically better than that given by unrelated people. Mothers who would not place their children in an organized child care setting will leave an infant or toddler with an older parent or relative. Interestingly, young children are not more securely attached to relatives than to nonrelative providers (Galinsky, Howes, Kontos, & Shinn, 1994). Quality is dependent on the circumstances and the individual giving the care. In some of these situations, grandmothers or aunts care for the infant while the mother returns to school or work. Others are more of an informal family child care situation that is run by a relative who, typically, also has young children. This arrangement is common for infants, children of mothers who work part-time, and for poor children (Clarke-Stewart, Gruber, & Fitzgerald, 1994).

Looking at this group more closely, 60 percent of the relatives were taking care of the children to help out the mothers, not because they wanted to. In addition, two-thirds of the children with relatives were living in poverty with its concomitant stresses (Galinsky et al., 1994). Intentionality was an important variable; that is, did the relative actually decide to care for children or was it viewed as "helping out?" "Intentional providers offer higher quality, warmer, and more attentive care that helps children achieve their fullest potential" (Galinsky et al., 1994, p. 60).

Family Child Care

In family child care a single provider cares for a small group of children (typically one to six) in her home. Family child care providers have a small business, caring for the children of others and often their own as well, in their homes. There are also large child care home providers where two or more providers (or one provider and one or more adult assistants) care for children in the residence of one of the providers (National Association for the Education of Young Children [NAEYC], 2004). These sites are usually located near the cared-for child's home and are easy to get to. Parents may feel that they have more control over what happens in this type of setting than they might have in a center-based program. In some states, family child care homes are licensed, in others they are registered. In some instances there are no state regulations or many providers do not follow through on licensing or registration.

Family child care providers have diverse experiential and educational backgrounds. They are primarily adult women, most of whom are or have been married and who have children of their own. Most care for their own children, or did at one time, while they care for the children of others. Many have participated in some type of in-service training, but the training varies greatly in content and duration, from the minimum requirements for a license to college degrees in early childhood education. Much like the director of a child care center, the family child care provider must administer and manage her own program. At the same time she is often the sole teacher. Family child care providers are among the loneliest and least appreciated of all professionals working with children (Trawick-Smith & Lambert, 1995).

In many instances family child care homes are not licensed. Kontos (1992) estimates that between 85 and 89 percent are not licensed. Galinsky et al. (1994) found that 81 percent of family child care homes were "illegally nonregulated." This confounds the reporting system and may mean that there truly are many more infants and toddlers in family child care than the surveys found and that we have even less control over quality than we thought. The NICHD study found that home child care settings that were licensed were of higher quality than unlicensed ones (Clarke-Stewart & Allhusen, 2005).

Because family child care providers are the proprietors of their business, parents can easily deal with the person making decisions relative to the care of their child. They do not have to go through a bureaucracy of teachers and program administrators to obtain information or to seek change. Family child care may provide more continuity of care for the infants and toddlers. Parents have fewer worries that a primary caregiver will be shifted from one room to another, or that, as caregivers change shifts, important information about their child will be lost. There are fewer children in the setting, so the children may receive more individual attention and there are fewer concerns about infection.

Family child care homes may be able to provide more flexibility in scheduling. Some families may need only part-time care, others may need full-time child care to allow the parents to work, which sometimes includes nights and weekends. Irregular working hours of some parents makes conforming to the requirements of a center difficult. Family child care providers make individual decisions about whether or not to accommodate their schedules to these types of demands. Some family child care homes also offer the potential for expanding the informal support network of the family by the addition of other parents and the family child care provider herself. Family child care creates relationships that can develop into friendships.

Most family child care providers care for children in a multi-age group with ages spanning five years or more. If they provide infant and after-school care, the age range can be even wider. This means that providers must be able to care for children at a variety of different developmental levels at the same time, as well as help children with different maturational levels interact with each other. Family child care providers often care for their own children within their home. At times the parenting and caregiving roles collide. With their own children, caregivers have to resolve issues such as autonomy and separation, which materials and equipment are shared and which are not, and differentiate between child care time and family time (Trawick-Smith & Lambert, 1995).

One concern about family child care is a backup system. A sick family child care provider needs to have another adult take her place. Many providers do not have these backup systems in place and instead close down their care. A related problem occurs if the family child care provider's children become ill, especially if it is with a communicable disease. If the setting is temporarily closed, parents must find alternate care for their child on short notice. Parents may also be concerned about the quality of care their child receives because there is usually no other adult in the setting.

Child Care Centers

Child care centers can be public or private, and either nonprofit or for profit. Some are individual centers; others are part of chains. About half of the child care centers in the United States are for profit. Approximately 40 percent of centers are administered by private community or charitable organizations, churches, or parent cooperatives. About 9 percent of centers are part of child care chains, and 10 percent of centers receive government funding. Government-funded centers usually offer a wide range of services, from meals to medical attention (Clarke-Stewart et al., 1994).

Child care centers vary in size, from small centers with as few as 12 children, to centers that have several hundred children. Some centers have their own building, whereas others may share a setting. Frequently the latter are located in churches, housing projects, community agencies, industrial buildings, or colleges and universities. Settings vary in the ages of children served. Some group settings do not include infants; other settings may have children as old as 11 in after-school care.

Child care centers must be licensed by the state and abide by their requirements. States vary widely in these requirements. Some states focus on health and safety regulations in their licensure requirements. There may be specific requirements relative to training of staff and administrators, and staff–child ratios based on the age of the child. Some states require a curriculum, while others suggest curriculum guidelines. The level of quality of child care centers is closely related to county and state requirements for licensing and their ability to monitor these requirements.

Child care centers have toys and equipment that allow toddlers to interact with each other as they play.

Other Care Arrangements

Families have a variety of other care arrangements. Some are informal, such as leaving children with a friend or neighbor; others are more organized, such as having a live-in nanny or someone who comes to the home on a regular basis. The least common type of care for infants and toddlers is to have an adult come into the child's home on a regular basis to care for the child or children. There are organizations that provide such services; however, there is no regulation for this type of care. Its quality is dependent on the person who is delivering the care; some is exceptionally good and some is not. Like care given by parents and relatives, we know less about the quality of this care and the qualifications of the individuals who provide it.

In-home care is the most expensive type of care on a per-hour basis—the cost has almost doubled since 1975—whereas other child care settings have remained relatively stable in cost (Hofferth, Brayfield, Deich, & Holcomb, 1991). However, for parents with several young children at home, this type of care may be particularly appealing as well as cost-effective.

Child care is increasingly being viewed as part of the larger issues that relate to the interface of work and family. Many corporations have become interested in child care as a way of increasing morale, stabilizing their work force, and reducing absenteeism. Issues continue to revolve around the quality of child care.

Quality in Early Care and Education

In addition to providing guidelines for programs, the NAEYC also provides guidance for families seeking quality programs for their infants and toddlers. NAEYC believes that parents should use the same standards for choosing a program for their infant or toddler that NAEYC uses for evaluating programs for accreditation. See Table 9–3 for NAEYC's (2006) 10 accreditation standards.

The director or program administrator plays an important role in ensuring high-quality programming. She is the one who develops and maintains written policies and procedures that are shared with families. She is the one who oversees the curriculum and ensures that group sizes and teaching ratios are appropriate.

Organizations such as the NAEYC set standards for the profession. "Research confirms what most people intuitively know: Quality child care that encompasses strong developmental experiences had a long-term positive impact on academic achievement and provides important social benefits for vulnerable children at risk of poor outcomes. For lots of kids, these early formed benefits extend through adolescence and into adulthood" (Annie E. Casey Foundation, 2006, p. 9).

Table 9–3 NAEYC Accreditation Standards

1. Promote **positive relationships** for all children and adults.

   If you were a parent or an evaluator, what would you look for to show evidence of that standard? Think about how children are greeted and how welcome you might feel visiting the program. Would you expect to see teachers supporting and facilitating children playing together? How would you expect teachers to help solve conflicts between children? Our expectations may be slightly different, but overall I think we would expect warm, positive relationships that value each child and are sensitive to the individuality and culture of each child. Like adults, children are part of a community of learners. Each brings a unique perspective to learning and each needs to be valued.

2. Implement a **curriculum** that fosters all areas of child development—cognitive, emotional, language, physical, and social.

   Having a planned curriculum helps ensure that there is balance to a program and that all curriculum areas are covered. Look at a center and see if there are enough toys and materials for infants and toddlers. Are experiences designed to help children solve problems, develop language skills, and work together? Do the infants sleep when they are tired, or are they all put to sleep on a schedule (not as good)? Is planning individualized? Is the infant or toddler the center of the planning? There are commercially available programs, such as the Creative Curriculum for Infants and Toddlers, Revised Edition (Dombro, Colker, & Dodge, 1999), which some centers use, or centers can develop their own curriculum. Either way, they must have a curriculum.

3. Use developmentally, culturally, and linguistically appropriate and **effective teaching approaches**.

   Infants and toddlers come into the world different and they learn differently. They need to have these differences acknowledged and they need to be responded to in a way that is responsive to their needs. They need to be respected and supported based on their needs, interests, and experience. Culture and language are such an intrinsic part of infant and toddlers development that home languages need to be honored if possible and cultural differences acknowledged and valued.

4. Provide **ongoing assessments** of child progress.

   To plan for infants and toddlers you need to know their developmental level, their individual strengths and needs, and their likes and dislikes. If you teach toddlers what they already know, you are not helping them learn. Likewise, if what you are teaching is so advanced that they do not understand what you are doing, you are not helping them learn. It is the ability to assess where children are and the knowledge of the next step in development and learning that impacts what is learned. Families need to know what their children are learning on a regular basis.

5. Promote the **nutrition and health** of children and staff.

   To learn, children need to be safe and healthy. Routines need to be in place that ensure that children and staff wash or sanitize their hands and all surfaces. Infants need to be on their backs to sleep and there must be a plan to care for ill children. Meals and snacks need to be a nutritious part of children's eating patterns.

6. Employ and support qualified **teaching staff**.

   Teaching infants and toddlers is not the same as teaching preschool children. Teachers need to have specialized training in this age group. They need to understand the ebb and flow of infants and empathize with the struggles that toddlers have as they assert their independence.

7. Establish and maintain collaborative relationships with **families**.

   Families must be treated with respect and trust. Programs must find a variety of ways to communicate with families as they are jointly raising infants and toddlers. Communication is necessary for everyday events as well as the larger policies that impact operating procedures.

(continues)

8. Establish and maintain relationships and use resources of the **community**.

Infants and toddlers need to be connected with their families and the larger community in which they live and grow. They need to visit the surrounding area as well as have individuals from the community visit them.

9. Provide a safe and healthy **physical environment**.

A well-equipped and well-maintained environment is more conducive to both learning and safety. Light levels need to be controllable and sound levels low enough to allow infants to sleep and toddlers to play. Air quality needs to be monitored.

10. Implement strong program management policies that result in **high-quality service**.

SOURCE: NAEYC (2006).

We know more about quality in child care centers than we do in family child care homes. Comprehensive programs, such as the Perry Preschool Project and the Carolina Abecedarian Project, improved child outcomes to the extent that for every dollar spent on child care, $17 was saved. Despite this knowledge, programs such as Early Head Start, which provides care and support for pregnant women and children ages birth to three, reaches less than 3 percent of the infants and toddlers who are qualified to receive it (Blank, cited in Annie E. Casey Foundation, 2006). "As a nation, we are far from providing the public funding required to make cost-effective, high-quality child care—whether it is center based or home based—broadly available to the children and families who need it most" (Annie E. Casey Foundation, 2006, p. 21).

There is no national system or consistent standards for the formal organization of family child care homes. Most providers have not been regulated or connected to community child care, but this is gradually changing. In some communities an infrastructure to support family child care is developing. Such supports include family child care associations, accreditation programs, the child care food program, child care resource and referral systems, education and training opportunities, and support organizations.

Measuring Quality in Early Care and Education Settings

We are concerned about the quality of child care in the United States. Several large studies have been done over the past 10 to 15 years that have attempted to look at the quality of early care and education, particularly as it relates to infant and toddler care.

There are few objective measures of quality of care; for infants and toddlers the most widely used measure is the *Infant/Toddler Environment Rating Scale, Revised Edition (ITERS-R)* (Harms, Cryer, & Clifford, 2003). This assesses group programs for infants and toddlers birth through 2 ½. The *Early Childhood Environment Rating Scale, Revised Edition, Updated (ECERS-R)* (Harms, Cryer, & Clifford,

up close and personal

I am the director of a large child care center. At capacity we have 22 classrooms and approximately 200 children. We serve children from 6 weeks to 11 years. We are committed to serving a high-risk population. Many of our children live at or near poverty, about 40 percent of our parents are single moms, and about 10 percent of the children have disabilities. This means there is a lot that goes on behind the scenes.

Sometimes it is subtle. A two-year-old said that his mother got spanked the night before. The teacher was concerned and told me. When the mother came to pick him up she had a slight limp, and wore heavy makeup and wraparound sunglasses. I joined the child's teacher at the time his mother usually picks him up. First, we asked her how she was. She, of course, said fine. We described her son's comments and told her that we were concerned about her son's safety as well as hers. She said things will be fine. I asked her again "What makes you think it is safe to go home today and to take your son with you?" As that point she broke down, cried, and talked. We called the police to come and support her. She told her story again. She went to a shelter with her son. We were there until eight. I lose teachers over this. Every day is stressful.

This story isn't that unusual. We become social workers. When I am concerned about a family I have them meet with the associate director once a week. We set up contracts with them. When things get really bad they meet with me. We serve children and families and it is hard work.

REFLECTIVE PRACTICE

What would you have done if you had been the director of that child care center? Should she have interfered? Describe some of the other problems you think she encounters. How would you handle these? Think about your education. Are you prepared to cope with situations such as this?

2005) assesses group programs for children 2 ½ through 5 years. The *Family Child Care Rating Scale, Revised Edition (FDCRS-R)* (Harms, Cryer, & Clifford, 2007) assesses programs conducted in a provider's home and encompasses infants through school-age children. The ITERS-R has seven subscales: space and furnishings; personal care routines; listening and talking; activities; interaction; program structure; and parents and staff (Harms et al., 2003). The scale requires that an outside observer rate items on a scale of one to seven, with one being inadequate and seven being excellent. When scoring an item the observer starts from the one (inadequate) and continues upward until the highest score is reached. At each point the observer indicates if all of the criteria at that level have been met. For example, in the area of health practices, even if the program meets all of the criteria for excellent (seven) but they do not wash toddlers' hands after toileting, they still receive an inadequate (one) score. See Table 9–4 for an example in the area of fine motor skills for what a particular score might mean.

These instruments are designed to be used in a single visit, which is good for research purposes. However, the "snapshot" is influenced by when the visit takes place and the particular staff who are observed. It is also difficult to judge the dynamic nature of the environment and how responsive it is to children's changing needs and desires.

The National Child Care Staffing Study (Whitebook, Phillips, & Howes, 1990), used multiple assessments to study 227 centers that served infants, toddlers, and preschool children in five major metropolitan areas. Some centers refused to participate, and one might conclude that these centers were of lesser quality than those that did agree to participate. The results were not encouraging.

Table 9–4 Fine Motor Scores on the ITERS-R

Inadequate: 1
1.1 No appropriate fine motor materials accessible for daily use.
1.2 Materials are generally in poor repair.
Minimal: 3
3.1 Some appropriate fine motor materials accessible for daily use.
3.2 Materials are accessible for much of the day.
3.3 Materials generally in good repair.
Good: 5
5.1 Many and varied appropriate fine motor materials accessible for much of the day.
5.2 Materials are well organized (e.g., similar toys stored together; sets of toys in separate containers; toys picked up, sorted, and restored as needed).
Excellent: 7
7.1 Materials rotated to provide variety.
7.2 Materials of different levels of difficulty accessible. (For example, some challenging and some easy for all children in group, including children with disabilities.)

SOURCE: Harms et al. (2003).

The authors stated that "the quality of services provided by most centers was rated as barely adequate" (Whitebook et al., 1990, p. 4).

The Cost, Quality, and Outcomes Study Team (1995) evaluated 400 child care centers and surveyed parents of 826 children. For infants and toddlers the outcome was devastating. Forty percent of infant classrooms were rated as poor quality, 52 percent as mediocre quality, and only 8 percent as developmentally appropriate.

In a newer study the State of Delaware was interested in learning more about the quality of child care for infants and toddlers in their state (Gamel-McCormick, Buell, Amsden, & Fahey, 2002). Although Delaware is a small state, it has urban, suburban, and rural areas. Because of the state's small size researchers were able get a representative sample of child care centers throughout the state. The centers had to be willing to participate, so the findings may be inflated. Overall, 113 infant/toddler groups in child care centers were rated using an earlier edition (Harms, Cryer, & Clifford, 1990) of the ITERS.

To the extent that the results from Delaware are representative of the nation, the forecast is still a gloomy one. The quality of child care for infants and toddlers continues to be mediocre to poor. Given the importance of early development for long-term growth, the outlook is not good. We need to enhance, expand, and support the systems of care for infants and toddlers. This includes hiring teachers with a passion for working with infants and toddlers and who have degrees in early childhood education (Gamel-McCormick et al., 2002). The findings are briefly summarized in Table 9–5 using the subscale categories.

A relative overarching issue is whether the amount and quality of individual attention provided is enough to meet the needs of infants and toddlers. Another major issue concerns the amount and the appropriateness of planning and following through on plans by providers.

Table 9–5 Child Care Quality for Infants and Toddlers

Subcategory	Good	Mediocre	Poor
Furnishings and display for children	22%	53%	25%
Personal care routines	13%	49%	38%
Listening and talking	34%	33%	34%
Learning activities	8%	46%	46%
Interaction	48%	31%	21%
Program structure	24%	33%	43%
Adult needs	30%	37%	33%

SOURCE: Gamel-McCormick et al. (2002).

What determines quality in child care for infants and toddlers? Parents and early childhood professionals agree that they want children in early care and education settings to be healthy, safe, have warm relationships, and to learn. They disagree about whether these conditions exist in a given setting and have different perspectives on achieving these outcomes.

Early Childhood Professionals' Criteria for Quality Care

Most early childhood professionals agree on a common set of elements when considering the characteristics of high-quality child care.

The Environment. Environments can support or impede relationships among caregivers, infants and toddlers, and their parents. All children need an environment that is safe, healthy, and comfortable. Environments need to include supports (place and flexibility of schedule) to encourage parents to visit, and to meet the needs of mothers who want to continue breastfeeding their infants. Pleasant surroundings help set a positive mood for young children and caregivers alike.

Group Size and Adult–Child Ratios. Children need to receive care in small groups. Recommended group size is dependent on the age of the children being cared for (the younger the child, the smaller the group). Table 9–6 summarizes the NAEYC-recommended relationship between the age of the child and the size of the group and number of caregivers. Infants and toddlers with disabilities can be included when group size is kept at these levels. In situations where there are mixed age groupings—for example, family child care homes—there should never be more than two children under age 2.

As groups get larger, adults not only have to respond to the caregiving demands of more infants and toddlers, but they also have to deal with the other adults in the room. This need for organization leads to more restrictive

Table 9–6 NAEYC Accreditation Criteria for Staff–Child Ratios and Group Size

Age of child	Size of Group				
	6	8	10	12	14
Birth to 12 months	1:3	1:4			
12–24 months	1:3	1:4	1:5	1:4	
24–30 months		1:4	1:5	1:6	
30–36 months				1:6	1:7

SOURCE: Willer (1990, p. 64).

Environments for children need to be indoors and outdoors.

management techniques and less social interaction and language stimulation (Howes, 1992). Infants and toddlers need an intimate environment where they can share and discover their world with the support of caring adults. For young children large groups have too many distractions, including increased noise level, stimulation, general confusion, and less intimacy.

Educated Caregivers. Adults who care for infants and toddlers need training in early care and education in general, and infants and toddlers specifically. The skills of the caregiver are paramount. Because infants and toddlers are so dependent on the adult in the environment, that adult must be well trained. Infants change so quickly that what is appropriate for a four-month-old is not appropriate for a nine-month-old. The caregiver needs to know how infants and toddlers change and grow from birth to three years, not only their physical and motor development but also their social and emotional development. Child care providers who had more specialized training in child development were more involved and affectionate with the children in their care, restricting them less and encouraging them more. A college degree in early childhood education is ideal (NICHD Early Child Care Research Network, 2002a, 2002b, 2002c).

Although there is diversity among states in group size and staff ratios, there is consistency in training requirements. Virtually all states allow infants and toddlers to be cared for by providers who have not completed high school, have no training specific to infant and toddler development, and have received less than six hours of annual in-service training. Few states have standards for the amount, content, or quality of training for individuals working in early care and education. "Many early care and education practitioners in America are not required to have any early childhood training to work with young children" (Morgan et al., 1994, p. 80). State governments do not consider training important, quite contrary to professionals and parents.

Designated Primary Caregiver. In addition to limitations on group size, there should be an adult who is designated as having primary caregiving responsibility for each infant; this should be someone who develops an intimate relationship with each infant and who learns his cues and patterns (Petrie, 2005). Toddlers will choose their own primary caregiver. This request should be honored when possible. This does not mean that one person is exclusively in charge of a particular child, but rather that there is a team, and each caregiver is primarily assigned to particular children. This gives parents a person to contact when they have a question about their child and means that fewer issues will fall between the cracks (Lally, Torres, & Phelps, 1994).

Continuity in Care. As infants and toddlers develop intimate relationships with caregivers, it is important that this relationship continues. Infants are developing trust. Security is a prime issue for them. The most serious threat to that security is the loss of a primary caregiver. From an infant's perspective, staff turnover or reassignments are viewed as loss. The national annual turnover rate among child care providers is 40 percent (Carnegie Task Force on Meeting the Needs of Young Children, 1994). New studies looking at the occupational turnover rate estimated it at 18 percent per year for center-based staff and family child care providers. Data is not available for other child care providers so this is probably a very conservative estimate (Burton et al., 2002). Although some of this cannot be prevented, child care settings need to be designed to allow infant–caregiver relationships to be maintained over time. Changes, when they happen, should be planned and gradual. A child care setting that moves children or caregivers every few months is not acting in the best interest of the child (Lally et al., 1994). A study of early child care found that almost all infants were in two care arrangements (child care and parental care), but 37 percent had three or more regular child care arrangements. Infants and toddlers who experienced multiple child care arrangements had more problem behaviors than those who had fewer child care arrangements (NICHD, Early Child Care Research Network, 1998a, 1998b, 1998c).

Each caregiver and infant brings unique cultural experiences and expectations to the child care setting.

Culturally Sensitive Care. The number of infants and toddlers from non-white, non-Anglo families is increasing in the United States. Ideally, there are caregivers who speak the same language and come from the same culture as the children in the setting (Garcia & Gonzalez, 2006). It is difficult to care for young children when caregivers cannot communicate important information to their parents. For the infant, cultural sensitivity is even more basic as he is developing a sense of self. A multicultural approach appreciates human differences as well as their similarities.

Newborns prefer their mother's smell and voice over all others. Infants come into the world ready to respond to differences. Infants become anxious around strangers because they know they are strangers. Infants and toddlers are astute observers of similarities and differences. If infants and toddlers are raised in diverse families and communities and child care settings, they learn that skin can be dark and light, language can sound different and have different intonation patterns. By age 3, children can verbalize their thoughts about skin color and know what their own skin color is. They can categorize people just as they categorize shapes (Ramsey & Williamson, 2003). Young children are not color blind. At as early as six months of age, children react consistently to racial differences (Katz, 2003).

Programs for young children must be responsive to the dynamics of cultural difference and power. Hiring people from different cultural and racial backgrounds is a first step, but the journey is a long one. Learning about different cultures is another step. However, actually interacting with a particular family and discussing cultural issues are also necessary. The result is you might not necessarily agree with the family's parenting methods, but you come away with an understanding that considering what this family has experienced what they are doing makes sense (Barrera, 2003). Cultural knowledge helps educators be aware of possibilities and increases the probability they will be ready to respond in an appropriate way. See Table 9–7 for guidelines in working toward cultural competency.

Parent Involvement. Good early care and education programs encourage parent involvement and input. Recognizing that parents also have other commitments, centers actively seek parents' advice about their child and about the setting in general. They find creative ways for busy families to be an active part of the system. Ideally, these programs are linked to a comprehensive "wellness" program, of which child care is only part of the support system available for families with young children. Unfortunately, this ideal is rarely realized. In the United States, child care is a fragmented system, if it is a system at all, with little regulation or support for either the child care setting or the families.

Table 9–7 Working toward Cultural Competency

- Engage in personal, respectful, and skilled conversations with families of infants and toddlers to try to gain a common understanding of the principles behind the behavior.

- Establish reciprocal interactions that equalize power and allow an equal voice for all perspectives.

- Be responsive and respectful of other's perspectives and work toward accessing the strengths of different perspectives.

- Acknowledge the tension that some families feel as they try to both maintain their cultural values and practices at the same that they are adapting to the dominant culture.

- Discrimination and marginal social position are conditions that many families face and that they feel powerless to do something about. Supporting cultural diversity lessens family fears and equalizes power.

- Review a range of possible behaviors based on cultural background, ask a parent where she falls in this range, and explain how some practices have changed based on new knowledge. Doing this well is an art, not a science.

- Strive to understand your own culture as if you were not a member of that culture.

SOURCES: Barrera (2003); Clark (2003); Lynch and Hanson (2004); Stott and Halpern (2003); Van Horn and Segal (2003).

up close and personal

It is hard. We try, but I don't really understand all of the nuances of culture. It can happen over something as simple as shoes. Maria is an unsteady walker at 14 months. She comes to our setting in patent-leather Mary Janes with a buckle and slippery soles. We take her shoes off because she falls less when she's barefoot. We have explained this to her mother numerous times, but her mother is still very upset with us whenever she arrives and finds that Maria is barefoot.

Although her mother's English is not great, we get the message. In Nicaragua there are parasites in the soil and children who go barefoot can get these parasites. Many of the homes only have soil floors. I get it. But we aren't in Nicaragua any more. We wouldn't let her go outside barefoot. This is the United States. Our child care setting has floors that are cleaned daily. We don't have parasites. I don't know how to make her get it.

REFLECTIVE PRACTICE

Obviously there is a cultural conflict. If you were the teacher how would you handle this? Is there any middle ground where the culture can be respected and Maria's emerging walking supported?

Parents' Criteria for Quality Care

Although parents and early childhood professionals share an interest in high-quality child care, their perspectives are different. Parents focus on their own child. They want caregivers to see their infant or toddler as special and to hold and cherish that child as if he were their own. They want their child to receive sensitive, individualized care. They want "good parenting" from a provider who delights in their child. Overall, they are interested in the caregiver as a person. Most parents believe that government regulations and standards are not related to quality. They see the government's role in setting health and safety standards but little else (Carnegie Task Force on Meeting the Needs of Young Children, 1994).

There is consensus among parents regarding aspects of high-quality child care. See Table 9–8 for common agreement.

Parents also differ from each other in what they want in child care. Some parents want a homelike setting with a "mom-like" caregiver. This situation can be viewed as an extension of the family; that is, it is identical to a home except that the provider cares for children other than her own. Other parents want a program of activities for their infants and toddlers that is provided by a caregiver who has had training in early childhood education. This situation can be thought of as a mini preschool, and the caregivers are often former teachers who have decided to stay home with their own young children. The third model is a combination of the two: a "mom-like" caregiver who provides an educational program, or a more extended family with planned activities.

Children's Perspective on Quality Care

In the United States we rarely think about children's views of quality, especially very young children. Such views have, however, been considered in Denmark. Denmark has a long-standing organized system of publicly funded

Table 9–8 Parent's View of High-Quality Child Care

• Attention to children's safety
• Provider's communication with parents about their children
• Cleanliness
• Attention children receive
• Provider's warmth toward children

SOURCE: Kontos, Howes, Shinn, and Galinsky (1995, p. 127).

early childhood services that include both centers and family child care homes. The Ministry of Social Affairs laid down a set of principles that all settings must observe:

1. Children's development, well-being, and independence must be encouraged.

2. Children must be listened to.

3. Parents must have influence.

4. Centers must be regarded as a resource in connection with preventive work; that is, the staff must, in cooperation with other professionals, ensure the special support that is needed for some families with children.

5. Centers must be regarded as one of each neighborhood's facilities for children; that is, the staff must cooperate with other facilities in the neighborhood, both public and private (Langsted, 1994, p. 30).

Following up on point number two, Denmark began an extensive program on "Children as Citizens" as a way of listening to and including children. Children's comments on their child care settings pointed out the need for some structural changes in centers. Children noted that they were not all hungry at the same time, that sometimes they did not want to go out to play at the designated time or they wanted to stay outside and play longer, and they felt it was unfair that children could only have water between meals while adults stood around with a cup of tea or coffee if they wanted it. Accommodations were made. Juice was always available, the playground was staffed with one adult throughout the day, and the common lunch time for all was dropped (Langsted, 1994).

Discovering the needs and desires of children under three was more challenging. Many programs for very young children had been preoccupied with rules and prohibitions. Where these rules were challenged, it was difficult for both caregivers and parents. Young children were given the right to say no. If a child did not want to eat he did not have to, and he could leave the table and do something that interested him. What he could not do was "yo-yo" back and forth. Rules that dealt with safety remained; most other rules were abandoned. One consequence was that there were fewer conflicts between adults and young children. There were, however, more conflicts among the children. This was viewed in a positive light—children had the right to try to solve their own conflicts. Parents were concerned that because their children were now allowed to jump on the furniture at the center, they would also want to do so at home. Meetings between staff and parents and observations over time helped parents realize that children are able to make more decisions for themselves than adults typically allow them to make. They were able to distinguish between home and center rules (Langsted, 1994).

REFLECTIVE PRACTICE

How do you feel about the Danish model? How do you think the programs you are familiar with would change if they included children's values?

Joining Parents' and Early Childhood Professionals' Criteria for Quality Care

Parents and professionals both want infants and toddlers who are happy, healthy, and learning in child care settings. Most parents find the quality of their children's child care "very good," whereas trained observers viewing the same setting evaluate the quality as mediocre to poor. There are several explanations for this discrepancy. One obvious one is different operational definitions of quality. Another explanation is that parents use different information to evaluate child care settings. Still another explanation is that parents do have concerns about the quality of care settings but they are reluctant to voice these concerns to themselves or others. From a parents' perspective, it would be very difficult to rate a child care setting as "poor" and then leave their child there. It is difficult to know what part each of these aspects plays in the different views of parents and early childhood professionals relative to high-quality child care.

"Research suggests that parents pay relatively little attention to the indicators of quality that professionals suggest they use to screen child care options, such as licensing and caregiver training" (Larner & Phillips, 1994, p. 51). Howes (1992) discusses the concept of quality child care, and also considers the different orientations of parents and professionals. She looks at quality as having two aspects: structural quality and process quality. "Structural quality generally refers to variables that can be regulated, including adult–child ratio, group size, and education and training of adult caregivers" (Howes, 1992, p. 33). On the other hand, "Process quality refers to the providers of developmentally appropriate activities and to warm, nurturing, and sensitive caregiving within the child care arrangement" (Howes, 1992, p. 33). Process quality is certainly more difficult to quantify than structural quality, but it is an equally important component of quality. Fortunately, the qualities overlap.

To support collaboration, early care and education personnel need training in working with parents as well as infants and toddlers. With a focus on viewing infants and toddlers in a culturally sensitive family-centered way, it is imperative that providers be sensitive to the needs of families as a unit. It is useful to start out with the assumption that most infants and toddlers are in early care and education so that their parents can work. This may limit the time when families can be involved as well as their preferences about involvement.

The ambiance of the setting itself influences levels of collaboration. Parents are more likely to become involved if they know they are welcome. Having an open-door policy as well as formal times when parents can get to know and talk to staff increases the likelihood that parents will be involved (Berger, 2004). One way of looking at parent involvement is to view the responsibility that early care and education settings have to enable families to be involved (see Table 9–9).

Educator/Caregiver Characteristics

Parents and professionals agree that the most important element in any early care and education setting is the teacher. The relevant structural characteristics of this individual include the amount and type of formal education she

Table 9–9 Responsibilities that Encourage Family Involvement

We have an obligation to provide families with the skills and knowledge they need to support their infant or toddler and to ensure that early care and education settings are safe and healthy, and to work out routines for continuity in care.
We must have a system of communicating with families to give and receive relevant information. This communication can take a variety of forms: notes, telephone calls, face-to-face as infants and toddlers arrive or leave the setting, conferences, take-home activities, newsletters, or e-mail. Communication must take place about positive events and sharing what is happening with infants and toddlers during the day, not just when they ate and slept, or when there are problems.
We need to encourage families to participate in the early care and education setting. Participation can range from attending parent meetings to volunteering. An expectation that parents can be regular volunteers is unrealistic and may cause stress if viewed as an essential part of parent involvement. However, we should welcome a visit from grandparents as they may want to understand how their grandchild spends his day.
Collaboration involves extending the learning into the home and making conscious decisions to support infant and toddler's learning at home. Depending on the setting, this may involve suggesting age-appropriate toys or recommending television viewing for infants (none), toddlers (none), and two-year-olds (1 to 2 hours a day).
Families should be involved in the governance or educational decision making in an early care and education setting. Having a parent advisory council for the setting also increases parent involvement and even parental satisfaction. A parent advisory council participates in the hiring process, determines hours the setting is open, costs, and so on. Having speakers on topics suggested by parents may make parents feel that the setting is responsive to their needs
Parents with young children, especially single parents, have many demands placed on them. If parent activities occur in the evening, the reality is that parents may be tired after working all day and that someone will need to stay home and care for the child or a babysitter will need to be hired if child care is not provided. If activities are held on the weekend, parents may feel that their only free days are being consumed. Expectations for parent involvement need to be couched in terms of the realities of dual-earner families and single parents. Levels of collaboration that do not require attendance at the center itself need to be acknowledged.

SOURCES: Berger (2004); Epstein and Dauber (1991).

has, whether it was related to infants and toddlers, and her experience in child care. To be effective, teachers of infants and toddlers need both formal education as well as specialized training in infants and toddlers.

It is very difficult to quantify the process quality of caregiving. It is hard to operationalize qualities like warmth, caring, and responsiveness. However, when these are agreed to be high, there is greater attachment and social play, and language scores are higher. The experience of the caregiver is not a good predictor of child outcomes. However, the long-term stability of the caregiver–infant relationship is an important variable that relates to child outcome. Infants and toddlers do better if caregivers are consistent. Children spend more directed time and have better language skills when the attachment aspect of child care is not at issue (Howes, 1992).

Parent-Educator Roles

The respective roles and expectations of parents and teachers or caregivers are much clearer with older preschool-age children than with infants and toddlers. With older children, parents are expected to provide love and affection, while teachers and caregivers provide support and stimulation. With infants and toddlers, the role distinctions are much less clear. Infants and toddlers need respect,

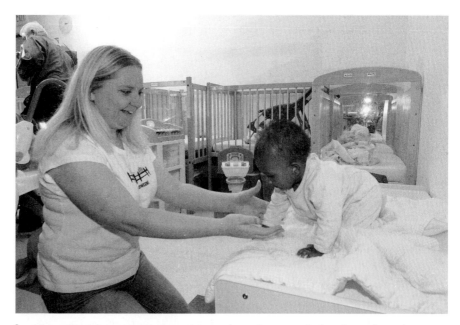

Sensitive, responsive, supportive caregivers make early care and education a place where infants can grow and thrive.

love, caring, and affection from all caregivers. Conflicts between parents and teachers may be based on this role confusion and the assumption that the traditional roles that educators play with older children are the same with infants and toddlers. Although caregivers do not usurp a parent's role, optimal child development requires a strong, loving relationship between infants and toddlers and their nonparental caregivers.

Parents and caregivers both approach the caregiving situation with expectations about their roles. Information must be communicated about these roles. As a parent places an infant or toddler in an early care and education setting, she may feel that caregivers are evaluating her as a parent and vice versa (Gestwicki, 2004). This influences the information each chooses to share. This may be a stressful time for a parent, as she attempts to help her child adjust to a care situation while experiencing pressure in returning to the "regular" work routine and adjusting to the added responsibility that an infant entails. Parents need support during this transition.

Parents want to know about the child from the caregiver's perspective, and caregivers need to know about the child from a parent's perspective to collaborate effectively. Good communication skills are essential for this exchange, whether they are used in a parent-teacher conference, on home visits, talking with parents about concerns, or providing information. Developing clear and open lines of communication and being specific about the roles that are expected of parents and caregivers benefit everyone. During the infant and toddler years, the distinctions between caregiving and parenting roles are overlapping, and may cause additional stress if they are not acknowledged.

Parents may worry that their child will love the caregiver more than them (Gestwicki, 2004). Parents play all roles related to the care and education of their child. For parents, having children is a marathon. They are in it for the long haul, and may have to pace themselves and balance concerns related to other children in the family, marital relationships, work, and other issues. Parents are expected to love their children unconditionally and to favor their child and to look out for him. Parents may find the level of the caregiver's emotional involvement a concern. They may also feel ambivalent or guilty about leaving their child in the care of someone else (Gestwicki, 2004).

Early childhood professionals interact with infants and toddlers only in the classroom or child care setting. They may see the child from the perspective of a sprinter. Their involvement is shorter; thus, what is not accomplished immediately may be gone forever. They may feel strongly about the infants and toddlers they care for, which can be problematic if their views differ from those of the parents. Caregivers are expected to love and care for young children but also remain somewhat removed and objective. They are expected to show no favoritism for a particular child. Caregivers sometimes feel that parents believe that their child is the only important child in the classroom (Gestwicki, 2004).

The differences in roles, as well as the ambiguity of the roles for early childhood professionals, may be a source of tension. Teachers in child care settings feel that they work very hard but that this is not appreciated by parents. Such feelings can cause tension in the parent and caregiver relationship.

Parental Stressors

Parents and teachers typically see each other at their worst times: in the morning when parents are trying to get to work on time, and at the end of the workday when they are both tired from a day's work and are going home to the "second shift." Some aspects of jobs increase parental stress. The more hours parents work, the more likely they are to feel conflict between their job and family responsibilities. Parents with little control over scheduling their work hours experienced more stress, as did parents with demanding, hectic jobs. When supervisors are not supportive of work/family needs, there is likely to be lower job satisfaction and a higher degree of stress (Galinsky, 1988).

Parents of young children may feel insecure about their parenting skills as they try to decide how to respond to the demands of their rapidly changing infant or toddler. They may also feel very possessive of their infant and are not sure they want to entrust anyone else with his care. They may not want their infant to form a strong attachment to the caregiver, as this makes them feel more insecure. They may even feel jealous of the caregiver who spends so much time with their child. Placing an infant or toddler in an early care and education setting may be very stressful for parents. According to Brazelton (1992), parents may protect themselves by not forming an attachment to their infant because it will hurt too much when they are not with the infant, or they may grieve, which may be displayed as blame, anger, guilt, or helplessness. Child care providers may interpret these behaviors very differently.

Early Childhood Educator Stressors

Early childhood educators experience stress from working long hours, and they feel more stressed when parents are detained or are unavoidably late at the end of the day. Taking care of infants and toddlers is physically demanding and hard work. It requires knowledge, intelligence, flexibility, creativity, and caring. While trying to be helpful to parents and responsive to their children, some caregivers begin to feel burned out as they find themselves trying to be "all things to all people" (Galinsky, 1988, p. 6). Staff working relationships are important to the health and well-being of caregivers. The same ambiguity about roles that affects parents also affects early childhood educators.

Some early childhood professionals feel that parents who leave children in care so they can work may think that caring for young children is not important—if it were important, then mothers would stay home with their children. Likewise, some caregivers feel that parents who leave their young children in care are abandoning them. These judgments get in the way of caregiving. If your personal philosophy includes feelings such as these, then you might want to care only for older children or find an aspect of the profession that does not include working directly with parents of infants and toddlers.

A provider's feeling that her work is not appreciated is further complicated by society's evaluation of the job status of those who care for infants and toddlers. This low job status with high levels of responsibility and low pay causes stress. As caregivers evaluate the differences in financial status between themselves and the parents, they may feel resentful that some parents are willing to spend money on a new car or expensive home, but are not willing to pay more for child care (Galinsky, 1988).

Early care and education professionals often receive little training in how to work with parents. This means that when everything is going well, there are few perceived communication problems. However, when there is a conflict with parents, caregivers have few skills to resolve these conflicts. Adults typically rely on methods that result in verbal aggression and defending, withdrawal without resolution, or blaming. Particularly if a teacher has had a difficult day, she does not want to take it out on the child but may well blame the child's parents or any available parent (Galinsky, 1988).

Although teachers may not do it openly, many of them make judgments about the parents of the children they care for. Generally, parents held in low esteem were those who limited their conversations with staff to talk about their children and were more authoritarian in controlling their children. They were also more likely to be single minority parents with low incomes. These parents are likely to be the most stressed, have the fewest resources, and in most need of social support. They are the least likely to receive support from the early care and education system (Kontos & Wells, 1986).

Parents and caregivers come with a history that needs to be acknowledged. Each has concerns, a perspective about the cause of those concerns, and some potential solutions. The communication skills of the teacher can exacerbate or allay these underlying tensions. Communication is the key to successful collaboration (Berger, 2004).

The quality issue does not appear to be what standards should be set, or whether parents or professionals should decide on the standards. Rather, the problem focuses on the cost of implementing those standards to provide quality child care that is affordable.

COST OF QUALITY CHILD CARE

Do parents with the most resources actually get the best child care? Is good child care basically dependent on the ability to pay? Family factors heavily affect child care outcomes for infants and toddlers. Table 9–10 provides information on what good experiences in early care and education are related to.

Even for parents with many resources, success in obtaining high-quality child care depends partly on luck; that is, finding the setting of choice in an acceptable location that has an opening for the age level of the infant or toddler who needs care. In general, families with the fewest resources have the most problematic child outcomes.

Research has shown a relationship between high-quality child care and cost. In 2006, high-quality care for infants and toddlers cost $200 to $260 per week in many communities. In Fairfax county Virginia, family child care for an infant was $180 to $200 a week and center care was $228 to $247. Assuming the cost is $225 per week the annual cost is $11,700 (Office of Children, 2007). The average cost for full-time infant care in Massachusetts was $13,480. However in the Boston area fees were $27,637 annually. (Contrast this with the average tuition at a public University in Massachusetts, which is $5,660.) These costs are out of reach for most families, particularly those with more than one child in care and for single-parent families. Comparing **accredited** program with those that were unaccredited, on average accredited programs cost $5,000 more annually (National Association of Child Care Resource and Referral Agencies (NACCRRA), 2006).

Child care costs vary by region and by age of the child (see Table 9–11).

One can also look at cost by the age of the child and type of care (see Table 9–12). Looking at these figures one might be tempted to decide that moving to the South would be a good idea. The reason costs are so much lower is the infant-to-staff ratio. In Massachusetts the infant care ratio is one caregiver

Accreditation
is a measure of quality that child care centers or family child care homes meet standardized criteria for quality.

Table 9–10 Characteristics of Families with Good Experiences in Early Care and Education

Parental knowledge of child development, which influences their choice of settings.
Family income, which allows them to choose among settings based on variables such as quality programs.
Stress levels, which are usually lower when parents have more resources.
Child-rearing values and practices, which usually coincide more with what early childhood professionals consider to be best practice in early care and education.

SOURCE: Howes (1992).

Table 9–11 Monthly Child Care Costs by Region and Age

Region	Infant	Toddler/Preschooler
Northeast	$794	$649
South	$479	$391
Midwest	$592	$476
West	$574	$463

SOURCE: NACCRRA (2006).

Table 9–12 Annual Cost of Child Care for Infants or Toddler and Preschool Children by Type of Setting

Type of Setting	Infants or Toddlers High	Infants or Toddler Low	Preschoolers High	Preschoolers Low
Family Child Care Homes	$13,100	$2,236	$8,761	$2,080
Child Care Centers	$16,061	$3,874	$9,874	$3,640

SOURCE: NACCRRA (2006).

for each three infants (1:3). In Arkansas and Georgia the ratio is one caregiver for each six infants (1:6). The NAEYC recommends either 1:3 or 1:4, depending on how many children are in the room (Willer, 1990).

According to the U.S. Department of Education (2001), child care costs in center-based programs for an infant or toddler averaged from $74 to $100 per week. Preschool costs averaged between $52 and $59 per week. On an annual basis most families pay between $4,000 and $6,000 per year for their infant and toddler care.

Child care is only one cost for families. Families who live below the poverty level spend 25 percent of their monthly income on child care, whereas those who made 200 percent above the poverty line or higher spend 6.5 percent of their income on child care (Johnson, 2005). This assumes that there is only one child in care. Obviously costs are higher when there are more children.

To move from a system of "barely adequate care" to one of "high-quality care" basically doubles to triples the cost of child care. The money goes into increasing the salaries of caregivers and lowering the teacher–child ratio. The result of low pay is a decline in the consistency and quality of care and high teacher turnover. Understandably, individuals with college degrees and experience in caring for infants and toddlers are not attracted to employment in most child care settings.

In 1992 the NAEYC reaffirmed its commitment to addressing the problem of inadequate compensation. "This statement affirmed that inadequate compensation, low status, and poor working conditions in many early childhood programs are rooted in three interconnected needs: *quality for children, equitable compensation for staff, and affordability for families*" (NAEYC, 1992, p. 43).

Its position statement on Quality, Compensation and Affordability (NAEYC, 1995) also supports these statements. Money matters! According to the Department of Labor (2006) child care workers are in the category of Personal Care and Service Occupations. It defines their role as "Attend to children at schools, businesses, private households and child care institution. Perform a variety of tasks such as dressing, feeding, bathing, and overseeing play." As of May 2006, they had an average hourly wage of $9.05 which results in an average annual wage of $18,820. The median hourly wage was $8.48 with the lowest 10 percent earning less than $6.21 per hour and the highest 10 percent earning more than $13.31. The federal minimum wage was $5.15 an hour. Money matters because it is a statement of value. It also relates to staff turnover. Those who were paid less than $4.00 an hour left at twice the rate as those who made $6.00 per hour (Clarke-Stewart & Allhusen, 2005).

GUIDING PRINCIPLES FOR EARLY CARE AND EDUCATION

In April 1993, a voluntary partnership of national organizations joined to share information and to develop a set of guiding principles for a unified and comprehensive system of early education and child care that they all could endorse. After working for more than a year, they developed a document that was endorsed by such diverse groups as the National Association for Family Child Care, the Children's Defense Fund, Child Care Law Center, Quality 2000, and Early Childhood Policy Research (NAEYC, 1995).

The Guiding Principles for a Child Care/Early Education System (NAEYC, 1995) endorses quality community-based care and an infrastructure necessary to support it, including a range of quality services, a well-compensated staff, and affordable prices for families. The principles affirm that child care and early education are a shared responsibility among the public and private sectors and families and providers. Table 9–13 highlights these underlying principles.

These principles reflect underlying concerns about quality and availability of child care. Quality is a relative concept, not an objective reality. Quality is also a dynamic concept that changes over time. Different stakeholders define

Table 9–13 Guiding Principles for an Early Care and Education System

- Families should be able to choose from a variety of diverse early care and education options, and have the primary voice in planning and delivery of services for their children.

- All options should be high quality with culturally competent, well-trained, stable staff who work with children in safe, healthy, age- and developmentally appropriate environments.

- Government regulation should serve as a consumer protection mechanism.

- Communities should offer a continuum of services beginning with parenting education and through supports for adolescents. Communities need to meet and serve families needs differently over time. Systems should be responsive to the unique needs of their community.

- The early care and education system should be integrated with other family support programs and should include children with disabilities and children from all income levels. It must provide resources and referrals, community planning, ongoing assessment, and evaluation.

- Leadership and staffing of the early care and education system should reflect the diversity of families in the community and nation. The staff should have adequate salaries that reward training, fringe benefits, effective mentoring, and career development opportunities. Leadership development should be promoted at all levels.

- Early care and education systems must be financed from multiple sources to provide high quality regardless of what families can afford to pay.

SOURCE: NAEYC (1995).

quality differently; quality has become an international buzzword. The quality of child care directly affects the welfare of children in care.

There is particular concern about the quality of care for children in the lowest income groups. They begin kindergarten with fewer pre-reading and pre-math skills than their middle-class peers This gap is greatest for minority children from low-income families. These differences are apparent by age 3 (Haskins & Rouse, 2005).

IMPACT OF CHILD CARE ON INFANT'S AND TODDLER'S DEVELOPMENT

Being in child care has an effect on children's development. However, it is difficult to determine exactly what that effect is for an individual child. Researchers interpret the data differently and have come to different conclusions about the impact of child care on infants and toddlers. In addition, we typically compare mothers who stay at home with their children to mothers who are employed and have their children in a child care setting. The differences we see are usually solely attributed to child care. However, the impact of maternal employment is rarely dealt with—but this is a confounding variable. Another concern is that the centers studied are biased toward high-quality centers, particularly those sponsored by universities.

Child care affects infants. When programming is developmentally appropriate and there is a specifically designated caregiver, the prospects are positive.

Studies of the impact of child care on infant and toddler development show some trends, but the studies are less conclusive than those with preschool children. Overall, child care offers opportunities for motor and physical development that children would not get in their own homes. It also exposes children to germs and illnesses. There is some concern about chronic ear infections with infants and toddlers that could lead to later language delays (Clarke-Stewart & Allhusen, 2005). Child care centers or family child care homes that have fewer children and that follow strict personal hygiene procedures may solve this problem.

Social class interacts with the impact of child care on infants and toddlers. A longitudinal study of 867 children in care during their first three years found that the effects of child care varied with the income level of the family. For infants from lower-income families, early care was associated with higher reading scores. Infants who were in center-based care also scored higher in mathematics. For middle- and upper-income children, the results are more variable. Children who began child care before one year, for example, were doing less well (Caughy, DiPietro, & Strobino, 1994). It appears that child care has the ability to compensate for the home environment of low-income children. However, entering care during infancy was not associated with gains for middle- and higher-income children, and in some cases the results were lower. When family income, mother's verbal ability, and positive parenting were controlled, children in child care were doing about the same in areas of intellectual development as child with exclusive maternal care. Advantages that were found were only for children in child care centers. Positive results occurred most frequently for children in high-quality model programs (Clarke-Stewart & Allhusen, 2005).

Quality matters. Infants and toddlers in high-quality settings did well. When caregivers were responsive and sensitive, children's scores in cognition and language went up. The frequency of language stimulation was particularly important during the first two years. There also an association between child care centers that meet standards and positive child outcomes (NICHD Early Child Care Research Network, 2005).

up **close** and **personal**

I know that I am a worrier, and one of the things I worried about a lot was placing Graciela in child care. I am the major breadwinner in the family and I had to go back to work. We found ways of dealing with things until Graciela was two months old. I think exhaustion was what drove us. I didn't want to face it, but I knew it was inevitable, so I visited a lot of child care settings. I went to those close to our home and those close to my work. I was appalled at many of them. At first I thought family child care was the way to go, but it was so dependent on one person. I wondered what would happen when I wasn't there. Graciela was there all alone. I finally began looking at centers. There was one new center that I decided on. It looked safe and clean and the adults seemed to genuinely like the children. But what I liked most was that for $10 a month I could have online access to real-time video of what was going on in Graciela's room. I could see her sleep and watch her play and really keep an eye on things. I worry less because I can take a break and check on her from my office. My mother checks on her as well. This has really made a difference to me.

REFLECTIVE PRACTICE

How would you feel about working in a center that had online real-time video? Do you think this is over the top? Do parents have any worries about their children in care? What criteria did this mother use to choose a center? Would you have reached the same conclusion?

The implications of child care for social and emotional development are less clear cut and are prone to different interpretations. Some studies have shown that preschool children in child care are more socially competent. They are more outgoing, assertive, self-sufficient, helpful, cooperative, and verbally expressive. Overall, infants and toddlers who were in child care showed some advantages in social competence, but this was not consistent across all assessments (Clarke-Stewart & Allhusen, 2005). Other data finds these children less polite, louder, more boisterous and rebellious, more likely to use profane language, and more aggressive. Interestingly, these data are not contradictory but reflect the experiences of two different groups of children. Apparently child care promotes social advancement in some children and behavior problems in others. The children whose social skills were developed also scored higher on tests of cognitive ability than children who displayed more negative social behaviors (Clarke-Stewart & Allhusen, 2005). Sensitive and responsive caregivers were also associated with positive skilled peer interactions. Apparently children in child care become more positive in their social play between 24 and 36 months. The child's experience in the family seems to be more important in explaining early social and emotional development than whether or not the infant or toddler was cared for routinely by someone other than his mother. Children who spent 45 hours of every week in child care for the first five years have a chance of becoming more aggressive and disobedient than those who spent less time in child care (Clarke-Stewart & Allhusen, 2005). The NICHD Early Child Care Research Network (2005) also found that infants and toddlers who spent more hours in child care had elevated levels of problem at age 4 ½.

The research that focuses solely on infants is less conclusive. There has been debate about whether or not child care is good for infants or whether it places them at risk for emotional insecurity and social maladjustment if they are separated from their mother for 8 to 10 hours a day (Clarke-Stewart & Allhusen, 2005). The standard way of evaluating attachment between infants and their mothers is the Ainsworth Strange Situation. Some researchers have questioned the validity of the Strange Situation for children in child care because they are accustomed to separations and reunions with their mother. Modifications were made in the procedure and the conclusion reached that child care does not lead to insecure attachment (Clarke-Stewart & Allhusen, 2005).

Most parents enroll their infants in child care before their first birthday, and of these children 75 percent enter before four months of age (NICHD Early Child Care Research Network, 1997). Belsky (1992) sees the age of entrance into care as a critical variable in the impact of child care. Being under one year of age when enrolled and being in nonparental care for more than 20 hours a week were seen as indicators of insecure attachment. His interpretation of the relative amount of insecure attachment moves from approximately 25 percent for young children in less than 20 hours of nonparental care, to about 40 percent for infants with more than 20 hours of care, to more than 60 percent for maltreated infants (Belsky, 1992). Belsky concludes that the detrimental consequences of poor-quality child care are greatest when such care is initiated in the first year of life (Belsky, 1992). He also found poor infant child care associated with attachment insecurity, aggression, and noncompliance. Other studies have not reached the same conclusions. They have found no consistent negative effects of infant child care on intellectual development, social competence, or attachment (Clarke-Stewart & Allhusen, 2005).

Overall, the evidence suggests that infants and toddlers are most likely to have positive and pleasant experiences in high-quality child care with sensitive and responsive caregivers. Centers that have higher-quality care include publicly sponsored centers, worksite centers, and centers with public funding tied to licensing standards—all have access to extra financial resources that they use to improve quality. High-quality centers hire educated staff and pay good wages that attract and retain good teachers, ensure that there are enough adults to pay close and caring attention to infants and toddlers, and train and retain competent directors.

The consequences of child care on development are not clear. However, no overall negative effects have been consistently documented. When well done child care holds the potential for having important gains for some children and providing consistent quality for others. Individual child differences play a role in the impact of child care, as does the quality of the care itself (Clarke-Stewart & Allhusen, 2005). Child care is and will continue to be a part of the way most children grow up. Professionals in early childhood continue to press for increasing the quality of child care to improve child outcomes and the need for federal regulation and a coordinated system for the delivery of services. The potential is there; the realization is not.

THE FEDERAL GOVERNMENT'S ROLE IN EARLY CARE AND EDUCATION

Although policy decisions about providing care for young children are provocative and bring forth deep-seated sentiments about the role of government and family, many laws that are passed both directly and indirectly affect child care programs. Many federal programs impact child care. Many programs provide subsidies in some specific formula to help defray the cost of child care for particular groups. In an effort to deal with child care in a more responsive, coordinated, systematic way, in January 1995, the federal government created the Child Care Bureau within the Administration for Children, Youth, and Families, which is part of the Department of Health and Human Services.

The primary government program for child care is a federal-to-state grant called the Child Care and Development Block Grant. Funding for this grant has been frozen since 2002. The process that families must go through to become eligible is also an obstacle (NACCRRA, 2006). Additionally, some child care settings will not accept **purchase of care** because it is usually far less than the cost of the care. For example, the cost of caring for a toddler might be $125 a week, but purchase of care pays only $75 a week. The child care setting either absorbs the cost or families must pay the difference.

Purchase of care is a voucher that eligible families receive to pay for child care.

Every state government has both federal and state funds for child care assistance. As of 2005, 17 states had waiting lists for this assistance (NACCRRA, 2006). Child care is a catch-22. Parents need child care so they can work, but child care consumes such a large part of the budget that they must decrease other household expenses to afford it. Child care is expensive, just like college. However, there are no scholarships or loans, and the price of child care is paid for by the parents, except for those who are eligible for government subsidies (purchase of care). The Center for Law and Social Policy estimated that 14 percent of children who were federally eligible for child care subsides received them in 2000; about one child in seven (Mezey, Greenberg, & Schumacher, 2002).

Infants and toddler care and education is not one the priorities of the federal government. The federal government budget allocate nearly seven times as much money per child for K–12 schooling as for prekindergarten (pre-K) early education and child care subsidies for three- to five-year-olds. U.S. Budget, Fiscal Year 2005, the United States now spends more than $530 billion a year on elementary and secondary schooling for children aged five and older and only about $18 billion on the Head Start program and child care subsidies, most of which go to preschoolers (Besharov, 2002).

Many see the goal for the federal government to look beyond the requirements of the child care necessary for the recipients of Temporary Aid for Needy

Families (TANF) to developing a shared vision of good child care choices for all families (Greenberg, 2007).

The federal government also sets regulations that affect who is included or excluded from child care. Legislation such as the Americans with Disabilities Act (ADA) supports the inclusion of children with disabilities in all child care settings. Additional support for inclusion is provided by the Individuals with Disabilities Education Improvement Act (IDEA) (2004). The intention of this legislation is that infants and toddlers with disabilities will be cared for in early care and education settings in their own neighborhoods, just like their siblings.

INCLUDING INFANTS AND TODDLERS WITH DEVELOPMENTAL DELAYS

Inclusion
supports having infants and toddlers in any setting they would expect to be in if they did not have a disability.

More early care and education programs include infants and toddlers with developmental delays and with diagnosed disabilities. **Inclusion** values the rights of all infants and toddlers to participate in natural settings within their communities. This includes early care and education settings. That is, infants and toddlers with developmental delays and disabilities can play and learn with their peers. Inclusive programs help all children understand diversity and become more accepting of those who are different from them (Han, Ostrosky, & Diamond, 2006).

There are many successful models for including infants and toddlers with disabilities in child care settings. The Bank Street Family Center uses a mixed age group of children six months to three years in groups of no more than 10, with one or two children with disabilities included (Balaban, 1992). Some programs such as Delaware FIRST and DelCare use a consultation model and invest heavily in both pre-service and in-service training for family and center care providers, whereas the Day Care Training Project in Connecticut developed a model curriculum for including children with special needs in child care (Bruder, Deiner, & Sachs, 1992). The issues around care for these infants and toddlers are the same issues that relate to quality of care for all children.

It comes back to teacher preparation and group size. When caregivers are well trained in early childhood education and early childhood special education and group size is small. Inclusion can be a positive experience for all.

WORK/FAMILY AND EARLY CARE AND EDUCATION

In the past the expectation was that an individual's work and personal life were separate. Studies of absenteeism have shown that this expectation is unrealistic. Causes of absenteeism include such things as staying home to care for a sick child, finding child care, and the breakdown of child care arrangements. Women are more likely to stay home than men. Economically, it makes sense for the woman to take the day off without pay if she earns less money than her spouse.

Work/family issues have become part of the total caregiving picture and these issues highlight the need for more reliable and responsive child care. **Dual-earner families** are the direct result of more women in the work force. With a 50 percent divorce rate, dual-earner families can turn into single-parent families. Work/family conflicts cause stress in most families with single working parents or dual-earner families. Some stress results from worrying about their child in child care. Some stress results from working more. Stress varies from day to day. When employed mothers have a high-stress workday they tend to withdraw from the family when they get home (Perry-Jenkins & Turner, 2004).

Large employers have taken the lead in improving their employees' access to affordable, quality child care. Initially, most employers used strategies, such as **Resource and Referral (R&R) services**, which helps employees locate child care, making **dependent care tax credits** available so child care may be paid with pretax dollars, or even an on-site center. Companies are beginning to develop more integrated approaches to work/family benefits that include adoption subsidies, creating and monitoring the quality of child care settings, training providers, and so on. Some companies are creating family-friendly workplaces. These companies provide a variety of innovative programs, such as family specialist hotlines, alternative work schedules (job sharing, working at home, compressed work weeks), and even seminars to sensitize management to work and family issues (Research and Policy Committee of the Committee for Economic Development, 1993). *Working Mother* is a magazine that rates companies based on their family-friendly policies.

Although many companies are responsive to their changing workforce and work/family issues, others do not acknowledge the obvious overlap and interaction among the work system, the family system, and the early care and education system. Something as simple as the particular hours that parents work or having to work overtime influences when they need child care. The interactions of work, family, and early care and education systems should be viewed as dynamic because a change in one greatly affects satisfaction with the others. For example, a change in work hours may not be accommodated by an existing child care arrangement or the addition of a new baby, or a change in work location may make an existing child care arrangement less satisfactory. Families might need to change what had previously been a satisfactory care arrangement in response to these situations. For infants and toddlers as well as families these changes are stressful and disruptive.

Dual-earner families are those in which both partners work.

R&R services help parents identify possible child care settings that fit their criteria.

Dependent care tax credit allows parents to allocate pretax dollars to pay for child care.

Parental Leave

In an effort to deal with some of the problems related to work/family issues, the Family and Medical Leave Act (FMLA) was passed in 1993. This federal legislation requires employers of 50 or more people to provide eligible employees 12 weeks of unpaid leave to care for a newborn infant with their job guaranteed at the end of this period and with a continuation of existing health benefits.

The FMLA is a step toward promoting parental care for newborns, but it only covers about half of the workforce. In addition, the unpaid nature of the leave does not solve the problem that most parents cannot afford to be without income for that length of time. Needing income, many parents return to work before the period of the leave is up.

PERSONNEL PREPARATION

The concept of professionalism can be used to distinguish between individuals who are engaged in an occupation and those who do similar tasks in a nonvocational way. Both parents and other adults care for infants on a regular basis. However, practitioners who work in early care and education are considered professionals, whereas parents are not. This concept, as defined, is unrelated to either skill or training.

Personnel preparation for those who work with infants and toddlers is considered part of early childhood education. Early childhood is usually defined as birth through eight years. Many different types of programs in early care and education include infants and toddlers, which include a variety of professionals within each type of program. This variety confounds the problem of a professional identity. Are we talking about child care providers, infant and toddler teachers, preschool teachers, early interventionists, educarers, or early care and education practitioners? Are we preparing individuals to work with children based on the projected need?

Regardless of label, looking at the age of children with whom these child care providers work is enlightening. Of paid child care providers 29 percent care for infants (0 to 18 months), 49 percent toddlers (19 to 36 months), and 22 percent preschool (3 to 5 years) children (Burton et al., 2002). At first glance one might question these figures, with some thought they make sense. Families in general are more reluctant to put young infants in child care and on a short-term basis they may figure out arrangements that keep young infants out of care. Relatives may be willing to watch nonmobile infants, parents might work part-time and through arrangements such as these fewer infants are in care. Overall, more toddlers are in care making sense of why the number went up. But why so many more toddler teachers than preschool. It goes back to the teacher–child ratios. NAEYC recommendations, depending upon group size, vary from 1 adult to 3 or 4 young toddlers with no more than 12 children in a group to 1 adult to 6 or 7 older toddlers and group sizes no larger than 14. Many child care settings do not following these guidelines, however, the reason for the need for so many toddler teachers is obvious. This is also why programs charge more for younger children. Caregiving skills for this age group should be a major focus of education and professional development.

High-quality early childhood education programs improve outcomes for children in school and in the community. Researchers estimate that for a few intensive early childhood programs the long-term benefits are as much as $8 to $14 for each dollar spent (Duncan, Ludwig, & Magnuson, 2007). The key to these programs included small child to teacher ratios, small class sizes and teachers who had college degrees, at least a bachelors degree.

Educational Attainment of Child Care Workforce

There is concern about the lack of requirements of those who teach in early childhood education that is not part of the public school system. Public school teachers are required to have a bachelor's degree and education in the disciplines in which they teach. Of those who teach or work as administrators in early care and education settings 2000–2004, 30 percent have a bachelor's degree or more. For those in home-based child care (family/group child care home or those who work in private homes) 11 percent have a bachelor's degree, 32 percent some college, and 56 percent high school or less (Herzenberg, Price, & Bradley, 2005).

Qualifications of those working in early care and education settings is low and has been decreasing over the past 30 years (see Table 9–14). These figures are only for teachers and administrators; they do not include paraeducators and other staff.

The problem is money. Teachers and administrators in early childhood education centers with a bachelor's degree earn only 52 percent of the median wage of other female college graduates ($10.00 compared to $19.23). In addition, two-thirds of female college graduates have employer-provided health insurance,

Table 9–14 Educational Attainment of Teachers and Administrators in Center-Based Early Childhood Settings: 1984 and 2004

Level of Education	1984	2004
High school or less	3%	4%
Twelfth grade	18%	26%
Some college	33%	41%
Bachelor's degree or higher	47%	30%

SOURCE: Herzenberg et al. (2005).

only a third of center-based teachers and administrators have job related health insurance. One in five have center sponsored pensions (Herzenberg et al., 2005).

Several professional organizations have issued a joint position paper on personnel standards for individuals working in early childhood and early childhood special education. This shared vision was developed over three years and recommends (a) a common core of knowledge and skills needed by all early childhood educators, and (b) a specific set of knowledge and skills that expands upon and exceeds the common core in relationship to children with significant learning needs (Smith, 1995, p. 2). The common core was developed by the NAEYC and endorsed by the Division for Early Childhood (DEC) of the Council for Exceptional Children and the Association of Teacher Educators (ATE).

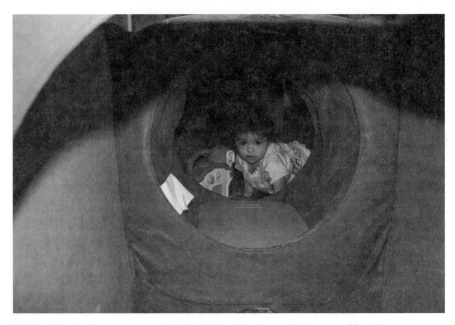

Adults design environments to promote children's active engagement and learning.

Personnel Standards

The Division of Early Childhood developed a set of standards that identify the knowledge and skills necessary for those who want to work in settings that include children with disabilities: *DEC recommended practices: A comprehensive guide for practical application in early intervention/early childhood special education* (Sandall, Hemmeter, Smith, & McLean, 2005). DEC believes that infants and toddlers are so different from older children that they need their own recommended practices. These recommended practices are evidence based. They address recommendations for five **direct service** strands and two strands of indirect support. There are 240 recommended practices in all (Sandall et al., 2005). These

Direct services are those practices which affect children on a person to person level.

are briefly detailed in Table 9–15. Two important areas that are not identified as strands but are embedded in each strand include cultural and linguistic sensitivity and the learning environment.

REFLECTIVE PRACTICE

If you are currently in a program that prepares students to work in inclusive settings with infants and toddlers, look the requirements for professional preparation and evaluate your own knowledge and program against these standards.

Table 9–15 Recommended Practices in Early Intervention

1. Assessment

   Professionals and families collaborate in planning and implementing assessment.

   Assessment is individualized and appropriate for the child and family.

   Assessment provides useful information for intervention.

   Professionals share information in respectful and useful ways.

   Professionals meet legal and procedural requirements and meet *Recommended Practice Guidelines*.

2. Child-Focused Practices

   Adults design environments to promote children's safety, active engagement, learning, participation, and membership.

   Adults use ongoing data to individualize and adapt practices to meet each child's changing needs.

   Adults use systematic procedures within and across environments, activities, and routines to promote children's learning and participation.

3. Family-Based Practices

   Families and professionals share responsibility and work collaboratively.

   Practices strengthen family functioning.

   Practices are individualized and flexible.

   Practices are strength based and asset based.

4. Interdisciplinary Models

   Teams, which include family members, make decisions and work together.

   Professionals cross disciplinary boundaries.

   Intervention is focused on function, not services.

   Regular caregivers and regular routines provide the most appropriate opportunities for children's learning and receiving most other interventions.

(continues)

5. Technology Applications

Professionals utilize assistive technology in intervention programs for children.

Families and professionals collaborate in planning and implementing the use of assistive technology.

Families and professionals use technology to access information and support.

Training and technical support programs are available to support technology.

Indirect supports are those activities that allow for high-quality direct services to happen.

6. Policies, Procedures, and Systems Change

Families and professionals shape policy at the national, state, and local levels.

Public policies promote the use of *Recommended Practices.*

Program policies and administration promote family participation in decision making.

Program policies and administration promote the use of *Recommended Practices.*

Program policies and administration promote interagency and interdisciplinary collaboration.

Program policies, administration, and leadership promote program evaluation and systems change efforts.

7. Personnel Preparation

Families are involved in learning activities.

Learning activities are interdisciplinary and interagency.

Learning activities are systematically designed and sequenced.

Learning activities include the study of cultural and linguistic diversity.

Learning activities and evaluation procedures are designed to meet the needs of students and staff.

Field experiences are systematically designed and supervised.

Faculty and other personnel trainers are qualified and well-prepared for their role in personnel preparation.

Professional development (in-service) activities are systematically designed and implemented.

SOURCE: Sandall et al. (2005).

SUMMARY

Child care grew out of the child welfare system, whereas nursery school grew out of education. As these concepts have merged child care has clearly become educational in orientation. There are many different types of nonparental care: relative care, family child care, child care centers, and other possible care arrangements.

Overall, we are concerned about the quality of child care and the impact that child care has on infants and toddlers. Although parents and professionals see quality in early care and education differently, they agree that children need safe, healthy environments in which to grow and learn. The cost of child care is high, so high that some families cannot afford good child care. There is often tension between the demands of work, child care arrangements, and the necessity of managing the home environment.

CHAPTER IN REVIEW

※ Child care is a reality and families choose from a variety of options as they consider care for their infant or toddler. Family resources, both human and financial, affect their decision relative to type of care.

※ Professionals and parents do not agree on what constitutes high-quality child care. Parents are more concerned with their own child and his individual teacher, whereas professionals are more concerned with teacher preparation, group size, regulations and licensing, and the curriculum that is planned for the children.

※ Child care is viewed in an ecological framework that includes work/family issues. Businesses and corporations are becoming more involved in child care. High-quality care is expensive. Costs would double or triple if care were brought up to a level recommended by early childhood professional organizations.

※ There is no comprehensive national system of child care; however, the government plays a role in providing child care subsidies

※ Infants and toddlers with disabilities are included child care settings.

APPLICATION ACTIVITIES

1. You are a parent of an infant and you must return to work when she is six months old. Decide on the type of setting you will use and what you will look for when you visit possible sites. What will be the basis of your decision regarding her placement?

2. There is concern about consequences of child care for infants. How will you cope with this at a personal level? What will you do to mitigate the negative effects, if any?

3. You are campaigning for election to the U.S. House of Representatives in your district. Describe your child care platform and how you will market it.

4. Go to the *Working Mother* Web site at http://vebranch.rgisolutions.com/web?service-vpage/106 and look at the top 100 companies rated as the most working-mother friendly. Look at the options these companies offer and decide which are the most important to you and why.

RESOURCES

Web Resources

※ The **Division for Early Childhood of the Council for Exceptional Children** offers recommended practices as well as a video to show how these practices can be implemented. www.dec-sped.org.

※ The **National Association of Child Care Resource and Referral Agencies** provides information on child care by state and serves as an advocate for high-quality child care. http://www.naccrra.org.

※ The **National Network for Child Care** has practical information and resources for working with children and parents. http://www.nncc.org.

☀ **Teaching for Change: Building social justice starting in the classroom** provides resources for early childhood equity in the form of books, articles, videos, and posters for children and teachers. http://www.teachingforchange.org.

☀ The **U.S. Department of Health and Human Services**, Administration for Children and Families has information about child care and child care subsidies at http://www.acf.hhs.gov.

Print Resources

☀ Annie E. Casey Foundation. (2006). *Kids count data book: State profiles of child well-being.* Baltimore, MD: Author.

☀ Clarke-Stewart, A., & Allhusen, V. (2005). *What we know about childcare.* Cambridge, MA: Harvard University Press.

☀ Harms, T., Cryer, D., & Clifford, R. M. (2003). *Infant and Toddler Environmental Rating Scale (ITERS-R)* (Rev. ed.). New York: Teachers College Press.

☀ Lally, J. R. (2001). Infant care in the United States and how the Italian experience can help. In L. Gandini & C. P. Edwards (Eds.), *Bambini: The Italian approach to infant/toddler care* (pp. 15–22). New York: Teachers College, Columbia University.

☀ NICHD Early Child Care Research Network. (2005). *Child care and child development: Results from the NICHD study of early child care and youth development.* New York: The Guilford Press.

☀ Sandall, S., Hemmeter, M. L., Smith, B. J., & McLean, M. (Eds.) (2005). *DEC recommended practices: A comprehensive guide for practical application.* Longmont, CO: Sopris West Publishing Co.

REFERENCES

Americans with Disabilities Act of 1990, Pub. L. No. 101–336, § 2, 104 Stat. 328 (1991).

Annie E. Casey Foundation. (2006). *Kids count data book: State profiles of child well-being.* Baltimore, MD: Author.

Balaban, N. (1992). The role of the child care professional in caring for infants, toddlers, and their families. *Young Children, 47*(5), 66–71.

Barrera, I. (2003). From rocks to diamonds: Mining the riches of diversity for our children. *Zero to Three, 23*(5), 8–15.

Bellum, D., Breuing, G. S., Lombardi, J., & Whitebook, M. (1992). On the horizon: New policy initiatives to enhance child care staff compensation. Child Care Employee Project. *Young Children, 47*(5), 39–42.

Belsky, J. (1992). Consequences of child care for children's development: A deconstructionist view. In A. Booth (Ed.), *Child care in the 1990s: Trends and consequences* (pp. 83–94). Hillsdale, NJ: Lawrence Erlbaum Associates.

Berger, E. H. (2004). *Parents as partners in education.* Columbus, OH: Pearson Merrill Prentice Hall.

Besharov, D. J. (2002). Testimony before the Subcommittee on 21st Century Competitiveness of the Committee on Education and the Workforce. Retrieved November 10, 2007, from www.welfareacademy.org/pubs/testimony-022702.pdf

Brazelton, T. B. (1992). *Touchpoints: Your child's emotional and behavioral development.* Reading, MA: Addison-Wesley.

Bruder, M. B., Deiner, P. L., & Sachs, S. (1992). Models of integration through early intervention—Child care collaborations. In S. Provence, J. Pawl, & E. Fenichel (Eds.), *The zero to three child care anthology 1984–1992* (pp. 46–51). Arlington, VA: National Center for Clinical Infant Studies.

Burton, A., Whitebook, M., Young, M., Bellm, D., Wayne, C., Brandon, R. N., et al. (2002). Estimating the size and components of the U.S. Child care workforce and caregiving population. Retrieved November 9, 2007, from http://www.ccw.org/pbs/woprkforceestimatereport.pdf

Carnegie Task Force on Meeting the Needs of Young Children. (1994). *Starting points: Meeting the needs of our youngest children*. New York: Carnegie Corporation of New York.

Caughy, M. O., DiPietro, J. A., & Strobino, D. M. (1994). Day-care participation as a protective factor in the cognitive development of low-income children. *Child Development, 65*(2), 457–471.

Clark, L. (2003). Making new choices possible: Understanding differences in infant feeding practices between Latina mothers and Anglo health care providers. *Zero to Three, 23*(5), 22–27.

Clarke-Stewart, A., & Allhusen, V. (2005). *What we know about childcare*. Cambridge, MA: Harvard University Press.

Clarke-Stewart, K. A., Gruber, C. P., & Fitzgerald, L. M. (1994). *Children at home and in day care*. Hillsdale, NJ: Erlbaum.

Cost, Quality, and Outcomes Study Team. (1995). Cost, quality and child outcomes in child care centers: Key findings and recommendations. *Young Children, 50*(4), 40–44.

CRS Issue Brief 98010. Head Start: Background and Legislation in the 105th Congress, by Karen Spar and Molly Forman.

CRS Report 98-541. Child Care: The Role of the Federal Government, by Molly Forman and Karen Spar.

Dombro, A. L., Colker, L. J., & Dodge, D. T. (1999). *The creative curriculum for infants and toddlers* (Rev. ed.). Washington, DC: Teaching Strategies, Inc.

Duncan, G. J., Ludwig, J., & Magnuson, K. A. (2007). Reducing poverty through preschool interventions. *The Future of Children, 17*(2), 143–160.

Epstein, J., & Dauber, S. (1991). School programs and teacher practices of parent involvement in inner-city elementary and middle schools. *The Elementary School Journal, 91*, 279–289.

Galinsky, E. (1988). Parents and teacher-caregivers: Sources of tension, sources of support. *Young Children, 43*(3), 4–12.

Galinsky, E., Howes, C., Kontos, S., & Shinn, M. (1994). The study of children in family child care and relative care—Key findings and policy recommendations. *Young Children, 50*(1), 58–61.

Gamel-McCormick, M., Buell, M. J., Amsden, D., & Fahey, M. (2002). *Delaware early care and education baseline quality study*. Newark, DE: Center for Disabilities Studies.

Garcia, E. E., & Gonzalez, D. M. (2006). *Pre-K and Latinos: The foundation for America's future*. Washington, DC: Pre-K Now Research Series.

Gestwicki, C. (2004). *Home, school and community relations* (6th ed.). Clinton Park, NY: Delmar Publishers.

Greenberg, M. (2007). Next steps for federal child care policy. *The Future of Children, 17*(2), 73–96.

Han, J., Ostrosky, M. M., & Diamond, K. E. (2006). Children's attitudes toward peers with disabilities: Supporting positive attitude development. *Young Exceptional Children, 10*(1), 2–11.

Handel, G., Cahill, S., & Elkin, F. (2007). *Children and society: The sociology of children and childhood socialization*. Los Angeles, CA: Roxbury.

Harms, T., Cryer, D., & Clifford, R. M. (1990). *Infant and Toddler Environmental Rating Scale (ITERS)*. New York: Teachers College Press.

Harms, T., Cryer, D., & Clifford, R. M. (2003). *Infant and Toddler Environmental Rating Scale, Revised Edition (ITERS-R)*. New York: Teachers College Press.

Harms, T., Cryer, D., & Clifford, R. M. (2005). *Early Childhood Environment Rating Scale, Revised Edition, Updated (ECERS-R)*. New York: Teachers College Press.

Harms, T., Cryer, D., & Clifford, R. M. (2007). *Family Child Care Rating Scale, Revised Edition (FDCRS-R)*. New York: Teachers College Press.

Haskins, R., & Rouse, C. (2005). Closing the Achievement Gaps. Policy Brief, The Future of Children. Accessed May 12, 2007, from http://www.futureofchildren.org/usr_doc/Policy_Brief_Spring_2005pdf.pdf

Herzenberg, S., Price, M., & Bradley, D. (2005). *Losing ground in early childhood education: Declining workforce qualifications in an expanding industry, 1979–2004*. Washington, DC: Economic Policy Institute.

Hofferth, S. L., Brayfield, S., Deich, S., & Holcomb, P. (1991). *The National Child Care Survey 1990*. Washington, DC: The Urban Institute.

Howes, C. (1992). *The collaborative construction of pretend: Social pretend play functions*. Albany, NY: State University of New York Press.

Individuals with Disabilities Education Improvement Act of 2004, Pub. L. No. 108–446, 118 Stat 2647, 20 U. S. C. 1400. 2004

Johnson, J. O. (2005). Who is minding the kids? Child care arrangements: Winter 2002. Current Population Reports, P70-101. Washington, DC: U.S. Census Bureau. Accessed May 11, 2007, from http://www.census.gov/prod/2005pubs/p70-101.pdf

Katz, P. A. (2003). Racists or tolerant multiculturalists? How do they begin? *American Psychologist, 58*(11), 897–909.

Kontos, S. (1992). Family day care: Out of the shadows and into the limelight. Research Monograph, 5. U.S.; District of Columbia: National Association for the Education of Young Children.

Kontos, S., Howes, C., Shinn, M., & Galinsky, E. (1995). *Quality in family child care and relative care*. New York: Teachers College Press.

Kontos, S., & Wells, W. (1986). Attitudes of caregivers and the day care experiences of families. *Early Childhood Research Quarterly, 18*, 77–94.

Lally, J. R. (2001). Infant care in the United States and how the Italian experience can help. In L. Gandini & C. P. Edwards (Eds.), *Bambini: The Italian approach to infant/toddler care* (pp. 15–22). New York: Teachers College, Columbia University.

Lally, J. R., Torres, Y. L., & Phelps, P. C. (1994). Caring for infants and toddlers in groups: Necessary considerations for emotional, social and cognitive development. *Zero-to-Three, 14*(5), 1–8.

Langsted, O. (1994). Looking at quality from the child's perspective. In P. Moss & A. Pence (Eds.), *Valuing quality in early childhood services: New approaches to defining quality* (pp. 28–42). New York: Teachers College Press.

Larner, M., & Phillips, D. (1994). Defining and valuing quality as a parent. In P. Moss & A. Pence (Eds.), *Valuing quality in early childhood services: New approaches to defining quality* (pp. 43–60). New York: Teachers College Press.

Mantovani, S. (2001). Infant-toddler centers in Italy today: Tradition and innovation. In L. Gandini & C. P. Edwards (Eds.), *Bambini: The Italian approach to infant/toddler care* (pp. 23–37). New York: Teachers College, Columbia University.

Meisels, S., & Shonkoff, J. (Eds.) (1990). *Handbook of early childhood intervention*. Cambridge, MA: Cambridge University Press.

Mezey, J., Greenberg, M., & Schumacher, R. (2002). *The vast majority of federally-eligible child did not receive child care assistance in FY 2000*. Washington, DC: Center for Law and Social Policy.

Morgan, G., Azer, S. L., Costley, J. B., Elliot, K., Genser, A., Goodman, I. F., et al. (1994). Future pursuits: Building early care and education careers. *Young Children, 44*(2), 52–56.

National Association for the Education of Young Children. (1992). NAEYC Governing board reaffirms commitment to addressing inadequate compensation in early childhood programs. *Young Children, 47*(5), 43–44.

National Association for the Education of Young Children. (1995). Reaffirming a national commitment to children. *Young Children, 50*(3), 61–63.

National Association for the Education of Young Children. (2004). Critical facts about the early childhood workforce. Retrieved November 9, 2007, from http://www.naeyc.org/ece/critical/facts3.asp

National Association for Education of Young Children. (2006). Quality programs nurture relationships to enhance young children's learning. Retrieved December 2, 2006, from http://www.naeyc.org/ece/2006/05.asp

National Association of Child Care Resource and Referral Agencies (NACCRRA). (2006). Breaking the piggybank: Parents and the high price of child care. Retrieved May 11, 2007, from http://www.naccrra.org/docs/policy/breaking_the_piggy_bank.pdf

NICHD Early Child Care Research Network. (1997). Child care in the first year of life. *Merrill-Palmer Quarterly, 43*, 340–360.

NICHD Early Child Care Research Network. (1998a). Early child care and self-control, compliance and problem behavior at twenty-four and thirty-six months. *Child Development, 69*, 1145–1170.

NICHD Early Child Care Research Network. (1998b). The NICHD Study of Early Child Care. *Psychiatric Times, 15*(3), 71–72.

NICHD Early Child Care Research Network. (1998c). Relations between family predictors and child outcomes: Are they weaker for children in child care? *Developmental Psychology, 34*, 1119–1128.

NICHD Early Child Care Research Network. (2000). Characteristics and quality of child care for toddlers and preschoolers. *Applied Developmental Science, 4*, 116–135.

NICHD Early Child Care Research Network. (2002a). Child-care structure>process>outcome: Direct and indirect effects of child-care quality on young children's development. *Psychological Science, 13*, 199–206.

NICHD Early Child Care Research Network. (2002b). Early child care and children's development prior to school entry: Results from the NICHD Study of Early Child Care. *American Educational Research Journal, 39*, 133–164.

NICHD Early Child Care Research Network. (2002c). The interaction of child care and family risk in relation to child development at 24 and 36 months. *Applied Developmental Science, 6*, 144–156.

NICHD Early Child Care Research Network. (2005). *Child care and child development: Results from the NICHD study of early child care and youth development*. New York: The Guilford Press.

No Child Left Behind Act of 2001, Elementary and Secondary Education Act, Pub. L. No. 107–110 (2002).

Office of Children. (2007). Child Care Costs, Fairfax County Virginia. Retrieved November 8, 2007, from http://www.fairfaxcounty.gov/ofc/AvCostCare.htm

Perry-Jenkins, M., & Turner, E. (2004). Jobs, marriage, and parenting: Working it out in dual-earner families. In M. Coleman & L. H. Ganong (Eds.), *Handbook of contemporary families: Considering the past, contemplating the future* (pp. 155–173). Thousand Oaks, CA: Sage.

Peterson, N. L. (1987). *Early intervention for handicapped and at-risk children: An introduction to early childhood special education.* Denver, CO: Love.

Petrie, S. (2005). The work of Emmi Pikler and Magda Gerber. In S. Petrie & S. Owen (Eds.), *Authentic relationships in group care for infants and toddlers—Resources for infant educarers RIE: Principles into practice* (pp. 17–33). London and Philadelphia, PA: Jessica Kingsley Publishers.

Ramsey, P. G., & Williamson, L. R. (2003). *Multicultural education: A resource book.* New York: Garland.

Research and Policy Committee of the Committee for Economic Development. (1993). *Why child care matters: Preparing young children for a more productive America.* New York: Committee for Economic Development.

Ring, B. (2001). *The child care disaster in America: Distain or disgrace?* Hamilton, NY: Nova Science Publishers, Inc.

Sandall, S., Hemmeter, M. L., Smith, B. J., & McLean, M. (Eds.) (2005). *DEC recommended practices: A comprehensive guide for practical application.* Longmont, CO: Sopris West Publishing Co.

Smith, B. (1995). DEC issues early childhood special education personnel standards. *Communicator, 21*(3), 3.

Spodek, B., & Saracho, O. N. (1992). Child care: A look to the future. In B. Spodek & O. N. Saracho (Eds.), *Issues in child care* (pp. 187–198). New York: Teachers College Press.

Stott, F., & Halpern, R. (2003). Listening to the voices of families: Thoughts, hopes, and fears in a Latino community. *Zero to Three, 23*(5), 16–21.

Trawick-Smith, J., & Lambert, L. (1995). The unique challenges of the family child care provider: Implications for professional development. *Young Children, 50*(3), 25–32.

U.S. Department of Education. (2001). *Guide to U.S. Department of Education Programs, 2001.* Washington, DC: Author.

U.S. Department of Education, National Center for Education Statistics (NCES). (2001). *The Condition of Education 2001. NCES 2001-072.* Washington, DC: U.S. Government Printing Office.

U.S. Department of Labor. (2006). Occupational employment and wages, May 2006. Retrieved November 8, 2007, from http://www.bls.gov/oes/current/oes_nat.htm#b39-000

Van Horn, J., & Segal, P. (2003). Talk to your baby: Honoring diversity while practicing from an evidence base. *Zero to Three, 23*(5), 33–39.

Whitebook, M., Howes, C., & Phillips, D. (1990). *The National Child Care Staffing Study–Who cares? Child care teachers and the quality of care in America.* Oakland, CA: Child Care Employee Project.

Willer, B. A. (1990). Public policy report federal comprehensive child care legislation: Much success in 1989 but more work ahead in 1990. *Young Children, 45*(2), 25–27, 49.

chapter 10

Partnering with Families of Infants and Toddlers

Chapter Outline
- Theories of Working with Families
- The Changing American Family
- Continuity and Discontinuity
- Parent Education
- Working with Families in a Cultural Context
- Culturally Diverse Families
- Partnering with Diverse Families
- Communicating with Families

Families' involvement in the care and education of their infants and toddlers is not a luxury, it is essential. Partnerships between families and early childhood educators set the stage for future involvement and is necessary for young children to thrive.

Renewed interest in working with families stems from two different aspects of our society. The first is the dramatic increase of mothers of very young children in the workforce and the resultant increase of infants and toddlers in child care. The second is our growing recognition of the importance of the first three years of life, the role that family plays in those years, and society's concern about a family's ability to play that role optimally. The first concern has led to interest in parent/educator collaboration, the second to interest in parent education and strategies to support families with young children.

WHY PARTNER WITH FAMILIES OF INFANTS AND TODDLERS?

- ☼ Families' relationships with educators begin with infants and toddlers. It is up to us to set the stage for partnering with families.

- ☼ Infants and toddlers must be viewed in the context of their families where they live and grow.

- ☼ To communicate with families we need to have a better understanding of their perspective on infants and toddlers and what they value and believe.

- ☼ Culture plays an important role in child rearing and caring for infants and toddlers. To work effectively with families you need to know the extent to which families embrace their culture and to educate their infants and toddlers in ways that are compatible with their values.

- ☼ A strong partnership between parents and educators supports all children's growth and development.

Regardless of the reasons for collaboration, parents and early childhood educators deeply care about and are committed to young children. They want to support the growth and success of all the children. Parents are the experts on their infant or toddler, and early childhood educators know about child development, curriculum, and ways of helping young children learn (Davis & Yang, 2005). Children whose parents are involved in their education have higher grades and test scores, regular attendance, better social skills and behavior, and adapt well to school. Family income or background did not influence these findings (Henderson & Mapp, 2002).

To the extent that families create home environments that support learning, communicate expectations about learning, and become involved with their child's education in school, the more likely their children are to achieve (National PTA, 2000). Your ability to provide parents with developmentally appropriate practices and ideas for playing with their infants and toddlers is the first step toward their involvement in their child's education.

To teach infants and toddlers we have to know them—really know them. We need to know where they are developmentally, but we also need to know what upsets them and what comforts them, how they go to sleep and what they like when they wake up, what they like to play with and how to play with them. We also need to know about their families and what their families want and expect from us. We need to be responsive to each family's values and culture. We need to know about the communities in which families live and what this means to families relative to transportation, safe neighborhoods and parks to play in, access to grocery stores, and the languages spoken.

Theories help us organize this information and make sense out of it.

THEORIES OF WORKING WITH FAMILIES

As with other areas, theories give us a framework or model to organize our thought and actions as we thing about building partnerships with families. Some theories move us away from just looking at the infant or toddler to a broader perspective that includes families, communities, and the global world we live in.

Ecological Model

The early chapters of this book have focused on different aspects of infant and toddler development. Although there were reminders that one cannot view the infant outside of the context of his family and community, the context was not the focus. In this chapter it is.

Until recently, when we looked at infants and toddlers and focused on their families, we actually meant their mothers. Increasingly we are including fathers, siblings, and even extended family members as "family." To understand infants and toddlers, we need to broaden our scope even further and look at the ecology or context in which infants and toddlers grow and develop. Bronfenbrenner's (1979, 1989) **ecological framework** provides a model for understanding, organizing, and making sense of the information about families and early care and education settings. He has helped us see that children grow up in a complex social environment (ecology) that is embedded in a larger social system. Bronfenbrenner argues that to understand an individual infant or toddler we must also understand the components of the larger social system that impact this child and her family. Culture plays an important role in that larger social system.

Ecological framework looks at an individual in the context of his family, community, and culture, to the society and the time in which he lives.

Bronfenbrenner (1979) sees the context of development as a set of concentric circles with the infant or toddler in the center. See Figure 10–1, which graphically shows how these systems interact with and influence each other. Although you may not think that the economy of Mexico or the political system in Guatemala will influence you, they do—to the extent that a Mexican

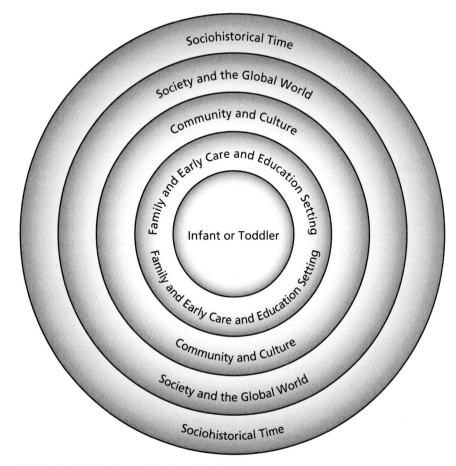

FIGURE 10–1 Ecological Model of Influence

worker earns five dollars a week and cannot feed his family influences his decisions about trying to come to the United States. Likewise, if you vocally opposed the current government, you might fear for your safety and need to leave the country

Let us start with the infant or toddler in the center. He is surrounded by his family and the early care and education setting where he spends time during the day. These are the parts of his world that he is an active part of, his face-to-face world, his **microsystem**.

At the next level, the focus is not on the family or early care and education but on the interaction between these two settings, as well as other settings in which young children participate, such as religious training, neighborhood play areas, and so on. This is called the **mesosystem**. Although the principles that Bronfenbrenner (1979) proposes apply to all relationships, the focus of this

Microsystems
are parts of system where an infant or toddler spends face-to-face time.

Mesosystems
focus on the relationships between members of the microsystem.

text will be primarily on the relationship between families and the early care and education settings. When these two systems are not interactive or connected or when there is conflict, this presents risks to the infant or toddler. For example, if a grandmother had been caring for a toddler, and the mother decided she was unhappy that her toddler spent most of his day watching television and decided to place him in an early care and education setting. There might be conflicts. These problems would be exacerbated if her son had problems adjusting to the center and the center was not responsive to or supportive of her situation, and the grandmother says, "I told you so."

Exosystems
are places where decisions are made that impact the infant or toddler indirectly through his parents or others.

Moving out to the next level, the **exosystem**, we find settings that the infant or toddler does not participate in, but someone from the child's microsystem, for example his mother, does. Let us go back to the previous example. The mother needs child care because she works. Let us say that she has been working from eight until five. She is notified that there will be a change in her work hours and she will now be working from 10 to 7. The child care center closes at six. Her boss says that if she cannot change her hours she should quit, the child care center is firm about their hours, and the grandmother, after a few choice words, is clear that she will not pick her grandson up and allow him to stay with her for the hour. She does not believe toddlers should be in child care and if that is her daughter's decision she wants no part of it. The exosystem affects infants and toddlers through others (in this example, the mother).

Macrosystems
are the attitudes, beliefs, and ideologies of a culture and how these are implemented.

The still larger system is called the **macrosystem**. The macrosystem consists of the attitudes, beliefs, and ideologies of the culture. Prevailing beliefs and practices in society at large impact families. The macrosystem also consists of the laws that govern society. For example, the Family and Medical Leave Act (FMLA) that allows some mothers to take 12 weeks of unpaid leave after the birth of a baby impacts the infant. If that infant were born in another country, the leave might be longer and paid. That would influence how soon mothers go back to work and the age at which infants enter early care and education centers.

Chronosystem
relates to time and takes into account world events.

Sociohistorical time
looks at what is happening in the world at a particular point in time.

The final system is the **chronosystem** or **sociohistorical time**. It looks at both patterns of stability and changes over time and also events (Bronfenbrenner & Morris, 1998). If this mother and toddler were seeking child care in 1940 so she could work to support the war effort, others might have found ways to be more supportive.

Bronfenbrenner also focused on the bidirectional aspect of development: Adults influence children and children influence the adults who care for them. Based on their individual traits and characteristics, children influence their environment in different ways. If the toddler I was referring to earlier were an easy going, quiet toddler, he would impact his environment very differently than if he were a difficult child with an irregular schedule who was frequently in a negative mood.

Bronfenbrenner (1979) was interested in formulating general principles or hypotheses to optimize relationships between microsystems. Although he proposed these almost 30 years ago they are still relevant today. Table 10–1 highlights his proposal.

Using Bronfenbrenner's model, it seems clear that one goal of family/educator collaboration is to look at the continuity between the home and early care and education microsystems. Of course, some discontinuity will always exist between the home and early care and education settings. We as educators need to focus on how to make the settings open to families and supportive of all infants and toddlers.

Table 10–1 Principles for Optimizing Relationships between Microsystems

- Frequent interaction and face-to-face communication between family and educators
- Communication designed to motivate and support the capacities of those who deal directly with children, not to degrade or undermine them
- Consensus on goals for children and roles for adults
- Both the family and the setting are supportive of each other, regardless of the family member's or child's competence, experience, race, or cultural background
- When a child enters a new microsystem he is accompanied by a familiar adult

SOURCE: Bronfenbrenner (1979).

THE CHANGING AMERICAN FAMILY

The days of the "Leave it to Beaver" family, with the father working and the mother at home baking cookies, while their two perfectly behaved children attend school are long gone. Today, in more than 70 percent of families, both parents work, the size of the American family has shrunk, and the divorce rate is about 50 percent.

Technology and increased population density make life more complex and impersonal. Gender roles have blurred and politicians and religious groups are questioning traditional family values. People can see this played out in debates about gay marriage, abortion, and stem cell research (McKenry & Price, 2005). Media has created images of lifestyles and expectations that may not be fulfilled. New patterns of work and leisure may increase stress, rather than reduce it. These changes in lifestyle and family structure influence infants and toddlers and they will influence your understanding of and interactions with families.

Family Structure

As shown in Table 10–2 family structure has changed dramatically since 1970. Twice as many women are in the workforce. Couples are marrying later and are choosing to cohabitate before marriage, after a divorce, or as a lifestyle choice. More women are choosing to have children outside of marriage, which has increased the number of children living with a single parent. Fewer households have children under the age of 18.

A variety of family structures are evolving in the United States because of economic and social changes and immigration patterns. In 2006, 67 percent of children lived with two parents, 23 percent lived with their mother, 5 percent lived with their father, and the remaining 5 percent lived in households with neither parent (Federal Interagency Forum on Child and Family Statistics, 2007).

Single-parent families have increased because of divorce, nonmarital child bearing and cohabitation. Most infants and toddlers raised in single-parent homes grow up healthy and happy. However, studies show that these children face more risks than others. Children raised in single-parent families face more risks than those raised in two-parent homes. Some problems relate to behavior problems, for boys particularly, externalizing problems such as aggression. Other concerns involve long-term effects such as increased risk of teen pregnancy. Single-parent homes are more likely to be economically disadvantaged and single mothers feel the strain of work and parenting (Martin Emery, & Peris, 2004). Extended family and child care personnel can provide a support system for these families.

Cohabitation is becoming increasingly common. By 1995, 40 percent of women ages 20 to 24 had cohabitated. Half of all first unisons were cohabitating unions (Bumpass & Lu, 2000). Cohabitating couples are parents because they have a child together, they live with children from a previous relationship,

Table 10–2 Changing Structure of the American Family

	1970	2001
Traditional Families (husband breadwinner, wife full-time mother)	60%	30%
Unmarried couple households	19%	31%
Married women in the labor force	30%	60%
Married couples with children under age 18	40%	24%
Children under 18 living with one parent	11%	27%
Births to unmarried women	11%	31%

SOURCES: Fields (2003); U.S. Census Bureau (2002).

or single women who become pregnant choose to cohabitate rather than marry the child's father before the baby is born. Six percent of all children live with a parent or parents who are cohabitating. Of children who live with single mother 10 percent also live with their mother's cohabitating partner; for children living with a single father 16 percent are in cohabitating relationships (Federal Interagency Forum on Child and Family Statistics, 2007).

Among children living with two parents, 90 percent live with biological or adoptive parents and 10 percent live with a biological or adoptive parent and a stepparent. Most of these are mother-stepfather families (Federal Interagency Forum on Child and Family Statistics, 2007). The family structure is even further complicated because about three-fourths of couples who are divorced cohabitate before a second marriage.

As an educator you must expect that the infants and toddlers you work with will come from a variety of family configurations and ensure that you are prepared to work with and honor this diversity.

Cultural Diversity

The cultural composition of the United States is becoming increasingly diverse. Those who teach infants and toddlers will see this diversity 20 to 30 years earlier than it is reflected in the population statistics (see Table 10–3).

The projection for 2020 shows that 40 percent of the population will be from non-Caucasian racial and cultural backgrounds. By 2050 it will be over 50 percent. This is the reality in infant care now.

Census data confirms that teachers are working in classrooms that include infants and toddlers from many different racial and ethnic backgrounds. And, this number is expected to increase. Demographers attribute the rising percentage to higher birth rates among nonwhite, non-Anglo women, increased immigration, and more women of childbearing age in the nonwhite groups.

Table 10–3 Projected Population of the United States: 2000 to 2050

Percent of Total Population	2000	2020	2050
White alone, not Hispanic	69.4	61.3	50.1
Hispanic (of any race)	12.6	17.8	24.4
Black alone	12.7	13.5	14.6
Asian alone	3.8	5.4	8.0
All other races	2.5	3.5	5.3

SOURCE: U.S. Census Bureau (2004).

Early care and education professionals need to develop cross-cultural competence so they can better educate the diverse groups of young children in their care (Lynch & Hanson, 2004). See Table 10–4 to look at the population of people over and under age 18 to confirm these trends.

Children in Immigrant Families

The United States is a nation of immigrants. In 1900, 80 percent of these immigrants came from Europe with only about 1 percent coming from Latin America and Asia (U.S. Bureau of the Census, 1999). Today immigrants come mainly from Latin America. See Table 10–5 for the place of origin of current immigrant families.

Children of immigrant parents
are under age 18, born outside the United States or have one foreign-born parent.

Children are considered to be **children of immigrant parents** if they are under 18 years of age and are either themselves foreign born or were born in the United States with at least one foreign-born parent. One child out of

Table 10–4 Annual Estimates of the Population by Age and Ethnic/Racial Characteristics for the United States: April 1, 2000 to July 1, 2006

	Under 18	Over 18	Median Age
White	56,234,845 (24%)	183,511,409 (76%)	38
Hispanic	14,966,364 (34%)	29,354,674 (66%)	27
Black	11,364,490 (30%)	26,978,059 (70%)	31
Asian	3,002,560 (23%)	10,156,783 (77%)	35
American Indian/ Alaska Native	847,390 (29%)	2,005,461 (71%)	30
Native Hawaiian/ Pacific Islander	151,234 (29%)	377,584 (71%)	30

SOURCE: U.S. Census Bureau (2007).

Table 10–5 Place of Origin of Immigrant Parents of Children Under Age 6

- 64% (3.7 million) are from Latin America and the Caribbean
- 39% (2.3 million) are from Mexico
- 25% (1.4 million) are from other Latin American and Caribbean countries
- 23% (1.4 million) are from Asia
- 7% (423,000) are from Europe and Canada
- 6% (363,000) are from Africa and the Middle East

SOURCE: Capps, Fix, Ost, Reardon-Anderson, and Passel (2005).

every five in the United States qualifies as a child of an immigrant parent. This is the fastest-growing segment of the nation's child population. In the 1990s this population of children grew at seven times the rate of native-born children (Capps et al., 2005).

up close and personal

I knew on our first date that José and I were going to get married. What I didn't know was how difficult that journey down the aisle would be. My husband is Guatemalan. I am from Delaware. We met at a bar in a tiny tourist town called Panajachel, in the highlands of Guatemala. He was a restaurant manager. I was a friend of one of the bands that played there frequently.

We fell in love. The only problem? We lived a continent and several countries apart. So I moved to Guatemala—living there for months at a time for almost three years. But then I realized that I wanted a career. I didn't want to live on $120 a month. And so I suggested that he come to the States and that we marry. Neither one of us thought the journey down the aisle would be quite as difficult as it proved to be. It took my husband almost a year for his visa to be approved. It was denied because papers were out of order, because I didn't make enough money, because a signature didn't appear to be original.

My husband went to the U.S. embassy 16 times and lined up and stood for seven hours in the cold (because even if you have an appointment they won't see more than 100 people a day) for a person who wasn't even a U.S. citizen to tell him "no."

There were times when I thought our relationship would crumble. Moments when I was so angry that I wanted to scream at my government and ask them what right they have to tell me who I can or can't fall in love with. Instances when both of us said this is just too hard.

My parents watched our struggle. They mostly stayed on the sidelines, but near the end they decided to intervene. It had gotten to the point of idiocracy. José's visa was being denied for no reason and their little girl was unhappy. Delaware is a small state and my parents had been active in politics. Soon our U.S. senators and representative were on a mission to bring José home. It took numerous phone calls, faxes, and e-mails, but with the help of a friend who is an immigration attorney and members of Congress, enough pressure was put on the U.S. embassy in Guatemala that José was granted a visa.

He came to Delaware six days later. He had a visa for 90 days. If we did not marry during that time he would return to Guatemala and could not come back to the United States for three years. We married one day before his visa expired.

REFLECTIVE PRACTICE

There is much concern about illegal immigrants in the United States. Have you thought much about the process of obtaining a visa to come here legally? How would you feel if you were the woman in this situation? From the first application for the visa to reapplying for a green card which will allow him to continue work in the United States and visit his family this couple paid almost $10,000. Reflect on what that means for immigrant families.

Most infants and toddlers in immigrant families are born in the United States and are thus American citizens (93 percent). Seven percent of children younger than six have foreign citizenship. The status of other family members is more complex. See Table 10–6 for the status of children less than six years of age.

Half of the children under six have a parent who came to the United States during the past 10 years and 86 percent of these children have only foreign-born parents (Capps et al., 2005; Schmidley, 2003). You might ask why this matters. It matters because many federally funded programs are not available to legal immigrants until they have been in the country five years or longer. If one member of the family is undocumented, the family may fear dealing with federal agencies even though the child is eligible for services. It means that the home language may not be English.

Over half of the immigrant families of young children are poor and they have access to fewer formal supports. This increases the probability of food insecurity and inadequate or crowded housing. These infants and toddlers may be facing extreme hardships and they have at least one parent in the workforce. The major reason for their poverty is the hourly wage the parent earns. These

Table 10–6 Status of Children Under 6 Years of Age Born to Immigrant Parents

- 19% are citizen children of naturalized citizen parents
- 48% are citizen children of legal noncitizen parents (permanent residents, people who have been granted asylum, and those with work permits)
- 26% are citizen children of undocumented parents
- 4% are legal noncitizen children (children who came to the United States due to a parent's work, people who have been granted asylum, or those awaiting citizenship)
- 3% are undocumented noncitizen children

SOURCES: Capps et al. (2005); Schmidley (2003).

Families immigrate to the United States for a variety of reasons. Some come to take advantage of educational opportunities for themselves and their children.

hardships are one reason Latino children enter kindergarten with fewer skills than other children (Takanishi, 2004).

Economics

Some of the greatest changes for all families are economic. A changing economy has introduced uncertainty and led to other changes. The United States has shifted from a manufacturing base to a service base. Although there are many jobs in the service sector, these jobs pay little. Other jobs require higher education and training. Many people entering these fields delay marriage and having children so they can have the opportunity to work in their chosen field before starting a family.

There has been little increase in household income over the past 15 years, which has resulted in over half of mothers with children under three in the workforce (Fields, 2003). In families where both parents work or in single-parent working households, many children are placed in early care and education settings at a very young age.

Families with Fewer Economic Resources

One of the most pervasive adversities facing infants and toddlers and their families is poverty. The human cost of poverty is high. It can rob infants and toddlers of their health, their education, their hopes and dreams, and even their lives.

Poverty increases the probability that risk factors (such as poor nutrition, little access to health care, and disabilities) will be present simultaneously in the child, the parent, the parent's informal support system, and the neighborhood. The disadvantages of poverty permeate all of life, from a parent's emotional availability, to quality of housing and neighborhoods, to educational opportunities. See Table 10–7 for the poverty rates of children.

Using a slightly different measure of poverty, the United Nations compared child poverty rates in the developed world. On this scale, the United States ranked 20th out of 21 countries, with only Mexico having higher rates of child poverty. Another comparison using industrialized nations again found the United States at the bottom of the scale, with only Russia having higher rates of child poverty (Annie E. Casey Foundation, 2003).

As of 2005, more children under the age of 5 were living in poverty (20 percent) than any other age group (Federal Interagency Forum on Child and Family Statistics, 2007). One-quarter of American families with young children earn less than $25,000 annually. Even if both parents work full-time at

Table 10–7 Percent of Children in Poverty in 2004

National Average	18
Non-Hispanic White	11
Hispanic/Latino	29
Black/African American	36
Asian and Pacific Islander	14
American Indian and Alaskan Native	31

SOURCE: Annie E. Casey Foundation (2006).

minimum wage jobs they will only earn $21,400 a year, which is $3,600 below the poverty line.

In 2005, 57 percent of children who lived below the poverty line had at least one parent employed full-time (Federal Interagency Forum on Child and Family Statistics, 2007). Although it would be possible for both parents to work in a two-parent household, the second salary, if minimum wage, would almost be negated by the cost of child care for one child and would be financially disadvantageous if there were more than one child. In 2005, high-quality care for infants and toddlers cost $200 to $260 per week in many communities (National Association of Child Care Resource and Referral Agencies [NACCRRA], 2006).

This is America's fifth child—the one child in five who lives in poverty. Contrary to public belief, this child is likely to live in a working family. Poverty affects all races of children; however, more than one in three black children and one in four Latino children are poor (Federal Interagency Forum on Child and Family Statistics, 2007). Poor children face risks other children do not see (see Table 10–8).

The number of people living in poverty fluctuates. In reality, many more people are poorer than the poverty rate suggests. Families living close to the poverty line may drop into poverty because of life changes such as an illness, birth of a child, divorce, separation, or disability (Annie E. Casey Foundation, 2003). In 2007, the poverty guidelines were $20,650 for a family of four and $17,170 for one parent with two children (U.S. Department of Health and Human Services, 2007).

Poverty adds to the stress experienced by all families. Families who are forced to spend their resources and energy on survival often do not have

Table 10–8 Risks Poor Children Face

They are:

- twice as likely to be born without prenatal care, have low birth weight, and to die before reaching their first birthday.

- twice as likely to repeat a grade, dropout of school, and require special education.

- more than twice as likely to be abused or neglected.

- frequently tired in school because they cannot sleep in their noisy, overcrowded apartment, house, or shelter.

- likely to fare better if they lived in another country. If they lived in 23 other industrialized nations they would be guaranteed health insurance, an income safety net, and a chance for a parent to stay at home with pay after childbirth.

SOURCE: Children's Defense Fund (2002, pp. 5, 6).

additional time or energy to encourage their infants and toddlers to develop language and other cognitive skills. When this happens children are more likely to experience emotional trauma and sustain injuries. Poverty increases the probability that children will be born with disabilities and that disorders that are preventable with timely medical intervention may become disabilities. Families who cannot afford regular medical care may wait until conditions become severe and then seek emergency room treatment. Nine million children, most of whom live in two-parent homes and 90 percent have a working parent, have no health insurance (Children's Defense Fund, 2007).

One of the reasons we are concerned about the relationship between families and early care and education is to look at how these environments are similar and ways in which they are different.

CONTINUITY AND DISCONTINUITY

Researchers are concerned about the effects of continuity and discontinuity on young children. **Continuity** refers to the linkages and congruence between families and early care and education settings. Linkages focus on the structural aspects of the relationship that look at the level, type, and frequency of communication between the settings as well as the amount of time that individuals from one setting spend in the other setting. It also refers to the substance of the relationship relative to the degree of similarity between the family and settings in such areas as child-rearing practices, values, goals, expectations, language, and adult-child relationships. For example, a family might have close linkages with their child's setting because an adult spends time there and communication is frequent. However, there might be little congruence if the families' home language is not English, they have few resources, and their ethnic heritage and cultural values focus on survival skills. Children from minority families with few resources are likely to experience **discontinuity** between home and school regardless of the ethnicity and social class of their teacher

Continuity and child care interact in a variety of ways. Parental values interact with child care decisions because, given a choice, parents choose settings that reduce levels of discontinuity. Shared values between the mother and caregiver increase maternal satisfaction with child care. Parents who value educational enrichment tend to choose settings where this is encouraged. Near-poor children received the lowest quality child care. These families are not choosing child care based on values, but based on what they can afford. Interestingly, poor children receive better child care than near poor children. This may be because poor children are attending subsidized settings, which have more regulation (NICHD Early Child Care Research Network, 2005).

Continuity
looks at the communication and the degree of similarity between the family and the early care and education setting.

Discontinuity
refers to the lack of congruency between the family and the early care and education setting.

We know less than we would like to about the impact of continuity and discontinuity on infants and toddlers. Discontinuity provides both opportunity and risk. Peters and Kontos (1987) suggest four variables that relate to the impact of discontinuity on young children. One variable relates to the *magnitude* of the discontinuity, with greater discontinuity posing a greater threat. A second variable is the *duration* of the discontinuity. A third relates to the *timing* of the event. To the extent that the discrepancy happens at a vulnerable or sensitive time, the impact is greater. Many people believe that infancy is such a period. The fourth variable relates to the *preparation* the child has had for understanding the situation and the communication that has occurred about the transition. Discontinuity may pose risks for infants and toddlers.

Parent education is one method that has been systemically used to increase continuity. Initially, the goal was to change family values to be closer to those of early care and education professionals. Current efforts are more collaborative, with families examining their values and early care and education settings reflecting on how they can modify their programs to better interact with and care for very young children.

PARENT EDUCATION

Needs assessment is a survey or questionnaire that asks parents what they want or would like relative to parent education.

Parent education is a form of collaboration. Parent education offers exciting possibilities for working with parents to potentially enhance the development of their children as well as giving them the support of others who are sharing a similar experience. Parent education can have many different goals. Successful parent education programs determine the needs and interests of the families they hope to serve. Designing a program that no one comes to is a waste of time and does not foster partnership. Depending on the goals, a formal or informal **needs assessment** is necessary. When establishing a new parent education program, a formal assessment is needed. For ongoing parent groups an informal assessment is probably enough (Berger, 2004). An opportune time for parent education is before the birth of an infant or during the first three years.

Evaluations of intensive family-oriented education programs have shown short-term positive effects in increased child competence and positive maternal behaviors as well as longer effects on increased levels of education, smaller family size, and an increased probability of the family being self-supporting (Powell, 1998).

Parent education groups vary significantly in their structure and purpose. They vary on a continuum, from parent groups in which a parent is the leader and there is little structure to groups where a professional runs the group. The meetings themselves can range from informal meetings designed to reinforce involvement, help understand ideas, and change attitudes, to formal meetings that may involve lectures on specific topics (Berger, 2004). In and of themselves, these different structures are neither inherently good nor bad, but the match between what the parents want and the structure influences participation and what is learned.

One challenge for parent education is the different value systems that parents may bring to the child-rearing situation. The academic field of child development has some clear guidelines regarding the types of parenting that are most likely to produce children who do well in school. Early childhood educators support reasoning over corporal punishment, authoritative rather than authoritarian parenting, responding to infants as quickly as possible in a gentle responsive way rather than letting them cry it out, and so on. These views are not accepted by all parents. It is often difficult to work with parents who hold different values. There is a fine line between supporting different ways of parenting and practices that could be damaging for infants and toddlers. These practices need to be addressed and changed. Parents do not want to be told how to raise their children. Parent education programs are adapting. The child development professional lecturing a group of mothers on how to raise their children is no longer an accurate portrayal of many of the programs (Powell, 1998). Supporting families who have children in early childhood settings requires us to rethink and reframe how we view our programs. See Table 10–9 for newer ways that we are reaching parents.

Table 10–9 Parent Education Programs

- Programs need to be designed to serve families, not just infants and toddlers.

- Programs must be responsive to the changing family demographics, specifically the families served by a particular program. Programs need teachers to be sensitive and respectful of the values of the families they serve. They also need some educators who speak the languages of the families served.

- Parents and educators need to have confidence in each other's ability. Parents want educators to be skilled, knowledgeable, and caring. Educators need to be confident in parents' abilities and clear about their own values about mothers who work outside the home. They need to value the strengths families have, especially when they are different from those of educators.

- Parent-educator relationships and communication must be individualized and personalized. They need to develop a shared vision and have common goals for the infant or toddler.

- Parents must be viewed as people with their own needs and identities apart from their roles as parents.

- Parents' beliefs about the usefulness of parent participation, and how what is learned at meetings can have a positive impact on their infant's or toddler's development needs to be apparent.

- Parents' beliefs about quality programming needs to be addressed in addition to the beliefs of professionals in the field.

- Educators need to hone their skills in working effectively with families.

SOURCE: Powell (1998).

WORKING WITH FAMILIES IN A CULTURAL CONTEXT

Individuals do not develop their language, rituals, rules, and beliefs in a vacuum. They are part of the cultural heritage handed down to them through their family. Culture is a way of life, a blueprint for living. It is both learned and internalized by being part of a particular culture (Berger, 2004). Infants and toddlers come to early care and education settings with a cultural background, as do their parents. Infants and toddlers and their families must be understood within the context of their cultural and ethnic background.

The analogy of the United States as a "melting pot" has been replaced by that of a "salad bowl." The overall percentage of children in the U.S. population is decreasing, but the proportion of children from non-Euro-American populations is increasing.

In developing cultural sensitivity, knowledge about different cultural groups is necessary. However, this limited knowledge may not be sufficient because all individuals and families are different and embrace different aspects of culture. Knowledge of culture has to be both generalized and individualized. To be culturally sensitive, you as a prospective teacher must accomplish several tasks, identified in Table 10–10.

Table 10–10 Clarifying Your Cultural Sensitivity

1. *Conduct a cultural self-assessment.* Before you can become aware of other cultures, you need to take a close look at your own culture and how this has shaped your values and beliefs about infants and toddlers. This is the lens through which you will view infants, toddlers, and their families. You need to be aware of the biases you hold. Other than Native Americans, we are all here through past immigration. This is an important part of our personal culture. Becoming aware of your own culture and its values increases the probability of becoming a culturally sensitive individual who can validate the differences among people and appreciate their commonality.

2. *Get acquainted with the community in which families live.* Gather and analyze ethnographic information regarding the cultural community. Meet them in their space. Recognize and understand the dynamics of difference. Cultural differences contribute to both obvious and subtle differences in individuals and communities. Obvious differences include such things as the language spoken, amount of eye contact, and body language used, whereas more subtle aspects of culture may influence the amount of self-disclosure someone is comfortable with. Avoid stereotyping.

3. *Determine the degree to which the family operates transculturally.* Honor diversity. Child-rearing practices are designed to socialize infants and toddlers into their own family and culture. Daily caregiving routines for infants and toddlers reflect a family's fundamental, deeply felt values and beliefs. Since infants absorb their culture as part of the caregiving process, the early care and education of infants and toddlers is important to parents. Child-rearing practices may provide the key to understanding socialization practices in different cultural contexts. However, if early care and education settings reflect only the values of the dominant culture, parents may be concerned about the practices used. Infants and toddlers may be deprived of a part of their own culture, or they may experience inexplicable discontinuity between care at home and that in a child care setting. You must examine each family's orientation to specific child-rearing issues while acknowledging and valuing diversity. This involves the recognition that there are cultural differences and that these differences play a role in what families believe about infants and toddlers and how they should be reared.

(continues)

4. Ensure that your program and curriculum have an anti-bias curriculum. Look around your classroom and evaluate it:

- Do the books reflect differences in gender, race, ability, culture, geographic location and socioeconomic status?

- Does the housekeeping area, equipment, and materials allow for diversity? Take a closer look at the dress-up clothing. Does it reflect the culture of the toddlers you serve? Is there diversity in the dolls?

- Is the music and art reflective of different cultures and countries?

SOURCES: Berger (2004); Cross, Bazron, Dennis, and Isaacs (1989); Derman-Sparks and A. B. C. Task Force (1989); Lynch and Hanson (2004).

REFLECTIVE PRACTICE

Answer these questions about yourself. Talk with parents if you are not sure about some of the answers.

ACQUIRING CULTURAL KNOWLEDGE

Learning about different cultures is an ongoing process. There are many books written that describe different ethnic groups, with some focusing on practices that relate to early childhood (Lynch & Hanson, 2004). This is the foundation from which more individualized knowledge must build. Additional family information is necessary about variations within a cultural group (see Table 10–11).

Table 10–11 Acquiring Cultural Knowledge

- *Reason for immigration.* What was the family seeking or leaving behind? Were they fleeing from political persecution, poverty, or war, or were they brought against their will as slaves?
- *Length of time since immigration.* How many generations has the family been in the United States?
- *Place of residence.* Does the family live in an ethnic neighborhood?
- *Order of migration.* Did the family come as a unit or did one member come first and others join later?
- *Socioeconomic status.* What is the socioeconomic status of the family and what are their attitudes toward education and upward mobility?
- *Religiosity.* What are the family's religious ties and are there strong political ties?
- *Language.* What languages are spoken by family members and what are their levels of comfort and fluency in different languages?
- *Intermarriage.* To what extent do family members have connections to other ethnic groups and how frequently have intermarriages occurred?
- *Attitudes.* What are the family members' attitudes toward the ethnic group and its values?

SOURCE: McGoldrick (1993).

Adapting to Diversity

The final element in cultural sensitivity is using the information and insights acquired to adapt early care and education practices to meet the needs of infants, toddlers, and their families. This may challenge you to expand your definition of "family" and their participation to include grandparents and various significant others in conferences. Focus on the strength that a particular cultural background brings to infants and toddlers and work with the strengths and priorities that families have set. At another level, adapting to diversity may cause you to look at the bulletin boards, books, and even dolls in the dramatic play area in a new light and to wonder about how comfortable families from various cultures feel in the early care and education setting.

REFLECTIVE PRACTICE

Reflect on your beliefs. If an infant or toddler comes from a family who is poor, they speak English haltingly, or the parents have little formal education, does that influence your expectations for the child? Are they influenced by the context? Support difference, not deficit; look for strength, not weakness. See families as a resource, not a liability. Many have had the strength to survive situation we cannot even imagine. Build on that strength. Move beyond celebrating holidays, singing the songs, and eating the food to more basic ideas that affect communication.

CULTURALLY DIVERSE FAMILIES

The United States is a multiracial, multicultural, and multilingual society. This needs to be acknowledged before effective strategies for interacting with diverse families can evolve. When trying to understand diversity it is easy to overgeneralize and oversimplify differences. Not all members of an ethnic group are alike in the way they embrace their culture's life style and values (Lambie, 2000). This section is not designed to be an exhaustive view of culture. It is designed to raise your awareness of the importance of recognizing cultural and ethnic differences and how they will influence your work with infants and toddlers and their families. All parents have goals and expectations for their children. However, differences in parental goals and expectations arise because parents and societies have different expectations for members of their communities (Okagaki & Diamond, 2000). We as educators need to be mindful of these differences.

Learning about culture is an ongoing process. It requires us to look at our own beliefs and values and to see how these influence how we look at others.

Families' views are influenced by their culture. What we think, how we act, the language we speak, and even what we eat are part of our wider cultural context. Looking at cultural diversity is a matter of validating the differences among us and appreciating our common humanity and finding the balance between the two.

Let us start with a common understanding of terminology. A **racial group** is a socially defined group distinguished by selected, inherited physical characteristics. An **ethnic group** is distinguished by a sense of peoplehood or "consciousness of kind" based on a common national origin, religion, or

Racial group is socially defined by selected and inherited physical characteristics.

Ethnic group is distinguished by a sense of peoplehood based on national origin, religion, or language.

language. If one's racial or ethnic group is subordinate to the majority in terms of power and prestige (not necessarily in terms of number of members), one occupies a **minority status** (Eshleman, 2000).

The key characteristics of any racial or ethnic group center on self and social definitions. In Hawaii and Jamaica, for example, the social meaning of Black is very different than in Kansas and Georgia. To have a particular skin color, speech pattern, or manner of dress may lead others to perceive and label someone, correctly or incorrectly, as a member of a specific racial or ethnic group (Eshleman, 2000).

There are five main groups of racial/ethnic families in the United States according to the U.S. Census Bureau: white, black, Hispanic, Asian or Pacific Islander, and American Indian and Alaska native. In many ways they are more similar than dissimilar to the dominant family forms that exist in the larger U.S. society. Children receive their basic identity and status within the family context. Parents ascribe to the basic achievement and mobility values that exist within the larger society. In other ways they are different. In the past, we did little to enhance children's understanding of their own culture. With growing cultural awareness and sensitivity, this should be changing. The following brief sketches provide some demographic information as well as information that is relevant to your teaching.

Latino Families

Latino families constitute the largest ethnic minority in the United States with a population of 41.3 million in 2004. Latinos includes people from all countries in Latin America as well as parts of the Caribbean that have Latin-based languages (Halgunseth, 2004). (*Note*: I use Latino and Hispanic interchangeably in this text.) They do not share a common racial background. The population is young, diverse, dynamic, and growing rapidly. The Hispanic growth rate of 3.6 percent from July 1, 2003, to July 1, 2004, was three times that of the total population (U.S. Census Bureau, 2005a). Nationally, 7 percent of the population is under the age of 5. Latinos had the highest proportion of children in this age range, at 11 percent. They are a community of first-, second-, and third-generation immigrants. Many have uprooted their families and left their homes and relatives for economic, political, professional, ideological, and educational reasons (Carrasquillo, Lantigua, & Shea, 2000). In the past, minority families were strongly encouraged to **assimilate** to be accepted. Assimilation required adopting U.S. customs and language as a way of being accepted and ignoring or not identifying with ones culture. **Acculturation** is different; it signifies the adoption of values of the host country but does not demand that cultural values be dropped. Typically this means learning English and accepting

Minority status is based on the power and prestige of a group relative to the majority.

Assimilation is the adoption of the majority culture's norms and views while rejecting the values of one's own ethnic/cultural group.

Acculturation supports the adoption of the host countries values without relinquishing ethnic/culture and values.

Bicultural adaptation involves honoring the home culture and adding experiences from the broader community to this base.

and promoting American ideals (Halgunseth, 2004). The third option is biculturalism. Bicultural adaptation incorporates aspects of the home cultural with the mainstream culture. Rather than replacing their home culture (their existing cultural values and behaviors) they add mainstream values and information. These individuals can function in both the home culture and the majority culture (Halgunseth, 2004). Families and settings can support **bicultural adaptation** by teaching children about their ethnic identity and about the special experiences they may encounter because of their ethnic background. This approach is related to higher self-esteem and proactive styles of coping with discrimination (Halgunseth, 2004).

Latinos are overrepresented in poverty groups. In 2005, 28 percent of Hispanic children lived below the poverty line. The poverty rate for all children was 18 percent at this time (Federal Interagency Forum on Child and Family Statistics, 2007)). In 2005, the median income of Latino families was $35,967 whereas for families as a whole it was $50,784. Among the Hispanic groups, Puerto Ricans (all of whom are U.S. citizens) have the lowest median family income and Cubans the highest (U.S. Bureau of the Census, 1998). The Latino population is the youngest with a median age of 27 compared to Whites who have a median age of 38. They also have the highest percentage of any ethnic/racial group of their population under age 18 (34 percent) (U.S. Bureau of the Census, 2007).

Hispanic families have high family cohesion and flexibility. Families are important to them and they frequently have supportive kin networks. Many families have a strong ethnic identity and, despite the stereotypes, most have equalitarian decision making.

Like African American families, they face many challenges. A primary challenge is increasing their level of education and overcoming economic discrimination to gain financial resources. Less than half of the foreign-born population from Latin America comes with a high school diploma (Hernandez, 2006).

Children from Latino families do not do well in U.S. schools. Over 20 percent of children between the ages of birth and eight are Hispanic. Although many are from immigrant homes, about 90 percent of the children are U.S. citizens. Hispanic children are five times *more* likely to have a mother who did not graduate from high school (compared to 9 percent for Whites) and three times *less* likely to have a mother who is a college graduate then White children (Hernandez, 2006). Hispanic children, particularly those from disadvantaged circumstances lag behind non-Hispanic Whites on measures of school readiness and school achievement. High-quality infant/toddler programs can contribute to greater school readiness. There is evidence that the use of both Spanish and English in infant/toddler programs and preschool contributes to greater school readiness for these children (National Task Force on Early Childhood Education for Hispanics, 2007).

The extended family plays an important role in Latino families. Siblings, cousins, and other relatives provide a support network that is helpful to families with infants and toddlers. The overall attitude toward infants and toddlers is one of acceptance, putting less pressure on them to achieve milestones early. They tend to be nurturing and permissive in early childhood. Because of family values, very young Latino children are less likely to be in early care and education settings. Mothers are generally expected to stay home and raise children. When this is not possible, the extended family frequently takes over the care of young children. Some families may see sending infants and toddlers to child care as a sign of deteriorating family values. They may need your help to see this as an alternative to extended family care. Help them feel they are still fulfilling their roles as parents.

Latino parenting styles foster interdependence and relational learning whereas European American parents emphasize independence and self-initiated learning. The major strategy that Latino parents use in teaching is modeling. If there are older siblings they may be the model for teaching younger children (Halgunseth, 2004). For example, if a Latino parent was teaching a two-year-old to set the table she would demonstrate how to do it and where the different utensils, cups, and plates go. A European American parent would use inquiry: "Where do you think the plate goes?" Then, if the child placed the plate in the right spot the parent is likely to say, "Great, you did that all by yourself." Because of their view of modeling as a way of teaching, they talk less to their children so Latino children have not heard as much language as others.

Maintaining harmonious relationships is important to most Latino parents. They support the development of interpersonal skills in their children. They want others to enjoy their children and find them pleasant. Negative emotions such as aggression, anger, and arguing are often distressing. They also monitor body language and facial expressions more than European American families. Being well educated includes not only the traditional three Rs, but also a sense of inner importance that includes tranquility, obedience, and courtesy. Some of these skills may make them more passive and dependent upon adult authority (Halgunseth, 2004)

Communicating with Latino families who do not speak English fluently may be challenging. Some families that speak Spanish may not read it. Children may come to school with good language skills in both languages or with only rudimentary knowledge of English or Spanish. If the parents speak little or no English, have bilingual/bicultural support for parent-teacher conferences and to translate forms that are to be sent home. Use parents as a resource to learn about the culture and to enrich the curriculum.

The overall Latino population is young. There are many distinctive differences among the Hispanic groups. Only a few of these will be highlighted but the differences are so great that it is important to know what specific group you are learning about and what aspects of the culture the individuals you are working with embrace.

Mexican American Families

Over 1 million Mexican Americans are descendants of the native Mexicans who lived in the southwest before it became part of the United States following the Mexican American War. They became Americans in 1848, when Texas, California, New Mexico, and most of Arizona became U.S. territory. There was also large-scale migration in the early 1900s caused by the chaos of the Mexican Revolution and the demand for labor on cotton farms and railroads in California.

High fertility rates and strong family ties typify the Mexican American culture. They often live near nuclear and extended family members and share interests and concerns about the welfare of the family unit. The needs of the family often supersede the needs of an individual family member. The theme of family honor and unity is strong throughout Mexican American society irrespective of social class or geographic location.

Godparents play an important role in families. Traditionally, expectant parents select a patron, a married couple, or an extended family member to be the child's sponsor. This is considered both a special honor and an obligation. The baptism ceremony establishes a social bond and godparents are thought of as being coparents. The relationship is expected to last a lifetime, although this tradition is less strong than it has been in the past (Halgunseth, 2004).

In the past, Mexican Americans adhered to the traditional ideal of manliness (*machismo*), which is equated with authority, strength, sexual virility, and prowess. The male was the patriarch who made important decisions. He was also the provider and protector for his family. He had the freedom of seeking other sexual partners; his wife could not. Decision making is becoming more egalitarian. In general, however, Mexican American males still exert power over their wives and the women still do the majority of child care and household tasks. Mexican American families have a high fertility rate and have an average of 3.2 children (U.S. National Center for Health Statistics, 2000). Fathers show a definite interest in their children and their behavior. Given the size of the family, along with minimal skills and low level of income, it is difficult for many Mexican American families to live above the poverty line. This is confounded by low levels of parental education. About 66 percent of fathers and 64 percent of mothers did not graduate from high school and about 40 percent completed only eight years of formal education (Hernandez, 2006).

Puerto Rican Families

Puerto Rican families are heavily concentrated in cities in the east, especially New York City. Many have low-paying full-time jobs, part-time jobs, or sometimes no job at all. Males previously came to the United States to work in manufacturing jobs that required little education and few skills. However, in today's economy there are few such jobs.

More than other Hispanic groups, Puerto Ricans form families without benefit of marriage and have a high proportion (60 percent) of female-headed households. In 1999, 27 percent of Puerto Rican households lived below the poverty line (U.S. Bureau of the Census, 2000). This poses challenges to these families. See Table 10–12 for ways of working with infants and toddlers in Latino families.

Please remember that this is just an overview for you to begin to think about different infants and toddlers and how families are both similar and different. You cannot assume that because a family came from Latin America that they will have the values and beliefs discussed. You need to work individually with families to determine what they want for themselves and their children.

up close and personal

I spent about four months in Costa Rica doing research and working with families who had young children with disabilities. Because I was in Latin America I was more conscious of issues relating to culture but it was still hard. I would try so hard to figure out how to get some of the services I thought the children needed. Then when I would talk with the families about what they could do with their young children. They were not interested in following through. Many mothers felt that it was a wiser use of their time to spend a half hour in church praying for their toddler to be well than to use that time working with the child or going to occupational therapy. I just didn't understand it.

REFLECTIVE PRACTICE

Reflect on how you might feel if you were the one working with these families. Can you think of ways to honor cultural beliefs and to work with families whose values are different from yours while also meeting the needs of infants and toddlers?

Table 10–12 Working with Latino Families with Infants and Toddlers

- Latino infants and toddlers come to educational settings with a broad range of language, cultural characteristics, and needs that affect their learning and cognitive development. They share some of the experiences of other Latino families in the United States, but they are, at the same time, a diverse group in a country that is just learning to value diversity.

- Look at yourself to determine your experience with culturally diverse people, especially those who speak English as a second language and those who have immigrated illegally.

- Assess your style of interacting with others, especially how you think about time. If you feel the pressure of time during your interactions and that documents must be signed *now*, families may interpret this as a lack of respect or concern.

- Learn to pronounce the children's names as the family does. Do not Americanize names unless the family requests that you do so. Talk to the infants and toddlers.

- Appreciate the opportunity you have been given to broaden your global knowledge and to look at your culture from another perspective. Learn some of the language the family uses and appreciate the challenge they face learning English. Honor and value children's native language.

- Find out from families what they want for their children. Some families want children to be respectful, polite, and loving and are less concerned about independent thinking and problem-solving skills than most European Americans.

- Have a culturally rich classroom that includes many artifacts and activities from other cultures and teaches the value of respecting others and their differences.

- If families have immigrated recently, they may need time to adjust to the culture and how they will meet their basic needs. There may be little energy left to focus on the needs of an infant or toddler. Particularly if the family is not legally documented, be clear about your role. Specifically how it relates to child welfare (you are not there to take their child away) and the *United States Bureau of Citizenship and Immigration Services (La Migra)* (you will not inform them). In paperwork do not reference their status. Educators need to know what resources can be used for illegal immigrants and what might jeopardize their legal status now or in the future.

- Learn about the immigrants' country of origin and area of the country the family emigrated from. If the area is rural, they may need support childproofing their home and adjusting to other basic issues that are different.

- Do not assume that families who speak Spanish and/or English can also read it. They may have learned words in English, particularly in relation to their child, that they have never seen or heard in Spanish.

- Learn more about the Latino culture in general, as well as the specific country from which the families come. Attend Latin American community celebrations and watch films from and about Latin America. Find out what community resources are responsive to and supportive of Latin Americans in general and specific countries or areas in particular

SOURCES: Carrasquillo Lantigua, and Shea (2000); Halgunseth (2004); Lynch and Hanson (2004).

African American Families

African Americans have a rich heritage with a strong sense of family, community, and culture. African Americans are the second largest distinct racial/ethnic group in the United States; they numbered about 39.2 million, or about 12 percent, of the population in 2004 (U.S. Census Bureau, 2005a). (I use the terms *Black* and *African Americans* interchangeably in this text.) The Black population has a median age of 31 compared to Whites who have a median age of 38. They have 30 percent of their population under 18 as compared to 24 percent of whites and 34 percent of Latinos (U.S. Bureau of the Census, 2007). Because of their unique historical and social experiences, many African Americans have lifestyles and value patterns that differ considerably from the European American majority. The establishment and development of their domestic units took many different paths (Tucker, Subramanian, & James, 2004). One path is the support of the single-parent family (50 percent) with 48 percent of children living with single mothers; the remaining 2 percent live with single fathers. Of these single parents 6 percent of the mothers and 30 percent of father live in a cohabitating relationship (Fields, 2003). Of mothers, 69 percent were not married at the time of their child's birth (U.S. National Center for Health Statistics, 2000). The median income for Black American families was $30,858 in 2005 (U.S. Census Bureau, 2005b). In 2006, 35 percent of Black children lived with two married parents. The poverty rate for Black children that year was also 35 percent. In 2005 62 percent of Black children lived in families with secure parental employment (Federal Interagency Forum on Child and Family Statistics, 2007).

The migration of African Americans from rural to urban areas has followed the general population trend. With the exception of California, there are fewer African Americans in the West and more than half live in the South. It is also a mobile population with 49 percent changing residences between 1995 and 2000 (Schachter, 2003). African American families, like white families, fit no stereotypic view. Most are doing well and thriving with increases in the numbers completing their education and entering the work force (Willis, 2004). Strengths such as strong family ties and flexibility in family roles, and caring parenting give some families and their young children a strong support network. African American families have a strong work orientation and motivation as well as a strong religious orientation. The African American family is an absorbing, adaptive, flexible, and amazingly resilient mechanism for the socialization of its children and surviving in society (Tucker et al., 2004).

African American families face challenges based on their history of racism and discrimination in the United States. Major disparities still exist between blacks and whites. A persistent problem is that of black females finding partners. Because black males experience higher rates of unemployment and underemployment, it is difficult to attain a family income level that allows them to provide adequately for their families. When families (regardless of ethnicity) are constantly worrying about financial problems, marital difficulties often follow.

WITH INFANTS AND TODDLERS

Learn more about the African American culture and incorporate this knowledge into your teaching. Examine your teaching materials. Do you have stories about African American children and representative dolls available? When you discuss families do you include a wide range of family configurations including multigenerational families, those who have others living with them, single-parent families, and those with working mothers? Do not ignore ethnicity and pretend that African Americans are the same as Whites but just happen to be Black. Value the strengths they bring to infants and toddlers. Use the information in Table 10–13 to work with infants and toddlers in African American families.

Although African American families are primarily nuclear families, they have a much stronger social support network than white families. The significance of such a support system is important to families with infants and toddlers. Relatives, particularly grandmothers, form a significant part of this network. The importance of religion in family life at all social levels is another difference between African American and White populations. The religious community provides a social life for African American families as well as giving emotional support and help in caring for infants and toddlers.

Within African American nuclear families, the typical pattern appears to be egalitarian relationships where roles are flexible and tasks are often interchanged. Parents are often more authoritarian than in white families and encourage independence and self-sufficiency earlier. Many African American women value child bearing and child rearing as a validation of their womanhood. Education is valued for upward mobility. Most women work either out of necessity or out of a desire to enhance family income. Some African Americans are asking for their differences as well as their similarities to be acknowledged and encouraged.

Like Latino families, some African American families embrace the values and lifestyles described, others do not. Learn from the families you work with what is important to them. Knowing an individual's culture does not mean you can predict their behavior (Gonzalez-Mena, 2005). See Table 10–13 for ways of working with infants and toddlers in African American families.

Asian and Pacific Islander Families

Over 4 percent of the U.S. population (14.0 million) was characterized as Asian or Pacific Islanders in 2005 (U.S. Census Bureau, 2005b). The Asian American population has doubled each decade since 1970. Most of this growth was the

Table 10–13 Working with African American Families of Infants and Toddlers

- Value the strengths of kinship bonds and included extended family members and friends who are involved with the family

- Work with the family's informal support network (friends, neighbors, church) whenever possible

- Begin by addressing people formally (Ms. Wapoles) until the individual asks you to change the form of address

- Learn about the family's beliefs relative to health and medical care and make suggestions that are congruent with their beliefs

- Learn about the resources in the African American community

- When evaluating assessment results be aware of potential bias in the assessment itself and the assessment process

- Honor the home language of the family and child while at the same time emphasizing the importance of standard English

- Avoid stereotyping

- Include African Americans on the infant or toddler's IFSP team if the child has an identified disability

- Learn more about the African American culture by talking and reading about it

SOURCES: Tucker, Subramanian and James (2004); Willis (2004).

result of immigration. Asian Americans are not a homogeneous group; they represent more than 28 subgroups. The major subgroups typically included in this category are: Chinese, Filipino, Japanese, Asian Indian, Korean, Vietnamese, Laotian, Cambodian, Thai, and Hmong. The Chinese American community is the largest Asian subgroup in the United States. Although the term Pacific Islander appears as a subcategory in the U.S. census, this does not represent an ethnic group. Included in this subcategory are Hawaiians, Samoans, and Guamanians; they constitute 980,000 people (U.S. Census Bureau, 2005b).

All of these groups had different ancestors, languages, customs, and recency of immigration. The Chinese, Korean, and Vietnamese cultures are rooted in some of the world's oldest civilizations and have been influenced by the doctrines of Confucianism, Taoism and Buddhism (Chan & Lee, 2004). Like African Americans and Latinos, they are concentrated in metropolitan areas and they reside in specific states: New York, Texas, Illinois, and New Jersey. Asian and Pacific Islanders marry at the same rate as the European American population (82 percent) and there is a high level of family stability. The Asian population has a median age of 35 compared to Whites who have a median age of 38. They have 23 percent of their population under 18 as compared to 24 percent of whites and 34 percent of Latinos (U.S. Bureau of the Census, 2007). They are better educated and have higher median incomes than all other groups. In 2005, the median family income was $61,094 (U.S. Census Bureau, 2005b). The poverty rate for Asian Americans was 11 percent in

2005 (U.S. Census Bureau, 2005c). Their strengths lie in family loyalty and a strong family orientation. They respect their elders and have high levels of mutual support between generations. Their children are well disciplined and they place a high value on education.

They, too, face challenges in the United States. One challenge is the loss of ties with kin, particularly for those who have come to the United States more recently such as those from Vietnam, Cambodia, and Laos. They may distrust those outside of their group and have a stigma against seeking help. They have high expectations for themselves and their children. They have very high academic expectations for their children, with a strong emphasis on self-control and academic achievement (Ishii-Kuntz, 2004).

Overall, Asian Americans value family highly and tend to initially solve problems within private family settings. Family needs and interdependence often have precedence over individual needs and independence. Family ties are close and divorce rates are low with few female-headed households. As a culture they avoid open confrontation, therefore they are unlikely to challenge educators even when they disagree with them. Communication is often indirect.

up close and personal

I am an international student from China. Strictly speaking, I am not an immigrant but a "non-immigrant alien" based on the categorization by the U.S. Immigration Office. Before I came to the United States, I had a stable job in Shanghai (one of the largest cities in China) and was married to my husband, a junior scientist working in a research institute. The idea of seeking better educational opportunities in a Western country was very attractive to us. A year after we got married, my husband left for the United States to study at a major university, but we never knew it would take us that long to see each other again.

Within 14 months I made four visits to the U.S. consulate to apply for a spouse visa. I was rejected the first three times because I was suspected of having immigration intentions. Each time, I cried my way back home and made tearful phone calls to my husband. I was literally hopeless when I went to the U.S. consulate for the fourth time. Luckily I was granted a visa this time. I was finally able to go to America to visit my husband.

A few months after I arrived in United States, I was also accepted at the University. To enroll as a full-time student, I needed a new visa. The fastest way to obtain a visa was to apply in a U.S. embassy or consulate outside the country. Otherwise it would take several months for a visa to be approved and mailed by the U.S. immigration office. I flew to El Paso, in Texas, crossed the Mexican border, and obtained my student visa in the U.S. consulate in Juarez, Mexico. Compared with my previous visa application experiences in China, this trip was easy and delightful!

So far I have studied in United States for five years and will graduate next spring.

If I choose to stay in America after graduation, I am allowed one year to look for a job and change my student visa to a different one. If that one year expires and I still do not have a decent employer, I will have to leave America. I really hope this is the last time I deal with a visa problem.

REFLECTIVE PRACTICE

Reflect on this woman's experiences. How are they similar to and different from the previous stories about immigration experiences?

Some of the traditional cultural norms fade, such as speaking the native language, patriarchal authority, and traditional role expectations for wives and children. By the second or third generation, children tend to accept English as their dominant language, they adopt the dress codes and musical preferences of their peers, and they pick up dating and sexual patterns that are at odds with traditional and parental values. They often intermarry with members of other ethnic groups (Chan & Lee, 2004). The family is seen as a harmonious group and anything that might disrupt this harmony, such as strong emotions, is expected to be suppressed. Children are expected to conform. To develop these values in children, parents may teach children that disobedience brings ridicule on the child and shame on the family. Traditional cultural values of patience and persistence are handed down. Family dependency is valued over independent achievement and cooperation over competition.

Asian American families place a high value on education. The parents generally show educators respect and expect their children to do the same. Children are expected to obey educators and not question what they say. Children may need to learn the skill of asking questions of adults without questioning the authority that adults have. Children may need support in learning skills for getting along with peers. Talk about the differences between feelings and how these feelings can be expressed. Children may need your help in learning to express themselves in ways that do not conflict with family values. As you work this out, consult with the parents for their ideas and use parents as a resource for expanding your knowledge of the Asian cultures. See Table 10–14 for working with Asian American families of infants and toddlers.

Table 10–14 Working with Asian and Pacific Islander Families of Infants and Toddlers

- To facilitate learning and be more relevant, materials and programming need to take the child's culture into account. Be aware, however, of the differences among Asian cultures. Japanese and Chinese people have both similar and different values. Even among members of one group, there is great variation. Learn about the particular families you interact with and decide which generalizations apply and which do not.

- When greeting family members (or saying good-bye), begin with the oldest family member and typically greet male members first. Use the appropriate title with either the last name (Chinese and Korean) or the individual's first name (Cambodian, Laotian, and Vietnamese), depending on the country of origin. Many women retain their own family name when they marry. It is appropriate to address her as Mrs. Onn (Miss Onn becomes Mrs. Onn when she marries Mr. Kim, not Mrs. Kim).

- Initiate interactions slowly and cautiously. Ask general, not personal questions, but do not ask about U.S. foreign policy, the internal politics of their country of origin, or religion. Expect to be asked personal questions; this shows interest and concern.

- In general, avoid initiating physical contact, particularly between men and women. This includes shaking hands or hugging another individual unless he or she initiates it.

- Keep your language and voice reserved and polite. Control your emotions and avoid direct confrontation. Do not show anger or criticize the family.

- Focus your attention on the family as a system rather than only on the child.

- Consider the degree to which the family embraces traditional values and beliefs, particularly as they relate to spirituality and healing.

- Assess the English proficiency of the family and modify your language to accommodate their level. Speak more slowly for families who are not as proficient. Do not correct their English. Do not assume that individuals who speak with an accent are not proficient.

- Become aware of your nonverbal communication. Avoid sustained eye contact and winking or batting your eyes. Do not touch a child on the head, wave your arms, beckon, or point your index finger. These are considered to be signs of contempt.

- Learn the body language that is associated with negative and affirmative responses. Some families will say yes to you even if they disagree with your suggestions. Learn when yes means no.

- When sitting in a chair, keep both feet on the floor and your hands visible; if on the floor, point your soles away from others.

- If the family does not wear shoes in the house, remove your shoes before entering. Expect to be offered food or drinks and enjoy the hospitality. Do not compliment or praise a particular household object; the family may feel compelled to give it to you.

- Families may offer you gifts. This frequently poses a dilemma as many agencies do not want you to accept these. If you do accept a gift, take it in both hands, express your gratitude, and do not open it in the presence of the giver.

- Include bilingual and bicultural professionals on the team.

SOURCES: Chan and Lee (2004); Mokuau and Tauili'ili (1998); Santos and Chan (2004).

Families embrace their culture in different ways. It is important to talk to parents about their beliefs and practices.

Early childhood programs need to be responsive to cultural differences and acknowledge these differences in the way they plan for infants and toddlers. It is important to know about differences as well as similarities in Asian cultures and to talk with parents about the aspects of culture that are important to them.

American Indian and Native Alaskan Families

There several hundred American Indian tribes or nations with 300 separate languages and dialects. Their population at the time Columbus landed (1492) was estimated to be about 10 million (Harjo, 1993). The 2000 census showed 4,119,301 people, or about 1 percent of the population of the United States, claimed American Indian or Alaska Native origins (U.S. Census Bureau, 2002). American Indians and Alaskan natives have a median age of 30 compared to a median of 38 for the white population. They have 30 percent of their population under age 18 compared to 24 percent of the white population (U.S. Bureau of the Census, 2007). Increasingly Americans Indians are moving into urban communities (78 percent) and leaving reservations, trust lands, or tribal designated areas (Kawamoto & Cheshire, 2004).

The largest group, the Cherokee, comprise about 19 percent of the American Indian population. The second largest group, the Navaho, comprise about 12 percent. Other groups, ranging from 6 to 2 percent, include the Chippewa, Sioux, Choctaw, Pueblo, Apache, Iroquois, Lumbee, and Creek tribes (U.S. Bureau of the Census, 1995). They live mostly in the western region of the United States: California, Arizona, Oklahoma, New Mexico, Washington, and Alaska. It is important to know the characteristics of the particular tribe the family belongs to, as there is much intertribal variation and danger in overgeneralization.

About two-thirds of all American Indian family households are comprised of married couples, with about 59 percent of mothers not married when they gave birth (U.S. National Center for Health Statistics, 2000). Interracial marriage is common. Elders play a special role. Grandparents actively participate in passing on the cultural heritage. Of particular relevance is the teaching of living in harmony with nature and having respect for the land. Overall, Americans Indians stress cooperation over competition and harmony with nature as opposed to trying to control nature. Personal strength is derived from knowing oneself and one's culture. Identity is associated with family roles, responsibilities, and relationships largely passed on by their mothers (Kawamoto & Cheshire, 2004). They are adult centered as opposed to child centered, and their time orientation is present instead of future.

Alaskan Natives represent approximately 16 percent of Alaska's residents, and represent a significant segment of the population in over 200 rural villages and communities. Many have retained their customs, language, hunting and fishing practices and ways of living since "the creation times." Alaskan Native people are divided into eleven distinct cultures, speaking 20 different languages (Alaskan Native Heritage Center, 2000).

The Athabascan people lived in the interior of Alaska along five major waterways. They have eleven linguistic groups. Athabascans are highly nomadic, traveling in small groups to fish, hunt and trap. All hunters are part of a kin-based network and are expected to follow traditional customs for sharing in the community. The Alaska Natives who live in the southwest are known as Yup'ik and Cup'ik. They still depend upon subsistence fishing, hunting and gathering for food. Elders tell stories of traditional ways of life, to teach the younger generations survival skills and their heritage. The Inupiaq and the St. Lawrence Island Yupik People, or "Real People," are hunting and gathering societies. They subsist on the land and sea of north and northwest Alaska. Their lives evolve around the whale, walrus, seal, polar bear, caribou, and fish.

The Aleut and Alutiiq peoples live in south and southwest Alaska, maritime peoples. They are water people, whether it is the creeks and rivers near villages, or the North Pacific and Bering Sea. The intensity of the weather on the islands governs activities more than any other factor. The Aleut and Alutiiq cultures were heavily influenced by the Russians, beginning in the 18th century. The Eyak, Tlingit, Haida and Tsimshian share a common Northwest Coast Culture although there are important differences in language and clan system. They have a complex social system consisting of moieties, phratries and clans. The region they live in is a temperate rainforest with precipitation ranging from 112 inches per year to almost 200 inches per year. Here the people depended upon the ocean and rivers for their food and travel (Alaskan Native Heritage Center, 2000).

The number of individuals choosing the designation Native American on census forms appears to be growing at a rate four times the national average. Primarily this is because many people who have previously called themselves European Americans are now identifying themselves as Native Americans (Eschbach, 1993). (Let me add a note of caution here. In collecting data, one graduate student observed that two males marked that they were Native Americans. When questioned, they said that they chose Native American because they were born here. Individuals have the right to claim any origins they choose on forms. To the extent that individuals do not fill out forms accurately, for whatever reason, our information will be misleading.) The census now uses the designation American Indian and Alaska Native populations for their categories.

Like other groups, American Indians are not a homogeneous people, although they share many values in common. A high rate of infant mortality, alcoholism, tuberculosis, obesity, diabetes, and other diseases, as well as psychological distress, suicide, crime, and accidental deaths all contribute to a lower life expectancy. However, it is now close to that of whites (Baldridge, 2001).

While other minorities have struggled to gain a place in the United States, the experience of the American Indians has been the opposite. They have struggled to avoid being subjugated and to preserve their land, water, traditions, and unique legal rights. Unlike any other minority group, American Indians have negotiated more than 600 treaties with the U.S. government and ceded billions of acres of land and untold natural resources (Harjo, 1993).

According to Harjo (1993), assimilation for American Indians has meant cultural genocide. There has been a concerted effort to destroy American Indian languages, traditions, customary laws, dress, religion, and occupation. This was done by encouraging Christian denominations to convert Indian nations, imposing an educational system that was designed to separate children from their families and instill non-Indian values, and by the federal government's breaking up tribal landholding in favor of individual landowners, and taxing the lands.

Education for American Indian children has often been run by the Federal Bureau of Indian Affairs. Traditionally, the schools have been boarding schools, located far from the children's homes, with European American educators. The focus of this education was to "de-Indianize" the children. It has not worked. American Indians have in many instances not wanted to have their children included, but instead have wanted to foster close ties with the tribe. They want to improve the quality of education for their children by changing the standard curriculum to be more responsive to another view of American history. Until the 1970s, American Indian children were taught in school that their traditions were savage or immoral (Harjo, 1993). Educators were actively trying to change and denigrate their way of life. Their school dropout rates are high. The 2000 census found that 11.5 percent of American Indians and Alaska Natives held bachelors' degrees compared to 24.4 percent of the total population (U.S. Census Bureau, 2002). See Table 10–15 for ways to include American Indian and Alaskan Native families in infant and toddler classrooms.

Table 10–15 Working with American Indian and Alaska Native Families of Infants and Toddlers

- Ask parents who they want to include in meetings. In some Alaska Native families the mother's brother takes responsibility for training and socializing his sister's children so they grow up knowing their clan history and customs. Once this is established, include and show respect for the entire group.

- Listen to the family's ideas and concerns and acknowledge them, show interest. Provide emotional support and respect for the family.

- Build trust. Many American Indian and Alaska Native families have a history of negative experiences with public agencies and hence distrust them.

- Learn about communication styles. Some families find periods of silence and reflection an important part of their interactions, move at a pace that is comfortable for the family.

- Find out what families want, particularly if they need support in interpreting an assessment and then explaining these results to other family members.

- If the family speaks English as a second language, offer the skills of an interpreter. Choose an interpreter with the advice of the family, sometimes an individual from the community is a good choice; in other instances, this might violate confidentiality.

- When you need a lot of information from families, set the stage by telling them you will be asking a lot of questions. Encourage them to ask for clarification if they do not understand and to feel free to consult with others before they answer.

- If you know little about the family's culture, admit it, show your respect, ask them to tell you if you offend them in some way, and make a sincere effort to learn more about the culture.

- Even after arranging to meet with families at a particular time, always check before entering if it is a good time; if not, honor their decision and reschedule.

- As families change and grow in their understanding of their child's situation, they may want or need information that they had previously been offered but did not seem useful then. Offer suggestions again, particularly opportunities to talk with other parents

SOURCES: Alaskan Native Heritage Center (2000); Joe and Malach (2004).

Some feel that one reason the dropout rate for Native American children is higher than for the rest of the population is because of the biased view that educators and textbooks present (Joe & Malach, 2004). For example, many Americans Indians' view Thanksgiving as a day of mourning, not one of cooperation, celebration, and feasting. Remember that cultural diversity may impact the ways in which you celebrate holidays. Of all cultures, we tend to most misrepresent this one.

Anglo-European American Families

As with other groups, we know descriptive information about this group. There were about 82 million White, non-Hispanic, family households in the United States in 2005 primarily of European American descent. Their median family income in 2005 was $50,784 (U.S. Census Bureau, 2005b). In 2005 approximately 6 percent of these families lived below the poverty line (U.S. Census Bureau, 2005b). Although we have many descriptive statistics, they shed little light on the culture and values of the "majority."

Traditional White Anglo-Saxon Protestant (WASP) values include such personal traits as control, personal responsibility, independence, individuality, stoicism, keeping up appearances, a "hard work" ethic, and moderation. Complaining is viewed negatively. Increasingly this dominant culture is embracing the importance of individualism, especially in gender-related issues. For their children, there is an emphasis on personal development such as being independent, self-reliant, self-assertive, self-controlled, and focusing on individual achievement. In contrast, many Asian and Latin American cultures emphasize interdependence, cooperation, collaboration, and being respectful and loving (Okagaki & Diamond, 2000). There are many subcultures of the dominant culture. One caution is in order: When discussing ethnic or cultural traits, we risk stereotyping people. My intention is to provide evidence of diversity. The 2000 census showed individuals from the following major groups: German (15 percent), Irish (11 percent), English (9 percent), Italian (6 percent), Polish (3 percent), French (3 percent), Scottish, Dutch, Norwegian, Scot-Irish and Swedish about 2 percent each (U.S. Bureau of the Census, 2000).

German Families

Germans were the most frequent immigrants to the United States and represent an estimated 60 million residents. The early waves of German immigrants came between 1880 and 1920 primarily for religious, economic, and political reasons (Lassiter, 1995). These early settlers migrated to rural areas, with later waves seeking out major cities.

Irish Families

There are approximately 38.5 million individuals in the United States of Irish background (Lassiter, 1995). Many came in large numbers in the 1840s because of the potato famine and the oppressive conditions in Ireland. They have often been here for four or more generations and think of themselves as American. Some traits this group shares are: They value language and poetry; they may believe that problems are a result of their sins and see problems as private matters and rarely seek help; they believe in suffering alone and in silence. Despite the "gift of gab," they rarely talk of feelings. They tend to have high rates of addiction, primarily alcoholism (McGoldrick, 1993).

Italian Families

The major Italian immigration to the United States was from the late 19th to the early 20th centuries. They continue to hold a strong cultural identity (Lassiter, 1995). Most are from southern Italy. Italians value family, both nuclear and extended, and the sense of security, affection, and relatedness that family brings. They have a strong ethnic attachment and may prefer to live in ethnic neighborhoods. The father is typically the undisputed head of the family and the mother its heart. Feelings are discussed, sometimes in colorful, expressive, and dramatic ways. There are often strong family boundaries and there is some information that is not talked about openly with individuals outside the family (McGoldrick, 1993).

Jewish Families

There are approximately 6 million Jewish people living in the United States (Lassiter, 1995). They tend to live in major cities. Most of the Jews in the United States came from Eastern Europe, beginning about 1900 through the 1940s. This group tended to be family oriented, value their culture, and take great pride in their children. Families are often democratic, even across generational boundaries. They seek information, respect wisdom, and then make decisions. They value artistic and educational achievement. Raising successful children is important and is a major responsibility of parents, particularly the mother. Parents make sacrifices for children and experience personal pleasure in their children's accomplishments. Life-cycle rituals play an important role in family life. Sharing suffering is seen as an expression of loyalty for those who have suffered in the past (McGoldrick, 1993).

Although there may be a set of values that reflect the dominant culture, it too is heterogeneous and it is just as difficult not to generate stereotypes about Anglo-European American groups as it is others. Learn your personal cultural background and where you fit in the culture. Value and respect the culture of others at the level at which they embrace it. See Table 10–16 for ways of working with Anglo-European families.

Working with families requires good communication skills and sensitivity to the needs and values of all parents based on their culture and the circumstances in which they live. Early childhood educators need to be respectful and, like they do with infants, read the cues the family gives them about what is important and the best way to convey this information.

Table 10–16 Working with Anglo-European Families with Infants and Toddlers

- Speak about issues directly and honestly without using jargon. Be aware of regional differences in terms and vocabulary.

- Families have a tradition of being involved in their children's education and expect to take an active role; they want to be informed and have input into the process.

- Many families have active complex lifestyles, so meetings need to be scheduled to accommodate these commitments. They should start on time and have a stated end.

- Even among the dominant culture, there are many individual differences and preferences. These must be respected and honored.

SOURCE: Hanson (2004).

PARTNERING WITH DIVERSE FAMILIES

The structure of the American family is changing. However, it is not the structure per se that poses the greatest challenges to infants and toddlers, but rather how the particular structure impacts the family processes.

Infants and Toddlers in Separating and Divorcing Families

One of the largest variations from the traditional family life cycle comes through separation and divorce. Not all separations move to divorce. Of white women 91 percent move from separation to divorce after three years compared to 77 percent of Latinas and 67 percent of black women (National Center for Health Statistics, 2002). Of these divorces, approximately three-fourths involve children (Berk, 2002). In divorcing families, the children are likely to be young.

Approximately 50 percent of first-time marriages end in divorce. Twenty percent of these separations or divorces happen during the first five years

(National Center for Health Statistics, 2002). Infants and toddlers who live in separating and divorcing families experience the divorce. If the separation or divorce is followed by a period of inept parenting by the custodial parent, the loss of the noncustodial parent, a decline in family income, conflict between parents, and residential instability, then the outcome is not likely to be a positive one for infants and toddlers. On the other hand, if the divorce is followed by attentive and authoritative parenting, the noncustodial parent is active, the household income remains stable, and there are few additional stressors, then it is likely to have a minimal effect on infants and toddlers. If there is a mixture, the effects on infants and toddlers will be a mix (Amato, 2004).

The average child spends approximately five years (a third of his childhood) with a single parent, usually the mother, but with a growing number of single-parent households headed by men. For many children this period is followed by new relationships, some informal, such as cohabitation, but after two to three years approximately 40 percent of individuals remarry and an additional 20 percent are in some type of nonmarital union. About half of these remarriages will result in divorce in about two to three years (Hetherington & Kelly, 2002). However, when children with difficult temperaments or other challenges have to cope with stressful life events such as family disorganization, divorce and remarriage, their problems are magnified (Lengua, Wolchik, Sandler, & West, 2000).

Parental conflict does not end with divorce and indeed is often escalated after a divorce. Conflicts often revolve around issues related to visitation rights and child support payments. Infants and toddlers can be caught in the middle of these conflicts. Older children seem to be able to adapt and negotiate, whereas young children do not have these skills, but they do experience the stress.

Women are more likely than men to be economically disadvantaged after divorce. The economic well-being of women and children plunges when compared to predivorce levels. In addition to the loss of one income, three-fourths of divorced mothers in the United States get less than the full amount of child support or none at all (Children's Defense Fund, 2000). The economic implications of divorce may mean that families have to move from their homes, reducing ties with neighbors and friends. After divorce, both parents' social networks become smaller and less dense. Women, especially those caring for infants and toddlers, have less time, energy, and economic opportunity to build a new friendship network. Because women typically interact more frequently with kin during the marriage, they are more likely to sustain this support network than men are. Ties to kin may become the major support network if relationships are positive.

There are few issues surrounding divorce that have generated more concern than those relating to children's adjustment to divorce and its aftermath.

Changes in a child's behavior may be your first indication that families are having problems.

It is difficult to make generalizations because the issue is a complex one. To some extent it is dependent upon the age, sex, and temperament of the child. The period of greatest challenge is from the separation until two years after the divorce. The cognitive immaturity of infants and toddlers makes it difficult for them to understand the issues related to their parent's divorce. One of the variables that impacts children's adjustment to divorce is the quality of children's relationship to their parents. Their adjustment is enhanced if they have a good relationship with at least one of their parents (Hetherington & Kelly, 2002).

Three major factors impact the infant or toddler's adjustments to divorce: (1) the effectiveness of the custodial parent in parenting the child; (2) the level of conflict between the mother and father; and (3) the relationship of the child with the noncustodial parent. When the custodial parent is effective, levels of conflict are low, and the relationship between child and the noncustodial parent is maintained, the outcome is more positive for children.

You, as an educator, will probably be told about the divorcing process when the physical separation takes place. This is when parents must make practical decisions about who will be picking children up and what emergency numbers need to be added or changed. Finding out about the divorcing process may help explain an infant's or toddler's behavior.

For infants and toddlers, divorce is a loss of a way of life. The predictable patterns of everyday life are replaced by different expectations and life experiences and a profound degree of uncertainty about what is happening. Household rules and routines change, and a single parent typically experiences task overload as he or she takes on the tasks that previously were shared by two. Young children are in a particularly vulnerable position as the people they would turn to most for comfort and to mediate the stress may be unavailable (Wallerstein, Lewis, & Blakeslee, 2000).

Although we frequently have parent conferences at this point, in many cases parents are too involved in their own feelings to be available and sensitive to their children. It is imperative that early childhood educators know the legal and informal agreements between parents regarding the care of the child. Infants and toddlers are almost always in the custody of their mothers.

WITH INFANTS AND TODDLERS

Infants and toddlers frequently regress and lose skills they had previously attained, such as toilet training. They may want to be held, they may bring an attachment object, such as a blanket that had been given up. They may need support to try new activities and materials. Infants and toddlers who had adjusted well may now cry when left and become anxious when it is time to leave.

Children in their early care and education setting need stability. They need familiar toys, familiar adults, and a familiar routine. They have problems handling change. Their world seems out of their control and they seem adrift. They need a setting to help them become stabilized. Be supportive of infant's and toddler's feelings of sadness, fear, and anger. Acknowledge these feelings and find ways to deal with them. Although children may test your limits, they need to know that limits exist. "You look like you are angry. You can kick the ball two more times, but then we need to put it away."

Infants and Toddlers in Cohabitating Families

Cohabitation is a living arrangement in which two adults who are not married to each other live in the same setting and have a sexual relationship. Cohabitation is less stable than marriage. The probability of a cohabitating relationship breaking up within 5 years is 49 percent (marriage is 20 percent) and after 10 years is 62 percent (first marriages are 33 percent) (National Center for

Health Statistics, 2002). There has been a significant increase in couples who make this choice. The number of unmarried couples living together constitutes almost 9 percent of all unions (Walsh, 2003). Nearly half of all adults live in a cohabiting relationship at sometime during their lives, with approximately three-quarters cohabiting before a second marriage.

Two out of five children will live in a cohabiting family during some of their childhood and 15 percent of children born are the biological children of cohabiting couples. Half of cohabiting unions last a year or less (Bumpass & Lu, 2000). Cohabiting fathers spend more time with their biological children than fathers who do not live in the same household, but less time than fathers who are married to the mother. Whether cohabiting is good or bad for infants and toddler depends upon the alternatives (Seltzer, 2004).

These relationships cut in half the median time (7 to 3.7 years) children live in a single-parent postdivorce household (Bumpass & Raley, 1995). About half of these cohabiting unions do not last (there is either a marriage or separation). This increases the number of transitions infants and toddlers experience (Seltzer, 2000). Nonmarital cohabitation appears to be difficult for many families and particularly boys. There is more cohabitation among previously married people than never-married people. Although this trend is too new to know what it means for infants and toddlers, it does mean that you are likely to have infants and toddlers in your setting living in cohabiting, but unmarried, families.

WITH INFANTS AND TODDLERS

Early childhood settings need to portray many family situations and provide opportunities for input from parents and significant others. When cohabiting relationships change, children need the stability of a setting that has familiar activities and people. Centers make individual decisions about who they invite to conferences and group meetings. It is important to talk with a biological parent and determine the roles of the adults in an infant's or toddler's life to be sure to include important figures.

Become familiar with the families of the children in your setting. If cohabiting families feel uncomfortable and judged as less than adequate they may not actively participate. When you plan activities, think about having children invite a "special adult" rather than specifying a mother or father (Kieff & Wellhousen, 2000). Be inclusive rather than exclusive. It is important to build bridges to all families.

Infants and Toddlers in Stepfamilies

Remarried families are formed when divorced men and women remarry or when a divorced individual marries a single or widowed adult. Only about half of these remarriages include minor children and are therefore defined as stepfamilies. Stepfamilies are also formed when a single, never-married mother marries for the first time. A stepfamily is defined as one in which at least one of the recoupling adults has one or more children from a prior relationship and the children spend some time in the adult's household (Crosbie-Burnett & McClintic, 2000). According to the 2000 census there are 4.4 million stepchildren under the age of 18 (Administration for Children and Families, 2003).

Stepfamilies are complex and highly variable. They include more than one household unit. All family members are affected emotionally, financially, and legally by the actions of another household. The coparenting team is complex: It includes biological parents and their respective spouses and/or committed live-in partners. The new extended family includes multiple grandparents and step-grandparents, and siblings consist of biological siblings, half-, and stepsiblings from both households. Approximately half of stepfamilies have a mutual child. If the child is born after the couple has formed a solid relationship, the birth of the child makes a positive contribution to the integration of the family; if before, there will likely be increased stress.

WITH INFANTS AND TODDLERS

Educators need to be open to discussions with toddlers who have siblings "some of the time." Conscious efforts need to be made to include diverse families in stories and celebrations. We need to acknowledge many types of families. Also, as an educator you need to be clear on who should receive notices and who should be included in conferences and invited to school events. You also need to know who is to pick up the infant or toddler and under what circumstances. Know for your emergency forms whom to contact and what to do if you cannot reach the identified person.

Remarried families are different from first-married families in a variety of ways. Stepfamilies form after a process of loss and change. Members of stepfamilies come together at different phases of their individual, marital, and family life cycles. Children and adults have experienced different traditions and ways of doing things. Parent-child relationships have preceded the couple relationship, rather than followed it. Infants and toddlers have a parent elsewhere, if not in reality, at least in memory. About half of children in stepfamilies have contact with their noncustodial parent; therefore there are shifts in household membership when the children move between households. There is little or no legal relationship between stepparents and stepchildren.

Infants and Toddlers in Single-Parent Families

Single-parent families are those with one parent and dependent children. The number of single-parent families has more than doubled since 1970. At any given time approximately 31 percent of children are living in a single-parent household, more than 21 million children in 2004 (Annie E. Casey Foundation, 2006).

Single-parent families are as diverse as two-parent families. Approximately 80 percent of all single-parent families are headed by women alone, with an additional 9 percent living with single mothers with a partner. About 9 percent of children live with a single-parent father and an additional 2 percent of these fathers live with a partner. Despite the increased number of single-parent families, there is still a tendency to look at these families as dysfunctional, deviant, or unstable. Society has not focused on the strengths of single-parent families or accepted them as viable family units with variability in style, structure, and values. Given the number of children living in single-parent families, it is important to view their strengths as well as their challenges. See Table 10–17 for the number of single-parent families.

Adolescent Single Mothers

Adolescent motherhood is a complex and serious situation. Although the national teen pregnancy rate is falling (84.5 pregnancies per 1,000 women ages 15 to 19), it is still the highest among most developed countries. The poverty rate of children who are born to mothers between 15 and 19 who are not

Table 10–17 Percent of Children in Single-Parent Families in 2004

National Average	31
Non-Hispanic White	23
Hispanic/Latino	35
Black/African American	64
Asian and Pacific Islander	15
American Indian and Alaska Native	47

SOURCE: Annie E. Casey Foundation (2006).

married and did not graduate from high school is 78 percent (Annie E. Casey Foundation, 2006). See Table 10–18 for the number of births to adolescent single mothers.

The move away from the marital dyad is increasing for all families in the United States. In 2000, 79 percent of all teenage mothers were not married at the time of delivery. Grandmothers or other family members often take on parenting responsibilities. This provides a collective responsibility for the child, but often adds stress to the household (Annie E. Casey Foundation, 2006).

The stresses of single parenthood are complicated by being an adolescent. During adolescence, women experience multiple biological, social, cognitive, and psychological transitions and challenges. If an event such as an unwanted or unintended birth occurs during adolescence, they are likely to be developmentally unprepared to adjust psychologically and socially to parenthood. The concern is not just for the unexpected pregnancy, but also its implications for the child. Between 74 and 95 percent of adolescent pregnancies are unintended (Advocates for Youth, 2004). Women with unintended pregnancies are less likely to have good prenatal care, less likely to reduce or end the use of drugs, alcohol, and smoking, and, after the child is born, less likely to follow up on immunizations. Correspondingly, the risks of child abuse and neglect, low birth weight, infant mortality, and disability are greater (Annie E. Casey Foundation, 2006).

Infants born to adolescents experience long-term consequences as well. They are 50 percent more likely to be born at low birth weight, 50 percent more likely to repeat a grade, and less likely to graduate from high school. If female, she is 83 percent more likely to become a teenage mother. Males are 13 percent more likely to be incarcerated. Regardless of sex, they are twice as likely to be abused or neglected and two to three times more likely to run away from home (Annie E. Casey Foundation, 2006; Florida State University Center for Prevention and Early Intervention Policy, 1997). Early intervention and high-quality child care can change these statistics.

Table 10–18 Births per 1,000 Females Ages 15 to 19 in 2003

National Average	42
Non-Hispanic White	27
Hispanic/Latino	82
Black/African American	64
Asian and Pacific Islander	17
American Indian and Alaska Native	53

SOURCE: Annie E. Casey Foundation (2006).

Adolescent mothers are less verbal and less supportive of their infant's social/emotional development. Negative long-term child development outcomes have been found in the areas of intellectual development, social/emotional development, and school achievement. Opportunities for learning and nurturing missed early in life cannot be fully regained; by 18 months, infants raised in impoverished environments have cognitive deficits that may not be totally reversible (Florida State University, 1996). However, early intervention and good early care and education can make a long-term difference. Talk about talking to infants and toddlers even when they do not understand. Help them think about talking and music and ways to connect.

WITH INFANTS AND TODDLERS

Take time to talk with young mothers and to learn about their life and their beliefs about child rearing. Do not make judgments. Find out what kinds of support systems they have, both formal and informal. Talk with them specifically about what you do in the classroom and why. Talk about reading to infants and toddlers and why you spend time doing it. Be matter of fact. Do not tell them how to raise their infants and toddlers, rather help them think about experiences related to raising infants and toddlers. Look at the support you might potentially provide such as a lending book or toy library.

Infants and Toddlers in Gay and Lesbian Families

Until recently, early childhood educators have dealt with sexual orientation by ignoring it. As more people are more openly expressing their sexual preferences, the intersection between early childhood education and the gay community must be addressed (Laird, 2003). Several million gay men and female lesbians are parents. Because of the stigma associated with being identified as gay or lesbian, we have little reliable data about numbers of gay and lesbian couples (Kurdek, 2004). Children of these unions often experience discrimination. Some child care settings refuse to accept children from lesbian, gay, bisexual, and transgender families. Some adults express biased attitudes when children talk about their families and show little understanding of the unique issues these children face on a day-to-day basis (Dispenza, 1999).

Three types of family structure typify gay- and lesbian-headed families: blended families, single-parent families, and couples having children together. As most gay fathers and lesbian mothers became parents through a heterosexual marriage, blended families are the most common type. Approximately

65,500 adopted and 14,100 foster children live with gay and lesbian parents (Gates, Badgett, Macomber, & Chambers, 2007). Lesbian partners who want to have children in the context of their relationship adopt children or use artificial insemination. This practice is new and we do not know a lot about it (Kurdek, 2004).

Contrary to concerns about children in these relationships, studies have found that children's development does not differ from that of children raised in a heterosexual relationship, and that attention, love, and support seem to be more important in rearing children than the gender of the parents. Children seem well adjusted and a large majority develop a heterosexual orientation (Chan, Raboy, & Patterson, 1998).

WITH INFANTS AND TODDLERS

Early childhood educators need to explore their own feelings for evidence of homophobia and for the assumptions they make about the children in their classroom. It is an opportunity to also look at gender bias in general and stereotypical sex roles in particular. It is important to teach tolerance and support of those who do not follow traditional gender roles.

Infants and Toddlers in Families with Fewer Economic Resources

There is concern over the increasing number of children who live at or near poverty. The number of families who are totally dependent upon welfare has fallen from 2.8 million in 1976 to 960,000 in 2001. However, the number of poor children who are living in families with earned income and no public assistance has risen from 4.4 million in 1976 to 6.9 million in 2001. Of all children living in poverty, only 22 percent receive cash assistance (Annie E. Casey Foundation, 2003).

Poverty is a leading risk factor in negative outcomes for young children. Poverty is complex and multifaceted. It undermines families and the well-being of infants and toddlers. Poverty affects parents who are overwhelmed by the work and cost of caring for young children. Substandard housing and crowded conditions increase the probability of infection, which may be compounded by poor nutrition and lack of medical treatment so that conditions that respond easily to medication at an early stage are left untreated and may become serious or chronic.

Medicaid is one of two federal programs started by President Johnson in his War on Poverty in 1965. Medicaid was designed to provide health insurance for families whose income falls below a certain standard. It is closely tied, in reality and in people's minds, to welfare. Although it is a federal program and the federal government creates minimum standards, the program is administered by the states and varies among states. Not all physicians will accept Medicaid patients because of the fee structure set for their services and because of the time it takes to get their reimbursement. Families who cannot get regular medical care may wait until things get "bad" before they seek emergency room treatment. Infants and toddlers may miss well baby checkups and ongoing medical monitoring.

Poverty increases the probability that risk factors will be present simultaneously in the child, the parent, the parent's informal support system, and the neighborhood. The disadvantages of poverty permeate all of life, from health care and nutrition to quality of housing and neighborhoods to educational opportunities. The cycle of poverty is associated with poor maternal nutrition, increased substance abuse by pregnant women and low birth weight in infants. These are all potential causes of developmental problems and additional potential stressors in an already stressed system.

Women with low incomes have the highest rate of depression of any group. Mothers who are depressed are less responsive and nurturing, less aware of their infant's or toddler's moods, and more restrictive. Children raised in extreme poverty are at risk for developmental problems. The causes are complicated, but include poor cognitive/language stimulation, poor nutrition, exposure to safety hazards, and poor health care. Adverse financial circumstances affect the entire family and include increased risk of marital dissolution, family disorganization, physical abuse, and neglect (Annie E. Casey Foundation, 2006).

As we look at areas like welfare reform, it appears that there will be more young children living in poverty in the foreseeable future. These children may not have their basic needs met. One outcome of poverty can be homelessness.

Homeless Families

The number of people who are homeless in the United States is a matter of debate. They are a very difficult group to identify and definitions of homelessness vary. It can be a transient condition or a long-term issue. Definitive figures on homelessness are difficult to find. It is estimated that over 1 percent of the population or somewhere between 2 and 3 million people experience homelessness during a year and that about 700,000 individuals are homeless on a given night (U.S. Department of Health and Human Services, 2003).

Most of the homeless population is adult men; however, the proportion of women, children, and youth has increased to about 38 percent of the population. Children who were member of homeless families made up a fourth of the total homeless population and were the fastest growing segment of this population. Homeless families are diverse, but young single females with young children are the most frequent family configuration. About half the children in shelters were under five years of age (A Status Report on Hunger and Homelessness in American Cities, 1998).

Many of these homeless families have experienced high rates of violence and report that family violence was the primary cause of the homelessness. Often the mother took the children and left an abusive situation without time, emotional strength, or financial resources to find another secure place to live. Concern about additional violence may make having a permanent address impossible. Living on the streets or in shelters impacts infants and toddlers and their families. There are physical health problems related to homelessness: colds, tiredness, generally not feeling well, and feelings of depression are the most frequent and common health problems. By 18 months infants demonstrate significant delays (Hart-Shegos, 1999).

Homeless infants and toddlers may be hungry, have poor nutrition, and increased health problems. When they are homeless their parents may not have safe places to put their children; therefore, there is little opportunity for them to play and explore their environment. For a young child, becoming homeless is devastating. Conditions related to homelessness frequently lead to developmental delays; these are most apparent in emotional, motor, cognitive, and language development. Homeless children may display problems by acting out, exhibiting aggression, depression, inattentiveness, hyperactivity, chronic tiredness, anxiety, and for younger children, regression. From toddlerhood on, these delays will influence later behavioral and emotional problems (Hart-Shegos, 1999).

Infants and Toddlers Living in Violent Environments

No one likes to think about violence and young children. When violence does occur, we want to believe that it is the exception and that it is reported to make headlines and sell newspapers. When we read these articles, we also want to believe that infants and toddlers do not understand what is happening and therefore would not remember the experiences. Research findings negate such optimistic views.

Witnessing violence threatens a young child's basic trust in adults. Young children show their reactions in four specific areas: emotional distress, physical complaints, regression, and loss of skills, particularly in the language area (Groves, Lieberman, Osofsky, & Fenichel, 2000). Restoring the parent-child

WITH INFANTS AND TODDLERS

Parental roles may change as families move, and parents may not be emotionally available to their infants and toddlers when they are trying to cope with problems related to food, shelter, and finances. Poverty and homelessness are inextricably tied to the family and community. In many instances, these problems are compounded by violence.

In the United States, an increasing number of early care and education settings are including homeless children. First and foremost, these programs need to feel safe for children. Schedules should be predictable and there should be many opportunities to use large motor skills and to participate in dramatic play. This is challenging, because although many of the children are in programs when their family is in a shelter, rules about how long a family can stay in a shelter vary, and programming may be based on unstable funding sources and whether or not space is available. Some shelters have on-site child care settings; others use settings within the community. Regardless, child care is seen as an essential element in helping young children whose families are homeless. Many young homeless infants and toddlers are fearful. They frequently display emotional and behavior problems such as short attention span, withdrawal, aggression, speech delays, sleep disorganization, difficulty in organizing behavior, regressive behaviors, awkward motor behavior, and immature social skills.

relationship, where possible, is the primary goal of intervention. The best way to help children is to help their parents. As stress to families' increases, the probability for violence increases. Young children are exposed to this violence and frequently are the victims of it. Infants and toddlers *do* experience violence and it influences their lives. Because they do not have the language to express their feelings, it is the professional's role to comprehend the meaning of this violence for young children. In addition to being the victims of violence, children are exposed to violence on television in their homes and in the community. The United States is the most violent industrialized nation in the world (Zero to Three, 2007).

Parents worry about their ability to protect their children from violence and to keep them safe even when they are home or in their own neighborhood. Low income and minority parents report the most worries. Protecting their children is a basic family function. When they cannot do this, parents feel helpless and threatened. Although infants and toddlers may not be aware of violence in the community, they are aware of their caregivers' fears and anxiety and will be influenced by the adults' coping strategies (Osofsky, 1994; Rice & Groves, 2005).

Parents who raise infants and toddlers in violent environments may be depressed, sad, and anxious. Adults who are depressed tend to talk to children less and to be less responsive to their needs. They have difficulty controlling their emotions and their children experience more scoldings and shouts than hugs and kisses. Young children reflect this same depression and smile less and begin to withdraw into themselves. Adults may cope with violent environments in a variety of ways, becoming overprotective as a way of keeping their children safe. They might put toddlers to sleep in bath tubs to avoid random bullets and rarely take them outside or allow them to play on the playground (Osofsky, 1994; Rice & Groves, 2005).

Young children who are exposed to violence think about their world differently. Repeated exposure to violence is likely to have an even more significant effect and it is likely to be more pervasive as infants' and toddlers' understanding of events changes with increasing age. It will be difficult for such children to learn to trust others or to think about their environment as dependable and predictable. Traumatic events in infancy continue to negatively affect social, emotional, and cognitive growth into adulthood. Children abused or neglected in early childhood were younger at the time of their first arrest and committed twice as many offenses. Being abused and neglected increased the likelihood of being arrested as a juvenile by 59 percent, as an adult by 28 percent, and for a violent crime by 30 percent. This data also showed that females were at increased risk of arrest for violence as juveniles and adults (Widom & Maxfield, 2001).

Unlike older children, infants and toddlers have a very small repertoire of behaviors with which to show their distress. The symptoms children display are related to their age, gender, and circumstances. Some very young children who have been maltreated or exposed to violence withdraw and may become depressed; others may become aggressive. Among young children who see parents fight, boys are more likely to become aggressive and girls to withdraw. Other symptoms may include disrupted patterns of eating and sleeping, fearfulness, and difficulties in attending (Cicchetti & Lynch, 1993).

WITH INFANTS AND TODDLERS

Infants and toddlers living in violent environments need to know that their early care and education setting is safe. If they cannot feel safe, they cannot participate in activities fully. Part of their energy is spent being watchful and waiting, not engaging. Children learn over time that they are safe and only then become available for learning. Experiences need to be repeated to gain control and mastery. Parents need to know that their children are safe before they can be concerned about their ongoing development.

Twins can make child rearing more complex and throw a family that was barely coping over the edge to a place where kinship care is necessary. Child care plays an important role in helping infants to have stability during times of stress.

Infants and Toddlers in Kinship or Foster Care

Sometimes, child rearing becomes so complicated by other stressful conditions, such as physical or mental illness, domestic violence, and abuse connected with alcoholism or drug addiction, that the social service system decides that a child's safety is threatened. At any given time in the United States there are more than 514,000 children in the formal foster care system; of these children, 311,000 entered the foster care system and 287,000 left it in 2005. Of the children leaving the **foster care** system, 52,000 were adopted (Administration for Children and Families, 2006) Many of the children awaiting permanent homes have special needs. Of children between two months and two years in foster care, over half were at high risk for developmental delays or neurological impairments (Vanidvere, Chalk, & Moore, 2003).

Abandonment and removal of children from their biological family is occurring more frequently. The increase in the number of children in out-of-home placements is related to increases in substance abuse, AIDS, homelessness, and child abuse and neglect (Green, 2004). Child removal is an emergency response for their safety.

Foster care
is a living arrangement for children who a court decided cannot safely live with their biological parents.

Kinship care
is when children who cannot safely live with their biological parents live in a foster home with relatives or other adults that they know.

Private kinship care
refers to all kinship care arrangements that occur without the involvement of a child welfare agency.

Kinship foster care
is when a child welfare agency places children in the care of relatives.

Voluntary kinship care
is when a child welfare agency tells parents they will seek a foster care placement for the child unless they place the child with kin outside of their house.

One reason **kinship care** has become the preferred placement is that it can provide continuity and connectedness for children who cannot remain with their parents (Green, 2004). Kinship caregivers receive less supervision and fewer services than non-kin caregivers. Kinship foster parents tend to be older, in poorer health, and have fewer resources. This makes caring for young children a challenge.

There are both formal and informal kinship care arrangements. The most common type, which takes place outside of the child welfare system, is referred to as **private kinship care**. Such children are not considered part of the foster care system (Green, 2004). Increasingly, child welfare systems turn to relatives to act as foster families—**kinship foster care**. The third arrangement is typically used in cases of child abuse and neglect when a case worker suggests that a relative take a child without the state taking custody to keep the child in a **voluntary kinship care** placement

In 1999 there were 2.3 million children living with relatives without a parent in the home. Of these 1,800,000 were in private kinship care arrangements, 200,000 in kinship foster care, and 285,000 in voluntary kinship care (Green, 2004). The families who accept these children into their families were often themselves at risk.

Children in kinship foster care differ in significant ways from those in non-kin care. They are more likely to be younger, Black, and live in the South. The most common kin caregivers are grandparents.

The attachment process is affected when infants and toddlers are removed from their homes. Attachment is based on day-to-day interactions and having needs met for physical care, nourishment, and affection. Families who cannot fulfill these functions place young children at risk. These young children are in double jeopardy. They live with caregivers who are unavailable to them and place them at risk, but removing them from their homes may have negative consequences relative to attachment. "As a practical guide, for most children between the ages of two and five, a separation for more than two months is upsetting to the degree that it may lead to psychological harm" (Solnit & Nordhaus, 1992, p. 16). Approximately 18 percent of the children in foster care are two years old and under. About 25 percent of children are in care for less than 6 months and another 29 percent had spent between 6 and 18 months in foster care (Administration for Children and Families, 2006). Kinship care is desired to support young children staying connected to their birth parents.

Although eligible, few of the families receive grants to care for these children, and only about half of the eligible children receive Medicaid (Ehrle, 2001). This is part of an ongoing debate about whether kin should be responsible for providing informal supports to relatives or whether they are part of the child welfare system. It comes down to money. If they are part of the formal

WITH INFANTS AND TODDLERS

Having an infant or toddler in an early care and education setting where there is a stable attachment figure available is important. Ensure that classrooms are safe and responsive. Help infants and toddlers think and feel positive things about themselves. Build their self-esteem by supporting their contribution to your classroom. Be positive and see yourself as a resiliency mentor. Support foster families in the same way that you support all families. Recognize the very challenging position they find themselves in. The goal of foster care is to return infants and toddlers to their biological families. As they care for these infants and toddlers and try to be a stable caring adult figure for them, they are at the same time trying to help these infants and toddlers reconnect with their families. Evaluate what you do in the classroom relative to what these infants and toddlers will do at home. If there are not safe places to play outside or if their families don't have the energy for physically active play, ensure that infants and toddlers have many opportunities for this at school.

welfare system, they need financial support for caring for this child. If these children were to formally enter the child welfare system, it is estimated that the cost would be over $4.5 billion (Butts, 2001). But the situation is something of a stalemate in that the children are not part of the formal welfare system and their individual risks and those of the families who care for them are not really being addressed.

Families Who Adopt Infants and Toddlers

The number of children living with adoptive parents in the United States is increasing. According to the 2000 census, there are 2.1 million adopted children living in U.S. households, and 12.6 million of these children were under the age of 18, about 2 million were under age 6 (Administration for Children and Families, 2003). Of these children, 87 percent were born in the United States. Of the 13 percent who were foreign born, about half (48 percent) were born in Asia, a third (33 percent) in Latin America, and a sixth (16 percent) in Europe. Korea is the largest single source of foreign-born adopted children but accounts for 15 percent of children under age 6, with China contributing 3 percent. Most of the European born adopted children under age 6 (82 percent) came from Russia and Rumania. The situation in Mexico is different. Mexico accounts for one-third of Latin American adoptions. Only 50 to 200 immigrant visas were issued to Mexican children during the 1990s. These children have

Householder
refers to the person in whose name the housing unit is owned or rented.

been primarily adopted by relatives or by the union of non-Hispanic Whites and Hispanics who adopt stepchildren. Young children adopted from Guatemala and Colombia fit the more traditional pattern of adoption. Seventeen percent of adopted children were of a different race than their family **householder** (Administration for Children and Families, 2003).

The number of foreign adoptions is increasing, and the situations of many of these children before adoption places them at risk for disabilities. Likewise, children who are adopted out of the child welfare system have also experienced separation and often neglect or abuse before adoption. Over 12 percent of adopted children have at least one identified disability, as opposed to 5 percent of biological children. Disability data was only collected for children ages 5 to 17. It is likely that infants and toddlers have a higher rate of disability, but that aggressive intervention in early childhood has resolved some of these issues. Families who choose to adopt children have a higher income and higher levels of education than families with biological or stepchildren (Kreider, 2003)

When families adopt internationally they have less knowledge of the health and development of the children they are adopting than families do who adopt domestically. Internationally adopted children have been reported to have a range of developmental and behavioral difficulties. Growth and developmental delays were common in children adopted from China. Seventy-five percent had significant delays in at least one domain. These patterns are similar to the growth and developmental patterns of other internationally adopted children (Miller & Hendrie, 2000). Overall, children adopted from Guatemala had similar patterns of growth and developmental delays as other internationally adopted children, but these were milder. Of infants and toddlers adopted from Guatemala, those who were raised in foster care had better growth and cognitive development scores than those who were raised in orphanages before adoption. The younger the children were at adoption, the better off they were (Miller, Chan, Comfort, & Tirella, 2005).

The goal for all adoption is to act in the best interest of the child. Some countries are questioning whether allowing children from their country to be adopted by families from the United States is in the best interests of the child and the birth parents. There is also concern about preserving the child's family and cultural background. Whether international adoptions increase or are dramatically curtailed by the countries is a concern (Johnson, 2005).

Some families knowingly adopt children with special needs. The definition of special-needs adoption is different than when the term special needs is used related to a specific child. **Special-needs adoption** includes children who are older (typically over seven years of age), are members of a minority group or are biracial, have an identified disability, and/or need to be placed as a sibling group of more than two.

Special-needs adoption
refers to children who are over age 7, are nonwhite or biracial, have an identified disability or need to be placed as a sibling group.

up close and personal

Just imagine the joy of your first anything. It is exceptionally special: your first date, your first car, your first house. We experienced an exceptionally special first last year: our first grandchild.

Our son and daughter-in-law were unable to have their own child biologically, so they began the process of international adoption. We were totally amazed at the amount of paperwork, visits, applications, interviews, and so on, that were necessary to provide a loving, bountiful home to an unwanted child who would otherwise possibly be subject to living in poverty. Listening to their anguish as they proceeded through this process was heart wrenching. We helped when we could. I was asked to write a letter of recommendation for the couple. I spent many hours painstakingly trying to select the correct words, terminology, and statements. I had numerous people edit and comment on this important document. After all, I did want them to be accepted to be parents of our first grandchild.

Then came the home visitation. The agency was to visit their home to see if it would "pass inspection." We went up and cleaned and decorated and worked very hard to make their home seem welcoming to a child. Even their next-door neighbor offered to come out with her children so that the inspector could see that their neighborhood was "child friendly." It certainly takes a town to even get a child!

Finally the day came. I was never so excited to get this wonderful e-mail of a child's picture and birth certificate, which I could not read. My boss' husband researched the birth certificate and determined that the area was poverty stricken and that the adoption would most probably go through. That bit of information gave us some peace of mind. They sent pictures each time the child was brought to the doctor's office for a checkup. We loved this child and had never seen or held him. In the back of our minds was the ever-present fear of the parent(s) reneging on the decision to give José (now David) up for adoption.

This adoption that was to take 4 to 6 months took 10 long months. It was one setback after another. It was paperwork and paperwork and signatures and more sign-offs. Then, at a crucial time for some paperwork to be signed, the one person (imagine, only one person in the whole country of Guatemala) who had the authority to sign the form to finalize the process decided to go to Italy for several weeks to see a soccer match.

My daughter-in-law wanted to go visit the baby, but my son was cautious because of the fear of the process not culminating in the desired end. Finally, when things seemed fairly certain, they went down to spend a week with our grandson. We were ecstatic that they could bond with this beautiful boy. Still apprehensive of the situation, we sent down all sorts of gifts (perfume, jeans, soccer shirts, cash) to be handed out to key players in the adoption process in the hopes that this might motivate them to move the process along.

Home they came without the baby. My daughter-in-law's work gave her a period of three months to get the baby so that she would be eligible for maternity leave. Time was ticking away while the ghastly bureaucracy of adoption still crept on. The frustrations mounted each day with the insane nature of this process and the slow actions of the Guatemalan governmental agencies. We were convinced that it was a monetary issue—the longer the child stayed in Guatemala, the more money would be sent to them. Finally, the day came that my son and daughter-in-law went to Guatemala and returned with our grandson.

Perhaps the most frustrating of all was to see the amount of effort it took to bring this child into a loving, prosperous family when so many American children are being harmed and abandoned by their parents in the United States. International adoption was definitely a learning experience for all of us.

REFLECTIVE PRACTICE

How do you feel about international adoptions? Do you believe that adults in the United States should be allowed to adopt children from other countries? Do you think parents should support the child's knowledge of his birth culture or just expose him to the majority culture? Do you think he will experience prejudice?

WITH INFANTS AND TODDLERS

Infants and toddlers are typically adopted after a period of stress and separation. They have been required to make many transitions in their short lives. Building security and trust is imperative. Working closely with families and individualizing planning is important. Creating an environment that depicts children of many races and from many cultures joining together conveys an air of acceptance and support. Talk openly with children about skin and hair color. Children's books about adoption should be included in the classroom literature. Educators also need to be watchful for social and emotional problems, particularly those relating to trust, self-esteem, and identity.

Families who adopt children with special needs may be better informed than other adoptive parents. Caseworkers may be more selective in matching children and families. Parents may have more realistic expectations based on education and information prior to the adoption. And parents may have a good external support network (Lambie, 2000).

INFANTS AND TODDLERS WHOSE PARENTS HAVE DISABILITIES

Parents with disabilities are as diverse as those without disabilities. However, they may need accommodations that other parents may not. They may have become disabled after their infant or toddler was born or the disability may have preceded the child. Like their children, we need to view these parents as individuals first, parents second, and then consider how we will adapt to include them as we might include any other parent. There are approximately 9 million parents with disabilities, or 15 percent of all parents (*Through the Looking Glass*, 2007). Parents with disabilities face two barriers—those that are physical or architectural and those that are attitudinal. Many people judge parents with disabilities as inadequate. They may experience discrimination.

Learning Disabilities

Given the prevalence of learning disabilities, it is likely that you will be interacting with parents who have learning disabilities. By adulthood, most parents know what they need in the area of accommodation and may directly ask for it. For example, they might ask you to put things in writing that you might not think necessary. There may be some fonts or colors that make materials easier for them to read. Parents may ask to tape record meetings so they can play them back when they have additional time to think about what is being said. Given what we know about the heritability of learning disabilities, it is important to observe infants and toddlers for early signs of learning disabilities. Some parents with learning disabilities will share knowledge of their disability with you, others will not.

Developmental Delays

Parents with developmental delays typically function at a lower level of cognitive understanding than most parents. They may live independently with support from their family or a social service agency. They need support in understanding the changing needs of their infant or toddler. As an educator, you need to provide parents with information that is clear and at a level they can understand. Check the reading level of your written material to see whether it is reasonable to expect that parents can comprehend it. Provide very specific information and, where appropriate, drawings or photographs to support the written word. Stress safety issues.

Early care and education settings will provide most of the stimulation that infants and toddlers will receive. Ensure that your program is strong in language and literacy and that children have many experiences in play as a support for problem solving.

Parents in these families may lack complex problem-solving strategies. They may need to be specifically told the importance of playing with and stimulating an infant as well as providing custodial care. Parents with developmental delays seem to be able to cope with one child with an adequate support system. The demands of two children often tax the system.

Physical Disabilities

Many physical disabilities involve a mobility impairment. Parents with spinal cord injuries, multiple sclerosis, cerebral palsy, and other disabilities may use wheelchairs or other mobility aids. Your environment needs to be accessible to these parents. You need to consider where you will hold meetings. Not only do parents need to get into the building, but you need to consider accessibility to restrooms and transportation. You also need to consider how you will handle a personal assistant who may come with the parent.

Other types of physical disabilities may make parents fatigued or make it difficult to sit for an extended period. Obviously, some physical impairments do not interfere with communications; however, it is important to be open and inclusive with families and acknowledge how they have adapted to the tasks of child rearing. Do not exclude these families from participating in classroom experiences; consider how they can be included.

Psychological Disorders

Comorbidity
refers to the presence of one or more diseases or disorders in addition to the primary disease or disorder.

Adults with psychological disorders vary as individuals and with the nature and severity of their particular situation. The National **Comorbidity** Survey found that 49 percent of their respondents (18 to 60-plus years of age) experienced a psychiatric disorder at least once in their life, and 28 percent had such an experience within the past year (National Comorbidity Survey, 2005).

Men and women differ in the prevalence of particular psychological disorders. Men show higher rates for substance abuse (25 percent compared to 14 percent) and impulse control disorders (29 percent compared to 22 percent). Men are more likely to self-medicate with alcohol and illicit drugs as a method of coping, so their rates maybe underestimated, especially as they relate to mood and anxiety disorders. Women show higher levels of **anxiety disorders** (36 percent

Anxiety disorders
cover abnormal anxiety, fears, phobias, and nervous conditions.

Mood disorders are conditions where the common emotional state is distorted or inappropriate to the circumstances; they include depression as well as alternating states of depression and mania.

Impulse control disorders are characterized by an inability to resist the impulse to take actions that are harmful to oneself or others.

Substance disorders are the inappropriate use of drugs, alcohol, or nicotine with or without dependence.

compared to 25 percent) and **mood disorders**, which include depression (25 percent compared to 18 percent). Fluctuations in hormonal levels during the female life cycle are seen as being related to anxiety and depression. Hormonal changes during pregnancy are also related to this. During the major childbearing years (18 to 29), in any given year 22 percent of women are diagnosed with an anxiety disorder, 13 percent with a mood disorder, 12 percent with an **impulse control disorder**, and 13 percent with a **substance disorder**. Overall, 38 percent of individuals 18 to 29 years old are likely to have a psychological disorder during any 12-month period (National Comorbidity Survey, 2005).

Some parents with psychological disorders have a paralyzing listlessness, dejection, and overall feeling of helplessness that impact not only them but their infants and toddlers as well. Some anxiety and mood disorders manifest themselves in young adulthood. Families may have young children when the parents discover the presence of these disorders.

Adults with psychological disorders may need, in addition to counseling and medication, specialized help in developing and maintaining relationships with their infants and toddlers. The episodic nature of some mental health problems makes it particularly difficult. Illness in one parent may contribute to the other partner's problems or the partner may be able to compensate. Other problems relate to unpredictability and inconsistency. It is difficult to know what is going on in the home. Marital discord is common as is separation and divorce.

WITH INFANTS AND TODDLERS

Parents may or may not tell you about their psychological disorders. You as a keen observer need to be aware of their behavior and that of their infant or toddler. You may inquire how things are going if they seem down. Sometimes infants and toddlers will give you behavior cues or you will notice a change in their behavior, either acting out or withdrawing. Talk with parents about this if you notice it and express your concern. Having a predictable routine and stable caregivers who genuinely care about infants and toddlers and are sensitive to their changing moods helps.

Sensory Impairments

Adults with hearing impairments may wear hearing aids to help their understanding of speech. Depending upon the amount of residual hearing and when they acquired their hearing loss, their own speech may be difficult to understand. If their loss is severe or their identification is with the deaf community, they may use Signed English or American Sign Language (ASL). If they sign it will be necessary to have a sign language interpreter at conferences or programs that depend on oral language. The parent may know someone she feels comfortable with or it may be necessary to hire a sign language interpreter. For telephone communication, Telecommunication Device for the Deaf (TDDs) or the more advanced teletypewriters (TTYs) can be used. Both locations must have the TTY. TTYs consist of a keyboard which between 20 and 30 character keys and a display screen. The TTY converts the typed letters into electronic signals that can travel over regular telephone lines. When they reach their destination the receiving TTY converts them back into letters that are displayed on the screen or printed. TTYs can be stationary or portable and can be used with digital cell phones. Depending upon the features they cost between $225 and over $1,000. They are easy to learn how to use. E-mail and instant messaging is certainly another method of communication that is useful providing both parties have computers.

Adults who have visual impairments vary greatly in their ability to use sight to comprehend their world. Again, as adults they know the mode that works best for them and the simplest thing to do is to ask. They may need written communications to be larger and bolder, or they may require a phone call to have information given verbally. Initially the adult may need to be oriented to the building and to where her child's belongings are to be kept. She needs to be consulted on how she prefers this orientation and under what conditions. If she uses a service dog, be clear with the children and others that the dog is working and is not there as a pet. Get her permission before approaching the dog.

WITH INFANTS AND TODDLERS

Talk with parents about what they do and how they adapt their routines to accommodate their disabilities. Find out what parts of this process will work in the setting and what is important to establish some continuity between home and the early care and education setting. Work out a system with them for communicating necessary information. Talk with parents about what they want from the setting and to determine if there are things that you could emphasize that would be difficult for them and how they want you to do this.

Chronic Illnesses

Chronic illness affects all aspects of family life. Depending upon the particular illness it will impact the family in different ways. Conditions that can affect functioning include epilepsy, diabetes, traumatic head injury, asthma, chronic fatigue syndrome, HIV (human immunodeficiency virus), multiple chemical sensitivities, multiple sclerosis, or environmental illness. The particular chronic illness they have and its severity will impact what they find difficult and what they are able to do. Learn something about the illness, in particular, if the illness is progressive, such as cancer, and whether or not it is life threatening. Find out if it is episodic and if there are times when a parent may be almost symptom-free and other times when the parent may be incapacitated. Other illnesses once diagnosed may be stable. Knowing the course of a particular chronic illness will help you understand the behavior of an infant or toddler and work better with her parents. Parents may or may not share this information with you. To the extent that they do, it is important to find out the accommodations they need and follow through with providing them.

WITH INFANTS AND TODDLERS

Some chronic illnesses have a stigma attached to them such as epilepsy and HIV. Ensure that you keep confidentiality and that you work with parents and their infants and toddlers without prejudice. Work to develop trust with both the parents and their children.

The rights of parents with disabilities are protected under the Americans with Disabilities Act of 1990 (ADA). Early care and education settings are required to provide reasonable accommodations to parents, just as they would for infants and toddlers. The accommodations vary with the parent's particular disability. The first and most obvious step is to learn what accommodations are necessary and the best ways to deliver information to the parents. This information may be obtained from the parents themselves, their partners, or other service delivery systems who work with these families. Examples of reasonable accommodations have been noted by general disability area. If more than one disability is involved, more adaptations may need to be made.

Educators need to challenge their own attitudes and beliefs about disabilities and inclusion. They also need to think about the assumptions they make about parents who have disabilities and how they can be included in early childhood programs.

INFANTS AND TODDLERS IN TRANSIENT FAMILIES

The United States is a highly mobile society. More than 39 million Americans, or 14 percent of the population, changed addresses in 2004 (U.S. Census Bureau, 2005d). In urban areas, elementary schools often experience a 50 percent turnover rate in a given year (Lash & Kirkpatrick, 1990). Families move for many reasons, such as the purchase of a house, the search for better educational opportunities, more secure employment and social services. Some families with wage earners in the military, sales, and consulting relocate annually (Plucker & Yecke, 1999).

Families who move frequently are diverse and range from migrant families who move with the crops to military personnel to high ranking company executives, to upwardly mobile individuals following job opportunities. Regardless of who they are, they and their children face a common set of problems. They are frequently in a state of leave taking and arriving at new places. This means not only looking at housing issues and friendship patterns, but it also involves looking at issues relating to continuity in medical and child care. Socially, families must reestablish their support network in a new place.

The importance of family during the relocation process is paramount. Open communication and viewing the move as a common goal increases the likelihood that the transition will be a smooth one. As with other traumatic life events, a child's resilience increases when caring adults mediate these experiences. Helping infants and toddlers reestablish familiar routines, and maintaining ties with extended family and friends helps the transition process.

In some situations, such as those with migrant children, it is tempting for educators to feel that it is not worth getting involved with these infants and toddlers because they will soon move on. There are over 2.8 million migrant

Child care can provide a support system for transient families. Good nutrition, supporting self-esteem and providing safe places to play increase children's feelings of control and safety.

children, mostly Hispanic, who live and move with their families. As a typical family of five, they may earn less than $5,000 annually (Rothenberg, 1998). Children as young as four may be working in the fields. These children tend to enter school later, have difficulty concentrating due to fatigue or illness, attend class irregularly, and have high dropout rates (Davis, 1997). Migrant Head Start programs are designed to serve these children whose families are often isolated from community resources. The programs are designed to be flexible. During harvest they may be open at 4:00 AM and run until midnight, and may be open seven days a week. They may run for only the six weeks that the families are working in their area. Health, education, and nutritional specialists may follow the children as their families follow the crops (Duarte & Rafanello, 2001).

Lack of prenatal care contributes to the poor physical and mental health of the children. Infants and toddlers have high rates of infectious diseases and chronic illnesses. Their greatest strength is their extended family. They often travel together (Duarte & Rafanello, 2001). Although some of the problems faced by migrant children are unique, others are the result of a lifestyle based on frequent relocation and poverty.

WITH INFANTS AND TODDLERS

Early childhood settings need to have procedures in place to welcome new infants and toddlers at any time of the year. Entering children have two challenges: the educational transition and the social transition. With infants and toddlers the educational transition is a minor one unless the child has an identified disability. Methods of obtaining information from the previous setting need to be in place. If an infant or toddler has an Individualized Family Service Plan, it may need to be scanned and e-mailed or faxed to maintain continuity in programming. If these processes take too long, infants and toddlers may lose some of their emerging skills if they are not focused on and reinforced. Socially, infants and toddlers may be tentative and fearful of the new setting or they may adjust quickly. This is difficult to predict because it is impacted by so many variables, including the child and his temperament, how long the family had lived in the previous location, the reason for the move, and even the response of the family and siblings to the move.

Working with parents who have experienced several moves can be challenging. Many parents have found that the only way to get services for their children is to be strong advocates. Most are not trying to be pushy or aggressive, but are concerned that with the frequency of moving, time lost in receiving services will impact their infant or toddler negatively.

The purpose of reminding you of the diversity of family types is not to provide exhaustive information about these families, but rather to encourage you to reflect on the assumptions you make about families and how these assumptions play out in the curriculum you plan, the books you choose, and the terms you use. For example, the term "special grownup" or "special adult" may be more appropriate than "mother" or "father," depending upon the children's living arrangements. As educators we need to look at and understand the complexity of family structures in our society and discover how we can use this diversity to enrich our classroom and the learning environment. In addition to valuing diversity as educators, we need to work with children in the context of their family and the cultural values of that family.

COMMUNICATING WITH FAMILIES

Communication is the process we use to get and give information. It refers to nonverbal as well as verbal processes and includes the social context in which the communication occurs. It is an indicator of interpersonal functioning. To get and give information, clear communication, both verbal and nonverbal, is essential.

Communication includes speaking, listening, reflection of feelings, and interpretation of the meaning of the message (Berger, 2004). Communication is a complicated process because it takes into account not only the words spoken, but also nonverbal information such as the tone of voice and the body language that accompanies the words. The message is also filtered through the values of the receiver, and his past experiences as part of the decoding process. Once interpreted the responder sends a message back with treads the same complicated path.

Relying only on the content of the spoken word is not effective. Researchers believe that when interpreting communication, only 7 percent of the meaning of a conversation is conveyed by the verbal message (spoken word); 38 percent of the information is gleaned from the way the words are spoken (the vocal and tonal quality of the message accounts for); and 55 percent of the meaning is gathered from the visual message, the body language (Miller, Nunnally, & Wackman, 1975). As early childhood professionals we need to be conscious of these factors and monitor ourselves as communicators.

Knowledge of the communication process requires that important information be conveyed face to face with parents and that telephone conversations should be limited to nonemotional factual information. In addition to the general aspects of the communication process, individuals filter messages through their culture, values, and past experiences. Different people may interpret the same information differently. See Table 10–19 for characteristics of good communicators.

Table 10–19 Characteristics of Educators Who Are Good Communicators

Educators who are good communicators:

- give their attention to the person speaking, using eye contact and body language, and focus on what is being said.

- listen to parents to gather both the feelings and meaning behind statements. They clarify, reframe, or restate parental concerns, and distinguish between factual information and feelings. They do not criticize, moralize, blame, or judge others.

- recognize parents' feelings and govern what they say in the context of the relationship they have with the parents. They discuss the infant's or toddler's positive qualities before bringing up concerns.

- match their style of giving information and the amount of information they share with the parents' ability to handle the information. They do not "dump" all the information on the parents at one time if they feel the parents will not be able to handle the information.

- emphasize that concerns are no one's fault. They work together to solve problems and plan for the infant's or toddler's future.

- focus on one topic and encourage parents to talk and share information and have enough specific information to document both concerns and progress, but keep the focus on strengths.

- become allies with parents, viewing them as partners and working to empower them to help their children.

SOURCE: Berger (2004, p. 208).

Words are abstractions which stand for ideas. They make communication possible, but also confound it. Clarity is especially difficult when people from different cultural backgrounds communicate. Context is important in determining the meaning of words. The word *orange*, for example, can be a fruit or a color. The way it is used allows us to distinguish between the two meanings. However, as ideas become more abstract, clarity is more difficult. A parent might consider herself to have been a "little" late for picking up her daughter. The caregiver may have considered her "very" late.

Communication Techniques to Avoid

There are some ways of communicating that are likely to be counterproductive with parents—or with anyone, for that matter. They are not dependent upon the family's income or culture they are based on communication that is respectful and that works.

Avoid Giving Advice. It is often tempting to give parents advice on how to solve problems that they are having with their infant or toddler; it is rarely wise. It is appropriate to offer constructive suggestions, but even these should be given with care. Before giving suggestions, follow these steps:

1. Gather enough information about a situation to make the suggestions relevant.

2. Find out about the problem: when it occurs, how frequently it occurs, what parents have already tried to do to solve the problem, and whether or not these solutions were effective. Try to get as much specific information as possible before you offer any suggestions.

3. Paraphrase your perception of the problem to see whether or not it is the same as the parents.

4. Support the parents in their efforts to solve the problem by commenting positively on what solutions they have tried (if this is appropriate).

If you do find the need to offer suggestions, do so in a casual, tentative, nonjudgmental way. Offer several suggestions (optimally four) rather than just one. If you just give parents one suggestion, they are likely to come back to you and say, "I tried what you said and it didn't work."

Avoid the Word "Understand". Sometimes educators respond to a parent's problem by saying, "I understand exactly what you mean." This response is likely to trigger in a parent thoughts such as, "How can she understand? She isn't me. She doesn't walk in my shoes. She isn't the one getting up in the middle of the night," and so on. People who respond by "understanding" convey the impression to others that they really do not understand. An empathetic response is far more appropriate: "It must be difficult to get up in the night when you know you have to go to work the next day."

Avoid Judging and Blaming. Although we consciously try not to judge parents, sometimes our language gives us away. When parents feel they are being judged or blamed, they frequently become defensive. Starting out a conversation with "As you know..." is almost always offensive. Using words such as "ought" or "should" also implies judgment. Saying "You should always make sure Chunga has a warm coat" is different from saying "Chunga couldn't go outside today because she didn't have a warm coat." The former statement is likely to evoke a defensive reaction from a parent. This can end up being a no-win situation that, with some thought, could easily be avoided.

Avoid Mind Reading. Mind reading is assuming to know what another person is thinking or feeling without asking. When a parent says, "Tell me what I need to know," she is assuming that you can read her mind. If you respond to that statement, you will tell her what you find interesting or what you would want to know if you were the parent. For example, you may tell her the particular activities that her son enjoys when what she really wants to know is whether or not he is a "behavior" problem. If he is not, you are unlikely to mention it. You may not figure out what the parent wants to know; ultimately, the parent will be dissatisfied with the exchange. It is more useful to help the parent clarify what it is she wants to know than to assume you can read her mind. Do this by asking the parent for more specific information: "I want to tell you about what concerns you have. Can you ask me questions about certain aspects of the day?" If the parent persists in wanting to know about what you think is important, you may have to offer her choices: "Would you like to know about his sleeping, his eating, or how he gets along with the other children? Help me decide where to start." This will usually get a parent to at least state a preference.

Being an active and explorative listener is a good way to avoid mind reading. A parent might ask, "Do you think Mario is happy here?" To simply say yes does not answer the question. It may take some exploration on your part to find out what the parent is concerned about, such as, "Can you tell me more specifically what you want to know?" The parent may say, "I worry because he always cries when I leave him and I wonder if he cries all day." Then you can appropriately respond: "Mario continues to cry for about five minutes after you leave. A teacher holds him and she walks around the classroom with him as she tries to figure out what may interest him. She typically finds something and he gets involved playing. He is involved until naptime, and then he frequently withdraws and gets a little weepy. We rub his back until he settles down. The other difficult time for him is when the other children's parents come to pick them up. He becomes anxious for you. I can see why you might think he was unhappy all the time when you only see his most difficult times. Do you have suggestions for ways of comforting him that work well for you that we might try?"

Suppose, on the other hand, you had said, "Mario really enjoys climbing through the cardboard box tunnels that we make. It keeps him happy for a long time." Although a truthful answer, the parent might come away from the interaction feeling that you did not answer her question (even though she never really asked it).

ETHICAL BEHAVIOR IN EARLY CARE AND EDUCATION

Ethics comes from the Greek word *ethikos*, meaning moral or ethical. Codes of ethics are statements about the right way to conduct oneself in a profession. Some might ask why ethics are important for individuals who work with and study very young children. The National Association for the Education of Young Children (2005) focuses on four aspects of the profession that give rise to ethical problems.

⁂ Multiplicity of Clients. Who is served by child care and early education? The off-the-top-of-the-head response is typically "the child, of course," However, if that were solely true there would be fewer concerns about the cost of child care. In reality, the parent may be the first client group served, and then the child. At another level, there are organizational concerns and the interest of the community at large. Sometimes these can be in conflict. Parents may want accommodations that the administration is unwilling to support, staff may feel that what parents request is not in the best interest of the child, and so on.

☀ Power and Status. The staff of early care and education settings, as well as all adults who interact with infants and toddlers, have tremendous power over them. An infant's self-protective repertoire is very limited. He is dependent upon the adults in his life for his care and safety. Power can also be an issue between parents and staff. Because individuals who care for young children do not have high status, parents may make demands on them that they would not make with other professionals, such as their pediatricians.

☀ Ambiguity of Database. The field of early childhood education has a set of beliefs and the science to back up what constitutes "best practice" in the field. However, there are still some areas where there is little evidence and in some cases where we know the evidence the costs may become prohibitive for many parents. When answers are not clear cut, a code of ethics is necessary.

☀ Role Ambiguity. Are teachers of infants and toddlers more motherlike or more teacherlike? To the extent that they responsible for the whole child, not just his academic life, it may be unclear where boundaries should be drawn. What happens when parents and caregivers disagree over issues related to child rearing, discipline, toilet training, socialization, and so on? From the child's perspective, if they do disagree, what are the effects of this discontinuity on his development?

These are truly dilemmas, and increased diversity in the population increases the concerns of all. Staff must decide how they will handle the parent who does not want her son to play with dolls, as well as the parent who wants her daughter disciplined for her "bad" behavior by being slapped. This parent agrees that you cannot do this at school, but requests that you keep her informed so that she can punish her when she gets home. Do you tell her when the child has misbehaved?

SUMMARY

Partnering with families is an essential part of working with infants and toddlers. They are the experts on their infant or toddler. Although there are many different ways to work with families, all take into account the changing American family, including families that have different structures and those for whom English is a second language. Because of different cultural and ethnic styles of child-rearing, parents and educators must communicate to ensure some continuity between the early childhood setting and the home environment.

Early childhood educators need skills to include diverse children and their families. Knowledge of culture in general and also of the ways particular families embrace their culture is a critical part of understanding families and what they value. Parent education is one way parents and educators learn about each other.

CHAPTER IN REVIEW

- Partnering with families is an essential part of early childhood education, but changing family structure and demographics make it challenging for parents to be as involved as they would like.

- Programs and philosophies of parent education are changing and are more responsive to the characteristics of the population served.

- Collaborating and communicating with parents are essential parts of working with infants and toddlers.

- Parents need information about their children and you need to know about the infants and toddlers from their perspective.

- Parents and teachers typically see each other on a regular basis at their worst times: in the morning rush and at the end of the workday.

- Caregivers who are good communicators listen to parents and attend to them, focus on issues, and become allies with them.

- Infants and toddlers come from a variety of ethnic and cultural backgrounds and these differences should be reflected in their care and education.

- Caregivers need to be aware of their own cultural values, be sensitive to those of others, and adapt their communication and programming to accommodate diversity.

- Families are the experts on their children, and through collaborating with them educators can build early childhood programs that meet the parents' goals in a developmentally appropriate way.

- Educators need to adapt their programming to include infants and toddlers with special needs and their families in a cultural context.

- Educators need to be aware of the special challenges some families face in addition to rearing an infant or toddler.

- Professionals in early childhood education have a great responsibility to both infants and toddlers and their families. To provide appropriate service, they need to find out what services families want and need. They need to coordinate these services in a useful fashion and help deliver the services in a way that is respectful of all families.

APPLICATION ACTIVITIES

1. American families have changed dramatically over the past 40 years. Reflect on these changes. Describe the families that you would expect to be working with in 2050.

2. Develop a plan for learning more about your cultural and ethnic background. Look at the ways you embrace your culture and operate within it as well as ways that you do not. Answer the questions in Table 10–11 Acquiring Cultural Knowledge about yourself.

3. Develop a plan for increasing your knowledge about diverse cultures and how you will use this information to increase your responsiveness to infants and toddlers and their families.

RESOURCES

Web Resources

- **Alaskan Native Heritage Center** provides information about Alaska Natives Cultures. http://www.alaskanative.net.

- The **Annie E. Casey Foundation** supports *Kids Count*, which provides up-to-date information about the welfare of children using state and national data or comparisons. http://www.aecf.org.

- **Child Care and Early Education Research Connections** provides full-text articles and reports, compares state policies, and has information about funding, employment, and educational opportunities. www.researchconnections.org.

- **Child Trends Data Bank** is a source of current information about children and their families. http://www.child-trendsdatabank.org.

- The **Future of Children** is a publication of Princeton University and the Brookings Institute. They publish articles that look at some of the economic implications of early care and education such as foster care, obesity, poverty, and quality early childhood education. http://www.futureofchildren.org/.

- The **National Task Force on Early Childhood for Hispanics** provides information about the Latino culture and the early childhood education of Latino children. www.ecehispanic.org.

- **Native Americans** provides information about the American Indians, their culture, and their concerns. http://www.native-americans.com/.

- **Native Americans—Internet Resources** provides links to a variety of internet resources about American Indians. http://falcon.jmu.edu.

- **Parents with Developmental Disabilities** shares information on the struggles parents face in raising their children. Videos make site this come alive and provide good information for discussing the rights of parents. http://www.developmentaldisability.org.

- The **Smithsonian** has information about African American history and culture. http://www.si.edu.

Print Resources

※ Berger, E. H. (2004). *Parents as partners in education: Families and schools working together* (6th ed.). Upper Saddle River, NJ: Pearson/Merrill Prentice Hall.

※ Lynch, E. W., & Hanson, M. J. (2004). *Developing cross-cultural competence: A guide for working with children and their families* (3rd ed.). Baltimore, MD: Paul H. Brookes Publishing Co.

REFERENCES

A Status Report on Hunger and Homelessness in American Cities. (1998). Washington, DC: The United States Conference of Mayors.

Administration for Children and Families. (2003). U.S. census counts adopted children for the first time. Retrieved May 17, 2007, from http://cbexpress.acf.hhs.gov/articles.cfm?issue_id=2003-10&article_id=717

Administration for Children and Families. (2006). Trends in foster care and adoption. Retrieved May 17, 2007, from http://www.acf.hhs.gov/programs/cb/stats_research/afcars/trends.htm

Advocates for Youth. (2004). *Adolescent pregnancy and childbearing in the United States.* Washington, DC: Author.

Alaskan Native Heritage Center. (2000). Information about Alaska Natives Cultures. Retrieved November 17, 2007, from http://www.alaskanative.net/2.asp

Amato, P. R. (2004). Divorce in social and historical context: Changing scientific perspectives on children and marital dissolution. In M. Coleman & L. H. Ganong (Eds.), *Handbook of contemporary families: Considering the past, contemplating the future* (pp. 265–281). Thousand Oaks, CA: Sage.

Americans with Disabilities Act of 1990, Pub. L. No. 101–336, § 2, 104 Stat. 328 (1991).

Annie E. Casey Foundation. (2003). *Kids count data book: State profiles of child well-being.* Baltimore, MD: Author.

Annie E. Casey Foundation. (2006). *Kids count data book: State profiles of child well-being.* Baltimore, MD: Author.

Baldridge, D. (2001). Indian elders: Family traditions in crisis. *American Behavioral Scientist, 44,* 1515–1527.

Berger, E. H. (2004). *Parents as partners in education: Families and schools working together* (6th ed.). Upper Saddle River, NJ: Pearson/Merrill Prentice Hall.

Berk, L. E. (2002). *Infants, children, and adolescents* (4th ed.). Boston, MA: Allyn & Bacon.

Bronfenbrenner, U. (1979). *The ecology of human development: Experiments by nature and design.* Cambridge, MA: Harvard University Press.

Bronfenbrenner, U. (1989). Ecological systems theory. In R. Vasta (Ed.), *Annals of child development* (Vol. 6, pp. 187–249). Greenwich, CN: JAI Press.

Bronfenbrenner, U., & Morris, P. A. (1998). The ecology of developmental processes. In W. Damon & R. M. Lerner (Eds.), *Handbook of child psychology: Theoretical models of human development* (5th ed., Vol. 1, pp. 993–1029). New York: Wiley.

Bumpass, L. L., & Lu, H. H. (2000). Trends in cohabitation and implications for children's family contexts in the United States. *Population Studies, 54,* 29–41.

Bumpass, L. L., & Raley, R. K. (1995). Redefining single parent families: Cohabitating and changing family reality. *Demography, 32,* 97–109.

Butts, D. (2001, April 3). *Kinship care: When parents can't parent.* First Tuesdays at the Urban Institute. Retrieved November 28, 2006, from http://www.urban.org/url.cfm?ID=900378

Capps, R., Fix, M., Ost, J., Reardon-Anderson, J., & Passel, J. S. (2005). *The health and well-being of young children of immigrants.* Washington, DC: The Urban Institute.

Carrasquillo, O., Lantigua, R. A., & Shea, S. (2000). Differences in functional status of Hispanic versus non-Hispanic white elders: Data from the medical expenditure panel survey. *Journal of Aging and Health, 12*(3), 342–361.

Chan, R. W., Raboy, B., & Patterson, C. J. (1998). Psychosocial adjustment among children conceived via donor insemination by lesbian and heterosexual mothers. *Child Development, 69,* 443–457.

Chan, S., & Lee, E. (2004). Families with Asian roots. In E. W. Lynch & M. J. Hanson (Eds.), *Developing cross-cultural competence: A guide for working with children and their families* (3rd ed., pp. 219–298). Baltimore, MD: Paul H. Brookes.

Children's Defense Fund. (2000). *The state of America's children yearbook.* Washington, DC: Author.

Children's Defense Fund. (2002). *The state of children in America's union. A 2002 action guide to leave no child behind.* Washington, DC: Author.

Children's Defense Fund. (2007). Nine million uninsured children need a solution now. Retrieved May 19, 2007, from http://www.childrensdefense.org/site/PageServer

Cicchetti, D., & Lynch, M. (1993). Toward an ecological/transaction model of community violence and child maltreatment: Consequences for child development. In D. Reiss, J. E. Richters, & M. Radke-Yarrow (Eds.), *Children and violence* (pp. 96–118). New York: Guilford Press.

Crosbie-Burnett, M., & McClintic, K. M. (2000). Remarriage and recoupling. In P. C. McKenry & S. J. Price (Eds.), *Families and change: Coping with stressful events and transitions* (pp. 303–332). Thousand Oaks, CA: Sage.

Cross, T. L., Bazron, B. J., Dennis, K. W., & Isaacs, M. R. (1989). *Towards a culturally competent system of care: A monograph on effective services for minority children who are severely emotionally disturbed.* Washington, DC: Georgetown University Child Development Center.

Davis, S. (1997). *Child labor in agriculture.* ERIC Digest (Las Cruces, NM): EDO-RC-96-10.

Davis, C., & Yang, A. (2005). *Parents and teachers working together.* Markham, Ontario, Canada: Pembroke.

Derman-Sparks, L., & the A.B.C. Task Force. (1989). *Anti-bias curriculum: Tools for empowering young children.* Washington, DC: NAEYC.

Dispenza, M. (1999). *Our families, our children.* Seattle, WA: Child Care Resources.

Duarte, G., & Rafanello, D. (2001). The migrant child: A special place in the field. *Young Children, 56*(2), 26–34.

Ehrle, J. (2001, April 3). *Kinship care: When parents can't parent.* First Tuesdays at the Urban Institute. Retrieved November 28, 2006, from http://www.urban.org/url.cfm?ID=900378

Eschbach, K. (1993). Changing identification among American Indians and Alaska Natives. *Demography, 30,* 635–652.

Eshleman, J. R. (2000). *The family* (9th ed.). Needham Heights, MA: Allyn & Bacon.

Federal Interagency Forum on Child and Family Statistics. (2007). *America's Children: Key national indicators of well being, 2007*. Author, Washington, DC: U.S. Government Printing Office. Retrieved November 18, 2007, from http://www.childstats.gov/americaschildren/index.asp

Fields, J. (2003). *Children's living arrangements and characteristics: March 2002*. Current Population Reports, P20-547. Washington, DC: U.S. Census Bureau. Retrieved November 28, 2006, from http://www.census.gov/prod/2003pubs/p20-547.pdf

Florida State University. (1996). *Teen pregnancy final report*. Tallahassee, FL: Author.

Florida State University Center for Prevention and Early Intervention Policy. (1997). *Florida's children: Their future is in our hands*. Tallahassee, FL: The Task Force for Prevention of Developmental Handicaps, Florida Developmental Disabilities Council.

Gates, F., Badgett, L. M. V., Macomber, J. E., & Chambers, K. (2007). Adoption and foster care by lesbian and gay parents in the United States. The Urban Institute. Retrieved November 17, 2007, from http://www.urban.org/publications/411437.html

Gonzalez-Mena, J. (2005). *Diversity in early care and education: Honoring differences* (4th ed.). Boston, MA: McGraw Hill.

Grieco, E. M., & Cassidy, R. C. (2001). Overview of race and Hispanic origin. U.S. Census Bureau. Retrieved October 31, 2005, from http://www.census.gov/prod/2001pubs/c2kbr01-1.pdf

Green, R. (2004). The evolution of kinship care policy and practice. *The Future of Children, 14*(1), 131–194. Retrieved May 18, 2007, from http://thefutureofchildren.org/usr_doc/8-green.pdf

Groves, B. M., Lieberman, A. F., Osofsky, J. D., & Fenichel, E. (2000). Protecting young children in violent environments—A framework to build on. *Zero to Three, 20*(5), 9–13.

Halgunseth, L. C. (2004). Continuing research on Latino families: El pasado y el futuro. In M. Coleman & L. H. Ganong (Eds.), *Handbook of contemporary families: Considering the past, contemplating the future* (pp. 333–351). Thousand Oaks, CA: Sage.

Hanson, M. J. (2004). Families with Anglo-European roots. In E. W. Lynch & M. J. Hanson (Eds.), *Developing cross-cultural competence: A guide for working with children and their families* (3rd ed., pp. 81–108). Baltimore, MD: Paul H. Brookes.

Harjo, S. S. (1993). The American Indian experience. In H. P. McAdoo (Ed.), *Family ethnicity: Strength in diversity* (pp. 199–207). Thousand Oaks, CA: Sage.

Hart-Shegos, E. (1999). Homelessness and it effects on children: A report prepared for the family housing fund. Hart-Shegos and Associates, Inc. Retrieved May 17, 2007, from http://fhfund.org/dnldreports/SupportiveChildren.pdf

Henderson, A. T., & Mapp, K. L. (2002). *A new wave of evidence: The impact of school, family, and community connections on student achievement*. Austin, TX: Southwest Educational Development Laboratory.

Hernandez, D. (2006). Young Hispanic children in the U.S.: A demographic portrait based on Census 2000. National Task Force on Early Childhood Education for Hispanics. New York: Foundation for Child Development. Retrieved May 15, 2007, from http://www.ecehispanic.org/work/September_update_2006.doc

Hetherington, E. M., & Kelly, J. (2002). *For better or worse*. New York: Norton.

Ishii-Kuntz, M. (2004). Asian American families: Diverse history, contemporary trends and the future. In M. Coleman & L. H. Ganong (Eds.), *Handbook of contemporary families: Considering the past, contemplating the future* (pp. 369–384). Thousand Oaks, CA: Sage.

Joe, J. R., & Malach, R. S. (2004). Families with American Indian roots. In E. W. Lynch & J. Hanson (Eds.), *Developing cross-cultural competence: A guide for working with children and their families* (3rd ed., pp. 109–139). Baltimore, MD: Paul H. Brookes.

Johnson, D. E. (2005). International adoption: What is fact, what is fiction, and what is the future? *Pediatric Clinics of North America, 52*(5), 1221–1246.

Kawamoto, W. T., & Cheshire, T. C. (2004). A seven-generation approach to American Indian families. In M. Coleman & L. H. Ganong (Eds.), *Handbook of contemporary families: Considering the past, contemplating the future* (pp. 385–393). Thousand Oaks, CA: Sage.

Kieff, J., & Wellhousen, K. (2000). Planning family involvement in early childhood programs. *Young Children, 55*(3), 18–25.

Kreider, R. M. (2003). Adopted children and stepchildren: 2000. Census 2000 special reports. U.S. Census Bureau. Retrieved May 18, 2007, from http://www.census.gov/prod/2003pubs/censr-6.pdf

Kurdek, L. A. (2004). Gay men and lesbians. In M. Coleman & L. H. Ganong (Eds.), *Handbook of contemporary families: Considering the past, contemplating the future* (pp. 97–115). Thousand Oaks, CA: Sage.

Laird, J. (2003). Lesbian and gay families. In F. Walsh (Ed.), *Normal family processes* (3rd ed., pp. 176–209). New York: Guilford Press.

Lambie, R. (2000). *Family systems within educational contexts: Understanding at-risk and special-needs students* (2nd ed.). Denver, CO: Love.

Lash, A. A., & Kirkpatrick, S. L. (1990). A classroom perspective on student mobility. *Elementary School Journal, 88*, 369–386.

Lassiter, S. M. (1995). *Multicultural clients: A professional handbook for health care providers and social workers.* Westport, CN: Greenwood Press.

Lengua, L. J., Wolchik, S., Sandler, I. N., & West, S. G. (2000). The additive and interactive effects of parenting and temperament in predicting problems of children of divorce. *Journal of Clinical Psychology, 29*, 232–244.

Lynch, E. W., & Hanson, M. J. (Eds.) (2004). *Developing cross-cultural competence: A guide for working with children and their families* (3rd ed.). Baltimore, MD: Paul H. Brookes.

McKenry, P. C., & Price, S. J. (2005). *Coping with stressful events and transitions.* Thousand Oaks, CA: Sage.

Martin, M. T., Emery, R. E., & Peris, T. S. (2004). Single-parent families: Risks, resilience, and change. In M. Coleman & L. H. Ganong (Eds.), *Handbook of contemporary families: Considering the past, contemplating the future* (pp. 282–301). Thousand Oaks, CA: Sage.

McGoldrick, M. (1993). Ethnicity, cultural diversity, and normality. In F. Walsh (Ed.), *Normal family processes* (2nd ed., pp. 331–360). New York: Guilford Press.

Miller, L. C., Chan, W., Comfort, K., & Tirella, L. (2005). Health of children adopted from Guatemala: Comparison of orphanage and foster care. *Pediatrics, 115*(6), e710–e717.

Miller, L. C., & Hendrie, N. W. (2000). Health of children adopted from China. *Pediatrics, 105*(6), E76.

Miller, S., Nunnally, E. W., & Wackman, D. B. (1975). *Alive and aware: How to improve your relationships through better communications.* Minneapolis, MN: Interpersonal Communications Programs.

Mokuau, N., & Tauili'ili, P. (2004). Families with Native Hawaiian and Samoan roots. In E. W. Lynch & M. J. Hanson (Eds.), *Developing cross-cultural competence: A guide for working with children and their families* (3rd ed., pp. 345–372). Baltimore, MD: Paul H. Brookes.

National Association for the Education of Young Children. (2005). Position Statement: Code of Ethical Conduct and Statement of Commitment. Retrieved November 17, 2007, from http://www.naeyc.org/about/positions/PSETH98.asp

National Association of Child Care Resource and Referral Agencies (NACCRRA). (2006). Breaking the piggybank: Parents and the high price of child care. Retrieved May 11, 2007, from http://www.naccrra.org/docs/policy/breaking_the_piggy_bank.pdf

National Center for Health Statistics. (2002). Cohabitation, Marriage, Divorce, and Remarriage in the United States. Series Report 23, Number 22. 103pp. Retrieved November 18, 2007, from http://www.cdc.gov/nchs/pressroom/02news/div_mar_cohab.htm

National Comorbidity Survey. (2005). Lifetime prevalence of DSM-IV/WMH-CIDI disorders by sex and cohort. Retrieved May 18, 2007, from http://www.hcp.med.harvard.edu/ncs/publications.php

National PTA. (2000). *Building successful partnerships: A guide for developing parent and family involvement programs*. Bloomington, IN: National Educational Service.

National Task Force on Early Childhood Education for Hispanics. (2007). Hispanic children gain an academic edge when their education starts early. Retrieved May 15, 2007, from http://www.ecehispanic.org/work/expand_PR.pdf

NICHD Early Child Care Research Network. (2005). Duration and developmental timing of poverty and children's cognitive and social development from birth through third grade. *Child Development, 76*(4), 795–810.

Ogunwole, S. U. (2006). We the people: American Indians and Alaska Natives in the United States: Census 2000 Special Reports. Retrieved May 15, 2007, from http://www.census.gov/population/www/socdemo/race/censr-28.pdf

Okagaki, L., & Diamond, K. E. (2000). Responding to cultural and linguistic differences in the beliefs and practices of families with young children. *Young Children, 55*(4), 74–80.

Olson, D. H., & DeFrain, J. (1997). *Marriage and the family: Diversity and strengths* (2nd ed.). Mountain View, CA: Mayfield.

Osofsky, J. D. (1994). Introduction. In J. D. Osofsky & E. Fenichel (Eds.), *Hurt, healing, hope: Caring for infants and toddlers in violent environments. Zero to Three, 14*(3), 3–6.

Peters, D., & Kontos, S. (1987). Continuity and discontinuity of experience: An intervention perspective. In D. Peters & S. Kontos (Eds.), *Annual advances in applied developmental psychology: Vol. II. Continuity and discontinuity of experience in child care* (pp. 1–16). Norwood, NJ: Ablex Publishers.

Plucker, J. A., & Yecke, C. P. (1999). The effect of relocation on gifted students. *Gifted Child Quarterly, 43*(2), 95–106.

Powell, D. R. (1998). Reweaving parents into the fabric of early childhood programs. *Young Children, 53*(5), 60–67.

Rice, K., & Groves, B. (2005). *Hope and healing: A caregivers' guide to helping young children affected by trauma*. Washington, DC: Zero to Three.

Rothenberg, D. (1998). *With these hands: The hidden world of migrant farm workers today*. Berkeley, CA: University of California Press.

Santos, R. M., & Chan, S. (2004). Families with Pilipino roots. In E. W. Lynch & M. J. Hanson (Eds.), *Developing cross-cultural competence: A guide for working with children and their families* (3rd ed., pp. 299–344). Baltimore, MD: Paul H. Brookes.

Schachter, J. P. (2003). *Migration by race and Hispanic origin: 1995 to 2000*. Census 2000 Special Reports. Washington, DC: U.S. Census

Bureau. Retrieved November 28, 2006, from http://www.census.gov/prod/2003pubs/censr-13.pdf

Schmidley, D. (2003). The foreign-born population in the United States: March 2002. Current Population Reports, P20-539. Washington, DC: U.S. Census Bureau.

Seltzer, J. A. (2000). Families formed outside of marriage. *Journal of Marriage and the Family, 62,* 1247–1268.

Solnit, A. J., & Nordhaus, B. F. (1992). *When home is not haven: Child placement issues.* New Haven, CT: Yale University Press.

Strong, M. F. (1999). Serving mothers with disabilities in early childhood education programs. *Young Children, 54*(3), 10–17.

Takanishi, R. (2004). Leveling the playing field: Supporting immigrant children from birth to eight. New York: Foundation for Child Development. Retrieved March 20, 2007, from http://fcd-us.org/uploadDocs/RTPackard06_11_04.pdf

Through the Looking Glass. (2007). Parents with disabilities. Retrieved May 18, 2007, from http://lookingglass.org/parents/

Tucker, M. B., Subramanian, S. K., & James, A. D. (2004). Diversity in African American families: Trends and projections. In M. Coleman & L. H. Ganong (Eds.), *Handbook of contemporary families: Considering the past, contemplating the future* (pp. 352–368). Thousand Oaks, CA: Sage.

U.S. Bureau of the Census. (1995). Top 25 American Indian tribes for the United States: 1990 and 1980. Retrieved May 15, 2007, from http://www.census.gov/population/socdemo/race/indian/ailang1.txt

U.S. Bureau of the Census. (1998). *Marital status and living arrangements: March 1996* (Current Population Reports, Series P20-496). Washington, DC: U.S. Government Printing Office.

U.S. Bureau of the Census. (1999). Region of birth of the foreign-born population: 1850–1930; 1960–1990. Retrieved May 19, 2007, from http://www.census.gov/population/www/documentation/twps0029/tab02.html

U.S. Bureau of the Census. (2000). *The Hispanic population in the United States: Current population characteristics, March 1999* (Current population Reports, Series P20-527). Washington, DC: U.S. Government Printing Office.

U.S. Census Bureau. (2002). Introduction to Census 2000 data products—American Indian and Alaska native. Retrieved May 15, 2007, from http://factfinder.census.gov/home/aian/mso01icd.pdf

U.S. Census Bureau. (2004). Projected population of the United States by race and Hispanic origin: 2000 to 2050. Retrieved May 19, 2007, from http://www.census.gov/ipc/www/usinterimproj/

U.S. Census Bureau. (2005a). Hispanic Population Passes 40 Million. Census Bureau Reports. Retrieved May 14, 2007, from http://www.census.gov/Press-Release/www/releases/archives/population/005164.html

U.S. Census Bureau. (2005b). Income, poverty, and health insurance coverage in the United States: 2005. Retrieved May 14, 2007, from http://www.infoplease.com/ipa/A0104688.html

U.S. Census Bureau. (2005c). Poverty: 2005 highlights. Retrieved May 14, 207, from http://www.census.gov/hhes/www/poverty/poverty05/pov05hi.html

U.S. Census Bureau. (2005d). Mobility. Retrieved May 18, 2007, from http://ask.census.gov/cgi-bin/askcensus.cfg/php/enduser/std_adp.php?p_faqid=366&p_created=1079983195&p_sid=TrUQBVBi&p_accessibility=0&p_redirect=&p_lva=&p_sp=cF9zcmNoPTEmcF9zb3J0X2J5PSZwX2dyaWRzb3J0PSZwX3Jvd19jbnQ9NTkm cF9wcm9kcz0mcF9jYXRzPSZwX3B2PSZwX2N

2PSZwX3BhZ2U9MSZwX3NlYXJjaF90ZXhOPU
51bWJlciBvZiBwZW9wbGUgbW92aW5nIGFu
bnVhbGx5&p_li=&p_topview=1

U.S. Census Bureau. (2007). Annual estimates of the population by age and sex for the United States: April 1, 2000–July 1, 2006 Retrieved November 10, 2007, from http://www.census.gov/popest/national/asrh/htm

U.S. Department of Health and Human Services. (2003). Ending chronic homelessness: Strategies for action. Retrieved May 17, 2007, from http://aspe.hhs.gov/hsp/homelessness/strategies03/

U.S. Department of Health and Human Services. (2007). The 2007 HHS poverty guidelines. Retrieved November 11, 2007, from http://aspe.hhs.gov/poverty/07poverty.shtml

U.S. National Center for Health Statistics. (2000). *Births: Final data for 1998.* National vital statistics reports, *48*(4). Washington, DC: U.S. Government Printing Office.

Vanidvere, S., Chalk, R., & Moore, K. A. (2003). Children in foster homes: How are they faring? Research Brief, Publication #2003023. Washington, DC: Child trends. Retrieved May 17, 2007, from http://childtrends.org/files/FosterHomesRB.pdf

Wallerstein, J., Lewis, J., & Blakeslee, S. (2000). *The unexpected legacy of divorce: A twenty-five year landmark study.* New York: Hyperion Press.

Walsh, F. (2003). Changing families in a changing world: Reconstructing family normality. In F. Walsh (Ed.), *Normal family processes* (3rd ed., pp. 3–26). New York: Guilford Press.

Widom, C. S., & Maxfield, M. G. (2001). An update on the "cycle of violence," National Institute of Justice research in brief. Office of Justice Programs. Retrieved May 17, 2007, from http://www.ncjrs.giv/txtfiles1/nij/184894.txt

Willis, W. (2004). Families with African American Roots. In E. W. Lynch & J. Hanson (Eds.), *Developing cross-cultural competence: A guide for working with children and their families* (3rd ed., pp. 141–177). Baltimore, MD: Paul H. Brookes.

Zero to Three. (2007). Research summary: Children exposed to violence. Retrieved May 17, 2007, from http://www.zerotothree.org/sit4e/DocServer/children_Exp_to_Violence.pdf?docID=2502

chapter 11

Inclusive Curriculum Planning for Infants and Toddlers

Chapter Outline

- Standards and Accreditation in Early Care and Education
- Curriculum Approaches in Early Care and Education
- Developmentally Appropriate Practice
- Curriculum for Infants and Toddlers
- Assessment and Record Keeping for Infants and Toddlers
- Adult Interactions with Infants and Toddlers

- Continuum of Teaching Techniques
- Multicultural Education
- Including Infants and Toddlers with Developmental Delays
- Safety, Health, and Nutrition
- Planning and Curriculum for Multiage Groups
- Developing a Philosophy of Working with Infants and Toddlers

The next four chapters focus on curriculum and planning for infants and toddlers. This chapter focuses on the principles that underlie all curriculum planning. Three chapters, one each on curriculum and planning for young infants (birth to 9 months), for mobile infants (8 to 18 months), and for toddlers (16 to 36 months), follow it. The first step in planning, regardless of the age of the child, is to clarify your philosophy of teaching. The topics that are part of your philosophy should be familiar to you. You have encountered them in other parts of the book. This chapter asks that you address a variety of topics for the specific purpose of clarifying your personal philosophy of working with infants and toddlers.

WHY STUDY INCLUSIVE CURRICULUM PLANNING?

※ Knowing about different curriculum approaches for educating infants and toddlers allows you to reflect on how these fit with your philosophy and how you can incorporate all or parts of them.

※ Clarifying your philosophy will help you know what positions to seek and will provide the basis for answering questions about early care and education.

※ Having a variety of teaching techniques gives you a repertoire to choose from as you educate infants and toddlers.

※ Making decision about the importance of content and process, inclusion, allocating time, and arranging the environment impact and are impacted by your philosophy.

※ Understanding developmentally appropriate practices and the principles behind them will support your understanding of infants and toddlers and how to work with them.

STANDARDS AND ACCREDITATION IN EARLY CARE AND EDUCATION

In all early childhood programs there are some qualities that are characteristic of high-quality programs. The National Association for the Education of Young Children (NAEYC) is dedicated to improving the quality of early childhood programs. It has developed a set of standards to acknowledge and improve the professional practices in early childhood education and to increase public knowledge about the importance of quality in early childhood education. The NAEYC (2006a) program standards focus on four areas: children, teaching staff, family and community partnerships, and leadership and administration. See Table 11–1 for the focus of the standards and the program standards under each foci.

This holistic approach is designed to have high-quality early care and education for infants and toddlers but also to acknowledge that infants and toddlers live in families and communities. Likewise, if infants and toddlers are going to have caregivers who care about them who are there for them, then standards must also address staff conditions to reduce staff turnover. There is wide agreement about what constitutes high-quality care. However, how different programs institute that care is very different. There are many curriculum models in early childhood education.

Table 11–1 Program Standards

Focus Area: Children

Program Standard 1:

Relationships: the focus is on developing positive relationships among all children and adults.

Program Standard 2:

Curriculum: the focus is on curriculum that has consistent goals for children and promotes learning and development in cognitive, emotional, language, social, and aesthetic development.

Program Standard 3:

Teaching: the focus is on adherence to developmentally, culturally, and linguistically appropriate teaching that results in children learning.

Program Standard 4:

Assessment of Child Progress: the focus is on ongoing systematic formal and informal assessment to document children's learning and development and to make sound decisions about children, teaching, and programs.

Program Standard 5:

Health: the focus is on the health, safety, and nutrition of children and staff.

Focus Area: Teaching Staff

Program Standard 6:

Teachers: the focus is on educationally qualified and committed staff.

Focus Area: Family and Community Partnerships

Program Standard 7:

Families: the focus is on establishing and maintaining sensitive collaborative relationships with families.

Program Standard 8:

Community Relationships: the focus is on knowing about and establishing relationships with resources in the community to support infants and toddlers' growth and development.

Focus Area: Leadership and Administration

Program Standard 9:

Physical Environment: the focus is on a safe, healthful environment both indoors and outdoors.

Program Standard 10:

Leadership and Management: the focus is on having effective policies, procedures, and systems to ensure that children, families, and staff have positive experiences.

SOURCE: NAEYC (2006c).

CURRICULUM APPROACHES IN EARLY CARE AND EDUCATION

Just as there are a variety of theories about developmental areas, there are different theories about what constitutes curriculum for infants and toddlers. High-quality programs share many qualities as well as many differences. There are many different models, but only a few will be characterized in this chapter.

The Creative Curriculum Approach for Infants and Toddlers

The Creative Curriculum for Infants, Toddlers & Twos, 2E (Dodge, Rudick, & Berke, 2006) was initially developed in 1997 and revised in 2006 by Teaching Strategies. It strongly supports relationships as the core of any infant and toddler program. It provides a practical and comprehensive approach that focuses on healthy development. It is one of the most widely used curriculums for infants and toddlers. It supports good observation skills. It has the potential for good staff training. The creative curriculum is strongly based on developmentally appropriate practices and these are an important part of the approach.

The creative curriculum views infants and toddlers in the context of their families and the community in which they live. The curriculum focuses on both activities and routines for infants and toddlers. Routines are a major aspect of the infant and toddler curriculum and there is information about diapering and toileting, eating and mealtimes, sleeping and naptime, dressing, and, of course, the hellos and goodbyes. The curriculum provides information on planning and individualizing planning as well as evaluating infants' and toddlers' learning and development. Health and safety is also emphasized. There is information on what is necessary in the infant and toddler environment and how to arrange the environment for both caregiving and learning.

The creative curriculum provides a framework for decision-making. It has models for many forms and checklists for health and safety procedures and is very user-friendly.

Loczy and the Pikler/Gerber Approach for Infants and Toddlers

Emmi Pikler was a pediatrician who became the director of Loczy after World War II, in 1946. Loczy was residential care facility for very young children in Budapest, Hungary. She was hired to care for 35 babies below age 3 until satisfactory living arrangements could be found. Given the legacy of past institutional care of young children, her first goal was to promote physical health and development. She was influenced by the work of John Bowlby and Mary Ainsworth, so one of the areas she concentrated on was attachment. One of the first things she did was fire the nurses. She felt they were giving the children custodial care and were more interested in paperwork than infants. She hired young women from rural areas who had little education but did have an interest in children (Petrie, 2005). She developed prescribed methods for tasks such as bathing and changing. Two hallmarks of her approach are not rushing and respectfully telling even the smallest infant what will happen before it does, then waiting for some response before proceeding. She also instituted daily observations of each child. She supported children's independence in a safe environment (Petrie, 2005).

Magda Gerber met Dr. Emmi Pikler because Pikler was Loczy's pediatrician and the women had children of the same age. She worked with Pikler until she left for the United States after the 1956 revolution in Hungary. She brought the ideas from Loczy with her. In 1979, she developed Resources for Infant Educarers (RIE).

"We should educate while we care and care while we educate. To emphasize this, I coined the words 'educarer' and 'educaring' to describe our philosophy" (Gerber, 1998, p. 1). The work of Emmi Pikler and Magda Gerber has influenced how we care for and work with infants and toddlers.

Gerber (2005) has been the voice for respectful care of infants and toddlers in the United States. She believes that infants need to be treated with respect and trusts their capacity to learn from their world. It is about working less with infants and enjoying them more, and giving infants time to establish their own rhythm and find how they want to be in the world rather than rushing about with them in car seats. She believes that infants need time to develop autonomy. She wants infants to become active participants in all of their care and believes we should have more trust in infant's abilities to explore and initiate their own learning.

> We provide an environment for the infant that is physically safe, cognitively challenging, and emotionally nourishing. We give her plenty of time for uninterrupted play. We do not teach her how to move or how to play, but rather observe her carefully to understand her communications and her needs (Gerber, 2005, p. 39).

Gerber (2005) sees infants as having the right to self-soothe. The best way they have of doing this is sucking. Sucking is a reflex and it is soothing. An infant's thumb is under her control. When she discovers it, she has the right to use it. The issue is one of control. Who is in control, the parent who gives and takes away the pacifier, or the infant who has a thumb as part of her body? If our goal is for infants and toddlers to learn about and explore their world, do we want them pacified?

The RIE approach to discipline is one of establishing a few simple, age-appropriate rules, expecting that they be obeyed, and consistently but not rigidly enforcing them. Children should be given choices within a secure framework and everybody needs to be able to save face (Gerber, 2005). Table 11–2 highlights the way an educarer would approach the classroom in contrast to how other caregivers might.

Table 11–2 Comparison of Caregivers and Educarers

- Caregivers might rush through routine care to allow more time for a planned curriculum; educarers would use the time in routine care as a potential source of learning.
- Caregivers rely on infant curricula to teach and build skills in developmental domains; educarers expect the infants to initiate their own activities.
- Caregivers teach and encourage postures that support locomotion (place in sitting position before the infant can get there); educarers provide space for the infant to move freely.
- Caregivers focus infant's response to particular stimuli (toy), educarers focus on the whole child and look at how the infant reacts to the environment, adults, and peers.
- Caregivers put objects or toys in infant's hands; educarers place objects or toys so the infant must make an effort to get them—work for what she wants.
- Caregivers encourage dependency by rescuing children in distress or solving their problems; educarers encourage autonomy by waiting to see if the infant can console himself or solve the problem.
- Caregivers use bottles or pacifiers to soothe crying children; educarers try to understand the child's reason for crying and encourage him to soothe himself with his thumb.
- Caregivers often restrict infant–infant interaction; educarers facilitate this and encourage it.
- Caregivers resolve conflicts by separating, distracting, or declaring who should get a toy; educarers comment on the fact that both toddlers want the toy.
- Caregivers control aggression by quickly dealing with the situation; educarers quietly touch the aggressive child saying calm, soothing words.
- Caregivers console victims of the aggressor; educarers stroke and console both so as not to reinforce the helplessness of the victim.
- Caregivers prefer to have more people or helpers in the room; educarers want to be the steady person for their small group.
- Caregivers may scoop children up to feed or change them; educarers tell the infant what will happen and wait for a response before doing an action.

SOURCE: Gerber (2005, pp. 49–50).

REFLECTIVE PRACTICE

Reflect on the role of the educarer and caregiver and the differences that Gerber sees. How do you see yourself in the classroom? If this were a continuum, where would you fall? As you work with infants and toddlers, reflect on your own behavior as it relates to these principles.

The Reggio Emilia Approach for Infants and Toddlers

Reggio Emilia is a town in Northern Italy. In 1945, at the end of World War II, there was a desire for change in Italy and a need to create a more just world. Loris Malaguzzi is the founder of the Reggio Emilia approach (Gandini, 2004). Like many approaches, it has since evolved and been influenced by scholars from different fields, such as Maria Montessori, Lev Vygotsky, Jean Piaget, and Erik Erikson, to name a few you are familiar with (Cadwell, 2003). It was a grass-roots effort started and built by parents. The Reggio Emilia infant-toddler centers are part of the public school system.

Some basic principles or ideas underlie the Reggio approach (see Table 11–3). Although given as separate points, "they must be considered as a tightly connected, coherent philosophy in which each point influences and is influenced by all others" (Gandini, 2004, p. 15).

Protagonist is the main figure or role.

Table 11–3 Ideas Underlying the Reggio Emilia Approach

*The child as **protagonist***: Children, including infants and toddlers, are viewed as powerful, strong, and capable. All children have potential and need experiences designed to tap into that potential.

The child as collaborator: Education focuses on the children in relation to other children, their family, teachers, and community. There is an emphasis on small group work based on the view that children construct their ideas of themselves through interactions. The infant-toddler center is a system in which all these relationships are interconnected and reciprocal.

The child as communicator: Children use many approaches to communication, including words, movement, drawing, painting, shadow play, and so on. To discover and encourage communication children need many materials to understand and wonder about, to feel and imagine. A teacher trained in the visual arts helps children explore their environment and use many languages to make thinking visible.

The three subjects of education: Children, teachers, and parents play the central roles in the educational process. Children's rights as well as their needs are recognized, and they have the right to the best that society can offer. Parents have the right to be involved in their infants' and toddlers' lives at home and at school. Teachers have the right to grow professionally.

The environment as third teacher: The design and use of space sends a message. The message is one of welcome that encourages encounter, communications, and relationships. The entryway should give ideas of what teachers and children do. Parents should feel accepted and welcome. Space should be flexible and change when the interests of the infants and toddlers change. Space follows the growth of the children. It should be beautiful and highly personal.

The teacher as partner, nurturer, and guide: Teachers listen and observe, they use theories to guide their actions, and they generate hypotheses and provide opportunities for discovery and learning.

The teacher as researcher: Teachers work in pairs, they discuss their work and the children. They see themselves as researchers who are supported and encouraged.

The documentation as communication: Teachers eagerly document infants and toddlers progress through transcriptions of their language and photographs of what they do and what they compose. This helps parents become aware of what their children do and allows teachers to evaluate their work. It creates a history.

(continues)

The parent as partner: Parent participation is essential. Exchanging ideas with parents provides for new ways of educating their infants and toddlers. Parents are an essential component of the system. They are part of advisory boards and play an active role in their children's learning.

Organization as foundation: Organization is not neat and tidy, it is intricate and complex. It is layered and involves everything from serving nutritious meals for children and educators to deciding how to create small groups of infants and toddlers.

SOURCES: Cadwell (2003); Gandini (1993); Rinaldi (2001).

REFLECTIVE PRACTICE

Think about these philosophies as you begin to develop your own. Identify aspects of approaches that you like. Figure out what intrigues you and learn more about the approaches that are a good match for you.

Programs for infants and toddlers focus on *time for families*. Having an infant can be an isolating experience, as parents feel tired and overstressed, especially if they both work. Individualized approaches help parents become more aware of their own needs and of their child's characteristics. Having an infant is a major adjustment, but with support, almost all families can have secure relationships. *Time with families* is a patient service that engages and supports families. Time is taken to assess individual family needs. Only families know what they want or need and they need to express these wants and needs. There are many ways to be good parents and parents need support to see this. Supporting families is an important part of the approach (Gandini, 2001).

The Emergent Curriculum Approach for Infants and Toddlers

The emergent curriculum takes advantage of infants' and toddlers' natural curiosity to focus the curriculum. Sometimes the educator plans curriculum based on her observations of the children, and sometimes the curriculum is in response to something that is happening in the environment, such as the parking lot of the child care center being paved. Like Reggio Emilia, the emergent curriculum is based on social constructivist theory. The theory is based on the work of Lev Vygotsky. The assumptions are that learning is a social process that takes place when toddlers are working with an educator or older child on something that intrigues or deeply interests them (Lewin-Benham, 2006). The role of the educator is to collaborate with the children and use her knowledge to scaffold their learning.

In the emergent curriculum, the infants and toddlers are the focus and the curriculum is built around their interests and desires. This does not mean that that there is no planning and no direction. Rather, the educator uses her knowledge and creativity to teach necessary concepts using the ideas and materials that interest the children. The curriculum is an active, fluid one that moves with toddlers. Most educators who embrace this philosophy use an interest- or center-based approach. There will always be an area for looking at books, but the particular books will relate to what the toddlers are interested in. The interest or focus of the emergent curriculum does not change on a daily basis, but rather plays itself out, and a wise educator listens to the children as they talk and observes their play to see where it is leading next and to know when to make the transition. Literacy, math, science, creative arts, and gross and fine motor activities are all woven into the fabric that interests the children. Digital photographs are often used to document experiences and to expand thinking by helping toddlers hold them in memory.

The advantage of an emergent curriculum is that the toddlers are motivated. It increases their ownership of their learning and provides opportunities for deeper, more complex learning.

REFLECTIVE PRACTICE

Reflect on the different curriculum approaches described. If you had to choose one, which would it be? If there are aspects of others that you like, think about those as well. How could you incorporate them into your philosophy of early care and education?

Although there are many additional approaches for educating infants and toddlers, they are beyond the scope of this book. However, if you find some that intrigue you, find out more about them. If these short descriptions have tickled your curiosity, follow up and learn more about them.

PROFESSIONAL PREPARATION FOR INDIVIDUALS WHO CARE FOR INFANTS AND TODDLERS

Although some people believe that caring for infants is an innate ability, they are missing the point. Educating and caring for infants requires as much skill, if not more, than teaching calculus. Students studying calculus can ask teachers questions to clarify what they do not understand. Infants have much less ability to demonstrate a mismatch between the material and the learner. Although they can show distress by crying, inappropriate program planning rarely causes that level of distress. The infant is dependent on the astute observations of adults to provide sensitive care that supports the development of trust and

Curriculum is more effective when it emerges out of what two-year-olds are interested in and want to learn about.

attachment. Adults also need to be committed, creative, bright detectives who are consumed with figuring out the clues that infants send. This is a Herculean task. Sometimes babies themselves do not know what they want. You need to be able to develop hypotheses about the probable wants and needs of infants beyond the wet, tired, hungry scenarios. Your focus should be on what intrigues them and when they are likely to be fascinated by what you have to offer.

Early childhood education is a profession and the adults are professionals and possess specialized knowledge and expertise. Being an early childhood professional is not like cramming for a test or memorizing the chemical formulas. It requires a strong knowledge base from which to guide decision-making (Freeman & Feeney, 2006). Although child development is a necessary knowledge base, it is no longer a sufficient one. Development provides the base for teaching, but early childhood educators need to be able to design stimulating learning environments for infants and toddlers and support their learning within their environments. They need strategies to help young children learn to regulate their behavior and to scaffold children's learning so that it builds on and extends infants' and toddlers' understanding of their world (Freeman & Feeney, 2006). Early childhood educators need to know how to establish meaningful relations with families, be knowledgeable about and use community resources to support children and their families, and work as part of a team to provide early intervention for infants and toddlers who have developmental delays.

DEVELOPMENTALLY APPROPRIATE PRACTICE

What is developmentally appropriate practice? How do you know it when you see it? The answer has been an undercurrent throughout this book and, although defined, it probably has not been explained thoroughly enough for you to truly use it. To explain developmentally appropriate practice, the NAEYC developed a position paper and guidelines in 1986, updated it in 1987, revised again in 1996 and again in 2006. These revisions reflect new knowledge, particularly in neurobiology; the inclusion of children with disabilities in regular classrooms, and the increasing number of infants and toddlers in group care. They also reflect a field that is changing and a professional commitment to keep up with these changes (NAEYC, 2006b).

Developmentally appropriate practice has three basic components: (1) knowledge about development and learning; (2) knowledge about individual children; and (3) knowledge about the social and cultural context in which children learn and grow (NAEYC, 2006b).

Knowledge about child development and learning requires you to understand patterns of growth and development. Knowledge of age-related characteristics allows you to make predictions about where children are developing within an age range and, given that knowledge, to design experiences and choose materials that are interesting and challenging and that infants and toddlers can achieve (NAEYC, 2006b).

Knowing about child development is necessary, but it is also necessary to know about the strengths, interests, and needs of each individual infant and toddler. This knowledge allows you to adapt and be responsive to individual variation (NAEYC, 2006b).

Infants and toddlers live in families, and to ensure that their learning experiences are meaningful and relevant, these experiences must be respectful of the children and their families. They must take into account the children's culture and language and social context of where they live and grow (NAEYC, 2006b).

Principles Underlying Developmentally Appropriate Practice

The principles underlying developmentally appropriate practice are based on what we reliably know about child development and learning. The principles are given below and an explanation follows each principle, focusing on infants and toddlers. These principles influence the beliefs and philosophy of education for all children. They too will become part of your philosophy. Principles of development and learning inform developmentally appropriate practice (NAEYC, 2006b) (see Table 11–4).

Table 11–4 Principles of Developmentally Appropriate Practice

1. *Domains of children's development—physical, social, emotional, and cognitive—are closely related. Development in one domain influences and is influenced by development in other domains.*

   The younger the child, the closer the curriculum is tied to the child's experiential base. Recently, scholars have focused more on functional interrelationships among the different domains. This multidomain approach increases the complexity of thinking about young children's development, which is further complicated by the need to look at the child as part of a family system that embraces certain cultural values and who lives in a specific geographic area at a particular time. However, once you get the hang of this it seems obvious. Thinking about multiple domains helps organize learning.

2. *Development occurs in a relatively orderly sequence, with later abilities, skills, and knowledge building on those already acquired.*

   Predictable changes occur in all developmental areas. Knowledge of these patterns provides the basis for designing the environment and planning for infants and toddlers. We use information about developmental patterns to decide what types of materials to use with children of various ages, as well as to determine whether children are showing delayed or atypical patterns of development. Planning needs to take into account children's patterns of growth and development.

3. *Development proceeds at varying rates from child to child, as well as unevenly within different areas of each child's functioning.*

   All children are unique, yet they share many commonalities in their sequence of growth and development. Children come into the world "prewired" to grow and develop in a certain predictable pattern. Understanding these patterns allows us to plan for children in developmentally appropriate ways and to make some predictions about whether future growth and development will fall within the normal range. Individual variation is expected and valued.

4. *Early experiences have both cumulative and delayed effects on individual children's development; optimal periods exist for certain types of development and learning.*

   Children's early experiences, both positive and negative, affect their development. As with patterns of development, isolated events may have a minimal impact, but events that occur frequently can have powerful lasting effects. Research supports the idea of broadly conceived *sensitive periods or cycles* when the child is more susceptible to change or where the impact of events is more pervasive than at other times. Birth to 3 years is the optimal period for the development of verbal language skills. Although children can and do learn language later, it requires specific intervention and more effort.

5. *Development proceeds in predictable directions toward greater complexity, organization, and internalization.*

   Infants and toddlers learn through their senses. As they enhance their knowledge base with hands-on experiences, they begin to acquire symbolic knowledge and move into thinking that can take place in the present, remember the past, and anticipate the future. Children grow in their ability to regulate their own behavior. The adult's role is to respond to this increasing growth by presenting a curriculum that motivates and challenges them and social situations that require skills for higher-level peer interaction. Knowledge of the universals in development and the uniqueness of each child support this curriculum.

6. *Development and learning occur in and are influenced by multiple social and cultural contexts.*

   Changing patterns have affected families and the children born into these families. Most infants and toddlers spend large parts of their day with adults other than their parents. Other patterns relate to the high divorce rate, single parents, and remarried families. The diversity of the population of children is increasing, forcing us to investigate the roles of nature, nurture, culture, and the complex intersections of these. Consequently, we must become more aware of families and culture, the role they play in early growth and development and assure that curriculum is responsive to this knowledge base. Infants and toddlers whose home language is not English should be able to learn English and also be supported in their home language.

(continues)

Table 11–4 *(continues)*

7. *Children are active learners, drawing on direct physical and social experience as well as culturally transmitted knowledge to construct their own understandings of the world around them.*

   We know that infants come into the world seeing, hearing, feeling, tasting, and smelling. They must use these senses to make their environment meaningful. Initially infants use trial and error to construct a knowledge base. Older infants and toddlers use cause-effect relationships to learn more about their world. Older toddlers and two-year-olds are moving into symbolic thinking and planning. Environments that support children as active learners encourage the construction of knowledge by offering experiences that are at the edge of a child's knowledge base and that encourage a child to generate and test out their hypotheses. Well-chosen new experiences help children modify, adapt, expand, and reorganize their working model of the world. When educators help children plan, act, and then reflect on experiences, this process is enhanced.

8. *Development and learning result from interaction of biological maturation and the environment, which includes both the physical and social worlds that children live in.*

   Probably the only "pure genetic moment" is at conception. From that moment on, there is an interaction between the organism and the environment. Information about the relationship between early experience and the brain has focused on birth to three as a prime time for development. An enriched environment helps brain cells form synapses and stabilizes these connections to support learning. Genetics may establish the upper and lower limits of development, but the environment determines where within this range a specific trait falls. If an infant is born preterm and has committed parents who nurture, talk to, and play with him and learn to read his signals well, the outcome will be very different than the same child born to parents who are annoyed with his shrill cry and cannot figure out what he wants and become so frustrated that they shake him.

9. *Play is an important vehicle for children's social, emotional, and cognitive development, as well as a reflection of their development.*

   Most early social interactions center on play and play activities. The quality and type or level of interaction that occurs among children in play activities develops sequentially, increasing with age and maturation. As children's play develops, their social interactions move away from adults to peers. One of the greatest aspects of play is that is that it is unpredictable. When children play, they do not know where it will lead. They have to respond to what happens. This means they have to put their cognitive processes in gear as well as using their social and emotional skills.

10. *Development advances when children have opportunities to practice newly acquired skills as well as when they experience a challenge just beyond the level of their present mastery.*

    Programming continually moves from what children know to the acquisition and consolidation of new knowledge. It moves from what children can do themselves to learning that requires the scaffolding of adults. Infants and toddlers come to learning experiences with different backgrounds; some have had a variety of experiences, others relatively few. Good curriculum planning and responsive adults meet infants and toddlers where they are and provide the scaffolding for them to take the next steps. Planning and experiences need to be flexible and allow for different learning experiences with the same activity. Experiences must be modified (made easier or more difficult) to meet the needs of infants and toddlers with diverse experiences and abilities.

11. *Children demonstrate different modes of knowing and learning and different ways of representing what they know.*

    Children come to understand their world in different ways. Most infants begin with a tactile-kinesthetic approach to their world and add information from the other senses. Over time, children develop preferred learning modalities and different styles of learning. They represent their world differently. They are good at different things. Sometimes this is due to personal experience and preferences. Other times it is because of sensory integration problems or a sensory impairment. Knowing how infants and toddlers represent their world, adults can present information in ways that make it easier for them to learn; likewise, they can give children opportunities to strengthen areas that may be challenging.

(continues)

12. *Children develop and learn best in the context of a community where they are safe and valued, their physical needs are met, and they feel psychologically secure.*

Infants and toddlers need to be in environments where they can develop trusting relationships with adults, establish their autonomy, and be empowered to continue to learn. They need to feel safe in early childhood settings both psychologically and physically. Prosocial behavior needs to be encouraged and supported.

SOURCE: NAEYC (2006b, pp. 1–8).

CURRICULUM FOR INFANTS AND TODDLERS

What kinds of goals do you have for working with infants and toddlers and for yourself as you interact with infants? Infants need a learning environment that supports all developmental domains. That sounds good, but what does it mean? Infants are entering a world that is new and strange. Picture an infant as Dorothy in the *Wizard of Oz*. She is dumped into a strange place and does not know how it works. The first thing she needs is friends. Then she needs a good queen to tell her how the place works. You are the good queen. She needs you to coach her on what is important, what matters.

You are the one who knows the skills she will need when she walks through the door to kindergarten that first day, as she approaches a group of children she would like to play with, and as another child takes something that is hers. The infant and toddler curriculum provides the prereading and premath skills that make her approach that door with confidence. Her self-regulation allows her to walk through the door. Her social and emotional skills will help her get along with both her peers and her classmates. She will be independent and competent, willing to give help and ask for it when she needs it. If you give her the foundation, she will take it from there. Without the foundation she starts out behind even before her first day of public school. The wicked witch may keep her broomstick and interfere with learning long after Halloween. How do you keep the wicked witch at bay? A good curriculum!

Many people have problems thinking about curriculum for infants and toddlers. They see children at this age as needing to sleep, to eat, and to be changed when wet. Curriculum is a planned challenging and engaging environment that is designed to promote positive outcomes for infants and toddlers (NAEYC, 2006c). Curriculum is more than interesting activities and routines. Curriculum is complex: It is goal-directed and supports particular practices with infants and toddlers. It provides cognitive challenges in developmentally appropriate ways that are designed to produce positive outcomes. Good curriculum for infants and toddlers is comprehensive and looks at growth in social and emotional development as being as important as cognitive and language development. Good curriculum provides cultural and linguistic continuity for infants and toddlers. For infants and toddlers the goal is to build positive relationships and informal language-rich sensory interactions (NAEYC, 2006c). Regardless of age, infants and toddlers learn more when they are actively engaged. They need firsthand hands-on experiences with real materials. In addition, they need to have choices.

There is agreement that curriculum should be evidence based; that is, that the long-term effects of using a curriculum will result in positive important outcomes for infants and toddlers. To do this we need studies that evaluate different curriculum models to determine their long-term impact on infants and toddlers. The goal is not to identify the best curriculum but rather to identify the features of curriculum that are likely to be most effective in producing particular outcomes. We additionally need to know for which particular infants and toddlers the curriculum works and under what circumstances (NAEYC, 2006c).

Curriculum provides the umbrella that guides decision making relative to what particular activities or experiences are appropriate for infants and toddlers. It ensures balance among curriculum areas and between children's interests and standards and curriculum goals. High-quality curriculum has clear goals and is based on knowledge of early development. That is why the beginning of this book was devoted to early development. Good curriculum requires you to use this knowledge to intentionally help infants and toddlers develop positive relationships, become competent communicators, and explore their physical world. Some of this learning is embedded in daily routines and experiences. Good curriculum supports home language learning and promotes security and social competence. This curriculum forms the foundation for later learning. There is no clear dividing line between what is academic and is not. Infants and toddlers learn through play and informal opportunities to develop academic knowledge. They do this from birth (NAEYC, 2006c). Obviously, to know whether the curriculum is effective, we must have goals and these goals must be assessed. Well-qualified educators who understand infant and toddler development are more likely to be effective than teachers who use a scripted curriculum that tends to be narrow. Early childhood educators need a variety of skills, including the ability to plan for and assess what infants and toddlers are learning.

How do we know that the curriculum is effective? (See Table 11–5).

Good curriculum for infants and toddlers is distinctly different from good preschool curriculum. The characteristics of infants themselves dictate how curriculum must be designed.

Infants and toddlers have a small repertoire of behaviors, but they are continually learning and adding to these behaviors. To establish a solid base they need to use the skills they have with small variations. Activities that are appropriate for an infant today may no longer be appropriate in a month. Planning for toddlers centers on the real world that toddlers know and love: the house,

Table 11–5 Indicators of an Effective Curriculum

- Infants and toddlers are active and engaged.
- Curriculum goals are clearly defined and share by all stakeholders.
- Curriculum is based on evidence about development, culture, and language.
- Important content is learned through play, planned experiences and exploration, and learning that is intentionally scaffolded by educators.
- Curriculum builds on what infants and toddlers know and do.
- Curriculum is holistic and comprehensive.
- Professional standards developed by scholars in particular areas of development are the basis for planning.
- The curriculum has evidence that it is likely to benefit the infants and toddlers who participate in it.

SOURCE: NAEYC (2006c).

the grocery store, and the toddler himself. You have to join toddlers where they are and move with them to where they want to go and can be.

Programming moves from what infants and toddlers know to the acquisition and consolidation of new knowledge. Toddlers work from what they know to what is new and different. They need a broad base of real experiences with real activities before they can role-play and pretend. They need to take walks around the neighborhood and look at the grass, trees, and bugs (if appropriate). They need to see a kiwi and taste it before seeing pictures of kiwi.

Infants and toddlers are active learners who learn from their errors as well as their successes. Toddlers want to do it themselves. It is rarely useful to tell them that something is too big to fit. They need to try it themselves. They learn from what does not work as well as from what does. They need to have a variety of materials as well as variations of the same materials to test out their learning.

Learning is a social experience. This experience varies from observing another child to the verbal and nonverbal scaffolding of an adult. Social interaction requires toddlers to acknowledge other children and their wants and needs.

WITH INFANTS AND TODDLERS

Infants and toddlers learn when you present them with variations on what they know. They may know that balls roll. They need to experience rubber balls, beach balls, waffle balls, koosh balls, yarn balls, tennis balls, soccer balls, basketballs, and so on. These variations in balls help them learn the principles behind force (cause and effect reasoning) and the relationship between speed, shape, and size.

Two-year-olds need to have a variety of experiences with balls, from large, light beach balls to small rubber balls.

Programming should include learning about sharing and taking turns and responding empathetically to those who are troubled.

Curriculum needs to support toddlers growing independence and competence. Toddlers are trying to be their own person. They need to view themselves as competent beings who have some control over their world. Adults need to support this by helping toddlers learn adaptive skills relating to dressing, eating, and toileting. Toddlers have preferences and, at least some of the time, these preferences need to be acknowledged.

Environments for toddlers need to be safe both inside and outside to prevent injuries. Health precautions, such as judicious hand washing, need to be followed conscientiously to keep infections from spreading. Toddlers also need to be psychologically safe in a supportive environment.

Curriculum and planning must be flexible. Although there should always be a written plan for the day and week, the plan should be flexible to accommodate infants and toddlers. The sequence of events should remain constant for toddlers, but the exact timing of events often reflects the day and how things are going.

Planning a good curriculum is a necessary first step. However, it must be implemented and assessed to determine whether it is effective. Record keeping is necessary to track development and to communicate with families.

ASSESSMENT AND RECORD KEEPING FOR INFANTS AND TODDLERS

Assessment serves a variety of purposes with infants and toddlers. First, it allows us to make decisions about teaching and learning. It provides a means for identifying infants and toddlers who may require focused intervention to support their learning. Finally, it provides a way for programs to evaluate their effectiveness (NAEYC, 2006a). The formal aspects of assessment have been addressed earlier. The informal ones that relate to the feedback loop between learning and assessment are covered in the next three chapters. Assessment for infants and toddlers is closely tied to the achievement of developmental milestones.

Most children follow a predictable pattern of development. Some follow at a slower or faster rate; a few do not follow the pattern at all. Growth itself is uneven, or asynchronous. One child may have a spurt in one area and lag in another. Some variations are related to the uniqueness of each individual child, others to family and cultural background. When assessing how a child is progressing, looking at developmental patterns is more useful than looking at isolated behaviors. We cannot assume that the infant who is on the slow track for walking is also on the slow track for talking. In fact, the opposite may be true. Value uniqueness in all children, as it provides a framework for including children with diverse abilities and respecting different cultural and ethnic backgrounds. However, be certain that development is unique and not an atypical pattern that may need early intervention.

USING DEVELOPMENTAL GUIDELINES IN CURRICULUM PLANNING

Developmental guidelines are used differently for programming purposes than for assessment. When you plan experiences and activities, it is important to know what skills are likely to emerge soon, what skills the infant or toddler is practicing, and what skills have been mastered. Developmental norms are used to determine when skills are most likely to emerge. For programming, the goal is to encourage the development of emerging skills. These skills are in the child's zone of proximal development. They are the skills a young child cannot

up close and personal

I was once asked to assess a toddler because she was not walking at 18 months. She was the youngest of six with brothers ranging from 6 to 16 years. The family wanted the assessment done in their home. From my perspective, this did not sound good. I knew all the family would be there. Eighteen months is late to walk, and I had also learned when setting up the appointment that she did not crawl or creep efficiently. She did sit.

Her parents greeted me warmly when I entered and took me to the family room. Sarah sat on the floor on a blanket. I never did get the boys' names straight, but one was on the blanket with her reading *Pat the Bunny*. Another was playing nearby. When the book ended, she said, "More book." A brother seemed to appear out of nowhere bearing more books. Another brother played peek-a-boo with her while he was doing his homework and she laughed.

I asked the parents how typical this scene was. Sarah's father said that the boys are upset when she cries, so they entertain her and bring her anything she wants. I asked what happened during the week when they were at school. Sarah's mother replied that she does a lot of cooking and packing lunches and so on in the kitchen, and that Sarah spends a lot of time in the kitchen playing with different toys in her highchair, and she likes to watch videos while her mother cooks.

REFLECTIVE PRACTICE

What would you do at this point? What do you think the problem is? I decided that the problem had nothing to do with Sarah's ability to walk, but rather how the household was reacting to Sarah. I suggested that the boys roll balls to her and not get them if they got away. I also suggested that they play hide-and-seek-type games to get her moving, and to scatter the toys she liked so she had to move to get them. I also thought the boys could encourage her to walk. I suggested they might join a playgroup. I agreed to come back in two weeks. They called and said that Sarah was walking and loved the playgroup. I did not go back.

do alone but can accomplish with adult scaffolding. Some infants and toddlers grow by the norms and their skills appear at the predicted times. Others, however, have unique patterns where some skills or behaviors may appear earlier and others later than predicted.

Emerging Skills

If a skill is likely to emerge in a given period, then it is important to provide experiences that support and encourage these skills. For example, if you know that infants sit with support at three months, then you would put an infant in a supported sitting position at about this time—not for long, but long enough to give her the opportunity to practice a skill that is emerging. You also know that at about three months infants follow moving objects with their eyes while in a supported sitting position. Therefore, you put the infant in a supported sitting position and then slowly move something that intrigues her across her field of visions so she can follow it with her eyes. If she loses it visually help her reconnect by tapping the object. This is not rocket science! It is curriculum. Adults provide experiences and scaffolding for learning.

Practicing Skills

Once skills emerge, they need to be practiced. When an infant can grasp one toy, then he need to practice using differently shaped toys—variations on a theme. Toys needs to be presented in different locations so that he has to reach up, down, left, and right. Adults need to vary materials so infants have a broad base of experiences to work from. Experiences must be designed and repeated many times with variations. The goal is to provide enough variation to broaden the skill base.

Mastering Skills

Infants and toddlers do not have to have completely master a skill to begin to learn other skills. This means that infants have some skills which are emerging, others they are practicing, and some they have mastered. (For a one-year-old, walking might be an emerging skill, creeping may be at the practicing stage, and sitting might have been mastered.) Infants and toddlers who have mastered a skill profit from using that skill in a variety of interesting ways or sequences with other skills they are learning. When skills are mastered, infants and toddlers need similar but more challenging opportunities to move on to related skills that are more complex. At the mastery level, infants and toddler are "grooving" the skill so it becomes automatic. In this instance, the goal is to provide opportunities for infants and toddlers to generalize their knowledge and use it in more complex goal-related sequences.

STRATEGIES FOR INDIVIDUALIZING LEARNING

Regardless of content or age, there is a cycle of learning that takes place, as new information becomes part of a child's repertoire. This learning framework has four broad aspects: awareness, exploration, inquiry, and utilization (Bredekamp & Rosegrant, 1992). Infants and toddlers come to child care with different experiences and they go home to families who spend time with them in different ways. Some toddlers may not have used markers before; others may have had many experiences with them. The first toddler may be fascinated that markers can make the paper a different color; those with more experience may want to draw or scribble with different colors of markers (see Table 11–6).

This learning cycle occurs repeatedly as children learn new information. It is important to know where individual children are in the cycle. When a toddler encounters information for the first time, he begins at an awareness level. Toddlers with previous experiences may be generalizing the information. Some children who live in families with fewer resources or children with diverse abilities may have less broad experiential backgrounds. They need time to experience and explore before they can participate in higher-level skills. Programs must be designed to allow infants and toddlers to profit from experience at all places in the learning cycle. With new knowledge, the cycle begins again.

ADULT INTERACTIONS WITH INFANTS AND TODDLERS

Adults need to be responsive and respectful of infants and toddlers. It means that adults should offer an infant two toys to see which he prefers. Early childhood professionals offer children choices. They watch where the infant looks

Table 11–6 The Learning Cycle

1. *Awareness* is the initial stage in the cycle of learning. Awareness grows out of experience. As infants and toddlers experience more and more of their world, they become aware of differences. Initially the awareness is at the sensory level. However, as children move into cause and effect reasoning, they become perplexed about how some things in their environment operate.

2. *Exploration* is the next level and requires the infant or toddler to observe and try to make sense out of an event or experience by exploring materials, gathering additional information, poking, prodding, or doing whatever seems to make sense to them. Although it is tempting to "explain" how something works, it is rarely useful; infants and toddlers need to find their own meaning. Explaining fosters dependency. Asking open-ended questions are more useful.

3. *Inquiry* involves the understanding of classes of information, the ability to generalize information, and to call up previous learning for comparison. Adults can help toddlers with more focused questions at this stage.

4. *Utilization* is a functional level of learning where information can be used in a variety of settings and applied to new information and situations.

SOURCE: Bredekamp and Rosegrant (1992).

and describe what is happening, rather than talking about what interests them. The adult lets the infant take the lead and then takes turns with the infant, listening, observing, and then talking; she does not lead, she follows.

Early childhood professionals are in general agreement about most issues related to a general philosophy. Individual variations in philosophy deal with the degree to which a particular practice is used. Exactly where an individual stands within the range of accepted practices is a matter of personal choice and one that frequently changes with time and experience.

REFLECTIVE PRACTICE

Think about where you stand on the aspects of philosophy that have been covered. Now, do more than think about it. Put pen to paper or fingers to keyboard and actually write it. Committing it to paper is a big step. The next step is to see how it influences your behavior in the classroom. Put your philosophy on a small index card (write small or use a small typeface). Choose one aspect of your philosophy and concentrate on that (or more, if you feel comfortable). Reflect on your actions and interactions in the classroom; were they consistent with your philosophy? If not, why not? What do you need to change, your behavior or your philosophy?

Toddlers interact with materials differently depending on where they are in the learning cycle.

The Role of the Educator/Caregiver

Many early childhood teachers feel that the roles of educators and parents should differ. The role of preschool teachers is clear; they are part of the child's world that revolves around playing and learning. If children falter they can be warm, loving, and supportive, but they are not parents. Working with infants is different. It is an intimate social relationship. Infants who are in the care of other adults need to develop secure attachments. They need adults who are responsive, respective, and fun. They need to be played with and cared for. Infants can form attachments to more than one adult. Secure attachment is a process, not a product. It is based on responsive interactions that are part of all good caregiving.

Levels of Involvement

The level of involvement of adults with children is one measure of quality. Klass (1987) characterizes these levels (see Table 11–7).

REFLECTIVE PRACTICE

Earlier in this chapter, you were asked to think about how you would plan time for children. Now the question is different: How much time do you expect to have in shared participation? How will you ensure that you spend some individual time playing with each infant or toddler? You may need to use times during routines to connect with each one in play, not just caregiving. You will need to plan other times as well.

Table 11–7 Levels of Adult's Involvement with Infants and Toddlers

Stabilizing Presence. Infants, when they are awake, always need an adult nearby to ensure their safety and to be available to them. An adult's presence has a stabilizing effect on an infant's or toddler's behavior. An adult fixing lunch or reading to an infant should be aware of what is happening to the other infants and toddlers around her.

Facilitative Intervention. At this level, the adult moves in and out of an infant's or toddler's play. It may be to pick up a dropped toy or to distract a toddler who seems intent on snatching a toy. This is not intrusive; rather, the adult involvement extends, redirects, expands, or clarifies what the children are doing.

Shared Participation. Adults actively participate in infants' and toddlers' experiences. These experiences may be initiated by infants and responded to by adults, or they may be planned by adults who take advantage of a quiet alert time to interact with an infant. Shared participation may be verbal turn-taking, helping a toddler exploring a new toy, or playing with a small group of toddlers. It may be looking at a book together, playing peek-a-boo, or searching for hidden toys.

SOURCE: Klass (1987).

Within the various levels of adult involvement, Klass (1987) delineates six distinct patterns of interaction: physical intimacy, spontaneous conversation, praise, assistance, structured turn-taking, and understanding and following rules. These patterns, occurring throughout the day in various situations, are central to quality adult–child interactions.

Physical Intimacy. Infants need frequent opportunities for physical intimacy with adults throughout the day. Infants need loving, supportive, responsive adults who are in tune with their needs. They need adults who hold, carry, and cuddle them frequently and respectfully. With increasing concern about child sexual abuse, both parents and caregivers are concerned about cuddling children. Many feel that it is safer to keep "hands off." For young children this concern creates a major problem. Infants need physical contact with caring adults as much as they need food and clothing. It is not a matter of allowing physical intimacy, but encouraging it.

Spontaneous Conversation. Infants need adults who look into their eyes when they talk to them, who use a soothing and pleasant voice, and who call each infant by name. They need adults who use simple language, "parentese," to explain what the infant sees, hears, and feels. Infants need adults who verbally prepare them for what is going to happen, describe what is happening, and then frame what will happen next.

Praise/Encouragement. A positive, appreciative atmosphere is more helpful for an infant's growth than a setting where negative, blaming comments are made frequently. Praise is one way of doing this. When praise is positive, general, and implies some judgment or evaluation of the infant's performance, it helps infants recognize their triumphs. Some examples of praise are, "Great job, Alexis," or, "Charday, you are getting so good you almost don't need any help." Adults use praise to make infants feel good about themselves, to encourage them to learn, and to promote appropriate behavior. Recent research, however, shows that indiscriminate praise does not always have these effects. Praise can sometimes even have negative effects if not used appropriately. Inappropriate praise may influence young children to rely on others' opinions rather than judging for themselves, and to decide that they are only "good" when they are pleasing adults (they have become externally motivated rather than internally motivated), thus encouraging dependence on adults rather than independence.

Encouragement may be a more appropriate word than praise. Encouragement refers specifically to responses to efforts or specific aspects of the infant's work or play. Encouragement does not place judgment ("You really dumped a lot of sand."). Encouragement focuses on effort rather than on an evaluation of a finished product ("You worked hard getting that piece in."). Encouragement is designed not to compare one infant with another but rather to note individual accomplishment and improvement. It is typically more specific than praise and provides some guidance about what aspect of behavior was well done.

Assistance. As unpredictable as infants are, they need adults who predictably come when they cry and soothe them patiently. Infants need adults who are responsive to their individual needs and rhythms for sleeping, eating, and elimination. They need adults who support their curiosity while keeping them safe and who model the behavior they want infants to develop. They need adults who like themselves and who cherish infants.

Adult-Supported Learning

Adult-supported learning offers infants and toddlers three kinds of support: environmental support, nonverbal support, and verbal support.

Adults play a very important role in supporting the learning of infants and toddlers. Although it is good for young children to learn to play independently, they will learn more if they spend time in **adult-supported learning**. This is particularly true of vulnerable infants and toddlers. It is through play that children learn. Children actively interact with their environment to learn about it. Infants who receive adult scaffolding during their play are likely to learn more. Adults can help children work through the questions and problems that arise during this learning process. They scaffold learning by talking about and playing with what interests the child, the emergent curriculum. An adult may introduce variations on activities, additional props, and new activities or ideas. The adult guides the child's learning and concentration but does not force it. She helps only when needed. By actively playing with young children, adults can make an ongoing assessment of where they are developmentally so that future appropriate learning activities can be planned.

Environmental Support

Environmental support involves arranging the space that children use to encourage active play and to allow mobile infants and toddlers to reach materials for play. This includes such things as providing a variety of materials for children to choose from and making sure there are enough materials to meet each child's needs and enough space for children to use materials. It involves planning an environment that meets and stretches children's understanding of their world.

Adults need to encourage and support independent play and exploration to allow the child to control and master his environment. It is important to allow toddlers to discover concepts and ideas on their own. This does not mean leaving them unattended but rather that adults arrange the environment in a developmentally appropriate way and then provide cues and suggestions when necessary. The child remains the "doer." They need many opportunities to participate in child-directed and child-selected play. See Table 11–8 for additional environmental supports.

Table 11–8 Environmental Supports

Supporting toddlers includes
- Avoiding interruptions, if possible and giving them adequate warnings before routine transitions.
- Providing an appropriate physical and emotional environment for play.
- Encouraging toddlers to help put away toys and materials they finished using.
- Bringing out a few toys at a time to keep activities novel and to maintain toddler as well as adult interest.
- Rotating toys and having duplicates of popular toys.

Nonverbal Support

Adults can do many things nonverbally to encourage play. Watching what infants and toddlers do with materials and then modeling and expanding their actions increases their attention span as well as their skill repertoire. Use materials yourself when you are with toddlers but don't get so involved that you are no longer paying attention to them. Avoid making models, but do model behavior. Model the process, not the product.

Use your body to express interest. Place yourself at the child's eye level. Listen to what he says and acknowledge his comments. For additional ways to show nonverbal support, see Table 11–9.

Table 11–9 Nonverbal Support

- Observe play to determine how children are playing, what toys and materials they are playing with, as well as the level of their development. This gives you a good opportunity to learn their individual characteristics.
- Show interest in what infants and toddlers are doing. Let them know and see that you value what they do.
- Be available to assist children when necessary. They sometimes struggle when playing with peers for a long time. Be nearby to help them learn to solve problems.
- Accept toddlers' statements and explanations. Sometimes adults tend to discredit toddlers' statements. When a toddler tells an adult that he is hot, the adult may respond with information that the room is not hot nor is the adult hot. Regardless, the toddler may actually be hot.
- Remain calm in the face of children's "mistakes." Most adults have no problem when a child spills the first glass of milk, but when a he spills a second glass, many lose patience, even when it is clear that the spill was accidental.

Verbal Support

There are many ways to verbally to support an infant's or toddler's learning and to encourage their language and cognitive development. Talk with them about what they are doing and ask questions that relate to their play. Encourage them to answer their own questions by saying, "What do *you* think?" See Table 11–10 for additional ideas.

Table 11–10 Verbal Support

Verbal support includes

- Acknowledging infants' and toddlers' actions and choices; responding to their answers and explanations helps infants and toddlers join words and actions.

- Reframing and repeating a toddler's language, as well as expanding and extending it, provides the foundation for understanding what is happening as well as language development.

- Referring toddlers to one another for problem solving and additional conversation supports social development and decreases their dependency on adults as the only source of information.

- Conversing with nonverbal children supports their understanding of language. Probably more than other children, those who do not yet have language need good language models. Adults find it more rewarding to talk to toddlers who respond by talking back. Talking with those who do not respond is extremely important.

- Expand play when appropriate. The adult might make verbal suggestions introduce new ideas or variations on what the toddler is doing. She can describe for and with them what they are doing and ask open-ended questions. She might add props to the play situation that encourage further play.

Children are curious about each other. It is important to encourage and verbally support this curiosity even if it feels uncomfortable by adult standards. You can stop children from asking questions, but not from being curious. Encourage children to satisfy their curiosity. Infants and toddlers benefit from adult support and attention. Those who receive support from adults during their play are likely to learn more.

CONTINUUM OF TEACHING TECHNIQUES

Teaching techniques need to be adapted to meet infants' and toddlers' learning needs. These techniques range from directive to nondirective, with many degrees in between. The goal is to match the technique to the material being learned and the infant or toddler who is learning. *All* teachers need *all* of these techniques. The skill is in matching the appropriate technique to the situation (see Table 11–11).

An educator's philosophy reflects how much time she plans to spend at each end of the teaching continuum. Early childhood educators are frequently criticized for being too nondirective to meet the needs of infants and toddlers with developmental delays, whereas special educators are criticized for being too directive. The solution is to be aware of the continuum, your personal philosophy, and to continually move from nondirective to more directive techniques as infants and toddlers need more direction in learning, but then to move into less directive strategies as they begin to master tasks. The goal is an appropriate

Table 11–11 Continuum of Teaching Techniques

- *Withholding attention or planned ignoring* is frequently used when adults know a toddler can accomplish a task without assistance, or as part of a behavior strategy for handling undesirable but nondangerous behavior. Ensure you give young children enough time to respond before you decide that they are not going to respond.

- *Acknowledging* is used to reinforce children's behavior, particularly when the goal is to have the behavior continue. Done intermittently and for pointing out specific aspects of behavior, it is a useful way to shape behavior. When overused or when acknowledgment is too general, it is less useful. "Good job" does not provide toddlers with a lot of information.

- *Modeling,* whether conscience or unconscious, is a way of teaching children which behaviors are appropriate and which are inappropriate. By their actions, adults show children how to interact with others or how to use a new material.

- *Facilitating* provides temporary assistance to a child. This can be verbal support, such as giving a suggestion for a different way of approaching a problem, or nonverbal, such as by reattaching a piece of paper that has come loose. It is specific and time limited and enables the child to continue independently.

- *Supporting* is similar to facilitating, but it is more general and lasts longer. The goal is independence, but the expectation is that it will take longer to achieve.

- *Scaffolding* works on the edge of a child's knowledge base. It provides the link between what a child can do independently and what she can accomplish with adult help. It is more directive than the previous techniques in that the adult provides more focus for the child's activity. This technique is frequently used with infants and toddlers because many experiences are new for them.

- *Co-constructing* involves participating with or collaborating with a toddler. This is a more directive technique and is useful when children don't know how to use particular materials. It is also useful to join with children. One can move momentarily from scaffolding to co-construction and back.

- *Demonstrating* is more directive than co-construction; the teacher shows what needs to be done and the toddlers typically watch. There are times when this is extremely useful and appropriate and other times when children can appropriately construct their own knowledge. Demonstrating is often followed by less directive techniques. The problem with demonstrating is that children often assume that there is only one way to do an activity rather than actively constructing a method of approaching a task.

- *Directing* involves telling a child specifically what to do. It also implies that there is one correct way to do something and that there is one outcome desired. This technique is frequently used when less directive techniques have not taught a desired task. There are concepts that must be directly taught, but these are rare with infants and toddlers.

SOURCE: Bredekamp and Rosegrant (1995).

match so that the strategy that provides the most learning for the child is employed. It is a dance.

My goal in identifying this teaching continuum is to have you become conscious of your behavior with young children and to reflect on where on the continuum you are spending your time. Then, to think about how the techniques you are using match your philosophy of teaching infants and toddlers.

In inclusive early childhood settings all children are welcomed and participate in the full program, with accommodations made only when the toddlers needs them.

MULTICULTURAL EDUCATION

Multicultural education begins with infants and toddlers.

> The term encompasses all of the issues young children encounter in their lives that can potentially create stereotypes and bias: race, ethnicity, handicapping conditions, language differences, class, gender, age, religion, and more (Williams & Cooney, 2006, p. 77).

Multicultural education is part of the entire curriculum and the value system of those who work in that system. The early childhood classroom provides messages about the program via the pictures on the walls, the books on the bookshelf, the music that is played, the food that is served, and the languages that are spoken.

Multicultural education uses diverse age-appropriate materials and activities and incorporates the strengths of the infants and toddlers' families and communities to enrich the curriculum. You do not have to ask whether a program embraces a multicultural philosophy—you can see it. The books are multicultural and nonsexist, showing different family structures, races, and ages, and including individuals with disabilities. They show families of various cultures living in the United States. Books in Spanish or other languages are on the bookshelves. These books are available to all infants and toddlers, and educators read these books to all children. The compact disks and other sources of music celebrate different cultures, languages, and styles of music. Songs are sung and fingerplays told in more than one language. American Sign Language might be used with all infants and toddlers.

The puzzles, although simple, are multicultural and nonsexist. The dolls are male and female and ethnically diverse. Clothes available for dress-up reflect the cultures of the infants and toddlers. Pictures, photographs, and artifacts represent diverse racial and ethnic groups. Food (snacks) provided include traditional foods from many cultures on a regular basis. The overall view is an additive one.

Developmentally, two-year-olds notice and ask about physical characteristics and specific cultural acts. They are trying to learn more about themselves and others. Although they do not yet know that gender and race are constant, they are curious about them and notice differences. Answer the questions they ask honestly. They are beginning to see themselves as part of their family, absorbing the rules and language of their home culture. They are influenced by societal norms and are vulnerable to negative societal messages about themselves (Williams & Cooney, 2006).

Multicultural education extends beyond the classroom to understanding what is important to parents in terms of cultural and educational values. It is important to know what they want for their infants and toddlers and what is offensive to them. All children and families need to be valued for their similarities and their differences.

INCLUDING INFANTS AND TODDLERS WITH DEVELOPMENTAL DELAYS

IDEA
is a public law that ensures the inclusion of children with disabilities in public education.

Most professionals in early childhood education and early childhood special education agree that the best setting for infants and toddlers with developmental delays is one that also includes other children without disabilities. The **Individuals with Disabilities Education Improvement Act (IDEA)**, Public

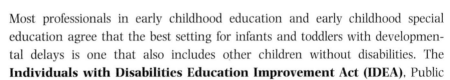

Law 108-446, was enacted on December 3, 2004. Part C of this law affirms that all infants and toddlers should have access to services that allow them to function in as "normal" an environment as possible; that is; they should be included in neighborhood schools (including child care settings) along with other children. Because programming for very young children is so individualized, planning for these children is not very different from developmentally appropriate planning for any infant. What is different is the form that planning takes and the individuals involved in the planning.

Part C of the IDEA provides states with grants to provides early intervention services for children from birth to 36 months who are (1) developmentally delayed; (2) at a substantial risk of delay due to diagnosed factors and conditions; or (3) at risk because of other factors (individual states can decide if they want to serve infants and toddlers who are at risk because of other factors). If a child is identified under Part C, he and his family will have an Individualized Family Service Plan (IFSP) (Sandall, Hemmeter, Smith, & McLean, 2005).

In the 2004 revisions to the IDEA, some changes were made to the Act. Relevant changes are summarized in Table 11–12.

The areas of evaluation and assessment have changed in the IDEA 2004 as well. There is an increased emphasis on the assessment being timely, comprehensive, and multidisciplinary. Assessment of child, family (if they agree) and service needs.

※ Child assessment refers to reviewing a child's pertinent records (health status, and medical history), observing the child and assessing him to identify his unique strengths and needs including his level of functioning in cognitive and physical development, including vision and

Table 11–12 Part C of the IDEA 2004

1. Emphasizes identifying underserved populations of infants and toddlers who have or are at risk of having developmental disabilities and specifies new screening regulations.

2. Clarifies that the IFSP is implemented as soon as possible once parent consent to intervention is obtained.

3. Increases accountability for the success of early intervention services

4. Ensures a seamless transition for children and families when they exit from the Part C program to other appropriate programs with planning and descriptions of available services at least 9 months prior to the toddler's third birthday

5. Provides states with flexibility to provide early intervention services to children with disabilities who are age 3 and older

6. Provides states with alternatives to dispute resolution under Part C's procedural safeguards

7. Clarifies certain definitions, including specific early intervention services, qualified personnel, and emphasizes that intervention services should be provided in natural environments

SOURCES: Individuals with Disabilities Education Improvement Act (2004); Keilty and Walsh (2007).

hearing, communication development, social or emotional development and adaptive development. These assessments must be based on objective criteria and must include informed **clinical opinion**.

※ Family assessment (if the parents concur) means the identification of the family's resources, priorities, and concerns, and the supports and services necessary to enhance the family's capacity to meet the developmental needs of the family's infant or toddler with a disability, as determined through child assessment and a voluntary personal interview with the family.

※ Service needs assessment, if the infant or toddler qualifies as a child with a disability, includes reviewing the assessment of the child and family as well as pertinent records and observations to identify the early intervention services appropriate to meet the child's unique needs in each developmental area.

※ Evaluation is the method used to review the assessments of the child and the family to determine if the child is eligible for services and his continuing eligibility (IDEA, 2004; Keilty & Walsh, 2007).

Infants and toddlers with developmental delays will have moderate to severe disabilities or characteristics that are recognizable at birth, such as Down syndrome or fetal alcohol syndrome. We are not as good at identifying infants and toddlers with mild delays. Other infants may be determined to be at risk because of low birth weight or because of their family situation. Some of the infants with developmental delays will look different from the other infants; others will not.

Individualized Family Service Plans

Infants and toddlers (birth to three) identified as having developmental delays or disabilities will have an **Individualized Family Service Plan (IFSP)**. This is a plan that is developed by the infant or toddler's parents together with a team that is working with the child. This team may have been instrumental in the selection of the early care and education setting for the child, it may have been the parents' choice, or the teachers in the center may have been instrumental in identifying the child's special needs. The purpose of an IFSP is to identify, organize, and facilitate the attainment of a family's goals for themselves and their infant or toddler. The components of this plan are laid out in **Part C** of the IDEA (2004). States have different definitions about what constitutes a developmental delay in infants and toddlers. If the child meets the state's definition, he will have an IFSP or it will be in the process of being developed. Although IFSPs vary, they all include the information found in Table 11–13.

Clinical opinion
is the opinion or recommendations of qualified personnel relative to the assessment of the child's present level of functioning.

IFSP
is a written document that includes the infant's or toddler's level of functioning and the plan of intervention.

Part C
is the portion of the IDEA that specifically applies to children from birth to 36 months.

In addition to the specific requirements of the law, most IFSPs also include the information given in Table 11–14, which is helpful in program planning.

A designated service coordinator will help gather the information needed to plan for the infant and his family. The family and other professionals, including early childhood educators, are part of the team. Infants and toddlers with developmental delays require more specific planning than other young children do. They are likely to have particular developmental areas that need additional programming. Therapists often work with educators and parents to design these experiences. Caregivers should be part of the team that decides on the plan for infants and toddlers with developmental delays so that it is not only appropriate for the infant or toddler, but is also one that the caregiver can carry out.

In an IFSP, the parents write the plan with the service coordinator. IFSPs are written based on the child's present level of function and the concerns, needs, and priorities of the family. See Figure 11–1 for significant parts of Bobby's IFSP. Ponder the differences between the test results and the family's inputs and concerns.

Table 11–13 IFSP Requirements

- A statement of the infant's or toddler's present developmental levels, including physical, cognitive, speech and language, psychosocial development, and self-help or adaptive skills.

- A statement of family strengths and needs relative to enhancing the development of their infant or toddler.

- A statement of major outcomes (goals) expected for the child and family, methods for achieving these, and a time line for measuring the degree to which desired outcomes are achieved and whether or not IFSP revisions are necessary.

- A statement of specific early intervention services necessary to meet child and family needs, including information about the frequency, intensity, and methods of service delivery.

- Projected dates for starting and ending (if appropriate) services.

- The name of the service coordinator who will be responsible for implementing and coordinating the plan.

- A statement about procedures and methods that will be used to produce the desired outcomes is a required part of the plan.

- A plan for supporting the child and family during the transition into programs for 3- to 5-year-olds.

SOURCE: IDEA (2004).

Table 11–14 Information That Can Be Included in an IFSP

- An emphasis on the infant or toddler's strengths and functional abilities and limitations as well as his needs.

- Information about all developmental domains (physical, cognitive, language and speech, psychosocial, and self-help), not just the ones where deficits are noted.

- Information on the infant's behavioral and temperament characteristics.

up close and personal

I was concerned about Bobby's language and decided to take him to Child Development Watch. It was horrible. I have never had such a bad experience in my life.

I called to get an appointment and waited to hear from them. They called on Friday to confirm the appointment for Monday. I didn't even know about the appointment, but since I had waited for a while I decided not to say anything, even though they scheduled it right at his naptime.

It didn't go well. Bobby and I were the first people there. It was a doctor's office with all kinds of cabinets and stuff. He was tired and he played with the stroller until we put it outside. Then they gave him toys, and instead of doing what they asked, he would put the toys in the cabinets.

There was a developmental nurse and a speech and language pathologist. The speech and language person couldn't get him to engage. They called him Bob, which is my husband's name, and then they said he didn't respond to his own name. I was getting upset but I didn't tell them we call him Bobby. I would have if they had asked if he had a nickname or something. They gave him the Peabody Picture Vocabulary test, but they couldn't get him to sit still to look at the pictures. He kept pulling my hand; he wanted to go home. We were there for 2.5 hours. We were both exhausted. When we got home he slept for three hours.

They kept saying things like, "Well, we know he's different," and, "He likes music; maybe he could do something in that." He's only two years old and they are already feeling that he's not going to make it. They didn't listen to anything I would say. I told them that he doesn't do what you tell him to do. But in 10 minutes she "knew" what was wrong with him. She kept pooh-poohing everything I said he could do. I was irrelevant in the doctor's room. Just because something happens in one situation doesn't mean it is true in all settings. The environment was producing some of this.

I was frustrated. I know that he has some problems, but not all the problems they are saying. I told them that he could go down four stairs independently (we have a split-level home), so they took him to the top of this long, dark staircase and the speech and language therapist stood at the bottom of the stairs and called to him. He shook and cried and grabbed me. She said, "Well, sometimes we see what we want to see when it is our child." I know he's not perfect—his temperament makes it difficult for him to sit still, but he is just 24 months old and he needed a nap. He knows what he wants to do and he does it. I do a lot of incidental teaching at home. He moves to learn; he is not a sitter. Bobby likes to play with his toys by running them on the couch or windowsill. When he was playing with the toys there, they said to me, "Don't you ever put toys on the floor for him?" Of course I do. What did they think? This was a strange place and his style is to explore it all.

When he's free to explore, he is like this. He likes his stroller and when we go to the market everyone in the market knows him. I went here for eight years before we had Bobby and I never knew anyone. They say things like, "Here come the boy." Everyone knows him. He really likes older men and tries to get their attention. Sometimes I'll hear him belly-laughing and see a man down at the end of the aisle making faces at him. He's very outgoing.

They gave me the results right there. They said they would give me the results in writing later, but they wanted me to know right away so we could get started. He's 24 months old and they said his adaptive skills were at 24 months, but that his cognitive skills were only at 11 months. He got 2 out of 12 questions on the Battelle. His receptive language was at 11 months and his expressive language at 13 months. His fine motor skills were at 12 months and gross motor at 21 months. His social and emotional skills were at 18 months.

I was devastated. I cried for two weeks and then I got angry. They wouldn't listen to me. They felt they knew more about my son than I did. They told me he needed a neurological evaluation and on my way out they gave me a card telling me when it was scheduled. They didn't even ask me if I wanted one. They told me he needed speech and language therapy, occupational therapy, and a feeding evaluation. (I guess that was because I said he was a picky eater.) He also needed a hearing test,

which was supposed to be done that day, but when we went to the audiologist she looked at us and asked if I was really worried about his hearing. I said I wasn't. She asked how likely it was that Bobby would cooperate. I said he wouldn't. She suggested we come back on another day.

I walked out of there shaking like a leaf. I wanted to shout, "How can you do this to parents?" I wanted to throw up for a week. My God, is there nothing you can do for me? If we give them early intervention, they can do more. Is there no hope? A kid is not a test case. We know more and how to help them better, but that wasn't how I felt when we left. We are doomed. I kept saying, "Don't worry about the tests, they are just test results." I felt like I needed to defend him. At two he looks like everyone else because they are all throwing tantrums. It is very disturbing that these are the people who are going to identify all the kids who need help. Their goal seems to be to scare people. They don't say things like, "Based on what we see today," or, "He qualifies for help because he does need help." I wanted someone to affirm what I was feeling. I wanted them to do it at my house. This felt like a medical model where they were making a diagnosis rather than trying to figure out what we could do to help him learn. My field is early childhood special education. I sought them out because I was concerned about his language development. I didn't need this. I called because I needed to talk to someone.

FIGURE 11–1 Individualized Family Service Plan for Bobby

Section 4. Developmental Strengths and Concerns for the Child Plan: Date: 2/18/07   Child's Name: Bobby

Present Levels of Functioning	Strengths/Resources	Concerns/Needs/Priorities
1. Cognitive (thinking and solving problems): Date: 8/14/07 Age at Evaluation: 24 months Test Tool: Bayley Scale of Infant Development III Developmental Age: 11 months	1. Will repeat an activity to get a laugh. Very inquisitive—wants to know how things work. Good problem-solving skills. Loves books. Imitates adult activities—engages in imaginary play.	1. None
2. Adaptive (self-help skills): Date: 8/14/07 Age at Evaluation: 24 months Test Tool: Early Learning Accomplishment Profile: 24 months	2. Can pull off and put on pants. Uses a spoon; learning to use a fork. Can brush teeth. Can put on shoes.	2. None
3. Social/Emotional (Interacting with others): Date: 8/14/07 Age at Evaluation: 24 months Test Tool: Early Learning Accomplishment Profile: 18 months	3. Great sense of humor. Does things to make people laugh. Good socially. Gets along with others at preschool. Can be independent and he engages in parallel play.	3. None
4. Communication (understanding and using language): Date: 8/14/07 Age at Evaluation: 24 months Test Tool: Preschool Language Scale 4th Edition Receptive Language: 10 months Expressive Language: 13 months	4. Makes his needs known by making sounds, pointing, eye contact, some signs, and can use some words. He seems to understand what is said. He has just started singing.No problem with food textures—balanced diet—loves fruit-eats meat.	4. Bobby should be saying more at this age and parents would like Bobby to express himself appropriately.
5. Physical (large body movement and ability to use hands): Date: 8/14/07 Age at Evaluation: 24 months Test Tool: Bayley Scale of Infant Development III Fine motor: 10 months Gross motor: 21 months	5. Good gross motor skills—runs, jumps, kicks ball—loves to roughhouse. Can unlock and open sliding glass door. Colors. Puzzles are energizing. Plays with playdough. Loves to dump/pour—loves to play with water.	5. Parents have no concerns about motor skills but have concerns about sensory integration.

(continues)

FIGURE 11-1 (*continues*)

Section 5. Health Strengths and Concerns for the Child Plan:	Date: 2/18/07 Child's Name: Bobby	
	Strengths/Resources	Concerns/Needs/Priorities
Present Level of Functioning		
Primary Care Physician	Dr. Amy Groll	
Vision:	Vision was tested: appropriate	
Hearing:	Tested 9/8/07: appropriate	None
Nutrition:	Picky eater—but has a balanced diet—takes a vitamin—typically two	
Significant Medical Findings:Cognitive CommunicationsMotor		

Section 6. Strengths and Concerns for the Family Plan:	Date: 9/18/07 Child's Name: Bobby	
	Strengths and Resources	Concerns/Needs/Priorities
Current Family Information		
Bobby currently lives at home with his mother and father and two dogs.	Supportive family with some family in the area and others in Florida.	None
	Mom gets to work part-time and be at home with Bobby.	

Section 7. Child and Family Outcomes Plan:	Date: 9/18/07 Child's Name: Bobby	
	Steps Toward Outcomes	Review Dates/Outcomes
Major Outcomes (To Address Concerns/Needs Priorities)		
1. Bobby will speak at an age-appropriate level.	1. Refer for speech and language therapy. Parents will convey all of the wonderful things they are doing.	
2. We will explore sensory integration.	2. Refer to an occupational therapist for a sensory integration evaluation. Mom will read *Raising your spirited child*.	

REFLECTIVE PRACTICE

Think carefully about this IFSP. Consider the discrepancies between the test results and the parents concerns. If this two-year-old were in your classroom, what concerns would you have? How would you plan to work with this child to support his needs and the parents' concerns? How would you decide to work with the differences between the assessment information and the parent's concerns as reflected in the IFSP?

The idea behind the IFSP is that services should be family-centered, not just infant- or toddler-centered. Families decide what they want as outcomes on the IFSP. This means that families and professionals jointly plan. The parents and professionals provide guidance and support for those working with the infant or toddler.

The previous information has concentrated on generalized information about developmentally appropriate practice and individualizing programming for infants and toddlers. There is some information that is essential for all infant and toddlers.

SAFETY, HEALTH, AND NUTRITION

A major consideration in setting up the environment for young children is safety. A safe, secure environment is essential for optimal growth and development.

Safety

Safety needs to be routinely evaluated based on the age and developmental level of the children. The roles of the adult in particular and the environment in general are transactional. Infants and toddlers influence them and are influenced by them. It is important that caregivers create a safe and inviting environment for infants and toddlers. As new mobility skills emerge, infants and toddlers need places where they can master them and feel safe and secure. They must use mobility skills to perfect them. However, they may have few inhibitions or concepts of safety.

The mobile infant is learning to get what he wants himself, although initially the energy and concentration that it takes to get there may make him forget the purpose of the venture before he reaches his goal. This mobility requires increased vigilance and "childproofing" the environment. Issues of safety are more easily solved in settings that are designed solely for infants and toddlers.

Indoor and outdoor areas raise different issues for child safety. Survey the learning environment visually. Look for obvious safety concerns: sharp corners or exposed edges on tables or chairs. Evaluate the tables, chairs, and shelves for sturdiness. Could an infant pulling up on them tip them over? If so, replace them. Now, get down on your hands and knees, or even lie down. Are there things you have overlooked, such as an exposed electrical outlet without a safety plug, a cord that could be pulled, a piece of a broken toy that could be swallowed? Are crib rails locked in the "up" position when children are napping? Is an adult always present when an infant is on a changing table?

Outdoor areas pose additional safety challenges, because older children frequently share them. Areas should be fenced in and functionally organized. Grass is the best surface area. Concrete and asphalt get very hot in the summer and are dangerous for infants who are sitting and creeping, and they are not very forgiving when children fall.

As infants and toddlers become more independently mobile, issues of health and safety take on new importance. Before taking infants or toddlers on walks or local field trips, teach safety concepts. While on walks, talk to them about safety practices while you pull them in a wagon or push them in a stroller: "The light is red; we have to stop until it turns green"; "Look both ways before you cross the path." Assess the classroom and outside environment for safety. See Table 11–15 for ways to evaluate the environment. Do this on a regular basis, particularly as infants' mobility skills increase.

Safety has a prevention component. Safety equipment such as smoke alarms and fire extinguishers should be operable and adults should know how to use them. Practice fire drills monthly so that all adults know the procedures. A current list of emergency services phone numbers—including poison control, the fire company, and medical help, as well as numbers for contacting parents—should be easily accessible. First-aid supplies should also be accessible and adults should know how to do basic first aid as well as how to handle choking.

Table 11–15 Evaluate the Environment for Safety

- Organize push-and-pull toys with trailing loops and cords and store them out of reach. Infants and toddlers should be taught never to put these loops or cords around the body, because they may cause tripping or choking. For safety reasons pull-strings should be no longer than 9 inches. Use these toys under adult supervision.

- Make sure riding toys have widely spread wheels and a low center of gravity to prevent tipping.

- Choose metal or plastic toys that have smooth, rolled edges. Avoid toys with jagged edges or with parts that are imperfectly fitted together, or toys that look as if they might break into sharp, jagged pieces.

- Spot-check toys occasionally for minor damage. Often a spot of glue, a tightened bolt, a few drops of oil, or even a bit of adhesive tape will prevent further damage that could lead to an accident.

Health

We track health in infants and toddlers by gains in height/length and weight and the achievement of developmental norms. Health is more than the absence of disease. It is a dynamic state of physical, social, and mental well-being. Preventive health care instills good health habits beginning in infancy. Inoculations are part of this prevention, as is hand washing. Planning the environment to avoid accidents and injuries is another aspect of prevention.

The role of early childhood educators working with infants and toddlers is to prevent harm to children from known risks and to promote good health practices. The greatest risk of physical harm comes from injury and **infectious** or **communicable disease**. The health component of child care settings must be planned and managed like other areas. All early childhood educators and families need to work together to implement healthy policies for infants and toddlers. Establishing positive early practices can set the stage for future personal health practices (Aronson & Spahr, 2002).

Aronson and Spahr (2002) identify five crucial steps for preventing infectious diseases (see Table 11–16).

The first defense against infection is hand washing! Clean and sanitize all surfaces as well as toys and furniture. **Sanitizing** is making a solution of one tablespoon of bleach per quart of water, made fresh daily, dispensing it from a spray bottle, wetting the entire surface and leaving it on for two minutes. Dry it with a paper towel or let it air dry.

Infants and toddlers are ill frequently. They get 8 to 10 colds a year, and then there is flu, diarrhea, rashes, cuts, bruises, middle ear disease, and on and on. Child care settings need written health care policies about when infants and toddlers are healthy enough to participate. This needs to be part of their parent handbook so all parents know the policy. Some programs have child health care consultants who help develop such policies (Cianciolo, Trueblood-Noll, & Allingham, 2004).

Infectious diseases are illnesses caused by viruses, bacteria, fungi, or parasites.

Communicable diseases are those infectious diseases that people can spread to one another.

Sanitizing is using a bleach solution to disinfect surfaces.

Table 11–16 The Child Care Provider's Five Commandments for Infectious Disease Control

1. Prevent infections from spreading
2. Require certain immunizations
3. Report some illnesses
4. Exclude some children
5. Prepare—Do not wait until an outbreak occurs

SOURCE: Aronson and Spahr (2002, p. 4).

Choking

As infants begin self-feeding and have the ability to purposefully put small things in their mouth, the probability of choking increases. About 90 percent of fatal choking episodes occurred in children under 4, and 16 percent of first-aid situations in child care involved choking (Aronson & Spahr, 2002). To prevent choking, children should eat sitting down with an adult who can engage them in conversation as well as observe them as they eat. See Table 11–17 for other ways to prevent choking.

If an infant or toddler is choking, first check to see that he can still breathe. If so, wait for the object to come up. If not, turn the infant so his head is facing down and is lower than his buttocks; then slap him firmly between the shoulder blades. If nothing happens, try again. If the infant still cannot breathe when upside down, try to remove the object with your finger. Chances are that one of these steps will remove the object. If the infant can breathe but continues to choke, rush him to the hospital. All people who care for children should know how to manage a blocked airway and perform rescue breathing. I believe that they should be certified in the Heimlich maneuver and infant cardiopulmonary resuscitation (CPR).

Some infants and toddlers have health care needs that go beyond the expected colds and ear infections. Educators need to learn about each child and his specific health condition. They need to be aware of subtle signs of illness and to work toward promoting all children's health development and learning. Children with special health care needs are unique. Flexible planning and collaboration with families is essential (French, 2004).

Table 11–17 Choking Prevention

• No objects smaller than 1 ¼ inches in diameter and shorter than 2 ½ inches in length should be accessible.
• Look at the seams of stuffed toys to ensure they are sturdy. Infants and toddlers can choke on stuffing. Check labels to see that toys are nonallergenic, and machine washable and dryable.
• Check toys to ensure small parts cannot break off.
• Do not use latex balloons in the classroom. They are treacherous for young children. They can be sucked into the windpipe and cause a child to choke. Covers for balloons to prevent this are becoming available, so this caution may need to be reevaluated.
• Do not use uncovered foam balls and blocks with infants. Because infants put everything in their mouths, they may ingest the foam and choke on it.
• Foods that are round, hard, small, thick and sticky, smooth or slippery should not be offered to toddlers. That means no hotdogs, grapes, dried fruits, hard candy, chewing gum, and raw vegetables. For infants, foods should be cut into ¼ inch cubes, ½ inch cubes for toddlers.
• Plastic bags are also a choking threat.

SOURCE: Aronson and Spahr (2002).

Chronic Health Problems

Asthma
is a chronic inflammatory lung condition.

Asthma is one of the most prevalent chronic diseases in childhood in the United States and is a major cause of childhood disability. Asthma may limit a child's ability to play, learn, or sleep. In 2005, 8.9 percent of children had asthma (6.5 million children). It affects 6.2 percent of children between birth and four years of age. These children are almost twice as likely as children between 5 and 17 to be hospitalized and to visit emergency rooms and doctors' offices because of asthma . The incidence of childhood asthma more than doubled from 1980 to the mid-1990s. It is still not clear why this happened (Akinbami, 2006).

Asthma is a disease that causes the airways of the lungs to tighten and swell. Wheezing is common among infants and toddlers, because their airways are small and more susceptible to anything that impedes airflow. They also have a high incidence of respiratory infections. Definitively diagnosing asthma in infants and toddler is difficult because there are many potential causes of wheezing. If the wheezing is intermittent, physicians are reluctant to diagnosis a young child with a chronic illness. The concern is that respiratory distress can be life-threatening. When a child has an asthma attack, the lungs do not get enough air to breath. About two-thirds of children with asthma have at least one attack a year (Akinbami, 2006). Things that cause asthma attacks are called **triggers**. Different children have different triggers. Common triggers are molds, pollen, smoke, dust and chalk dust, fibers, and feathers. Other triggers include food allergies, laughing or crying hard, exercise and upper respiratory infections. Ask parents to provide you with a list of their child's triggers.

Triggers
are substances that cause asthma episodes.

All infants and toddlers with asthma should have an action plan. Physicians and parents typically write action plans. Although plans differ, they have two sections: a daily program and a rescue program (Environmental Protection Agency, n.d.). The daily action should list the child's asthma triggers, daily medicines and how to use them, and a **peak flow meter** chart. A peak flow meter is a small, hand-held device used to measure airflow through the lungs and the degree of restriction in the airways. The peak flow meter measures the infant's or toddler's best ability to expel air from the lungs. Peak flow readings are higher when infants or toddlers are breathing well, and lower when the airways are constricted. Changes in recorded values help determine how well the lungs are functioning, the severity of asthma symptoms, and treatment options. The rescue program should list the child's warning signs, his peak flow meter readings, names of rescue medicines used to treat an asthma attack, steps to take if the child has an asthma attack, when to call the parents, and when to take the child to the emergency room. They should also include emergency numbers for family, health care provider, and/or an asthma specialist.

Peak flow meter
is a hand-held device that measures airflow through the lungs.

Nutrition

Good nutrition is essential in child care. Programs vary with how snacks and meals are provided. Some programs have parents provide snacks; others provide the snacks. Some programs provide lunch; others have parents send it with their child. Regardless of the source, children should have a variety of foods offered each day, regular times for meals and snacks should be part of the routine. Food portions should be appropriate for infants and toddler, and snacks should be nourishing. Infants and toddlers are learning lifetime food habits (Aronson & Spahr, 2002). Although caloric levels based on **estimated energy requirements** have not been set for infants, two- and three-year-olds are estimated to need between 1,000 and 1,400 calories a day depending on where they are in their age range and activity level. This is about half of the 2,200 calories required for a moderately active 19- to 25-year-old female (U.S. Department of Agriculture, 2005). Think about how this relates to portion size and your expectations about how much toddlers should eat. The major determinant of energy intake (food consumption) is the amount served by their caregivers (Mrdjenovic & Levitsky, 2005). Start with small servings.

Estimated energy requirements are calorie levels needed to grow at an appropriate rate based on age and activity level.

Between four and six months, infants begin solid foods. Actually, the food is not solid—it is semisolid—and is typically an iron-fortified rice cereal. This is mixed with breast milk or formula. By eight months, infants' families begin to introduce fruits, vegetables, and other pureed foods. New foods are added one at a time with about a week in between to determine if an infant has an allergic reaction to a food before adding others. Feed infants solids with a small spoon, and have the infant suck the food off the tip. Do not put solids in a bottle unless the infant has a condition such as reflux. Toddlers eat a diet that is much more similar to that of adults, but serving sizes are smaller. See Table 11–18 for examples of appropriate servings for meals and serving sizes.

The Child and Adult Care Food Program which is administered by the Department of Agriculture provides funding for meals and snack for approximately 3 million children in early care and education. Centers that receive these funds must plan meals based on the Table 11–18. Providers can give children more food, but they must give them the minimums listed. Some feel that these standards are too loose and that centers should be required to have meals and snacks that meet specific nutrient-based standards (Story, Kaphingst, & French, 2006). One concern about what and how much infants and toddlers are fed is related to early childhood overweight and obesity.

Early Childhood Obesity

With the current concerns about obesity, there is a renewed interest in nutrition for very young children. Nutrition during the first three years of life influences growth patterns and may prevent some diseases. The patterns established during

Table 11–18 Meal-Pattern Requirements and Serving Sizes for Children 1 and 2 Years of Age

Breakfast	
Milk (must be fluid)	½ cup
Vegetable, Fruit, or 100% Juice	¼ cup
Grains/bread (enriched or whole grain)*	½ slice or ¼ cup serving
Snacks, two per day, select two of the four components for each snack	
Milk (must be fluid)	½ cup
Vegetable, Fruit, or 100% Juice	½ cup
Meat or meat alternative	½ ounce
Yogurt**	2 ounces
Egg	½ large
Grains/bread (enriched or whole grain)*	½ slice or ¼ cup serving
Lunch/Supper	
Milk (must be fluid)	½ cup
Meat/poultry/fish/cheese	1 ounce
Cooked dry beans or peas	¼ cup
Egg	½ large
Vegetables and/or Fruits (two or more)	¼ cup (total)
Grains/bread (enriched or whole grain)*	½ slice or ¼ cup serving

SOURCE: U.S. Department of Agriculture (2002).

these years may program preferences into the brain that influence adolescent and adult nutrition. Causes of obesity are complex. They include genetic, environmental, and social features. For example, infants who are low birth weight or heavy at birth are more likely to become overweight. With low birth weight infants the emphasis is on gaining weight, with large infants parents may inadventently restrict their food intake. Both of these patterns can lead to overweight (Milano, 2007; Statter, 2005).

Obesity causes an increased risk of health problems in early childhood and later. Increases in asthma and sleep disorders occur early. Risks for type 2 diabetes, heart disease, high blood pressure and cholesterol, liver disease, orthopedic complications, and mental health problems can occur later. However, although many of these diseases take years of damage to develop, obese children

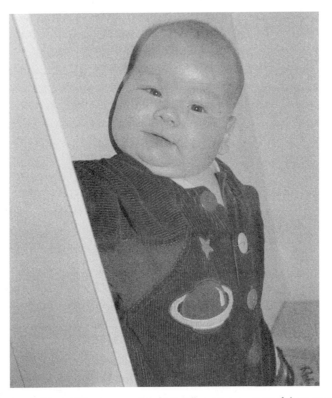

In some cultures chubby toddlers are preferred, but there is a concern if they are over-weight at age 3.

Energy balance is energy intake being equal to energy expenditure.

develop them at a younger age than their parents would despite advances in medicine (Daniels, 2006).

Obesity prevention involves maintaining a healthy weight while meeting health and nutritional needs. **Energy balance** means that energy input is equivalent to energy expenditure. Young children need a slightly positive energy balance to grow. With young children, the goal is healthy eating. Obesity prevention involves helping normal-weight children maintain their weight and helping children who are overweight to prevent further excess weight gain (Koplan, Liverman, & Kraak, 2005). Data from the Feeding Infants and Toddlers Survey found that infants 4 to 6 months averaged 61 calories per day over their estimated energy requirements; infants 7 to 11 months were 173 calories per day over their estimated need; and 1 to 2 year olds averaged 299 calories per day over their estimated requirements (Devany, Ziegler, Pac, Karwe & Barr, 2004). We may have to reevaluate the concept of "picky eaters" and think about the possibility that young children are not picky but full. Because of the number of infants and toddlers in early care and education settings, they are seen as ideal places to both provide nutritious food and model good nutrition; they also hold the potential for parent education (Story et al., 2006).

Food is part of our culture and the way we live. To reduce the risk of obesity and other chronic diseases, we need to take cultural feeding practices and socioeconomic levels into account (Mennella, Ziegler, Briefel, & Novak, 2006). Many Latino mothers prefer a chubby baby. A physically heavy baby is often preferred in cultures where levels of infant mortality are high. For many families, memories of food scarcity and high rates of infant mortality linger even when food is plentiful (Clark, 2003). More Hispanic infants began to eat pureed baby food around four to five months and to drink fruit juice or fruit-flavored drinks or eat fresh fruit than non-Hispanic infants. These differences were still true at 6 to 11 months with infants eating fresh fruits and drinking fruit-flavored drinks. They also ate more baby cookies, soups, and rice and beans. These differences continued into 24 months, with tortillas added as a noted difference. Why the emphasis on Latino infants and toddlers? They are three times more likely to be overweight or in danger of becoming overweight as Caucasian children (Mennella et al., 2006).

Although fruit juice contains good nutrients, it also contains high levels of sugar (fructose). Likewise, most fruit contains high levels of fructose. Many Hispanic cultures routinely feed infants sweetened drinks to prevent or treat infant colic (Mennella, Turnbull, Ziegler, & Martinez, 2005). The concern is that infants and toddlers will develop a heightened preference for sweet-tasting foods. Mexicans are genetically programmed to prefer even higher levels of sweet tastes. When this genetic tendency is combined with liberal feeding of sweetened beverages, gelatin, canned fruit, soft drinks, and juice, heightened sweet preferences are developed in early childhood and last a lifetime (Pepino & Mennella, 2005).

Increases in overweight after age 2 suggest that the infant and toddler years provide a window of opportunity to target nutritional messages and initiate healthful eating practices (Mennella et al., 2006). As adults help children establish eating habits, it is important to choose food for snacks and meals wisely. The best foods are those that are low in fat and salt and high in complex carbohydrates. Snacks are a major part of the toddler's diet. When you make snacks with children, make sure they adhere to good nutritional standards. Find ways of celebrating special events that do not always include cupcakes and candy.

Educators need to maintain a safe and healthy environment and to have the knowledge to design space that is intriguing to infants and toddlers. This can be particularly challenging when teaching infants and toddlers in a multi-age group.

PLANNING AND CURRICULUM FOR MULTI-AGE GROUPINGS

Often, individuals who work with infants and toddlers find themselves in the position of needing to plan curriculum for different ages of children at the same time. For example, a family child care home may have an infant of 6 months, toddlers at 18 and 28 months, and two preschoolers 3 and 4 years of age. This can be challenging because older children often enjoy toys with small parts that could be dangerous to infants and toddlers. Here are a few suggestions for working with children in multiage groupings:

* Separate the infant, toddler, and preschool materials. For example, have infant toys (rattles, soft balls, and blocks) on the floor and preschool materials such as crayons and paper up on a table where infants cannot reach them.

* Have some time during the day when the older children can help the younger ones. For example, an older preschooler may enjoy building a block tower that a toddler knocks down repeatedly. Do not overdo the helping role. Make sure that older children have time to play, experiment, and explore on their own with activities appropriate to their age.

* Plan some activities for the older children while allowing the younger children a choice about participating. Support their participation in an age-appropriate way. For example, encourage preschoolers to move to the musical directions on a record while you support crawlers and walkers just moving their bodies to the music but without following the directions in the song. If an infant is awake, hold her and move with her to the music.

* If older children wake up early from a nap, take advantage of the opportunity to play a game with them, talk, cuddle, or do an activity of their choice that is more difficult to do when both infants and toddlers are awake.

* While feeding an infant, tell riddles or play a guessing game with older children.

* When teaching multi-age groups that include toddlers, it is important to adjust your expectations to their developmental level.

※ Do not expect toddlers to sit for a long time in a group situation. If you are doing a long activity, allow toddlers to come and go as they please.

※ When a disruptive behavior cannot be prevented, anticipate when it will happen. If a toddler typically has a difficult time leaving her parents, plan to have an adult available who can give the toddler undivided attention to help this transition go more smoothly.

※ Remember age-appropriate expectations. Different strategies are effective with different ages of children. Infants and toddlers are more easily distracted than older children.

※ Match children's developmental level in an age-appropriate way. Even if a toddler is functioning at a much younger level, try to find toys and materials appropriate for him, not a young infant.

※ Redirect children to more appropriate activities when possible. This may be difficult with a persistent toddler who is fascinated by a particular object and cannot be distracted. You might find a special time when you can give this child your full attention and let him touch the delicate object with your close supervision. This will often decrease rather than increase the level of stress you are comfortable with. Try not to go much beyond that level.

※ Occasionally allow children the option of not participating. They will often watch for a while and then join you when they are ready. Everyone, including children, needs to have control over their environment and letting them choose when they will participate is one way of doing this. Watch, on the other hand, for a child who does not want to participate. Find ways of regularly including this child.

A well-managed setting is not always quiet and neat. Decide what levels of noise and clutter you can tolerate and make decisions that will maintain those levels. The previous sections have focused on curriculum and information related to teaching. Decide how a philosophy of teaching might incorporate them. Now it is time for you to actively reflect on this and begin to develop you philosophy of teaching including your preferred teaching techniques.

DEVELOPING A PHILOSOPHY OF WORKING WITH INFANTS AND TODDLERS

What do *you* believe about infants and toddlers? How and where should they be cared for? Do you think that anyone can care for an infant, that it is "natural," and that it requires no training? Do you think that all infants need is to be is safe, warm, and dry? Do you think all infants are pretty much the same? Do you think toddlers are little adults who just have a lot to learn? Your answers to these questions will influence how you plan and form your philosophy of working with infants and toddlers.

You already have a philosophy for working with very young children. It may not be well articulated, but it exists, and it influenced how you answered the questions above. It will also influence how you will interact with families, how you set up the environment, the type of preparations you make, and the degree to which you individualize planning. Developmentally appropriate practices are necessary regardless of your personal philosophy. There is no single correct philosophy, but it is important to be able to articulate your philosophy, to know how it developed, and to continually evaluate and modify it with your personal growth. It is also important to compare it with what early childhood educators and researchers have found. This is true whether this is your first experience with infants and toddlers or whether you have taught for 30 years. It is true whether you are childless or have raised 12 children.

Developing a philosophy for working with infants and toddlers is a dynamic process. Your philosophy is dependent upon many different variables. One variable is you as a person, your experiences as a child, and the decisions you have made based on these experiences. These personal experiences may be through working at an early care and education setting, babysitting for young children, or having children yourself. Those who teach you about infants and toddlers also affect it. Your personality, temperament, and way of being in the world influence your philosophy. Related to this are your attitudes toward young children in general and the role you believe that families and early care and education settings play in caring for and educating very young children. This combines with what you know about a variety of specific content areas: child development, particularly as it relates to infants and toddlers; early childhood education; early childhood special education; and family studies. These knowledge bases interact and affect your philosophy.

Scholars in the field emphasize different aspects of development. Some emphasize the social and emotional aspects of early development; others emphasize cognitive development. This emphasis may influence your philosophy and how much time you plan to devote to different curriculum areas. If professionals voice opinions about aspects of the field, such as breast- versus bottle-feeding, placing young infants in early care and education settings, and discipline, these too may influence your philosophy. This textbook, and others you have read, may have affected the focus of your philosophy.

You will modify and change your philosophy with your personal growth and development and changing ideas about infants and toddlers. As you interact and plan for infants and toddlers your increasing knowledge base expands and influences your philosophy. Your philosophy evolves as you change, learn, and try out what you know and reflect on the outcome.

The question then becomes how does your personal philosophy determine what happens in the classroom? Can you implement what you believe in the classroom? The reality of the early care and education setting will affect the answer to that question. Your philosophy will influence the actual setting that you choose to work in. To the extent that a setting's philosophy lacks congruence with your philosophy, you may not seek employment there. Once you are working in a setting, you may find that there are differences between your philosophy and the way the classroom is organized. You might believe that young children should eat when they are hungry and sleep when they are tired, and the setting might have set times for eating and sleeping. How you cope with these differences depends on your philosophy and how flexible it is, and even perhaps, how badly you need the job and the availability of other employment. States also have regulations with regard to child care licensing.

Developing a philosophy is ongoing, and you need to bring it up to a conscious level so you can reflect on it and continuously reevaluate it relative to your practice. Because infants change and grow quickly, it is useful to focus your philosophy on three distinct periods: young infants (birth to about 9 months), mobile infants (8 until about 18 months), and toddlers (16 to 36 months) (Lally et al., 1997). Note that the age ranges overlap to allow for individual differences in development. The curriculum chapters in this book reflect these age divisions. The following sections will help you clarify your philosophy.

Purpose of Early Care and Education

Is early care and education a service for parents or a stimulating, enriching environment for infants and toddlers to grow and develop, or can and should it be both? Is it the way a village would raise a child? If you care for very young children, you need to decide what type of care children need. Although this is *your* philosophy, it needs to be grounded in what we know about infants and toddlers and what is best practice in the field. If you have reached this point in the book, my philosophy is probably clear if you reflect on what you have read. However, you may not have thought about it. For me, the goal of early care and education is to give infants and toddlers the most ideal environment conceivable at a cost their parents can afford. To do this means that some of the costs of child care would need to be subsidized as they are in many other countries.

Let us start with the basics: Infants should be able to eat when they are hungry, sleep when they are tired, be changed when they are wet, and comforted when they are distressed. Beyond the basics, the goal is to be respectful and responsive to infants and to follow their lead. This means being able to read their cues and to match their biological state with an appropriate response. It also means delighting in their smiles, suffering when they cry, and doing whatever is in your power to create a safe, predictable environment for them.

As infants become toddlers, they need more structure in their environment. Their emerging self-sufficiency needs to be supported as well as their independence. Toddlers need to learn to play by themselves and with others and to regulate their emotions and behavior. All young children need to participate in all curriculum domains: cognitive, language, motor, sensory, science, and creative arts.

REFLECTIVE PRACTICE

Stop a moment and reflect on where you are in the development of your philosophy. You are clearer about my beliefs. What are yours?

Content and Process

The issue of whether content or process is most important has been debated for years. The overall conclusion is that they are both necessary and important. In reality, content and process support each other. However, with infants and toddlers the emphasis is mostly on process. If toddlers are going to scribble (process), they need something to scribble about (content). Relevant content that is integrated across a broad range of activities supports learning. A heavy emphasis on content learned through drill and practice is inappropriate.

Child-Initiated and Teacher-Initiated Learning

The proportion of time allocated to teacher-directed versus child-directed tasks should be thought about and addressed in your philosophy. Toddlers increase their knowledge by acting upon the environment and by reacting and organizing the feedback they receive. They want to know about what interests them at the moment they are interested, and this interest may be fleeting. They can learn from adults, but in small doses. Obviously, there is a relationship between content and teacher-initiated instruction and process and child-initiated instruction. There is a bridge. If teachers are willing to teach about what toddlers want to learn, there is a perfect match. Teacher-initiated instruction is informal and used on an individual or small group basis.

Time Allocation

Think about your day with toddlers. The first broad plans you develop divide the day into segments that have particular purposes. Toddlers, like infants, have a significant amount of time devoted to routines like diapering and toileting, sleeping, and eating. The decisions you make about how you allocate the remainder of the time reflect your philosophy. Toddlers and most two-year-olds are too young for group times to be effective. Remember, for mobile infants, 3 to 5 minutes is a long time, and for toddlers, 10 minutes may seem like forever. Most of the time infants and toddlers are in care they should be able to choose the experiences in which they want to participate in their indoor or outdoor environment.

The National Association for Sports and Physical Education (NASPE) recommends that toddlers accumulate at least 30 minutes of daily structured physical activity and at least 60 minutes or more of unstructured physical activity (NASPE, 2002). Aerobic exercise improves cardiovascular fitness. However, children at a very young age are not ready for long uninterrupted periods of strenuous aerobic activity. They need bursts of energy output. Developmentally appropriate aerobic activities for young children include moderate to vigorous play and movement (Graham, Holt-Hale, & Parker, 2007). If toddlers are really going to accumulate 30 minutes of structured (teacher-led) physical activity, this time needs to be planned into the day. It needs to be considered much like routines. Although 30 minutes does not sound like a long time, it actually is and needs to be done in two- to four-minute increments. To meet this requirement in an all day program this means that you need to schedule 8 to 10 planned energy bursts. This may mean two minutes of baby yoga for a young infant after diapering, supporting the infant to "kick, kick, kick," or bicycle their legs. For mobile infants it may be moving objects (or you) for them to creep after, rolling, throwing or kicking balls, or jumping over a line taped on the floor. For toddlers it may be a dance party, follow the leader (you are the leader), or variations on movement (Deiner & Qiu, 2007). The goal is for children to move until they are breathless. They need your support to do this.

REFLECTIVE PRACTICE

If toddlers are really going to get 30 minutes of structured physical activity in a full-day program, how will you accommodate this in your philosophy of teaching? Decide when and how you can work this time into your daily schedule, what role you will play in selecting and leading these activities, and the types of activities that are developmentally appropriate for toddlers.

Number of Activities

How many activities are available for toddlers to choose from? They need choices, but not so many that they are overwhelmed. Toddlers need to practice making decisions about what interests them and how long they stay. It is inappropriate to require them to stay a specific amount of time at an activity or to all participate in the same activity with identical outcomes. On the other hand, if one goal is to help them become more socially aware of their peers, you don't want so many different activities that each child can do his own thing without having to interact with others.

Toddlers and two-year-olds need 30 minutes of structured, teacher-led moderate to vigorous physical activity. Even with equipment designed to stimulate physical activity, children rarely achieve that level. They need to move until they are breathless.

WITH INFANTS AND TODDLERS

Start with have an activity or experience for every two to three toddlers. See what happens. If your goal is to increase sharing and turn-taking, is this accomplishing your goal? If not, experiment with the ratio of children to activities until it does what you want.

Balance of Activities

Look at the choices you give toddlers to see the balance between active and quiet ones, and teacher-directed and child-directed activities. Do these match your philosophy? That is, if you believe that toddlers need choices, can they choose among five or so different activities in a two-hour span? Can toddlers make their own choices for at least 75 percent of the time? Look at the complexity of the activities you offer to ensure that toddlers who are gifted as well as those who learn more slowly still have choices. Did you plan for the energy bursts? If toddlers are to get 30 minutes of structured physical activity, you need to divide these into about 10 to 15 time slots of two to three minutes each and ensure that they are scattered throughout the day. Plan them or they will not happen. Transitions are an easy time to include some of them. As children move from inside to outside, they can march (it may not look like marching). You can have a dance party to music with a strong, fast beat. Nevertheless, include these in your plans.

Inclusion

Including infants and toddlers with disabilities in early care and education settings has a legislative base. However, you need to look at your personal feelings about inclusion. Some feel that *all* children should be included; others feel that only infants and toddlers with mild to moderate disabilities should be in regular early care and education settings. Who do you believe should be included? Once you are clear about your feelings, you can then go to the next stage and look at how all children will be included and the supports necessary for inclusion, if any.

SUMMARY

Curriculum determines what infants and toddlers do during the time they are in early care and education. There is general agreement that infant and toddlers and their families need to be treated respectfully. The role of developmentally appropriate practices is also an accepted part of planning. However, different curriculum approaches use these concepts in very different ways. Curriculum and assessment provide a feedback loop to educators so they know what skills are emerging, what skills infants and toddlers are practicing, and those that have been mastered.

To work effectively with infants and toddlers, adults need a variety of teaching techniques and the knowledge of matching the particular technique to the particular infant or toddler and in what particular situation. Adults support learning in a variety of ways: environmentally, verbally, and nonverbally.

Infants and toddlers with developmental disabilities and other chronic illnesses are included in early care and education settings. Infants and toddlers who have been identified as having a developmental delay will have an IFSP. Health, safety, and nutrition are critical aspects of all programming for infants and toddlers.

One goal of learning about different curriculum approaches and ways to work with infants and toddlers is to develop a philosophy of working with infants and toddlers. This philosophy supports decision making at many different levels from what happens in the room to what positions to apply for.

CHAPTER IN REVIEW

- Different approaches to early care and education emphasis different areas of development and how they believe infants and toddlers learn best.
- Developmentally appropriate practice underlies all curricular approaches.
- Assessment and record keeping are an integral part of all curriculum.
- A philosophy of early care and education guides an adult's behavior in the classroom.
- All teachers have a philosophy of education and it is important to clarify it and reflect on it frequently.
- The years from birth to three are important for brain development, and early childhood educators and early childhood special educators need to use this prime time to help children learn.
- Curriculum for infants and toddlers includes social, emotional, physical and motor development, as well as cognitive and language development.
- Curriculum must have age and subject matter integrity. It moves from what children know to what they can learn with adult scaffolding.
- Programming balances active and quiet play; it emphasizes process and play that is more child-directed than teacher-directed.
- Infants with identified developmental delays will have an IFSP.

APPLICATION ACTIVITIES

1. Write your philosophy of early childhood education for infants and toddlers.

2. The term "developmentally appropriate practice" has been used throughout this book, but especially in this chapter. Discuss what that means to you and how you would know it if you saw it.

3. People have different feelings about which infants and toddlers with disabilities should be included in early childhood programs. Where do you draw your limits and why?

4. Go to your state's website for child care licensing (typing "child care licensing" and the name of your state into Google is the easiest

way to find it). Look at its policies and procedures. Look at what aspects of early care and education are addressed and what are not. Analyze the document. Reflect on the amount of space in the document devoted to curriculum and planning versus facilities and health care.

RESOURCES

Web Resources

❋ **Caring for Our Children: National Health and Safety Performance Standards: Guidelines for Out-of-Home Child Care Programs** written by the American Academy of Pediatrics, American Public Health Association, and National Resource Center for Health and Safety in Child Care and Early Education, provides a wealth of information relative to health care requirements for child care programs. This site also provides a variety of other material for early care and education in the area of health and safety at this site. http://nrc.uchsc.edu.

❋ The **English Learning for Pre-schooler Project**, although designed for preschool children, has some helpful hints about strategies to use with children whose home language is not English. http://www.edgateway.net/pub/docs/pel.

❋ **Teaching Strategies** has curriculum materials and parenting resources for infants and toddlers. www.teachingstrategies.com.

❋ The **U.S. Department of Agriculture** has a food pyramid for kids and even simplified, it is too complex for infants and toddlers, but it can serve as a guide for choosing healthy snacks and or helping parents learn about young children's nutritional needs. http://www.mypyramid.gov/kids.

❋ **WestEd** is a national nonprofit research and service agency working with education and human development communities to promote excellence, achieve equity, and improve learning for all children. It has a variety of support materials for new teachers with a special emphasis on English language learners. http://www.wested.org.

Print Resources

❋ Aronson, S. S., & Spahr, P. M. (2002). *Healthy young children: A manual for programs.* Washington, DC: National Association for the Education of Young Children.

❋ Gandini, L., & Edwards, C. P. (Eds.) (2005). *Bambini: The Italian approach to infant/toddler care.* New York: Teachers College Press.

❋ Petrie, S., & Owen, S. (Eds.) (2005). *Authentic relationships in group care for infants and toddlers—Resources for infant educarers RIE: Principles into practice.* London and Philadelphia, PA: Jessica Kingsley Publishers.

※ Sandall, S., Hemmeter, M. L., Smith, B., & McLean, M. E. (2005). *DEC recommended practices: A comprehensive guide for practical* application in early intervention/early childhood special education. Missoula, MT: Division of Early Childhood.

REFERENCES

Akinbami, L. J. (2006). *The state of childhood asthma, United States, 1980–2005. Advance data from vital and health statistics; No. 381*, Hyattsville, MD: National Center for Health Statistics.

American Academy of Pediatrics, American Public Health Association, and National Resource Center for Health and Safety in Child Care and Early Education. (2002). Caring for our children: National Health and Safety Performance Standards: Guidelines for Out-of-Home Child Care Programs (2nd ed.). Elk Grove Village, IL: American Academy of Pediatrics and Washington, DC: American Public Health Association. Retrieved November 20, 2007, from http://nrc.uchsc.edu/CFOC/index.html

Aronson, S. S., & Spahr, P. M. (Ed.) (2002, Edition). *Healthy young children: A manual for programs*. Washington, DC: National Association for the Education of Young Children.

Bredekamp, S., & Rosegrant, T. (Eds.) (1992). *Reaching potentials: Appropriate curriculum and assessment for young children* (Vol. 1). Washington, DC: NAEYC.

Bredekamp, S., & Rosegrant, T. (1995). Reaching potentials through transforming curriculum, assessment, and teaching. In S. Bredekamp & T. Rosegrant (Eds.), *Reaching potentials: Transforming early childhood curriculum and assessment* (Vol. 2, pp. 15–22). Washington, DC: NAEYC.

Cadwell, L. B. (2003). *Bringing learning to life: The Reggio approach to early childhood education.* New York: Teachers College Press.

Cianciolo, S., Trueblood-Noll, R., & Allingham, P. (2004). Health consultation in early childhood settings. *Young Children, 59*(2), 56–61.

Clark, L. (2003). Making new choices possible: Understanding differences in infant feeding practices between Latina mothers and Anglo health care providers. *Zero To Three, 23*(5), 22–27.

Daniels, S. R. (2006). The consequences of childhood overweight and obesity. *The Future of Children, 16*(1), 47–67.

Deiner, P. L., & Qiu, W. (2007). Embedding physical activity and nutrition in early care and education programs. *Zero to Three, 28*(1), 13–18.

Devany, B., Ziegler, P., Pac, S., Karwe, V., & Barr, S. (2004). Nutrient intakes of infants and toddlers. *Journal of the American Dietetic Association, 104*(1), S14–S21.

Dodge, D. T., Rudick, S., & Berke, K. (2006). *The creative curriculum for infants, toddlers & twos.* Washington, DC: Teaching Strategies, Inc.

Environmental Protection Agency. (n.d.). Help your child gain control over asthma. Retrieved May 22, 2007, from http://www.epa.gov/asthma/pdfs/ll_asthma_brochure.pdf

Freeman, N. K., & Feeney, S. (2006). The new face of early care and education. Who are we? Where are we going? *Young Children, 61*(5), 10–16.

French, K. (2004). Supporting a child with special health care needs. *Young Children, 59*(2), 62–63.

Gandini, L. (1993). Fundamentals of the Reggio approach to early childhood education. *Young Children, 49,* 4–8.

Gandini, L. (2001). Reggio Emilia: Experiencing life in an infant-toddler center. In L. Gandini & C. P. Edwards (Eds.), *Bambini: The Italian approach to infant/toddler care* (pp. 55–66). New York: Teachers College Press.

Gandini, L. (2004). A brief Reggio Emilia story. In J. Henrick (Ed.), *Next steps toward teaching the Reggio way: Accepting the challenge to change* (2nd ed., pp. 2–12). Upper Saddle River, NJ: Pearson Education, Inc.

Gerber, M. (Ed. J. Weaver) (1998). *Dear parent: Caring for infants with respect.* Los Angeles: Resources for Infant Educarers.

Gerber, M. (2005). RIE principles and practices. In S. Petrie & S. Owen (Eds.), *Authentic relationships in group care for infants and toddlers—Resources for infant educarers (RIE: Principles into practice)* (pp. 35–50). London and Philadelphia, PA: Jessica Kingsley Publishers.

Graham, G., Holt-Hale, S. A., & Parker, M. (2005). *Children moving: A reflective approach to teaching physical education* (7th ed.). New York: McGraw-Hill.

Individuals with Disabilities Education Improvement Act of 2004, Pub. L. No. 108–446, 118 Stat 2647, 20 U. S. C. 1400, 2004.

Keilty, B., & Walsh, S. (2007, October). What's new with the IDEA Part C regulations? *Paper given at the annual conference of the Division for Early Childhood,* Niagara Falls, Ontario, Canada.

Klass, C. S. (1987). Childrearing interactions within developmental home- or center-based early education. *Young Children, 42*(3), 9–13, 67–70.

Koplan, J., Liverman, C. T., & Kraak, V. I. (2005). *Preventing childhood obesity: Health in the balance.* Washington, DC: National Academics Press.

Lally, J. R., Griffin, A., Fenichel, E., Segal, M., Szanton, E., & Weissbourd, B. (1997). Development in the first three years of life. In S. Bredekamp & C. Copple (Eds.), *Developmentally appropriate practice in early childhood programs* (Rev. ed., pp. 55–69). Washington, DC: National Association for the Education of Young Children.

Lewin-Benham, A. (2006). One teacher, 20 preschoolers, and a goldfish: Environmental awareness, emergent curriculum, and documentation. *Young Children.* Retrieved May 25, 2007, from http://www.journal.naeyc.org/btj/200603/LewinBTJ.asp

Mennella, J. A., Turnbull, B., Ziegler, J., & Martinez, H. (2005). Infant feeding practices and early flavor experiences in Mexican infants: An intra-cultural study. *Journal of the American Dietetics Association, 95,* 908–915.

Mennella, J. A., Ziegler, P., Briefel, R., & Novak, T. (2006). Feeding infants and toddlers study: The types of foods fed to Hispanic infants and toddlers. *Journal of the American Dietetic Association, 106*(1 Suppl 1), s96–s106.

Milano, K. O. (2007). Prevention: The first line of defense against childhood obesity. *Zero to Three, 28*(1), 6–11.

Mrdjenovic, G., & Levitsky, D. A. (2005). Children eat what they are served: The imprecise regulation of energy intake. *Appetite, 44,* 273–282.

National Association for the Education of Young Children. (2006a). New NAEYC Early Childhood Program Standards and Accreditation Performance Criteria. Retrieved May 24, 2007, from http://www.naeyc.org/about/releases/20050426.asp

National Association for the Education of Young Children. (2006b). Developmentally appropriate practice in early childhood programs serving children from birth through age 8. Retrieved May 21, 2007, from http://www.naeyc.org/about/positions/dap7.asp

National Association for the Education of Young Children. (2006c). Early childhood curriculum, assessment, and program evaluation: Building an effective, accountable system in programs for children birth through age 8. Retrieved November 20, 2007, from http://www.naeyc.org/about/positions/pdf/pscape.pdf

National Association for Sports and Physical Education. (2002). *Active start: A statement of physical activity guidelines for children: Birth to five years.* Reston, VA: Author.

Pepino, M. Y., & Mennella, J. A. (2005). Factors contributing to individual differences in sucrose preference. *Chemical Senses, 30,* 319–320.

Petrie, S. (2005). The work of Emmi Pikler and Magda Gerber. In S. Petrie & S. Owen (Eds.), *Authentic relationships in group care for infants and toddlers—Resources for infant educarers RIE: Principles into practice* (pp. 17–33). London and Philadelphia, PA: Jessica Kingsley Publishers.

Rinaldi, C. (2001). Reggio Emilia: The image of the child and the child's environment as a fundamental principle. In L. Gandini & C. P. Edwards (Eds.), *Bambini: The Italian approach to infant/toddler care* (pp. 49–54). New York: Teachers College Press.

Sandall, S., Hemmeter, M. L., Smith, B., & McLean, M. E. (2005). *DEC recommended practices: A comprehensive guide for practical application in early intervention/early childhood special education.* Missoula, MT: Division of Early Childhood.

Statter, E.(2005). *Your child's weight: Helping without harming.* Madison, WI: Kelcy Press.

Story, M., Kaphingst, K. M., & French, S. (2006). The role of child care settings in obesity prevention. *The Future of Children, 16*(1), 143–168.

U.S. Department of Agriculture. (2002). *Menu planning guide for child care home: Menu Magic for Children.* U.S. Department of Agriculture Child and Adult Care Food Program. University of Mississippi: National Food Service Management Institute.

U.S. Department of Agriculture. (2005). My Pyramid food intake pattern calorie levels. Retrieved May 24, 2007, from http://www.mypyramid.gov/downloads/MyPyramid_Calorie_Levels.pdf

Williams, K. C., & Cooney, M. H. (2006). Young children and social justice. *Young Children, 61*(2), 75–82.

chapter 12

Curriculum and Planning for Young Infants: Birth to Nine Months

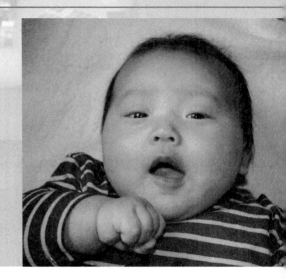

Chapter Outline

- Developmentally Appropriate Planning for Young Infants
- Implementing Curriculum for Young Infants
- Methods and Materials for Working with Young Infants
- Schedules, Routines, and Transitions
- Including All Young Infants
- Observing and Recording Infant Behavior

What is curriculum for young infants? They just "are" until they begin to move and talk, or are they? Young infants have a surprising number of skills, likes, and dislikes, and can express both pleasure and disappointment. They like human faces, sounds, and smells. They see adults as objects of interest and a novelty in their environment. They may even favor them with a smile or a laugh, or babble at them. They like to look at them and then stop looking when they decide they have had enough. Although young infants have a limited repertoire of skills, they do have them, and the objective of planning is to enjoy infants, develop relationships with them, and support their development.

WHY STUDY CURRICULUM AND PLANNING FOR YOUNG INFANTS?

- ☀ Young infants are dependent on adults to provide them with interesting experiences.

- ☀ Young infants need support in regulating their state to enable them to be available for learning.

- ☀ Young infants' skills develop rapidly and they need adults to support emerging skills and to provide opportunities to practice and master more developed skills.

- ☀ Young infants need responsive and respectful care from adults to develop trust and attachment to the adults in their environment.

- ☀ Young infants need caregivers to know if their development is following a typical pattern.

Infants from birth to nine months are dependent on adults, not only to plan experiences but also to bring the materials to them and often to play with them. Experiences for infants this age are designed as lying or sitting experiences.

DEVELOPMENTALLY APPROPRIATE PLANNING FOR YOUNG INFANTS

This is it! The time when babies are not sleeping, eating, or getting their diaper changed. Optimally, this is a time when they are alert and interested in learning about their world. Young infants are not in this state for very long, so it is important to "catch" it. With increasing age, infants spend more time in the quiet alert state and less time sleeping and crying. Young infants are just learning how to interact with others so their interactions may last only a moment or two. These interactive times alternate with times when babies play alone. All infants need some planned play time with an adult every day. They also need to be cared for, supported, and played with throughout the day.

Planning for nonmobile infants is very different from planning for toddlers or preschool children, yet many professionals do not realize the degree of expertise necessary. Planning for very young infants is very individualized and developmentally based. Experiences are usually one on one, are planned for a particular infant, and executed when that infant is interested. Very young infants have such a small range of behaviors that experiences with slight variations are repeated until the infant reaches another developmental level, which is within a week or two. For example, "teethers" can be repeated many times by using different teethers and talking about their characteristics.

Because planning for infants is so closely related to their developmental level, it is most efficient to initially organize planning based on age and then to individualize it. The interaction of development, experiences, and learning forms the foundation for planning.

Planning for infants is more holistic than planning for older children. Their ability to attend to a task is dependent on their state and your ability to choose the appropriate time and experience to engage the infant. The ability to excel as a teacher of infants is dependent on accurate observations of infants, knowledge of development, and the ability to bring these two sets of information together in a joyful, fun way.

For purposes of planning, early infancy can be divided into three functional phases based on large- and small-motor development. In general, the motor requirements of an experience determine which experiences are appropriate for which infants (see Table 12–1).

Developmental differences between a one, a four, and an eight-month-old infant are so vast that experiences for one are inappropriate for the other. Infants need to be the center of the planning process. From birth to about eight months infants focus their attention on developing a sense of security (Lally & Mangione, 2006).

The best materials encourage active involvement. Active involvement differs by age; just looking is active involvement for a very young infant, but not for an older infant. Routine care and transitions take up a major part of the young infant's day. Think about these as potential learning experiences while making them enjoyable and having one-on-one time with infants. A diaper change can be enhanced with a short massage. But remember that the curriculum for infants is learning to build secure relationships.

Planning That Keeps the Young Infant in the Center

Webbing is a technique that is used to generate ideas about a particular topic. When educating preschool children, a particular theme is put in the center of the web; for example, *transportation* might be at the center of the web. Working

Table 12–1 Motor Requirements of Young Infants

- Infants from birth up until about 4 or 5 months of age do not have good antigravity skills. Therefore, experiences are designed for an infant who is lying either prone (on the stomach) or supine (on the back) or in a supported sitting position. These experiences are also appropriate for older infants who have these developmental skills.

- Beginning at about 4 months of age, infants need less support sitting (head control is greatly improved) and they are moving toward independent sitting. Their hands are now free to explore the environment and they play more independently.

- At about 7 to 8 months purposeful mobility begins to emerge. The infant begins to move independently by rolling, crawling, creeping, hitching, scooting, or perhaps walking.

from there you generate ideas about different types of transportation pre-schoolers might be familiar with and expand on these. You would then look at the different curriculum areas and see how you could incorporate each into the learning goals you have for the children.

When planning for infants and toddlers, put the infant in the center. Use the webbing technique to first note the infant's development and what skills are emerging. Write the infant's name in the center of a blank piece of paper. Then make a web around the infant noting her developmental levels, needs, and interests. From this, experiences can be identified that are likely to interest the infant and also provide a sound basis for curriculum planning (Sutton & Buell, in press). Planning for young infants is probably best classified as emergent curriculum, because it truly emerges out of what infants know and are interested in doing (See Figure 12–1).

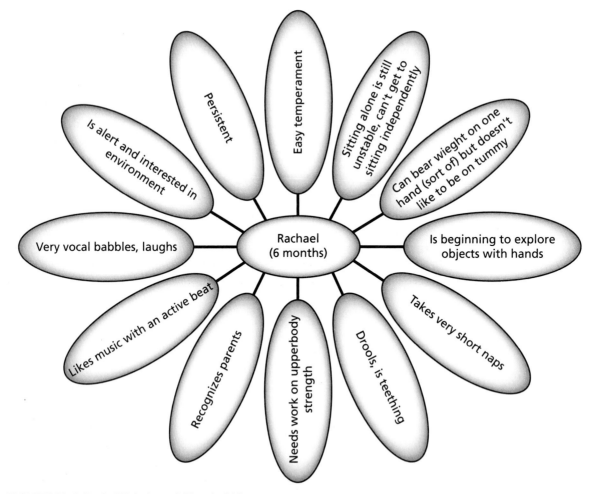

FIGURE 12–1 Basic Web for a 6-Month-Old

WITH INFANTS AND TODDLERS

Rachael is a six-month-old infant. From this basic web, what might you do based on her need to work on upper body strength? To build upper body strength she needs to be on her tummy with her head up and supporting her weight with her arms. I might lie down beside her on my tummy and read her a book. I would stop reading if she put her head on the mat. Start when she shows interest again. I might put her on a textured mat, lie beside her on my tummy, play music with a beat, and use one hand to tap the rhythm on a particular texture square so she uses one arm to support her weight and one to tap with me. I would talk about what was happening. What might you do?

With young infants the basic webbing process ends with a single infant. However, you will need to redo your web as their development changes. By increasing her upper body strength you are affecting the age at which she will begin to crawl and then creep. What you are doing now will be inappropriate in a month or even a week. Planning starts with a basic web, but as we look at different curriculum areas, the key to planning is to look at the infant in relation to the norms in the field, analyze them, and then, using the curriculum areas, plan experiences to support her development. The infant is still in the center, but we will have to add the curriculum and what we know about the norms of development to the web. We will explore each developmental domain, the norms, and then finalize Rachael's web.

When you plan for infants under four months, calculate the age in weeks; for infants between four and nine months, knowing the age within two weeks is fine, or knowing that an infant is 6 ½ months old. Adults need to remember that their planning must be reevaluated as infants learn new skills and reach developmental milestones. Certainly learning occurs that is not part of a written plan, but it is important to plan specific learning experiences for each infant and to have these in some written form. Start planning with the infant in the center. If you prefer a more traditional format for your written plans, use something like Figure 12–2.

Experiences for Young Infants

Experiences and materials for very young infants are chosen because they are interesting to look at or listen to. At about two to three months of age, infants begin to reach for and grasp small toys. For infants older than three months, materials and experiences are designed to withstand active exploration,

FIGURE 12–2 Planning for a Single Infant for a Week

Infant _____ Age_____ Date_____

Interests		
Strengths		
Needs		
Emerging skills		
Developmental Areas	Materials	Methods
Social and Emotional Including Self-Help/Adaptive		
Sensory and Motor		
Communication, Language, and Literacy		
Cognitive		
Aesthetic		
Comments		

(This is a weekly record; make one for each week for each child.)

particularly mouthing, as well as constant washing. For infants to practice their skills, having a variety of similar toys is helpful and varying their use is the key for planning. Observe infants and respond to their changing skills.

WITH INFANTS AND TODDLERS

If you want to play with a six-month-old infant, start by observing him. He is sitting and you notice that he looks at a particular toy. Voilà! You get the toy and hold it slightly out of reach (motor). You encourage him to reach for it. Tell him what it is (cognitive) and verbally support his exploration of the toy (language); as he tires, you show him a different way to use the object (cognitive). He led; you followed (social). You did not expect him to get the toy because you knew he could not crawl yet but that his sitting was stable enough that he could manipulate the toy with his hands (physical/motor). You supported his choice of objects and you provided him with an experience responsive to his interests (emotional). You encouraged his exploration of the object by talking about what he was doing (language) and providing additional possible ways to play enriching his cognitive experience.

The nonmobile infant is dependent on the adults in her environment to choose developmentally appropriate experiences. When infants are able to sit, they have their hands free to explore materials and manipulate them. You need to ensure that they have interesting materials to play with. As infants approach mobility, experiences are used that encourage infants to pivot and to want to approach intriguing materials and people.

Experiences That Support Social and Emotional Development

Babies are social at birth. It is one of their survival skills. How adults respond and interact with their overtures sets the stage for infants' later social skill development. Infants take the cues and examples adults demonstrate for them and use them in their own interactions. Appropriate and positive social interactions will lead to the development of good social skills and a positive self-image. Infants are not ready to learn social etiquette, but they are ready to learn the foundational skills that will lead to later social skill development. The key to the development of early foundation skills is social interaction.

Opportunities for social interaction skills occur during all of the experiences that take place between adults and infants. The process begins when an adult answers an infant's cry, talks to the infant during feeding, looks at the infant during diapering, waits to interact during an infant's quiet times, and initiates interaction when appropriate. Though adults may not feel they are actively "teaching" children social skills, their respectful styles of interaction are powerful **incidental learning** experiences.

Incidental learning is informal learning that occurs from observation or experience.

When adults answer an infant's cry, it instills a sense of safety and security, knowing that someone is available to help when needed. Infants need to trust and feel secure with the adults who care for them. Infants are different. Each has a basic way of being in the world. Temperament influences a variety of behaviors in the infant: activity level, mood, persistence, and distractibility, and the ability to adjust to change. Caregivers should be sensitive to these differences in infant temperament.

Although infancy may seem to be stress-free to an adult, to the infant it can very stressful. Being separated from his parents and adjusting to new caregivers is stressful. Different surroundings, routines, and other children cause stress. Even adjusting to their own emerging skills, especially locomotion, places infants in stressful situations. Infants need to be viewed as legitimately having stress. Therefore, caregivers need to reduce that stress where possible as well as help infants learn to cope with stress. Being responsive to infants and giving them your attention supports their development. See Table 12–2 for ways to support an infant's social and emotional development.

As infants become more competent, rather than initiating the cues, respond to the infant's cues. If he quiets when you are approaching his crib or infant seat, say, "You know I'm going to pick you up." Then do it. As infants learn that their world is predictable, they are willing to wait longer for events to happen because they are developing trust. Developing a secure relationship with an adult is critical to the infant's health and competence.

Table 12–2 Supporting Young Infant's Social and Emotional Development

- Catch and maintain eye contact with infants, smile at them. When infants begin to stir from a nap, talk to them in a soothing voice.
- Lift infants to your shoulder, rub their back, and help them to focus on an interesting object or your face when they cry.
- Play a gentle game of pat-a-cake or peek-a-boo using infants' hands when they notice their hands and have fun making them move.
- Place an infant on your lap facing you when she is quietly alert. Smile and say "ah-boo" as you lean forward and gently bump your forehead to hers. Repeat this as long as the experience seems enjoyable.
- Carry on conversations with infants. Use parentese. Say the infant's name frequently; it is familiar and gives her a marker in the jumble of "noise" that she hears.
- Play turn-taking games. Play a babbling game with infants. It works best if they start, but if they do not, then you start. Babble or coo and then wait; you will get more and more responses as time goes on. Play verbal ping pong.
- Respond to infants' cries! This does not spoil them. Crying is their way of expressing that something is not right. Not responding to cries can lead to children who do not initiate communication because they think no one will respond!
- Talk to infants. Tell them what you are about to do *before* you are going to pick them up, put them down, change their diaper, or place them in an infant seat. This signals when a change is to occur. It is respectful and important in their development of trust.
- Learn each infant's unique signals and their meaning. Be alert to the subtle movements of infants to communicate thoughts or feelings.

WITH INFANTS AND TODDLERS

Before beginning an event such as giving an infant a bottle, picking him up, or changing him, offer the infant verbal information and a visual cue about what will happen. Show the infant the bottle and say, "Are you hungry? I have your bottle ready. Do you want it?" Then pause to give the infant time to respond. (Do not expect him to say "yes." You are giving him the time and respect to process information rather than just putting the bottle in his mouth.) Before picking up an infant, hold out your arms and say, "I'm going to pick you up," then pause so the infant can anticipate what will happen. Then follow through on your action. Keep the gestures and words you use consistent so the infant knows what to expect. Follow through with the action quickly; that is, if you show him the bottle and he responds, then feed him right away, and do not wait several minutes.

Self-Help and Adaptive Development. For infants, self-concept begins with self-awareness. Infants need to feel accepted for who they are. They need to be respected as individuals who have their own wants and needs. Infants need your support in developing these skills. Sometimes respecting infants means that we need to give them the privilege of struggling. We are often too quick to rescue infants. When we do it for them they lose the satisfaction and learning that come from doing it themselves. Provide necessary support and encouragement, but allow infants to do what they are capable of doing. Provide materials that encourage **adaptive** behavior and independence. See Table 12–3 for additional ideas.

Adaptive
behavior is the same as self-help skills. The term is used in early childhood special education.

Table 12–3 Supporting Self-Help/Adaptive Development

- Support infants in holding their own bottle, but you hold them.
- Give infants cups and spoons to explore and play with.
- Encourage emerging mobility.
- Give infants choices and show delight and support when they chose.
- Enthusiastically support infants as they learn to control their body and make it function in the way they want it to.
- Help young infants find their hands and gently guide the hand to the mouth if this is something that will bring the infant comfort and is supported by their family.

Locomotor
skills are movement patterns that support the exploration of space by allowing movement from one place to another.

Nonmanipulative
skills are movement patterns where the body operates from a stable base while different body parts move.

Stability
skills are similar to nonmanipulative skills.

Manipulative
skills are movement patterns that support gross and fine muscle contact with objects.

Experiences That Support Sensory and Motor Development

The development of movement requires a complex interaction between an infant's biology and experience. Movement requires different areas of the brain to communicate with each other. New motor skills initiate interactions between the parts of the brain that control senses to those that initiate movement (Zero to Three, 2006).

Plan experiences that include **locomotor**, **nonmanipulative** or **stability**, and **manipulative** skills. These skills are foundational movement patterns that are essential for later motor development. See Table 12–4 for a classification of the skills for infants that are in each of those areas. Infants must use both the large and small muscles in their body. They must gain control over the core muscles of the back and neck that support stability to be able to sit and stand; the arm and leg muscles, which are used in creeping and walking; and the small muscles related to manipulation of objects, such as reaching, grasping, and releasing. Infants must integrate the information from their senses with their motor skills to understand that something to look at is also something to touch. They need to

Table 12–4 Classification of Motor Skills

Locomotor skills:
Crawling
Creeping
Walking
Nonmanipulative skills:
Controlling neck, head, and trunk
Bearing weight while prone
Reaching
Pulling
Pushing
Body awareness
Stretching
Pivoting
Turning
Twisting
Rolling
Balancing
Transferring weight
Manipulative skills:
Grasping
Releasing
Throwing
Kicking
Catching and collecting

SOURCES: Gallahue and Ozmun (2002); Graham, Holt-Hale, and Parker (2005); Haywood and Getchell (2005).

integrate the use of muscles with information they receive from their senses to know how to move around objects without bumping into them and to know how far to reach to grasp a desired object.

The large muscles of the body, such as those in the neck, trunk, arms, and legs, are necessary for all antigravity postures such as sitting and standing. They also are necessary to stabilize the body to perform finer movements. Infants differ in the rate they acquire motor skills, but the pattern and progression of development is the usually the same. See Table 12–5 for methods of supporting locomotor skills.

The equipment for infants has become so sophisticated that they have become containerized. The car seat is also the stroller. While this is a great convenience, infants are being moved less, so they use fewer muscles. The insert

Table 12–5 Scaffolding Locomotor Skills

To encourage locomotor skills
• Place objects at a greater distance so the infant has to move to get to the object while prone.
• Use push toys to encourage infants to pivot and move forward.
• Move with infants, dance and walk with them so they are intrigued with movement and can feel your body moving and share your enjoyment of moving.

inside the car seat supports their head so they do not use their muscles to keep their head upright. They need to practice using their muscles just as any athlete would to be prepared to explore their world. Providing tummy time is particularly important because so many infants are sleeping on their backs as a way of helping to prevent Sudden Infant Death Syndrome. However, many infants who slept on their backs showed delayed motor development by six months of age (Majnemer & Barr, 2005). It is not sleeping on the back that is truly the problem; it is that they are not placed on their tummies while they are awake.

Tummy time is any activity that keeps infants from lying flat in one position on a hard, supportive surface. Tummy time is adaptable and changes as infants grow and gain strength. To make tummy time more interesting, play with infants on the floor or put them on your tummy or across your lap or even on large balls.

In addition to developing the muscle strength to control their body, infants also need to become more aware of where their body is in space, how far they can lean without toppling, how to shift weight, how to extend and contract their body, and how to turn, twist, and pivot. See Table 12–6 for methods of scaffolding nonmanipulative skills.

Table 12–6 Scaffolding Nonmanipulative Skills

To encourage stability skills

- Place infants on their tummy to give them experience controlling their head, neck, and trunk By 2 months infants should have at least 30 minutes of tummy time daily.
- Put scrunchies, bright socks, or commercially purchased wrist and ankle bands on the infant's wrists and ankles. Some of these make noise. Encourage infants to move their arms and kick their legs.
- Place a desired object slightly out of reach so that the infant has to stretch (but not move) to get the object while prone.
- Place a desired object to one side of an infant so the infant has to transfer weight to one hand or arm to reach with the other.
- Play music or sing and model moving to the music while prone (rolling back and forth to the beat or tapping your hand).
- Provide interesting things for infants to look at and touch while prone.
- Call to infants so they have to twist and turn to visually make contact with you.
- Place or hold objects so infants have to stretch, bend, and balance to reach them while sitting.

WITH INFANTS AND TODDLERS

When infants can sit, sit in front of the infant and do the following "warm up" exercises. Encourage the infant to copy what you do (but do not really expect him to). Talk about what you are doing as you do it.

Look over your right shoulder, then left; look at the ceiling, then the floor
Roll your shoulders
Put your arms out at shoulder height and flap them
Touch your toes
Pivot your shoulder left and then right
Look at the child and call his name
And so on.

The infant will not be proficient in following you, but it is good exercise. If the infant begins to slump, sit behind her and place your hands around her hips and lower back for a minute or two. This will give added support. Help move her body gently as you talk about what you are doing.

Gradually increase the amount of time and the number of opportunities infants have to sit independently. Trunk muscles need to be used to develop. Sometimes infants need encouragement to continue to develop these muscles. They need something to do while they sit. So be sure there are toys available to play with. If an infant is encouraged to use her hands to play with toys or copy your motions, she is less likely to need them to help with balance.

The small muscles of the hands and fingers need to be engaged. The development of fine motor skills is dependent on other related skills. Although vision is not a prerequisite for fine motor development, the ability to see objects motivates infants and directs their reaching. Reaching is also dependent on the infant's core muscle development: neck and trunk control, and adequate balance. Reaching is a prerequisite to grasping and picking up objects. An infant must be able to pick up and release objects for finer eye–hand coordination skills to develop.

Picking up an object or holding an object is just the first step. Infants first do this with one hand, but by about four to five months infants often reach with both hands. Eventually infants need to be able to hold an object in one hand and use the other hand to explore the object. This happens by about eight months (Haywood & Getchell, 2005). See Table 12–7 for ways to increase infants' manipulative skills.

WITH INFANTS AND TODDLERS

Encourage infants to reach, grasp, and mouth a teether. Say, "This is a 'foot' [if foot-shaped] teether. Do those toes taste good?" Touch the infant's foot and toes and say, "Here's your foot. I have your toes!" Wiggle them. If the infant has trouble grasping, gently guide his arm from the shoulder area to help him grasp the teether and bring it to his mouth if necessary. Tell the infant about your actions as well as his. Confirm that it is comforting to suck on something even without hunger.

Encourage infants to explore the teether in ways other than mouthing, such as banging, shaking, and throwing. Try to support the infant in simple imitation skills. For example, put the teether in front of your face and then say, "You do it." Or transfer it from one hand to the other. Encourage infants to try. Tap the teether on the surface or clap while holding the teether in one hand. This uses a natural form of exploration (mouthing) to interest infants and expands their exploration. Have a variety of teethers so infants have experience with different shapes, colors, and textures. (Be sure to wash and disinfect them after use.)

Table 12–7 Scaffolding Manipulative Skills

To encourage manipulative skills
- Give infants toys such as teethers that are easy to grasp.
- Provide a variety of objects to grasp that have different shapes, sizes, and textures.
- Provide objects to grasp that make interesting noises.
- Gently guide an infant's hand to feel materials of different textures. Talk about the textures as you help him grasp them.
- Hold an object for an infant and encourage him to explore it with his hands.
- Vary the position, size, weight, texture, and shapes of objects to be grasped. As infants approach 8 months be sure that some objects can be grasped with one hand and others require two hands. With young infants these need to be large and soft objects. As infants develop more precision, the toys can be harder and smaller.
- Encourage infants to both grasp and release objects. Asking infants to give you what they have grasped helps them learn to release.
- Give infants objects that are safe to drop and throw and encourage them to do so.

Young children, particularly infants, learn about their world through exploring with their senses—looking, hearing, touching, tasting, and smelling. Motor skills are often used in conjunction with sensory information. In sensory integration both sensory and motor components of behavior are integrated in the brain to facilitate smooth movement and the ability to learn new skills. Infants need experiences that encourage the development of both large and small motor skills and opportunities for integrating these skills with sensory input. They need a variety of materials that encourage all types of movements and reflect a developmental progression for skill building. Infants are very active. They want to practice emerging skills. Know and encourage the movements that infants are capable of. Be sure these movements are safe.

Experiences That Support Communication/Language/Literacy Development

Learning to communicate is a major task for infants. Learning the underlying concepts of language and its usefulness begins in infancy. Adults who respond to the infant's language initiations increase the likelihood of his continuing and increasing his language skills. Communication also requires listening skills and someone to listen. As the infant is learning to talk, he is also learning to use language as a way of internalizing and organizing information.

In the first few weeks of life infants are learning to distinguish different sounds; that is, noise versus the human voice. By one month, infants respond differently to speech than to other sounds and even begin to show awareness of the different speech sounds that people make. Young infants can hear speech sounds, but they are not yet able to make them because they lack the muscle coordination for speech. By the time the infant is six to seven months old, he begins to practice sound formation by babbling. Talking to him and imitating the infant's babbling are good ways to foster language during this stage. One of the easiest and most important things you can do for infants is use their name. As you use their name over and over again it becomes a marker for them in the jumble of language they are trying to decipher.

As infants begin to babble, they also initiate verbal contact with others. Infants need verbal stimulation at this time. You can support language development by responding to infant's attempts at conversation (babbling). Introduce new words, but take turns with him. Infants are continually learning how to say new sounds and eventually new words. See Table 12–8 for ways to support communication and language development.

Humming, singing, and talking are ways to help infants listen, make sounds, and begin to understand the give and take that is so important in communication. By providing stimulating materials for infants to listen to, touch, and play with, you give them many opportunities to listen and to make sounds.

Table 12–8 Scaffolding Communication and Language Skills

- Initiate language with an infant with the expectation that she will respond, whether or not she does.
- Talk to infants and encourage their communication efforts.
- Use the infant's name as your talk with her.
- Model language by verbally labeling experiences and pictures for infants in addition to extending and expanding the infant's language.
- Encourage infants to coo, babble, make sounds, and say words by talking directly to them while you play. Describe in simple words what you are doing as well as what they are doing. Describe the materials you are using.
- Communicate with infants during caregiving routines, such as feeding, changing, and dressing. Respectfully tell them what you are going to do and then what you are doing. These are great times to tell each infant how special he is.
- Play or sing lullabies, or read nursery rhymes or poems.
- Respond to words that are repeated often (opening arms with palms out while saying "all gone" or "so big").
- Imitate their motions and initiate them (waving bye-bye).
- When the infant makes noise, pay attention and look interested.

One of the most important methods of encouraging infants to make sounds is by interacting with them.

Infants make sounds with objects by hitting, banging, shaking, and even crumpling. They experience a wide range of sounds and noises, including voices of adults and other infants, doors opening and closing, kitchen noises, music, and outside noises. There are many ways to encourage infants to make sounds. Think about playing "ping pong"; that is, the baby makes a sound and sends it to you; you repeat the sound and send it back to her. Watch and listen for her reaction!

Although infants this age are not going to read, the foundation for reading begins at birth. Read to babies. When you read, the cadence of your voice is different than when you are talking. See Table 12–9 for ways to support literacy.

Now that you know the right books, curl up and read them to a baby. Put him on your lap look at the front of the book and point to the title. Read it. Look at the cover and point out some salient details. Continue reading or adapting the book to meet the infant's needs. Make reading a positive experience for you and the infant. Read to each infant every day.

Table 12–9 Scaffolding Literacy

• Choose books with simple black-and-white illustrations for very young infants.
• Choose books with simple photographs or designs with bright colors.
• Choose books made of stiff cardboard that can be folded out or propped up while infants are on their tummies. Cloth and soft vinyl books can be washed or go in the bath.
• Choose books that have large, clear, colorful photographs or illustrations, ideally one per page of topics that interest babies: other babies, toys, animals, nursery rhymes, familiar experiences, and food.

Experiences That Support Cognitive Development

Infants begin with reflexive actions that develop into more organized and coordinated movements. These movements are then repeated intentionally and variations are added. About four months infants become fascinated with what objects do. They now explore materials to see what they can do. Previously, the goal was simply motor action. Now, an infant who "discovers" he can make a toy rattle will repeat the shaking action again and again to hear the rattle. This is the beginning of means-end behavior. This is also science. The first signs of object permanence begin in the middle of the first year. So infants need many experiences with hidden objects and people. Sometimes the objects should be partially visible. Then, as the infant's skill improves, hide the object completely.

See Table 12–10 for ways to support cognitive development.

Table 12–10 Scaffolding Cognitive Development

- As infants are developing object permanence, play games that involve looking for objects and hiding and seeking. Hide toys for the infant to find.

- When the infant drops objects from his high chair, see if he looks for them. Repetition is important, so the adult needs to retrieve the objects. This helps infants learn what predictably happens.

- Talk to infants when you are out of their sight. Disappear and reappear in the same or different places.

- Play simple repetitive games such as patty cake, open shut them, and peek-a-boo.

- Provide for repetition as infants are developing their memory skills and learning that certain things happen (predictions), and that they can act on things and the response is the same over and over.

- Note the senses an infant uses to explore objects. It should be eyes, mouth, and hands by about 6 months.

- As infants learn about the effects of their actions, give them objects they can act on, such as a ball that moves when they hit it. Encourage them to vary their actions (Push it harder), point out the effect actions have on the object (The harder you push it, the farther it goes).

WITH INFANTS AND TODDLERS

With the infant sitting, offer a ring (about six inches in diameter) to the infant to reach and grasp. Encourage the infant to explore the ring by mouthing or shaking it. Place the ring on the floor where the infant can just grasp it. Place a desired toy inside the ring and see if the infant will pull the ring to get the toy. If the infant does not pull the ring, move the ring closer and demonstrate how to pull the ring to get the toy. Place the ring and toy out of reach and verbally encourage the infant to reach for them. Place the ring on a small towel and place the toy in it. Encourage the infant to pull the towel to get the toy. Infants need many opportunities to practice means-end behavior. Work on variations of this. See if infants will pull a washcloth or small towel to get a toy. Infants need experience seeing causal relationships and stretching their minds.

Experiences That Support Aesthetic Development

It may be difficult to imagine aesthetic development in an infant, but just like reading to infants sets the foundation for later reading, so too do early experiences in the creative arts. Babies learn to love music by listening to music and being sung to. Most adults who hold infants while trying to get themselves organized sway as they hold the baby and even hum or whisper soothing words. Start singing to babies at birth. It does not matter that you are not a great singer, it matters that you sing. Like reading, singing is a learned behavior. The repetitive nature of many songs that we sing to infants helps them learn language. Infants need exposure to a variety of musical experiences. Although nonmobile infant's cannot dance, you can. Dance with infants to music that you enjoy.

Infants are too young to use tools, but they can enjoy art. Talk about art to infants and show them pictures on walls as well as illustrations in books. Discuss the quality of art and how it makes you feel. See Table 12–11 for ideas on scaffolding aesthetic development.

Table 12–11 Scaffolding Aesthetic Development

- Play music for infants, not just musical scores that are written for infants but Mozart, Jazz, and music from around the world such as the Putumayo kids series.
- Play music sung in different languages, but especially those that are representative of the infants in your classroom.
- Sing. Singing is like reading, the cadence is different, so, even if you do not have a good voice—sing.
- Hold infants and dance with them to many different types of music.
- Show infants a variety of art forms. Point out salient features. Talk about color and form.
- Support infants' efforts to be with other infants. Let them safely explore each other when you are there to guide this. Talk about playing together and what infants are doing.
- Talk to infants about their families and what is happening when they are in your care and what happens when they go home.

IMPLEMENTING CURRICULUM FOR YOUNG INFANTS

Curriculum for infants is individualized. In Figure 12–1 we started with a six-month-old infant's basic developmental level and strengths and needs. Now let us add the curriculum to show how individualized planning might look for this infant (see Figure 12–3).

Learning Environments for Young Infants

Infants need a variety of learning environments. Learning environments are indoors and outdoors, and are at floor, stroller, lap, and shoulder levels. Learning environments change during the day as infants play on the floor, are picked up and carried, are read to in a rocking chair, are walked outside in a stroller, and bask on a blanket on the grass. Their environment should contain both soft and hard elements. They need cuddly stuffed toys and mirrors. Young infants like bright, high-contrasting colors and interesting patterns.

FIGURE 12–3 An Individualized Curriculum for a 6-Month-Old Infant

REFLECTIVE PRACTICE

Look at Figure 12–3 in comparison with Figure 12–1. Reflect on the process of using an individual developmental web to one that supports curriculum for an individual infant. Think about what you might add or change. How would this be different if you knew the infant?

They need cheerful, friendly pictures of infants, children, and adults hung at different levels. These pictures should depict a variety of cultures and ethnic groups and include children with visible disabilities. Infants need space to be alone and space to interact with other infants. They need space to pivot, roll over, and crawl, as well as sturdy furniture to practice pulling up on. The learning environment should include varied equipment and materials that are developmentally appropriate, and these materials should be organized in a useful way so that the materials are readily available, but are rotated so they are not all out at once.

Beyond the obvious safety considerations, the environment should seem like a soft cozy place to play and relax. Infants need their own cribs and bedding, and objects that are of special comfort to them. Child-size furnishings and materials are appropriate for infants, such as textured mats and objects to crawl over and through. Diapering, feeding, sleeping, and play areas need to be separated. Different types of music can be played some of the time. The infant environment should be "shoe-free." Adults should either put covers over their shoes (like hospital personnel do) or take off their shoes in the infant room. Infants need to be on the floor and the floor needs to be clean.

Adults too are affected by the environment. Furnishings should encourage adults to hold and cuddle children. Adults should be with infants on the floor, in rocking chairs, and swaying and dancing with infants in their arms. Adults need to see all of the infants so they can keep visual contact with one infant while playing with another. They need to respond quickly if an infant is hurt or frightened. Environments support the curriculum.

Adult-Infant Interactions

Relationships between adults and infants are the most important aspect of the curriculum. Infants need adults to meet their basic needs, but they need far more than that. They need loving, caring, respectful relationships with adults. The adult's role is to scaffold the infant's development. Adults are infant's play partners. Adults help structure play with infants. Sensitive adults help to maintain an infant at an optimal level of arousal, neither bored nor overwhelmed. They provide individualized intense social interaction.

How Young Infants Learn

You know *what* you want to do and the materials to do it with; the question is *when* do you do it? It is challenging to decide when babies are ready to play. Early care and education centers are busy places with lots going on. Sometimes there is so much going on that babies are not ready to play. You are the one

Learning environments are at shoulder level as well as on the floor and lap.

who will read their cues to know when to play with babies and when to just help them to calm down and get organized (see Table 12–12).

Are there times when babies will not be ready to play? Absolutely! It is your knowledge of ways to help them change states that makes a difference.

METHODS AND MATERIALS FOR WORKING WITH YOUNG INFANTS

Methods
are the behaviors, strategies, and techniques adults use to interact with infants and toddlers.

Materials
are the toys or objects infants or toddlers use.

Methods are the behaviors, strategies, and techniques adults use to interact with infants and toddlers. **Materials** are the toys or objects that infants and toddlers interact with. The methods adults use require a knowledge base that includes the ability to assess an infant's developmental level and state, a repertoire of behaviors, strategies, and techniques, and the ability to match these appropriately to a particular infant at a specific point in time. Then, the adult must evaluate whether the "match" was a good one by observing the infant's behavior and reflecting on her own behavior. This is ongoing.

Since infants change and grow by interacting with their environment, materials are an extremely important part of planning. Nonmobile infants are dependent upon adults to provide these materials. Infants learn through their senses. They need materials that can be held, dropped, thrown, mouthed, and shaken. They need materials of different textures, colors, weights, and sizes.

Table 12–12 Deciding When to Play with Infants

Infants are ready to play when they

- are quiet and look alert

- are active and alert (maybe, if they are not too active)

- look at you

- reach out to you

- hold their hands near their chest or mouth

- shape their mouth like the letter "O"

Infants are not ready to play or want to stop playing when they

- start crying, fussing, or spitting up

- turn their body or face away

- break eye contact or close their eyes

- arch their back or neck

- have rapid, shallow breathing

- change color and become red

- hold their arms out straight and to the side

You can help infants get ready to play by

- giving them some quiet time alone

- placing your hand gently on their chest

- talking to them in a quiet voice

- holding their hands in yours close to their chest

- changing their position

- placing one hand on their head and one hand on their feet to help them tuck their body

- swaddling them

- remaining quiet and turning your eyes away

- helping them find something to suck on

- rocking them

- putting them to your shoulder and swaying

SOURCE: Parks (1988).

Adults must choose appropriate materials to support infant learning. The following diagram (See Figure 12–4) depicts this process of materials-methods/ adult-child interaction.

As you interact with very young infants, remember that you are the most important "material." Because you can be responsive and adapt to the infant,

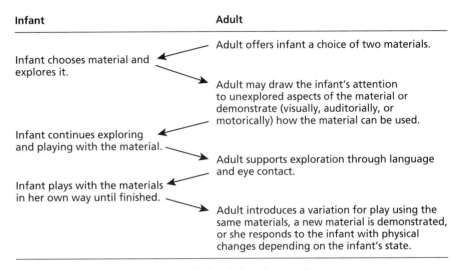

Infant	Adult
	Adult offers infant a choice of two materials.
Infant chooses material and explores it.	
	Adult may draw the infant's attention to unexplored aspects of the material or demonstrate (visually, auditorially, or motorically) how the material can be used.
Infant continues exploring and playing with the material.	
	Adult supports exploration through language and eye contact.
Infant plays with the materials in her own way until finished.	
	Adult introduces a variation for play using the same materials, a new material is demonstrated, or she responds to the infant with physical changes depending on the infant's state.

FIGURE 12–4 Materials-Methods/Adult-Infant Interactions

your simple games such as "ah boo" and your verbal turn-taking may be more relevant than any toys the infant might play with.

The materials you choose and the methods you use are components of the learning environment. Materials are specific to young infants; they are listed here along with guidelines for selection. Appropriate materials can enhance learning and encourage exploration. See Table 12–13 for questions to ask when selecting materials for young infants.

Table 12–13 Questions to Ask when Selecting Toys for Young Infants

- Is the toy safe and durable? Watch for sharp edges or small parts that infants could swallow or choke on. Consider whether the toy will stand up to banging, dropping, chewing, and so forth.

- Is the toy washable? Infants enjoy and learn from putting toys in their mouth. Washability is a must to prevent the spread of germs.

- Is the size, weight, and shape of the toy appropriate? Consider how easy or difficult it will be for an infant to hold and manipulate the toy. If the toy is heavy and hard to grasp, an infant is less likely to play with it. If it tips over easily or rolls away, the infant may become quickly frustrated. (Toys with suction cups on the base may avoid this difficulty.)

- Is the toy bright, colorful, and appealing?

- Does the toy stimulate more than one sense? For example, is the toy soft and textured *and* does it make noise?

- Is the toy appropriate for the infant's developmental level? In general, infants need experiences with toys they can successfully play with, but they also benefit from being challenged by toys and tasks slightly above their level of development.

Some categories and examples of possible materials to consider when making selections are given in Table 12–14. In looking at your overall variety of materials, include some from several categories rather than having more toys in just one or two areas.

Table 12–14 Categories of Materials for Young Infants

- Materials that encourage awareness of self and others: mirrors, dolls, and puppets.
- Materials with varied textures: textured mats, rattles, blocks, and fuzzy puppets.
- Materials that make noise: musical toys, rattles, and squeaky toys.
- Materials that reflect ethnic diversity.
- Materials for cuddling: soft stuffed dolls, animals, toys, and other huggables.

Even the best materials are not a substitute for adult interaction. Although infants benefit from periods of independent play, their play with toys is almost always enhanced by an adult talking about what the infant is doing and offering encouragement and assistance as needed.

For infant's birth through nine months, see Table 12–15 for recommended materials.

Table 12–15 Recommended Materials for Young Infants

- Mobiles (evaluate them from underneath, because that is where infants will be). Ensure infants cannot reach them.
- Rattles
- Teethers (some of which are easy to grasp)
- Musical toys
- Unbreakable mirrors
- Soft-fabric toys of different textures that are sturdy and washable
- Fabric dolls or animals (huggables) with limbs that are easy to grasp
- Balls (soft, textured, clutch, and some that make noise when they roll)
- Toys with suction cup bases
- Toys that roll, or can be pushed or pulled
- Plastic measuring spoons and cups
- Soft vinyl or board books
- Water toys

Novelty is an important variable. Infants are attracted to new and different objects. Toys with different colors, designs, and actions add differences. Caregivers can provide novelty by adding to and changing crib mobiles and having a variety of similar toys so they can be rotated.

Organizing Materials for Young Infants

To rotate toys effectively they must be organized. There are a variety of ways to organize materials for infants. The choice is dependent on personal preference and planning style (see Table 12–16).

Over time you will find the method that best fits your needs.

Table 12–16 Methods of Organizing Materials for Young Infants

1. Materials can be organized by general developmental levels. Materials might be categorized for infants' from birth to 4 months and 4 through 9 months. Materials themselves might be categorized; for example, all rattles might be placed together with the age noted (4 to 9 months).

2. Organize similar materials (all the suction-cup toys) in baskets, boxes, or other containers. This makes it easier to grab exactly what you want quickly.

3. Keep most toys out of sight, bringing out one or two at a time. Bring out a few toys at a time to keep experiences novel and to maintain the infant's interest. And to control how many different toys you need to wash each time they are used by an infant.

Many experiences for infants are variations on caregiving routines or are implemented during routines. They are included to show how to vary these routines and also the types of experiences that are appropriate for young infants. It is important to think of these as experiences and vary them, otherwise care can become solely custodial.

SCHEDULES, ROUTINES, AND TRANSITIONS

Schedules
refer to the order of events during the day and when they will be done.

Schedules refer to who will do what and when they will do it. There are two schedules that impact the day: the infant's and the adult's. Each infant has an individual schedule that responds to her physical and biological needs. This schedule changes over time (older infants sleep less than younger infants). Some infants have relatively regular internal schedules and settle into a routine easily, while others have difficulty and do not seem to have a pattern. With increasing age, almost all infants develop more predictable schedules. Adults must develop a schedule that coordinates the caregiving for each infant. The key to schedule planning is *flexibility* and organizing general time blocks that respond to infants' needs. Ideally, timing is flexible, but sequences are predictable. This helps infants learn what will happen next. The younger the infant, the more imperative it is to respond to the infant's biological clock than to preset schedules. In good infant care the schedule is based on the infant.

Routines are events that the must be completed on a regular basis and often involve a series of responses (Ostrosky, Jung, Hemmeter, & Thomas, n.d.). Much of the time spent providing care to infants is made up of important and essential routines such as changing diapers, preparing meals, giving bottles, or helping infants settle down for a nap. These routines offer an opportunity for spending time individually with an infant and provide chances to communicate how much you like that infant by making eye contact, talking, singing, imitating the infant's sounds, or saying nursery rhymes. Routines give infants a sense of security and trust, as their most basic needs are being met in a consistent caring manner. Thinking about routines as part of the learning environment incorporates planning into the physical caring aspect of routines.

For young infants, try to make routines as similar as possible between home and child care. If an infant is sung a particular song at home before she takes a nap, sing it. The more you can follow established routines, the easier it will be for you and the infant.

Transitions are the time between the end of one event and the beginning of another. The time between when the parent arrives with her infant until she walks out the door is a transition. These are often difficult times. With infants the transition is far clearer to the adults than it is to the infant.

Routines
are events that happen on a regular basis and require a series of responses.

Transitions
are times between events.

Arrival Time

This is the time when infants make the transition from parent care to other care. Adults need to be available to make this transition easier for infants. I sometimes think of this as the "hip-to-hip" transfer. This may be a difficult time for some infants, and it is likely that even infants who readily transfer will have some difficult days. Adults, too, may have trouble with this process. Mothers or fathers, concerned about leaving a child in care, often find this transition difficult. They need a caring adult to reassure them that their infant will be well cared for while they are gone.

Arrival time is a time for parents to share information with caregivers about the infant's time at home and any concerns, joys, or unusual events that have taken place. For example, "Josh's grandparents visited last night and he didn't get to bed until very late and had trouble quieting down." Now, if Josh takes a longer than usual nap, you will have an indication as to why that happened. Parents should be encouraged to put complex information in writing. When the parent actually leaves, infants need one-on-one time with an adult to settle into the new situation. What the infant does next is dependent on his age and his particular schedule. If he has gotten up early, he may sleep; if he is not tired, he may want to play.

It helps if the caregiver and parent are each clear about who has what responsibilities, such as who puts on or takes off the infant's outside clothing. Either the caregiver or the parent should regularly initiate the transition and leaving. If both adults are undecided, the infant is likely to become restless and fussy, making it difficult for the adults to communicate.

Routines such as napping consume a large portion of the young infant's day.

Naptime

Setting up a routine for sleeping is important. Soothing and calming infants helps them go to sleep. They have different preferences. Helping infants develop positive sleep patterns is crucial to the adults in their world. Some problems in this area derive from **sleep associations**. There are events or patterns of events that become paired with sleep so that the infant associates these events or patterns with sleep and cannot go to sleep without them. A particular pacifier or blankie, being rocked or patted, or being walked are some of the common associations. The result of these sleep associations is that if an infant awakens she does not have the skill to get back to sleep herself and so she needs adults to help.

Infants can *learn* to go to sleep at about four months. They can be put to bed awake, the adult saying something like, "Have a good sleep," and moving out of their range of vision. If infants cry, they should be checked on every five minutes. Unless there is some reason that they need to be picked up, it is not a good idea to do that. They need love, reassurance, and support, but they also need to learn to go to sleep. However, infants need to sleep on their schedule, not the schedule of the adults. At any given time in a child care center some infants will be asleep and others will be awake and playing. Remember, back to sleep, front to play.

When infants are having problems in this area, the adults need to agree on a routine to help the infant learn to go to sleep and to comfort himself if he awakens at inappropriate times. **Swaddling** young infants frequently helps them sleep. See Figure 12–5 to learn how to swaddle an infant. Cribs are for sleeping. When they are not sleeping infants should be on the floor, although an occasional swing is fine. Beware of placing infants in any position where they cannot freely move their arms and legs. Infants are typically fed when they awaken from sleep.

Feeding

Very young infants eat every two to four hours. The time is counted from when they start eating to when they start eating again, so it may seem like one or two hours. There is little doubt when they want to eat, as they fuss and cry to let you know. Most, however, have a pattern, and if you learn it you can feed them before they cry. Infants need to be held while they are fed. Eating should be a relaxed, leisurely, social time. When feeding the infant, gently massage her head, fingers, and shoulders. Consider singing softly during feeding. This is a great time for working on eye contact, as infants will look at your face while you're talking or singing.

Sleep associations are objects or behavior patterns that become paired with going to sleep.

Swaddling is the process of wrapping an infant so his arms and legs are contained.

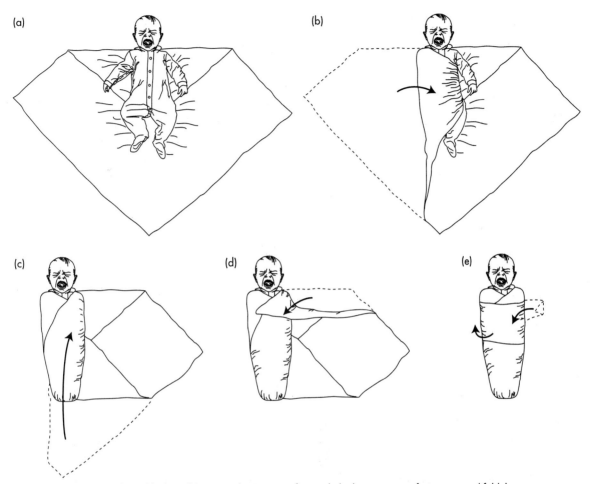

(a) Place a large square baby blanket (about 40 inches) on a surface with the bottom corner facing you and fold the top corner down. Place the infant on the blanket with his neck on the folded edge.

(b) While holding the infant's right arm against his side, pull the blanket across his body and tuck it underneath. Stretch it tight. It will be snug.

(c) Straighten his left arm and put it against his side. Bring the bottom corner up to his left shoulder and tuck the blanket behind it.

(d) Bring the remaining blanket down a little over his shoulder and pull it hard to the right while holding the part near his breastbone with your left hand.

(e) Then bring it around his body at waist level, pull tight, and tuck it in.

FIGURE 12–5
How to Swaddle an Infant. (Karp, H. (2002). *The happiest baby on the block*. New York: Bantam Dell.)

With increasing age, infants eat more at each feeding and the feedings become further apart. Up until about one month, infants typically take two to six ounces of fluid 6 to 10 times a day. Between one and three months, the volume increases to four or six ounces and the feedings decrease to six to eight. By six months, the infant has four to six feedings of about six ounces each (Lowdermilk & Perry, 2003).

Feeding is essential for nutrition, but like other routines is an essential part of infants developing the skills of self-regulation. Although infants are born with some ability for self-regulation, it is primarily the adults in their lives who help them handle strong emotions (Gillespie & Seibel, 2006). **Self-regulation** is the infant's or toddler's ability to gain control of his bodily functions, develop the skill to manage powerful emotions, and learn to maintain focus and attention (National Research Council and Institute of Medicine, 2000). Adults structure feeding but it requires self-regulation on the part of the infant. The infant must coordinate sucking, swallowing, and breathing. He cries to alert caregivers that he is distressed, and he needs to stay focused on the task of feeding until he is full (Gillespie & Seibel, 2006). To develop self-regulation, he needs manageable challenges. Adults provide manageable challenges when they hear a baby cry and say, "Rainuka, you're hungry, aren't you? Let me get your bottle. Your mother pumped breast milk into this bottle so I could feed you when she isn't here. It's hard to pump breast milk. She must love you so much. Good, I think we have it now." She then picks her up and feeds her. With time Rainuka will stop crying when she knows her needs will be met and does not wait until the bottle is in her mouth.

Propping a bottle—that is, placing an infant in a crib with the bottle propped so it is in his mouth—is not recommended for both social and medical reasons. Socially, infants need the close skin-to-skin contact with caring adults. Medically, infants who go to sleep with a bottle risk developing **bottle-mouth syndrome**, which is characterized by a high rate of tooth decay. Although teeth are not visible, they are there and susceptible to decay. Propping a bottle can also lead to ear infections if the bacterial growth in the pooled liquid travels from the infant's mouth to the Eustachian tubes and into the ears. Allowing an infant to lie down with a bottle also increases the danger of choking.

Breast milk or formula contains all the nutrients needed by the infant for the first four to six months of life. Six months is a real demarcation in infant eating. Around this time infants begin to produce enzymes that can digest complex carbohydrates and proteins other than those found in breast milk or formula. This is when additional foods are usually introduced. Typically, iron-enriched cereals are introduced first (the infant's iron stores are exhausted by about six months). Teeth begin to erupt at about six months. This is stressful for infants and may disrupt their eating pattern. They want to use their teeth and may prefer foods that can be chewed, such as dry toast or teething biscuits. The diarrhea that often accompanies teething is not caused by the teething process itself but by infectious organisms from items that the infant is mouthing and chewing. If an infant is mouthing an item, put that item in the dishwasher or disinfect it or both.

Self-regulation
is the ability of control bodily functions, manage emotions, and maintain attention.

Bottle-mouth syndrome
is a dental condition which involves the rapid decay of many or all the baby teeth of an infant or child.

Diapering

Infants' diapers are changed many times each day. Some days caregivers feel that all they do is feed infants and change their diapers. "If a child is changed six times a day until he is 30 months old, he will have had his diaper changed more than 5,400 times. Anything a child experiences 5,400 times is an important part of his life and those who change him" (Dombro, Colker, & Dodge, 1999, p. 179). Diapering is one-on-one time when the infant is awake and available. Often, the stimulation of being partially naked will make an infant alert and interested. It is a wonderful time to talk to him, sing, or play. Talk about body parts or what the infant was doing or will be doing next. The infant may look away occasionally; give her time to get herself organized, do not "chase her face." She is sending you a message that she needs a break. She will come back to you.

When you are changing the infant, take the opportunity to develop body awareness by massaging her arms, legs, and feet with gentle pressure and light touches. Be sure to have pictures or a mirror at a height the infant can see while being diapered. **Keep one hand on the infant at all times. Never leave an infant alone on the changing table**. There should be a set procedure for diapering that everyone in the center follows. Wash your hands before you diaper and immediately after diapering before doing anything else. This is true even if you use gloves.

Infants urinate as frequently as often as every one to three hours; it is important that infants urinate at least seven times a day. The darker the color, the more concentrated the urine. The stools of breast-fed infants are a light mustard color, whereas those of formula-fed infants are more tan or yellow and smellier. They are also firmer than those of breast-fed babies, about the consistency of peanut butter. The frequency of bowel movements varies widely from one infant to another, with breast-fed infants having fewer, as there is very little solid waste to be eliminated. Infants frequently pass a stool after feeding as a result of a gastrocolic reflex, which causes the digestive system to activate whenever the stomach is full.

If formula-fed infants do not have at least one bowel movement a day, or have very hard stools, they may be constipated. As solid food (cereal) is added to an infant's diet, the first few stools may be very difficult for the infant to pass, which is an important reason to have good communication with parents. Infants can also get diarrhea, which is characterized by high liquid content in the stool and an increased frequency of bowel movements. This can be caused by a change in the infant's or mother's diet (if breast-fed), or it could be an indication of an intestinal infection. The major concern with diarrhea is that the infant could become dehydrated. Noting urination and bowel movements is part of the record-keeping system for infants. When stools are hard or very watery, parents should be informed.

Departure Time

Departure time is a major transition. Some infants are overjoyed to see their parents, others seem nonchalant about the transition, and others may find the transition a difficult one. All infants need support and reminders of the routine. Toward the end of the day most caregivers reflect on the day and decide what information needs to be shared with an infant's parents. Important information should be written down. If there is more than one caregiver, all relevant information should be collected and communicated prior to departure. Know who has permission to pick up the child so there is no tension if someone besides the parent comes to get the infant. Have clear rules about when infants can be picked up and dropped off and be sure you and the parents know what the emergency backup system is and how to use it. Again, established rituals will help make this time an easier transition.

Routine Record Keeping

Daily record keeping is an important part of care for young infants. There is typically a part for parents and a part for caregivers. The parent section includes when the infant woke up, ate, and last had his diaper changed. There should also be a place to add other important information. The caregiver's portion contains times of diaper changes and whether the infant was wet, dry, or had a bowel movement. It may also include a request for additional supplies such as diapers, extra clothes, bibs, jars of food, and so on. The infant's feeding schedule and the type of food eaten is noted. There should also be a place to note the planned activities of the day. See Figure 12–6 for a sample schedule. These reports are often written on paper that automatically makes a carbon copy so both the parent and the caregivers have a copy. Parents bring a new one each morning and take a filled-out one home each time they pick up their infant.

INCLUDING ALL YOUNG INFANTS

Some young infants are vulnerable because of their environment or their biological makeup. Infants born to parents living in poverty, infants born too soon, and infants who do not weigh enough are at risk for developmental disabilities (Guralnick, 2004). Some infants are doubly vulnerable as they have both identified disabilities and live in poverty. An estimated 35 percent of children between birth and age 5 fall within this category (Bowe, 1995).

early learning center

Infant's Daily Report

Infant's Name:_____

Date:_____

Parent Section:

Woke up at:_____

Ate at:_____

Diaper changed at:_____

Other important information:_____

_____

_____

I NEED MEDICINE: YES/NO

Items I need:

❑ Extra Clothes

❑ Diapers

❑ Wipes

❑ Socks

❑ Cereal

❑ Bibs

❑ Jar Food: Fruit_____

Veggies_____

❑ Other_____

Diaper Changes	Naps
_____W/D/BM	_____
_____W/D/BM	_____
_____W/D/BM	_____
_____W/D/BM	_____
_____W/D/BM	_____

Feeding Schedule

Time	Type of Food

MY ACTIVITIES TODAY

❑Social/Emotional ❑Sensory and Motor ❑Communication/Language/Literacy ❑Cognitive ❑Aesthetics

_____

_____

_____

_____

_____

_____

_____

FIGURE 12–6 Sample Infant Daily Report

States differ in the criteria they use to make an infant eligible for early intervention services. We classify infants as having a developmental delay rather than trying to pinpoint a specific disability, unless a specific disability is apparent, such as Down syndrome. Unless the delay is serious it is unlikely that an infant will be classified before nine months. It is often unclear whether delayed development is just an individual growth pattern and the infant will "catch up" in his own time, or whether the delay is of a more permanent nature. However, if an infant cannot hold his head up when on his tummy or he cannot push up with his arms by three months, you should talk with his parents and encourage them to consult their pediatrician or contact the local **Child Find**. Infants identified as having a developmental delay have an early intervention team and an Individualized Family Service Plan. This team will provide guidance in planning for these infants. The following general information will help you plan.

Child Find is a process of public awareness activities, screening and evaluation designed to *locate, identify, and refer as early as possible* all young children with disabilities and their families who are in need of early intervention (Part C).

Low-Birth-Weight and Premature Infants

Some infants who are born with low birth weight are initially classified as having a developmental delay and need individualized programming planned by an early intervention team. Early intervention increases the probability that premature infants will catch up to their peers. As with all infants, planning is based on developmentally appropriate practice. For young infants an adjusted age may be most useful in planning. That is, an infant who is currently five months old and was born two months premature may be more appropriately planned for as a three-month-old.

Infants born prematurely have an especially limited repertoire of skills, so a variety of materials at the same developmental level is particularly important. Although many low-birth-weight infants catch up with their peers, at this young age there are predictable differences. The cues that these infants give are often subtle. With practice, these can be interpreted and responded to. The task of interpretation and response may not be easy. See Table 12–17 for characteristics of premature infants.

Table 12–17 Characteristic of Premature Infants

- Premature infants may have trouble establishing a pattern of wake and sleep; their cry is often more high pitched and frequent.

- A disorganized premature infant often cries 6 hours a day. (Full-term newborns often cry 2 to 3 hours a day for several months.) Colicky crying typically begins right after feeding and frequent burping is useful. Random patterns of crying are difficult to interpret. They may be just a discharge of excess energy, boredom, or overstimulation.

- Many premature infants have a low tolerance for stimulation. Therefore, a child care setting with much activity may tax their system. When they become fussy and irritable, try less, as opposed to more, stimulation.

Decreasing the stimulation as much as you can is helpful. Swaddling is a good way to help them get organized.

Young Infants with Developmental Delays

Infants with disorders such as Down syndrome or Fetal Alcohol Syndrome may be identified at birth. Early intervention has changed the trajectory of their development and it begins shortly after birth. See Table 12–18 for ways to adapt the environment. Because working with infants is so individualized, accommodations are easy to implement.

Table 12–18 Adapting the Environment to Include Infants with Developmental Delays

- Provide a visually stimulating environment, particularly mobiles, until the infant begins reaching and grasping. (Watch the infant, what is stimulating to some is overstimulating to others.)
- Use a great deal of variation and repetition of experiences, especially those that intrigue the infant; it is likely to take these infants longer to "groove" an idea or skill.
- Encourage the efforts that the infant makes.

Young Infants with Physical Impairments

Most physical disabilities involve damage to the central nervous system. Although these cannot be cured through early intervention, alternative pathways may be developed through exercise, massage, appropriate positioning, and the use of prostheses (see Table 12–19).

Table 12–19 Adapting the Environment to Include Infants with Physical Impairments

- Provide toys that are interesting to look at and listen to.
- Bring objects to the infant and experiment to see if there is a way she can hold or control the object herself.
- Use soft or textured objects that are easier to grasp.
- Use toys with suction cups so the toys stay in one place if the infant has coordination problems.
- Positioning of the infant is very important. There are some positions infants should not be in and ways of carrying them that are not helpful. Talk with the physical therapist or parent about positioning.

Young Infants with Hearing Impairments

Early intervention can help infants use residual hearing. Infants with hearing impairments use signs in much the same way that hearing infants babble. With the support of parents these signs should be encouraged as one would encourage babbling. Also be aware of infants who pull on their ear. Although early, some infants begin to have middle ear disease because of allergies (see Table 12–20 for adaptations).

Many families are using signs with infants who do not have hearing losses. Infants are capable of making simple signs before they can talk.

Table 12–20 Adapting the Environment to Include Infants with Hearing Impairments

- Support the infant's signs and learn the meaning of gestures that the infant and his parents typically use for communicating.
- Use signs with all infants beginning around 4 to 6 months. This helps all infants communicate their needs when they do not have the ability to speak.
- The sense of hearing and balance are related. Give infants many opportunities for large-motor experiences that require and develop balance.
- Offer stimulation through other senses: sight, smell, taste, and touch.
- Use songs and finger plays that have motions to go with the words.

Young Infants with Visual Impairments

Blindisms are unusual behaviors made by some individuals with severe visual impairments.

In infancy the role of vision is to motivate and guide behavior. It also plays a major role in incidental learning and it extends the infant's world beyond his reach. Because infants with severe visual impairments do not use eye contact to express and maintain interest, caregivers must use other senses to motivate infants to explore their world. The classic work of Fraiberg (1965) showed the importance of early intervention, including touch, to prevent **blindisms** or secondary autistic-like behaviors in infants with severe visual impairments and the necessity of physical stimulation during critical periods of two to three months and again from seven to nine months for the development of attachment behaviors (see Table 12–21 for adaptations).

Table 12–21 Adapting the Environment to Include Infants with Visual Impairments

- Find out the infant's degree of vision and under what distance and lighting conditions she sees best.
- High-contrast colors such as black and white are usually easiest to see and developmentally appropriate for this age.
- Use real three-dimensional objects to support concept development.
- Work through the infant's strengths by offering stimulation through other senses: sound, smell, taste, and touch.
- Keep in verbal contact with the infant because she will use your voice to know you are near if she cannot see you. Be sure to identify her by name when you talk to her.
- Provide as much verbal stimulation as the infant can adapt to.

Work with the parents and vision and mobility specialists to ensure that the infant has an environment that meets her needs.

Young Infants Whose Home Language Is Not English

The infant's first language, or home language, is the language that the infant heard and overheard her parents speak before and after her birth (Genesse, Paradis, & Crago, 2004). It is the language she was exposed to. Infants who are exposed to two languages at the same time are called dual-language learners (Genesse et al., 2004). Although young infants from immigrant families are less likely to be enrolled in early care and education than infants of native-born parents it is important to think about continuity when these infants are in care.

Young infants depend upon schedules and routines to feel safe. To the extent that these are extremely different infants can become confused and disorganized. Creating some level of continuity is important and yet challenging when the infant's home language is not English. It is more of a challenge when neither the parents nor the caregivers are fluent in a common language. In situations where many infants come from homes where the caregivers do not speak English, it is imperative to have at least one child care provider who speaks the home language. Although an obvious strategy is to send important information home in both English and the home language, it may not be possible. Additionally, adults may not be literate in either their home language or English. See Table 12–22 for more ideas to support young infants whose first language is not English.

One goal for all young infants is to become more neurologically organized, which is often seen in the establishment of more predictable patterns of behavior.

Table 12–22 Adapting the Environment to Include Young Infants Whose Home Language Is Not English

- Find out as much as possible about the infant's routines at home and, when possible, ensure that there is continuity between home and the child care setting.

- Be honest about your desire to communicate with families on a daily basis and be creative about making this happen. Find out from parents what works for them.

- Use a digital camera and photographs to share with families what their infant is doing during the day. Encourage families to bring you (or e-mail you) photographs about how they do things at home. If they do not have a camera, see if it is possible to loan them one. Photographs give you a common ground on which to base a discussion, even one that may consist of a lot of nodding and smiling.

- Ensure that the music you play, the picture books you look at, and the toys and materials that are available reflect the cultures of the infants in the room.

- Celebrate the ways in which infants and families are alike and different.

up close and personal

When I work with very young babies I see my role as helping them get organized. It's like coming into a messy room and you don't know where anything is. You want something but you don't know where to begin looking, so you just stare in amazement, and the disorganization of the room makes you disorganized. One way to help babies get organized is to swaddle them. This way they don't have to worry about where their arms and legs are and what they are doing. Then look at what is going on in the environment. Is it too much? What can be eliminated? Is there a quiet corner where a baby can work on getting organized? I think babies cry sometimes because they are just disorganized and overwhelmed. The role of the adult is to help them organize themselves. As they get older they get disorganized less frequently.

REFLECTIVE PRACTICE

This is one opinion about why babies sometimes cry. What do you think your role is when an infant is unhappy? Given your opinion, what do you do for babies when they cry but you know they are full and dry? How do you make sense out of it for yourself?

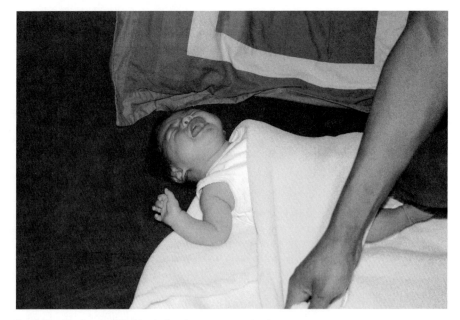

Swaddling disorganized babies helps them get organized.

The way to determine an infant's organization is through interacting with and observing the infant and his behavior. To identify patterns of organization and disorganization, you need to record the information and look for trends.

OBSERVING AND RECORDING INFANT BEHAVIOR

Planning is infant-centered. Thus, to learn about infants, you need to observe them and write down your observations. Although it may seem that you are only noting eating, sleeping, and elimination patterns, it is important to establish a pattern of observation. You will have both formal and informal observations. Formal observations should be arranged on a regular, rotating basis for all infants. Because infant behavior changes so quickly, it is important that these observations happen weekly for young infants and biweekly for older infants. For young infants formal and informal observations may be similar in format, with the major distinction being that the formal observations occur on a regular basis and are part of the record-keeping system.

With young infants, one of the first uses of observation and record keeping is to determine the infant's biological rhythms. One way to determine the patterns of a young infant is to keep a round-the-clock chart of what the infant does at various times of the day and night. It is frequently easier to determine patterns when you have information for 24 hours than just the hours that the infant is in care. This is also a way of sharing information with parents and they with you. Although it is not necessary to keep a chart every day, it may be useful to do it for three consecutive days or until you can determine a pattern. Knowing patterns helps planning. If an infant is particularly fussy at a specific time of day, you may be able to arrange to be with him then, or you may find out that he is fussy because there is a lot of stimulation going on at that particular time, and you can modify the environment. Infants' patterns change predictably around one and four months, and unpredictably at any time.

If you make up a chart, you can include information that is useful to you and the parents. The easier the form is to fill out, the more likely it will be completed. Figure 12–7 is a sample of how you might collect this information. By using 15-minute intervals, you get enough information to establish the patterns you are looking for. Often parents do not fill in the chart at night, but in the morning will check what time they got up to feed their infant and for how long.

Certain data is essential for all observations. It may be useful to duplicate observation sheets so that you will routinely record the information. Such data includes: infant's name, birth date, current date, and so on. Note on the form who made the observation and the infant's state at the beginning of the observation. Infants have different patterns at different times of the day. Most infants are more

FIGURE 12–7 Round-the-Clock Observation and Recording Chart of Infant Behavior

Name _____ Birth date _____ Date _____ Recorder _____

Time	Sleeping	Eating (Amount)	Diapering	Quiet Alert	Active Alert	Crying	Fussing
8:00							
8:15							
8:30							
8:45							
9:00							
9:15							
9:30							
9:45							
10:00							
10:15							
10:30							
10:45							
11:00							
11:15							
11:30							
11:45							
12:00							

alert in the morning, and if you are looking for optimal behaviors it is sensible to choose times when the infant is likely to be at her best. Note that the first three columns are the same as the daily behavioral record. It is the last four columns that are different as these are particularly important for programming purposes.

Different forms of record keeping are used for different purposes. Informal observations occur more frequently and mostly focus on events that are markers (Amelie rolled from her back to her stomach today for the first time), or that deviate from the usual pattern (Juan took an unusually long nap today). In these cases, anecdotal notes are probably the most efficient way to record behavior.

Probably the most common form of nonsystematic observation is keeping anecdotal notes on an infant's behavior. You might have a card for each infant, a notebook with a page for each infant, or a folder for each infant. When you write your notes indicate where the infant is during the observation, such as on his tummy in the middle of the rug, who else is present (both children and adults), and what playthings the infant has available. Additional information can be added, evaluative comments included, and so on.

Regardless of the level of formality, there are two important aspects to observation: detail and objectivity. To note that "Kaiyan had a hard day" is not useful. You need details to both understand what happened and to see what modifications might help Kaiyan. You should also be aware of your subjectivity in saying that whatever happened was "hard." It is more useful to note that "Kaiyan cried for 20 minutes after he was dropped off this morning. He also woke up from his afternoon nap crying."

Observations made during the course of the day are part of the ongoing teaching/caregiving process. You need to continuously monitor the match between infants and their environment and note where modifications are necessary. In addition, your attention may be drawn to behaviors that are unusual for a particular infant; for example, an infant who had a loose bowel movement, fussed more or less, wanted to be held more than usual.

Interesting behaviors should be briefly noted and a method of discussing them with parents should be developed. Parents want to know what happened during their infant's day, and, because the infant cannot tell them, a system needs to be in place to convey this information on a regular basis. Taking photographs with digital cameras helps. Likewise, you need to have a system of incorporating information from parents' observations that might influence your day. The methods you choose for recording the information gathered from your informal observations is dependent on both the setting and the purpose of the observations and the desires of the parents.

Because of parents' interest in what happens when they are away, digital cameras and photographs are a great way of reassuring parents about what their baby is doing and that the behavior they see as they leave their baby is not what happens for the entire day. Digital assessment can show not only what the infant can do, but also how he does it. It also provides a permanent record that can be shared.

Observations are made for a variety of purposes. The goal of this type of observation is to share information with parents and to plan and individualize programming for infants.

SHARING OBSERVATIONS WITH PARENTS

Some caregivers find it effective to exchange information verbally with parents at the beginning and end of the day. This method is most effective when there is one caregiver and few parents who stagger both their arrival and departure times. When there are changes in the caregivers over the course of the day, information may fall through the cracks. Even when the major method of communicating information is verbal, some system of written record keeping should be developed for each infant. Developmental milestones should be recorded and photographed, as should general information about development that might be shared with parents at more formal parent-teacher conferences.

Information for parents of an infant typically falls into one of two categories: temporary (daily) concerns and permanent records. Typical information that is exchanged on a daily basis includes eating (both time and amount), sleeping (beginning and end time noted), toileting (with bowel movements noted), and qualitative comments about the infant. Permanent record keeping focuses on entries related to developmental areas and reflects the infant's abilities and preferences. These observations are part of formal record keeping.

Two different systems of record keeping are necessary. If there are multiple caregivers, they should use the same systems and have some general agreement about what falls into each category and how the information will be recorded. For daily concerns some caregivers use a message board where both they and parents can write each other brief notes that are erased at the end of the day. Some find that sending index cards home is useful; others send a notebook back and forth with each child; and still others develop sheets with categories already written on them and with categorized information filled in on a daily basis. Permanent records are usually filed in an office and include more generalized information, written observations, as well as photographs and videotapes.

RECORDING OBSERVATIONS FOR INDIVIDUALIZING PROGRAMMING

Infants are dependent on the observations and insights of adults to choose toys that match their developmental level and their individual preferences. Noting what materials an infant likes is a necessary part of programming. It is also important to note the infant's ability level in playing with different materials in different developmental areas. Infants may be mastering some large motor skills while other skills are just emerging. Planning needs to be responsive to such individual differences.

It is useful to compare your observations to a set of norms, such as those in the HELP Charts (Furuno, 1994). Comparison will help you focus on skills that are expected for a particular age. Charts such as these are used differently for programming than for assessment. For programming purposes it is useful to look at the age at which skills begin to emerge so that you can support the development of those skills with the materials you choose and the methods you use with a child. These are experiences that require adult scaffolding.

A recording device such as Figure 12–8 can be used with six-month-old infants. It contains only skills that are likely to emerge beginning at about six months. It frequently takes skills a month, or even two or three, to emerge. Similar charts from earlier months would overlap this one. This chart might be used at two-week intervals as a guide for deciding on the types of experiences to use

FIGURE 12–8 Emerging Skills at 6 Months

Name _____ Birth date _____	Date	Date	Date	Date
Follows trajectory of fast-moving objects				
Retains two of three objects offered				
Looks for family member or pet when named				
Slides object or toy on surface				
Finds hidden object behind 1, 2, and then 3 screens				
Plays peek-a-boo				
Responds to facial expressions				
Plays 2 to 3 minutes with a single toy				
Says "dada" or "mama" nonspecifically				
Waves or responds to "bye-bye"				
Holds weight on one hand in prone position				
Gets to sitting without assistance				
Stands, holding on				
Pulls to standing on furniture				
Brings one knee forward beside trunk in prone position				
Manipulates toy actively with wrist movements				
May show fear and insecurity with previously accepted situations				
Shows anxiety over separation from mother				
Responds playfully to mirror				
Cooperates in games				
Struggles against supine position				
Feeds self a cracker				
Drinks from cup held for him				

SOURCE: HELP Charts (Furuno, 1994).

with an infant this age. Develop a simple code such as plus /+/ for observing the behavior, minus /−/ for no observation, and /N/ for no opportunity.

Given the information in this chart, you would probably not be surprised when an infant who had previously separated easily from his mother now began to cling, or when a parent proudly tells you that her son calls her "mama" or that he is now pulling up on furniture. Knowing that an infant at this age may play two to three minutes with toys, you might encourage the infant who is distracted after one minute to play longer, whereas if an infant played for four or five minutes you might note what interested him for this length of time. You might make funny faces in the mirror with an infant, play peek-a-boo, and help him wave bye-bye to his parents. You might offer a prone infant a small toy so he has to support his weight with one hand while he reaches for the toy with the other and even dance with him as you provide the balance and sing music to bounce to. These are emerging developmentally appropriate behaviors. The adult's skill is to make them individually appropriate. The infant would not reach for a toy that does not intrigue him or play longer if he has no interest in the materials. He needs to be invited to participate and the play needs to be both fun and respectful of the infant's needs and desires. For some infants this is too much too soon. If you systematically use charts such as this and many of the skills are still being mastered, you may not want to move to the next chart until the infant is 6 ½ or even 7 months old. There may be some developmental areas that are developing more quickly than others. Infants grow unevenly. The skill in teaching is the ability to individualize programming.

It is not enough to plan and program well; being an acute observer and keeping records of these observations is an important part of teaching and the basis for future planning.

SUMMARY

Developmentally appropriate planning for young infants keeps the infant at the center. Infants are planned for based on their strength and needs. Experiences are planned that support their social and emotional development. Infants are placed on both their stomach and back to allow them to move their body freely in preparation for locomotor skills. Both manipulative and nonmanipulative skills are planned for as well as the integration of motor and sensory information. Communication and language are supported by adults talking to infants about with they are doing and playing sound games with the caregiver following the infant's lead. Literacy begins at birth and infants are read to on a daily basis. Infants are problem solvers; they should be allowed to become intrigued with their world and actively learn about it. Infants can enjoy illustrations in books and the art on the walls. They particularly enjoy music, especially when they are sung to.

The learning environment for infants is on the floor, in laps, and at shoulder height. Infants are ready to learn when they are in a quiet alert state. It is the role of the adult to help them attain that state and stay in it. Materials for infants are related to their developmental level. As infants have such a small repertoire of behaviors it is important to have a variety of similar materials to give them a firm foundation.

Schedules are very individualized with young infants. Routines consume a large portion of the day and need to be part of their learning process.

Transitions need to be planned to make them easier for parents, educators, and infants. All infants are included in a setting. Because planning for infants is so individualized, fewer adaptations are necessary. Observing infants and recording the information is the best way to track an infant's patterns. These records allow planning to be individualized and information to be shared with parents. Photographs are a great way to show families what their infant is doing when they are not there.

CHAPTER IN REVIEW

- Planning for young infants is different from planning for mobile infants or toddlers.

- Planning for young infants is individualized and designed to meet the infant's changing interests and skills.

- Young infants are dependent on adults to choose developmentally appropriate materials and bring these materials to them when they are in a quiet alert state.

- Adults need skills to include premature infants and infants with developmental delays in their planning.

- Routine care consumes a large part of the young infant's day. Caregivers should make this quality time for social and emotional development as well as language stimulation.

- Adults must develop both formal and informal observational and record-keeping skills.

- Infants cannot tell their parents about their day, so caregivers must convey information about the infant's day, as well as other relevant information about what transpired in the infant's life while he was not home.

- Planning provides the framework for working with young infants, but it does not provide the experiences.

- Experiences and planning are designed to be age-appropriate, culturally appropriate, and individually appropriate.

APPLICATION ACTIVITIES

1. Make a web for a young infant with some type of developmental delay or whose home language is not English after observing the infant and talking with the caregiver. Compare

your web to more traditional methods of assessment and planning. What conclusions did you reach?

2. Develop a written lesson plan for the infant you observed based on your web and carry out the plan. Evaluate the lesson and reflect on how the webbing influenced the plan. Decide how you could convert the web into an IFSP for this infant and how your would

go about discussing this with the infant's parents.

3. A friend has just had a baby and you want to buy a baby present. Describe what type of toy you would buy and what you would tell your friend about using the toy with her infant. Reflect on how you might explain to her when babies are ready to play and how to support their emerging skills through play.

RESOURCES

Web Resources

※ **Child Find** has a variety of resources for the early identification of children who may have developmental delays. http://www.childfindidea.org/.

※ **Mind in the Making**, developed by Family and Work Institute and New Screen Concepts, is a collaborative effort that supports the science of early learning through print and multimedia. http://mindinthemaking.org.

※ The**National Center for Cultural Competence (NCCC), based at Georgetown Univeristy**, is dedicated to increasing the capacity of health and mental health programs to design, implement, and evaluate culturally and linguistically competent service delivery systems. It has checklist for self-assessing ones cultural competence. http://www11.georgetown.edu.

※ **Our Kids** is a devoted to improving and disseminating what we know about the importance of early childhood to the

community at large. http://www.ourkidsnetwork.ca.

※ **Pathways Awareness Foundation** has produced an inexpensive compact disk, *Is my baby OK?*, which highlights typical and atypical development in the young infant. It also has other resources. 800-955-2445 or www.pathwaysawareness.org.

Print Resources

※ Karp, H. (2002). *The happiest baby on the block: The new way to calm crying and help your baby sleep longer.* New York: Bantam.

※ Koralek, D., with Dombro, A.L. & Dodge, D.T. (2005). *Caring for infants and toddlers* (2nd ed.). Washington, DC: Teaching Strategies.

※ Koralek, D., with Dombro, A. L., & Dodge, D. T. (2005). *Skill-building journal: Caring for infants and toddlers* (2nd ed.). Washington, DC: Teaching Strategies.

REFERENCES

Bowe, F. G. (1995). Population estimates: Birth-to-5 children with disabilities. *The Journal of Special Education, 20,* 461–471.

Dombro, A. L., Colker, L. J., & Dodge, D. T. (1999). *The creative curriculum for infants and toddlers.* Washington, DC: Teaching Strategies, Inc.

Fraiberg, S. (1965). *The magic years.* New York: Scribner.

Furuno, S. (1994). *HELP Charts based on the Hawaii early learning profile.* Palo Alto, CA: VORT Corporation.

Gallahue, D. L., & Ozmun, J. C. (2002). *Understanding motor development: Infants, children, adolescents, adults* (5th ed.). New York: McGraw-Hill.

Genesse, F., Paradis, J., & Crago, M. B. (2004). *Dual language development and disorders: A handbook on bilingual and second language learning.* Baltimore, MD: Paul H. Brookes.

Gillespie, L. G., & Seibel, N. L. (2006). Self-regulation: A cornerstone of early childhood development. *Young Children, 61*(4), 34–39.

Graham, G., Holt-Hale, S. A., & Parker, M. (2005). *Children moving: A reflective approach to teaching physical education* (7th ed.). New York: McGraw Hill.

Guralnick, M. J. (2004). Effectiveness of early intervention for vulnerable children: A developmental perspective. In M. A. Feldman (Ed.), *Early intervention: The essential readings* (pp. 9–50). Malden, MA: Blackwell Publishing, Ltd.

Haywood, K. M., & Getchell, N. (2005). *Life span motor development* (4th ed.). Champaign, IL: Human Kinetics.

Lally, J. R., & Mangione, P. (2006). The uniqueness of infancy demands a responsive approach to care. *Young Children, 61*(4), 14–20.

Lowdermilk, D. L., & Perry, S. E. (2003). *Maternity nursing* (6th ed.). St. Louis, MO: Mosby.

Majnemer, A., & Barr, R. G. (2005). Influence of supine sleep positioning on early motor milestone acquisition. *Developmental Medicine and Child Neurology, 47,* 370–376.

Ostrosky, M. M., Jung, E. Y., Hemmeter, M. L., & Thomas, D. (n.d.). *Helping children understand routines and classroom schedules.* Center on the Social and Emotional Foundations for Early Learning. What Works Briefs. Retrieved November 23, 2007, from http://www.vanderbilt.edu/csefle/briefs/wwb3.pdf

National Research Council and Institute of Medicine. (2000). *From neurons to neighborhoods: The science of early childhood development.* Committee on integrating the science of early childhood development. In J. P. Shonkoff & D. A. Phillips (eds.). *Board on Children, Youth, and Families, Commission on Behavioral and Social Sciences and Education.* Washington, DC: National Academy Press.

Parks, S. (1988). *HELP … at home.* Palo Alto, CA: VORT Corporation.

Sutton, T., & Buell, M. (in press). Weaving a web that keeps children in the center: A new approach to emergent curriculum planning for young preschoolers. *Young Children.*

Zero to Three (2006). Where it all begins: Movement and the brain. *Young Children, 61*(4), 39.

chapter 13

Curriculum and Planning for Mobile Infants: 8 to 18 Months

Chapter Outline

- Developmentally Appropriate Planning for Mobile Infants
- Implementing the Curriculum for Mobile Infants
- Materials and Methods for Working with Mobile Infants
- Schedules, Routines, and Transitions
- Including All Mobile Infants
- Supporting Self-Regulation
- Transitioning between Settings

In just nine months infants have made tremendous strides in growth and development and what they can learn about their world. Infants are now sitting and moving beings who have a definite personality and are ready to make some new demands on their world. Many of them have been in the care of adults other than their parents for several months; others will be entering into care for the first time.

WHY STUDY CURRICULUM AND PLANNING FOR MOBILE INFANTS?

✸ Mobile infants make unique demands on caregivers. They have mobility and amazing curiosity, but few skills in evaluating the safety of their environment.

✸ Mobile infants' newfound independence allows them to make more choices and to seek out materials and toys that are of interest to them.

✸ Mobile infants' knowledge of self makes them more vulnerable when left in the care of others, as they are more certain of who they are and who their family is.

✸ Mobile infants between 8 and 18 months reach major milestones in motor and communication skills. Knowing the expected milestones is necessary for planning.

✸ Mobile infants are born preprogrammed to survive and thrive in their world. The role of the early childhood educator is to be responsive to these internal drives and plan to provide mobile infants with opportunities to master their developing skills and their environment.

✸ Mobile infants who do not meet major milestones need the support of caregivers and an early intervention team.

With emerging mobility (8 to 18 months) the focus is on motion. Infants need both incentives to move and something to do when they get where they are going. Moving still requires concentration and effort. Infant's skills develop at differing rates: The competent creeper may be late in walking because she finds walking to be an inefficient mode of transportation. Crawlers and early walkers may concentrate so much on the process of getting where they want to go that they forget why they wanted to be there. Planning is still very individualized.

DEVELOPMENTALLY APPROPRIATE PLANNING FOR MOBILE INFANTS

All individuals are curious and driven to learn about things that intrigue them. This function is present in infants, but it is more specific than in older children. Infants are born with their learning agenda preprogrammed. Infants and toddlers are genetically programmed to learn some things: language, motor control of large and small muscles, knowledge about the function of people and things in their world, and relationship building (Lally & Mangione, 2006). Infants are born seeking to learn these skills because they have survival value. Older children may want to learn how to sail because they live by

Genetically wired is an inborn drive to learn essential developmental skills.

the beach and it is what their friends are doing. Environmental opportunity, interest, and some form of socialization motivate older children to pursue particular interests. Young children are **genetically wired** to learn the skills that are important for their survival. The needs of infants and toddlers become the curriculum (Lally & Mangione, 2006).

Learning is more holistic with infants and toddlers than with older children. As you look at how the curriculum is designed, the infant is still in the center and experiences are built around what the infant wants. Experiences, not activities, are planned. These are broad based because infants receive information from each domain simultaneously regardless of what we wish to emphasize (Lally & Mangione, 2006). With mobility, infants who have developed a sense of security and safety in their surroundings explore their environment by moving through it and manipulating the items they find. They actively explore their world. This not only changes how they are, but it also necessitates a change in the behavior of their caregivers. You are their secure base. Contact need not always be physical—eye contact and an encouraging smile may be enough for a mobile infant to continue his exploration. You need to encourage the exploration of infants. If you constantly hover over them and do not give them the freedom to solve some of their own problems and allow them to explore, you are sending a powerful message: You do not support their developing competence (Lally & Mangione, 2006).

Planning That Keeps the Mobile Infant in the Center

As with young infants, the mobile infant is in the center of the web. Because programming is still so individualized and the infant remains the focus, this is an excellent way to plan for mobile infants. Responsive curriculum planning focuses on each infant's unique thoughts, feelings, needs, and interests. More generalized programming emerges out of the overlapping interests of mobile infants. Webs not only offer the opportunity to focus on these, but can also serve as a record about the infant's development. Good planning puts the caregiver in the role of facilitator of learning. She must excel at reading the infant's cues as these provide the basis for adapting and individualizing learning experiences. Webbing is also easy to share with parents, particularly when it is fleshed out with digital photos.

See Figure 13–1 for a basic web for two mobile infants. I have purposefully included an infant with an identified disability so that you can see how easy it is to include infants with disabilities. You can meet their specific needs and respond to their strengths while you are planning for all of the infants in the room.

Mobile infants need a combination of materials and experiences that are nearby. Toys should be arranged on low shelves so infants can go to them and

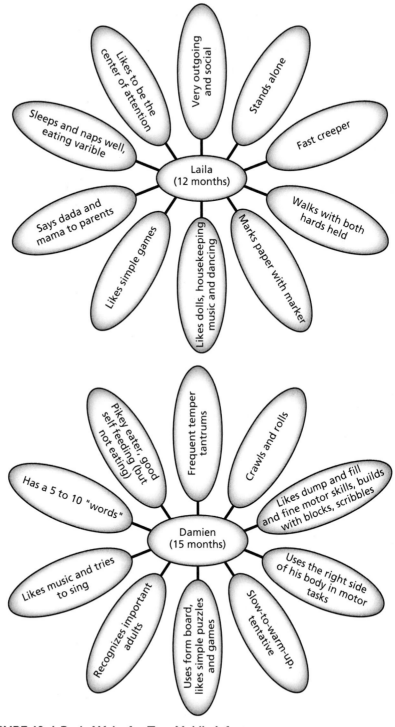

FIGURE 13–1 Basic Webs for Two Mobile Infants
Damien was diagnosed with cerebral palsy at 9 months.

choose the ones that attract them. Be sure that toys are accessible, as mobile infants will creep to an area, sit, make a choice, and then play. Be prepared that this process may be repeated several minutes later (if that long). If the infant initiates the choice of toy, it will probably take place directly on the floor; if an adult prepares an experience, older infants may be at a low table but it will be his choice to be there.

Experiences That Support Social and Emotional Development

Mobile infants first develop self-awareness and then awareness of others and the roles those significant others play in their lives. This is the beginning of social awareness. First, they learn about their family and caregivers. As they enter an early care and education setting, they expand their awareness of roles of adults. They may need to learn new ways to be with adults when they enter an early childhood program. They must learn the different expectations of staff and parents, and also the different expectations of the early childhood program versus home. They need to find ways of sharing adult attention. Likewise, they need to develop methods of interacting with peers. Throughout this process they are learning about themselves. These are challenging areas of growth.

As infants move out into their world they need manageable challenges to develop self-regulation. Infants are moving from external regulation to self-regulation. Infants and toddlers have different temperaments (Chess & Thomas, 1977). Self-regulation is less of a challenge for mobile infants with easy temperaments than for feisty ones. The match between adult and child temperaments makes a difference as well. Understanding your temperament and those of the mobile infants you are educating can help you select strategies that support self-regulation (Gillespie & Seibel, 2006).

When an infant's self-regulation is not working, adults provide external support for self-regulation until infants can regain control. Strategies for helping infants and toddlers self-regulate must be individualized. They are closely based on your ability to accurately observe an infant and read the cues that he is sending. It is supported by a developmentally appropriate environment that sets age-appropriate limits and by caregivers who genuinely love, respect, and empathize with the infants they care for.

Playing simple social games is an important learning tool at this stage. The rules are simple, but the possibilities are endless. One element is turn-taking. The adult engages an action, then stops and waits for the infant to act. The earliest of these games involves the infant dropping something and the adult picking it up. Young infants are more interested in the toy, whereas mobile infants are showing interest in the social aspect of the game. The games are played over and over. The adult stacks blocks; the infant knocks them down. The adult wiggles her fingers; the infant puts his hand over them to make them stop. And on and on. Mobile infants are struggling but learning to wait their turn and to adapt to the pace of the other person. They also need to focus and pay attention to their partner's actions. These are positive interactions that also support language development. Adult-infant games appear earlier than peer interactions because the adult structures and scaffolds the infant's play (Hughes, 1999). Table 13–1 provides ideas for supporting social and emotional development.

Table 13–1 Supporting Mobile Infants Social and Emotional Development

• Include materials that encourage awareness of self and others, such as toys with mirrors, dolls, and puppets.
• Provide materials for cuddling, such as stuffed dolls and toys, as well as a cozy area to cuddle in.
• Make bulletin boards or wall displays that include pictures of infants and toddlers from different racial/ethnic groups and of children with assistive devices (eye glasses or wheelchairs) and visible disabilities.
• Play simple social games with mobile infants.

Self-Help/Adaptive Development

Mobile infants are developing skills that allow for increasing independence. They can feed themselves finger foods, drink from a cup, get objects that interest them, and cooperates in routines such as dressing and undressing. Napping is becoming more regular and mobile infants may nap twice a day or they may begin to refuse the morning nap and just take a longer afternoon nap. Young mobile infants sleep about 12 to 14 hours a night. By the end of this period their sleep typically decreases to 10 to 12 hours and their afternoon nap is between 1 and 3 hours.

This is a time when parents and caregivers are often concerned about eating. Between 12 and 18 months infants may begin to refuse food. Their appetite decreases as their energy demands also decrease. Their rate of growth is decelerating so the demand for energy is less. They are becoming more competent at eating independently and can feed themselves with a spoon with some spilling by the end of this period. Bowel and bladder control are beginning to show a pattern. See Table 13–2 for ways to support mobile infants adaptive development.

Table 13–2 Scaffolding Self-Help/Adaptive Skills

• Provide mobile infants with a variety of plastic cups, plates, and spoons to explore and then use.
• Ask mobile infants if they are wet or their diapers are soiled. Respond to their assessment (Let's see.) Help them build the connection between how they feel (wet, soiled or dry) and their bodily function.
• Be responsive to mobile infant's changing nap schedules and accommodate those in your planning.

(continues)

Table 13–2 *(continues)*

- Chart when mobile infants are wet or soiled to determine a pattern.

- Give mobile infants time to self-feed and set up the environment so that cleaning up the mess is not an onerous task. (Consider putting the high chair on a plastic shower curtain so you can just scoop it up and shake it.)

- Build more time into transitions so infants have time to practice their emerging undressing and dressing skills.

- Put clothing in the dramatic play area that is easy to put on and take off and encourage mobile infants to "dress up."

Experiences That Support Motor Development and Sensory Integration

Developing motor skills and integrating these with sensory information is most rapid during infancy. Mobile infants are programmed to move. They are active explorers who are captivated by what they see, and they want to learn more about what intrigues them. This is the exploratory stage: The focus is on movement. Motor skills emerge and are refined with practice. The pattern of motor development dictates that gross motor development precedes fine motor development. Mobile infants who cannot pick up a large ball and lift it over their heads cannot be expected to print letters recognizably regardless of the amount of time spent practicing printing. The motor skills they are practicing need to be progressively challenged. As their sense of balance and strength improves, they progress from standing to walking, and to walking on a line taped on the floor. They need many opportunities to integrate information that comes in from the senses with both large- and small-motor movement. Encourage mobile infants to use the motor skills available to them, regardless of competence. They need the most practice in areas in which they are the least able. So emphasize process over product and be ecstatic in your encouragement. Remember that mobile infants are born to crawl and walk; give them many opportunities to practice safely inside and outside. See Table 13–3 for ways to support mobile infants' locomotor development.

WITH INFANTS AND TODDLERS

Choose a push toy for a crawler or a pull toy for a walker. First, allow the infant to explore the toy then roll the toy slightly out of his reach. Encourage him to creep after the push toy. As he reaches it, push it a little farther, then encourage him to push it rather than retrieve it. (Do not do this to the point of frustration.) When the infant understands about pushing toys, introduce toys that can be pulled as well. Initially choose toys that move slowly. As infants become more proficient, use toys that move more quickly, such as balls or push toys that you walk behind.

Table 13–3 Scaffolding Locomotor Skills

- Support emerging motor skills by providing crawlers with moving toys that can be pushed or pulled on the floor, and toys they can creep or crawl after.

- Support emerging walkers with toys that give them some support as they walk, such as heavy baby carriages. (If they are likely to tip, add some weight to them.)

- Play games like "Ring around the Rosie," and then play them again.

- Dance to music with a beat. Have a 2-minute dance party.

- Push and kick balls and retrieve them.

- Put a wide tape line on the floor and encourage toddlers to walk it, holding their arms out for balance.

- Take materials outside to play, such as simple riding toys, large balls, large trucks and cars, and so on.

Beginning walkers enjoy pushing toys as they practice their emerging skill.

Although infants are interested in moving, they also need to increase awareness of their body and where it is in space. They need to stretch, twist, turn, squat, and balance as well as move. Table 13–4 provides ideas for supporting stability skills. The goal for the development of nonmanipulative or stability skills is body awareness.

Table 13–4 Scaffolding Nonmanipulative Skills

- Play music (rock and roll works well) and have mobile infants twist and turn their bodies to the music.
- Play music and have infants sway to the music first side to side then front to back. They can do this sitting or standing.
- Play easy games of mirroring and following the leader as you stretch high and then reach low. Squat down and jump up. Encourage the infants to do what you do.
- Play easy games where infants try to make their bodies a big as they can and as small as they can.

Although large motor skills overshadow small motor development, there are just as many changes going on in infant's manipulative skills as there are with the locomotor skills. Fine grasp involves the use of the fingers independently and the ability to use the thumb and index finger together to pick up small objects. Experiences with finger foods, large crayons, and large wooden beads facilitate the development of these skills. Infants need to develop motor-planning skills to precisely pick up and release these objects when finished. When they have time, mobile infants are interested in exploring small objects with their hands. In addition, they now have the ability to use **tools.** They can now make marks with crayons or markers, stack blocks, use a spoon, and drink from a cup. See Table 13–5 for ways to support manipulative skills.

Tools is a generic term for objects that children use to mark with, including markers, crayons, paintbrushes, and so on.

Mobile infants need to engage their senses to learn about their world. One area of manipulative skills we refer to as dump and fill. Dump and fill typically

Table 13–5 Scaffolding Manipulative Skills

- Provide young toddlers with many opportunities to practice reaching, grasping, and releasing. Give them small objects such as measuring cups, blocks, spoons—safe but small toys to manipulate.
- Provide form boards and simple wooden puzzles with knobs.
- Encourage stacking by providing toys that fit inside each other (for younger infants take out every other one to make the task easier).
- Provide large balls to kick, throw, and roll.
- Introduce cardboard blocks for building.
- Provide opportunities for infants to "dump and fill."

involves a substance put in a plastic wash basin and then the toddler fills up a plastic measuring cup or other object and then dumps it into the container and fills it up again. It is clearly possible to use water, sand, or birdseed for dump and fill. They need to "dump and fill" from many different objects using many different substances. They need to feel water, sand (if the janitor does not go berserk), birdseed, oatmeal, rice, noodles, and so on. There is a controversy here. Infants often eat what they are playing with. Many people feel that because there are people who do not have enough food that we should not use something that could be eaten as a sensory experience. This is your call. For me, the concern about infants eating the sensory materials outweighs the other considerations. However, as children become old enough to not eat the sensory materials, I change to non-food options. I believe this is both respectful and practical.

REFLECTIVE PRACTICE

How do you feel about using substances that could be eaten? Would you let young toddlers use rice in "dump and fill? What about finger paint with pudding?" Reflect on this practice and take a stand.

Experiences That Support Communication, Language, and Literacy Development

Language permeates the curriculum. For mobile infants the opportunities for language input abound. A formal language arts program would be out of place for infants. However, the foundation for language and literacy are an important part of the curriculum. For mobile infants, a major component of language involves learning the meaning of words. Often a child's first words depend on context for exact meaning. For example, when an infant says "ball," it is usually easy to understand from the situation whether he means "get me the ball" or "play with the ball" or "look what I found—a ball!" It's not until about 18 months that toddlers begin to string words together, such as "ball gone." See Table 13–6 for ways to support communication and language development.

Literacy
is a system of marks that fixes language in place to save it.

Literacy is a system of marks that represents language and fixes it in place so it can be saved. It involves the reading, writing, and thinking necessary to produce and comprehend it. To be literate one also needs to understand the rules that govern languages, such as spelling and punctuation (Roskos, Tabors, & Lenhart, 2004). Depending on their family literacy environment, infants and toddlers begin to form ideas about books and print. In early childhood, learning to use oral language is an important step toward literacy. Infants and toddlers are

Table 13–6 Scaffolding Communication and Language Skills

- When an infant talks to you, wait until her "sentence" is over before you respond. This helps foster the give-and-take rhythm of normal conversation. Do not interrupt, wait for her to finish.
- Point to what you are talking about to support infants in learning the names of objects.
- Give mobile infants the vocabulary they need by labeling objects and actions for them. See yourself as a language model, and model good language usage.
- Ask mobile infants to bring you different objects. Then thank them for their help.
- Play games where the infant points to his nose, head, eyes, foot, stomach, and so on. Or have him point to yours. Play "I'm going to get your (body part)." Laugh and enjoy yourself as you play.
- Give mobile infants time to respond to your requests. Language is new to them and it takes a while to process.
- Use the infant's name frequently in conversations. He recognizes his name and it helps him understand conversations better.

very dependent on the illustrations in a book to understand it. Mobile infants need to be able to relate the story to their lives and past experiences and identify with the characters. Books need to be short, with few words and action-packed (Roskos et al., 2004). See Table 13–7 for ways of supporting literacy.

Table 13–7 Scaffolding Literacy

- Use singing, rhyming, and simple storytelling to set the stage for literacy.
- Use books about hellos and good-byes.
- Use books that have a touch-and-feel component.
- Use books about familiar topics: children, families, animals, or events in infant's lives such as eating, sleeping, or playing.
- Choose books with only a few words on each page (or only read a few words).
- Choose books with brightly colored photographs or engaging illustrations.
- Choose books with simple rhymes, repetitions, and predictable text.
- Select durable books. Many infant/toddler books are available with pages of heavy coated cardboard, cloth, or plastic. Expect to read these books in one-on-one situations, again, again, and again.
- Provide scribbling materials for mobile infants such as large nontoxic crayons and markers.

Experiences That Support Cognitive Development

In an emergent curriculum holistic approach, cognitive skills naturally flow out of development. It is not drilling infants on numbers, shapes, and the alphabet. If they have an enticing environment they will explore and learn. Adults need to provide opportunities for learning about the world as well as the language labels that make these experiences meaningful to young children. This combination of experience and language is necessary to develop scientific and mathematical thinking.

Although from an adult's perspective, mathematics may seem mundane, the experience of hearing songs and nursery rhymes that include numbers and that designate quantity and size are initial mathematical concepts. Math develops out of real-life mathematical relationships. Discovery experiences support a mobile infant's natural learning processes. Provide opportunities for children to actively learn about their environment on a regular basis. Provide a variety of materials to facilitate self-discovery so children can construct their own knowledge. Mobile infants learn competence when their behaviors have a predictable outcome. They need practice discovering this in relation to both objects and people. See Table 13–8 for ways to support mathematical development.

Table 13–8 Scaffolding Mathematics

- Ensure that schedules and routines are orderly and consistent if flexible so mobile infants can predict what will happen next. They are working on memory skills.

- Make requests of mobile infants using simple one-step directions with supporting gestures if necessary.

- Continue playing simple repetitive games, especially games like peek-a-boo.

- Provide toys that have predictability as a consequence of their actions: cause and effect toys, push buttons and levers, as well as windup toys, busy boxes, and jack-in-the-boxes.

- Support cause and effect learning by providing a variety of sound toys: shakers, bells, rattles, and clackers

- Give mobile infants an opportunity to stack blocks to support their concepts of spatial relationships; larger blocks will be easier to stack, but may be hard for small hands to manage.

WITH INFANTS AND TODDLERS

Play many variations of simple games such as peek-a-boo. Using your voice, get the infant's attention, make eye contact, then hide behind a blanket or a piece of furniture. Reappear and say, "Peek-a-boo, I see you." Put a book between you and the infant and peek around the corners of the book. Put a handkerchief or tissue over your face and then pull it off and say, "Peek-a-boo." Put your hands over your face to cover it and then move them and say, "Peek-a-boo, I see Jerrod."

Games such as peek-a-boo play an important role in cognitive development. They help toddler learn that what they cannot see still exists (object permanence). Because the game is similar every time, toddlers develop the ability to predict what will happen next.

Science experiences for mobile infants are based on what they do naturally. They look at things, touch them, taste them, smell them, and manipulate them. These skills are exactly what young scientists need to know in order to learn about the properties of the world around them. With mobile infants supporting cognitive development is viewed as discovery. They are learning to persist in order to make sense out of their discoveries. Real science begins with curiosity, which leads to discovery and exploration. Science is integrated into all aspects of the day. Notice what the mobile infant notices and seize the moment: Go outside and catch snowflakes, have a windy day party, find bugs after the rain. For more ideas of ways to scaffold science see Table 13–9.

Table 13–9 Scaffolding Science

- Explore with children as they are learning about their world. Provide opportunities to explore new places and talk to them about what they are doing and seeing.
- Provide many sensory opportunities, indoors and out, to pat, push, mound, and squish as well as to mix, fill, pile, and dump.
- Provide many opportunities for mobile infants to imitate behavior. You need two toys to play. Shake a rattle and see if the child shakes it. Put a block in a cup and take it out.
- Learning about the properties of gravity as children stack and knock down cardboard boxes.
- Provide opportunities for mobile infants to think things out and problem solve, do not interfere so soon that they do not have the opportunity to solve the problem.
- Continue to add cause and effect toys and experiences. Young toddlers can predict what will happen (splash water with a flat hand and it comes up) they will be surprised when these things do not happen.

Experiences That Support Aesthetic Development

All children are unique. Each has his own special style of working, learning, and creating. Creativity is dependent upon the developmental level of the child and his past experience with various media. What is creative for infants is not for mobile infants, and what is creative for a young toddler who has never experienced a particular media is not creative for toddlers who have had much experience with it.

There is not any hard-and-fast rule about when to introduce art experiences into the planning process; however, children from about one year old can participate in simple art experiences. First art experiences are characterized by exploration and experimentation. They focus on the use and texture of the materials. Mobile infants are intrigued with what materials can do and what they can do with the materials. It is important to have a variety of media so they can discover the most important qualities of each.

Art for mobile infants is also a sensory experience. Scribbling develops from the first faint markings of an infant until about two years of age when toddlers begin random scribbling. These are jerky, erratic marks on paper. They may be just as interested in getting crayons out of the container or the tops off markers as they are in making marks. Because of their lack of concern about the product, the boundaries of paper are seen as arbitrary and are rarely acknowledged. Mobile infants need large sturdy crayons, chalk, and paintbrushes. The paper, too, needs to be large enough to accommodate broad movements. Young children need to explore and use many different art media. They can paste collage materials and they can help tear them into pieces. They enjoy fingerpainting as well as using thick tempera paint or playdough. Mobile infants are interested in exploring the media itself at first. Art activities provide them with opportunities to develop and use their senses in a satisfying, constructive way (see Table 13–10).

Table 13–10 Scaffolding Art

• Provide the mobile infants with enough materials, space, and time to be creative.
• Provide mobile infants with large markers or crayons and vary the color, size, and shape of paper used (but do not make it too small). Begin to add accessories such as stamps.
• Use wet or dry chalk on paper and a chalkboard. Use sidewalk chalk and let the children see what happens when it gets wet or it rains.
• Have easel painting or coloring available on a regular basis. Using an almost vertical surface is different than a horizontal one.

Young children enjoy and learn from a variety of musical experiences. They learn new words, develop memory skills, and develop a sense of rhythm as they sing and listen to music. You can make up the words. They especially enjoy having their name included in the song. Songs can be as simple as "I'm going to get Sara's bottle, bottle, bottle. I'm going to get Sara's bottle, bottle, bottle. I'll be back in a minute." Even if you do not have a good voice, they will like your singing (see Table 13–11).

When introducing mobile infants to dramatic play, start with the housekeeping area. This is familiar and is the easiest to facilitate. Do not put all your props out at first, but rather watch the play and gradually add materials in response to their interest. Mobile infants will spend most of their time reenacting the adult roles they are most familiar with, and situations that are meaningful

Table 13–11 Scaffolding Music

- Sing simple songs throughout the day. You can make up the words. Sing; you do not need to be an opera star but you need to engage the children. Having more personality than tune works.
- Use music to help transitions such as waiting to go outside, eating lunch, or cleaning up.
- Sing songs or play "following directions" games. Ask children to "touch their nose" or "clap their hands." Sing songs like "Put your finger in the air." Take advantage of these opportunities to add to children's learning and their self-esteem.
- Jump or dance to music if toddlers are standing waiting.
- Have a dance party. Although toddlers are active, many get very little play that is in the moderate to vigorous activity level. They need small bursts of energy (2 to 3 minutes) to support their long-term health.
- Add scarves to dance with.
- Play simple cooperative games like ring-around-the-rosy.
- Pair music and movement to encourage young children to move in different ways and to explore body awareness.

to them. As awareness of the environment expands, these new roles will be incorporated into play. A trip to the grocery story or a visit to a relative or friend may expand play (see Table 13–12).

Table 13–12 Scaffolding Dramatic Play

- Provide dolls and places for them to sleep as well as blankets to wrap them in
- Have a kitchen with pots and pans and plastic food
- Provide dress-up clothes that have been cut short enough that mobile infants will not trip
- Add props as play demands

Despite his new skills, the mobile infant is fragile. He can look as competent as many preschool children one minute and in the next he will fall apart and cling and cry like a young infant. He is curious about his world, but he needs to satisfy this curiosity in a safe environment with caring adults. Mobile infants are some of the most satisfying and frustrating children to work with. As they learn about themselves, they teach us about ourselves.

Emergent Curriculum Planning for Mobile Infants Using Webs

Starting with a web that is hand-written spontaneously helps you evaluate your perceptions of mobile infants and the areas you focus on (see Figure 13–1). It will be neither complete nor perfect. But it will help you think about each infant. The second step in the process is to look at the webs you have developed, to pull out the information and place it in a developmental framework. The developmental information is essential for planning at the appropriate level, the likes and dislikes ensure that what you plan will be motivating for the infants. The table below is another version of Figure 13–1. In the initial web information was added as it occurred to the teachers making the web. Now it has been organized into a framework. At this point it might become apparent that some information is missing and needs to be added or a particular domain has not been covered and perhaps additional observation is needed. The notes that are in italics were added to the original web. In a typical toddler classroom you would have more toddlers and your planning would grow out of their individual development and likes and challenges as you put them into a developmental framework

Damian was diagnosed with cerebral palsy at nine months. In his case it affects the left side of his body. Note how many of the observations relate to movement. This is clearly what focuses attention. For this age group the emphasis on motor development is appropriate. After you organize your observations, and add additional information you are ready to move onto more curriculum-based decisions. Routines and transitions are added to the planning, as these times provide great opportunities to work with mobile infants on a one-on-one basis.

In additional to the materials that are used in the classroom on a regular basis, the web helps you decide what materials and experiences to add to the basics. Although these are divided by developmental area, there is clearly overlap. For example, repeat and respond to language is an example of turn-taking. It could also be communication, language, and literacy. Including all developmental areas is important, but worrying about exact placement of experiences is not. Planning is still very individualized and holistic (Table 13–13).

Table 13–13 Placing Mobile Infants Webs Into a Developmental Framework

Development, Likes, and Challenges	
Laila (12 months)	Damian (15 months)
Social and Emotional	
Sleeps and naps well, eating variable	Slow to warm up, tentative
Likes to be the center of attention	Says "no," many temper tantrums
Very outgoing and social	
Motor and Sensory Integration	
Fast creeper	Crawls and rolls
Stands alone	Uses form board, likes simple puzzles
Walks if both hands held	Likes dump and fill, builds with blocks

(continues)

Table 13–13 *(continues)*

Marks paper with marker	Scribbles
	Uses right side of body in motor tasks
Communication, Language, and Literacy	
Says "dada" and "mama" to parents	Has 5 to 10 "words"
Likes books about animals	Likes books about trains
Cognitive Development	
Likes simple games	Recognizes important adults
Understands cause and effect	Follows one-step directions
Aesthetic Development	
Likes dolls, housekeeping, music and dancing	Likes music and tries to sing

Social and Emotional

※ Play games that require turn-taking—rolling the ball back and forth, asking for toys and giving them back, repeating and responding to language, stacking covered foam blocks and letting the infants knock them down.

※ Make a photographic sequence of the day's plan and post it at a low level so infants can see it. Talk with them about this sequence.

Motor and Sensory Integration

※ Add 3-6 piece train puzzle.

※ Set up a soft obstacle course (infants will crawl, creep, or pull themselves through the course) using covered foam blocks, short tunnels, rolled-up towels, and so on.

※ Add larger easy-grip balls with polka-dot nobs (by Gertie).

※ Add wooden doll carriage; add weight if necessary to support walking.

Communication, Language, and Literacy

※ Play a short game of "Simon Says" with small groups.

※ Read board book *The rooster struts.* (2004). New York: Random House.

※ Read *Thomas and friends: Blue train, Green train* (2007) or *A crack in the track* (2004) by W. Rev Awdry (Bright and Early Board Books published by Random House Books for Young Readers, Board Book edition).

Cognitive Development

- Add trains to the blocks.
- Add ethnically diverse dolls to housekeeping.
- Play simple repetitive games (patty cake, open shut them, peek-a-boo).
- Add more cause and effect toys: those with push buttons, pulls, levers, or handles that make something happen.
- Add cardboard blocks.

Aesthetic Development

- Add scented playdough and scented markers.
- Dance creatively to different types of music.
- Play a variety of music, including classical music such as Mozart for babies and children.

Routines and Transitions

- *Laila*: When she arrives, take the opportunity to hold her hands and walk her to an area that interests her. Do this after each diaper change as well.
- *Damian*: After talking with his parents and physical therapist, develop a ritual that you can build into the program. If appropriate, use materials and equipment that require the use of two hands. For example, rolling a large ball back and forth or using a jack-in-the-box.

REFLECTIVE PRACTICE

Look at the relationship between the additions to the curriculum and the interests, challenges and developmental level of the infants. Provide a rational for the additions. Decide what you might add and why.

IMPLEMENTING THE CURRICULUM FOR MOBILE INFANTS

Mobile infants are now actively exploring and playing with toys and other materials. Although they have more skills, they still need to practice the ones that are developing. A variety of similar toys and experiences that have many variations are useful. Being able to sit steadily frees the hands, and with increasing fine motor skills infants need toys to grasp and hold. Mobile infants need sturdy toys. They will hold, shake, bat, kick, bang, drop, throw, as well as bite and taste their toys. As they become more mobile they need toys that move—pushed or pulled.

Learning Environments for Mobile Infants

In a responsive curriculum for infants and toddlers, most of an educator's time is taken up in preparing the environment for learning rather than making up lesson plans to teach specific concepts.

Select toys and activities that stimulate the young toddler's imagination and help to develop skills. Choose some toys that can be used independently. It is important to reexamine toys to make sure they are safe. The concern is no longer small parts that might accidentally fall off, but rather, parts that can be pulled, dropped, or chewed off. The ability and interest of the young toddler in putting objects in her mouth causes some safety concerns. As small objects can easily become lodged in the throat and cause choking, keep small objects away from young children. Increased but unstable mobility adds new safety considerations.

Planning for mobile infants is different from planning for either young infants or toddlers. This is a transitional time emphatically marked by developmental milestones: the first step and the first word! Children have a growing sense of self and an increased interest in their peers. They are interested in listening to adult language, but may not be happy around unfamiliar adults. Sitting is old hat; crawling is being replaced by creeping and standing. Walking is emerging, to be followed by the toddler's version of running and even walking backward.

Receptive language far outstrips expressive language. Toddlers are beginning to have two-word utterances and their vocabulary is increasing. There are often long babbled sentences that "ought" to make sense, but it is as if they are in a different language. Self-help skills are emerging as children want to dress and feed themselves, although they may be happier undressed and self-feeding is often very messy. Emotions are becoming more specific. There are smiles and hugs for affection, anxiety at separation, and anger at both people and objects that do not do what they are "supposed" to do.

Mobile infants have a heightened awareness of the world around them and the ability to explore more of that world. But they lack experience. Planning concentrates on the consolidation of emerging skills and building a foundation of trust in the world around them. With predictable mobility, mobile infants are moving into toddlerhood.

Adults are responsible for setting the stage for young children's play. To provide quality play experiences, adults must arrange time, space, materials, and preparatory experiences. Mobile infants need space to play to practice emerging large-motor skills. A good program should have areas for mobile infants to create messy artwork, a dramatic play corner for simple familiar play (primarily variations on housekeeping), a block corner for constructive play, a cozy book and language area for quiet reading, a fine motor manipulative area, and a sensory area for exploring the properties of sensory materials.

Adult-Mobile Infant Interactions

Multitasking
is doing two or more tasks at the same time.

Caregivers often find themselves needing to **multitask** most of the time. They may be talking to one infant while they are preparing a snack and periodically reminding other children that they need to clean up the toys they were playing with as well as monitoring who has had their hands washed and who still needs to accomplish this task. Although this is necessary some of the time, it is also necessary to have mindful, relationship-based practices. **Mindfulness** is the purposeful act of being attentive, of being in the moment with infants and toddlers. It is being aware of infants and toddlers and being totally present with them (McMullen & Dixon, 2006). Mindfulness is also part of a cycle where one plans, observes the results of the planning, reflects on these results, and then modifies the plans based on what was learned.

Mindfulness
is being in the moment with infants and toddlers.

See Table 13–14 for principles of mindful, relationship-based practices.

Table 13-14 Principles of Mindful, Relationship-Based Practices

- Be fully present with the children and adults you are working with.

- Be respectful of infants, toddlers, and their families, honoring their knowledge, strengths, and needs in the context of the lives they are living and the culture they live it in.

- Engage in reflective practice as you interact with infants and toddlers.

- Learn about your own culture, values, and beliefs and know that these serve as a filter as you work with infant, toddlers, and their families. Reflect on how they influence what your do and challenge yourself to learn more about the culture, values, and beliefs of the infants and toddlers you educate and their families.

- Listen, truly listen to words, intonation patterns, and body language. Ask questions to gain understanding and listen and reflect on the answers and what they mean in the context of the infants and toddlers you work with.

- Support positive relationships between all of the settings in which young children live and grow: their homes, the early care and education setting they attend, their neighborhood, and community.

SOURCE: McMullen and Dixon (2006).

Mobile infants enjoy one-on-one interactions from supportive and responsive adults.

How Mobile Infants Learn

Mobile infants learn through active exploration of materials and objects. They learn through the use of their senses. They continuously absorb the sights and sounds of the world around them, whether events are planned or happen spontaneously. Building on what they have previously learned, they add new ideas, words, and thoughts. This building process results in learning. Learning happens during the active experiences children are involved with on a daily basis and when there are adults in the environment who provide the necessary scaffolding to support learning.

Play is the work of childhood. The curriculum is play. Through play, children learn cognitive, social, emotional, language, motor, and adaptive skills. They perfect motor skills, they learn to cooperate and share ideas, and they learn practical aspects of math, science, reading, social studies, and communication skills. The secure play environment allows them to make mistakes and take risks without feeling pressure to be perfect. Play fosters a lifelong attitude whereby children learn to use play to relax. Play develops these skills well because it is so unpredictable. It constantly requires infants, toddlers and educators to reevaluate and to not only go with the flow but make the flow into individualized learning experiences.

Experiences can help young toddlers express their feelings in actions when they do not have the vocabulary to use words. It is important to think about play and the characteristics of play. Play is fun. Play is done for the process, not the outcome. However, there is more to play than mere fun. Play needs to be challenging, but not impossibly difficult, to hold interest. Play takes place in a relaxed environment.

From a Piagetian viewpoint, by playing with objects, exploring their different uses, and thinking about them, children come to understand objects and cause-and-effect relationships. They construct their own knowledge. Children's active involvement is an important aspect of play. Understanding and knowledge develop when the child discovers "new" ways to accomplish something through manipulating the objects in her world. Play occurs when the child suspends reality-based uses for objects and creates unique uses for these objects based on her needs or desires. For example, the toddler who uses a block as a telephone is playing rather than exploring the properties of blocks.

Mobile infants need more than nice toys and equipment to play with. They need to have warm, caring interactions with adults. Knowledgeable adults expand play by imitation, then modify and provide scaffolding for the play. They respond to the child's play, demonstrating that his behavior has consequences. If a mobile infant is using playdough, the adult might expand the play by initially manipulating the playdough and then making a pancake, snake, or little balls out of it. The infant can decide whether or not to add these actions to his repertoire of playdough behaviors. A modification might involve adding a rolling pin or cookie cutters to help the infant use the dough in a different way if he has completed his exploration process.

Mobile infants are learning many things about their world. They may not understand at first that the water from the faucet sprays when they hold their hands too close. They require time to experiment as well as verbal scaffolding that helps them understand the relationship between where they hold their hands and what the water does. Likewise, if they are playing with the playdough, they will learn that the harder they roll the thinner the dough gets.

They also need to learn that if they hit someone and hurt him he may cry or bite. They learn more when adults elaborate on their play and are responsive to them.

Verbal interactions with adults encourage the child's language, problem solving, self-esteem, and social skills. Acknowledgment of a child's actions and choices helps focus his attention, and repeating his verbalizations increases the likelihood of his verbalizing again. Talk with mobile infants about what they are doing and ask them questions that relate to their play even though they may not answer them. Demonstrate different ways to play with an object. If children are hitting beach balls with their hands, casually demonstrate how to hit the beach ball with an elbow, head, foot, or cardboard tube. This is the type of scaffolding Vygotsky feels is necessary for young children to learn in their zone of proximal development.

On busy days it is easy to forget how important individual time with a mobile infant is. Spending time alone with a young child communicates to him that you like him and that he is important to you. This is an important time for learning. Take advantage of special time you have with one child before the other children arrive, or when a child wakes early from nap. As in families, individual time is important for all children in early care and education. Mobile infants just learning to move about independently may want to spend their whole time crawling, cruising, or walking. An adult can follow them about and talk about what they are doing. The adult should spend some time working on developing skills. Try to achieve a balance, however, of planned activities that are responsive to the child's interests and of following the child's immediate choice or lead.

Adults are responsible for planning children's play. This includes generating goals and objectives for the group as well as individual mobile infants, gathering appropriate materials, planning how time will be spent and the procedures that will be used. It also includes organizing materials so that only one or two special experiences are available at a time. For instance, have several trucks and cars with play people to put in and take out of the vehicles. When interest wanes, add something such a gas station to make the play more complex. Ask questions that increase the complexity. If the interest is gone, bring out a new activity, such as large interlocking blocks. Mobile infants need choices, so have other options available if some mobile infants are not interested in the main one, but do not have so many choices that they get overwhelmed.

Part of all child care programs are patterns and routines. Although they are an essential part of care, they also guide social development and provide opportunities to teach behavior regulation and help children regulate emotions (Butterfield, Martin, & Prairie, 2003).

MATERIALS AND METHODS FOR WORKING WITH MOBILE INFANTS

Mobile infants need toys to support their newfound mobility, their autonomy, and their emerging skills at imaginative play. They need toys to push, pull, and climb on and over. They need toys for solo play and some toys that are more social. There should be a variety of toys from several categories rather than just one or two types. See Table 13–15 for selecting toys for mobile infants.

Even the best toys are enhanced by adult interactions. Mobile infants need to play alone, but they also need your encouragement, assistance, and scaffolding.

Select some toys and materials from all the areas listed in Table 13–15. The actual materials will depend on the age and developmental level of the group and what they are interested in. Mobile infants vary greatly in skill level and need a variety of materials to choose and use. Adults must provide enough materials for each child; have duplicates of popular toys; and provide enough space for mobile infants to use materials. Educators should select toys that are safe, durable, cleanable, appealing to mobile infants, realistic, versatile, and developmentally appropriate.

Whatever the play experience, the purpose of the interaction with toys and materials is to be fun but educational. Learning occurs at the point where mobile infants are challenged between what they already know and what they can learn with adult support: Remember Vygotsky's zone of proximal development.

Table 13–15 Selecting Toys for Mobile Infants

- *Toys that encourage movement:* pull toys, push toys (including ones that do not tip easily for beginning walkers), balls, small vehicles

- *Toys with pieces that fit together:* shape sorters, simple puzzles (three to six pieces with and without knobs), blocks, stacking rings

- *Toys that require pressure to put together or take apart:* large interlocking blocks that fit together, "pop" beads, rubber puzzles, pegboards and plastic-knobbed pegs, giant blocks or links that snap together

- *Toys with varied textures:* texture rattles, balls, and blocks, fuzzy puppets

- *Toys that make noise:* musical toys, squeaky toys

- *Toys that involve cause-and-effect relationships:* wind-up toys, "busy boxes," building blocks

- *Toys with hidden parts:* jack-in-the-boxes

- *Toys that encourage talking:* toy telephones, puppets, cardboard boxes

- *Toys that encourage pretending:* play dishes, picnic supplies, hats, dolls, pounding benches

- *Toys for cuddling:* stuffed dolls and huggables

SCHEDULES, ROUTINES, AND TRANSITIONS

A schedule for mobile infants includes time for free play, indoors and outside, and for routine events such as eating, napping, and diapering. Providing mobile infants with a predictable schedule and consistent approaches to routines such as sleeping, diapering, and eating helps them develop self-regulation (Bronson, 2000). When temporal and behavioral patters are consistent, repetitious, and frequent they become internalized. They allow mobile infants to anticipate events and learn behaviors that support development (Butterfield, 2002). They provide a sense of safety and security. They make the unknown known.

Much of the planning for transitions and routine care are continuations of patterns developed for younger infants.

Arrival Time

As with infants this is a time for the transitions from parent care to other care. Information is exchanged, daily schedules brought in, and then the impending separation. Ritualizing separations can make them easier. It again allows mobile infants to be part of a predictable sequence. Rituals are very individual and usually grow out of how parents and infants traditionally separate. Infants need support from both caregivers. Rituals may involve the reading of a favorite book. Hanging up a coat and then washing hands before standing quietly by a favorite adult as she talks about experiences of potential interest. The ritual, whatever it is, provides security for the child and his move into care.

Young children are often interested in learning self-help skills such as dressing and undressing themselves. The natural opportunities for dressing and undressing typically come during arrival and departure times, or other transition times when children are going outside or coming inside. These times are frequently stressful. Sometimes the thought of putting mobile infants in snowsuits, boots, and mittens is enough to make even the staunchest believer in outside play stay inside. The long-term solution is to have mobile infants become more self-sufficient and independent in these tasks. To do this they need unhurried time. If this can be built into a ritual after the parent leaves, this is a great time for settling in.

Undressing is easier than dressing, so begin with undressing. For undressing, have the child do just the last part of the task, such as taking off her coat when it is unzipped and loosened. Gradually have the child do more of the task. Encourage the mobile infant for her efforts. Starting with something the infant can feel successful about encourages her to continue learning these skills and to try more difficult sequences. Providing specific feedback builds skills. Work on the mobile infant's body awareness *and* motor planning skills as she figures out which leg goes where, how hats and mittens fit, and how to pull shoes off.

Naptime

A much larger portion of the child's day is spent playing and proportionately less in routines, particularly sleeping. Sleep patterns are gradually changing. However, sleep patterns and schedules are still very individual. Setting up a routine for naps is important. When infants are about a year old or so their sleeping becomes more predictable and naptimes become more uniform. There is a general expectation that most mobile infants will take two naps during the day: one in the morning and one in the afternoon. However, some may be moving toward only taking a longer afternoon nap that begins earlier. It truly depends on the infant. And the transition from one to two naps is often challenging for everyone. Good programs are respectful of these differences. Mobile infants may nap on low cots instead of in cribs.

Some toddlers have problems going to sleep. Soft soothing music may help some toddlers. Put toddlers to sleep in the same place each day. This adds a sense of security. They need clean blanket and sheets as well as some **attachment object** from home.

Attachment objects are items such as blankets or a particular stuffed animal that help the infant feel secure.

up close and personal

Sleep was a nightmare with our youngest daughter. She was what we expected as an infant. But instead of getting better, it began to get worse when she was about 15 months old. Because she had climbed out of her crib once, she slept in a very low bed. She would wake up between 2 and 22 times a night. She would walk out of her room and walk to ours and call our names. If she wanted me, my husband went. Then we took shifts. We bought a king-size bed in hopes that one of us would be able to sleep through the night. I talked to her pediatrician. He suggested we lock her in her room. I couldn't do that. Her brother and sister were older and practiced their musical instruments every night right after she went to sleep. We had the rule, "You wake it, you take it." She never woke to their music. It was always later. She had ear infections almost constantly. First the infections were bacterial, then viral. We had her hearing tested and they said she had fluid in her ears and suggested we see an allergist. Ultimately what we discovered was that she was allergic to almost everything. So, when she would lie down to sleep she was fine. As time went on, however, she couldn't breath. Getting vertical solved the problem for her. Allergy medicine solved the problem for us. It really didn't matter what we did in response to her demands, it was a medical problem, and her sleep problem was solved once we discovered this. It was solved in a very different way than we expected. But that year is a still a blur in our lives.

We tried to put her in child care during this year. She didn't take long enough naps. She would sleep and then get up. The child care center told us that if we couldn't figure out how to make her sleep she couldn't stay. She didn't. It was a problem.

REFLECTIVE PRACTICE

If parents talk about infants who do not sleep, consider a variety of possibilities. What could cause an infant not to sleep through the night by 12 to 14 months? What are some possible hypotheses or alternatives? Think broadly. Decide on the questions you might ask parents as they struggle with being tired and having a child who does not sleep.

Eating and Mealtimes

Mobile infants are usually starting to have teeth and bite, instead of just mouthing objects. With teeth and better arm and finger control they can drink from a cup independently or with some adult assistance, and they can feed themselves using both their fingers and a spoon. Fingers are still more reliable. As physical growth slows, children may eat less than previously.

Cereal is introduced, then fruits and vegetables, followed by meat or meat substitutes. Initially, individual foods are introduced rather than mixtures, so if food allergies develop they can be more easily identified. Finger food such as dry bread and crackers are also introduced around this time. Although infants prefer sweet foods and then salty ones, with the concerns related to early childhood obesity this is not a preference to encourage. At the beginning, all foods are new to infants and they may reject these new foods.

Rather than deciding that an infant does not like a particular food that is rejected, the key is to continue to offer a particular food. Looking and smelling is not enough. The infant actually has to eat the food before it enters the familiar category and is accepted (Birch, Johnson, & Fisher, 1995). This may have a biological, adaptive base. Putting food into the body is risky. What if you eat something poisonous and die? As you eat and stay healthy, you eat the same foods again. When you consider the vast variety of foods that infants eat throughout the world, there is some credibility for this position. But it means that infants have to offered foods as many as 15 times before they are accepted.

Eating should be a relaxed social experience, even for infants. Talk or sing to infants when they are eating. Name the foods they are eating, describe the tastes and textures. Encourage them and support their competence as they begin to feed themselves with finger foods. Encourage infants to explore and play with empty cups and spoons. If mothers are still nursing, ensure that they are comfortable and feel supported.

Diapering

Diapering should follow the routines of young infancy. This should also be taken as an opportunity to have some one-on-one time with a mobile infant. This is also a time when infants can work on dressing and undressing as well as instilling habits about hand washing. Singing songs such as "Mary Had a Little Lamb" while washing hands teaches mobile infants (and caregivers) how long they need to wash hands to ensure that they are clean.

Mobile infants are learning to feed themselves. Although they can often use a spoon when they are really hungry, they rely on their fingers.

Departure Time

Follow the general procedures detailed for young infants. Mobile infants may be involved in what they are doing when parents come to pick them up and may be reluctant to leave. Other mobile infants will be eager to go as soon as they spot their parents. Again, having a ritual helps make the transition an easier one. It is also a time when parents and educators talk briefly about the day, noting how it went and if there any unusual occurrences, highlights, or concerns.

Routine Record Keeping

Although it is necessary to keep records and have a daily report, the information for mobile infants falls between infants and toddlers and the most useful forms are dependent on the organization of the child care setting. For mobile infants from 8 to 12 or 13 months, the forms used for young infants (see Chapter 12) work best. As they are eating more solid food and drinking milk and are more regular about sleeping, forms become less focused on exact quantities eaten and more on evaluative comments such as how well they ate. With meals and snacks at more predictable times, parents have a better idea of when things are happening. Naptimes are noted by length and often include a qualitative statement about how naptime went. There needs to be a place for communicating things that are needed and information about what went on during the day. A form that is typically used for toddlers is given in Chapter 14.

Communicating with parents remains an important area. With mobile infants, parental concern begins to move from biological functions to social, emotional, and cognitive development. Although parents of mobile infants will want to know generally about sleeping and eating, they are often more concerned about the social and emotional aspects of their child's day. Because children are so variable, knowing whether or not theirs had a "good" or "bad" day is important for parents. The following information is useful as a guide for informal regular communications (see Table 13–16).

Table 13–16 Communicating with Parents on a Daily Basis

- Parents need information about the daily experiences of children.
- Parents want a consistent system of recording information on a daily basis. This may be a message board, a notebook that travels with the child, or any system that works for you.
- Parents want to know that you accept and like their child in all of his quick-shifting moods. It is imperative that you show these feelings to both the child and the parents, even on "bad" days.
- Parents need to hear information from you about their child and his successes on a regular basis, no matter how small the accomplishments may seem.

INCLUDING ALL MOBILE INFANTS

Inclusive programs are the norm. One expects to see children with disabilities in the classrooms they would be in if they did not have a disability. Teaching in an inclusive classroom requires additional skills. Adults must be aware that social interactions may not occur spontaneously. Adults must often facilitate positive social interactions between children with disabilities and those without. Ways to encourage positive interactions include: supporting the achievements of all infants, even when these accomplishments are different; modeling appropriate behavior for infants; and encouraging empathy and prosocial behaviors in children (see Table 13–17).

Table 13–17 Supporting All Mobile Infants

• Say the infant's name (this serves as a marker for getting his attention), then tell him what he has done in short, simple language, and that it pleases you.
• Be responsive to cues from mobile infants that indicate understanding, interest, frustration, or fatigue.
• Provide many opportunities to manipulate and explore objects and materials. Give mobile infants time to explore materials before expecting then to use the materials.
• Provide experiences that are developmentally appropriate for the skills and goals of each individual infant in the program.

Adapting Toys for Mobile Infants with Disabilities

Most of the toys and materials you would use for any mobile infant can be used with infants who have disabilities; others may require minor modifications. If there are major modifications, parents or specialists will typically provide this equipment (see Table 13–18 for adaptations).

Table 13–18 Adaptations to Include All Mobile Infants

• Slightly deflated beach balls are easier than regular rubber balls for mobile infants to grasp, throw, and catch.
• Toys can be hung above a child who is not moving independently but is interested in looking at or reaching for and grasping the toys. Toys can be hung from the upright handle of an infant seat, above a changing table, or (if you are really ambitious!) you can attach a pulley to the ceiling and hang toys from a rope. Use of the pulley allows you to easily adjust the height of the toys for various children. If infants are grasping toys and pulling them, be sure that this equipment is strong enough to be safe.
• Toys with several parts (such as simple puzzles) can be adapted by gluing magnetic strips onto the back of each piece. Use a cookie sheet as a base. Just moving the pieces and taking them on and off the cookie sheet provides some resistance.
• Cut pop beads open and put them over small handles, such as those on a jack-in-the-box, to make them easier to hold. Foam hair curlers can be placed over paint brushes or crayons to make them easier to hold.
• Experiment with different adaptations to see what works. Remember that young children change and grow quickly so that adaptations have to be monitored and evaluated on a continuing basis to be sure that they are developmentally and socially appropriate and are still necessary.

Mobile infants with physical disabilities may need support when sitting to free their hands for play.

If there is no need to modify an experience, then do not. When modifications are necessary, the toys and materials should be appropriate for the child's developmental level and chronological age, promote age-appropriate social and communication skills, and not interfere with regular routines or call undue attention to the child. Although alternative activities may be used, they should be interesting, varied, and available to all the children in the class. In reality, they are not alternatives but activities that are good for all children. Adaptations are useful to all infants who are challenged by an activity.

Mobile Infants with Developmental Delays and Intellectual Disabilities

With increasing age, differences among children become more apparent. Children with developmental delays may have deficits in a variety of areas so that a particular disability is not yet apparent. Mobile infants with intellectual disabilities may also have deficits in other areas but it is clear that intellectual functioning will be involved. They require some modifications in your planning and activities, but these are minor and usually easy adaptations. Depending upon the specific infant, there are also areas that you will want emphasize more than for other infants. Embedding these needed skills into routines in one way to ensure that they are supported (see Table 13–19).

Table 13–19 Adapting the Environment to Include Mobile Infants with Developmental Delays and Intellectual Disabilities

- Use simple direct language and directions.

- Break down difficult activities into small steps. (If you are playing with pop beads, start with two and see if the child can pull them apart. It is far easier to pull them apart then put them together.)

- Model what you want the child to do. Then give her a turn and support her attempts at imitating you. Reflect on her response and decide how effective your scaffolding was. That will determine your next response.

- Emerging skills need to honed by working on variations of that skill. If the infant has learned to roll an orange rubber ball, then have the child roll a tennis ball, a wiffle ball, a yarn ball, a soccer ball, a football, a beach ball, and any other ball you have. She will need more practice than others to master skills.

- Keep activities short. Children with developmental delays have short attention spans and need more support and redirection. They may need more cues to interact with materials.

- Support their social interactions with other infants by cuing them on appropriate responses, modeling behavior, and scaffolding their interactions.

Mobile Infants with Physical Impairments

Children with physical impairments need materials that support the development of their large and small muscles. When other children are beginning to crawl and walk, it is important that you think about other forms of mobility, such as a creeper of some kind where the child can lie on his stomach and roll (or be pushed) if this is appropriate. Professional literature is increasingly focusing on the importance of movement not just for motor skill development but for cognitive development. Scaffolding motor tasks may be challenging. Talk to parents and other professionals who work with the infant to find the best way to do this.

Holding and positioning children with physical impairments is important. Specific information should come from the infant's parents or the physical or occupational therapist (see Table 13–20 for additional ideas).

Table 13–20 Adapting the Environment to Include Mobile Infants with Physical Impairments

- Encourage mobile infants to use all the movements they are capable of.

- Be alert to subtle movements that indicate communication of thoughts or feelings.

- Movement is both internal and external. Infants whose muscles do not move as they want can begin to develop internal neural connections by being in a classroom where they can observe other children moving in ways they want to move.

- Support children's exploration of materials. Ensure that they can reach, touch, and explore the materials.

- Mobile infants are still light enough to carry so ensure that you dance and move with this infant so he experiences movement.

- Have a variety of toys that can ensure movement even for those who cannot move (wagons, creepers, carriages sturdy enough for mobile infants, etc.).

Mobile Infants with Mental Health Challenges

Children with social and emotional disorders cover a broad area and with young children it is sometimes difficult to accurately identify all of the important variables. These problems and disorders fit in the broad area of infant mental health and, at this age, are frequently related to sensory integration and self-regulation. The goal of programming is to identify infant's internal response to sensory input and then to program in a way that is compatible with their internal being. Children can have either high or low sensory thresholds, and within these limits some overreact to small stimuli whereas other children try to avoid stimulation. Some children with high sensory thresholds take a lot of stimulation to get their attention, whereas others seek stimuli. Consult with the psychologist, parents, and occupational therapist on the best ways to adapt programming and to include these mobile infants in your program. You may need to look at the "goodness of fit" between the child's needs and your environment (Williamson & Anzalone, 2001) (see Table 13–21 for additional information).

Identifying mobile infants and meeting their needs is a challenge and takes skill. Too often these children are not identified as having a genuine problem but are just seen as unusual or difficult children.

Table 13–21 Adapting the Environment to Include Mobile Infants with Mental Health Challenges

- For mobile infants with a very low threshold for sensory input, the littlest thing can bother them, like a tag in their clothing. They are distractible, their affect is often negative, and they are impulsive. (Does this sound like the feisty child with the difficult temperament?) If a child is overly sensitive to stimuli, evaluate your environment in this respect. Noisy vacuum cleaners or other children playing noisily may disturb some mobile infants.

- Other mobile infants with low thresholds for stimuli may try to avoid sensory input. They are often quiet and hypervigilant, scanning the environment for someone who might come too close or touch them. Respect the child's concerns and create areas that are safe for him to play without other children getting in his space. Be sure to find ways of letting this child know you like him. Verbal support, such as saying, "Brett, I'm glad to see you this morning," is wiser than a hug. If you do touch the child, do it firmly.

- Some children have high thresholds of arousal. These children may be difficult to arouse and may miss opportunities because they do not engage. Their affect may appear flat or depressed. We often miss these children because they are "good." A light touch may alert this child. Loud music with a varied intensity might get their attention as well.

- Other children with high thresholds seek sensory input. They may be impulsive and take risks for the sensory feedback. They can become overly excited. These are the mobile infants who pull up on shelving, not to see what is on the shelf but to get to the top. For these children, classical music is a better choice; swinging and rhythmical rocking decrease stimulation. A pacifier or thumb sucking also can decrease sensory input.

Mobile Infants with Hearing Impairments

If a hearing impairment has not been identified at birth, it is often during this period that it is suspected. When infants and young toddlers do not meet milestones in the area of speech, they are often referred for a hearing evaluation. Consult with the child's parents and the speech and language pathologist for additional information on how to accommodate and adapt your programming. The accommodations will be based on the degree of the hearing loss and its cause, as well as the parent's decisions on how they plan to have their child educated and the form of language they wish to pursue. For some general accommodations, see Table 13–22.

Table 13–22 Adapting the Environment to Include Mobile Infants with Hearing Impairments

• Use vision and visual cues as the primary input source with appropriate verbal information. Show the child what you want her to do. Model behavior.
• Provide activities that encourage the child to use the hearing she has. Find out what the child is most likely to hear and incorporate these sounds into your curriculum.
• Be aware of extraneous noise in the classroom. Hearing aids amplify all noise, so the child may actually have a hard time concentrating on specific sounds if there is loud background noise.
• Use signs with this child and all the children to communicate some information. Many children who have hearing impairments do not have the language skills to tell you what they want or need.

Mobile Infants with Visual Impairments

With the advent of locomotion, mobile infants with visual impairments may need additional accommodations. Consult with a vision specialist, orientation and mobility specialist, or others involved in providing services to the child about room arrangement, appropriate experiences, and so on. These specialists have information about long-term expectations for the child; that is, whether the child will read using large print or Braille, and useful hints as well. If infants have less severe visual impairments this may be the time your concern heightens when infants do not move toward toys or try to grasp objects in some positions (see Table 13–23 for additional information).

Table 13–23 Adapting the Environment to Include Mobile Infants with Visual Impairments

• Use materials that make sounds when manipulated. Toys that make a noise when they move help children focus on and reach for them.
• Help children locate sound. Make a noise, and when the child turns to the sound, encourage him and give him the noisemaker. Verbally encourage him as well. "Friedrich, I can't fool you. You know where that noise is coming from, don't you. Here is the ball." This supports locating skills through sound.

(continues)

Table 13–23 *(continues)*

- Use whatever sight the mobile infant has available. If she can make distinctions only among toys with high contrast, like black and white, be sure you have toys like this.

- Locomotion is challenging for infants with visual impairments. They frequently walk later than other children and they often use hitching as a means of locomotion instead of creeping or crawling. (Children hitch when they scoot on their bottom. This is very adaptive because they will run into something with their feet, not their head.)

- Provide materials such as large manipulative toys that require two hands, or activities that prohibit self-stimulation behavior, if this is a problem.

Mobile Infants Whose Home Language Is Not English

Locomotion makes all infants able to explore their world. This provides greater potential for learning as well as greater challenges. If families are recent immigrants to the United States, they may have come from regions where the threats to a mobile infant's safety were very different. Mobile infants of immigrant families are more likely to live in crowded housing (more than one person per room) and live in a household that includes people in addition to their parents and siblings (Hernandez, 2004). Crowded conditions may make it difficult for mobile infants to safely explore their environment.

This is a time to reevaluate your learning environment to ensure that it is supportive of the children in the setting. The early childhood classroom constantly provides messages about what the program values, and who is valued, from what hangs on the walls to the experiences educators offer. Bilingual teachers are a tremendous asset in language learning and also in communicating with parents. Research supports infants' ability to learn two languages simultaneously. Settings need to make decisions about how they will support second-language learning. Obviously the choices made are dependent on the goals and philosophy of the program and the available resources (human and material) (see Table 13–24 for additional ideas).

Table 13–24 Adapting the Environment to Include Mobile Infants Whose Home Language Is Not English

- Provide information about childproofing environments and child safety for mobile infants.
- Ensure that mobile infants are encouraged to explore their environment. Provide safe places to crawl, creep, and explore.
- Use CDs that celebrate different cultures, languages, and styles of music.
- Sing songs and use fingerplays in the languages of the infants in the setting.
- Develop effective ways to communicate with families. This may include sharing photographs as a method of communication and assessment.

(continues)

- Value all languages spoken in the classroom, whether or not you can speak them. As infants are learning first words, learn with them. Ask parents to write down the words infants know and how they use them. Develop your own pronunciation code.

- Provide language input. In some Latin American cultures the expectation is that infants and toddlers learn by modeling the behavior of others. In these cultures infants may not have been exposed to much spoken language. Talk to infants.

SUPPORTING SELF-REGULATION

Mobile infants move. Adults need to evaluate their feelings about what young children should or should not be allowed to do and how they will deal with challenging behavior. Feelings about conflict and its resolution need to be incorporated into your philosophy as you expand it to include mobile infants. There is inherent conflict between the mobile infant's growing need for autonomy and the adult's need to maintain control and inculcate values and socially acceptable behavior. One might view this inherent conflict as a continuum between giving the child complete autonomy and breaking his will. This conflict appears first with mobile infants. Adults make a conscious or unconscious choice about where they stand on this issue. Your philosophical position about dealing with conflict has both short- and long-term implications for the children you work with. The skills children learn in dealing with conflict set the groundwork for conflict resolution during their later school years.

Setting limits is part of an adult's commitment to children, not just a reaction to an immediate behavior. Behavior management should fit the child and the situation, and should be accompanied by a conviction that setting limits is an important part of caring for young children. When caring accompanies discipline, it is positive; when there is no caring, it is just punishment. The goals of discipline, then, are two-fold: stopping inappropriate behavior as it occurs and developing long-term inner controls, self-regulation of behavior. Adults can facilitate the development of these inner controls by using positive discipline effectively.

How children act or respond affects the way adults interact with them. Children are different, and some are easier than others. These differences in temperament are relatively permanent and affect adult-child interactions. One key to discipline is the "goodness of fit" between adult expectations and what the mobile infant is emotionally and developmentally capable of doing. What is easy for one child may be close to impossible for another. The infant himself is a variable.

Easy children (those who show moderation in intensity, are adaptable, approachable, have generally positive moods, and a sense of rhythmicity), may stop an inappropriate behavior with only a "teacher look." Slow-to-warm-up

Learning to play together is a challenge for most mobile infants.

children (those who have low activity and intensity levels and take longer to adapt than easy children) may initially require physical cues, such as the adult moving close to them, but as they become aware of the rules, they will become more self-controlled. Teachers need to realize this and pull back to give them more opportunities to establish self-control.

Difficult children (those who have intense reactions, are slow to adapt, nonrhythmical, and often have negative moods) may require physical prompts to stop the same behavior and they may continue to need these prompts. Physical prompts include behaviors such as holding a child, physically helping him put a toy away, placing your hand over his to accomplish a task. Regretfully, children who have difficult temperaments need more adult understanding, yet may actually receive fewer positive responses from adults who do not understand them or know how to work with feisty children.

Sometimes mobile infants, especially difficult ones, will make adults angry, particularly when they hurt another child. Sometimes it is appropriate to tell the infant that her actions made you angry. However, it is imperative to *discipline*, not punish the child's behavior. For example, say firmly to Rochelle, "I don't like it when you bite Carter. It hurts him and it makes me angry." Talking to her at this point is useless. Her emotions were hijacked before the incident occurred. Find something safe for her to do playing alone. It may take as long as 10 minutes for her hormones to come back to a reasonable level so

up **close** and **personal**

Amy had many issues with being grouchy and inflexible. She would have weeks of being difficult to mange and having lots of tantrums. This happened on and off for what seemed like forever. I thought that it could be problems with her ears, but there were never any symptoms other than being grouchy, poking at her ears, waking up many times crying during the night. Then when school began in September and I put her in child care, she got a cold that continued until February. She would get over it, then a few days later it would come back. Antibiotics were not effective at getting rid of it entirely. Finally the doctor recommended going to an ear, nose, and throat specialist. The doctor agreed that tubes were warranted. After receiving the tubes, Amy's speech became clearer and her language exploded. She has not had any more ear infections and her demeanor has changed greatly. The temper tantrums decreased and she has an easier time adjusting to things.

REFLECTIVE PRACTICE

Are there any indications you might have had that some of Amy's behavioral issues might have been related to physical problems? When children are having problems, consider a wide range of possibilities. If the problem is related to the child's health, most behavioral solutions will not solve the problem.

she can listen. Talk to her then and coach her on the skills she should have used when she resorted to biting. It is important to follow up with a child and teach her what the acceptable behavior is. However, you need to give the child time to calm down to hear what you want to say. Even after a situation such as this, reflect on why and how it happened. Is there some way you could change the environment to decrease the probability of this happening again? Infants learn from experience. Learning how to handle conflict is part of what they need to learn. If there is no conflict to be managed, they will have no skills to cope with conflict in the future.

As infants move from infants into mobile infants, their interest in expressing their growing autonomy sometimes impinges on the rights of others. Although early care and education settings have few rules, the ones they have need to be followed and they should focus on the safety of all of the children and ensuring that the setting is a positive learning environment for all mobile infants (see Table 13–25 for guidelines that may be useful).

Table 13–25 Guidelines for Working with Mobile Infants

- Keep a child's developmental level in mind. Expect behavior that is appropriate for his developmental level.

- Take into account a child's cultural and environmental background when deciding how to deal with particular behaviors. In some instances it may be necessary to preface rule statements with reference to a behavior. "When you are in school you must wash your hands before you may have a snack."

- Be firm, persistent, and consistent. Being firm lets children know you are serious and what they are doing is inappropriate. Be persistent—follow through with your consequences. Be consistent—every time the child rips pages from a book, there should be consequences, and they should be the same. (If the adult is firm and persistent, a child usually will only try an inappropriate behavior a few times.) If the adult is wishy-washy, a child is likely to try the behavior more often because he has not learned the limits for his behavior.

- Set reasonable limits. Mobile infants are just learning to share. It is not realistic to expect them to share an especially desirable toy with a friend.

- Let children know that you care for them and are proud of who they are and what they can do. Reinforce them when they act appropriately, or make attempts to please. For example, "Kaitlin, I'm so proud of you. You put the blocks away all by yourself."

- Set up the room so the physical space encourages appropriate behavior. Avoid long paths that encourage running.

- Help children label their feelings verbally when they are upset, angry, or hurt. You might say, "Shawntell, you're really angry because Jacy took your doll."

- Provide reasons for the limits you set. "Marco, you need to walk when you are inside, because the floors are slippery."

- Use patterns and routines to guide positive behavior. Structure provides mobile infants with guidelines.

- Think of rules as instructions, they help focus what has to be done.

Anticipatory Guidance

Following the adage that it is better to prevent spilled milk than to clean it up; consider a preventive approach to discipline. Prevention, or anticipatory guidance, is broad based. It ranges from developmentally appropriate planning to who sits beside whom in a small group. It includes reinforcing appropriate behavior and knowing the cues individual infants give before they "lose it." Rules and limits vary in an infant's home and are based on values, culture, and even time. Some families have predictable mealtimes and bedtimes; others do not. Early care and education settings can help mobile infants learn rules through well-planned routines that provide them with a sense of security and knowledge that parts of their life are predictable. When mobile infants understand patterns, they increase their safety and decrease conflict and anxiety. They have made their world more predictable (Butterfield, 2002).

Reinforcing Appropriate Behavior

One aspect of anticipatory guidance is looking for "the good stuff"; that is, catching children doing something good. The magic is for adults to comment on the desired behaviors they see as much as they can. Children want attention and tend to repeat the behaviors for which someone gives them attention. So, if many comments are made on positive behaviors, children should be showing more of those behaviors.

Comment on the behavior you want to reinforce in a specific but matter-of-fact way. "What a good idea! You got a puzzle for José so that you and he could each have one." Think carefully before making a comment to see if you can turn a potentially negative comment into one that looks at the positive part of what the child is trying to do. When one child takes a toy from other child do not say, "Don't grab that from him, Mikayla." Try instead to reframe the situation and say, "Oh, I see you want to play with a puzzle. Let's see if we can find one for you," or, "Were you trying to help Chris put that puzzle piece in? It looks like he wants to do it by himself. Let's find a puzzle for you." By interpreting part of a behavior as positive, the child can look at himself in a more positive light also. He may feel a relief that an adult saw what he really wanted and helped him get it.

Labeling the Behavior, Not the Infant or Toddler

It is better to label the *behavior* as "bad" rather than the child. For instance, say, "I don't like it when you bite Jamie," rather than, "Only bad girls bite." The child will eventually learn that you do not like her behavior (biting), and not that you do not like her.

Mobile infants are just beginning to understand that others have feelings. You can help them with this process. One way is to give the child who was bitten a lot of caring attention rather than paying negative attention to the child who did the biting. You may also want to verbalize the hurt infant's feelings to increase awareness in others of how it felt. For instance, "Oh, Jamie, that bite must have hurt. How can we make you feel better?" Hold and cuddle the hurt child and attend to her needs. Give less attention to the child who did the biting (if you think the purpose of biting was to gain attention). Try to be understanding of both children's feelings, and try not to make a big deal of the child who did the misdeed. Rather, include that child in the conversation of figuring how to make the hurt infant feel better.

Another way to help infants understand others' feelings is to notice and label different feelings, expressions, and behaviors during the day as you see them occur. For example, "Ryan, you look angry. Do you want *that* truck? You can play with *this* one now or wait until Anna's turn is over." "Oh, Brennan, how thoughtful of you to bring Paten's blanket to her. You know that makes her feel good and helps her go to sleep."

Adults need to actively look for and comment on the positive (good) things infants do every day. Mobile infants like attention and want to please adults. If they are rewarded with positive comments and hugs, they will feel good about themselves. If, however, they only hear from adults when they do something they are not supposed to do, then expect that they will continue to behave negatively to get attention. Children will have conflicts occasionally. You cannot prevent all negative experiences. However, if you are positive most of the time and turn conflicts into learning experiences, more positive behavior is likely to follow. One particular area that is of concern to many is biting.

When an Infant or Toddler Bites

Biting is a relative common experience in that one out of 10 infants or toddlers does it; however, it is disturbing and potentially harmful (National Association for the Education of Young Children [NAEYC], 2006). Understanding why infants bite has implications for how to prevent it. Biting may occur as a way to relieve stress. Although we think about motor and language milestones as positive events to mobile infants they are stressful. To walk and fall or to want to say something others do not understand makes this time stressful. Children may bite because they lack the ability to respond to a situation appropriately (Ramming, Kyger, & Thompson, 2006).

Some infants are experimental biters. They are trying to understand their world and mouthing is one of their ways of doing this. When they have teeth, mouthing turns into biting. They need appropriate things to mouth or bite, but when they bite people they should receive a clear, sharp "no." Experimental biters typically bite their mother's breast or a caregivers' shoulder (NAEYC, 2006).

Frustrated biters are toddlers who lack skills to get what they want. They use biting as a strategy to attain their goal. Tend to the victim and then clearly show the child that biting is not an appropriate behavior and is not allowed. Support this toddler in learning communication skills and finding ways to get his needs met that do not include biting. Positively reinforce children when they communicate effectively, but be alert to times when frustration mounts (NAEYC, 2006).

The threatened biter bites in self-defense. This toddler may be overwhelmed and bites as a way of getting some control. Family situations may make the child feel unsafe, another child may try to take something that is important and the mobile infant fights back with this weapon. Use the techniques described above (NAEYC, 2006).

Some biting may relate to sensory needs; a child's sense of touch and the integration of touch with other senses. A mobile infant may need more texture or stimulation from food choices, such as something crunchy in her diet. As mobile infants are adding foods to their diet chewy snacks, cut into small pieces to prevent choking and under adult supervision, may help (Ramming et al., 2006).

Think broadly for reasons why mobile infants might bite. Work with families for their ideas and look for patterns.

OBSERVING AND RECORDING MOBILE INFANT'S BEHAVIOR

The techniques described for observing and recording young infant's behavior work well for mobile infants. Recorded information is important for curriculum planning and communicating with parents.

COMMUNICATING WITH PARENTS

Sometimes informal parent communication provides the impetus for a closer look at the match between the child and the program, including comments such as, "Jason seems to be bored with school right now," or, "Shaleen used to be eager to go to school and now she seems reluctant to go." Although problems might not be related to the program, that is one alternative that should be considered.

Parent contacts range from the informal greetings and exchanges at arrival and departure to regularly scheduled and specialized conferences. Sometimes important information can be communicated in a matter of moments. However, that does not obviate the need for regularly scheduled conferences to sit back and look carefully at each infant, how he is growing and developing, and how the programming is adapting to these changes. Typically as infants become mobile there is a change in their child care placement. Infants may move from one room to another in the same child care setting or move from a family child care setting to a center-based setting or from home-based care to a child care setting.

TRANSITIONING BETWEEN SETTINGS

I have chosen to use NAEYC guidelines relative to programming for young children and have divided the age ranges into birth to 8 months, 8 to 18 months, and 18 to 36 months. These divisions are based on children's development. Child care settings often have a more practical approach. Their concerns are based on safety and staff-child ratios. In some settings children would experience no transitions in classrooms or teachers for their first three years. This is usually true in family child care and in some child care centers. Other centers may have as many as three planned transitions that are unrelated to staff turnover. For safety reasons many child care centers like to move infants when they become predictably mobile, at about a year. In addition, the ratio of children to teachers increases so that it is economically advantageous to move infants at this time. In reality, although I have divided the programming information to end at 8 months, it is likely that you will use the information relative to transitions when infants are around 12 months and then again as they reach 24 or 36 months.

Decisions as to when to move children out of a particular grouping are made for a variety of reasons. Some of these decisions are based on expediency (there is space); others have a more philosophical base. Mobile infants are typically moved out of an infant setting between 12 and 18 months, perhaps before this if their large-motor skills are very good. If moved in the younger age range, it is typically to a "tweenie" group of toddlers about 12 to 24 months; if the move is later; the age range is often 18 to 36 months.

As infants and toddlers get older, they often move to new rooms or settings and new children join the original group. It is frequently difficult for the young children to leave familiar surroundings and people to face an unknown situation. It may also be stressful for an adult when a mobile infant she likes very much leaves and is replaced with an unknown child with whom she has to build a relationship. Changing just one child in a group can change the entire group's dynamics. When children are moving from one group to another within the same setting, for example, from an infant to a toddler group, there are steps you can take to make the move easier. Similarly, these procedures can be taken when a child first joins the group.

Infant and toddler programs are different. Infant programs are more individualized and personalized and there are fewer infants and more adults. In infant programs, typically an adult is assigned to an infant as a primary caregiver. Mobile infants typically choose their own primary adult based on their preferences. Toddler programs have more complex social demands from peers and a different daily routine.

Changes in settings cause stress for all the individuals involved: the mobile infant joining the group, the parent leaving the child with different caregivers, and the caregivers receiving the new child. To make this transition easier for everyone, see Table 13–26.

Entering a new room is a difficult time for all, especially as it is accompanied by internal growth in the mobile infant himself. It is unwise to begin this

Table 13–26 Supporting Transitions

- Encourage parents to visit the new room before the transition and talk with staff about the transitioning process.

- Expect the transition to take 4 to 6 weeks. Begin the transition gradually with a short visit (about half an hour) to the new room with a trusted adult. This time is gradually extended and the mobile infant is drawn into the new group. The familiar adult may leave, but will return for the child. When all feel comfortable, the mobile infant will become a permanent member of this new group.

- When possible, have mobile infants who know each other go through this group transition at the same time.

- Borrow some toys the mobile infant is familiar with, particularly ones that are huggable and more "homelike," from the infant room.

- Support mobile infants in dramatic play. They may "play out" their concerns, or give you insight into what it is that they are concerned about.

- Read stories about children beginning school, or about the beginning of any new event.

process at a time when other major changes are happening in the family (the birth of a new baby, family separations, vacations, etc.). The transition should be made either before or after these events. And clearly it should not be tied to the event if it is a negative event (from the mobile infant's perspective).

Although these suggestions would not entirely eliminate problems at transition times, they should reduce them. Anticipating possible problems and planning strategies to avoid them is useful. Some thoughtful planning that deals with your individual situation and the needs of the toddlers is likely to be helpful as well. Having mobile infants understand exactly what you expect of them during transition times is a first step. They need to feel secure and know that there are rules and that the adult is in control. Expect some testing behavior at transition time. A calm but firm response is reassuring.

SUMMARY

Mobile infants make tremendous strides between 8 and 18 months. The first step and the first word are an indication of what is to come. Planning is still very individual, but as infants get closer to 18 months there is more planning for small groups of two or three infants. Relationships are still the most important part of the curriculum. Mobile infants are struggling with social behaviors such as turn-taking. Simple games that adults play with toddlers help this learning process.

Mobile infants are born to move. Their energy is in locomotion. Infants' ability to move changes curriculum planning and how the classroom is set up. The ability to talk also changes the curriculum as mobile infants are beginning to express their wants and needs to a far greater extent than young infants. A well-equipped developmentally appropriate environment and well educated, respectful early childhood educators are the best tools for learning for mobile infants.

Schedules and routines take up less of the day, making mobile infants more available for play. Including all infants in a setting requires some general adaptations and some that are based on a specific child's needs. All mobile infants are struggling to learn self-regulation, which is why well-trained educators are so important. Communicating with parents on a daily basis continues. Mobile infants who are in early care and education settings will typically transition to another room at some point during this time span.

CHAPTER IN REVIEW

- ※ As young children become mobile, planning must support their emerging mobility and the fact that they can make more active choices regarding the experiences they want to engage in and how long they chose the stay.

- ※ Environments need to be evaluated in light of mobility and sensitive adults need to set limits to keep mobile infants safe.

- ※ Planning is a combination of offering choices and planning specific experiences for individual children or small groups.

- ※ At 8 months, infants need adults to actively support their play; by 18 months, mobile infants can play side by side with adult scaffolding.

- ※ Adults support the mobile infant's learning by arranging the environment so it is developmentally appropriate and available to them.

- ※ Transitions and routine care take up less time and mobile infants have more time to engage in play.

- ※ Transitions between classrooms need to be well planned and gradual to allow the toddlers, parents, and educators time to adjust.

- ※ With increasing age, planning becomes less individualized and more oriented to groups of two or three children.

APPLICATION ACTIVITIES

1. Explain to the mother of a mobile toddler who is concerned about his decreased food intake and his picky eating why this might be happening. Share with her what you know about obesity prevention and how she might evaluate her concerns in light of this information.

2. Explain to a parent or colleague the value of play and its importance to the mobile infant. Include information as to why play teaches infants more than direct instruction.

3. Describe how you would modify the curriculum and classroom for a mobile infant with

   a. Low threshold for sensory input who is overly sensitive to stimuli

b. Low threshold for stimuli input who tries to avoid sensory input

c. High threshold of arousal who only responds to varied intensity of input

d. High threshold of sensory who seeks sensory input.

4. Given the basic web you have in Figure 13–1 how would you begin to program for these two mobile infants?

RESOURCES

Web Resources

※ **Best Children's Music** provides reviews and commentary on music by age group, including infants and toddlers. You can even listen before you choose to buy something. http://www.bestchildrensmusic.com/.

※ The **Early Head Start National Resource Center** has a variety of information available about Early Head Start as well as health and safety and useful multimedia. www.ehsnrc.org

※ The **High/Scope Educational Research Foundation** supports an Infant-Toddler Curriculum based on the principle that children learn best through direct, hands-on experiences with people, objects, events, and ideas. Learning and development are anchored by long term, trusting relationships with caregivers. Adults scaffold further learning as they interact with infants and toddler throughout the day. http://www.highscope.org.

※ **Mother Goose Programs for Children's Education and Preschool Reading**, supported by the Vermont Center for the Book, has an extensive list of books for infants and toddlers as well as other materials to support literacy. http://www.mothergooseprograms.org.

※ The **National Infant and Toddler Child Care Initiative** at Zero to Three works collaboratively with the Administration for Children and Families to provide information on child care and the development of the infant/toddler specialist. http://www.nccic.org.

Print Resources

※ Bardige, B. S., & Segal, M. M. (2005). *Poems to learn to read by: Building literacy with love.* Washington, DC: Zero to Three Press.

※ Lally, J. R., & Mangione, P. (2006). The uniqueness of infancy demands a responsive approach to care. *Young Children, 61*(4), 14–20.

※ Williamson, G. G., & Anzalone, M. E. (2001). *Sensory integration and self-regulation in infants and toddlers: Helping very young children interact with their environment.* Washington, DC: Zero to Three.

REFERENCES

Birch, L. L., Johnson, S. L., & Fisher, J. A. (1995). Children's eating: The development of food acceptance patterns. *Young Children, 50*(2), 71–78.

Bronson, M. B. (2000). *Self-regulation in early childhood: Nature and nurture.* New York: Guilford.

Butterfield, P. M. (2002). Child care is rich in routines. *Zero to Three, 22*(4), 29–32.

Butterfield, P. M., Martin, C. A., & Prairie, A. P. (2003). *Emotional connections: How relationships guide early learning.* Washington, DC: Zero to Three.

Chess, S., & Thomas, A. (1977). Temperamental individuality from childhood to adolescence. *Journal of Child Psychiatry, 16*, 218–226.

Gillespie, L. G., & Seibel, N. L. (2006). Self-regulation: A cornerstone of early childhood development. *Young Children, 61*(4), 34–39.

Hernandez, D. J. (2004). Demographic change and the life circumstances of immigrant families. *The Future of Children, 14*(2), 17–39.

Hughes, F. P. (1999). *Children, play, and development* (3rd ed.). Needhan Heights, MA: Allyn & Bacon.

Lally, J. R., & Mangione, P. (2006). The uniqueness of infancy demands a responsive approach to care. *Young Children, 61*(4), 14–20.

McMullen, M. B., & Dixon, S. (2006). Building on common ground: Unifying practice with infant/toddler specialists through a mindful, relationship-based approach. *Young Children, 61*(4), 46–52.

National Association for the Education of Young Children. (2006). What to do about biters. Retrieved May 31, 2007, from http://www.naeyc.org/ece/2003/05.asp

Ramming, P., Kyger, C. S., & Thompson, S. D. (2006). A new bit on toddler biting: The influence of food, oral motor development, and sensory activities. *Young Children, 61*(2), 17–23.

Roskos, K. A., Tabors, P. O., & Lenhart, L. A. (2004). *Oral language and early literacy in preschool: Talking, reading, and writing.* Newark, DE: International Reading Association.

Williamson, G. G., & Anzalone, M. E. (2001). *Sensory integration and self-regulation in infants and toddlers: Helping very young children interact with their environment.* Washington, DC: Zero to Three.

chapter 14

Curriculum and Planning for Toddlers: 16 to 36 Months

Chapter Outline

- Developmentally Appropriate Planning for Toddlers
- Implementing the Curriculum for Toddlers
- Materials and Methods for Working with Toddlers
- Schedules, Routines, and Transitions
- Including All Toddlers
- Supporting Self-Regulation
- Managing Challenging Behavior

The changes that occur between 16 and 36 months are dramatic. Toddlers move from tentative walking to running, climbing, jumping, and twirling around. They learn to throw and sometimes catch a ball, to pick up small objects with their fingers, to scribble, and to feed themselves. They learn to dress themselves in easy-to-put-on-and-take-off clothing and most learn to use the toilet. They can talk and they are learning to share and take turns. They know they can impact their world and they want to. Most of all they are learning about themselves.

WHY STUDY CURRICULUM AND PLANNING FOR TODDLERS?

- ☀ Toddlers are reaching real milestones in self-definition and have a clearer understanding of self and others.

- ☀ Toddlers focus on self-definition sometimes makes them resistant to adult direction.

- ☀ Educators' role becomes one of setting boundaries to ensure the safety of toddlers and to be there for them when boundaries are breached.

- ☀ Educators' roles remain that of the facilitator who plans appropriate environments for learning, allows children to choose and scaffolds their learning and not the teacher who instructs toddlers; toddler are not taught they learn.

- ☀ Curriculum planning must offer toddlers more choices to allow for individual differences and to anticipate developmental learning.

- ☀ Curriculum planning must keep the toddler in the center yet find common interests so toddlers can build skills in peer relationships.

Infants move through three major developmental stages during their first three years. From birth until about six to eight months the focus is on developing a sense of security. With mobile infants internal needs focus on moving and exploration. Between 16 and 36 months the focus changes again. Most toddlers are proficient movers and now their need to explore is replaced by a drive to define the self. "Interactions and negotiations with others lead to learning about themselves as independent, dependent and interdependent beings" (Lally & Mangione, 2006, 17). Again, the role of caregivers must change. The role of caregivers is one of setting boundaries to help toddlers learn about themselves and the societal rules that govern interactions. Adults must supportive but also provide security for the toddler and enforce boundaries that are set.

Toddlers build their sense of self through interactions with others. Infants who are picked up when they cry have a different sense of self than those who are not responded to. The sense of self is not taught it is learned. Toddlers who are given choices learn to choose. Toddlers who are listened to learn to listen. The sense of self is defined through relationships. And, with infants and toddlers these relationships need to be warm, caring, and responsive.

DEVELOPMENTALLY APPROPRIATE PLANNING FOR TODDLERS

Toddlers are challenging to adults in very different ways than young infants and mobile infants. Some adults feel very comfortable working with toddlers. For these adults it is like being able to watch a person unfold and develop with all of the trials and tribulations that are inherent in the process. Others prefer to work with infants; they like the dependency and the caring of this age more than the budding autonomy of toddlerhood. See Table 14–1 for some characteristics that make toddlers challenging for adults to deal with.

Table 14–1 Characteristics that Make Toddlers Challenging

- Toddlers have a high need to practice their emerging independence. This is often characterized by the word "No!"

- Toddlers show intense emotional swings for no apparent reason.

- Toddlers are messy. They lack adult coordination, so they are often clumsy, spill things, and knock things over. They learn by doing.

- Toddlers are active, they appear to be in constant motion, and they do not slow down.

- Toddlers are egocentric. They can only understand their own perspective. This is different from being selfish.

- Toddlers have limited language skills. They cannot put their feelings into words.

- Toddlers also have limited knowledge. Adults may make requests of them that are outside their range of knowledge. An adult may ask a toddler to handle a pet gently, and when he handles the pet roughly the adult may decide that he was not responding to the request. In reality he may not know what gentle means and an adult may have to show him how to act gently.

- Toddlers periodically have separation anxiety as their increasing knowledge of object permanence and long-term memory increases. They know their parents exist when they cannot be seen and they miss them.

- Toddlers learn about their world by grabbing, hitting, biting, and pushing both animate and inanimate objects. These are *normal* behaviors for toddlers, but they are not pleasant nor acceptable behaviors.

- Toddlers have a very limited understanding of time. This makes it difficult for them to wait for things and also difficult to delay gratification. Asking a toddler to wait 10 minutes for lunch does not mean much to him as he has no concept of 10 minutes.

These characteristics make toddlers a particularly challenging and rewarding group of children to work with. They have mobility but lack many of the "common sense" attributes that adults typically assume goes with it. For me, interacting with toddlers is better than reading all the brain research in understanding how children think, problem solve, and learn.

Planning That Keeps Toddlers in the Center

Although it is tempting to move into theme and unit plans that are frequently used for preschool children, toddlers are not there yet. If there is a theme for toddlers it is a consistent one: "All about Me!" Toddlers are struggling with self-definition so the curriculum must reflect their interest in themselves, what they do and how they do it, how they are different from and the same as others. The curriculum still emerges from what and who they are and who they are trying to be.

See Figure 14–1 for a basic web for four toddlers. I have purposefully included a toddler with an identified disability so that you can see how easy it is to include him. You can meet his specific needs and respond to his strengths while you are planning for all of the toddlers in the room. You also have his family's experience in the identification and evaluation process and the IFSP that was designed for him in Chapter 11.

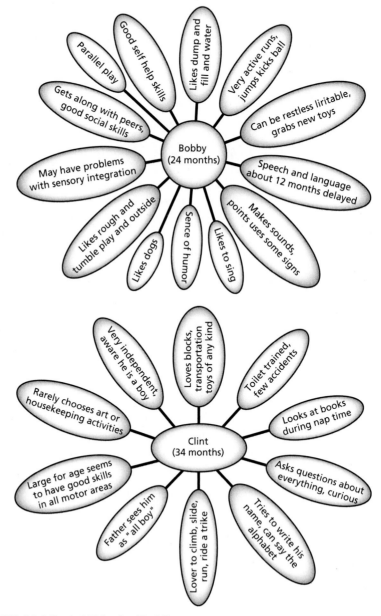

FIGURE 14–1 Basic Webs for Toddlers

FIGURE 14–1 *(continued)*

Although planning is still individualized it is important to include at least one activity from each of the planning areas each day. Because toddlers need choices, it is even better to include more than one if you can support this. Some emergent curriculum favors one area over another, so be sure to think creatively of ways to incorporate all **developmental domains**.

Developmental domains are the areas of social, emotional, motor, language, cognitive, and aesthetic development.

Experiences That Support Social and Emotional Development

Toddlers are emotional beings. They are learning to identify, label, and demonstrate their feelings. They display a range of emotions, from pure delight to utter frustration and sadness, from open curiosity and gregariousness to extreme shyness, from happy cooperation to obstinate noncompliance, and from tender loving to hurtful anger.

Toddlers are beginning to understand themselves as separate individuals with rights and privileges. However, they are only beginning to see that others have these same rights. They are more aware of their own feelings than the feelings of others. This is the stage of increasing independence and possessiveness. You will hear exclamations such as "mine!" "me do it," and "no!" as toddlers try to assert control over their environment. They notice other children in their world and struggle with building social play skills, sometimes eager to share toys with another child and sometimes hoarding all toys for themselves.

Toddlers who feel good about themselves can accept themselves as they are. They can also accept others, for social awareness involves the toddler's growth as a member of a community of learners. To be part of the group, toddlers must learn to share materials, take turns, listen at appropriate times, work independently, and also join the group.

With increasing age, self-awareness grows. Two-year-olds can tell you their name, their gender, the members of their family, and their ethnic background. They know where they live. They also become aware of ways in which they are similar to and different from others. They become aware of their strengths and limitations. They learn about themselves by the way others respond to them.

Toddlers gradually become aware of their nearby environment, their home and early care and education setting, and the community in which they live. They do this by taking short field trips, going to the grocery store, and visiting others. They see people who look different than they do. They see adults performing many different tasks. Going out into the community helps toddlers learn about the complexities of their environment.

One aspect of social awareness for toddlers is learning about their own cultural and ethnic background. Early childhood programs can consciously promote an awareness of the positive aspects and similarities of all individuals regardless of race, ethnicity, gender, or disability. Toddlers need to learn who they are and who their friends are. They need opportunities to explore similarities and differences with the goal of learning mutual respect and cooperation.

Toddlers do not need multicultural "lessons." They do need the opportunity to interact with friends and adults from different backgrounds, to be exposed to good role models, and to feel good about themselves as human beings. Good programs incorporate many of the ideas detailed in Table 14–2.

Table 14–2 Supporting Toddlers' Social and Emotional Development

- Recognize and treat each toddler as a special person. Acknowledge cultural differences and discuss them as an ongoing, normal integrated part of the day. Although not supporting the "holiday curriculum," take advantage of different celebrations to learn about different customs.

- Include books in your library that have pictures of young children of different ethnic backgrounds and stories about different cultures. If your center includes children whose home language is not English, ensure that you have some books in each toddler's home language.

- Invite parents to share their cultural heritage with toddlers. This may be through traditional dress, ethnic foods, photographs, art, or stories and songs.

- Talk with toddlers about ways in which they are similar to others, as well as characteristics that make them unique. Celebrate each child's specialness.

- Pair toddlers with a "new friend" to accomplish a task during a small-group experience. This expands friendship patterns and allows you to include all children.

Health, Safety, and Nutrition

Health, safety, and nutrition are aspects of social and emotional development and are both matters of concern and areas of study. As toddlers become aware of what it means to be healthy and develop the knowledge and vocabulary to describe where they hurt, there is less likelihood of undetected illness. When they learn to recognize signs of danger and act appropriately, the environment will be safer for them. Only healthy toddlers who feel safe and secure can participate fully in early childhood programs.

As toddlers learn to label their body parts and become more aware of their body, they can take a more active role in their health care. This is also a time when toddlers are curious about their own bodies and those of others. You may need to discuss "good" touch and "bad" touch. Toddlers need to know that when touch makes them feel uncomfortable they should talk to an adult that they trust. Toddlers can learn health routines early, such as washing their hands before eating and after toileting. They can learn about appropriate clothing for different types of weather and about good nutrition (see Table 14–3).

Table 14–3 Supporting Toddlers' Health, Nutrition, and Safety

- Point out the differences between warm weather and cold weather clothing as well as clothing for rain and protection from sun as children are dressing to go outside or as they come in, to help toddlers learn the relationship between clothing and weather.
- Teach toddlers basic health practices as part of daily routines (such as washing their hands after toileting and before snack).
- Present toddlers with healthy snacks to choose from, such as vegetables (microwave briefly); cutup fresh, frozen, or canned fruit; whole-grain bread; yogurt; cheese cubes; apples; bananas; or rice cakes. Fruit juice has too much sugar to be a substitute for fruit. Offer milk and water. (*Note*: The purpose of microwaving some fresh vegetables such as fresh carrots is to soften them so they are not a choking threat, but they can be included if they are cut up small enough. Do not microwave bottles of milk.)
- Plan for toddlers to help prepare their snacks occasionally. They are often willing to try new foods that they have helped prepare.
- Talk with toddlers about relevant safety issues such as walking inside, looking for children at the bottom of the slide before sliding, and ensuring that no one is on the path where they are riding a Big Wheel or tricycle.

Self-Help/Adaptive Development

Adaptive or self-help skills for toddlers are a part of social and emotional development and need time allocated for them. Dressing and undressing, toileting, washing, and cleaning up all involve the use of fine motor skills, sensory integration, motor planning, and sequencing. These skills also support autonomy and self-esteem. While taking off and putting on clothes, especially during the winter, can easily become drudgery, think of ways you can make it a fun learning experience.

Task analysis breaks tasks down into their component parts so that each part can be taught individually if necessary.

Analyze tasks and then break them down into their component parts. Use **backward chaining** to teach adaptive skills. That is, if you are teaching a toddler to wash his hands, the FIRST thing you teach him is to hang up the towel or throw the paper towel away. Then he dries his hands and deals with the towel, then turns off the water, and so on. He gets the satisfaction of completing the task successfully without being required to do the entire task from the beginning. For more ideas on how to support toddlers' adaptive skills, see Table 14–4.

Backward chaining uses the task analysis and instead of starting with the first step of the task it starts with the last step.

Taking a few extra minutes to encourage children to help with dressing and undressing and other self-help skills will make the experience more pleasurable and relaxing for all. Thinking about self-help skills in relationship to other areas of development may make you feel more comfortable about it as part of the curriculum for toddlers. Educating toddlers is holistic; they learn about themselves as their independence grows. This is part of self-definition.

Table 14–4 Supporting Toddlers Self-Help/Adaptive Development

- Routinely involve toddlers in cleanup. When a toddler spills some milk, offer the child a sponge to assist you in wiping it up.

- Build a sense of independence as toddlers become increasingly capable of dressing themselves and capable of other self-help tasks.

- Sneak in cognitive skills during dressing by encouraging toddlers to find their own clothing and match pairs of mittens, boots, and scarf and hat sets.

- Give toddlers practice with dressing skills, such as zipping and buttoning. Use dolls, books, or dressing frames designed for this purpose. Start with big buttons and zippers.

- Develop language skills as you describe what you or they are doing ("Erin, look how you put your legs in your snowsuit!").

- Help develop social and emotional skills, as you give specific encouragement to toddler's to help guide their efforts. This, in turn, will make the toddler feel good about her accomplishment.

- Putting on coats is difficult for toddlers. Teacher "lore" suggests that the easiest but not most conventional method is as follows:

  1. Place the toddler's coat on the floor with the inside facing up and the collar or hood by the toddler's feet.

  2. Have the toddler put both arms partially in the sleeves.

  3. Then assist the toddler in flipping the jacket over her head, while her arms stay partially in the sleeves.

  4. Slip arms into sleeves the rest of the way, help start the zipper for her if necessary or assist with buttoning, and she's ready!

Experiences That Support Motor and Sensory Development

Children learn about their world through their senses. Infants and young toddlers often use their mouth to learn about their environment. As children get older, they more frequently use their hands. One of the areas of greatest concentration of sensory (tactile or touch) receptors on the human body is the hands. These sensory receptors give toddlers a great deal of information about their world and how to interact with it. For example, if something is solid and smooth (a firm hug or a smooth toy), the child generally gets a pleasurable feeling. Some sensations, such as light touch (or tickling), may feel uncomfortable and the child may avoid them.

Many sensory experiences come from everyday activities, such as having the toddler play on different play surfaces (grass, vinyl, carpet, fleece, etc.) and giving toddlers different-textured objects with which to play. Toddlers need space and objects to push, pull, carry, and lift. This develops strength in the core trunk area of the body. They need safe places to slide and swing. Music encourages toddlers to dance either alone or with others. This is not ballet, this is moving! Use tapes and compact discs that encourage children to move, especially when you cannot go outside.

Outside is the ideal place to practice large-motor skills. Although toddlers should not be outside when it is *very* hot or *very* cold, they need to play outside daily. There is more space for active gross motor play and a different place to play helps keep a toddler's interest. A variety of outside play activities will keep up not only the children's interest and learning, but also their heartbeat. Toddlers need vigorous activity, this means they need to play long enough and hard enough so they become breathless. Moderate to vigorous activity is also a way to purposefully use up some of that exuberant toddler energy. Except for playing in the snow, cold-weather toddler activities are similar to what you might plan for warmer weather.

Early childhood educators think about motor development in terms of gross and fine motor development. Those who specialize in motor development and early childhood physical education think in terms of fundamental movement skills and the base for these skills. The concern is that when the emphasis is on game playing or just letting young children do their own thing, some fundamental motor skills are not learned. Toddlers do what they enjoy. If they become proficient at a particular skill like riding a tricycle, given a choice, that is what they do. If fundamental motor skills are not developed in the early years

Toddlers need to practice locomotor skills. Having them creep through a tunnel is a fun way to support this basic movement skill.

then children tend to avoid activities that require these skills (Graham, Holt/ Hale, & Parker, 2005). With our growing concern about obesity it is imperative that toddlers develop necessary skills to support fitness and that you plan in such as way that ensures that the necessary skills are developed. Many people believe that young children automatically develop motor skills through matura- tion. Maturation only means that toddlers are capable of performing the skills (Pica, 1995). They need both practice and coaching to attain motor skills. They will not attain proficiency during these years but they do need a broad founda- tion. And, they need to learn the love of movement. Provide them with safe chal- lenges. Toddlers are learning a lot about how their body moves. As they are moving, build in concepts about *how* they are moving: fast, slow; high, low; for- ward, backward; stopping, going. There also need to learn *where* they are mov- ing: over, under; up, down; in front of, behind. Incorporate these ideas to help toddlers expand their locomotor skills.

Toddlers are at the precontrol level of proficiency. They are not able to re- peat movements in succession and the same movement looks different each time they do it. They include movements that are not part of the skill. They seem awkward and it may not be clear exactly what skill they are trying to per- form. They may be surprised when they succeed. When they use a ball it seems to control the toddler rather than the toddler controlling it (Graham et al., 2005). They need many different opportunities to explore and discover how to do new movements.

Locomotor Skills

Locomotion requires an understanding of space because all movement takes place in space. Understanding space is a safety issue. Toddlers who do not under- stand spatial concepts and know where their body is in space bump into other children or trip over toys (see Table 14–5).

Table 14–5 Scaffolding Locomotor Skills

- Play a game of "chase" with toddlers outside. Play with them as they run off and you slowly chase after them. If they get away, they will probably giggle a lot and end up feeling quite successful. For variation have them chase and "catch" you.

- Take walks in the neighborhood; talk about seasonal changes.

- Make soft obstacle courses where toddlers crawl over pillows, through cardboard boxes, and on mats and even mattresses if there is room. If not, use foam.

- Play music and have toddlers march, dance, or just move to the music. Play the music for 2 to 3 minutes and keep the pace vigorous.

- Climbing a tree or a jungle gym helps toddlers develop strength and coordination.

Nonmanipulative Skills

Nonmanipulative or stability skills are the second group of skills that toddlers need to practice. Muscle and joint stability is a prerequisite for fine motor control. It is difficult for toddlers to perform fine motor tasks such as buttoning or using crayons or markers without the necessary trunk stability. Toddlers need many experiences with turning, twisting, bending, and stretching to develop these skills (see Table 14–6).

Table 14–6 Scaffolding Nonmanipulative Skills

- Play "follow the leader." You are the leader. Encourage toddlers to stretch their hands as high as they can and wave like a tree in the breeze, bend their knees so their hands touch the ground, then spring like a tiger. Make up other simple routines that use these skills.
- Do the twist to music or without music. Twist fast and slow, gently and strongly.
- Encourage children to roll like a log (keep legs together, arms overhead, or close to chest).
- Use yoga designed for young children.
- Encourage children to balance on different body parts.
- Sing songs with movements.

Toddlers are learning about their bodies and what they can do with them. Locomotor and nonmanipulative can be done with just the child's body, manipulative skills involve the exploration or manipulation of objects or tools. Manipulative skills include both small and large motor skills. Virtually all require sensory motor integration.

Manipulative Skills

Small- or fine-motor development involves the toddler's ability to use the small muscles of the arms, hands, and fingers for reaching, grasping, and manipulating objects. With toddlers a real emphasis in the small-motor area is adaptive or self-help skills, such as dressing and undressing, toileting, washing and drying hands, and even cleaning up. The ability to care for oneself is an important building block in developing independence and self-esteem.

Toddlers need opportunities to practice manipulative skills. Small-motor manipulative skills are impacted by the motor systems of the brain. During the second year the motor system has more myelin. Young infants do not have a myelin sheath, a protective fatty coating of glial cells, covering their axons in the brain. The development of the myelin sheath is necessary for the development of voluntary fine motor movement and gross motor movement. Myelin helps the system run faster and more clearly, allowing the toddler better control and coordination. It is truly a two-way street, with practice supporting the myelination process and the increases in the myelin sheath allowing for more speed and coordination. The development of the cerebellum also helps the timing and coordination of motor tasks. When focusing on large motor movements, most of the time that toddlers play should be devoted to locomotor and stability skills. Toddlers also need opportunities to perform manipulative skills (see Table 14–7).

Table 14–7 Scaffolding Manipulative Skills

To support small motor manipulation
- Provide toddlers with many opportunities to explore objects with their hands. Point out salient features about shape, texture, weight, and so on.
- Provide simple wooden or rubber pegs and pegboards and puzzles (four to 12 pieces). Be sure to include some with knobs.
- Provide toys to stack. Encourage stacking by providing toys that fit inside each other, such as nesting toys, measuring cups, and small blocks.
- Provide beads to string.

To support large motor manipulation
- Provide balls to kick, throw, and roll.
- Introduce cardboard blocks and unit blocks for building.

To practice the fundamental movement skills toddlers need to play with materials and then to do the same thing with materials that differ in size, weight, shape, texture, and other relevant qualities. This allows them to extract the underlying principles of motor movements such as space awareness, effort, and relationships.

Sensory Integration

Toddlers need play that supports their sensory integration. Messy play experiences provide much tactile sensory stimulation and should be a daily part of toddlers' experiences. Setting up a sensory table or having a sensory area ensures that toddlers have sensory experiences that continue to wire the brain and ensures that these pathways remain and are efficient.

Mud, finger paint, sand, water, and playdough are a few examples of sensory play materials that provide tactile experiences important for the overall development of all toddlers (see Table 14–8).

Table 14–8 Scaffolding Sensory Integration

- Toddlers enjoy playing in a container of water—a wading pool for several children or a dish pan for one child. Add a few inches of water and plastic cups and a tablespoon, or a few floating and sinking items such as a cork, a stone, pieces of paper, a clothespin, and so on.

- Toddlers enjoy sand play. You can use the same container for sand play that you use for water play. Add cups, spoons, cars, and wooden or plastic people. You can add a little water to the sand to change the texture and make it firm to mold. Watch that toddlers do not eat the sand.

- Good old-fashioned mud play is a dirty but interesting sensory experience. If you have a corner where there is dirt to dig, add some water to make mud. On warm days, strip toddlers down to diapers or shorts and let them play. Mud washes off easily with soap and water! Be sure to use sunblock before they go outside.

Experiences That Support Communication, Language, and Literacy Development

Toddlers are talkers. They use two-word phrases, and even full sentences. By their second year, most children are capable of holding conversations unfamiliar adults can understand.

Toddlers need opportunities to both talk to adults and listen to adults talking to them. They need exposure to prereading and prewriting activities. In addition to the naturally occurring occasions when language is used, there need to be special times during the day when language arts experiences are highlighted. Although the four main aspects of language arts (speaking, listening, reading, and writing) can be differentiated, overall curriculum planning would treat them as interrelated and interdependent.

Expressive Language

Toddlers understand the meaning of many words before they are actually able to speak them. Helping them build an expressive vocabulary is an important goal. Toddler conversations are not the same as adult conversations, so you will need to continue to rely on situational cues for the meanings of toddlers' words. Different toddlers develop language skills at different rates. Some are early talkers and some are not. Almost all toddlers have problems pronouncing certain sounds or words. Developmentally, children cannot physically make all the sounds necessary for the English language until about age 6 or 7.

Toddlers not only need experience talking, they also need experiences to talk about. Offer toddlers a wide range of experiences and talk with them during and following these experiences. Experiences as simple as a stroll around the block, a trip to the grocery store, or looking at and touching a visiting pet are very important. Point out the flowers you pass on your walk, name different fruits as you place them in the grocery cart, and label the kitten's fur as "fluffy" while the toddlers pet her. See Table 14–9 for some ways to support expressive language development.

Table 14–9 Scaffolding Expressive Language

- Model good language skills when you talk with children.

- If a toddler mispronounces a word, repeat the word correctly in your next sentence. For example, if she says, "Here's a poon," you might say, "Oh, you found the *spoon*." Do not correct the toddler.

- When giving toddlers a choice, encourage them to tell you which one they want or to describe what they want, not just answer "yes" or "no."

- Keep sentences simple, but refrain from using the "parentese" that adults use with infants.

- Listen to what toddlers say. Having someone listen encourages their talking.

- Provide materials that encourage talking: toy telephones, puppets, dolls, board books.

- Encourage toddlers to label their own body parts and point to and then name these parts on dolls. Talk with children about the function of these parts.

- Toddlers learn best from concrete experiences. They learn more about the concept of "apple" when they can see, touch, taste, and smell a real apple. However, they need an adult to support their apple experience with language telling them the apple is red, it is crunchy to bite, and it tastes tart.

- Expand concrete experiences by using a variety of objects (if the objects are apples, use Granny Smith, Golden Delicious, and Macintosh apples). Be sure to label the apples and their characteristics (color, taste, and shape). But do not expect them to remember the labels. Encourage toddlers to see, touch, smell, and eat the apples.

- Say or read nursery rhymes, use simple finger plays, and play easy rhyming games.

Expansion
takes the meaning of an utterance and puts it in a more complete form.

Extension
is broadening the context of an utterance.

Remember to use expansion and extension. **Expansion** extracts the meaning of a toddler's utterance and puts it into a more complex form. For a toddler, using telegraphic speech such as, "Me go," the expansion might be, "Where do you want to go?" or, "Are you ready to go now?" The objective is to provide a language model, not just an answer that says "OK."

Extension involves putting the toddler's statement in a broader context; that is, extending the meaning of the phrase. If the toddler says, "Me go out," you might respond, "If you want to go outside you need to get your coat on." Using these techniques is particularly effective as the toddler has initiated the "conversation" and is prepared to listen to the response, as it is meaningful to him.

Receptive Language

We rarely think about listening as a skill. It is obvious that toddlers are learning to speak and must be taught to read and write, but we often think that children are born already knowing how to listen. Listening is a complex component of learning. It involves hearing and processing that allows for auditory identification and discrimination of sounds. Then what is heard must be stored in either short- or long-term memory. As with speaking, toddlers are most likely to develop good listening skills if you are a good model. When you are listening to a toddler, *listen*. If you always repeat what you say, toddlers learn *not* to listen the first time around.

Despite the need to prepare toddlers to listen, an adult's immediate goal is often to have toddlers be quiet so she can speak. Additionally, we rarely think of the skills involved in listening. One of the questions we as adults must consider is how much of what we say do toddlers find worth listening to? Would we be willing to sit spellbound for several hours each day listening to boring information? For toddlers to practice good listening skills, they need something stimulating to listen to that lasts for a very short time. Although they need to develop good listening skills, toddlers learn by doing. Table 14–10 provides guidelines for listening.

Table 14–10 Scaffolding Receptive Language

- Use toddlers' names to get their attention; they are still figuring out what is relevant and is not.

- Use a signal to focus toddlers' attention on listening, such as a particular song, finger play, or flicking the lights.

- Develop simple rules about listening to others, taking turns speaking, not interrupting others, raising your hand before speaking when in a group, and so on.

- You might have some speaking rules that relate to listening, such as talking loud enough to be heard and speaking clearly. You cannot expect toddlers to listen when it is not possible to hear.

- Fingerplays can help prepare toddlers for listening by zipping their mouths closed, or having them "put on their listening cap."

- It is helpful to rephrase what you say to a toddler if he appears not to understand. Requesting a child to "tell me in different words" is useful if you do not understand what a toddler is saying to you. This way both you and the child have a second chance to process the information.

Having a cozy place to look at books with a friend supports prereading skills as well as social development.

Good listening skills allow toddlers to receive more useful information from their environment.

Prereading

Programs specifically aimed at helping toddlers become good readers are very controversial. Programs for toddlers that use an academic approach, such as letter and word flash cards, have been criticized for placing undue pressures on them and not letting them "be children" and learning through play experiences. They are not developmentally appropriate ways of teaching prereading skills. There are, however, very appropriate ways to work with toddlers to set the stage for reading.

Have a daily time for reading. Toddlers enjoy sitting on your lap in a rocking chair or on the floor as you slowly turn the pages in a book, and talk about the pictures, or read the book. The close physical contact provided is often as important as the book itself. Independently, toddlers may chew on books, attempt to turn the pages, screech and slap pages, or carry books with them as they toddle about. Such playful manipulations of books provide positive early experiences which enhance learning language. Toddlers can enjoy books in small groups of two or three. See Table 14–11 for ways to help toddlers develop prereading skills.

Table 14–11 Scaffolding Prereading Skills

Choose books
- With clear illustrations or photographs of people, especially children, doing familiar things. If there are words, they should be simple and brief.
- With simple stories about "calamities," such as making a mess, breaking something, or getting dirty.
- That can be manipulated, such as "touch-me" books, dress-up books with zippers, scratch-and-sniff books, and squeeze-and-squeak books.

When using books with toddlers
- During or after reading a story, ask toddlers what they think about the story. Be aware that toddlers might have some unusual ideas!
- Encourage toddlers to talk about the pictures in books.
- Expect toddlers to bring their favorite book to you to be looked at or read again and again. They like the repetition and the predictability this brings as they are trying to master their environment.

Prewriting

In the area of prewriting, the major objectives are to introduce toddlers to the concept of a written language, and for them to understand that there is a connection between written and spoken language. There is no expectation that children this age will write. However, they can learn from an early age that writing is different from creative media. See Table 14–12 for ideas about introducing prewriting skills.

Table 14–12 Scaffolding Prewriting Skills

- Provide writing materials for toddlers such as nontoxic large crayons and markers.
- Introduce words informally as you write the toddler's name on his paper. (Say something like "this says Inti" each time you write his name.)
- As children begin to label their drawings, for instance calling their scribbles a "ball," write the label on the paper, whether or not it looks anything like what they say it is. This will help toddlers make the connection between spoken and written words.

Experiences That Support Cognitive Development

Toddlers need to learn about the world they live in. They need many real-life experiences to serve as a foundation for scientific and logical mathematical reasoning. For toddlers to discover these relationships and ideas they need to be actively engaged with their environment. They must have a variety of experiences from which they can abstract ideas. Most things fascinate toddlers—from rain to how the toilet flushes, and the garbage truck to the bug that crawled in. All of these present learning opportunities.

Mathematics

Toddlers begin math with an understanding of the concept "more." They have awareness of numbers and the concept of counting and sizes and shapes. Toddlers can make size distinctions between what is big and little, so they can put large pegs in pegboards as adults count them. They can sing counting songs. They may be able to "count," but it is unlikely that they will truly have number concepts at this age. They have some understanding of different shapes and can do simple (three-piece) form boards and wooden puzzles.

Blocks. Blocks are one of the most versatile materials to help young children understand mathematical concepts. Blocks can be used in a variety of ways by children of varying ages. Toddlers enjoy building with blocks. Both unit blocks and cardboard blocks are useful. Blocks have the potential for teaching many mathematical concepts. See Table 14–13 for more specific ideas about what can be learned from blocks.

There are certainly many other ways that toddlers are learning mathematical knowledge. Toddlers are moving out of Piaget's sensorimotor stage and into

Table 14–13 Scaffolding Block Play

- Toddlers learn about cause-and-effect relationships by knocking down block towers. They come to understand that when they hit the tower with their hand, the tower falls and makes a loud sound. They may want you to build towers over and over again as they test to see if the same thing happens each time.

- Toddlers may enjoy matching blocks to help them gain concepts of shape and size. Give the toddler two blocks of vastly different sizes and keep two blocks that match the child's. Hold up one block and say, "Do you have one like this?" As the child is successful, gradually make the task more difficult by using blocks which are closer to each other in size. Stack blocks and comment on their size and how this affects stacking.

- Support toddlers in finding answers to their own problems as much as possible. Let them figure out why their building fell over and how to prevent it happening again. You might ask good questions that gets them thinking on the right track but telling them why it fell is rarely useful.

- Sometimes simple open-ended statements such as, "I wonder why that happened," give toddlers the opportunity to think and respond without putting them on the spot.

- Blocks can be used to encourage pretend play with toddlers. Start initially by using one block to represent an object such as a car. Push the "block car" across the floor and say "beep-beep." You can gradually support toddlers in building more complex structures. You can also provide accessories, such as cars, animals, or people, to extend the play.

- Store blocks in groups by size and shape on a low open shelf. This will give toddlers a chance to practice shape and size sorting as they help clean up.

One-to-one correspondence is the understanding that one group has the same number of things as another group.

preoperational thinking. See Table 14–14 for the types of experiences that toddlers need to expand their mathematical concepts. Toddlers are beginning to learn **one-to-one correspondence** which is the most fundamental component of the concept of number. They are learning to count and can usually count two objects. They are learning to sort and classify objects, match them, as well as compare them (Charlesworth & Lind, 2002).

Table 14–14 Scaffolding Mathematical Concepts

- Provide materials such as cupcake tins and small toys so toddlers can put one toy in each hole of they want to. Small plastic containers, such as the ones yogurt comes in, and small toys work as well. Set tables with chairs and plates and napkins to give toddlers the opportunities to discover one-to-one correspondence.

- Sing songs, say rhymes, or read books that include numbers and counting.

- Give toddlers enough materials to play with that they have the opportunity to sort and classify them into groups. Do not be surprised if their categories are very different from yours.

- Provide materials that are big and little, heavy and light, long and short. Materials that invite comparison and exploration.

- Read books about shapes, have puzzles or form boards, draw or cut out shapes and help toddlers label and sort them.

Science

Science for toddlers involves investigating the world they live in. The process of finding answers is more important than the answers themselves. Science is a way of thinking. For toddlers, science is informal, nondirected, free investigation by the toddler. The adult's role is to plan an intriguing environment that invites exploration.

Some adults may think the idea of planning science experiences for toddlers is a little farfetched. But science experiences are easy to plan and carry out. Science for toddlers includes experiences learning about how plants grow, how animals grow and change, how our own bodies grow and develop, different kinds of weather, foods we eat, how colors mix, and the properties of water. Science is not memorizing facts but carrying out the process of inquiry, which involves asking question, making observations and gathering, organizing, and analyzing data (Charlesworth & Lind, 2002). There is no expectation that toddlers can do all these things, but there is an expectation that this is how science is approached. Many of the mathematical concepts also support scientific inquiry (see Table 14–15).

Table 14–15 Scaffolding Science Concepts

- Explore the outdoors with toddlers during different seasons or weather conditions. Being outside regularly helps children learn about nature and the environment in which they live. It provides both freedom and a challenge to observe and understand nature. Continue outdoor science experiences inside.

- Take simple field trips to a park or wooded area to learn about new plant growth, rocks, old plants or trees, possibly even about animals such as rabbits or squirrels, and definitely about insects and spiders.

- Let toddlers plant seeds in individual cups (beans are easy to handle and grow fast) and watch the changes that occur as the plants grow. Or let them help plant a garden patch in the play yard.

- Catch insects or spiders and let toddlers observe them for a day or two. Then have a "born free" time to return the insects to their natural habitat.

- Purchase an ant farm. Toddlers are fascinated by the busy nature of ants.

- Bring back different rocks and set them around your garden or play area. Encourage the toddlers to feel the different textures and talk about and compare the different colors and weights of the rocks. (Also be sure there are rules about not throwing rocks.)

- Use a cordless hand-mixer for cooking/baking with toddlers. You can mix anywhere (low table, on the floor on a tray, outside, etc.) and not have to worry about a cord. Plus there's only one beater to worry about! If the batter is not too thick, have toddlers take turns mixing with a wooden spoon. Remember, however, that taking turns is not their strength. And some of what you are mixing may not stay in the bowl.

WITH INFANTS AND TODDLERS

We have a large early care and education center, and when they decided to tear up the parking lot and repave it I thought it would be a nightmare. For the adults it was. The toddlers, however, loved it. They took longer to get into the center as they wanted to watch all the men and the equipment. The men running the equipment were great. They smiled and waved to the children. The toddlers in classrooms with windows facing onto the parking lot stood and watched. We were unsuccessful in getting them to do what was planned. It took us a day or two, but we finally got it. I went on eBay to find Tonka trucks. The plastic ones were not realistic enough. I bought eight trucks and some other construction equipment as well as hard hats.

The toddlers built parking lots. We rolled over things, scooped things up and moved them into trucks to be taken away. We took walks to watch what was happening. We smelled the macadam. The workers continued to smile and wave. An embarrassed foreman talked to the toddlers about building parking lots. He stammered but they hung on his every word. He left and the kids built more parking lots. The play continued long after the parking lot was completed. We met the toddlers' individual goals in the context of this play. This is what emergent curriculum is all about. You work with what the child is interested in. For us, it was parking lots.

REFLECTIVE PRACTICE

If you were the educator in one of the classrooms in this center, how would you feel about the parking lot taking over your planning? How would you make this into a learning experience for the toddlers? Discuss some of the individual goals you could meet while honoring the toddlers' interest in the parking lot construction.

Experiences That Support Aesthetic Development

Creativity is a process of thinking, acting, or making something that is new or different. It does not mean that the person has to be the first to produce or do something, but rather that it is a new experience for the particular person. For example, finger painting is not new, but it can be a creative experience for a toddler as he explores the texture and qualities of fingerpaint. And it can be a creative experience for a toddler as he experiments with new ways to apply the paint to the paper or table. Toddlers will deal with fingerpaint very differently, but each can use it in a creative capacity.

Creativity helps to develop a good self-concept. It encourages toddlers to think, to express their own ideas, and to find alternative solutions to problems. It supports toddlers in learning to take risks and to develop new skills. Support toddler creativity in your curriculum as well as providing toddlers with an aesthetic appreciation of their environment and the elements in it.

Creative experiences are usually unstructured opportunities for exploration. They are typically process-oriented at this age. So they present the opportunity for learning about oneself as well as the materials involved. Toddlers need to be supported and acknowledged for their creative activities. By objective standards, the products are rarely good; the importance, however, lies in developing a creative style of thinking. Toddlers need the opportunity to freely explore graphic media, move to music and learn simple songs, and play through familiar roles.

Art

Toddlers progress through several predictable developmental stages as they interact with art materials. By about 2 ½, toddlers begin more refined scribbling that includes repetitive patterns and circles. At some point, they discover the connection between their movements and the marks on the paper. They are now in control. The product may not look different, but the experience is different for toddlers. Control is motivating. It is also generalized. If they know they made a mark on the page, they also know their finger made the hole in the dough. Art now becomes a different experience for them. Although toddlers differ, this usually happens close to age 3. Finally, at about three years, they begin to name their scribbles, even though they may not look like anything to others. By three, children have the fine motor skills and eye-hand coordination for more purposeful drawing.

Art for toddlers is messy, fun, free exploration with different materials. It is putting paint on paper, at the easel, or on the table. It is watching paint drip from a squeeze bottle. It is finger or hand painting. It is squishing paint-filled sponges in one's hands. It is rolling and pounding playdough. It is gluing scraps of paper, cloth, or macaroni on paper. It is coloring or scribbling with crayons, chalk, or water-based markers.

Art is not a toddler watching the teacher glue precut pictures onto a piece of paper. It is not making something look exactly like everyone else's or the teacher's. It is not crayoning within the lines of a coloring book or ditto. And it is not a one adult–one child activity. Art is not the nice picture the toddler takes home; it is the experience the toddler has in making the product, whatever it looks like, and what the toddler learned in the process. There may not even be a product! Art affects toddlers in a variety of way. See Table 14–16 for what toddlers gain through interacting with art materials and participating in art activities.

Table 14–16 The Benefits of Art for Toddlers

- Learning how to create something from "raw" materials
- Exploring materials with their senses
- Learning different ways to express thoughts and ideas
- Learning to make decisions
- Developing the ability to share materials and appreciate others' work
- Developing a positive self-concept
- Developing and refining fine motor and cognitive skills.

Because art for toddlers is messy, it is important to plan for that aspect. Plan to set out a large plastic tablecloth on the floor or cover a child-size table with newspaper. Protect children's clothes with an art smock (old adult-size shirts work fine).

The adult role is to ask toddlers to describe what they are doing or making, or the adult can give a verbal description of what the child is doing, if she is too young to talk. It is rarely wise to ask what something "is." Comments should support the process, not the end product. See Table 14–17 for additional ideas about toddlers and art.

Table 14–17 Scaffolding Art

- Provide opportunities to paint, draw, glue, color, or mold dough each day. Do *not* provide a model for toddlers to copy.
- Keep art activities for creative arts; talk about colors and make comments about their use but do not interrupt the creative process to directly teach color names or match colors
- Show interest in what toddlers are doing and display all original art work regardless of quality.
- Play with toddlers to encourage their participation. As you play, model the process, not the product; that is, squeeze the dough, roll it, pound it, break it up into smaller pieces, but do not make a smiley face out of it.
- Use your language to support creative thinking. Instead of "What did you make," say, "Tell me about your picture." Instead of giving a direct answer to every question, occasionally ask, "What do you think might happen?" Ask *why* and *how* questions: "Why do you think that happened?" or, "How did you make that?"
- Give toddlers a variety of materials to explore (e.g., if gluing, give toddlers torn paper, wood chips, cloth, etc.).
- Use variations of a single media. Have toddlers paint using large brushes, rollers, sponges, and so on. Vary texture by adding sand to tempera paint. Paint on a table and/or easel.
- Have toddlers' fingerpaint directly on a table and then have them help clean up. (Be sure to plan enough time for the cleanup and have enough adult supervision.) Because of the probability of it going into their mouth, consider how edible the fingerpaint is.

(continues)

- Make playdough using a variety of different recipes that influence the consistency and texture of the dough (an edible variety is recommended). Encourage toddlers to squash, roll, pat, pinch, or shape playdough. Add cookie cutters and popsicle sticks (children use these to cut). Playdough is available commercially or you can make it yourself from one of the many different recipes. If you make it yourself, it is not a problem if children taste it, and they can even participate in making it.

- Paint with water. On a warm day, fill a couple of buckets with water and add a couple of old paintbrushes. The toddlers can harmlessly "paint" outside walls, sidewalks, fences, and so on.

Music

Toddlers respond to the mood of music. Quiet singing and rocking sets the tone for sleep whereas a fast drum beat encourages movement. Toddlers can use tools to produce sound. They can hit a xylophone with a mallet or a piano with their fingers. Toddlers experiment with sound by hitting different instruments with different objects to discover different sounds. By about 18 months toddlers enjoy music and dancing. By two years they can learn simple songs and want to sing them again and again. They like simple songs and nursery rhymes that you can sing or chant together. Toddlers enjoy and learn from a variety of musical experiences. They learn new words, develop memory skills as they recall songs or parts of songs, and develop a sense of rhythm as they sing and listen to music. Toddlers need time to explore, interpret, and understand musical sound. Toddlers should be immersed in singing, speaking rhythmically, moving expressively, and playing musical instruments (Humpal & Wolf, 2003).

Music also impacts the mind, but you need complex music just as you need complex language to help children build better language skills (Hart & Risley, 1995). Complex music is typically classical music from the baroque era (from about 1600 to 1750). It features the music of Bach, Mozart, and others. If you plan to do this, ensure that you do not get versions that are so watered down for children that the complexity is lost (Shore & Strasser, 2006). See Table 14–18 for ways to include music.

Table 14–18 Scaffolding Music

- Use musical cues as a signaling system to let toddlers know it is time to move to another experience (cleaning up) or to welcome toddlers to a small group.

- Play prerecorded music at a variety of times throughout the day. Children's songs will be enjoyed, but classical or popular tunes will be appreciated as well. Fit the music to the activity. Play quiet, relaxing music at naptime and louder, bouncier music for dancing on a rainy day when toddlers cannot go outside.

- Use fingerplays to teach toddlers language skills, including listening, remembering, sequencing, and saying words to songs, as well as to increase sensory motor integration.

(continues)

- Include clapping and taping to a beat and then walking or marching. Clap children's names.

- Sing counting and alphabet songs to support learning.

- Use music to teach toddlers social skills. Since they usually participate in songs and finger plays with at least one other child, they learn to pay attention to something that interests them and to imitate actions of adults and other children.

Creative Movement

As movement comes more under toddlers' control, they begin to experiment. At about age 2 they like songs with motions and moving to music. They are not ready for prolonged periods of strenuous movement. However, they do need to accumulate 30 minutes of moderate to strenuous activity a day. This means that you need to include about 5 to 10 bursts of energy that last about two to three minutes each. You need to move with the toddlers or it is unlikely that they will keep moving that length of time. While movements are still being mastered, toddlers are not as free to be creative.

Creative movement is a personal statement about one's inner self. This is what differentiates it from functional movement, which has a practical purpose. Because it is a personal statement, there is no right or wrong way to move. It is important not to judge movement as being silly or awkward. All movements should be seen as equally appropriate for boys and girls. The goal of creative movement is to avoid demonstrating movements, because the toddlers may decide that they must do what you do, and then it is no longer creative movement. If the goal is aerobic movement then modeling the behavior is great. Music is often used to set the tone for movement. Combine music and movement with small group games like the "Hokey Pokey" or "Ring around the Rosie" or by singing songs with motions like "If you're happy and you know it." Ask the children for input into movement activities.

Dramatic Play

With the advent of language skills, toddlers' play becomes richer and more imaginative. They begin to pretend with toys and materials and imitate the adults in their world, often playing "mommy" or "daddy." Toddlers use dramatic play to try out and consolidate the adult roles with which they are most familiar. These are usually roles that revolve around the home. Child care, cleaning, and cooking are typical housekeeping themes. Toddlers also play through situations that are meaningful to them. One can often learn about the toddlers' feelings by watching and listening to their play. Toddlers as young as 16 months should have dramatic-play experiences. By adding a few props, and perhaps initiating the play, adults can provide toddlers with many rewarding dramatic-play activities. Between two and three, children expand their use of mental representations and symbolic thought. Words become signifiers of objects and events. Toddlers can classify based on function. This allows their play to be more creative. They can pretend.

Dramatic play is grounded in what toddlers know and have done. The way to expand dramatic play is to increase the toddlers' knowledge base with real experiences. Field trips are difficult with toddlers, but they are the best way to increase their learning and also enhance their dramatic play. They need to visit a real farm, or at least a petting zoo, to begin to understand animals and what they do. A book about the farm really does not do it for toddlers.

Toddlers learn from watching others and then trying activities on their own. They may show their first signs of pretend play by moving a spoon around a bowl in imitation of daddy cooking or by pretending to feed a doll or a stuffed animal. Encourage these behaviors. If toddlers are not yet doing any pretend play but show an interest in dolls, stuffed animals, or other possible pretend toys, encourage the toddler to imitate you. Say, "I'm combing," as you pretend to comb the doll's hair, and then say, "Now you do it." Help the toddler by gently guiding her hand if the child does not follow through on her own (a physical prompt). Encourage any attempts the toddler makes. However, if she does not seem interested, she may not yet be at that developmental level and you may need to come back to pretend activities at a later point. Both boys and girls need time to pretend. Boys need chances to feed dolls and cook and girls

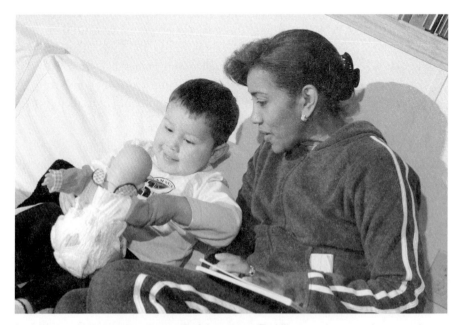

As dramatic play emerges it may need adult support. Toddlers use dramatic play to work through some of what is happening in their lives.

need chances to push trucks and fire engines, as well as practicing the more traditional roles. If you show acceptance of boys pretending to cook and girls pretending to drive trucks at a young age, toddlers will grow up with fewer limitations on their future roles.

One way toddlers learn to be social is to imitate or "try on" the actions of adults. That is why their favorite roles are the people they know best. Watch-

up close and personal

Toddlers fascinate me. When teaching a classroom of toddlers I was fascinated by one toddler who consistently stayed in the housekeeping area. She set the table and then ran away. She would come back and then run away again. She did this for several days. I tried to ask her some questions about what was going one but nothing made any sense to me. Then the light dawned. When her mother came to pick her up I asked her if she were pregnant? She hemmed and hawed and finally said yes but they had not told anyone yet. I explained her daughter's behavior and she laughed. She said that she had awful morning sickness. She said that perhaps they should rethink their decision.

REFLECTIVE PRACTICE

Observing toddlers behavior tells you a lot about toddlers' lives. What would you do if you observed unusual consistent behavior by a toddler? What would you have done in this case?

ing toddlers at pretend play is true pleasure for adults. Sometimes they imitate "mommy," "daddy," or "teacher" more realistically than we would like. It is interesting to watch, but what do toddlers learn from pretend or dramatic play? Toddlers rarely pretend to be superheroes or "good guys/bad guys" until they are close to three years old. Toddlers need to experience events or situations in order to understand them. Since most toddlers experience mommy making dinner or daddy doing the dishes, these events are often the toddler's first dramatic play activities.

Toddlers can learn how to interact with others through dramatic play. Many toddlers have a difficult time playing with peers. With practice and maturation they begin to learn to share, communicate, and negotiate. In dramatic play activities, toddlers have to resolve conflicts over who is going to play mommy (or daddy, big sister, baby), what each role means—just what do they do—and the general theme behind the play situation. See Table 14–19 for some suggestions for encouraging dramatic play with toddlers.

Table 14–19 Scaffolding Dramatic Play

- Set up the dramatic play area as a housekeeping arrangement. Include a play kitchen set (stove/refrigerator), child-size table and chairs, play dishes and pots, and empty food boxes. (Vary by adding play cleaning supplies or add playdough and turn it into a bakery.) Provide child-size brooms and dishpans and let toddlers help you when you sweep. Expect that they will spread the dirt around at first rather than gather it together, but with practice, they will get the idea!

- Put a grocery store in the dramatic play area. Collect lots of empty food containers, paper bags, a cash register, baskets, and shelves for stocking the food. Parents are often willing to bring in empty containers.

- Make the dramatic play area into a shoe store. Collect old pairs of shoes from parents (child and adult size). Add shelves for displaying make a pretend foot-size measurer and set up child-size chairs for children who are customers. Add shoe boxes and bags.

- Try turning the dramatic play area into a nursery. Provide baby dolls, doll clothes, cribs (use cardboard boxes), bottles, blankets, a dishpan and cloth for the baby's bath, empty powder containers, and diapers.

- Encourage toddlers to dress up in oversized clothes that are easy to take on and off to support some of their dramatic play.

Dramatic play activities increase language skills. Toddlers must talk to resolve conflicts constructively in order for play to continue. Dramatic play builds cognitive skills as toddlers learn how different people do things. One child's mother may work outside the home, so part of her "mommy" role includes going to the office and being the boss. Another child's mother may work in a fast food restaurant, so this presents a different role of the working mother. Another child's mother may not work outside the home, so that child's "mommy" role may be different. Through dramatic play, each child gets to learn about different roles that mothers may have.

Dramatic play is also a safe way for toddlers to express negative feelings. It is not uncommon (or harmful) for a toddler who has a new baby brother or sister to hit the baby dolls because "they are bad." Toddlers can release their anger, hurt, or jealousy on inanimate objects rather than hurting the real source of their feelings.

IMPLEMENTING THE CURRICULUM FOR TODDLERS

Parallel play
is playing with the similar materials as others but not exchanging materials or ideas.

Toddlers are predictably mobile. Although they frequently play alone, they participate in **parallel play** with others in small groups. More of their work is at tables, but the floor is a convenient play space as well. Their skills in the areas of language and gross and fine motor have expanded their interest in their world and their ability to interact with it. They are moving out of the sensorimotor period and into preoperational thought, which supports pretend play and symbolic thought. Although individualized, the play is more oriented toward small groups.

Emergent Curriculum Planning for Toddlers Using Webs

Because there are more toddlers in a classroom this may seem like a laborious process, but once you have the initial webs they only need to be updated. These are your working notes; they do not have to be pretty, just functional. Again, after you have organized your webs into developmental areas, check if you need additional information. You may need to observe more to obtain this information or just jog your memory. Then use this as a planning document. For individual children you read the document down, for planning you read it across. Bobby (24 months) has a speech and language delay and his IFSP is in Chapter 11. Note how easily his planning is included (see Table 14–20).

REFLECTIVE PRACTICE

Look at the emergent curriculum webs of a young infant, Chapter 12, the mobile infant, Chapter 13, and the toddlers. As you look across these webs, what commonalities do you see? What are the differences? How does this inform your practice with infants and toddlers?

Table 14–20 Placing Toddlers Webs into a Developmental Framework

Development, Likes and Challenges Center	
Amber (20 months)	*Bobby (24 months)*
Social and Emotional Including Health, Safety and Nutrition, Self-Help Skills	
Watches for a long time before joining groups or using new toys.	Can be restless, irritable, grabs new toys. Gets along with peers, good social skills.
Easily frustrated.	Good sense of humor.
Shy.	Participates in parallel play.
Usually plays alone.	Good self-help skills.
Mom is concerned about weight and eating habits.	Picky eater.
Wants adult attention.	
Likes adults to play with her.	

(continues)

Table 14–20 *(continues)*

Motor and Sensory Integration Including Locomotor, Nonmanipulative, and Manipulative Skills	
Walks, but asks to be carried.	Likes rough and tumble play.
Scribbles with crayon.	Likes playing outside.
Has appropriate skills, doesn't like to use them.	May have problems with sensory integration. Likes dump and fill and water play. Very active runs, jumps, kicks ball.

Communication, Language and Literacy Including Expressive and Receptive Language and Prereading and Prewriting Skills	
Likes nursery rhymes and fingerplays.	Language about 12 months delayed.
Uses two-word sentences and jargon.	Makes sounds, points, uses some signs.

Cognitive Development Including Mathematics and Science	
Sorts and matches objects.	

Aesthetic Development Including Art, Music, Creative Movement, and Dramatic Play	
Likes to paint and use play dough.	Likes to sing.
Likes housekeeping and dolls.	
Rosa (30 months)	*Clint (34 months)*

Social and Emotional Including Health, Safety and Nutrition, Self-Help Skills	
Likes almost everything and everybody.	Father sees him as "all boy."
Wakes up smiling, usually happy, adaptable.	Very independent.
Working on toilet training.	Aware he is a boy.
Likes to do things herself but will accept adult help.	Toilet trained, few accidents.
Likes animals.	
Wants to be a princess when she grows up.	

Motor and Sensory Integration Including Locomotor, Nonmanipulative, and Manipulative Skills	
Walks, runs, hops, jumps, dances.	Large for age.
Likes riding toys.	Has good skills in all motor areas.
Beginning to use scissors.	Loves to climb, slide, run, ride trikes.

Communication, Language and Literacy Including Expressive and Receptive Language and Prereading and Prewriting Skills	
Talks frequently and well, sings, loves to be read to and to read to herself.	Tries to write his name. Can say the alphabet.
Good understanding of language.	Looks at books during naptime.

(continues)

Cognitive Development Including Mathematics and Science	
Likes to play games, use puzzles.	Loves blocks, transportation toys.
Can count to 10.	

Aesthetic Development Including Art, Music, Creative Movement, and Dramatic Play	
Likes housekeeping and creative movement.	Rarely participates in these areas.

Compare the webs of toddlers to those of mobile infants. Notice how much more complex they are and how there is far more detail. They have more skills and the planning process is becoming more group based although it still responds to individual differences (See Table 14–21).

Table 14–21 Placing Toddlers' Webs into a Curriculum Framework

Social and Emotional Including Health, Safety and Nutrition, Self-Help Skills

- Ensure that pictures, photographs, and artifacts represent diverse racial and ethnic groups and that they are nonsexist.

- Talk about turn taking, provide some visual (egg timer) or auditory (timer) way of deciding how long turns are. Support toddlers who are waiting.

- Talk about ways to include others in play.

- Support good nutrition and health with the snacks that are served. Drinks should be primarily milk or water. Snacks should be fruits, vegetables, and whole grains. Yogurt can be a great dip, and toddlers love to dip.

- Encourage toddlers to help each other. Talk about feelings, particularly facial expressions and what they mean. Encourage toddlers to learn skills to include all toddlers.

Motor and Sensory Integration Including Locomotor, Nonmanipulative, and Manipulative Skills

Outside

- Ensure that toddlers are outside for at least an hour (in an all-day program) each day unless weather does not allow this.

- Move some equipment outside, such as easels.

- Add hopping trails with colored chalk.

- Add hula hoops and have toddlers jump into and out of hula hoops on the ground.

- Add a variety of riding toys.

- Plan for outside time in the same way you do inside to ensure active play and learning.

- Create interesting ways of walking—like animals, sideways, backward, clapping, and so on.

Inside

- Add yoga on a regular basis.

(continues)

Table 14–21 *(continues)*

- Vary the materials used in dump and fill to provide different sensory experiences.

- Add plastic fruits and vegetables to basins filled with water or the water table for toddlers to wash, dry, and talk about.

- Add 2- to 3-minute dance breaks to increase the amount of moderate to vigorous activity. Play songs from compact disks such as *Jazz for kids: Sing, clap, wiggle, and shake,* various artists (2004) Verve; or *Animal playground,* various artists by Putumayo World Music; or music by the Wiggles, such as *Let's wiggle* (2003) or *Toot toot* (2001).

Communication, Language, and Literacy Including Expressive and Receptive Language and Prereading and Prewriting Skills

- Use finger plays and nursery rhymes daily.

- Expand and extend toddlers' language.

- Add board books and other books that show diverse racial and ethnic groups and are nonsexist and show men and women doing nontraditional work. Read books about children who are toilet training. Read to them daily.

- Read books about food and eating, such as . *From head to toe* (1997) and *The very hungry caterpillar* (1969). New York: Philomel Books. Talk about food and what toddlers eat and like to eat and what is healthy.

- Read alphabet books.

- Use toddlers' names frequently to help focus their attention.

- Ask toddlers to "tell you in a different way" if they have repeated what they want and you do not understand. Likewise if they do not understand you, restate your request.

- Provide a variety of different types of paper and stamps.

Cognitive Development Including Mathematics and Science

- Add small transportation toys and people to the block area.

- Encourage toddlers to help set the table for snack and help them work on one-to-one correspondence.

- Provide a variety of small transportation toys that can be sorted and classified.

- Sing songs and read books about numbers, sizes, and shapes.

- Add form boards and wooden puzzles with knobs.

- Help toddlers explore the outdoors and observe the plants and animals around.

- Take a walking field trip for a particular purpose (look for insects or birds).

Aesthetic Development Including Art, Music, Creative Movement, and Dramatic Play

- Sing songs that require motions (Johnny hammers with one hammer; Head shoulder, knees and toes; This is the way we wash our cloths; etc.) and then sing them a second time, making the motions larger and/or faster and with more vigor.

- Play music that supports creative movement; the Putumayo kids' series has many movement possibilities.

- Combine dolls and blocks while supporting symbolic play.

- Sing songs that include toddlers' names.

- Introduce multiethnic diversity in the music and materials.

Individualizing Routines and Transitions

Amber: When she arrives, encourage her to join children in either art or dramatic play. Redirect her to peers as a problem-solving strategy. Respect her need for time, but encourage her participation with peers and decrease her dependence on adults. When children are participating in planned energetic play, verbally encourage her to move at a moderate to vigorous activity level.

Bobby: Talk with parents and speech and language pathologist for ways of supporting his language development. Develop a greeting and departure routine that is language based. When Bobby makes sounds, points, or uses signs, verbalize what you think he wants and ask for clarification. When using sensory materials, observe Bobby's reactions: Is he hyper- or hyporeactive? Does he seek or avoid sensory input? Is it mixed? Check out the sensory profiles developed by Williamson and Anzalone (2001) and determine if he fits any of them. Talk with parents regularly about their concerns.

Rosa: Ensure that she gets her share of teacher time. She is so easy that children who are more demanding may take up most of the adult time.

Clint: Support his independence and gender knowledge as you present a nonsexist view of the world. Entice him into the aesthetic arts by specifically showing him what is available when he arrives.

Learning Environments for Toddlers

Curriculum and setting up learning environments for toddlers is different from planning for young infants or mobile infants. Although developmentally based, planning for toddlers is typically experience-related and organized along more traditional subject matters areas. A good toddler curriculum provides toddlers with choices of experiences. Toddlers play with what interests them at any given moment and might reject a particular experience an adult has planned. If given choices, the toddler can choose the toys or materials she wants to play with from the preselected, developmentally appropriate experiences the adult provides. This is most easily accomplished by having low open shelves with safe toys that toddlers can use. Choices also provide toddlers with the opportunity to assert their independence and autonomy. Choosing for oneself builds self-esteem.

Good toddler planning provides experiences that are self-paced and open-ended. A toddler is finished playing when he wants to leave an area. Forcing or coaxing a toddler to "finish" his art project only causes frustration for the adult and the toddler. The adult should accept the individual differences in toddler's interests and attention spans. Some toddlers will paint for 20 minutes, others for

20 seconds. Even the same toddler might paint for a long time one day and not show any interest in painting the next.

Good planning provides toddlers opportunities to learn through sensory, creative, physical, and problem-solving experiences. Experiences are the building blocks of planning. As you think about the experiences, think about areas of development and how these can be incorporated into your plan in a developmentally appropriate way. One way to do this is to label the different areas of the room such as dramatic play or language arts. Space should be allocated for sensory play, easel painting, creative arts, playdough, simple dramatic play, books, blocks, music, language, and manipulative experiences. There should be enough materials for toddlers to use without causing undue frustrations; that is, there should be at least duplicates of some toys and enough other materials so sharing is not a problem.

Toddler experiences are designed for children who can get to places and can choose what they want to do. See Table 14–22 for characteristics that indicate a classroom with good planning and high-quality care for toddlers.

Table 14–22 Characteristics of High-Quality Curriculum for Toddlers

- Warm, personal contact with adults (verbal and nonverbal) who are active, enthusiastic, and enjoy playing with toddlers.

- Experiences that are mostly self-directed and a few that are teacher-directed including active physical play.

- A comprehensive program that includes developmentally appropriate experiences that meet the interests of individual children as well as the group. Planning includes physical, emotional, social, language, creative, sensory, and cognitive areas of development.

- A regular and stable schedule that allows for flexibility in meeting the needs of toddlers, including planned times for quiet and active periods.

- Consistent rules and guidance techniques that preserve self-esteem.

- Opportunities to play alone, near peers, with peers, and with adults.

- A safe classroom environment that encourages active play.

MATERIALS AND METHODS FOR WORKING WITH TODDLERS

Toddlers need a variety of toys that are safe and durable. Toys can be anything from dolls and dump trucks to pots, pans, and wooden spoons. Toddlers invent uses and play based the props that are provided. See Table 14–23 for guidelines in choosing play materials for toddlers.

Table 14–23 Guidelines for Choosing Toys for Toddlers

- **Authenticity**. Realism is important to toddlers. Does the toy look like what it is supposed to be? For truck play, a small wooden truck is more realistic than a wooden block, although both can be used similarly. The younger the child, the more realistic the toys need to be.

- **Degree of structure**. Toddlers' ideas are concrete and certain materials can create concrete structures. Certain toys suggest certain play. Examples of structured toys are cars and play dishes; unstructured materials are playdough and blocks.

- **Interactiveness**. Does the material encourage children's participation? Materials that encourage interaction support play and learning. Toys that move, make sounds, and change in a toddler's hands discourage participation from the toddler.

- **Complexity**. Consider the complexity of a toy. How many different uses does a toy have? A simple toy such as a ball is functionally complex because toddlers can do so many things with it. People are the most functionally complex playthings; therefore, adult-child or child-child interactions increase the complexity of any type of play.

- **Plasticity**. Can the toy be used in more than one way by more than one child over a wide span of ages? Blocks are a good investment because children will play with them in different ways as they grow and develop. Infants may use them to practice grasping, mouthing, and bringing objects together. Mobile infants may use them as objects to place in and out of containers as they develop spatial relationships and motor control. Later they may be used for stacking and the beginnings of pretend play. Blocks may also encourage more than one toddler to become involved in the play. Many art materials such as paint, crayons, and playdough fall into this category.

- **Independence**. Will the toy encourage independence or will the toddler always be dependent on an adult for assistance with the toy? Although play is usually enhanced by an adult, you do not want the play dependent upon the adult.

SCHEDULES, ROUTINES, AND TRANSITIONS

The schedule for toddlers includes time for free play, indoors and outside, and for routine events such as eating, an afternoon nap, and diapering/toilet training. A predictable schedule and consistent approaches to routines provide a sense of safety and security. Some of the planning for transitions and routine care are continuations of patterns developed for mobile infants; other aspects are different. The schedule is more consistent and may be posted. For a sample schedule, see Figure 14–2.

I did not include a large group time in the above schedule, and probably would not until toddlers are about 30 months. Or, you can plan one but not require that all children participate. Even then it would only be about five minutes. I am more comfortable singing and reading and allowing those who are interested to join and others can do different things. Sometimes, when toddlers are ready, the schedule evolves and then I would include them as a regular program.

FIGURE 14–2 Sample Toddler Schedule

Early Morning	Arrival of parents and children
	Encourage toddlers to use materials set out
Two to three minutes of teacher-directed planned energetic play, more singing and movement, book reading, hand washing, snack	
Mid-Morning	Change diapers and use toilet, wash hands
Get ready and go outside, including 5 to 10 minutes of planned energetic play (2 to 3 minutes each)	
	Come inside, take off outdoor clothing, and wash hands
	Eat lunch
Early Afternoon	Change diapers and use toilet, wash hands
Help toddlers get ready for naps, read stories, play music	
One-on-one time as toddlers wake up	
Change diapers and use toilet, wash hands	
Snack	
Late Afternoon	Play indoors and outside, including 5 to 10 minutes of planned energetic play (2 to 3 minutes each)
	Read stories, quiet play
	Help parents and children reunite

SOURCE: Dombro, Colker, and Dodge (1999).

Arrival Time

For toddlers who have been in care, the rituals are down and the transition is usually easy unless something unusual has happened. That would obviously be discussed between the parents and educators. Time to support self-help skills should continue to be part of the transition.

WITH INFANTS AND TODDLERS

Talk with toddlers briefly about what they do from when they get up until they come to school. Tell them that you are all going to sing about what they do. At first make up the motions to go with the song. You can ask older toddlers for suggestions. Sing as long as toddlers are interested and make up verses that match your needs. Sing to the tune of "Here We Go Round the Mulberry Bush."

This is the way we get out of bed, get out of bed, get out of bed.

This is the way we get out of bed so early in the morning.

Wash our hands	Brush our teeth
Put on our clothes	Take off our clothes
Come to school	Eat our breakfast

Substitute an activity such as cleaning the house

Sweep the floor	Vacuum the rug
Make our beds	Wipe the table

Use songs such as this to support self-help skills. Sing "this is the way we take off our shoes (jacket, hat, and so on)" while toddlers are participating in the activity.

Naptime

Toddlers typically take one afternoon nap. The length of the nap varies with the toddler. Some toddlers go to sleep or rest easily; others have a difficult time. This is often a pleasant quiet time to rock younger toddlers and to rub backs and talk quietly with older toddlers.

Eating and Mealtimes

Young toddlers may still be in high chairs for lunch, but older toddlers are probably seated at a low table to give them the opportunity to make eating a social time as well as a time to eat nutritious food. Some programs have families send in lunchs; other programs prepare it. Family-style eating, with an adult and two to four toddlers at the table, is considered best practice if the food is prepared by the center. Toddlers should be allowed to serve themselves from small dishes that are passed. Have the food ready when the toddlers arrive so there is little waiting time. Encourage toddlers to try new foods, but bribing them for forcing them is not productive. If dessert is a normal part of the meal, be sure it is nutritious and that there is no requirement that toddlers clean their plate to be allowed to have dessert. Make snack and mealtimes pleasant. Talk with families about food allergies and preferences. Culture plays a large part in the food we eat. Ensure that the cultures of the children are reflected in the food that is served. Encourage parents to join you when this is possible.

Diapering and Toileting

Diapering offers one-on-one time which is often pleasant to both the child and the educator. As children become toddlers, parents decide when the child should begin using the toilet. This is usually between two and three years. Learning to go to the toilet takes time and patience. Typically, the earlier it is started, the more time and patience are required. It also takes teamwork, because the person with toddler must remain with him but continue to be aware of what is happening in the group. There are regular times to check if a toddler's diaper is wet. If it is wet, it is changed then.

Ideally centers have child-size toilets. Potty chairs that sit on the floor are difficult to maintain in a center. If potty seats are placed on adult-size toilets, they must be secured and have cleanable steps leading up to them. Make the bathroom a pleasant place for both two-year-olds and adults, because you will be spending time there.

Parents and educators may have strong feelings and even different strategies for going about toilet training. Parents who train children young (about 12 months) believe that it is the adult's responsibility to get the child to the potty. This may be done for a variety of reasons, including the fact that diapers are expensive. Others wait until the child is ready to assume responsibility for toileting, so they do not begin about 24 to 30 months.

People have different ideas about when children should be toilet trained. However, all agree that having a child-sized toilet supports the process.

Look for indications that the toddler is ready to learn about toileting. Signs might include staying dry for longer periods of time, awareness of being wet, having a somewhat regular schedule of voiding, talking about poop and pee, and sitting on the toilet with their clothes on (Dombro et al., 1999).

Teaching children to use the toilet requires time and organization. When planning toilet training parents and educators try to determine if there is a pattern. If there is no pattern the decision may be to wait. Toddlers need to be encouraged to use the toilet frequently. There are logical times to go. Watching others going to the potty may encourage toddlers. Toddlers need to be encouraged when they successfully do go to the potty but not out of proportion. All children will have accidents; these should be handled matter-of-factly. Allow toddlers to see what they have done, flush the toilet, and wash their hands.

up close and personal

We were going to be traveling in Argentina with our daughter. She would be 14 months when we left and we planned to be there for about six months. Because we would be moving frequently, I knew we needed disposal diapers. At that time they cost five times as much as they did in the United States (about $1.00 for each diaper). We couldn't afford them. We decided that the simplest solution was for her to learn to go to the toilet. We began when she was about a year old. I had tried to figure out what her schedule was. We would go to the bathroom on a regular basis. She would sit on the potty; I would sit on the floor. I would sing, read to her, and frequently check to see if anything happened. When it did, I was appropriately excited. I discovered that washable shoes were a necessity and that when she wore dresses there was less to change. Ultimately it worked—but I was trained, she wasn't, at least not then. I still seemed to spend an inordinate amount of time in the bathroom, because she had my undivided attention and enjoyed this time. Do I recommend this? No. But it is possible.

REFLECTIVE PRACTICE

What do you think the role of the early childhood educator should be relative to toilet training? Do you feel that is something that you should be responsible for if you teach infants and toddlers? How would you respond to a parent who wants their child trained early? How much of your time do you think you could spend with an individual child? Is there a way you could make this time learning time?

Cleanup Time

Make the cleanup of toys a regular part of your routine with toddlers. With young infants and mobile infants, educators talk about cleanup time and may even sing about it. The responsibility of cleaning up lies primarily with the teacher. Toddlers can and should be involved in the cleanup process. Set low expectations at first (such as having a young toddler put two blocks in the box) and raise the standards as they become more able. Having a particular song that signals cleanup time is useful. It can be a tape or CD or a song you sing each day. This lets toddlers know what is happening. The song can be a simple tune you have made up or you can put new words to a familiar tune.

WITH INFANTS AND TODDLERS

Sing songs to support cleanup time.

Sing simple songs such as

This is the way we pick up our toys, pick up our toys, pick up our toys
This is the way we pick up our toys, so early in the morning.
(Sung to the tune of "Here We Go Round the Mulberry Bush")

Or

It's time to put our toys away, toys away, toys away;
It's time to put our toys away, for another day.
(Sung to the tune of "Mary Had a Little Lamb")

For variation, substitute the name of the toy a child is putting away, substitute a child's name, the name of the setting, or name what will happen next.

This is the way Jack picks up the blocks, picks up the blocks, picks up the blocks.
This is the way Jamelia picks up the blocks, and they put them all away.

Departure Time

As with arrival time rituals make this time less stressful. If toddlers have been in a child care setting for a long-time departure time has probably turned into a predictable pattern. Information is still passed between parents and educators, daily sheets still go home about how toddlers spent their day. If the toddler is learning to use the toilet, this may dominate the conversation.

Figure 14–3 provides an example about the type of information that is recorded about a toddler's day.

early learning center

Daily Toddler Report

Child's Name: _____   Date: _____

"Let me tell you about my day..."

Meals & Snacks

"I ate my breakfast:
◆ Well ◆ Fair ◆ Not at all"

"I ate my lunch:
◆ Well ◆ Fair ◆ Not at all"

"I ate my snacks:
◆ Well ◆ Fair ◆ Not at all"

Comments: _____
_____
_____

Bathroom / Diapers

_____ am/pm
◆ Dry ◆ Wet ◆ BM ◆ Used toilet
_____ am/pm
◆ Dry ◆ Wet ◆ BM ◆ Used toilet
_____ am/pm
◆ Dry ◆ Wet ◆ BM ◆ Used toilet
_____ am/pm
◆ Dry ◆ Wet ◆ BM ◆ Used toilet
_____ am/pm
◆ Dry ◆ Wet ◆ BM ◆ Used toilet
_____ am/pm
◆ Dry ◆ Wet ◆ BM ◆ Used toilet

Things I need to brings:

Nap Schedule

_____ am to   _____ pm
◆ Slept peacefully   ◆ Woke often

MY ACTIVITIES TODAY

❏ Social/Emotional   ❏ Sensory and Motor   ❏ Communication/Language/Literacy
❏ Cognitive   ❏ Aesthetics
_____

_____

_____

Comments: _____

_____

FIGURE 14–3 Daily Toddler Report

Transitions

I have not addressed transitions in the previous two chapters because with infants the transitions are more in the minds of adults than time that affects children. When toddlers have a schedule that all the children in the group use, the transitions become more apparent to the children and are sometimes more problematic.

Transition is the label given to the time between the end of one event and the beginning of another. This can be the time between experiences, the beginning or end of the day, before and after lunch, snacks, and naps, or moving from inside to outside. Transitions are difficult times for toddlers, teachers, and parents. Even at home, the transitions before meals, bedtime, and the like can be stressful. Changes required by transitions cause tension regardless of the physical location. As there are many transitions in a single day, it is important to think of and plan for transitions as a time of learning. Stress created in these transitions can carry over into the next event, so thought must also be given to decreasing the stress.

Transition
is the time between an experience or activity ending and another starting.

What Makes Transitions Stressful?

Transitions are more obvious to the adult than to toddlers. Because toddlers are just learning about sequences, they may view each event, including the transition, as a discrete event unrelated to what went before or to what will follow. A calm but firm response to children is reassuring. Children need to feel secure and know that there are rules and that the adult is in control. The younger the children, the more likely it is that transition periods will take longer. (Compare the time it takes for a five-year-old vs. a two-year-olds to put on boots and a coat.) Likewise, the wider the age ranges of children, the longer the transition. The longer the transition, the more likely it is to be a difficult one. Transitions are difficult for a variety of reasons. Table 14–24 identifies some of these and some possible solutions.

Table 14–24 Transitions

Boredom. Transitions often involve waiting. Toddlers who have "nothing to do" will usually find something to do, and it is rarely what you would choose.

Combating boredom. Eliminate as much waiting time as possible. When you cannot eliminate it, help toddlers by singing a song with them, do a fingerplay, tell or read a story. Do not move from one experience until you have the next one prepared; that is, do not have toddlers clean up for lunch until lunch is on the table. Do not wait until all the children are present before starting an experience. Slower toddlers may speed up if they think they are missing something.

Change. Toddlers, like adults, like to change experiences when they are finished, not by the clock. They may feel uncertain about what will happen next.

(continues)

Make changes easier. Warn toddlers about upcoming changes. "In five minutes it will be cleanup time." Follow a schedule. They cannot tell time, so it is not important whether you allow experiences to run a little longer or shorter, but rather that you follow the same sequence of events. Encourage toddlers to think about what will happen next.

Rules. Toddlers may feel uncertain about the "rules" or expectations for them during transition times.

Make rules easier to follow. Help toddlers to understand exactly what you expect of them during transition times. To aid cleaning up, for example, you could have a picture or outline of an item on the shelf where it belongs if it is important that it be returned to the right place. Expect some testing behavior at transition time.

Control. Toddlers are trying to gain control over their world and exert their independence and autonomy.

Give toddlers some control. It often helps transitions to give toddlers control of some decisions. Be sure they are choices you are willing to live with. A toddler can decide which book she wants to look at during naptime, not whether she will nap.

Separation. Many transitions involve separation, whether from a parent, caregiver, sibling, playmate, or the place itself.

Make separation easier. If a toddler is having a difficult time separating from his parents, talk with them about the issue and jointly develop a plan. A picture schedule is particularly helpful for toddlers who are having problems adjusting to care, as they can see that the final picture is a parent picking them up.

Emerging skills. Transitions require toddlers to use skills that are new to them, such as dressing and undressing, toileting, and self-feeding, in a relatively short time frame.

Allow time for practicing emerging skills. Part of the transition process is learning adaptive behavior or self-help skills. Rushing transitions puts pressure on toddlers who are mastering these emerging skills. This often results in children who resist what you want. Additional time is an asset to a toddler who is striving for competence. Try dismissing slower toddlers first to give them more time, or plan an experience following the transition that is easy for them to join when they are ready.

Lack of planning. Transitions are an important part of the day and need to have a purpose as well as advanced planning to make them work.

Plan for transitions. Transitions are an opportunity for learning as well as a necessary part of the day. Have toddlers pretend they are cleaning up for a party, or as they move between experiences have them jump like bunny rabbits, move as softly as the wind, march, dance, and so on.

Testing Limits during Transitions

Occasionally all adults get involved in a situation when a toddler is testing the rules. Let us suppose a toddler gets upset because it is time to clean up the toys and he is not finished playing. He cries, throws toys, and refuses to clean up. The adult, after trying to deal with his behavior for several minutes, becomes angry and tries to force the child to comply. What develops is a power struggle; someone wins and someone loses after a fairly lengthy dispute. Everyone loses because time and energy was wasted on a potentially preventable situation.

Given an opportunity to do it again, what could you change? Two or three minutes before cleanup time, give the toddler a warning that he will need to finish soon and alert him to what is coming next. Then, at cleanup time, give him a choice of what he wants to put away: "You can put the blocks on the shelf or help me put the paints away." If the toddler ignores you, repeat your direction and walk away to start clean up. Generally, the toddler will begin to clean up or leave the area. If he leaves the area, stop him and put something in his hand that needs to be put away and say, "Thanks for helping to clean up, that goes on the shelf. We need to get ready for snack now." Positive directions—that is, telling children what to do—almost always work.

One key for handling toddler outbursts is to remain calm and in control. If the adult is thinking and planning ahead rather than reacting emotionally, tantrum situations will be less likely to occur, or at least will be of lesser intensity. A second key is to have realistic expectations. Toddlers' cleanup will be haphazard and rushed. Remember it is the effort that counts and effort should be praised.

INCLUDING ALL TODDLERS

As toddlers become aware of the ways in which they are different from each other, the skill of a sensitive teacher determines the long-term outcome of this awareness. Children look to you as a model. Examine your feelings about including young children with disabilities in your early childhood program. Also check out your feelings about having children from different ethnic, racial, and language backgrounds, and your expectations based on gender, to discover if you have personal values that might make working with some children difficult. Table 14–25 provides some techniques for including toddlers with disabilities.

Table 14–25 Techniques for Including All Toddlers

- Provide an atmosphere where issues about race, gender, language, and disability can be freely discussed. Young children are very aware of these differences. Toddlers learn respect and caring for others who are different from themselves by modeling adults' interactions with the child.

- Support diversity in your classroom through experiences, materials, and curriculum planning. Toddlers learn about differences by firsthand experience. If a toddler wears braces, the other children may be curious about the braces. With the support of a physical therapist who has access to supplies such as crutches, braces, walkers, and wheelchairs, children can learn more about how braces and others prosthetic devices work.

- Teach toddlers specific ways of handling situations involving staring or making unkind remarks. Make all toddlers aware of how children who are stared at feel. Teach all children socially acceptable ways of learning about others.

- Teach children specific skills to use in approaching others and entering groups. If other children tease or make unkind remarks about the toddler with a disability, serve as the child's ally. Stop teasing and explain that words can hurt people's feelings. Give correct information: "Ernesto speaks Spanish at home. He does not know this word in English." Over time, help children build the skills necessary to stand up for themselves.

- Help all toddlers find roles to play and facilitate accommodations and adaptations that allow all children to play together.

If you pity toddlers with disabilities or are overprotective or condescending toward them, the other children will react the same way. If you celebrate only holidays that a majority of the children share, then those who have different beliefs may feel excluded. If you always choose boys to go to the block area and expect girls to use the dramatic-play area, you are supporting stereotypic gender differences. Awareness is important for *all* children. Toddlers are egocentric. They need support in viewing events from another's perspective.

Adults can successfully facilitate the inclusion of toddlers with disabilities into their programs if they plan to meet the individual needs of all the children in the group. Sometimes special toys or materials will be needed to allow the toddler with a disability the opportunity to learn a new skill. Often, the special toys can be used by other children in the program. By including young children with disabilities in a setting there is potential gain for all children in the classroom.

Including toddlers with disabilities requires more individualized planning. Typically, these needs are very compatible and need only variations on the general plans. The recommendations for including toddlers with disabilities reflect developmentally appropriate practices for all children this age, but may require some adaptation to meet individual toddlers' needs.

Toddlers with Developmental Delays and Intellectual Disabilities

Involve toddlers actively in the learning process, but expect to repeat this process with variations many times for learning to take place. Have the toddler crawl *under* the table when you are teaching that concept. Point out when he is using an obstacle course that he is *under* the ladder. You may need to use more direct teaching, rather than just assuming the toddler will discover what to do from incidental learning. You may also have to provide more scaffolding for learning to occur (see Table 14–26).

Table 14–26 Adapting the Environment to Include Toddlers with Developmental Delays and Intellectual Disabilities

• Keep a consistent daily schedule so toddlers will know what will happen next. Provide a picture chart to support the schedule.
• Limit choices to two or three experiences during free play time or provide some guidance in choosing appropriate experiences.
• Limit the potential for distraction, especially during small-group times, by seating the child close to you and facing away from busy areas.
• Add cues such as carpet squares to indicate where toddlers should sit.

(continues)

Table 14–26 *(continues)*

- Provide safe outlets for the release of excess energy and feelings. Children may need punching bags or silly time when they are encouraged to use up excess energy.

- Sequence tasks from easy to hard and try to match the toddler's developmental level. Use backward chaining where appropriate.

- Be specific about your rules for experiences and post these with pictures. Show the toddlers the rules as well as telling them.

- Help toddlers organize their experiences. For example say, "What will you do first? ... What comes next?"

- Use a variety of teaching techniques, including modeling what you want the child to do. Toddlers often learn appropriate behavior by imitating others.

- Toddlers with developmental delays may have a limited repertoire of behaviors, and modeling can increase this repertoire. You may have to point out the salient features you want them to attend to.

- Help shape a toddler's behavior by breaking an activity down into smaller steps and then leading the toddler through progressively more of the steps, providing many prompts until he can do it alone.

- The opposite technique of shaping is fading. As the toddler begins to master a skill, gradually give fewer cues and less information so that he becomes more responsible for doing the skill independently.

Toddlers with Physical Impairments

Toddlers need materials that encourage the development of large- and small-motor skills. The adult's role is to provide an adequate supply of a variety of materials that encourage all types of movements and reflect a developmental progression for skill building. The nature of the disability and information from parents and therapists will determine the most appropriate accommodations (see Table 14–27).

Table 14–27 Adapting the Environment to Include Toddlers with Physical Impairments

- Use adaptive equipment that allows the toddler to participate as normally as possible.

- Use larger, lighter versions of manipulative toys.

- Be aware of equipment in the classroom that can tip or roll.

- To encourage self-help skills, attach a carry-all or basket to the child's walker, or have the child wear a light carry-all around her neck if she is using crutches.

- Encourage the toddler to use her motor skills. Many children shy away from art or manipulative experiences because these are difficult for them, but they need the experience using the muscles and there is no right or wrong for these activities.

Toddlers with Mental Health Challenges

An organized, predictable, safe environment will help toddlers to be better organized. A consistent structure provides stability and helps with self-regulation. These children need adult support, warmth, and attention. Social norms and patterns are learned in families and child care settings. Families have different social norms based on their culture and social expectations for their children. It is sometimes difficult to tell if the differences in toddler's social and emotional behavior are based on different expectation or are behaviors that need mental health consultation

Children whose behavior falls on the autism spectrum disorder are often identified during this time. Some infants have seemingly normal development for about the first 12 to 15 months of life. Other infants have characteristic behaviors may seem unusual, but by age 2, the failure to develop nonverbal aspects of social behavior (facial expression, looking at the speaker) and lack of interest in peers become apparent.

Some toddlers begin to show oversensitivity or becomes less reactive to sounds and touch. Language development stops and existing language seems forgotten. (Greenspan & Wieder, 2006). Communication deficiencies are also noted, particularly the lack of spontaneous communication, and the inability to use language symbolically. If there is language, it may be immature or idiosyncratic so that only those familiar with the child know what is meant.

Each toddler has a unique profile relative to communication, sensory reactivity, sensory processing, muscle tone, and motor planning or sequencing. One role of early childhood educators is to be aware of these possibilities and work with parents in the identification of children with mental health needs (see Table 14–28).

Table 14–28 Adapting the Environment to Include Toddlers with Mental Health Challenges

- Provide toddlers with many opportunities to run, jump, climb, and swing in a secure environment.
- Develop with the parents a consistent plan for handling disruptions and targeting behaviors to concentrate on.
- Find many opportunities to give positive feedback and help toddlers develop the skills necessary to enter small groups and play with or near other children.
- Use pictures to communicate necessary information. Toddlers with autism spectrum disorders are visual learners.
- When you talk to toddlers ensure that your facial expression and tone of voice match (if you are happy, look and sound happy).
- Find out what toddlers find rewarding and use that for behavior you want to reinforce.
- Be clear, precise, and patient.

up close and personal

Luisa had difficulties with feedings around three weeks of age. She would cry for food and then, when drinking her bottle, she would scream and claw at the bottle as if in extreme pain. My husband and I took her to the doctor, who diagnosed her with acid reflux. The solution was to hold the baby high on an incline when feeding her, give gas relief drops, and try to get as much air out of the bottle as possible before feeding. This alleviated some of the crying, but not all.

She continued to cry while eating for six more weeks. This was extremely stressful to me. Listening to her cry for hours on end was frustrating and anguishing because I could not do anything about it. She hurt, I hurt. When she began eating solid foods she no longer cried when drinking her formula, but now made strange noises when eating the baby foods. The noises sounded as if she was not enjoying the food, but she never made any gestures to avoid the food or refused to eat it. This continued from when she was around five months old to a little over two years of age. The doctor thought there was something else going on. I attribute this behavior to her having sensory integration issues. She had problems with loud noises and too many people in one room. She had extreme responses to new and different environments and adults she didn't know getting too close to her. Her response would be to cry and try to escape.

REFLECTIVE PRACTICE

With the information you have, what do you think? If Lusia were to join your classroom of toddlers, what would you expect? How would you prepare for her? How would you support her development? What supports would you want for yourself?

Toddlers with Hearing Impairments

Parents will decide how they want communications skills to be taught to their toddler. Your role is to support this decision. When possible, incorporate the toddler's preferred communication mode into regular experiences (see Table 14–29).

Place the toddler in a good visual position during small-group time or snack time; across from you and not looking into the sun.

Table 14–29 Adapting the Environment to Include Toddlers with Hearing Impairments

- Remove barriers that may block the toddler's vision of the classroom, provided such removals do not create runways. Encourage the toddler to look over the choices of what has been set up in the room on any given day before deciding what to do.
- Encourage the toddler to attend to a speaker's face. Look at the child when you talk to her; remind the other children to do the same: "Look at Sofia when you talk to her; it makes it easier for her to understand you."
- Support what ever method parents have decided to use as a communication system for their toddler.

Toddlers with Visual Impairments

Help the toddler locate the different areas of the room and help her develop safe ways to get to each area. Keep these areas consistent to encourage independent movement. Providing consistent routines helps toddlers know what to expect and supports their independence. Keep chairs pushed in and do not have toys lying around on the floor (see Table 14–30).

Table 14–30 Adapting the Environment to Include Toddlers with Visual Impairments

- Be aware of the toddler's location in the room.
- Use objects the toddler can feel and pair words with the objects she is feeling: "Chunga, this is a ball. Feel how round it is. Drop it and it bounces back up." Using pictures of objects is dependent upon the child's level of vision.
- Be aware of lighting needs. Some toddlers actually see better in dim light. If she sees better in some lighting conditions than others, adapt your classroom.
- Use language that is comfortable for you. Do not eliminate the words "see" and "look" from your vocabulary, but describe what you see to the child in the most concrete way you can.
- Use high contrasting colors to help toddlers identify boundaries (put white paper on a black background or outline the edges of the paper with a black marker).
- Add texture to materials (sand in the paint) so they can be felt as well as seen.

Toddlers Whose Home Language Is Not English

As mobile infants move into toddlerhood, language becomes a more important vehicle of communication and learning. Supporting early language learning is an important aspect of all early childhood programs. When toddlers are learning two languages, the process is more challenging, but also more rewarding. How this process actually works is dependent on how particular programs are set up. In some settings, the toddlers spend their day in the second language. Depending on the multicultural commitment of the program, there may be few cultural supports for children whose first language is not English. This situation is both stressful for toddlers and not supportive of the home language; in fact, it devalues the home language. Culture and language are part of the curriculum for toddlers.

Ideally, programs have bilingual educators who are representative of the languages and cultures in the setting. It is easier to build relationships and to understand schedules, routines, and transitions in the home language. If one teacher speaks each toddler's home language and other teachers speak English, all children are immersed in a rich language environment. However, this may not be possible in settings where there are five or six different home languages and no educators who are from the culture or speak the language or even if toddlers speak one language that none of the educators speak. If toddlers will not be taught in their home language then it is imperative that the setting reflect the cultures of the toddlers who attend. A play-based environment and small groups support language learning. A long large-group time in one language does not support language-learning goals (DeBey & Bombard (2007).

As toddlers are learning two languages, there may be words they know in one language but not in the other. It is natural for them to use the words they know from both languages (code-switching). As you talk with them, include the words they are trying to learn. Provide a language-rich environment (See Table 14–31).

Table 14–31 Adapting the Environment to Include Toddlers Whose Home Language Is Not English

- Provide board books in the home language, and other picture books that show different cultural and ethnic groups.
- Support both the home language and English in the classroom.
- For English-language learners, use visual cues, repeat and restate language, use simpler language.
- Label materials in the classroom in the languages of the toddlers in the setting and in English. If there is more than one language label some materials in the home language of each toddler. Point out the distinctions in the labels. This is not because you expect toddlers to read, but because you are respecting their language and honoring your commitment to support first-language learning.
- Support toddlers' talking and do not comment when they switch between English and another language.
- Have dress-up clothing and props that reflect the language and cultural groups in the class.
- Encourage families to talk with you about what they want for their toddlers.
- Have discussions about childproofing the house given the toddlers' increased mobility skills.
- Provide time for active play inside and outside.
- Use music (singing and compact discs) to support play and language learning. Select music that reflects the languages and cultures of the toddlers in the classroom.

SUPPORTING SELF-REGULATION

As mobile infants become toddlers, they increasingly need adult guidance to help them determine the difference between acceptable and unacceptable behavior. This guidance includes using gentle redirection, acknowledging feelings, giving positive feedback, and providing appropriate experiences. Toddlers can be difficult as well as charming. They are emotional beings and one of their developmental tasks is learning how to control the emotions they feel. One expects that toddlers will have emotional outbursts and be noncompliant at times. How adults handle these situations affects their frequency, duration, and intensity.

Many adults have questions about when and how to discipline toddlers. When does discipline start? Typically, adults begin to discipline children at the end of the first year, when an infant becomes mobile. Most toddlers behave—in their own minds, they do not misbehave; misbehavior is, to some extent, an interpretation by adults. Sometimes adults are prompted to discipline toddlers because of their growing independence and interest in doing things for themselves. Their seemingly constant activity and their hands-on approach to life can lead adults to take measures to try to control toddler behavior.

Guidance
is teaching self-regulation and appropriate behavior.

Punishment
is designed to stop an unwanted behavior.

Many use the words **guidance** and **punishment** as though they were interchangeable. However, each means something slightly different and their use affects children differently. Guidance is behavior that is designed to encourage self-control and self-regulation. That is, guidance involves any actions or words that help someone learn to self-monitor his behavior so that it is appropriate and acceptable in a given situation. The purpose of guidance, then, is to teach a child what to do in a given situation rather than what not to do. Guidance is teaching a toddler appropriate or acceptable behavior.

Punishment is an action taken by an individual designed to stop another's particular behavior. Punishment is not concerned with teaching appropriate behavior; the only concern is stopping unwanted behavior. Punishment generally involves the infliction of some negative consequence for a behavior that is deemed inappropriate or wrong. Punishment usually succeeds in stopping unwanted behavior, but may have some negative effects. Toddlers may learn when they can "get away" with negative behavior, usually in the absence of the controlling adult, or they may come to fear adults as harsh and uncaring. There is concern that some active boys are having a difficult time finding classrooms encouraging. There are few male teachers and some early childhood educators are more comfortable with compliant girls than boys who test limits (Gartrell, 2006).

Positive discipline, or guidance, is designed to facilitate the development of good self-concepts, prosocial behaviors, and an ability to control one's behavior. It is a process approach designed to guide a toddler's behavior rather than a "one-shot" act. Guidance involves awareness of children's feelings, developmental level, and the ability to set and keep sensible limits. When a toddler behaves in an unacceptable way, the logical consequences for his behavior are presented in a way that preserves his self-esteem. As toddlers begin to learn that there are consequences for behavior (positive ones for acting appropriately, and negative ones for inappropriate actions), they will begin to learn to act responsibly and control their own behavior. The goal of guidance is to help toddlers learn socially acceptable limits and to develop internal controls. Guidance involves facilitating children's social development and prosocial skills (Gartrell, 1987).

Most toddlers do not intentionally misbehave. Toddlers are just beginning to think logically about the consequences of their behaviors. The toddler who is ripping pages from the book is not doing it to destroy the book, but because ripping the pages is fun and interesting. We, as adults, often ascribe negative intentions to children's behavior and that is why we get angry. We know ripping pages in a book is inappropriate, but a toddler may not (see Table 14–32).

Table 14–32 Using Guidance with Toddlers

- If you are angry, use your anger constructively. Let toddlers know you are angry and model appropriate ways to handle that anger. It is important for toddlers to learn how to handle anger, too. For example, "Ricardo, it makes me angry when you hurt Brie. You need to go to another area of the room."

- Tell the toddler what behavior is unacceptable *and* what they can do instead that is more appropriate: "Noel, you may not climb on the fence. I'll walk you to the jungle gym where you may climb."

- Help toddlers learn to solve their problems themselves. Give younger or more inexperienced toddlers the words to say at first, but eventually they will learn how to talk out their problems. "Regan, tell Irma you don't like it when she hits you."

- If a toddler is having a "bad day," give her some space to work out her feelings. Adding sensory materials often provides a good outlet.

- If a toddler has a tantrum, allow him to calm down in a safe place. Being out of control is scary, so an adult should be nearby. Although one might think that the best way to calm a distraught toddler down is to say in a soothing voice that as soon as he is calm, the two of you will talk about what happened, that may not be the best approach. You need to reach toddlers where they are. Do not try to reason with a toddler while he is screaming and thrashing.

- Provide enough interesting experiences and smooth transitions to keep toddlers actively involved in constructive play with minimal time wasted in waiting.

- Provide an atmosphere where exploration is encouraged. This often means putting valuables or other "untouchables" out of reach. If you are spending a lot of your time telling toddlers that they cannot touch things, exploration behavior (an important way in which toddlers gain information and learn) will be discouraged.

- Arrange your space to go along with your goals for positive behavior management. For example, if you would like to encourage more independence in toddlers, arrange some carefully selected materials on low open shelves that toddlers can choose from on their own, and have duplicates of the most popular toys when possible.

- Help toddlers realize that their actions and words affect others. For example, "Darren, did you see Orlando's face? He was really angry when you knocked down his blocks."

Teaching toddlers appropriate behavior is an important task for adults. The long-term goal of guidance is for toddlers to self-regulate their social and emotional behavior. Guidance, not punishment, supports the development of self-control in toddlers.

MANAGING CHALLENGING BEHAVIOR

The principles for positive management of challenging behavior are similar to all guidance principles for toddlers, but focus particularly on aggressive behaviors. Aggressive and antisocial behaviors for toddlers include hitting, biting,

Toddlers are struggling to find their own identity. Sometimes their goals come in conflict with adults ideas about what should be done in a given situation. Toddlers are still trying to understand the rules. Positive guidance not punishment is important.

throwing objects at others, hurting others, not sharing, swearing, and name-calling. In general, there is a victim involved as well as the toddler who is exhibiting these behaviors.

As in all guidance, you first need to consider the individual toddler and his needs, and his chronological age. Positive behavior management is based on respectful treatment of all children. Your consistent modeling of respectful treatment of toddlers is a powerful behavior management tool. Toddlers who feel loved and respected are more likely to cooperate and comply with well-thought-out rules.

To combat aggressive and antisocial behavior effectively, it is important to know some specific information. Take three days to watch the toddler and plan a strategy. This is difficult because there is an urge to want to do something about it "now." However, what you have been trying has probably not been working, so the usual approach may not be sufficient. See Table 14–33 to ask the right questions about the behavior.

If the behavior is really unusual for that particular child, determine if the toddler is feeling well. Sometimes the only sign of an ear infection, for example, is a negative change in the child's behavior.

Table 14–33 Questions to Ask about Challenging Behaviors

- *Pattern.* Is there is any pattern to the behavior that is causing the problem?

- *Time of day.* Does it happen when the toddler first arrives? When the toddler is leaving? Before snack or lunch time? During naptime? Or at any time of day?

- *Experiences or routines.* Does it occur during specific experiences or routines? If so, do some additional thinking about the experiences. Are they structured or free choice, group or individual? Are the children sitting or active?

- *Place.* Is there a particular place where the behavior occurs? Is it outdoors or indoors? Does it occur in a particular area of the room, such as where the blocks are or where dramatic play is set up?

- *Causes.* What seems to cause or trigger the behavior? What happened immediately before the incident? Did another child take something away from the toddler, or did the toddler ask for something to which another child said no or an adult said no? Was the toddler in an argument with another child, or were the children "fighting" or pretend fighting at the onset? Was the toddler tired? Are there changes occurring in the toddler's life? Is there a new sibling, a grandparent visiting, a parent away? A toddler may just need a soft lap to be held and cuddled on, and an understanding smile rather than hearing that she should be a "big girl" and stop throwing the doll.

- *Who is the victim?* Is the victim anyone who happens to be there, or is it usually a particular child or a few certain children? If it seems to be a variety of children, determine if they are mostly boys or girls or both. Are they bigger or smaller children? Are they older or younger children? Are they the aggressive children or the shy, more timid children?

- *How does the toddler act after the behavior?* Does the toddler deny or admit to the behavior? Is the toddler upset by the victim's crying (if that is what happens)? Does the toddler get upset if the victim returns the behavior (e.g., bites or hits back)? Does the toddler look to see if an adult is watching before proceeding with the behavior? Does the toddler walk away? Does the toddler apologize and seem concerned about the victim?

The answers to these questions will help develop some strategies for intervention. When you are faced with a situation that you must deal with, it is important to develop a strategy that is followed by all the adults involved. It should be jointly agreed to and consistently followed.

Dr. Harvey Karp (2004, 2006), a pediatrician, has developed some intervention techniques that are a bit off the beaten track but hold some potential for being effective. He starts with the assumption that toddlers are really pint-size cavemen and act like it. They stomp their feet, wipe their noses on their sleeve, and act like uncivilized wild men (and women). He sees adults in the role of the ambassador who is coming from this civilized world to tame them. And the first thing than any good ambassador needs to do is learn the language—in this case, toddlerese. Karp analyzed the way toddlers talk and came up with two characteristics that he feels are important, particularly when they are upset: their phrases are one to three words long and they repeat them over and over. If you think about a toddler who wants to retain possession of a favorite toy, can you picture him saying "mine!" Does he stop with one "mine" or one "no?" Typically he does not.

So, in response to a child who does not want to clean up, Karp (2004, 2006) might say to the child, "You don't want to clean up; you don't want to clean up. You aren't done playing. You don't want to clean up." While he is doing this he mirrors the child's face and values. He echoes at the same level of energy the toddler is feeling. Like the toddler, he points and grunts. He goes ape! He refers to this as the "Fast Food Rule." When you pull up at a fast food restaurant, you place your order. The first thing that the person on the other end of the line does is repeat your order, your agenda. Next, she gets to her agenda, would you like to add a drink, a special, or whatever. Then you move on to pay. Karp posits that toddlers have to know you have heard them before they can listen to you. The way they know is if you speak their language. Distracting a toddler may work in the short run, but because it does not acknowledge the toddler's feelings in the long run it tells toddlers not to pay attention to their feelings.

Karp (2004, 2006) joins the toddler in the jungle and guides him back to civilization. When this technique does not work as well as you would like, he suggests offering a hug, a solution to the problem, or a distraction. Or, ignoring the child by respectfully walking away and returning in 30 seconds to a minute to begin again.

Karp also has advice on preventing tantrums. The first is to avoid problem situations where possible and to use good communication—again, toddlerese. He talks about "feeding the meter." He believes that we need to be responsive to toddlers on a regular basis just as you would think about feeding quarters to a parking meter so you do not get a ticket. Toddlers thrive on attention, play, high-fives, praise, massage, and all of the good ways we make them feel special. We need to make toddlers feel special and to make them feel like they are competent and they can do things. Karp's work has been primarily with families, not early care and education settings. However, his work is being generalized to these settings. For a more traditional approach, see Table 14–34.

Table 14–34 Handling Challenging Behavior

- Quickly check on the victim; if possible, have another adult do this.
- Firmly tell the aggressive toddler that you will not tolerate the behavior. (Think through this statement so that you know exactly what you will say ahead of time.) "I will not allow you to hurt other children."
- Help the toddler find an activity that is of interest. Toddlers are struggling with issues relating to independence at a time when they do not have the language skills to understand and support the complex reasoning related to situations. Alert caregivers can help prevent conflicts and help mediate them when they do occur.

WITH INFANTS AND TODDLERS

What do you think of this approach? Is it too off the wall or might it work? Would you be willing to try it out?

SUMMARY

Toddlers continue to grow and learn. They are into being themselves and spend energy trying to determine the boundaries of that self as well as to regulate their behavior. Their competence in motor skills requires increased vigilance by educators. They are very interested in doing things by themselves, including learning to dress and undress as well as feed themselves, and are moving into learning to control body functions.

Mobility is taken for granted and fine motor and manipulative skills are beginning to play a larger role in development. Toddlers are able to express more of their thoughts and are moving into symbolic play. They are building skills that lay the foundation for reading and writing. Early math and science skills are learned by interacting with well-planned environments. Toddlers learn through play, and dramatic play helps them integrate thoughts and ideas. Art, music, and creative movement provide avenues of expression.

Accommodations and adaptation to include all toddlers are still relative easy because curriculum relies on individual and small-group planning. As toddlers move to a more uniform schedule, transitions are more apparent and can be a challenging time. The environment is making more demands on toddlers, and taking part in cleanup time and other routines may be difficult. Toddlers tend to test the limits. They continue to struggle with self-regulation as they are seeking self-identity.

CHAPTER IN REVIEW

❋ Toddlers are actively exploring their world and trying to learn about it.

❋ Toddlers need to have all the content areas included daily in a developmentally appropriate way.

❋ Planning for toddlers uses simpler and more concrete concepts than for pre-schoolers and provides time for learning self-help skills, as developing independence is an underlying theme of the curriculum.

❋ With toddlers, process is more important than product.

❋ Transitions are particularly stressful for toddlers, so evaluate and perhaps modify transitions to be valid learning experiences as well as less stressful.

❋ Guidelines for discipline practices are important because toddlers are expected to test limits as they explore their environment.

APPLICATION ACTIVITIES

1. Guidance or punishment? A toddler is looking at a book and begins to rip the pages from the book. Discuss how you would handle this behavior and the rationale behind your decision.

2. Plan a week in September for a group of 12 toddlers. Describe how you would modify this plan for this same group if you repeated the week in March (they would be six months older). What would you have expected them to learn and what developmental changes would impact your planning?

3. Describe developmentally appropriate practice and what it means for adults who work with young children ages birth to 3. Visit an early care and education setting and evaluate it against your ideas about developmentally appropriate practice.

RESOURCES

Web Resources

❋ The **American Academy of Pediatrics** (AAP), in collaboration with the Department of Health and Human Services, the Child Care Bureau, and the Maternal and Child Health Bureau, sponsors the Healthy Child Care America Campaign. It has resources for parents and early childhood educators. http://www.healthychildcare.org.

❋ The **Book Vine for Children** categorizes books in a variety of different ways including by age. Their selections are evaluated by a children's librarian. They sell both individual books and packages of books about particular topics. http://www.bookvine.com/.

☀ **Dr. Harvey Karp** provides information about his philosophy of raising happy infants and toddlers as well as resources for implementing this philosophy. It also has information on *The happiest toddler on the block.* http://www.thehappiestbaby.com/.

☀ The **International Reading Association** (IRA) lists culturally diverse books for children, including infants and toddlers and provides professional development resources, IRA has position statements on reading instruction, as well as resources on teaching strategies for teaching in diverse classrooms. http://www.reading.org.

☀ The **Red Leaf Press** has a variety of books that are specifically written for infants and toddlers as springboards for discussing social issues (*Feet are not for kicking, Hands are not for hitting*). http://www.redleafpress.org.

☀ The **World Bank Early Child Development** (ECD) focuses early childhood from a global and economic perspective. It has links to international and regional sites; resources, and links to data and statistics from various international organizations. http://www.worldbank.org.

Print Resources

☀ Brown, W. H., Odom, S. L., & McConnell, S. R. (2008). *Social competence of young children. Risk, disability, and intervention.* Baltimore, MD: Paul H. Brookes Publishing Co.

☀ Gartrell, D. (2007). *A guidance approach for the encouraging classroom with professional enhancement booklet* (4th ed.). Clifton Park, NY: Delmar Thompson Learning.

REFERENCES

Charlesworth, R., & Lind, K. K. (2002). *Math and science for young children* (4th ed.). Clifton Park, NY: Delmar Thomson Learning.

DeBey, M., & Bombard, D. (2007). An approach to second-language learning and cultural understanding. *Young Children, 62*(2), 88–93.

Dombro, A. L., Colker, L. J., & Dodge, D. T. (1999). *The creative curriculum for infants and toddlers.* Washington, DC: Teaching Strategies, Inc.

Gartrell, D. (1987). Punishment or guidance? *Young Children, 42*(3), 55–61.

Gartrell, D. (2006). Guidance matters. *Young Children, 61*(3), 92–93.

Graham, G., Holt/Hale, S. A., & Parker, M. (2005). *Children moving: A reflective approach to teaching physical education* (7th ed.). New York: McGraw Hill.

Hart, B., & Risley, R. (1995). *Meaningful differences in the everyday experiences of American children.* Baltimore, MD: Brookes.

Humpal, M. E., & Wolf, J. (2003). Music in the inclusive environment. *Young Children, 58*(2), 103–107.

Karp, H. (2004). *The happiest toddler on the block.* New York: Bantam Dell.

Karp, H. (November, 2006). *The happiest toddler on the block.* Presentation at the annual meeting of the National Association for the Education of Young Children. Atlanta, GA: .

Lally, J. R., & Mangione, P. (2006). The uniqueness of infancy demands a responsive approach to care. *Young Children, 61*(4), 14–20.

Pica, R. (1995). *Experiences in movement with music, activities and theory.* Clifton Park, NY: Delmar Learning.

Shore, R., & Strasser, J. (2006). Music for their minds. *Young Children, 61*(2), 62–67.

Williamson, G. G., & Anzalone, M. E. (2001). *Sensory integration and self-regulation in infants and toddlers: Helping very young children interact with their environment.* Washington, DC: Zero to Three.

subject index

author index

M